# BERLITZ

# COMPLETE GUIDE TO CRUISING AND CRUISE SHIPS

by
DOUGLAS WARD

President
The Maritime Evaluations Group (MEG)

Berlitz Publishing Company Inc.
New York, New York

Berlitz Publishing Company Ltd
Oxford, England

**ACKNOWLEDGEMENTS**

The ship silhouettes and cabin layouts were drawn by Susan Alpert and Oxford Illustrators.

The black and white photographs were kindly supplied by the cruise lines concerned.

Designed by Fox and Partners, Bath, England

Editors: Donald Greig, Kate Targett

*1995 Edition*

**PUBLISHER'S NOTE**

The Maritime Evaluations Group (MEG) has evaluated cruise ships since 1980, issuing annual reports on the world's cruise fleet. All professional opinions and ratings are strictly those of the author and not of the publisher, Berlitz, which makes this survey available in bookstores.



ISBN 2-8315-1327-8

Printed in the United States of America

*INTERNATIONAL ACCLAIM FOR THE BERLITZ COMPLETE GUIDE TO CRUISING AND CRUISE SHIPS*

"One way to find the right cruise is to get a copy of Berlitz...which rates all cruise ships in the world, the facilities they offer and the kind of passengers you can expect to meet."

*International Herald Tribune*

"...helps you pick a ship that most closely meets your needs."

*The Travel Agent, New York*

"...indispensable for choosing a ship the first time, or for experienced cruisers wanting to try a new ship."

*Tourist Echo, Paris*

"...a variety of knowledgeable advice and opinion."

*Chicago Sun-Times*

"Only once in many years does one find a book so very well done."

*The Travel Store, Los Gatos, CA*

"...informative about all aspects of cruising...sensible and comprehensive."

*Sunday Telegraph, London*

"...required reading when selecting a cruise ship."

*Travel & Enjoyment, Hamburg*

"...the do's and don'ts of taking a cruise."

*The Houston Post*

"...includes simply everything you ever wanted to know about...cruise ships."

*Knight-Ridder Newspapers*

"...extensively describes ships in a chart format and evaluates oceangoing vessels, giving star ratings and numerical scores to each."

*Chicago Tribune*

# STOP PRESS

As this book was going to press, some changes to ships, owners and operators took place. The latest known changes are included here.

For more updates throughout the year, I invite you to read *PortHole Magazine* (see the questionnaire page at the back of this book for details).

### American Family Cruises

This company will cease operating as of September 1994. Its ship *American Adventure* is expected to revert to the Costa Cruises fleet.

### *Aurora I/Aurora II*

These ships have been sold to Singapore interests, and are expected to operate from that port in 1995 and beyond.

### *Ayvasovskiy*

This ship is now chartered by the UK-based company Eurocruises to operate 7-night cruises from Trieste, Italy, during the summer months.

### *Columbus Caravelle*

This ship stopped sailing on her 1994/95 schedule on 3 August 1994, following the sale of the vessel to Singapore interests.

### *Crown Monarch*

This Cunard Crown Cruises' ship, chartered by Lines International, is to be renamed *The Nautican* for short cruises based on Singapore.

### *Star/Ship Majestic*

Premier Cruise Lines' *Star/Ship Majestic* has been chartered by London's CTC Cruises and will be renamed *Southern Cross*, effective March 1995.

### *Holiday*

This Carnival Cruise Lines ship will be repositioned to Los Angeles for 3/4-night cruises, effective May 1995.

### *Illiria*

This ship has been sold to P&O Spice Island Cruises. She will operate 3/4-night Indonesia cruises and has been renamed *Sea Dancer*, effective fall 1994.

### *Regent Jewel*

This ship is expected to be repositioned to Singapore for 7-night cruises in South East Asia.

### *Regent Rainbow*

This ship will operate 7-night Alaska cruises in 1995.

### *Royal Viking Sun* and Royal Viking Line

In June 1994 this world-renowned ship and the brand name Royal Viking Line were purchased by Cunard. The purchase did not include sister ship *Royal Viking Queen*, which will be transferred to Royal Cruise Line fleet on January 1, 1995, and renamed *Queen Odyssey*.

All evaluations of cruise ships in this book were made without bias, partiality, or prejudice. In almost all instances the ship has been visited recently by the author in order to update earlier ratings or assess current status. Much of the information contained in the profiles in Part Two was supplied and checked by the cruise lines and shipowners themselves. Any errors, modifications, or comments with regard to present or future editions should be addressed directly to:

**Douglas Ward, 1521 Alton Road, Suite 350, Miami Beach, FL 33139-3301, U.S.A.**

# Contents

# Foreword

by James G. Godsman, President
Cruise Lines International Association

## Relax, Your Ship Has Come In

In this fast-paced world, where there's a big premium on relaxation and worry-free vacationing, cruise vacations fulfill the desire to sit back, and just say "ah-h-h."

You work hard all year, so when you go on vacation, it's to get away from it all—ideally in comfort and style. You wistfully dream of a vacation where you will be wined and dined, pampered and spoiled ...one where you can indulge your every whim and come home rejuvenated, refreshed and floating on top of the world ...and in true '90's fashion, you expect to get the most for your money.

This explains why 1995 is shaping up to be another record-breaking year for the cruise industry. It continues to grow at almost double-digit levels, and is the fastest-growing vacation option in the world today. And with more than 20 new ships of all shapes and sizes to be added to the fleet over the next few years, the industry is expected to continue its dynamic growth well into the 21st century.

## Just Sit Back and Say "ah-h-h"

One big reason for the industry's success is cruise vacationers' high satisfaction level. The majority of cruise vacationers rate a cruise higher than other vacations because it allows them to relax and be pampered in a stress-free environment. But relaxation and pampering aren't the only reasons that cruisers sail repeatedly. Today's cruise-goers also attach a high degree of importance to the destinations that ships visit.

Cruises exceed—and often greatly exceed—the expectations of the traveler, especially in the areas of hospitality, activities, entertainment, ports of call, learning experience, meeting new people and romance. Passengers are so enthuisiastic about the places they visit that the industry is continually investigating new and exotic cruising areas. This year finds cruise lines delivering millions of eager and prospective tourists to destinations around the world, while at the same time, creating millions of "hot prospects" for return tourism among cruise vacationers.

Five out of six first-time and veteran cruisers believe that cruising is a convenient and affordable way to indulge in a spot of "destination sampling" on one trip, and an ideal way to try out a possible future vacation spot. Fully half of cruise passengers intend to return to a place they first visited by ship.

## Destined for Success

During 1995, cruise passengers will have the greatest choice of destinations and itineraries ever offered—nearly 500 ports in more than 100 countries.

Imagine scouting the Amazon River by zodiac landing craft, flightseeing the volcanoes of Hawaii, or standing on Alaska's Mendenhall Glacier and listening to it "crack" as it moves slowly towards the sea. Remarkably, these are just a few of the adventures available to the modern cruiser.

While the Caribbean remains the number one cruise destination (more than 50 per cent of cruisers travel here), Alaska will also continue its popularity, with more ships being deployed here than ever previously. In addition, one of the world's greatest adventures—transiting the Panama Canal—is now one of the most popular cruise vacations, having increased capacity a whopping 78 per cent in the last year alone. Cruises to the Pacific Rim, especially South East Asia—where fleet expansions and a cruise clientele eager for new destinations have contributed to growth—will continue to increase as well.

Other "in" destinations include: the southern, deeper Caribbean's exotic and less frequented islands; Europe and the Mediterranean; Bermuda (a top cruise itinerary and one of the few that visits just one port); and New England's scenic coastline, which provides a dramatic backdrop for the celebrated "Fall Foliage" sailings between New York, Boston and Montreal.

What's more, new destinations are continually coming on line as politics permit. Consider such cruise ports as Ho Chi Minh City (formerly Saigon), Warnemunde in former East Germany, and Riga in Latvia.

## Trend Watch

Aside from exotic itineraries, industry trends include more families cruising together, more theme cruises and more early booking discounts.

With a noticeable increase in family cruisers, many cruise lines have developed a variety of innovative programs to appeal to every type of family, with some catering to the family market almost exclusively.

In addition, after years of building on and perfecting the theme concept, cruise lines are now embracing an even wider range of special interests. One line will offer no less than 60 theme cruises, each designed to enhance the cruise experience. As travelers look for vacations that are an extension of their fondest pursuits on land, cruises which offer everything from gardening to arts and antiques are now available.

A host of lines now offer early booking discounts, some that include free cabin upgrades for passengers booking six months in advance. Many are also offering free passage to children under 16 traveling with two adults on selected sailings.

Other top attributes that will keep cruise vacationers coming back for more include: the excellent value of a cruise vacation versus a comparable land-based vacation; the fact that cruises appeal to a wide demographic mix, from couples to families to singles; the diversity of cruises available (I can confidently say that there's a cruise for everyone!); and the stress-free nature of a cruise.

As new capacity is added and adjustments and enhancements are made, the industry continues to attract a tremendous and relatively untapped market of new cruisers. New destinations, high levels of customer satisfaction, and the perception of value in the cruise purchase also continue to help maintain the cruise industry's trend of growth and set the pace in the travel market.

All of this is good reason for optimism and why we look forward to 1995 and beyond with great expectations.

*James G. Godsman is President of Cruise Lines International Association (CLIA), one of the world's largest and most influential industry associations. With 32 member cruise lines and over 22,000 travel agency affiliates in North America, it is the largest such association in terms of agency affiliate representation.*

# How to Use this Guide

Ever since my first transatlantic crossing, in July 1965, on the largest passenger ship ever constructed, Cunard's giant 83,673-grt RMS *Queen Elizabeth*, I have been captivated by passenger ships and the sea. More than 700 cruises, 130 transatlantic crossings and countless Panama Canal transits, shipyard visits, maiden voyages and ships later, I am even more fascinated by and absorbed in every aspect of cruising and passenger-ship travel.

For the discerning vacationer, there is simply no better way to get away from it all than on a cruise. Those who have cruised before will be unstinting in their praise of it. They may talk about a specific ship, line or cruise, but always with enthusiasm. So will you—that is, if you choose the "right" ship for the "right" reasons.

That brings me to the purpose of this book: it is intended to be a primary and comprehensive source of information about cruising and the ships and companies that offer to take you away from the pressures, stresses and confines of daily life ashore. When you first start looking into the possibilities of taking a cruise you will be confronted by an enormous and bewildering choice. Don't panic. Simply read through this book carefully. At the end you will be nearer to making the right choice and will leave for your cruise as well informed as most specialists in the industry! In fact, cruise consultants, travel agents and personnel connected with the industry will also find this book a valuable reference source on ships and cruising.

The book is divided into two distinct sections. Part One comprises 21 chapters and various charts and diagrams; introduces you to the world of cruising; helps you define what you are looking for in a cruise; tells you how and where to book and what kind of accommodations to choose; and provides valuable advice on what you should know before you go. There is a complete picture of life aboard ship and how to get the best from it: the world-famous cuisine, the evolution of cruising, nautical terminology, amusing anecdotes, who's who on board, and advice about going ashore. If you are looking for the cruise with a difference—along a river or an adventurous expedition—there is a survey of these aspects, too, culminating with that ultimate travel experience: the world cruise, and other grand voyages.

Part Two contains profiles of 210 oceangoing cruise ships of the world (including expedition, "soft" expedition cruise vessels and sail-cruise vessels). From large to small, from unabashed luxury to moderate and economy, old and new, they're all here. The ratings are a painstaking documentation of my personal work, much of it undertaken in strict secrecy. To keep this book up-to-date and accurate, I travel throughout the world constantly (this translates to approximately one million air miles every year) and inspect hundreds of ships (including areas that passengers don't normally see, but which are a necessary part of the total evaluation), and this involves, quite naturally, much on-board cruising as well.

The ratings are best used selectively—according to your personal tastes and preferences. If cuisine is important to you, or your concern is for entertainment, then these aspects of the ratings will obviously be more significant for you than the overall score or number of stars awarded. You may find the Pick-a-Ship chart at the beginning of Part Two useful. This gives you an idea of the type of passenger to expect on board, the ambiance and whether the tone and style are formal, informal or casual. For instance, you might be looking for a young, single, active disco crowd, or perhaps want to avoid one. The attraction of cruising is in the variety of opportunities available. This book is intended to help you make an informed choice, given the differences between ships today.

As soon as new ships enter service, a survey is undertaken for the next edition of this book. This edition covers the state of the cruise industry through the end of 1994 with a look at 1995 and beyond.

This book is a tribute to everyone who has made my seafaring experiences possible, and to everyone who helped make this book a reality. In addition, I would like to give a brief mention to my mother and father, without whom I would never have gone cruising. With my love.

**Douglas Ward**
*June 1994*

---

During the early part of his sea-going career, starting in 1965, Douglas Ward worked on some 15 well known liners (some of which are no longer in service) as follows:

*Andes*, 25,689 grt; scrapped in 1971

*Black Watch,* 11,209 grt; withdrawn

*Blenheim*, 10,420 grt; now *Discovery I*

*Calypso*, 20,204 grt; now *OceanBreeze*

*Cunard Countess*, 17,593 grt

*Cunard Princess*, 17,495 grt

*Franconia*, 22,637 grt; now *Fedor Shalyapin*

*Kenya Castle*, 19,904 grt; now *Amerikanis*

*Ocean Monarch*, 22,552 grt; withdrawn in 1966, scrapped at Kaohsiung in 1975

*Oronsay*, 27,632 grt; withdrawn in 1973, scrapped at Kaohsiung in 1974

*Queen Elizabeth*, 83,673 grt; withdrawn 1968; caught fire in Hong Kong under suspicious circumstances 9 Feb. 1972

*Queen Elizabeth* 2, 66,451 grt

*Queen Mary*, 81,237 grt; withdrawn in 1967, moored at Long Beach, California

*Reina del Mar*, 21,501 grt; withdrawn in 1975, scrapped at Kaohsiung in 1975

*Southern Cross*, 20,204 grt; still in service as *OceanBreeze*

PART ONE

# The World of Cruising

# The Evolution of Cruising

## A Brief History

It was a French sailing ship, the *Deux Frères*, that first introduced a regular passenger service, between Le Havre, France, and New York, on December 17, 1784, eight years after the Declaration of Independence of the United States. However, cruising did not become established until the following century.

In 1835 a curious sample advertisement appeared in the first issue of the *Shetland Journal.* Under the heading "To Tourists," it proposed an imaginary cruise from England round Iceland and the Faroe Islands, and went on to suggest the pleasures of cruising under the Spanish sun in winter. The journal's founder, Arthur Anderson, is thus said to have invented the idea of cruising.

Two years later, along with his partner, Brodie Wilcox, Anderson founded the Peninsular Steam Navigation Company (later to become P&O).

Sailing for leisure soon caught on. Writers such as William Makepeace Thackeray and Charles Dickens boarded ships for the excitement of the voyage, and not necessarily just to reach a destination. The Victorians had discovered tourism, and they promoted the idea widely in their own society. Indeed, Thackeray's account of his legendary voyage in 1844, from Cornhill to Grand Cairo by means of P&O ships of the day, makes fascinating reading, as does Dickens' account of his transatlantic crossing in a Cunarder in 1842. P&O's *Tagus*, which journeyed from London to the Black Sea in 1843, was the subject of Mark Twain's book *The Innocents Abroad* (published 1869).

In 1881 P&O's 2,376-ton ship *Ceylon* was sold to the newly formed Oceanic Yachting Company for conversion into a commercial pleasure yacht capable of sailing round the world—the first passenger ship to do so. The ship continued its cruising career after being sold to the Polytechnic Touring Association.

Cruising in its more modern sense got underway on March 12, 1889, when the 33,847-ton Orient liners *Chimborazo* and *Garrone* were redeployed from their normal services to Australia to undertake seasonal cruises to the Norwegian fjords. By 1893 seasonal cruises were also being offered to the Mediterranean, and in 1895 a third vessel, the *Lusitania*, was sent on a 60-day cruise around the West Indies, Madeira, Tenerife and the Azores. From then on, both the Orient Line and the Royal Mail Steam Packet Company featured regular cruises for the wealthy. In 1912 the former Orient Line's *Ortona* emerged after refit, operating under Royal Mail as the 8,939-ton *Arcadian.* With beds for 320 first-class passengers (there were no others), facilities included a 35-ft.-long swimming pool and a three-deck-high dining room.

The first vessel built exclusively for cruising was the Hamburg America Line's two-funnel yacht, the 4,409-ton *Prinzessin Victoria Luise.* It even included a private suite for the German Kaiser.

After World War I there was a shortage of tonnage, and cruising activities were curtailed, with one notable exception—Royal Mail's *Arcadian*, which built up an enviable reputation as a British cruise vessel. Her facilities included a tiled swimming pool and hot and cold running water to every cabin.

The first *official* round-the-world cruise was pioneered by the Cunard Line in 1922-3 on the *Laconia* (19,680 grt)—a three-class ship that sailed from New York. The itinerary included many of the ports of call still popular with world-cruise passengers today. The ship accommodated 350 persons in each of its first two classes, and 1,500 in third class, for a total capacity of 2,200 passengers—more than most ships of today.

In the 1920s, cruising became the thing to do for the world's well-to-do. Being pampered in grand style was "in" and is still the underlying concept of cruising. The ship took you and your belongings anywhere, fed you, accommodated you, relaxed you, and entertained you. At the same time, it even catered for your servants who, of course, accompanied you.

The cruise idyll was helped greatly by Prohibition in the 1930s. After all, just a few miles out at sea, liquor could be served in unlimited amounts. Cheap three- and four-day weekend "booze cruises" from New York were a good alternative to "bathtub gin." Then came the introduction of short cruises with destinations, as well as drink. Subsequently, the short cruise became one of the principal sources of profit for the steamship companies of the day.

During the late 1920s and well into the 1930s ships became floating luxury palaces, offering every amenity imaginable in this era of social elegance. One of the most beautiful flowing staircases ever built was on board the French liner *Paris* (35,469 grt), constructed in 1921. It is reported that seagulls made this ship their five-star favorite because of its *haute cuisine* garbage.

The 1930s saw a battle of the giants develop, with Great Britain, France, Germany and the United States building liners of unparalleled luxury, elegance, glamor, and comfort. Each country was competing to produce the biggest and best afloat. For a time, quality was somehow related to smokestacks: the more a ship had, the better. Although speed had always been a factor, particularly on the transatlantic run, it now became a matter of national ambition.

The first ship designed specifically for cruising from the U.S.A. after World War II was the *Ocean Monarch* (Furness Withy & Company Ltd.), which was awarded a gold medal by the US Academy of Designing for "outstanding beauty and unusual design features of a cruise ship." Her maiden voyage was from New York to Bermuda on May 3, 1951. I worked aboard her for a short time.

One of the most famous cruise liners of all time was Cunard's lovely *Caronia* (34,183 grt), conceived in 1948. She was designed and built to offer a transatlantic service in the peak summer months only and spend the rest of the year doing long, expensive cruises. She had a single giant mast and one smokestack—the largest of her time—and her hull was painted four shades of green, supposedly for the purposes of heat resistance and easy identification. Known for extensive world cruises, she was one of the first ships to offer a private adjoining bathroom for every cabin—a true luxury. Lovingly known as the "Green Goddess," she was sometimes called the "millionaires' ship."

In June 1958 the first commercial jet aircraft flew across the Atlantic and completely altered the economics of transatlantic travel. It was the last year that more passengers crossed the North Atlantic by sea than by air. In the early 1960s passenger shipping directories listed more than 100 oceangoing passenger ship lines, with more than 30 ships featuring transatlantic crossings for the better part of each year. Up until the mid-1960s, it was cheaper to cross the Atlantic by ship than by plane, but the jets changed that rapidly, particularly with the introduction of jumbo jets in the early 1970s.

Today, one major superliner alone still offers a regular transatlantic service—the elegant, modern Cunard liner *Queen Elizabeth 2* (69,053 grt). Built in 1969, re-engined and extensively refurbished in 1987, and with a mini-refit in 1992/3, the *QE2* offers more than two dozen crossings each year between New York and Southampton, with occasional calls at Cherbourg, Baltimore, Boston and Philadelphia. Besides the *QE2*, several cruise ships offer occasional transatlantic crossings, usually twice each year when relocating between cruise areas.

The success of the jumbo jets created a fleet of unprofitable and out-of-work passenger liners that seemed doomed for the scrap heap. Even the big "Queens," noted for their regular weekly transatlantic service, found themselves in jeopardy. The *Queen Mary* was withdrawn in September 1967. Her sister ship, the *Queen Elizabeth*, the largest passenger liner ever built, made her final crossing in October 1968. I was aboard for the last few voyages of this great ship.

The transatlantic shipping companies searched desperately for new employment for their aging vessels, but few survived the ever-successful growth of the jet aircraft. Ships were sold for a fraction of their value, and many lines simply went out of business.

Those that survived attempted to mix transatlantic crossings with voyages south to the sun. The Caribbean was appealing. Cruising became an ideal alternative. An entire new industry was born, and new lines were formed exclusively for cruising.

Then came smaller, highly specialized ships, which were capable of getting into the tiny ports of developing Caribbean islands, and which were built to carry a sufficient number of passengers in a single class arrangement to make money.

Instead of cruising long distances south from northerly ports such as New York, the new lines established their headquarters in Florida. They based their ships there not only to escape the cold weather and rough seas, but also to cut fuel costs in sailing to the Caribbean ports. Cruising was reborn.

California became the base for cruises to the Mexican Riviera, while Vancouver on Canada's west coast was the focus for summer cruises to Alaska.

Flying passengers to the ports of embarkation was the next logical step, and there soon emerged a working relationship between the cruise lines and the airlines. The air/sea package therefore came into being with the cruise lines using the jumbo jets for their own purposes. The concept of fly-cruising was first featured in the Mediterranean in 1960 by Chandris Cruises; these days passengers are flown to join up with cruises almost anywhere in the world.

Then came the "sail 'n' stay" packages, joint cruise and hotel vacations that were all included in the cruise fare. Cruising had become an integrated part of tourism, with ships and hotels offering comfort and relaxation and airlines providing quick access.

Some of the old liners came out of mothballs—purchased by emerging cruise lines. Refurbished for warm-weather cruising operations, these ships are often almost completely new in internal design and fittings.

One of the finest examples of refurbishment of a famous transatlantic liner is the *Norway* (Norwegian Cruise Line), formerly the *France*, which has been converted into a Caribbean cruise liner and occasional visitor to Scandinavia. The French can hardly recognize their former transatlantic flagship, which first entered service in 1962— just as passenger traffic on the North Atlantic was declining. Other excellent examples of this type of conversion are seen in Celebrity Cruises' *Meridian* (ex-*Galileo*), and Princess Cruises' *Fair Princess* (the ex-Cunarder *Carinthia*), which is now classical and elegant after refurbishment in 1984.

By the late 1970s the cruise industry was growing at a rapid rate. It is still expanding today and is, in fact, the fastest-growing segment of the travel industry. Several brand new cruise ships enter service each year, and new-building growth is expected to continue well into the late 1990s.

## Cruising Today

Today's cruise concept hasn't changed a great deal from that of earlier days, although it has been improved, refined and expanded. Cruises now place more emphasis on destinations and feature more ports. Modern ships are larger, on the whole, than their counterparts of yesteryear, yet cabin size has decreased in order to provide more space for entertainment and other public facilities.

Today's ships boast air-conditioning to keep heat and humidity out, stabilizers to keep the ship on an even keel, an excellent level of maintenance and safety, and more emphasis on health and fitness facilities.

Cruise ship design has moved from the traditional, classic, rounded profiles of the past to much more boxy shapes with squared-off sterns and towering superstructures. Although ship lovers may bemoan the changes in design, they were brought about by a need to fit as much as possible in the space provided: you can squeeze more in a square box than you can in a round one, although it may be less aesthetically appealing. Form follows function, and ships have changed in function from ocean transportation to floating vacation resorts.

With new ships being introduced at the rate of almost one every five months to cater for the increase in demand for cruises, and old tonnage being constantly converted, reconstructed or upgraded in order to comply with the latest international safety and hygiene standards, the choice for cruise vacations has never been more comprehensive.

Whatever you enjoy doing, you'll find it on a cruise. Although ships have long been devoted to eating and relaxation (promulgating the maxim "Traveling slowly unwinds you faster"), cruise lines now offer all sorts of activities, learning and life-enriching experiences that were not available in previous years. Also, the places you can visit on a cruise are unlimited: from Antarctica to Acapulco, Bermuda to Bergen, Dakar to Dominica, Shanghai to St. Thomas, or if you wish, even *nowhere at all*. All told, more than 500 ports are visited by the world's cruise fleet (including 115 ports in the Aegean/Mediterranean and 145 ports in Northern Europe alone).

Although small when compared to the figures for tourism in general, the cruise industry is now a $12 billion business worldwide, with over $6.5 billion in the United States alone and growing at a rate around 10 per cent each year (although the growth rate slowed slightly following the intrusion of the Persian Gulf War). Clearly, cruising is now in the mainstream of the vacation industry, and has virtually taken over from the increasingly regulated packaged vacation so popular in the sixties.

With over 4 million gross registered tons of ships, the global cruise industry provides employment to an increasing number of personnel, both directly (there are over 50,000 shipboard officers, staff and crew, and approximately 12,000 employees in the cruise company head offices) and indirectly (such as in the suppliers of foodstuffs and mechanical and electrical parts, port agents, transport companies, and a wide variety of other peripheral workers).

The spin-off effect on tourism in areas that are adjacent, or close to, the world's principal ports for the embarkation and disembarkation of cruise passengers is tremendous, with direct and indirect benefit being brought to both mainland and island nations, airlines, railways, bus firms, other transportation systems, hotels, car rental companies, and so on. For example, on the small island of Bermuda, in the North Atlantic, the in-port expenditure per passenger aboard Celebrity Cruises' *Horizon* in 1990 was $182—the highest such figure of the four regularly scheduled ships which cruise to the tiny island nation each week.

In 1992 over 5.5 million people worldwide took a cruise, packaged and sold by cruise lines through tour operators and travel agents or cruise consultants. The greatest number of passengers were Americans, followed by Germans and British. Most cruising is undertaken from North American ports. While four times as many Americans still prefer to visit Europe on vacation than opt for a cruise, the latter is clearly emerging as the ultimate value-for-money escape.

The most recent (1992) breakdown of passengers by nationality aboard cruise ships is as follows:

| | |
|---|---|
| United States | 4,250,000 |
| U.K. | 275,000 |
| Germany | 190,000 |
| Canada | 175,000 |
| Rest of Europe | 175,000 |
| France | 125,000 |
| Australia | 100,000 |
| Far East | 100,000 |
| Italy | 100,000 |
| Japan | 20,000 |
| **Total** | **5,510,000** |

In terms of popularity, the Caribbean (including the Bahamas and Bermuda) is still at the forefront of warm-weather cruising, followed closely by the Aegean and Mediterranean (both of which offer not only sunshine but also historical, cultural and archaeological interest). There is also a proliferation of short cruises from Florida and California—excellent for a short break and for introducing people to the idea of a longer cruise. Today, as more and more ships are built, it is likely that some will have to move out of the Caribbean and develop new ports of call or home bases. This promises to make a wider range of cruises available to cruisegoers everywhere.

Cruising has come of age. No longer the domain of affluent, retired persons, the industry today is vibrant and alive with passengers of every age and socioeconomic background.

## Constructing a Modern Cruise Ship

More than any other type of vessel, a cruise ship has to fulfill fantasies and satisfy exotic imaginations. It is the job of the shipyard to take those fantasies and turn them into a steel ship—without unduly straining the laws of naval architecture and safety regulations, not to mention budgets.

While no perfect cruise ship exists, turning owners' dreams and concepts into ships is the job of specialized marine architects and shipyards, together with consultants, interior designers, and a mass of specialist suppliers. The job has been made simpler with today's extensive use of computers. It is a complex process that, thank goodness, seems to be mostly successful, although shipboard management and operations personnel often become frustrated with shoreside designers who are more idealist than they are practical.

Ships used to be constructed in huge building docks by putting them together from the keel (backbone) up. Today's ships are built in huge sections and then joined together in an assembly area—as many as 45 sections for one of the current mega-ships. The sections may not even be constructed in the shipyard, but they will be assembled there.

Cost is certainly a predominant factor in ship design and size. The larger the ship, the more cabins can be incorporated, hence the greater the potential in earnings, both in bookings and on-board revenue. A 2 per cent increase in cabin capacity on a 1,400-passenger ship could mean an increase of \$1–\$1.5 million in annual income. Yet adding more facilities and cabins adds up to an increase in weight and cost.

Every ship today represents a compromise between ideals and restrictions of space and finance, and the solution, according to some experts, is to design ships for specific conditions of service. That means tailor-making a ship to fit an operating niche and cruise area, rather than for general use.

So, where to build? Shipyards that can offer state subsidies, such as the Italian yards, where subsidies of 28 per cent are available to a member of the European Union (EU), are of course attractive to shipowners and their bankers.

Traditionally, passenger spaces have been slotted in wherever there was space within a given hull. Today, however, computers provide the possibility of highly targeted ship design.

Computer-aided design (CAD) was first applied to a ship's interior by John McNeece of London, on the *Horizon/ Zenith* projects for Celebrity Cruises. His own CAD system was interlinked with that of Meyer Werft, the shipyard in Papenburg, Germany, that constructed the new sister ships (delivered in 1990 and 1992 respectively).

Maximum acceptable noise and vibration levels in the accommodations spaces and recreational areas are stipulated in an owner's contract with the shipyard. Global vibration tests are carried out once the ship is built and launched, using what is termed a finite method element of evaluation, which embraces analyses of prime sources of noise and excitation: the ship's propellers and main engines.

In the outfitting of a large cruise ship today, prefabricated cabin modules, including *in situ* bathrooms with toilets, are used. When the steel structure of the relevant deck is ready, with main lines and insulation already installed, a cabin module is then affixed to the deck, and power lines and sanitary plumbing are swiftly connected. All waste and power connections, along with hot/cold water mixing valves, are arranged in the service area of the bathroom, and can often be reached from outside the cabin module from the passenger hallway.

While accommodations modules in ships can be successfully systemized, the public spaces cannot. Areas such as food preparation galleys and pantries can, however, be supplied on a turnkey basis by outside contractors. They install these highly specialized areas during the fitting out period. Electrical wiring is another area normally subcontracted today. In the building of the ss *France* (now called the *Norway*; see p.17), for example, some 18,000 miles of electrical cabling had to be installed.

Numerous contractors and subcontractors are involved during the fitting out period of one of today's cruise vessels, the whole being a massive effort of coordination and timing. If just one or two contractors or subcontractors are late, it can put the entire shipbuilding and delivery process behind, causing as many problems as, say, a fire or strike.

## Cruising Tomorrow

The Maritime Evaluations Group (MEG) reports that less than 10 per cent of any national population has discovered cruising, but more ships are being constructed every year because of the expected increase in popularity. This has led to an overcapacity of (or rather, less demand for) berths in certain cruising areas, which has kept prices modest and extremely competitive for passengers (in 1994 several cruise lines offered 2 for 1 discounts). Since 85 per cent of people who take cruises are eager to go again, the overcapacity should decline as the margin increases.

The average age of all cruisegoers is decreasing, with almost 40 per cent of new passengers under the age of 35. Clearly, this has meant a revamping of on-board facilities and activities for many ships, the provision of more and better health and fitness facilities and programs, and a higher, more international standard of entertainment.

There is a definite trend toward "specialty" cruising, on smaller ships which are equipped to cater to young, active passengers pursuing their hobbies or special interests, such as watersports. Cruise areas are developing for the islands of the South Pacific, the Far East, South America, and East and West Africa.

As for ship design, current thinking in the industry follows two distinct avenues, both based on the "economy of scale" and market forces. The economy of scale helps the operator to keep down the cost per passenger. This is the reason for the move toward either large ships that can carry 2,000 passengers or more (*Ecstasy, Fantasy, Imagination, Majesty of the Seas, Monarch of the Seas* and *Sensation*, for example), or smaller luxury vessels that accommodate no more than 250 passengers.

This presumes that some passengers will think "bigger is better," while others will "think small." Somehow, mid-sized ships are difficult to make a profit on in an economically variable climate; ships that have been delivered during the past few years are either large-capacity mega-ships or small-capacity yacht-like vessels, with only a sprinkling of mid-sized ships.

Although mega-ships that can carry 5,000 passengers (or more) have been on the drawing board for some time, no purchase orders have been written yet.

One such giant ship under consideration (which has been in the planning stage for several years) is the *Phoenix World City* project. This is a 250,000-grt vessel that will be 1,246 feet long, with a beam of 252.6 feet and a draft of 32.8 feet. There will be accommodations for 5,600 passengers in some 2,800 cabins located in three huge, eight-deck-high tower blocks atop a monohull, split at the stern by huge portals which open on to a large marina within the hull. This will house four 400-passenger, high-speed tenders that can be deployed to and from ports and a wide variety of destinations within a 50-mile radius of the mother vessel.

The *Phoenix World City* does indeed promise to be the ultimate conference vessel. Other features include 13 swimming pools, 92,000 sq. ft. of convention and meeting space, a 2,500-seat theater, 14 international restaurants, twenty 400-passenger lifeboats, and 1,800 single staff cabins. It will take an estimated 15 million work-hours to build, in an American shipyard, and will operate under the American flag, which means that the vessel could be of use in times of national need. The ship has been designed to convert easily into a 9,000-bed hospital ship, with nine times the capacity of the U.S. Navy's newest ships, including 57,000 sq. ft. of treatment and operating facilities, plus space to drive on 124 ambulances. The ship has the capacity to carry 24,000 troops (equal to an entire division, plus a brigade), and it can also serve as a movable rest and relaxation facility.

There are, of course, practical limitations to such giant ships, however, such as draft restrictions and the viability of attracting the numbers needed to fill the accommodations. Large ships can offer more facilities than small ships, but can't get into many ports; and a metropolis at sea, while it might be good for huge conventions and meetings, poses a challenge for the individual cruise passenger who simply wants a quiet, restful vacation.

The "small is beautiful" concept, on the other hand, has now gained a strong foothold, particularly in the luxury category. New specialist lines offer very high quality ships of low capacity. A small-draft vessel can enter ports larger ships can't even approach, and it can provide a highly personalized range of quality services. However, small ships aren't as stable in bad weather, which is why they tend to follow itineraries close to shore.

Some lines have expanded by "stretching" their ships. This is accomplished by taking a ship into dry dock, literally cutting it in half, and inserting a newly constructed midsection. This gives the vessel an instant increase in capacity, more accommodations space and enlarged public room facilities, with the bonus of maintaining the same draft.

Besides the traditional monohull construction of all but one cruise vessel to date, a switch to multihull and "swath" (small water area twin hull) vessels could well dominate the small- to medium-size designs of the late 1990s. Multihull vessels provide a sound, wide base on which a platform can be constructed, with both accommodations and public areas lying well above the water line. The *Radisson Diamond* is one such example of this new type of vessel.

Whatever direction the design of cruise vessels takes in the future, ships, together with the companies that operate them, will have to become increasingly environmentally friendly, and passengers will need to be taught to behave accordingly. With growing concern about the environment, particularly in eco-sensitive areas such as Alaska and the South Pacific, better safeguards against environmental pollution must be built into the vessels themselves.

## Safety

Safeguards for cruise passengers include lifeboats and life rafts. Since the introduction of the 1983 amendments to Chapter III of the *Safety of Life at Sea* (SOLAS) *Convention 1974* (which actually came into effect in 1980), much attention has been given to safety, particularly to ships' lifeboats, their design and effectiveness. All cruise ships built since July 1, 1986 have either totally enclosed or partially enclosed lifeboats. The totally enclosed lifeboats have diesel engines that will still operate when inverted.

The latest life rafts, called Hydrostatic Release Units (HRU), were designed in Britain and approved by the Royal Navy, and are now compulsory on all British-registered ships. Briefly, an HRU is capable of automatically releasing a life raft from its mountings when a ship sinks (even *after* it sinks), but can also be operated manually at the installation point, saving precious time in an emergency.

The 1990 SOLAS standards on stability and fire protection (mandating the installation of sprinkler systems) for new ship construction are taking effect in 1994. Existing ships have another five years to comply (the retro-fitting of sprinkler systems is an expensive measure that may not be considered viable by owners of older ships).

A lifeboat drill must be conducted on board within 24 hours of leaving port. You will hear an announcement from the bridge, which goes something like this:

"Ladies and Gentlemen, may I have your attention, please. This is the captain speaking to you from the bridge. In fifteen minutes time, the ship's alarm bells will signal emergency lifeboat drill for all passengers. This is a mandatory drill, conducted in accordance with the requirements of the *Safety of Life at Sea Convention*. There are no exceptions.

"The emergency signal is a succession of seven or more short blasts followed by one long blast of the ship's whistle, supplemented by the ringing of the electric gongs throughout the ship. On hearing this signal, you should make your way quickly but quietly to your cabin, put on some warm clothing and your lifejacket, then follow the signs to your emergency boat station, where you will be kept fully informed over the loudspeakers through which I am speaking to you now."

# Choosing Your Ship and Cruise

So, you've decided your next vacation will be a cruise. Good choice! But the decisions don't stop there. Bombarded with glossy cruise literature tempting you with every imaginable lure, and the overly prolific use of the word "luxury," you may find choosing the right cruise for you difficult.

Despite company claims that theirs has been named "Best Cruise Line" or "Best Cruise Ship," there is *no* best cruise line or best cruise ship, only what's best, and *right*, for you.

## What a Cruise Is

A cruise is a vacation, a complete change of scenery, environment and people. It is an antidote to the stresses and strains of contemporary life ashore. It offers you a chance to relax and unwind in comfortable surroundings, with attentive service, good food, and a ship that changes the scenery for you as you go—and you don't even have to drive. It is virtually a hassle-free, and, more importantly, a crime-free vacation.

## What a Cruise Is Not

Some cruises simply aren't relaxing, despite cruise brochures proclaiming "that you can do as much or as little as you want to." Watch out for high density ships—mega-ships that carry 2,000 or more passengers—or older ships with limited public room space; they tend to cram lots of passengers into small cabins and provide non-stop activities that do little but insult the intelligence and taste buds, and assault the pocket.

How do you begin to select the right cruise for the right price? Price is, of course, the key word for most people. The cost of a cruise provides a good guideline to the type of ambiance, passengers and degree of luxury, food and service you'll find on board.

The amount you are prepared to spend will be a determining factor in the size, location and style of your shipboard accommodations. You should be wary of cruise lines that seem to offer huge discounts, for it either means that the product was unrealistically priced at source, or that there will be a reduction in quality somewhere. Remember, discount the price, and you end up with discounted quality. Aside from cost, ships are as individual as fingerprints: no two are the same and each can change its "personality" from cruise to cruise, depending on the make-up of passengers.

## Where To?

With approximately 500 destinations available to cruise ships, it's almost certain that there's a ship to take you wherever you want to go. Because itineraries vary widely, depending on each ship and cruise, it is wise to make as many comparisons as possible by reading the cruise brochures and their descriptions of ports visited. If, for example, you would like a Caribbean or Mediterranean cruise, you can choose from over 100 itineraries.

Several ships may offer the same, or similar itineraries, simply because these have been successfully tried and tested. You can then narrow the choice further by noting the time spent at each port, and whether the ship actually docks in port or lies at anchor. Then compare the size of each vessel and its facilities.

## Caribbean and Mediterranean Cruises

If you want to cruise around the Caribbean or Mediterranean, what you'll notice when choosing your cruise is the trend and marketing strategy of some companies to offer more ports in a week than their competitors. Indeed, there are several ships that feature seven or more ports in a week, which works out to at least one port a day on some of the Greek Isle cruises.

Such intensive "island hopping" leaves little time to explore a destination to the full before you have to be back on board for a quick ride to the next port. While you see a lot in a week, by the end of the cruise you may need another week to unwind. Ultimately, this is not the best way to cruise, unless you wish to cover a lot of ground in a short space of time.

Several cruise lines that offer Caribbean cruises have their own "private" island—a small island in the Bahamas close to Nassau that is outfitted with all the ingredients to make an all-day beach party a memorable occasion. Cruise lines have their own inventive names for these islands, such as Blue Lagoon Island (Dolphin Cruise Line), Princess Cays (Princess Cruises), Royal Isle (Majesty Cruise Line). Some out-islands sometimes change names, depending on what day of the week it is, and what ship is in.

## European Cruises

If you're thinking about going to Europe (including the Baltic and Mediterranean areas), then go by cruise ship. Many of Europe's grandest cities—Amsterdam, Barcelona, Copenhagen, Genoa, Helsinki, Lisbon, London, Monte Carlo, Nice, Oslo, St. Petersburg, Stockholm and Venice—are on the water, and it is much less expensive to take a cruise than to fly and pay enormous rates to stay in decent hotels. Another advantage is that you won't have to contend with different languages aboard ship as you would ashore.

You should be aware that small- or medium-sized ships are better than large ships, as they will be able to get berthing space (large ships may have to anchor). On some itineraries, one company may give you more time ashore than another, so it pays to compare cruise brochures.

## Alaska Cruises

For Alaska cruises, be advised that the ships of several lines, such as Regency Cruises and Holland America Line, anchor in most ports of call, whereas other lines such as Cunard and Princess Cruises may pay more in fees so that their ships can dock alongside, making it easier for passengers to go ashore; this is particularly useful in inclement weather.

Unfortunately, cruise brochures don't indicate which ports are known to be anchor (tender) ports.

Holland America Line and Princess Cruises both have such comprehensive shoreside facilities—hotels, tour buses, and even trains—that they will be committed to Alaska for many years. Other lines have to use what's left of competing local transportation for shoreside tours.

### Transcanal Cruises

Transcanal cruises will take you through the wonders of the Panama Canal, which was started in 1880 by Ferdinand de Lesseps (who also built the Suez Canal in 1860-69) and finally opened in 1914. The canal traverses from north to south (not east to west as many believe), and the best way to experience this feat of engineering is from the privileged position of a cruise ship. Cruising from the Caribbean to the Pacific, your ship will be lifted almost 80 feet by three locks (at Gatun), negotiate the narrow Gaillard Cut, a series of six reaches cut through a range of green hills, and then be lowered again by two more locks (at Miraflores), just by the forces of nature. Mechanical "mules" are attached and pull your ship through the locks. Most ships start in Fort Lauderdale or San Juan and end in Acapulco or Los Angeles, and vice versa.

### Australasia and Orient Cruises

If you like the idea of Australasia, South East Asia and the Orient, and you live in Europe or North America, be aware that the flying time to your ship will be long. It is advisable to arrive at least two days before the cruise, as the time changes and jet lag can be quite severe to those not used to long distances. The whole area has so much to offer, however, that it's worth taking a cruise of a minimum of 14 days in order to make the most of it.

Choose an itinerary that appeals to you, and then read about the proposed destinations and their attractions. The public library or your local bookstore are good information sources, and your cruise or travel agent will also be able to provide background on destinations and help you select an itinerary.

## How Long?

On many cruises, the standard of luxury is generally in direct proportion to the length of the cruise. Naturally, in order to operate long, low-density voyages, cruise lines must charge high rates to cover the extensive preparations, high food and transportation costs, port operations, fuel and other expenditures. The length of cruise you choose will depend on the time and money at your disposal and the degree of comfort sought.

The popular standard length of cruise is seven nights, although trips vary from a one-day gambling jamboree to an exotic voyage around the world lasting over 120 nights. If you are new to cruising and want to "get your feet wet," you might try a short cruise of three or four nights first. This will give you a good idea of what is involved, the kind of facilities and the lifestyle on board. While a three- or four-night cruise from a Japanese port should be quite relaxing, be warned that a three- or four-night cruise from an American port such as Miami, Ft. Lauderdale or Los Angeles, or from the Greek port of Piraeus, could end up as more of an endurance test. It's fine if you like non-stop activities, noise and razzle-dazzle stimulation, but hardly the thing if all you want is to relax.

Although in the past three- and four-night cruises have often been on the older, less elegant ships, spectacular new ships, such as Majesty Cruise Line's *Royal Majesty*, Norwegian Cruise Line's *Seaward* and Royal Caribbean Cruises' *Nordic Empress*, are now in the Miami-to-Bahamas marketplace, while Carnival Cruise Lines' *Fantasy* cruises to the Bahamas from Port Canaveral. Then there are the three- and four-night cruises featured by Premier Cruise Lines, particularly for families and children, where out-island beaches provide an attraction.

## Which Ship?

There really is a cruise line, cruise and ship to suit virtually everyone, so it is important to take into account your own personality when selecting a ship.

Ships are measured (not weighed) in gross registered tons (grt) and come in a variety of sizes, from intimate (up to 10,000 grt), small (10,000–20,000 grt), medium (20,000–30,000 grt) to large (30,000–60,000 grt), and mega-ship size (60,000–77,000 grt). But whatever the dimensions, all ships offer the same basic ingredients: accommodations, food, activities, entertainment, good service, and ports of call, although some do it better than others.

## Ship Size Comparisons

### Ships under 10,000 grt

Andaman Princess
Antonina Nezhdanova
Argonaut
Astra
Aurora I
Aurora II
Ayvasovskiy
Berlin
Bremen
Caledonian Star
City of Rhodos
Columbus Caravelle
Daphne
Explorer
Funchal
Hanseatic
Hebridean Princess
Jason
Klaudia Yelanskaya
Konstantin Simonov
Kristina Regina
Mikhail Sholokhov
Nantucket Clipper
Neptune
Oceanic Grace
Orient Star
Orpheus
Polaris
Princesa Amorosa
Princesa Cypria
Princesa Marissa
Regent Jewel
Renaissance One
Renaissance Two
Renaissance Three
Renaissance Four
Renaissance Five
Renaissance Six

Renaissance Seven
Renaissance Eight
Romantica
Royal Star
Royal Viking Queen
Sea Goddess I
Sea Goddess II
Seabourn Pride
Seabourn Spirit
SeaSpirit
Song of Flower
Stella Maris
Stella Oceanis
Vistamar
Yorktown Clipper
World Discoverer
Le Ponant
Sea Cloud
Sir Francis Drake
Star Clipper
Star Flyer
Wind Song
Wind Spirit
Wind Star

## Ships of 10,000–20,000 grt

Aegean Dolphin
Americana
Amerikanis
Arkona
Atalante
Ausonia
Azerbaydzhan
Black Prince
Club Med I
Club Med II
Crown Dynasty
Crown Jewel
Crown Monarch
Cunard Countess
Cunard Princess
Dimitri Shostakovich
Dolphin IV
EnricoCosta
Gruziya
Ilich
Illiria
Island Princess
Italia Prima
Kareliya
Kazakhstan
Kazakhstan II
La Palma
Leisure World
Lev Tolstoi
Mermoz
Odessa
Odysseus
Pearl
Princesa Victoria
Radisson Diamond
Regent Spirit
Silver Cloud
Silver Wind
Song of Norway
Southward
Star/Ship Majestic
Starward
Stella Solaris
Sun Viking
The Azur
Triton
Universe
World Renaissance

## Ships of 20,000–30,000 grt

Achille Lauro
Albatros
Asuka
CostaAllegra
CostaMarina
Enchanted Seas

Fair Princess
Fairstar
Fedor Dostoyevsky
Fedor Shalyapin
FiestaMarina
Fuji Maru
Golden Princess
Ivan Franko
Kapitan Khlebnikov
Leonid Sobinov
Marco Polo
Maxim Gorki
Monterey
Nippon Maru
Nordic Prince
OceanBreeze
Orient Venus
Pacific Princess
Regal Empress
Regent Rainbow
Regent Sea
Regent Star
Regent Sun
Royal Odyssey
Sagafjord
Sea Princess
SeaBreeze I
Seawind Crown
Shota Rustaveli
Sovetskiy Soyuz
Star Odyssey Taras Shevchenko
Vistafjord
Yamal

Crown Odyssey
Crystal Harmony
Crystal Symphony
Dreamward
EugenioCosta
Europa
Festivale
Holiday
Horizon
Independence
Jubilee
Langkapuri Star Aquarius
Maasdam
Meridian
Nieuw Amsterdam
Noordam
Nordic Empress
Rotterdam
Royal Majesty
Royal Princess
Royal Viking Sun
Ryndam
Seaward
Sky Princess
Song of America
Star/Ship Atlantic
Star/Ship Oceanic
Statendam
Tropicale
Viking Serenade
Westerdam
Windward
Zenith

## Ships of 30,000–60,000 grt

American Adventure
Canberra
Celebration
Constitution
CostaClassica
CostaRomantica

## Ships over 60,000 grt

Century
Crown Princess
Ecstasy
Fantasy
Fascination
Imagination

Legend of the Seas
Majesty of the Seas
Monarch of the Seas
Norway
Oriana
Queen Elizabeth 2
Regal Princess
Sensation
Sovereign of the Seas
Star Princess
Sun Princess

There are some "all-inclusive" ships where there really are no bar bills to pay, nothing to sign for, no gratuities to give, and no standing in line to sign up for shore excursions, but these are usually the small "luxury" cruise ships that cost upwards of $500 per person, per day (although suites on larger "standard" market cruise ships can easily cost that). Once you're on board, you may never have to say "how much?" Most of the larger cruise ships, however, will entice you to spend money on board, which is one way that cruise lines manage to support those low fares.

If you like or need a lot of space around you, it is of little use booking a cruise on a small, intimate ship where you knock elbows almost every time you move. If you like intimacy, close contact with people and a homey ambiance, you may feel lost and lonely on a large ship, which inevitably will have a more impersonal atmosphere. If you are a novice in the world of cruises, choose a ship in the small or medium-size range. For an idea of the amount of space you'll have around you, look closely at the Passenger Space Ratio given in the evaluation of each ship in Part Two of this book. A Passenger Space Ratio of 40 and above is the ultimate in terms of space per passenger; 30 and above can be considered extremely spacious; between 20 and 30, moderately so; between 10 and 20 would be high density; and below 10, extremely cramped, as in "sardine-style."

A ship's country of registry or parent company location can be a clue to the atmosphere on board, although there are many ships that are registered, for financial reasons, under a flag of convenience, such as Liberia or Panama. The nationality of the officers or management often sets the style and ambiance.

You can estimate the standard of service by looking at the crew to passenger ratio. Better service will be found on ships that have a ratio of one crew member to every two passengers, or higher.

Except for those ships with a single-nationality crew (such as the Greek Epirotiki Lines and Sun Line Cruises or German-speaking Hapag-Lloyd Cruises), the crew mixture can be like a miniature United Nations. On a ship with a multi-nationality crew, you can expect something like the following: 38% European, 36% North/South American, and 26% Asian (Celebrity Cruises).

If the crew is a happy one, the ship will be happy too, and passengers will certainly be able to sense it. The best way for any cruise ship to have a happy crew is for the cruise line to provide good accommodations, food and relaxation facilities for them. The finest ship in the world, from the point of view of crew living and working conditions, is the *Europa* (Hapag-Lloyd Cruises), followed closely by the *Crystal Harmony* (Crystal Cruises), *Asuka* (NYK Cruises), *Royal Viking Queen* and *Royal Viking Sun* (Royal Viking Line), and *Seabourn Pride/Seabourn Spirit* (Seabourn Cruise Line). At present, few other ships come close. Indeed, both Hapag-Lloyd Cruises and Crystal Cruises even have pension plans for their crew members.

## New vs Old Ships

Some executives in the cruise industry, whose fleets comprise new tonnage, are often quoted as saying that all pre-1960 tonnage should be scrapped. Yet there are many passengers who like the older-style ships. While it is inevitable that some older tonnage cannot match up to the latest in high-tech section-built ships, it should also be noted that ships today are simply not constructed to the same high standards, or with the same loving care, as in the past. Below are some advantages and disadvantages to both.

### New Ships—Advantages:

- They meet the latest safety and operating standards, as laid down by international maritime conventions.
- They offer more public room space, with public rooms and lounges built out to the sides of the hull, as open and closed promenade decks are no longer an essential requirement.
- They have public room spaces that are easier to convert if necessary.
- They offer more standardized cabin layouts and fewer categories.
- They are more fuel efficient.
- They incorporate the latest advances in technology, as well as in passenger and crew facilities and amenities.
- They have a shallower draft, making it easier to enter and leave ports.
- They have bow and stern thrusters, so seldom require tug assistance in many ports, thus cutting operating costs.
- The plumbing and air-conditioning systems are new—and work.
- They have diesel engines mounted on rubber to minimize vibration.
- They are usually fitted with the latest submersible lifeboats.

### New Ships—Disadvantages:

- They do not "take the weather" as well as older ships (sailing on a new mega-ship across the North Atlantic in November can be unforgettable). Due to their shallow draft, they roll—even at the slightest puff of wind.
- They have smaller standard cabins, with narrow—and often short—beds.
- They have thin hulls and do not withstand the bangs and dents as well as older, more heavily plated vessels.
- They have decor made mostly from synthetic materials (due to stringent fire regulations), and therefore could cause problems for passengers who are sensitive to such materials.
- They are powered by diesel engines, which inevitably cause some vibration; although on the latest vessels, the engines are mounted on pliable, floating rubber cushions and are virtually vibration-free.
- They have cabin windows that are completely sealed instead of portholes.

### Older Ships (pre-1970)—Advantages:

- They have strong, plated hulls (often riveted) that can withstand tremendous wear and tear. They can "take the weather" well.
- They have large cabins with long, wide beds/berths, due to the fact that passengers of yesteryear needed more space, as voyages were much longer.
- They have a wide range of cabin sizes, configurations and grades which are more suited to families with children.
- They are powered by steam turbines, which have virtually no vibration or noise and are considerably quieter and smoother in operation.
- They have portholes that, in many instances, actually open.
- Their interiors are built from more traditional materials such as wood and brass, with less use of synthetic fibers (and are therefore better for anyone who is allergic to synthetics).

### Older Ships (pre-1970)—Disadvantages:

- They are less fuel efficient, and therefore are more expensive to operate.
- They need a larger crew, due to more awkward labor-intensive layouts.
- They have a deep draft (necessary for a smooth ride), but need tugs to negotiate ports and tight berths.
- They have increasing difficulty in complying with today's international fire, safety and environmental regulations.
- They are usually fitted with older-type open lifeboats.
- Any ship 10 years old or more is likely to have plumbing and air-conditioning problems in cabins and public areas.

The International Maritime Organization (IMO), which is a United Nations agency, was formed in the late 1940s to pass legislation among its 130-plus member nations regulating the safety of life at sea. The IMO Safety Committee has voted to bring older ships up to date by making various safety features—including smoke detectors—mandatory in all cruise vessels. Starting in 1994, and covering an 11-year period, all vessels will be required to fit sprinkler systems (an expensive retrofit for many older ships).

## Maiden/Inaugural Voyages

There's something exciting about taking the plunge on a maiden voyage of a new cruise ship, or an inaugural voyage on a refurbished, reconstructed, or stretched vessel, or in a new cruising area. But although it can be exciting, there is usually an element or two of uncertainty in any first voyage, as with, for example, Orient Lines' *Marco Polo*, whose maiden voyage was postponed until its programed second voyage, due to the ship being unfinished. Things can, and invariably do, go awry. Some maiden voyages are faced with no major problems, of course, but, on most, Murphy's Law prevails: "if anything can go wrong, it will."

If you are a repeat cruiser who can be flexible, and don't mind some inconvenience, or perhaps slow or non-existent service in the dining room, fine; otherwise, it is best to wait until the ship has been in service for at least two or three months. Then again, if you book a cruise on the third or fourth voyage, and there is a delay in the ship's introduction, you could find yourself on the maiden voyage! One thing is certain—any maiden voyage is a collector's item. Bon Voyage!

So, what exactly can go wrong?

- A strike, or fire, or even a bankruptcy at a shipyard can delay a new ship or a completely new cruise line about to embark on its first venture. Ship introductions such as *Club Med I*, *Crown Monarch*, *Crown Dynasty*, *Ecstasy*, *Fantasy*, *Marco Polo*, *Nieuw Amsterdam* and the eight small Renaissance vessels were all delayed by shipyard strikes and bankruptcies, while the *Astor* (which is now called *Arkona*), *Crown Dynasty* and *Monarch of the Seas* were delayed as a result of extensive fires while still being fitted out.
- Service on new or recently refurbished ships or a new cruise line is likely to be unsure at best, and could be a complete disaster. An existing cruise line may well use experienced crew from its other vessels to help "bring out" a new ship, but they may be unfamiliar with the ship's layout and have problems training other staff.
- Plumbing and electrical items tend to cause the most problems, particularly on reconstructed and refurbished vessels. For example: toilets that don't flush, or don't stop flushing; faucets incorrectly marked, where "hot" really means "cold" and vice versa; room thermostats fitted with reverse wiring; televisions, audio channels, lights and electronic card key locks that don't work; electrical outlets incorrectly indicated; "automatic" telephones that simply refuse to function; and so on.
- The galley (kitchen) of any new ship causes maybe the most consternation. Even if everything does work, and the Executive Chef has ordered all the right ingredients and supplies, they could be anywhere apart from where they should be. Imagine if they forgot to load the seasoning, or if the eggs arrived shell-shocked!
- "Software" items such as menus, postcards, writing paper, or remote control units for television and/or video systems, door keys, towels, pillowcases, glassware, and even toilet paper may be missing—lost in the bowels of the ship, or simply not ordered.
- In the Entertainment Department, something like spare spotlight bulbs may not be in stock, or there may be no hooks on which to hang the costumes backstage—if such an area is provided, for many ships don't even have dressing rooms. Or what if the pianos arrived damaged, or the charts for the lectures didn't show up? If the ship was supplied with German sound and light equipment, the operating manuals might be in German, so what does the American stage technician do? In the Entertainment Department, many things can go wrong.

The Pick-a-Ship chart at the beginning of Part Two will help you not only to compare the differences between the ships and lines, but will also indicate the ambiance and type of passengers you can expect to find aboard, and the level of quality and "luxury."

At the real luxury end of the market, where the best in luxury and personal service corresponds to a per day cost of over $500 per person, the choice is either of large ships, which, because of their size, have more facilities and entertainment for passengers, or small ships, which can feature a much greater degree of personal service.

## Large Luxury Ships vs Small Luxury Ships

Large ships (measuring over 30,000 grt) have the widest range of public rooms and facilities—but no large ship has yet been constructed with a watersports platform/marina at its stern. The very finest in personal butler service is featured in the top penthouse suites on ships such as *Crystal Harmony*, *Queen Elizabeth 2*, and *Royal Viking Sun*.

Small (country club) ships (measuring under 10,000 grt) may lack space and some of the facilities that larger ships offer, but they usually have a hydraulic marina watersports platform in the stern. They also carry equipment such as jet skis, windsurfers, a waterski power boat, scuba and snorkeling gear, and, in the case of two particular ships, a swimming enclosure for use in areas where waters may be unsafe. Small ships can also truly cater to the highest degree of culinary excellence. On *Sea Goddess I* and *Sea Goddess II*, those seeking the ultimate in decadence can revel in Beluga caviar, champagne and fine wines whenever they want—and all at no extra cost.

## Theme Cruises

If you still think that all cruises are the same, the following list will give you an idea of special theme cruises available:

| | |
|---|---|
| Adventure | Exploration |
| Archaeological | Fashion |
| Art Lovers | Food & Wine |
| Backgammon | Holistic Health |
| Big Band Bridge | Jazz Festival |
| Chess Tournament | Maiden Voyage |
| Chocoholics | Movie Buffs |
| Classical Music | Murder Mystery |
| Computer Science | Naturalist |
| Cosmetology | Photographic |
| Country & Western | Singles |
| Diet & Nutrition | Square Dancing |
| Educational | Theatrical |

Perhaps the most successful theme cruise is the annual Classical Music Cruise aboard the *Mermoz* (Paquet French Cruises), which is organized by Andre Borocz, himself an accomplished musician. Famous musicians who have played (or sung) on the cruise include Annie Fisher, Isaac Stern, James Galway, Jean-Pierre Rampal, Mystislav Rostropovich, Schlomo Mintz, Tamas Vasary, Maurice Andre and Vladimir Ashkenazy. Shore excursions consist of concerts in some of the world's most beautiful settings.

For Jazz enthusiasts, the most comprehensive cruise is the Annual Floating Jazz Festival in October each year aboard the *Norway* (Norwegian Cruise Lines), in which artistes such as Clark Terry, Joe Williams, Jimmy McGriff, Lee Konitz, Lou Donaldson, Jimmy Giuffre and Dick Hyman can be found.

# Comparing the Small Luxury Cruise Ships

Almost every ship owner wants to be a "luxury" cruise operator, and most passengers want to sail on one of the top-rated "luxury" ships. Not everyone can, however, and few operators can really deliver a five-stars-plus product. It is therefore refreshing to find that there *are* ships to cater for more discerning travelers, who want only the finest quality.

These are the 15 "boutique" cruise ships. They are more specialized, the latest breed of small luxury vessels—under 10,000 grt, carrying less than 250 passengers in great comfort, and providing an unstructured lifestyle which caters to the needs of each individual. They offer a level of luxury and service not found on most larger ships, and which is better than many five-star hotels on land.

## Comparing the Ships
(in company alphabetical order)

### Cunard Sea Goddess Cruises

*Sea Goddess I*/*Sea Goddess II* (4,260-grt; 116 passengers; PSR: 36.7)

These two ships started the ball rolling in the early eighties, by featuring "yacht-harbor" destinations that were not accessible to larger cruise ships. Each of the ships offers a setting of fine luxury and a standard of culinary excellence and creativity unmatched by any other ship. The atmosphere is that of an exclusive country club, with all drinks included. The highly personal service is practiced as an art form, and nearly all staff remember passengers' names—no mean achievement, but one that is most appreciated.

### Renaissance Cruises

*Renaissance 1/2/3/4* (3,990-grt; 100 passengers; PSR: 39.9)
*Renaissance 5/6/7/8* (4,280-grt; 114 passengers; PSR: 37.5)

These eight ships offer in-depth, destination-intensive cruises. Itineraries are planned to avoid crossing large stretches of open ocean, where the ship size and hull configuration would be vulnerable to poor weather. The company frequently charters ships to tour operators and alumni groups, so it could be that only four are operating regularly scheduled cruises at any one time. Check with your travel agent or cruise line to see which ships are operating on which itinerary.

### Royal Viking Line

*Royal Viking Queen* (9,975-grt; 212 passengers; PSR: 47.0)

The smaller of two ships in the Royal Viking Line fleet, almost identical in size and features to the two Seabourn ships (see below), with which it vies for exclusivity. The *Royal Viking Queen* places more emphasis on entertainment, however, giving passengers a scaled-down big-ship feeling while taking them in luxury—with the latest high-tech features—to well-programed destinations.

### Seabourn Cruise Line

*Seabourn Pride* (9,975-grt; 204 passengers; PSR: 48.8)
*Seabourn Spirit* (9,975-grt; 204 passengers; PSR: 48.8)

These two ships, dating from later in the eighties, carried the *Royal Viking Queen* theme further: they are larger ships, with more facilities and some entertainment, but no drinks included (the company believes that passengers who don't drink needn't subsidize those who do). Comparatively, for the number of days and identical or similar itineraries, fares can be higher than those on *Sea Goddess* cruises. Seabourn Cruise Line, however, has achieved an impressive level of panache, notably with fine food, but the level of personal service is slightly lower.

### Seven Seas Cruise Line

*Song of Flower* (8,282-grt; 214 passengers; PSR: 38.7)

Seven Seas Cruise Line's only ship features destination-intensive cruises in relatively luxurious surroundings, with a wonderful level of service. The staff—many have been with the ship since her maiden voyage—learn passengers' names and favorite drinks. The cabins are not as luxurious as the Sea Goddesses' or Seabourns' (the price is much lower), but the food displays creative excellence.

### Showa Line

*Oceanic Grace* (5,218-grt; 120 passengers; PSR: 43.4)

Showa Line's only ship features cruises around the coast of Japan—a wonderful, relaxing way to see the country—calling at such places as Abaratsu, Abashiri, Funukawa, Hiroshima, Hofu, Ishigaki Island, Kobe, Kochi, Miyako, Nagasaki, Oki Islands, Rishiri Island, Sendai, Uwajima, Yokohama and Yoron Island amongst many others. Whale-watching cruises around Ogasawara Island are also offered. The majority of the passengers are Japanese.

## Comparable Features

All the above ships have similar facilities and features, including an "open bridge" policy—which means you can visit the bridge at almost any time. They also have almost totally unstructured environments, which means you are not asked to participate in any scheduled activities. Instead, you can have total privacy, should you so wish.

All ships feature outside cabins only (usually called suites by most "upscale" cruise companies, although they really are luxury cabins), and all have two beds, which, when placed together, form a queen-sized bed. Cabin accessories such as fluffy cotton bathrobes, hairdryer, color television and video cassette player (VCRs), and flowers and fruit (replenished daily) are also common to all. On most of these small ships, you can go from your cabin to other parts of the ship (particularly to the health spa and outside decks, but not the restaurant) in your bathrobe. After 6p.m. however, they become more formal.

In cabins on the *Oceanic Grace*, *Renaissance 1-8*, *Royal Viking Queen*, and *Seabourn Pride/Seabourn Spirit*, the lounge area is adjacent to a large picture window. On *Sea Goddess I/Sea Goddess II* the bedroom is adjacent to the window and the lounge area is adjacent to the picture window. Both have cabins with similar appointments, but *Royal Viking Queen* has six suites that are enormous in size and regally equipped.

Bathrooms on *Song of Flower* are smaller—and more difficult to maneuver in—than on the other ships. The "half-tubs" are also more difficult to get into and out of. Bathrooms on *Seabourn Pride/Seabourn Spirit* have two washbasins, while those on *Oceanic Grace*, *Renaissance 1-8*, *Royal Viking Queen*, *Sea Goddess I/Sea Goddess II* and *Song of Flower* have one.

Cabin windows on *Seabourn Pride/Seabourn Spirit* have electrically operated blinds, while those on *Sea Goddess I/Sea Goddess II* and *Royal Viking Queen* are manually operated (pull-down). *Oceanic Grace*, *Renaissance 1-8* and *Song of Flower* have no blinds.

On *Sea Goddess I/Sea Goddess II* and *Song of Flower*, all liquor, champagnes, wines, and soft drinks are included in the cruise fare. On the more expensive *Royal Viking Queen*, only wines, spirits and soft drinks for in-cabin use are included when you first embark. Soft drinks are provided free afterwards, while everything else consumed in public rooms is charged for (at reasonable prices). The *Sea Goddess* aims to deliver an all-inclusive product—which it does—although port taxes and insurance are extra.

Afternoon Tea on *Sea Goddess I/Sea Goddess II* is superior to that on all the other small luxury ships, notably due to the choice of around eight different teas (the others feature only one main type of tea, plus a few herbal teas).

The health spa/sauna/steam room complex is open 24 hours a day on *Sea Goddess I/Sea Goddess II*, and from 6am to 9pm on the *Royal Viking Queen*, and *Seabourn Pride/Seabourn Spirit*.

*Royal Viking Queen* offers entertainment, including full mini-production shows, classical concerts and cabaret acts, while *Seabourn Pride/Seabourn Spirit* and *Song of Flower* offer cabaret only. *Oceanic Grace*, *Renaissance 1-8*, and *Sea Goddess I/Sea Goddess II* offer no such entertainment, but have a small band for dancing.

All the ships have watersports facilities, but only *Royal Viking Queen* and *Seabourn Pride/Seabourn Spirit* have a floating, enclosed aft marina pool, as well as air-conditioned, mahogany shore tenders. The two tenders on *Oceanic Grace* have a shower as well!

In the dining room, tableside flambeaus are featured on all ships apart from *Oceanic Grace*, *Renaissance 1-8* and *Song of Flower*. All ships usually offer full room-service breakfast, even on the day of disembarkation. This is not the case on large ships.

If you are considering a long cruise on one of these smaller vessels, remember that they are like a small village rather than a large town. Any cruise in close quarters for more than 14 days may bring out more "cliques" than on larger ships. If you enjoy being with people, cruising on the smaller ships can be the epitome of fine living at sea.

## Product Comparison Chart (Small Luxury Ships)

| **What's Included** | A) | B) | C) | D) | E) | F) |
|---|---|---|---|---|---|---|
| Leather ticket wallet: | No | Yes | No | Yes | Yes | Yes |
| All beverages: | No | No | No | Yes | No | Yes |
| Wines with dinner: | No | No | No | Yes | No | Yes |
| Shore Excursions:* | No | No | Yes | Yes | No | No |
| Gratuities: | No | Yes | Yes | Yes | Yes | Yes |
| Port Taxes:** | No | No | Yes | No | No | No |
| Insurance: | No | No | No | No | No | No |
| In-cabin dining: | No | Yes | No | Yes | Yes | No |
| Open seating dining: | Yes | Yes | Yes | Yes | Yes | Yes |
| Tableside flambeaus: | No | Yes | No | Yes | Yes | No |
| **Product Comparison** | | | | | | |
| Food quality: | 7 | 9 | 8 | 10 | 10 | 8 |
| Menu choice: | 6 | 10 | 7 | 10 | 10 | 8 |
| Special orders: | 6 | 9 | 6 | 10 | 9 | 8 |
| Food service: | 7 | 10 | 8 | 10 | 10 | 9 |
| Activities: | 6 | 9 | 6 | 5 | 9 | 8 |
| Lecturers: | 3 | 10 | 4 | 6 | 9 | 7 |
| Entertainment: | 5 | 9 | 5 | 6 | 8 | 9 |
| Officers: | 4 | 9 | 8 | 10 | 9 | 8 |
| Tender operation: | 4 | 9 | 7 | 10 | 9 | 8 |
| Watersports: | 6 | 9 | 9 | 10 | 9 | 8 |
| Accommodations: | 7 | 10 | 7 | 9 | 10 | 8 |
| Staff Friendliness: | 6 | 7 | 8 | 10 | 8 | 10 |

### KEY

| | |
|---|---|
| A) *Renaissance 1-8* | D) *Sea Goddess I/Sea Goddess II* |
| B) *Royal Viking Queen* | E) *Seabourn Pride/Seabourn Spirit* |
| C) *Oceanic Grace* | F) *Song of Flower* |

*Sea Goddess I*, *Sea Goddess II*, *Seabourn Pride*, and *Seabourn Spirit* include some shore excursions on selected itineraries. *Sea Goddess II*, for example, includes all shore excursions (except any overnight stays) on all South East Asia cruises, but not on either *Sea Goddess I* or *Sea Goddess II* in Europe.

* Most shore excursions are included, but those in Northern Europe are not.

** Port taxes must, by law, be included in all brochure prices for passengers who are resident in any country of the European Union (EU) which is participating in the new EU Travel Directive.

# Booking Your Cruise

## Travel Agents

Many people think that travel agents charge for their services. They don't, but they do earn commission from cruise lines for booking their clients on a cruise.

Can you do your own booking direct with the cruise line? Yes and no. Yes, you can book your cruise direct with a small number of cruise lines (mostly in Europe/Asia/Japan), and no, because most cruise lines do not generally accept personal checks, thus in effect requiring you to book through a travel agent; in the United States, 95 per cent of cruise bookings are made by travel agents.

A good travel agent will probably ask you to complete a profile questionnaire. When this is done, the agent will go through it with you, perhaps asking some additional questions before making suggestions about the ships and cruises that seem to match your requirements.

Your travel agent will handle all matters relevant to your booking, and off you go. You may even find a nice flower arrangement in your cabin on arrival, or a bottle of wine or champagne for dinner one night, courtesy of the agency.

Consider a travel agent as your business advisor, not merely as a ticket agent. As a business adviser, a travel agent should have the latest information on changes of itinerary, cruise fares, fuel surcharges, discounts, and any other related items, and should also be able to arrange insurance (most important) in case you have to cancel prior to sailing.

Some cruise lines now have a totally automated booking system by computer, much like those used for booking air tickets. The best known is Royal Caribbean Cruises' CruiseMatch 2000 system, which allows agents access to almost all shipboard information, and even displays details such as cabin dimensions and if there is a porthole or window.

## Cruise Consultants

A number of cruise-only agencies—often called "cruise consultants"—have sprung up in the last five years. While most are reputable, some sell only a limited number of cruises. These are "preferred suppliers" because they may be receiving special "overrides" on top of their normal commission. If you have chosen a ship and cruise, be firm and book exactly what you want, or change agencies. In the United States, look for a member of NACOA—the National Association of Cruise Only Agents. In the U.K., look for a member of PSARA—the Passenger Shipping Association of Retail Agents.

Many traditional travel agencies now have a special cruise section, with a knowledgeable consultant in charge. A good agent will help you solve the problem of cabin choice, but be firm in the amount you want to pay, or you may end up with a larger and more costly cabin than you had intended.

In the United States, CLIA (Cruise Lines International Association), a marketing organization with about three dozen member lines, does an admirable job providing training seminars for cruise/travel agents in North America. Agencies approved by CLIA (there are about 25,000) display a blue, white, and gold circular emblem on their door, and can gain one of two levels of certification status for their training. In the U.K., a similar scheme is run by the Passenger Shipping Association, via PSARA. U.K. Passengers should also note that cruise and tour packagers registered under the Passenger Shipping Association's bonding scheme are fully protected in case a cruise line goes into bankruptcy (there is no similar scheme in the United States).

## Cruise Brokers

Cruise brokers are useful for last-minute bookings. They often have unsold cabins at substantially discounted rates. Most brokers have low overheads, using only a phone and automated message services.

If you're looking for full service, then a cruise broker isn't for you; but if you *can* book at the last minute, a cruise broker may save you a substantial amount of money. What you gain in price advantage you may lose in choice—of dinner sittings, cabin category and location, and other arrangements. You may also have to pay your airfare to join the cruise.

## Reservations

Rule number one: plan ahead and book early. After choosing a ship, cruise, date, and cabin, the agency will ask for a deposit—roughly 10 per cent for long cruises, 20 per cent for short cruises.

When you make your initial reservation you should also make any special dining request known, such as your seating preference, whether you want the smoking or nonsmoking sections or any special dietary requirements (see page 58). Prices quoted in cruise brochures are based on tariffs current at the time the brochures are printed. All cruise lines reserve the right to change these prices in the event of tariff increases, fluctuating rates of exchange, fuel surcharges, or other costs beyond their control.

Confirmation of your reservation and cruise fare will be sent to you by your travel agent. The balance is normally requested 45 to 60 days prior to departure, depending on individual line policy. For a late reservation, you have to make payment in full as soon as space is confirmed. Shortly after full payment has been received by the line, your cruise ticket (if applicable) will be issued, along with baggage tags and other items.

When it arrives, check your ticket. In these days of automation, it is prudent to make sure that the ship, date, and cruise details you paid for are correctly noted. Also verify any connecting flight times.

## Extra Costs

Despite brochures boldly proclaiming that "everything's included," in most cases you'll find this isn't strictly true.

Your fare covers ship transportation, landing and embarkation charges, cabin accommodations, all meals, entertainment, and service on board. With few exceptions, it does not include alcoholic beverages, laundry, dry cleaning or valet services, shore excursions, meals ashore, gratuities, port charges, cancelation insurance (this covers you only if the cruise itself is canceled by the cruise line or the tour operator), optional on-board activities such as skeet shooting, bingo or horse-racing and casino gambling, or special features or conveniences not mentioned in the cruise line's brochure.

On most cruise ships, expect to spend about $25 per day per person on extras, plus another $10-$12 per day per person in gratuities. This can add up to as much as $500 per couple on a seven-day cruise. Genuine exceptions are *Sea Goddess I* and *Sea Goddess II* (Cunard), where everything *is* included, and *Royal Viking Queen* (Royal Viking Line), *Seabourn Pride* and *Seabourn Spirit* (Seabourn Cruise Line), where everything *except* bar drinks and wine is included.

Here are some examples of extra costs:

| | |
|---|---|
| **Dry-Clean Dress** | $3.00-$7.50 |
| **Dry-Clean 2-Piece Suit** | $4.50-$7.50 |
| **Hair Wash/Set** | $17.00-$28.00 |
| **Haircut (men)** | $20.00 |
| **Ice Cream** | $1.00-$2.50 |
| **Massage** | $1.00 per minute (plus tip) |
| **Satellite Phone/Fax** | $15.50 per minute |
| **Souvenir Photo** | $5.00-$8.00 |
| **Trapshooting (3 or 5 shots)** | $5.00, $8.00 |
| **Wine with Dinner** | $7.00-$500 |

In order to calculate the total cost of the cruise you've chosen, not including any extra-cost services you might decide you want once on board, read the brochure and, with the help of your travel agent, write down a list of the costs involved. Here are the approximate prices per person for a typical seven-day cruise on a well-rated medium or large cruise ship. This estimate is based on an outside two-bedded cabin:

| | |
|---|---|
| Cruise fares | $1,500 |
| Port charges | $100 (if not included) |
| Gratuities | $50 |
| **Total per person** | **$1,650** |

Divide this by seven and you get a rough cost of $235 per person per day.

## Discounts and Incentives

Looking at the fares listed in current cruise line brochures is only the starting point. Because overcapacity exists in certain cruise markets, at specified times of the year (such as the beginning and end of the summer) discounts and special incentives are widespread. It is wise to enlist the eyes and ears of a good travel agent and check out current discounts.

One way of saving money is to book well ahead, so that you can profit from one of many variations on the "super savers" theme. Some cruise lines are now offering larger discounts for those that book the farthest ahead, with discounts decreasing as the date of the cruise comes closer. Another method is to reserve a cabin grade, but not a specific cabin—booked as "tba" (to be assigned.) Some lines will accept this arrangement and may even upgrade (or possibly have to downgrade) you on embarkation day if all the cabins in your grade have been sold. It is useful to know that the first cabins to be sold out are usually those at minimum and maximum rates.

Another way of economizing is to wait for a "stand-by" cabin on sailing day or shortly earlier. Some lines offer stand-by fares 30 days before sailing (60 days for transatlantic crossings). They may confirm a cabin (some lines even assign the ship) on the day of embarkation.

Those who can go suitcase-in-hand to the dockside might be lucky enough to get on at minimum rate (or less) and be assigned a last-minute cancelation of a high-grade cabin.

For cruises to areas where there is year-round sunshine, there is an "on" and an "off" season. Naturally, the best cruise buys are in the off-season, while the on-season commands the highest prices. Some lines offer a "shoulder" season, which is somewhere between the on and off seasons. Peak season is during the Christmas and New Year vacation. Check with your travel agent to get the best rate for the time you wish to go.

Many cruise lines offer highly reduced rates for third and fourth persons sharing a cabin with two full-fare adults. Individual policy varies, so ask your travel agent for current rates. On some sailings, they might even go free.

Many cruise lines also have their own versions of "frequent passenger" clubs. You can join most without a fee (some, like Celebrity Cruises' Captain's Club, make a charge of $25), and you will be notified first of any special offers. Discounts can often be as high as $1,500 per cabin, so it's worth belonging, especially if you like cruising with a particular line.

Most cruise fares are listed as "per person double occupancy" or "ppd." If you are single and wish to occupy a double cabin on your own, you may have to pay a single supplement (see *Cruising for Romantics,* page 74).

However, many lines will let you share a cabin at the standard ppd rate. The line will find you a cabin partner of the same sex, and you can both save money by sharing. The line cannot, however, guarantee you'll like your partner, and will invariably specify which cabin categories are available for sharing.

For those wishing to take their children on a cruise, there are some excellent bargains available for families (see *Cruising for Families,* page 78).

## Cancelations and Refunds

It is highly recommended that you take out full cancelation insurance, as cruises (and air transportation to and from them) must be paid in full before your tickets are issued. Without such insurance, if you cancel at the last minute, even for medical reasons, you will generally lose the entire amount. Insurance cover can be obtained from your travel agent for a nominal charge.

Cruise lines usually accept cancelations notified more than 30 days before sailing, but all charge full fare if you don't turn up on sailing day, whatever the reason. Other cancelation fees range from 10 to 100 per cent, depending on the cruise and length of trip. Curiously, many lines do not return port taxes, which are *not* part of the cruise fare.

If you cancel with sufficient notice due to serious medical problems, a doctor's letter should be obtained. This is usually regarded sympathetically by cruise lines.

## Insurance

If you intend to travel overseas and your present medical insurance does not cover you, you should look into extra coverage for your cruise. A "passenger protection program" is usually prepackaged by the cruise line, and the charge for same may be on your final invoice. This is worth every penny, and it covers such things as evacuation by air ambulance, high-limit baggage, and baggage transfers.

## Port Taxes

These are assessed by individual port authorities and are generally shown with the cruise rates for each itinerary. Port charges will be part of the final payment for your cruise, although they can be changed at any time up to the day of embarkation. The most expensive port charge at time of press was Bermuda, at $60 per passenger.

Remember to ask about port charges as only a handful of North American-based lines show them in their brochure prices. They all should! By contrast, *all* lines advertising cruises in the European Union (EU) countries *must* include port taxes in their brochure rates.

## Air/Sea Packages

Where your cruise fare includes a one-way or round-trip air ticket, airline arrangements cannot usually be changed without paying considerably more toward the fare. This is because cruise lines often book space on aircraft on a special group basis in order to obtain the lowest rates. Changing your air ticket or flight within 30 days of your cruise will mean a surcharge, payable to the cruise line (Regency Cruises, for example, charges $30 for this "service.")

If you do change, remember that in the event of the airline canceling your flight, the cruise line is under no obligation to help you or return your cruise fare if you don't reach the ship on time. If you are joining a ship in a far-off country, allow extra days (particularly in winter) in case your domestic airline connections don't work or are canceled.

Because of the group-fare ticket basis by which cruise lines work, be aware that this can also mean that the airline routing to get you to your ship may not always be direct or non-stop. The airlines' use of the hub-and-spoke system is invariably frustrating to cruise passengers. Because of changes to air schedules, often cruise and air tickets are not sent to passengers until a few days before the cruise. A small number of upscale cruise lines include business-class air tickets.

In Europe, air/sea packages generally start at a major metropolitan airport, while some include first-class rail travel to the airport from outlying districts. In the United States, it is no longer necessary to depart from a major city, since many cruise lines will include connecting flights from small suburban airports as part of the whole package.

There are many variations on the air/sea theme, but all have the same advantage of offering passengers an all-inclusive price, even down to airport-to-ship transfers and port charges.

Most cruise lines offer the flexibility of

jetting out to join a ship in one port and flying home from another. This is especially popular for Mediterranean, transcanal (Panama Canal) and long cruises. Cunard even has a transatlantic program that lets you cruise one way and then fly back. They have taken the idea even further by allowing you to return on specially selected, supersonic Concorde flights for a small additional charge.

Another advantage of almost all air/sea packages is that you only have to check in your baggage once—at the departure airport—for even the baggage transfer from plane to ship is handled for you. This does not, however, include intercontinental fly/cruises, where you must claim your baggage at the airport on arrival in order to clear customs.

You may be able to hold an open return ticket, allowing you to make either a pre- or post-cruise stopover. This depends on the type of contract that exists between a cruise line and its airline partner. Usually, however, you have no stopovers en route, nor can you even change flights.

When the price of an air/sea package is all-inclusive, it is often presented as "free air" in publicity material. Of course, there is no such thing as a free air ticket—it is simply hidden in the overall cruise fare.

However, air tickets are not always included. Some lines simply don't believe in increasing their rates to cover "free air" or they wish to avoid subsidizing airline tickets. These are, for the most part, upmarket lines that operate long distance cruises to some of the more exotic destinations.

## Read the Fine Print

If you book through a large consolidator or packager, you should know exactly who is responsible for getting you where you are supposed to be at the right time.

The cruise line/operator/packager may seem initially responsible, but there is *no* set standard within the industry at present. The best advice is to read the fine print when booking. If you have complicated travel arrangements, make sure the cruise line provides you with a list of contacts for every stage of your journey.

## Sail 'n' Stay Programs

A reasonably recent concept in the cruise industry is that of going to a specific destination by ship, enjoying the cruise on the way. You then disembark (on an island in the Caribbean or South Pacific, for example) and stay a week or two, before rejoining the ship when it makes its return weekly or biweekly call. The idea has been adopted by an increasing number of cruise lines in conjunction with hotel and resort properties.

Sail 'n' stay programs are on the increase as cruise lines diversify their offerings to cater to those who like to have the best of both worlds. It is also likely that cruise lines currently operating short cruises to the Bahamas will build resorts on Bahamian out-islands, so that their passengers can extend their cruise into a sail 'n' stay vacation.

The sail 'n' stay concept has yet to take hold in the Mediterranean, although cruise vacation add-ons at resort or city hotels are increasingly popular.

# Accommodations

Selecting your accommodations is the single most important decision you will have to make. So choose wisely, for if, when you get to the ship, you find your cabin (incorrectly called a "stateroom" by some companies) is too small, you may not be able to change it or upgrade to a higher price category, as the ship could well be completely sold out.

Although you may request a specific cabin when you book, most lines now designate cabins only when deposits have been received and confirmed. They will, however, guarantee the grade and rate requested. If this is not done automatically, or if you come across a disclaimer such as one spotted recently—"All cabin assignments are confirmed upon embarkation of the vessel"—then I would advise that you get a guarantee in writing that your cabin will not be changed upon embarkation.

Here are some tips which you should take into consideration when choosing your accommodations.

## How Much to Pay

The amount you pay for accommodations on most cruise ships is directly related to the size of the cabin, the location within the ship and the facilities provided. Some other factors are also taken into consideration when cruise lines grade their accommodations.

There are no set standards within the cruise industry; each line implements its own system according to ship size, age, construction, and profit potential. It is unfortunate that cruise lines neglect to give cabin sizes in their brochures, but you'll find the sizes in *The Ratings and Evaluations*, starting on page 195.

Before you select your cabin, decide how much you can afford to spend—including airfare (if applicable) and onboard expenses (don't forget to include the estimated cost of shore excursions, port charges, and tips)—since this will determine the cabin categories available to you. It is advisable to choose the most expensive cabin you can afford, especially if it's your first cruise, as you will spend some time there. If it is too small (and most cabins are small), you might suffer from "cabin fever," and the cruise might fall short of your expectations. Alternatively, it is better to book a low-grade cabin on a good ship than a high-grade cabin on a poor ship.

If you are in a party of three or more and don't mind sharing a cabin, you'll achieve a substantial saving per person, so you may be able to go to a higher grade cabin without paying any extra.

In general, with regard to cabins, you will get precisely what you pay for.

## Size of Cabins

Ships' cabins should be looked upon as hotel rooms in miniature, providing more or less the same facilities. With one difference—that of space. Ships necessarily have space limitations, and therefore tend to utilize every inch efficiently.

Viewed by many owners and designers as little more than a convenient place for passengers to sleep, shower and change for dinner, space is often compromised for large public rooms and open areas.

There is no such thing as an average cabin, as cabin size will depend on the space that is allocated to accommodations within a ship of given tonnage measurement and principal dimensions. New ships have more standardized cabin sizes, because they are made in modular form. They also have integrated bathrooms, often made from noncombustible phenolic-glass-reinforced plastics, and fitted into the ship during construction.

Generally, the larger the ship, the more generous it will be with regard to cabin space. Cabins can vary from the compact 117 sq. ft. standard cabins on Royal Caribbean Cruise Line ships to a magnificent 1,125 sq. ft. penthouse suite on Holland America Line's *Maasdam*, *Ryndam*, and *Statendam*.

Remember that cruise ships are operated both for the pleasure of passengers and for the profit of the cruise companies. This is why cabins on many new or modern ships are on the small side. The more cabins a ship can provide, the more fare-paying passengers can be carried.

Ships of yesteryear offered passengers more spacious cabins simply because there were more days at sea, fewer ports of call, generally less speed, and fewer entertainment rooms. Thus many people spent a great deal of time in their cabins, often entertaining other passengers.

Although most modern ships have smaller cabins, they are certainly adequate for standard-length cruises, and allow maximum space in public rooms for entertainment and social events.

Some cruise brochures are more detailed and specific than others when it comes to deck plans and cabin layout diagrams. Deck plans do not normally show the dimensions, but they are drawn to scale, unless otherwise noted.

You can get a good idea of the space in a cabin by examining the cabin plan of the category you are interested in. By looking at the beds (each twin being between 2 ft. and 3 ft. wide and 6 ft. long), you can easily figure out how much empty or utilized space (bathroom, closets and so on) there is.

If the cabins appear to be the same size on the deck plan, it's because they *are* the same size, with the exception of suite rooms, which will be substantially larger. This is particularly true on some newer ships, where cabins are standardized.

Ask the cruise line, via your travel agent, for the square footage of the cabin you have selected, if it is not indicated on the deck plan. This will give you some idea of its size. Pace out a room at home as a means of comparison.

## Location of Your Cabin

An "outside" cabin is preferable by far, especially if this is the first time you have been cruising. An "inside" cabin has no portholes or windows, making it more difficult to orient yourself or to gauge the weather or time.

Cabins located in the center of a ship are more stable, and they tend to be noise- and vibration-free. Ships powered by diesels (this applies to most new and modern vessels) create and transmit some vibration, especially at the stern.

Consider your personal habits when choosing the location of your cabin. For example, if you like to go to bed early, don't pick a cabin close to the disco. If you have trouble walking, select a cabin close to the elevator (and not on a lower deck, where there are none).

Generally, the higher the deck, the higher the cabin price and the better the service—a carry-over from transoceanic days, when upper deck cabins and suites were sunnier and warmer.

Cabins at the bow (front) of a ship are slightly crescent-shaped, as the outer wall follows the curvature of the ship's hull. They are usually roomier and cheaper. However, these forward cabins can be subject to early morning sounds, such as the anchor being dropped at ports where the ship cannot dock.

Connecting cabins are fine for families or close friends, but remember that the wall between them is unusually thin, and both parties can plainly hear anything that's being said next door.

If you book a deluxe upper-deck cabin, check the deck plan carefully; the cabin could have a view of the lifeboats. Many cruise lines now indicate these "obstructed-view" cabins in the brochure. Make sure to read the fine print. Similarly, cabins on promenade decks may have windows which can easily be looked into by passing strollers on deck.

If you select a cabin that is on one of the lower decks, be warned that engine noise and heat become more noticeable, especially at the aft end of the vessel, and around the engine casing.

## Facilities

Cabins will provide some, or all, of the following features:

- Private bathroom (generally small and compact) with shower, wash basin, and toilet. Higher-priced cabins and suites often have full-size bathtubs—some may even have a whirlpool bath and/or bidet, a hairdryer, and considerably more space.
- Electrical outlets for personal appliances, usually U.S. standard, sometimes both 110 and 220 volts.
- Multichannel radio; on some ships, television (regular or closed circuit); video equipment.
- Two beds, or a lower and upper berth (plus, possibly, another one or two upper berths) or a double, queen- or king-size bed (usually in suites or deluxe accommodations). On some ships, twin beds can be pushed together to form a double.
- Telephone, for inter-cabin or ship-to-shore communication.
- Depending on cabin size, a chair, or chair and table, or sofa and table, or a separate lounge/sitting area (higher-priced accommodations only).
- Refrigerator and bar (higher-priced accommodations only).
- Vanity/desk unit with chair or stool.
- Personal safe.
- Closet space, some drawer space, plus storage room under beds for suitcases.
- Bedside night stand/table unit.
- Towels, soap, shampoo and conditioner. (Many ships, and particularly the more "upscale" ones, will provide a greater selection of items.)

## Typical Cabin Layouts

The following rates are typical of those you can expect to pay for (a) a 7-day and (b) a 10-day Caribbean cruise on a modern cruise ship. The rates are per person, and include free roundtrip airfare or low-cost air add-ons from principal North American gateways.

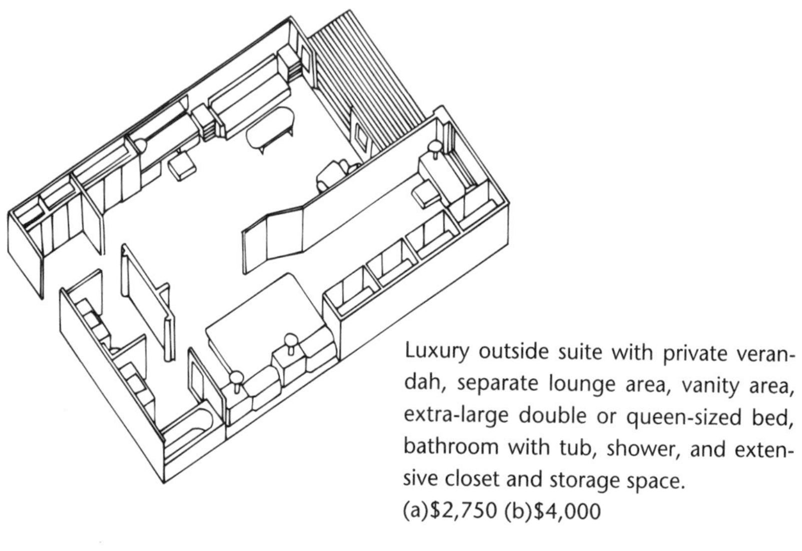

Luxury outside suite with private verandah, separate lounge area, vanity area, extra-large double or queen-sized bed, bathroom with tub, shower, and extensive closet and storage space.
(a)$2,750 (b)$4,000

Deluxe outside cabin with lounge area, double or twin beds, bathroom with tub, shower, and ample closet and storage space.
(a)$2,250 (b)$2,850

Note that on some ships, third- and fourth-person berths are available for families or friends wishing to share. These upper Pullman berths, not shown on these cabin layouts, are recessed into the wall above the lower beds.

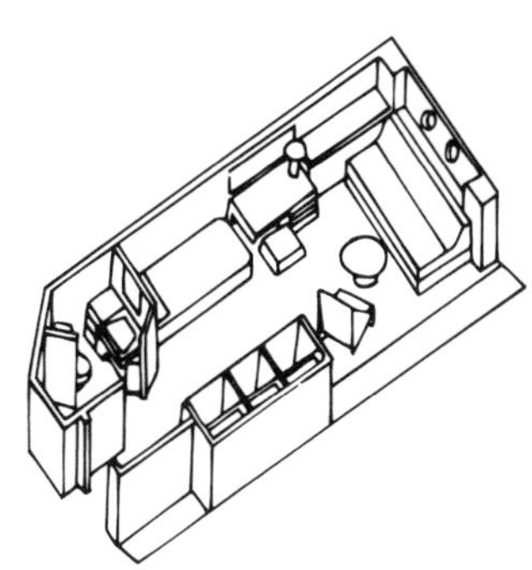

Large outside double with bed and convertible daytime sofabed, bathroom with shower, and good closet space. (a)$1,750 (b)$2,450

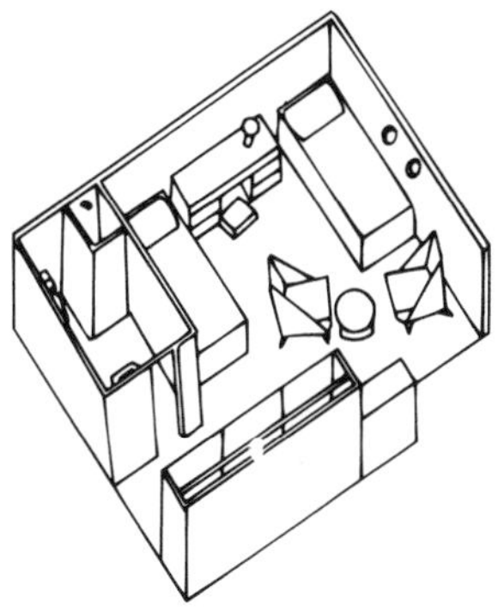

Standard outside double with twin beds (plus a possible upper 3rd/4th berth), small sitting area, bathroom with shower, and reasonable closet space. (a)$1,450 (b)$1,975

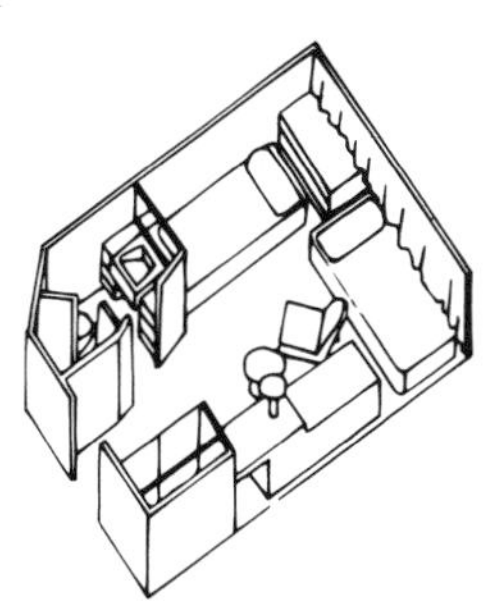

Inside double with two lower beds that may convert into daytime sofabeds (plus a possible upper 3rd/4th berth), bathroom with shower, and fair closet space. (a)$1,250 (b)$1,750

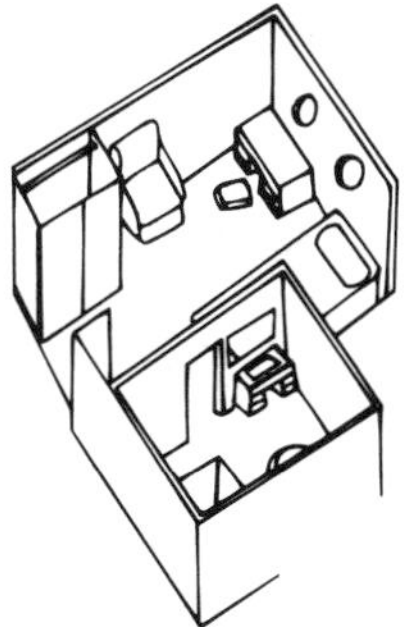

Outside or inside single with bed and small sitting area, bathroom with tub or shower, and limited closet space. (a)$1,650 (b)$2,450

Many first-time cruisers are surprised to find twin beds in their cabin. Double beds were a comparative rarity on cruise ships except in the higher-priced suite rooms, at least until recently. On some newer ships, the twin beds convert to sofas for daytime use, and at night are converted back by the steward.

The two beds are placed in one of two configurations: parallel (with little space in between) or, preferably, in an "L" shape, giving more floor space and the illusion that the cabin is larger.

On some ships (especially older ones), you'll find upper and lower berths. A "berth" is a nautical term for a bed held in a wooden or iron frame. A "pullman berth" tucks away out of sight during the day, usually into the bulkhead or ceiling. You climb up a short ladder at night to get into an upper berth.

## The Suite Life

Suites are the most luxurious and spacious of all shipboard accommodations. They usually comprise a separate lounge or sitting room and a bedroom with a double, queen- or king-size bed, or large, movable twin beds.

The bathroom will be quite large (for a ship) and will have a large bath tub (often with a Jacuzzi whirlpool tub) and shower, plus a toilet, deluxe wash basin and even a bidet. Today, some ships boast gold bathroom fittings in their best suites! Although this is the exception and not the rule, the bathrooms attached to the suites are usually superb.

Suites often contain a stereo system, television, VCR video unit, refrigerator and a partially or fully stocked bar, and occupants can command the very best of service round-the-clock.

On ships like the *Crown Odyssey* and *QE2*, each suite is decorated in its own style, with authentic or reproduction period furniture, beautiful drapes, and fine furnishings. On the *Crystal Harmony*, *QE2* and *Royal Viking Sun*, you'll be attended by a personal butler.

Suite rooms are best for a long voyage, when the ship might cross stretches of ocean for five or more days at a time. They are wonderful for impressing a loved one and for entertaining in.

Most suites have their own balcony or veranda, although it's wise to check the deck plan in case the veranda faces the lifeboats or other apparatus. Suites are usually sheltered from noise and wind and should provide considerable privacy.

## 19th-Century Cruising

Cruising today is not the same as it used to be; on the first cruise ships there was little entertainment, and passengers had to clean their own cabins! Yes, it's true! Opposite is an extract of orders that were enforced on all ships sailing from Great Britain in 1849.

## Reading a Deck Plan

Learning to read a deck plan is a relatively easy matter. It is always laid out so that the bow (front part of the ship) faces to your right or to the top of a page.

Traditionally, ships have designated the central deck (equivalent to the main lobby of a hotel) as the Main Deck. This

## Meals/Bedtime

1) Every passenger to rise at 7:00 am unless otherwise permitted by the Surgeon, or if no Surgeon, by the Master.

2) Breakfast from 8:00 am to 9:00 am   Dinner at 1:00 pm   Supper at 6:00 pm

3) The passengers to be in their beds at 10:00 pm.

## Fires/Lights

4) Fires to be lighted by the Passengers' Cook at 7:00 am and kept alight by him until 7:00 pm, then to be extinguished unless otherwise directed by the Master or required for the use of the Sick.

5) The Master to determine the order in which the Passengers shall be entitled to the use of the Fires for Cooking. The Cook to take care thatthis order is preserved.

6) Three Safety Lamps to be lit at dusk, one to be kept burning all night in the Main Hatchway, the two others may be extinguished at 10:00 pm.

7) No naked light to be allowed at any time, or on any account.

## Cleaning Berths and Etc.

8) The Passengers, when dressed, to roll up their Beds, to Sweep the Decks (including the space under the Bottom of the Berths) and to throw the Dirt overboard.

9) Breakfast not to commence until this is done.

10) The Sweepers for the day to be taken in rotation from the males above the age of 14 in the proportion of five for every 100 passengers.

11) Duties of the Sweepers to be to clean the Ladders, Hospital and Roundhouse, to sweep the Decks after every meal, and to dry-holystone and scrape them after breakfast.

12) But the Occupant of each Berth to see that his own Berth is well brushed out, and Single Women are to keep their own compartment clean in Ships where a separate compartment is allotted to them.

13) The Beds to be well shaken and aired on Deck, and the bottom boards, if not fixtures, to be removed any dry-scrubbed and taken on deck at least twice a week.

14) Two days in the week to be appointed by the Master as Washing Days, but no Clothes to be washed or dried between decks.

is where you'll find the Purser's Office and other principal business offices. Some modern ships, however, do not use the term "Main Deck," preferring a more exclusive- or attractive-sounding name. All ships also have a Boat Deck, so called because this is where the ship's lifeboats are stowed.

In the past, many ships also had a Promenade Deck—an enclosed walkway along the length of the deck on one or both sides of the ship. This was popular with passengers crossing the Atlantic, for when the weather was cold or foggy, they could still take their stroll. It is located between the Main Deck and the Boat Deck, except on some modern ships where Boat and Promenade are interchangeable. When the new generation of specialized cruise ships came into being in the 1970s, the Promenade Deck disappeared in favor of public entertainment lounges across the full beam of the ship, and the name of the deck was changed. Some ships built recently have returned to the idea of a Promenade Deck.

The uppermost decks are usually open and feature sunning space, multisports areas and running or jogging tracks that may or may not encircle the ship.

The Restaurant Deck has undergone a metamorphosis too. It used to be buried on one of the ship's lower decks so as to avoid the rolling motion of nonstabilized ocean liners. Even on the most luxurious liners, there were often no portholes, because the deck was placed below the waterline. As cruising replaced transportation as the prime source of revenue, newer ships were designed with restaurants set high above the waterline. Big picture windows give diners a panoramic view of the port or surrounding sea. The Restaurant Deck can thus be either above or below Main Deck.

Traditionally, popular-priced cabins have been below Main Deck, with high-priced suites occupying space on one or two of the uppermost decks. Suites are always located where the view and privacy are best and the noise is least. In the latest ship designs, however, almost all accommodations areas are located above Main Deck in order to cut down on disturbing engine noise and vibration. Older ships designated their accommodation decks A, B, C, D... and so on, while most modern ships have given these decks more appealing names, such as Acapulco, Bimini, Coral, Dolphin, and so on, using the deck letter as the first letter of a more exotic name.

On a deck plan, cabins are generally shown as small rectangles or blocks, each with its number printed on it. Public rooms will either be drawn in detail or left as blank spaces. Elevators are usually indicated by the British term "lift," while any stairs will be shown as a small series of lines set closely together.

# Cruise Cuisine

Without doubt, food is still the single most talked and written about aspect of the cruise experience. One of the most sensual pleasures in life is eating; show me the person who is not aroused by the aroma of food being prepared, or charmed by a delicious, satisfying meal.

There is a special thrill that comes with dining out in a fine restaurant. So it is on board a luxury cruise ship, where gracious dining in elegant, friendly, and comfortable surroundings enhances an appetite which is already sharpened by the bracing sea air. Some passengers take shipboard dining to the limit, however. Indeed, I've seen many people eat more in one meal than most others do in two or three days!

Constant attention to presentation, quality, and choice of menu in the tradition of the transatlantic luxury liners has made cruise ships justly famous. Cruise lines know that you'll spend more time eating on board than doing anything else, so their intention is to cater to your palate in every way possible, within the confines of a predetermined budget.

Expenditure on food ranges approximately between $7.50 and $30.00 per person per day, depending on the cruise line and standard of cuisine required, although there are exceptions at the higher end, particularly in the Japanese market, where fresh fish and seafood costs are exorbitantly high. Most cruise ships catering to the general (mass) market spend anything between $7.50 and $15.00 per person per day.

Cruise lines put maximum effort into telling passengers how good their food is, often to the point of being unable to deliver what is anticipated. Generally, however, the level of food provided is good. The best rule of thumb is, if you were to eat out in a good restaurant, what would you expect relative to what you are paying? Does the ship's dining experience meet or exceed your expectations? Would you come back again for the food? If you would, then that cruise line has met its promise of fine food. While gourmet cuisine is enjoyed by a small percentage of people ashore, few ships have the facilities or availability of fresh foods to equal even those of a one-star Michelin-rated restaurant.

The cuisine will vary, inevitably, depending on the nationality and regional influence of the executive chef, his staff and the ship's country of registry or ownership. Thus, choosing a cruise and ship also involves thinking about the kind of food that will be served on board—and how it is served.

Some ships have full place settings that include 10 pieces of cutlery, while others provide the correct cutlery before each course is served. If you find it bewildering, or don't know which knife and fork to use for which course, the rule is always start at the outermost pair and work towards the innermost pair. The knife and fork closest to where the plate is set will be for the entree (main course). Some ships have special knives for fish courses; others do not, requiring you to use a standard (flat) knife.

While on the subject of place settings, if you are *left-handed*, make sure you tell your waiter at your first meal exactly how you want your cutlery placed, and to make sure that tea or coffee cup handles are turned in the correct direction. It would even be better if right- or left-hand preferences were established at the time of booking, and the cruise lines passed on the information.

Menus for luncheon and dinner are usually displayed outside the dining room each morning so you can preview the day's meals. On some of the more upmarket ships, menus will be delivered to your suite or cabin each day. When looking at the menu, one thing you'll never have to do is to consider the price—it's all included.

Depending on the ship and cruise, you could sit down to gourmet specialties such as duck à l'orange, beef Wellington, lobster thermidor, or prime roast rib of Kansas beef. Or maybe French châteaubriand, Italian veal scaloppini, fresh sea bass in dill sauce, or rack of roast English lamb. To top off the meal there could be crème brulée, chocolate mousse, kiwi tart, or that favorite standby of mass meringue—Baked Alaska, not to mention tableside flambé items such as Cherries Jubilee or Crêpes Suzette. And you can always rely on your waiter to bring you a double portion, should you so wish! Of course, these specialties may not be available on all ships. But if you would like something that is not on the menu, see the maitre d', give him 24 hours' notice (plus a small tip) and, if the galley can cope, it may well be all yours.

Despite what the glossy brochures say, however, not all meals on all cruise ships are gourmet affairs. In general, cruise cuisine can be compared favorably to the kind of "banquet" food served in a good-class hotel or family restaurant. For a guide to the standard of cruise cuisine, service, and presentation on a particular ship, refer to the ratings in Part Two, but remember that the rating of cruise cuisine is always determined in relation to the per diem cost averages paid by passengers.

One reason that the food on ships cannot always be a gourmet experience is that the galley (ship's kitchen) may have to turn out hundreds of meals at the same time. What you *will* find is a very fine selection of highly palatable, pleasing, and complete meals served in very comfortable surroundings, in the company of friends (and *you* don't have to do the cooking!). Add to this the possibility of large picture windows overlooking a shimmering sea, and perhaps even dining by candlelight. Dining in such a setting is a delightful and relaxed way to spend any evening.

## Caviar and Champagne

If it's the best caviar you're after, you might want to know that Cunard's *QE2* prides itself on being the world's largest single purchaser of Beluga caviar (spending about half a million dollars annually), after the Russian and Ukrainian governments. There are no mother-of-pearl caviar spoons on the *QE2*, however, but you *will* find them on *Sea Goddess I* and *Sea Goddess II*, and *Song of Flower*.

Although it might seem like it from menu descriptions, most ships do not serve Beluga caviar, but the less expensive, and more widely available Sevruga and Sevruga Malossol (low salt) caviar. Even more widely served on less exclusive ships, such as those of Dolphin Cruise Line or Royal Caribbean Cruises, is Norwegian lumpfish caviar—quite different from the highly prized Beluga caviar. The price of caviar is a reflection of the growing rarity of the sturgeon, the fish from which it is derived.

Caviar goes quite naturally with good champagne, but good champagne (like anything else of high quality) doesn't come cheap. What most ships use as champagne—for the Captain's Welcome Aboard Party for example—is only just passable as champagne. Some ships (for example, the newer ships of Princess Cruises) have a caviar and champagne bar, which offers several varieties of caviar at extra cost. Champagne making is a real art (in France the production of Champagne is restricted to a very small geographical area). Unlike wine, it is bottled in many sizes, ranging from the minute to the ridiculous, with a variety of names to match:

| | |
|---|---|
| Quarter bottle: | 18.7 centiliters |
| Half bottle (split): | 37.5 centiliters |
| Bottle: | 75 centiliters |
| Magnum: | 2 bottles |
| Jeroboam: | 4 bottles |
| Rehoboam: | 6 bottles |
| Methuzelah: | 8 bottles |
| Salmanazar: | 12 bottles |
| Balthazar: | 16 bottles |
| Nebuchadnezzar: | 20 bottles |

Although the Champagne area has been producing wines of renown for a long time, its vintners were unable to keep their bubbles from fizzling out until a monk in the Abbey of Hautvilliers, whose name was Dom Perignon, came along. The bubbles—escaping carbonic acid gas—had always escaped until the right bottle was developed. Until Dom Perginon's work on the refinement of champagne, exploding bottles were a common occurrence in local cellars. Because of the work done by this clever monk, the champagne bottle is the strongest bottle made today. Its thickness is concentrated around the bottle's base and shoulders. Dom Perignon's bottle was aided by the coincidental development of the cork.

## Healthy Eating

Today, with more emphasis on low-cholesterol and low-salt diets, many ships feature "spa" menus—where the heavy, calorie-filled sauces have been replaced by *nouvelle cuisine* and spa cuisine.

Among the best cuisine available on a "general market" cruise is that featured on the ships of Celebrity Cruises—the *Horizon, Meridian,* and *Zenith*—where three-star Michelin chef Michel Roux is in charge of the menus and overall food product. In the general market, however, you won't get caviar. Going smaller in size but higher in price, the ships of Renaissance Cruises provide an "800 Club" menu for lunch and dinner—a complete meal that together adds up to 800 calories. This is an excellent idea for those on a diet.

At the upper (expensive) end of the spectrum, meals on ships like the *Royal Viking Queen*, *Royal Viking Sun*, *Sea Goddess I* and *II*, *Seabourn Pride*, and *Seabourn Spirit* can be memorable—always cooked to order individually.

The difference between the most expensive and the least expensive cruises can often be found in such details as the provision of high quality biscuits made for eating with cheese, or the provision of cappuccino and espresso coffees in the dining room without charge, or the variety of fresh and exotic fruits and the general quality of meats and fish used.

## National Differences

Passengers of different nationalities have their own needs and requirements. Here are a few instances of national characteristics which I have noticed and which you may come across:

- British, German and other European passengers like real china egg cups for their boiled eggs for breakfast. When North Americans eat boiled eggs, which is infrequently, they are often put into a bowl and eaten with a fork.
- German passengers like breads (especially dark breads) and cheeses for breakfast. They also prefer German draught or bottled beers rather than American canned beers.
- French passengers like soft, not flaky, croissants, and may request brioche and confitures.
- Japanese passengers will be looking for a "bento box" breakfast of fresh steamed Japanese rice, salmon and eel, and vegetable pickles.
- Most passengers agree that cruise coffee is appalling, but often it is simply the chlorinated water that gives it a different taste. Europeans like strong coffee, usually made from African coffee beans from countries like Kenya. North Americans usually drink coffee from Colombia or Jamaica.
- European tea drinkers like to drink tea out of tea cups, not coffee mugs.

## The Dining Room

On many ships, the running and staffing of dining rooms are contracted to an outside catering organization specializing in cruise ships. Ships that are continually in waters away from their home country find that professional catering companies do an excellent job, and provide a degree of relief from the operation and staffing of their dining rooms. The quality is generally to a very high standard. However, ships that control their own catering staff and food are often those that go to great lengths to ensure that their passengers are satisfied.

Catering companies do change occasionally, so a complete list would probably soon become obsolete. However, here are just a few examples of the principal maritime catering companies:

| | |
|---|---|
| Apollo Catering | USA |
| CFCS | Italy/USA |
| Century Catering | USA |
| Ligabue Catering | Italy |
| Stellar Maritime | USA |
| Trident Catering | USA |
| World-Wide Catering | USA |
| Zerbone Catering | Italy |

## Dining Room Staff

The maitre d' is an experienced host, with shrewd perceptions about compatibility; you can trust him when he gives you your table seating. If a table reservation has been arranged prior to boarding, you will find a table seating card in your cabin when you arrive. If this is not the case, you will need to make your reservations with the maitre d' or one of his assistants. If you wish to reserve a table or location in the dining room, do so as soon after boarding as possible.

Unless you are with your own group of friends, you will be seated next to strangers in the dining room. Tables for two are a rarity, except on some small ships and on some of the upmarket liners. Most tables seat six or eight people. It is a good idea to ask to be seated at a larger table, for if you are a couple put at a table for four and you don't get along with your table partners, there's no one else to talk to. Remember, too, if the ship is full, it may be difficult to change tables after the start of the cruise.

If you are unhappy with any aspect of the dining room operation, the earlier you complain the better. Don't wait until the cruise is over and send a scathing letter to the cruise line, for then it is too late to do anything positive. See the people in charge—they are there to help you enjoy your meals during the cruise. They want your comments—good or bad.

Each table has at least one waiter and one assistant waiter or busboy. On some ships, up to 30 nationalities may be represented by the dining room staff, who are courteous, charming, and helpful.

Many ships run special incentive programs, such as a "waiter of the month" competition. This helps keep staff on their toes, especially if they want to reach the "best" tables. The result is that passengers really do get fine service.

The best waiters are without doubt those who have trained in the exclusive European hotels or in hotel and catering schools—like the Maritime Catering Institute in Salzburg, Austria. These highly qualified individuals will excel in silver service, and will always be ready with the next course when you want it. They will also know your likes and dislikes by the second night of the cruise. They normally work on the upmarket ships, where dignified professionalism is evident everywhere in the dining room.

## Smoking/Nonsmoking

A few ships feature totally nonsmoking dining rooms. At press time these were *Azerbaydzhan*, *Belorussiya*, *Dreamward*, *Gruziya*, *Hebridean Princess*, *Jubilee*, *Kareliya*, *Kazakhstan*, *Norway*, *Regent Sea*, *Royal Majesty*, *Seaward*, *Sensation*, and *Windward*. All others have dining rooms that separate smokers and nonsmokers, and most ask passengers not to smoke cigars or pipes.

Nonsmokers who wish to sit in a special section should tell the maitre d' or his assistants when reserving a table. You should know that at open seating breakfasts and luncheons in the dining room (or informal buffet dining area), smokers and nonsmokers may be together. If smoke bothers you, be adamant—demand a table in a nonsmoking area.

## The Captain's Table

The captain usually occupies a large table in or near the center of the dining room, seating eight or ten people picked from the passenger or "commend" list by the maitre d'. Alternatively, the captain may ask personal friends or important company officials to dine with him. If you are invited to the captain's table for dinner, it is gracious to accept and you'll have the chance to ask all the questions you like about shipboard life.

The captain will not attend meals if he is required on the bridge. When there are two sittings, he may have dinner at the first sitting one night, and at the second the next night. On some ships, the captain's guests are changed daily so that more people can enjoy the experience.

Senior officers generally also host tables, and being seated with them can be a fascinating experience, especially as they tend to be less formal.

## Which Sitting?

The best ships feature an open, or single, sitting for meals, where you may dine in unhurried style. "Open sitting" means that you can sit at any table with whom you wish, at whatever time you choose within dining room hours. "Single sitting" means you can choose when you wish to eat, but have regularly assigned tables for the entire cruise.

The majority of ships operate on a two-sitting basis. The first, or main, sitting is for those who like dining early and do not wish to linger. The second sitting is a more leisurely meal. Those at the late sitting may not be hungry enough to eat again at the midnight buffet, since it begins about two hours later.

Standard meal times for a two-sitting ship are:

| | |
|---|---|
| Breakfast: | 6:30a.m./8:30a.m. |
| Lunch: | 12:00noon/1:30p.m. |
| Dinner: | 6:30p.m./8:30p.m. |

Note that some ships that operate in Europe (Mediterranean) may well have even later dinner sittings. Costa Cruise Lines, for example, has its second dinner sitting at 9:00p.m. instead of the usual 8:15p.m. or 8:30p.m. Dinner hours may vary when the ship is in port in order to allow for the timing of shore excursions.

You may also find that some of the better seats for the shows and at the movie theater have been taken by those on the first sitting. Most ships get around this problem by scheduling two performances for all shows at night.

Most ships request that you enter the dining room 15 minutes after the meal has been announced, out of consideration for your fellow passengers, table companions, and the dining room staff. This is especially true for those on the first sitting, but provides little time to sit and linger over cocktails or after-dinner drinks—one of the drawbacks of the two-sitting arrangement.

## Special Requirements

If you are counting calories, are vegetarian or require a salt-free, sugar-restricted, macrobiotic or other diet, let the cruise line know when you first book.

The line will then pass the information to the ship, so that your needs can be met. Some of the larger cruise lines, including Carnival Cruise Lines and Royal Caribbean Cruise Lines, now feature a vegetarian entree for every dinner.

Because the food on cruises is considered "international" or French cuisine, be prepared for dishes that are liberally sprinkled with salt. Vegetables are often cooked with sauces containing dairy products, salt, and sugar. A word with the maitre d' should suffice.

## First and Second Nights

For new and experienced cruisers alike, the first evening at sea is exciting—like an opening night at the theater. Nowhere is there more a feeling of anticipation than at that first casual dinner when you get a foretaste of the feasting to come.

By contrast, the second night of most cruises is formal, for it is usually the captain's welcome-aboard dinner. For this the chef will pull out all the stops to produce a gourmet meal. The dinner follows the captain's cocktail party, which takes place in one of the ship's larger lounges and is an excellent opportunity to meet fellow passengers and the ship's officers. Toward the end of the party, the captain will give his welcome aboard speech and may introduce senior members of staff.

## Theme Nights

Other nights of your cruise may be designated as special theme nights, when the waiters dress up fittingly and the menu is planned to suit the occasion.

## A Typical Day

From morning till night, there's food to the point of overkill on even the most modest cruise ship. In fact, on some ships you can eat up to seven meals a day.

Early risers will find piping hot coffee and tea on deck from about 6a.m.

A full breakfast, of up to six courses and as many as 60 different items, can be taken in the main dining room. For a more casual meal, you may wish to sit al fresco or buffet style at the outdoor deck café (ideal after an early swim or if you don't wish to dress for the more formal dining room). The choice is naturally more restricted than in the main dining room, but good nonetheless. Times will be given in your daily program.

A third possibility, especially for romantics, is to have breakfast in your cabin. There's something rather special about waking up and eating breakfast without getting out of bed. Some ships offer a full choice of items, while others opt for the more simple, but usually well-presented, continental breakfast.

On many ships, mid-morning bouillon is an established favorite, often served on one of the open decks—a carry-over from the grand days of the transatlantic steamships. Bouillon aboard *Sagafjord* and *Vistafjord* is served right to your chair-side from trolleys that parade around the promenade deck.

At lunch time, there are at least two choices: a hot lunch with all the trimmings in the dining room, or a buffet-style luncheon at the outdoor café, featuring light meals, salads, and one or two hot dishes. On some days, this could well turn into a lavish spread, with enough food for a feast (special favorites are seafood and tropical fruits). And on some ships there will be a separate hot dog and hamburger stand or pizzeria, where everything is cooked right in front of you, but usually presented with less style than at a McDonald's.

At around 4p.m. there will be another throwback from the heyday of the great liners: afternoon tea—in the best British tradition—complete with finger sandwiches and cakes. This is often served in one of the main lounges to the accompaniment of live music (it may even be a "tea-dance") or recorded classical music. Afternoon tea usually lasts about an hour (although on some ships it is only half an hour, in which case it is best to be on time so as not to miss out).

Dinner is, of course, the main event of the evening, and apart from the casual first and last nights, is formal in style.

If you enjoy wine with your dinner, you'll find an excellent choice on board. Upmarket ships may carry a selection of wines far more extensive than you'll find even in the better restaurants ashore, while other ships will provide some excellent inexpensive wines from the country of the ship's registry or ownership. It is wise to order your wine for the evening meal at lunch time, or at the very latest as soon as you are seated; the wine stewards tend to be extremely busy during the evening meal, and need to draw their stock and possibly have it chilled.

A few hours after dinner, there's the midnight buffet—without doubt the most famous of all cruise ship meals. It

## Food Statistics

The amount of food and drink consumed during an average cruise is mind-boggling. Here is an idea of what is carried aboard Cunard's *QE2* on a 10-day round-trip transatlantic sailing.

| | | | | | |
|---|---|---|---|---|---|
| Beef | 25,000 lb. | Milk | 2,500 gallons | Dog biscuits | 50 lb. |
| Lamb | 6,000 lb. | Cream | 3,000 quarts | Champagne | 1,000 bottles |
| Pork | 4,000 lb. | Ice cream | 5,000 gallons | Assorted wines | 1,200 bottles |
| Veal | 3,000 lb. | Eggs | 6,250 dozen | Whiskey | 1,000 bottles |
| Sausages | 2,000 lb. | Caviar | 150 lb. | Gin | 600 bottles |
| Chicken | 5,000 lb. | Cereal | 800 lb. | Rum | 240 bottles |
| Turkey | 5,000 lb. | Rice | 3,000 lb. | Vodka | 120 bottles |
| Fresh vegetables | 27,000 lb. | Herbs/spices | 50 lb. | Brandy | 240 bottles |
| Potatoes | 30,000 lb. | Jam/marmalade | 700 lb. | Liqueurs | 360 bottles |
| Fish | 1,400 lb. | Tea bags | 50,000 | Sherry | 240 bottles |
| Lobsters | 1,500 lb. | Tea (loose) | 500 lb. | Port | 120 bottles |
| Crab | 800 lb. | Coffee | 2,000 lb. | Beer | 12,000 bottles/cans |
| Canned fish | 1,500 cans | Sugar | 5,000 lb. | Cigars | 4,000 |
| Fresh fruit | 22,000 lb. | Cookies | 2,000 lb. | Cigarettes | 2,500 cartons |
| Frozen fruit | 2,500 lb. | Kosher food | 600 lb. | Tobacco | 1,000 lb. |
| Canned fruit | 1,500 gallons | Baby food | 600 jars | | |

really is at midnight (until 1a.m.), and is a spread fit for royalty. Like dinner, it may feature a different theme each night: a King Neptune seafood buffet one evening, an oriental buffet the next, a tropical fruit fantasy the third, and so on. And the desserts at each of these buffets are out of this world.

On one night (usually the penultimate evening) there will be a magnificent gala midnight buffet, for which the chefs pull out all the stops. Beautifully sculpted ice-carvings will be on display, each fashioned from a 300-pound block of ice. Some ships also demonstrate ice-carving.

Even if you are not hungry, stay up to see this display of culinary art—it's something most people never forget.

In addition—or as an alternative—to the midnight buffet, pizza may be served for the late-night disco or casino crowd.

During a typical day at sea, the ship's bars will open from about 10a.m. to late into the night, depending on the bar, its location, and the number of patrons. Details of bar hours are given in the ship's *Daily Program.*

## The Executive Chef

Each ship has its own executive chef who is responsible for planning the menus, ordering sufficient food (in conjunction with the food manager), organizing his staff and arranging meals.

When a cruise line finds a good executive chef, it is unlikely that they will part company. Many of the best ships have European chefs who are members of the prestigious *Confrérie de la Chaîne des Rôtisseurs*, the world's oldest gourmet society. Top food and beverage experts work together with their executive chefs, striving for perfection.

One of the principal aims of any good executive chef will be to make sure that menus are never repeated, even on long cruises. He will be inventive enough to offer his passengers dishes that will be new gastronomic experiences for them. On long voyages, the executive chef will work with specially invited guest chefs to offer passengers a taste of the best in regional cuisines. Sometimes, he may also obtain fish, seafood, fruit, and local produce in "wayside" ports and incorporate them into the menu with a "special of the day" announcement.

## The Galley

The galley ("kitchen" for landlubbers) is the very heart of all food preparation on board. At any time of the day or night, there is activity here—whether baking fresh bread at 2a.m., making meals and snacks for passengers and crew around the clock, or decorating a cake for a passenger's birthday celebration.

The staff, from executive chef to pot-washer, must all work together as a team, each designated a specific role—and there is little room for error.

The galley and preparation areas consist of the following sections:

### Fish Preparation Area

This area contains freezers and a fully equipped preparation room, where fish is cleaned and cut to size before it is sent to the galley.

### Meat Preparation Area

This area contains separate freezers for meat and poultry. These are kept at approximately 10°F. There are also defrosting areas (35°F to 40°F). Meat and poultry is sliced and portioned before being sent to the galley.

### Soup, Pasta, and Vegetable Preparation Area

Vegetables are cleaned and prepared here, pasta is prepared and cooked, and soups are made in huge tureens.

### Garde Manger (Cold Kitchen)

This is the area where all cold dishes and salads are prepared, from the simplest sandwich (for room service, for example) to the fine works of art that grace the most wonderful buffets. The area contains mixing machines, slicing machines and refrigeration cabinets where prepared dishes are stored until required.

### Bakery and Pastry Shop

This area provides the raw ingredients for preparation, and will contain dough mixers, refrigerators, proving ovens, ovens, and containers in all manner of shapes and sizes. Dessert items, pastries, sweets, and other confectionery are prepared and made here.

### Dishwashing Area

This area contains huge conveyor-belt dishwashing machines. Wash and rinse temperatures are carefully controlled to comply with public health regulations. This is where all the special cooking pots and pans are scrubbed and cleaned, and where the silverware is polished.

## Standards of Hygiene

Galley equipment is in almost constant use. Regular inspections and maintenance help detect potential problems.

Hygiene and correct sanitation are also vital in the galley, and there is continual cleaning of equipment, utensils, bulkheads, floors, and hands. All personnel are required to wear rubber-soled shoes or boots, and senior officers conduct regular inspections of galleys, equipment and personnel.

Passenger ships sailing from U.S. ports or visiting them are all subject to sanitation inspections by officials from the United States Public Health (USPH) Department of Health and Human Services, under the auspices of the Centers for Disease Control. It is a *voluntary*, and not a *mandatory*, inspection, and the whole program is paid for by the cruise lines. A similar process takes place in Britain under the Board of Trade.

On board many ships, a hygiene officer oversees health and sanitation standards. A tour of the galley has proved to be a highlight on some smaller ships. On larger vessels, passengers are not usually allowed into the galley, due to constant activity and insurance restrictions. A video of *Behind the Scenes*, for use on in-cabin television, may be provided.

According to internationally accepted standards, the potable water brought on board, or produced by distillation on cruise ships, should contain a free chlorine or bromine residual equal to or greater than 0.2 ppm (parts per million). This is why the drinking water served in the dining room often tastes of chlorine.

## Menus

These typical cruise ship menus show the different presentation and cuisine between various lines.

### Breakfast

*Constitution* (American Hawaii Cruises)

**Fresh Fruits**

Island Fruit, Sliced Pineapple, Half Papaya, Melon (in season), Stewed Prunes, Grapefruit Half, Sliced Bananas (in cream), Strawberries (in season)

**Chilled Juices**

Orange, Pineapple, Grape, Grapefruit, Prune

**Cereals**

Corn Flakes, All Bran, Shredded Wheat, Puffed Wheat, Granola, Bran Flakes, Rice Krispies

**Fresh Farm Eggs**

Served with Hash Browns or potato du jour
Scrambled eggs, served plain, with stewed tomatoes or green onions
Fried Egg, sunny side up, or over easy; Soft Boiled Eggs
Omelette, plain, mushrooms, diced ham, or cheese

**Grill**

Minute Steak with Mushrooms, Link Sausages, Canadian Bacon
Portuguese Sausage, Grilled Ham, Country Bacon

**From the Griddle**

French Toast, Pancakes, Waffles

**Toast, Rolls and Pastries**

Macadamia Nut Muffins, English Muffins, White Toast, Croissants, Toasted Bagel, Raisin Toast, Whole Wheat Toast, Assorted Danish

**Health Food Breakfast**

Natural Apple Juice, Yogurt Smoothie, Hawaiian Fruit Plate, Herbal Tea

**Beverages**

Kona Coffee, Kona Decaf, Hot Chocolate, Herbal Tea, Tea, Postum, Milk/Low fat milk

## Cabin Service Menu

*Queen Elizabeth 2*

(Cunard)

*The Cunard Club* triple decker sandwich with bacon, turkey, tomatoes, lettuce and mayonnaise on toast

*Quiche Lorraine* served with raw celery sticks and green olives

*Hot Pastrami* thinly sliced on American rye bread with mustard, coleslaw and dill pickles

*The All American Hamburger* served with coleslaw, tomato and dill pickle and cheddar cheese

### Cold Snacks

*Herring platter* with sour cream, onion rings and bread rolls

*Croissantwich* filled with ham, Swiss cheese, lettuce, tomatoes, pickled vegetables and potato chips

*Sliced Roast Chicken* served with salad garnish and toast, mayonnaise on the side

*Pita Bread* with a filling of cottage cheese, sliced avocado and bean sprouts

*Tuna Fish* with celery and spring onions on whole wheat bread, served with boiled eggs and lettuce

*Sliced Smoked Salmon* served with bagel and cream cheese

### Short Orders

*French Onion Soup* au Gratin

*Minute Fillet Steak* served plain or with herbed butter "Cafe de Paris" salad garnish and toast

*Chicken in the Basket* or *Fillet of Fish in the Basket* deep fried, and accompanied by French fries, coleslaw; sauce tartar served with fish

*Small Country Sirloin Steak* served plain or with fried egg, baked beans, French fries and grilled tomato

*Grilled Veal Scaloppini* served with fresh, hot vegetable garnish and poached pear

*Omelettes* with ham, cheese, herb, mushroom or plain

### Choice of Accompaniment

*Hot*: French fries, onion rings

*Chilled*: Pickled vegetables, dill pickles, olives, relish, kosher pickles

*Dry*: Potato chips, corn chips

### Crudite Platter

Fresh raw vegetables in season with sour cream dip

Fresh Fruit Platter with cottage cheese or yogurt

Whole Fresh Fruit in season

Selection of cheese and crackers with celery and grapes

Feta Cheese Cubes in olive oil and oregano

## Dinner

*Horizon/Meridian/Zenith*

(Celebrity Cruises)

### The Chef Presents

*Smoked Salmon Claudine* an envelope of smoked salmon filled with smoked trout and salmon mousse

*Cream of Broccoli* prepared with fresh broccoli and herbs

*Finlandia Salad* crisp garden greenery with red cabbage, topped with tomato, cucumber, apple and hard-boiled egg – the Chef suggests vinaigrette dressing

*Veal Scaloppine "Celebrity"* presented with a sweet Marsala wine sauce

*Swan Puff* delicate profiterole filled with pastry cream and served with chocolate sauce

### Beverages

Freshly brewed regular or decaffeinated coffee or iced coffee

Tea, herbal tea and iced tea

Hot chocolate, milk

### Appetizers

Fruit Supreme Amaretto

Country pâté

Smoked salmon Claudine

Feuillete of mushrooms in port wine sauce

### Soups

Cream of broccoli

Consommé with vegetables brunoise

Chilled apricot with almond

### Salads

*Finlandia* mixed seasonal lettuces with red cabbage, apple, egg and fresh vegetable garnish

*Pomodori con Basilico* sliced ripe tomatoes with scallions and fresh basil

*Dressings* Creamy garlic, Thousand Island, Vinaigrette

### Entrees

*Chicken Fines Herbes* roast spring chicken seasoned with fresh herbs and enhanced by a creamy bread sauce

*Grilled Mahi Mahi Caprice* pan sauteed with pureed spinach and a choron sauce

*Brochette King Neptune* grilled scallops, shrimp and assorted fish on a skewer and served with linguine and sauce vierge

*Veal Scaloppine "Celebrity"* presented with a sweet Marsala wine sauce

*Entrecôte à l'Échalotes* grilled New York strip steak with herbed shallor butter, garnished with watercress and straw potatoes

Bundle of Vegetables; Cauliflower Gratin; Cretan Potatoes; Straw Potatoes

**Desserts**

Swan puff with chocolate sauce

Fresh fruit in light phyllo pastry

Strawberry cake

Raspberry mousse, red fruit coulis

Burgundy cherry, vanilla or rum raisin ice creams

Today's Sherbert

Fruit and Cheese

Fresh seasonal fruit complemented by fine cheese: Roquefort; Brie de meaux; Swiss Emmental; Edam

### West Indies and South-America Cruise

What is was like in the "old" days. Here is a 1939 dinner menu from Holland America Line's *Nieuw Amsterdam*, Wednesday, 1st February 1939

**Hors d'Oeuvre**

Iced Hearts of Table Celery – Norwegian relishes

Salmon Salad – ripe and green Californian olives

Smoked Sturgeon – sliced black and red radishes

Canapés Danoise – pickled herring

**Soups**

Cream Solférino

Consommé Châtelaine

Potage Cormeilles

**Fish**

Suprême of red snapper singalaise

Broiled porgies with salmon butter

**Relevés**

Roast sirloin of beef Floréan

Roast rack of pork à la Rochambeau

**Hot Entrée**

Stuffed chicken à la Parisienne

**Cold Entrées**

Noisettes of venison à la Cumberland

Chaud-froid of oxtongue Palermo

**Grill (15 min.)**

Sirloin steak (single or double)

Escallops of lamb

Split pork sausages on toast

Grenadins of veal

**Vegetables etc.**

Broccoli with melted butter – peas and carrots

Buttered lima beans – steamed Caroline rice

Potatoes: boiled, duchesse, straw, baked Idaho

**Sherbert**

Mousse Malmason

**Roast**

Philadelphia capon roasted on spit with watercress

Roast barded partridge on toast with bread sauce

**Salads and Compotes**

Hearts of lettuce, Sliced tomatoes

French, Ohio, Russian and Roquefort dressing

Pears, sweet pickled, pineapple, prunes, apple sauce, mixed

**Cakes**

Barquettes Frangipane

Chocolate roll cake

**Ice-Cream**

Coupe Frascati

Chocolate Parfait, Vanilla

**Pastry**

Glazed chestnuts – Friandises

**Fruit**

## Environmental Concerns

Cruise ships refine oil, treat human waste, and incinerate garbage, but that's not enough today. Due to ever increasing regulations and concern about the environment, many cruise lines are replacing plastics with more biodegradable and recyclable materials. For example, plastic plates used in certain areas on general market ships should be replaced by china plates, or washable and re-usable hard plastics. Plastic laundry bags should be replaced by paper bags. Plastic bottles used for in-cabin amenities should be replaced by containers made of recyclable or re-usable materials. Efforts should be made to purchase products made from recycled paper.

## Waste Disposal

Today's cruise ships need efficient handling of garbage and waste materials. While some are equipped with "zero-discharge" facilities, other, older cruise ships still have a way to go when it comes to garbage handling. One method of dealing with food waste is to send it to a waste pulping machine which is partially filled with water. The cutting mechanism reduces the waste and allows it to pass through a sizing ring and be pumped directly overboard or into a holding tank or an incinerator when within three-mile limits. Whichever method is chosen, it, and the ship, must meet Annex V of MARPOL international regulations (see below).

For those interested, here are the present regulations defined:

| Garbage Type | Outside Special Areas | In Special Areas* |
|---|---|---|
| • plastics, including synthetic ropes, fishing nets, plastic garbage bags | disposal prohibited | disposal prohibited |
| • floating dunnage, lining and packing materials | 25 miles off shore | disposal prohibited |
| • paper, rags, glass, metal, bottles, crockery | 12 miles off shore | disposal prohibited |
| • comminuted or ground paper, rags, glass | 3 miles off shore | disposal prohibited |
| • food waste, cooked, not comminuted or ground | 12 miles off shore | 12 miles off shore |
| • general food waste | 12 miles off shore | 12 miles off shore |
| • fresh fish remains | 3 miles off shore | 12 miles off shore |

* Special areas are the Baltic, Black Sea, Mediterranean, Persian Gulf, and Red Sea.

# Cruising for the Physically Challenged

Cruise lines, port authorities, airlines and allied services are slowly improving their facilities to enable those who are wheelchair-bound or otherwise handicapped to enjoy a cruise to the full. At last count, in the United States alone, some 43 million people—or one out of every five people over the age of fifteen—was registered physically handicapped, while in the U.K. over 6 million persons were registered disabled. Not all are in wheelchairs of course, but all have requirements that the cruise industry is (slowly) working to meet.

The very design of ships has traditionally been discouraging for mobility-limited people. To keep out water or prevent it escaping from a flooded cabin or public area, raised edges (known as "coamings" or "lips") are frequently placed in doorways and across exit pathways. Furthermore, cabin doorways are often not wide enough to accommodate even a standard wheelchair.

Bathroom doors are particularly troublesome in this regard, and the door itself, whether it opens outward into the cabin or inward into the bathroom, compounds the problems of maneuvering within a cramped space. Remember, too, that bathrooms on most ships are normally small and are full of plumbing fixtures, often at odd angles—extremely awkward when you are trying to move about from the confines of a wheelchair. Bathrooms on new ships are more accessible, except for the fact that their plumbing is often located beneath the complete prefabricated module, making the floor higher than that in the cabin, which means a ramp must be fitted in order to "wheel" in.

It was once the policy of almost all cruise lines to discourage the mobility-limited from taking a cruise or traveling anywhere by ship for reasons of safety, insurance and legal liability. But it is now becoming clear that a cruise is the ideal holiday for a physically challenged person because it provides a relaxed environment with plenty of social contact, and organized entertainment and activities. However, despite the fact that most cruise brochures state that they *accept* wheelchairs, few ships are well fitted to accommodate them. Some cruise lines, such as Carnival Cruise Lines, openly state that all public restrooms and cabin bathrooms are inaccessible to wheelchair-bound passengers.

While on the subject of bathrooms, note that many ships have bathroom doors that open inward instead of outward, providing even less space. An inward opening bathroom door is hard even for ambulatory passengers, but absolutely useless for anyone in a wheelchair. Many suites have bathroom doors that open inward, while standard-size cabin bathroom doors open outward. Ask your travel agent to check which applies to your ship and cabin chosen.

The Pick-a-Ship chart on page 164 rates each ship according to the facilities it provides for the physically handicapped, and the accessibility to most public rooms. Once you've decided on your ship and cruise, the next step is to select your accommodations. There are many grades of cabin, depending on size, facilities and location. Select a cruise line that permits you to choose a specific cabin, rather than one which merely allows you to select a price category, then assigns you a cabin immediately prior to your departure date or, worse still, actually at embarkation.

The following tips will help you choose wisely:

- If the ship does not have any specially equipped cabins for the handicapped, book the best outside cabin in your price range.
- Choose a cabin that is close to an elevator. Remember that not all elevators go to all decks, so check the deck plan carefully. For example, cabins for the physically challenged on the *Radisson Diamond* are located as far away from the elevators as possible. Smaller and older vessels may not even have elevators, making access to many areas, including the dining room, difficult and sometimes almost impossible.
- Avoid, at all costs, a cabin down a little alleyway shared by several other cabins, even if the price is attractive. The space along these alleyways is extremely limited and entering one of these cabins in a wheelchair is likely to be frustrating.
- Since cabins that are located amidships are less affected by the motion of the vessel, look for something in the middle of the ship if you're concerned about rough seas, no matter how infrequently they might occur.
- The larger (and therefore more expensive) the cabin, the more room you will have to maneuver. Nowhere does this assume more importance than in the bathroom.
- If your budget allows, pick a cabin with a bath rather than just a shower, because there will be considerably more room, especially if you are unable to stand comfortably.
- Ships over 20,000 grt will have more spacious alleyways, public rooms and (generally) cabins. Ships under 20,000 grt tend to have cabins and passageways that are somewhat confining and therefore difficult to maneuver in.
- Meals on some ships may be served in your cabin, on special request—a decided advantage should you wish to avoid dressing for every meal. There are, however, few ships that have enough actual space in the cabin for real dining tables.
- If you do want to join the other passengers in the dining room and your ship offers two sittings for meals, choose the second rather than the first. Then you can linger over dinner, secure in the knowledge that the waiter won't try to hurry you.
- Space at dining room tables is somewhat limited on many ships. When making table reservations, therefore, tell the maitre d' that you would like a table that leaves plenty of room for your wheelchair, so that it is not an obstacle for the waiters and there is room for them—or other passengers—to get past.

- Even if you have found a cruise/travel agent who knows your needs and understands your requirements, try and follow up on all aspects of the booking yourself so that there will be no slip-ups when the day arrives for you to travel.
- Take your own wheelchair with you, as ships carry a very limited number of wheelchairs that are meant for emergency hospital use only. An alternative is to rent an electric wheelchair, which can be delivered to the ship on your sailing date.
- Hanging rails in the closets on most ships are positioned too high for someone who is wheelchair-bound to reach (even the latest ships seem to repeat this basic error). There are certain ships, however, which have cabins specially fitted out for mobility-limited passengers, in which this and similar problem areas have been dealt with. The cabins on *Royal Viking Sun* have walk-in closets, for example. In Part Two of this book, the ships which have special cabins are marked with a "Yes" under Cabins for the Physically Challenged.
- Elevators on many ships are a constant source of difficulty for passengers in wheelchairs. Often the control buttons are located far too high to reach, especially those for upper decks.
- Doors on upper decks that open onto a Promenade or Lido Deck are very strong, difficult to handle and have high sills. Unless you are ambulatory, or can get out of your wheelchair, these doors can be a source of annoyance, even when there's help around.
- Advise any airline you might be traveling with of any special needs well ahead of time so that arrangements can be made to accommodate you without last-minute problems.
- Advise the cruise line repeatedly of the need for proper transfer facilities, in particular buses or vans with wheelchair ramps.

## Embarkation

Even if you've alerted the airline and arranged your travel accordingly, there's still one problem area that can remain when you arrive at your cruise embarkation port to join your ship: the actual boarding. If you embark at ground level, the gangway to the ship may be level or inclined. It will depend on the embarkation deck of the ship and/or the tide in the port.

Alternatively, you may be required to embark from an upper level of the terminal, in which case the gangway could well be of the floating- loading-bridge type, such as those used at major airports. Some of these have floors that are totally flat, while others may have raised lips an inch or so in height, spaced every three feet. These are rather awkward, especially if the gangway is made steeper by a rising tide.

I am constantly pressing the cruise lines to provide an anchor emblem in their brochures for those ports of call where ships will be at anchor instead of alongside. If the ship is at anchor, be prepared for an interesting but safe experience. The crew will lower you and your wheelchair into a waiting tender (ship-to-shore launch) and, after a short boat-ride, lift you out again onto a rigged gangway. If the sea is calm this performance proceeds uneventfully; if the sea is choppy, your embarkation could vary from exciting to harrowing. Fortunately (or not) this type of embarkation is rare unless you are leaving a busy port with several ships all sailing the same day.

Passengers who do not require wheelchairs but are challenged in other ways, such as the sight-impaired, hearing-impaired and speech-impaired, present their own particular requirements. Many of these can be avoided if the person is accompanied by an able bodied companion, experienced in attending to their special needs. In any event, some cruise lines require physically handicapped passengers to sign a waiver.

The advantages of a cruise for the handicapped are many: ideal place for self-renewal; pure air at sea; no smog; no pollen; no packing and unpacking; spacious public rooms; excellent medical facilities close by; almost any type of dietary requirements can be catered for; helpful staff; relaxation; good entertainment; gambling (but, as yet, no wheelchair accessible gaming tables, or slot machines); security; no crime on board; different ports of call and so on.

## Wheelchairs

Wheelchair users with limited mobility should use a collapsible wheelchair. By limited mobility I mean a person able to get out of the wheelchair and step over a sill or walk with a cane, crutches or other walking device.

The chart on the next page indicates the 24 best cruise ships for wheelchair accessibility. To locate cabins for the physically handicapped on each ship (something most cruise lines do not do in their brochures), especially in relation to principal access points, the cabin numbers for the ships are also listed.

Finally, remember to ask questions before you make a reservation. Here are some of the most important to ask:

- Does the ship's travel insurance (cancelation/trip interruption) cover you if any injuries are incurred while you are aboard ship?
- Are there any public rooms or public decks that are inaccessible to wheelchairs (for instance, it is sometimes difficult to obtain access to the outdoor swimming pool deck)?
- Will you be guaranteed a good place in the main showroom from where you can see the shows, if seated in a wheelchair?
- Will special transportation be provided to transfer you from airport to ship?
- If collapsible wheelchairs are required, will the cruise line provide them?
- Are passengers required to sign a medical release?
- Do passengers need a doctor's note to qualify for a handicapped cabin?
- Will crew members be on hand to help, or must passengers rely on their own traveling companions for help?
- Are the ship's tenders accessible to wheelchairs?
- How do you get from your cabin to the lifeboats (which may be up or down several decks) in an emergency, if the elevators cannot be used?

## Top 24 Ships for Wheelchair Accessibility

| Ship | GRT | Passengers | Company | Cabin numbers |
|---|---|---|---|---|
| Celebration* | 47,262 | 1,896 | Carnival Cruises | M76, 77, 78, 79, 80, 81, 94, 95, 96, 97 88, 89, 92, 93 |
| Crown Odyssey | 34,242 | 1,221 | Royal Cruise Line | 8052, 8053, 8054, 8055 |
| Crown Princess*** | 70,000 | 1,910 | Princess Cruises | D101, 103, 104, 106 |
| Crystal Harmony** | 46,621 | 1,010 | Crystal Cruises | 1042, 1043 |
| Ecstasy* | 70,367 | 2,594 | Carnival Cruises | E52, 53, 56, 64, 65, 66, 67, 68, 69, 70, 71, 72, 73, 80, 81, 116, 119, 120, 123 |
| Europa | 37,012 | 600 | Hapag-Lloyd | 159, 161, 170, 172 |
| Fantasy* | 70,367 | 2,634 | Carnival Cruises | E52, 53, 56, 64, 65, 66, 67, 68, 69, 70, 71, 72, 73, 80, 81, 116, 119, 120, 123 |
| Horizon | 46,811 | 1,660 | Celebrity Cruises | 5048, 5049, 5060, 5061 |
| Jubilee* | 47,262 | 1,896 | Carnival Cruises | M76, 77, 78, 79, 80, 81, 94, 95, 96, 97 88, 89, 92, 93 |
| Majesty of the Seas | 73,941 | 2,744 | Royal Caribbean | 2007, 2507, 9034, 9035 |
| Monarch of the Seas | 73,941 | 2,744 | Royal Caribbean | 2007, 2507, 9034, 9035 |
| Nieuw Amsterdam | 33,930 | 1,350 | Holland America | 100, 101, 102, 103 |
| Noordam | 33,930 | 1,350 | Holland America | 100, 101, 102, 103 |
| Nordic Empress | 48,563 | 2,020 | Royal Caribbean | 4548, 4550, 4605, 4607 |
| Norway | 76,049 | 2,370 | Norwegian Cruises | O-49, O-58, O-59, V-123, V-124, V-131, V-220, 0-67, 0-68, P-031 |
| Queen Elizabeth 2 | 69,053 | 1,870 | Cunard | 2113, 2120 |
| Regal Princess*** | 70,000 | 1,910 | Princess Cruises | A105, 109, 122, 124, 125, 129 |
| Royal Princess | 44,348 | 1,275 | Princess Cruises | A459, 465, 467, 471, 473, 475, P203, 205, 217, 219 |
| Royal Viking Sun | 37,845 | 814 | Royal Viking Line | 420, 422, 423, 425 |
| Sensation* | 70,367 | 2,594 | Carnival Cruises | E52, 53, 56, 64, 65, 66, 67, 68, 69, 70, 71, 72, 73, 80, 81, 116, 119, 120, 123 |
| Sky Princess | 46,314 | 1,350 | Princess Cruises | C207, 208, D136, 137, 160, 161 |
| Star Princess | 63,564 | 1,620 | Princess Cruises | C136, 137, 140, 141, D101, 102, 118, 119 |
| Viking Serenade | 40,132 | 1,863 | Royal Caribbean | 4035, 5073, 5547, 5549 |
| Zenith | 47,255 | 1,796 | Celebrity Cruises | 5048, 5049, 5060, 5061 |

* These large Carnival Cruise ships have double width entertainment decks accessible to wheelchair passengers, but public restrooms and cabin bathrooms are not, although cabin bathrooms are equipped with shower stalls and grab bars.

** This ship is the only one with special long access ramps from an accommodation deck directly to the ship's lifeboats.

*** This ship has large outside cabins for the handicapped, but all have obstructed views.

## Sailing as One of the Crew

For something really different and adventurous, how about sailing yourself? The square-rigged sts *Lord Nelson*, constructed in 1988, is a specially built barque sailing ship with three masts and a total of 18 sails. Designed for the physically challenged and able bodied to share the challenge of crewing a ship at sea, the 141-foot-long ship sails in both the Mediterranean and Caribbean areas.

Aptly named after arguably Britain's most famous sailor, the ship was built at Wivenhoe, England, at a cost of $5 million for the Jubilee Sailing Trust, headquartered in Southampton, England. All decks are flat, without steps, and there are special lifts to get between them, as well as up the ship's side to get aboard. There is even a lift seat to go up the main mast for a seagull's eye view!

Navigation aids include an audio compass and bright track radar screen for the blind or partially sighted, ship to shore radio and hydraulic-assist steering.

Down below, all accommodations are accessible to all physically challenged or able bodied crew, with specially fitted cabins and bathrooms. In addition, there is a saloon/bar, launderette, library and workshop. Special yachting-type clothing is available on loan. The *Lord Nelson*'s flat decks, powered lifts, wide companionways and other facilities enable everyone on board to take part on equal terms as part of the ship's crew.

On each voyage, under a professional captain and sailing master, six permanent crew, including a qualified medical purser, guide and instruct the 40-strong crew on each "cruise."

## Hearing Impaired

More than 6 million Americans suffer from hearing loss. Some 1.5 million Americans suffer from a hearing loss of more than 40%. Those affected should be aware of problems on board ship:

- hearing announcements on the public address system
- use of telephone
- poor acoustics in key areas (boarding shore tenders)

Remember to take a spare battery for your hearing aid. Increasingly, new ships feature cabins specially fitted with colored signs to help the hearing impaired. NCL's *Dreamward* and *Windward* provide special cabins for the hearing-impaired—the first to do so.

# Cruising for Romantics

## Singles and Solos

In the early 1950s Howard Hughes presented Jane Russell in an RKO movie called *The French Line*, which depicted life on board one of the great ocean liners of the time—the ss *Liberté*—as being exciting, frivolous, promiscuous and romantic! The movie was, in fact, made on board the great ship. Today in the United States, that same romantic attraction is still very much in vogue.

With more and more singles and solos (those who like to travel alone) in the world today, the possibility of a shipboard romance affords a special attraction. While you may not believe in mermaids, it does happen—frequently. Cruise lines, long recognizing this fact, are now trying to help by providing special programs for single passengers. Unfortunately, many singles are put off cruising because they are unable to understand why so many lines charge a solo occupancy supplement to the fare.

The most precious commodity aboard any cruise ship is space. Every square foot must be used for essential facilities or revenue-earning areas. Since a single cabin is often as large as a double, using the same electrical wiring, plumbing and fixtures—and thus just as expensive to build—cruise lines naturally feel justified in charging supplements or premiums for those occupying single cabins. Singles would probably not mind a smaller cabin, but don't like being charged a supplement or given a poor location.

Where they do exist, single cabins are often among the most expensive, when compared with the per-person rates for double occupancy cabins. They are also less flexible. From the point of view of the crew, it takes as much time to clean a single cabin as it does a double. And there's only one tip instead of two.

One answer is to build double cabins, and, when possible, sell them as single-occupancy units—something that only a handful of cruise lines do. Guaranteed singles rates are offered by several lines, but the line and *not* the passenger picks the cabin. If the line doesn't find a roommate, the single passenger may get the cabin to themselves at no extra charge. Ideally, all lines would offer guaranteed singles rates, with no supplement.

Cruise lines are only now realizing that about a quarter of calls to travel agents (in the United States) are made by singles, single parents, and solos. Singles tend to test the waters by taking short cruises at first. There are lots of singles on the three- and four-day cruises from several U.S. ports, and also from Piraeus (Greece). Cruises to *nowhere*, often known as "party cruises," are popular.

Some cruise lines or tour operators advertise special cruises for singles, but remember that the age range could be anything from 7 to 70. One cruise line in Australia (CTC Cruises) operates 18 to 35 cruises—a nice touch for singles.

Single supplements, or solo occupancy rates, vary between lines, and sometimes between ships. As cruise lines are apt to change such things at short notice, it's best to check with your travel agent for the latest rates, and read the fine print.

The supplement applicable can be found in the ship profile information in Part Two (supplied by the cruise line and correct at the time of going to press).

Some lines charge a fixed amount—$250, for example—as a supplement, no matter what cabin category, ship, itinerary, or length of cruise you require.

## Cruising for Single Women

Single women, career women—whether single or married—and widows can take a cruise vacation knowing they are in an encapsulated, safe environment. There is perhaps no better way to de-stress, and if you are seeking that special someone, cruising somehow brings people closer together. There's always someone to talk to, whether it be couples or other singles, and cruising is not a "meat market" where you are constantly under observation. In the dining room, the maitre d' will seat you with other singles, or a mix of singles and couples, as you wish.

## Cruise Hosts

Because the female to male passenger ratio is high (as much as eight to one on some long cruises), especially for cruisers of middle to senior years, some lines feature male social hosts, generally about half a dozen of them, specially recruited to provide dance partners for passengers. These gentlemen, usually retired, enjoy traveling around the world for nothing and acting as escorts and social hosts.

If you are thinking you'd like such a job, do remember that you'll have to dance just about every kind of dance well, and dance for several hours most nights! Cunard, Crystal Cruises, Ivaran Lines, Regency Cruises, Royal Cruise Line, and Royal Viking Line all provide male social hosts, especially on longer voyages or world cruises.

## *The Love Boat* Connection

The famous television shows *The Love Boat* (U.S.) and *Traumschiff* (Germany) have given a tremendous boost to the concept of cruising as the ultimate romantic vacation, although what is shown on the screen does not quite correspond to reality. Indeed, the captain of one of the ships featured on television, after being asked the difference between his real-life job as captain and that of master of *The Love Boat*, remarked: "On TV they can do a re-take if things aren't quite right first time around, whereas I have to get it right first time!"

Ships are indeed romantic places. There is nothing quite like standing on the aft deck of a cruise ship with your loved one—hair blowing in the breeze—as you sail over the moonlit waters to yet another island paradise. Of course, a full moon only occurs once a month, so you'd better get the calendar out if you want the timing of *your* moonlit cruise to be perfect.

But there is no doubt that cruises are excellent opportunities for meeting people of similar interests. So if you're looking for romance, and if you choose the right ship, the odds are in your favor.

## Getting Married Aboard Ship

Unlike in all those old black and white movies, the ship's captain can no longer marry you, *with one exception—in Japan*—where the law still allows couples to marry at sea. If you can't go on a Japanese-registered ship, you should know that cruise ship captains *can* conduct a marriage vows renewal ceremony.

You *can* get married aboard ship, provided you take along your own registered minister. Some lines, such as American Hawaii Cruises and Carnival Cruise Lines, have a whole package which includes the services of a Minister to marry you, wedding cake, champagne and leis for the bridal party, a band to perform at the ceremony and an album of 24 wedding photos. Carnival Cruise Lines' program includes a marriage ceremony on a beach in St. Thomas. Majesty Cruise Lines offers weddings aboard ship in Miami, and each of five price levels ($375–$825 at time of going to press) includes Notary Public services, witnesses and a beautifully designed certificate.

Even if you can't get married aboard ship, why not have your wedding reception on one? Many cruise lines offer outstanding facilities and complete services to help you plan your reception. Contact the director of hotel services at the cruise line of your choice, and you'll be pleased with the way cruise lines go out of their way to help, especially if you follow the reception with a honeymoon cruise.

UK-based passengers should know that P&O Cruises has a series of cruises called the "Red-Letter Anniversary Collection" specially for those celebrating 10, 15, 20, 25, 30, 35, 40, 45, 50, 55 and 60 years of marriage. Gifts you'll receive with the compliments of P&O Cruises include a brass carriage clock by Taylor & Bligh, leather photograph album, free car parking at Southampton or free first class rail travel from anywhere in the UK (details correct at time of going to press, but check with your travel agent for the latest details).

A cruise also makes not only a fine, no-worry honeymoon vacation, but a delightful *belated* honeymoon getaway if you had no time to spare when you were married. You'll feel like you're in the middle of a movie set as you sail away to fairytale places, though actually, you'll find the ship a destination in itself.

## Cruising for Honeymooners

There's no doubt that cruising is becoming ever more popular as a honeymoon vacation. In fact, U.S.-based Premier Cruise Lines says that more than five per cent of its cruise passengers are honeymooners. There are some real advantages to a honeymoon cruise: you pack and unpack only once; it's a completely hassle-free and crime-free environment; and you'll get special attention, if you want it. What's more, it's also easy to budget in advance, as one price often includes airfare, the cruise, food, entertainment, several destinations, shore excursions, and pre- and post-cruise hotel stays and other arrangements. And, once you are married, some cruise lines often offer discounts if you should book a future anniversary cruise.

Even nicer is the thought that you won't have to think about cooking meals, as everything will be done for you. You won't have to think about where to eat, or what choice you will have. *You can* think of the crew as your very own service and kitchen staff.

Although no ship as yet provides bridal suites, many ships do provide cabins with queen-sized or double beds. Some, but by no means all, also provide tables for two in the dining room.

Some cruise ships feature Sunday or Monday departures (from Miami, San Juan, Venice), which allow couples to plan a Saturday wedding and reception, and leisurely travel to the ship of choice. Pre- and post-cruise hotel stays can also be arranged by the cruise line.

While most large ships accommodate honeymoon couples really well, if you want to plan a more private, intimate honeymoon, then try one of the smaller, yacht-like cruise vessels, where you'll feel like it's your own private ship and you've invited another 50 couples as guests. Highly recommended for a supremely elegant, utterly pampered honeymoon would be those of Renaissance Cruises, Cunard Sea Goddess Cruises, Seabourn Cruise Line, Seven Seas Cruise Line, Showa Line (whose *Oceanic Grace* specializes in weddings, with huge electric chimes built in to the topmost outside deck), and Windstar Cruises. All have an open bridge policy, so you can join the captain on the bridge at almost any time.

While most passengers like to socialize in the evenings, it can be more romantic to take your new spouse outside on deck, to the forward part of the ship, above the ship's bridge. This will be the quietest (except perhaps for some wind noise), and most dimly lit part of the ship, ideal for star gazing and romancing. Almost all ships have such places.

Cruise lines provide a variety of honeymoon packages, just as hotels and resorts on land do. Here's a list of some of the things you can expect (note that not all cruise lines provide all services):

- Private captain's cocktail party for honeymooners
- Tables for two
- Set of crystal champagne or wine glasses
- Honeymoon photograph with the captain, and photo album
- Complimentary champagne (imported or domestic) or wine
- Honeymoon cruise certificate
- Champagne and caviar for breakfast
- Flowers in your suite or cabin
- Complimentary cake
- Special T-shirts

Finally, before you go:

- Remember a copy of your marriage license or certificate, for immigration (or marriage) purposes, as your passports will not yet have been amended.
- Remember to allow extra in your budget for things like shipboard gratuities (tips), shore excursions, and spending money ashore.
- If you need to take your wedding gown aboard for a wedding along the way—in Hawaii, or Bermuda, for example—there is usually space to hang it in the dressing room adjacent to the stage in the main showroom—especially on larger ships.

# Cruising for Families

Yes, you *can* take children on a cruise. In fact, once you get them aboard, you'll hardly see them at all, if you choose the right ship and cruise. Whether you share a cabin with them or whether they have their own separate, but adjoining, cabin, there's plenty to keep them occupied. On several of the ships which cruise in the Caribbean, you'll even find favorite life-sized cartoon characters on board.

Some cruise lines have token family programs, with limited activities and only a couple of staff allocated to children, even though their brochures might say otherwise. But the cruise lines that are really serious about family cruise programs dedicate whole teams of children's "tweens and teens" counselors, who run special programs that are off-limits to adults. They also have specific facilities such as high chairs in the dining room, cots and real playrooms. Most children's entertainment is designed to run simultaneously with adult programs. For those who cruise with very small children, baby-sitting services may also be available (Cunard's *Queen Elizabeth 2*, for example, has full-time children's nurses and even real English nannies).

There's no doubt that families that cruise together, stay together! There's no better vacation for families than a cruise—especially at holiday time—be it at Christmas and New Year, Easter or during the long summer school vacation. Active parents can have the best of two worlds—family togetherness, social contact, and privacy. Cruise ships provide a very safe, crime-free, encapsulated environment, and give junior cruisers a lot of freedom without parents having to be concerned about where their children are at all times. Cruising has never been more child-friendly or affordable, as the emergence of new lines catering specifically to families has proven. Destinations, too, provide a veritable palette of participation excursions for both parents and children to enjoy.

A cruise also allows junior cruisers a chance to meet and play with others in their own age group. And because days are quite long on board ship, youngsters will also be able to spend time with their parents or grandparents, as well as with their peers.

A cruise for children is an educational experience. They'll tour the ship's bridge, meet senior officers and learn about the navigation, radar and communications equipment, as well as seeing how the ship operates. They will be exposed to different environments, experience many types of food, travel to and explore new places and participate in any number of exciting activities.

Cruise ships can be literally crawling with kids, or they can provide quiet moments, shared pleasures, and wonderful memories. But on the busiest ships, such as those of American Family Cruises or Premier Cruise Lines, adults will rarely get to use the swimming pools alone—they will be overcome with children having a truly good time.

Many cruise lines, recognizing the

needs of families, have added a whole variety of children's programs to their roster of daily activities. Some ships have separate swimming pools and play areas for children, as well as playrooms, junior discos, video rooms and teen centers. One cruise company—Carnival Cruise Lines—has created a "Camp Carnival" on its ships. Royal Caribbean Cruises has junior counselors on almost all sailings. Other cruise lines generally have counselors sailing during the summer and other special holiday periods.

Cruise lines that are serious about children split them into five distinct age groups, with various names to match, according to cruise line and program: Toddlers (ages 2-4); Juniors (ages 5-7); Intermediate (ages 8-10): Tweens (ages 11-13); and Teens (ages 14-17). Notably, it often seems to be children under 12 who get the most from a cruise vacation.

Children and junior cruisers are usually not permitted to participate in adult games, tournaments, quizzes and so on, but have their own versions of them. Also, in compliance with international law, as well as with the policy of most cruise lines, casinos and bars are reserved strictly for passengers aged 18 and over.

The company that perhaps best caters to families with children is a new company, founded by Bruce Nierenberg (ex-Premier Cruise Lines), who is himself the father of four children under the age of 10. It's called American Family Cruises and has currently converted one ship, the *American Adventure* (ex-*Costa Riviera*) into a floating theme park, with another, *American Pioneer* (presently operating as the *EugenioCosta*), scheduled to follow at the end of 1994. It's rather like being in summer camp, but all year long and on water. The line boasts that hot meals are available 24 hours a day. For dinner, the dining room is for kids only from 5 to 7p.m. An American-registered pediatrician travels with all cruises.

Then there is Premier Cruise Lines, which carries an abundance of children's counselors on every cruise, on each of its three ships *Star/Ship Atlantic*, *Star/Ship Majestic*, and *Star/Ship Oceanic*, as well as such famous cartoon characters as Daffy Duck and Sylvester. Carnival Cruise Lines features a water slide at the swimming pool on its five largest ships.

In South East Asia there is a new company, Star Cruise, based in Singapore, with one ship, the *Langkapuri Star Aquarius* (the first of a planned fleet of 12) that has incredible facilities for families and children, including a children's video arcade that is unmatched by anything else at sea. There are also seven restaurants/dining places to choose from.

Parents with babies can rest assured that they *will* find selected baby foods on board ships that cater to children (along with cribs and high chairs—but do ask your travel agent to check first). If you need something out of the ordinary, or that special brand of baby food, *do* let your travel agent know well in advance. Most cruise lines are very accommodating and will do their best to obtain what is needed, provided enough notice is given, but for parents using organic baby foods, such as those obtained from health food stores, you should be aware that cruise lines buy their supplies from major general food suppliers and not the smaller specialized food houses.

Many ships have really full programs for children during days at sea, although these may be limited when the ship is in port. Ships expect you to take your children with you on organized excursions, and sometimes (though not always) there are special prices for children. If the ship has a playroom, it might be wise to find out if it is open and supervised on all days of the cruise. Don't expect your travel agent to know everything. Either ask them to find answers to your questions, or do some researching yourself.

When going ashore, remember if you want to take your children swimming or to the beach, that it is wise to phone ahead to a local hotel with a beach or pool. Whether it is in the Caribbean, Mediterranean or the Orient, most hotels will be delighted to show off their property, hoping for future business.

While the sun and sea might attract juniors to the warm waters of the Caribbean, children aged seven and over will find a Mediterranean or Baltic cruise a delight. They will find it easier to understand, remember and compare the differences between ports of call. They will also have a fine introduction to history, languages and different cultures.

## Children's Rates

Most cruise lines offer special rates for children sharing your cabin, often lower than third and fourth person share rates. To get the best possible rates, however, it is wise to book early. And don't overlook booking an inside cabin—you'll rarely be in it anyway.

You should note that while many adult cruise rates include airfare, most children's rates do not! Also, although some lines say children sail "free," they must in fact pay port taxes as well as airfare. The cruise line will get the airfare at the best rate, so there's no need to shop around for the lowest fare.

Unless they have plenty to keep them occupied, even the most placid and well-behaved children can become bored and restless. So choose a cruise where there are lots of other children, as they will be best equipped to provide entertainment. See the Pick-a-Ship chart on page 164.

## Single Parents

Single parents traveling with their child(ren) have their own special needs, and needn't feel left out, either. In fact a cruise provides a safe, convenient way for a single parent and child to be together but also have their own space in a vacation environment and, in some cases, a guarantee of peer companionship for the child. A handful of cruise lines have now introduced their own version of the "Single Parent Plan." This offers an economical way for single parents to take their child on a cruise, with parent and child sharing a two-berth cabin, or parent and children sharing a three-berth cabin. Single parents pay approximately one third the normal single person rate for their children, and there will be plenty of activities for both parent and child to enjoy.

American Family Cruises and Premier Cruise Lines are good places to start. Ask your travel agent for the latest details.

**Top:** *The 37,845-grt, 814-passenger* ***ms Royal Viking Sun*** *(Royal Viking Line), one of the highest-rated cruise ships in the world.*
**Rating:** ★★★★★+

**Above:** *The 37,012-grt, 600-passenger* ***ms Europa*** *(Hapag-Lloyd Cruises), the highest-rated cruise ship for German-speaking passengers.*
**Rating:** ★★★★★+

**Below:** *The 48,621-grt, 1,010-passenger* ***ms Crystal Harmony*** *(Crystal Cruises) provides cruising in grand style.*
**Rating:** ★★★★★+

**Bottom:** *The 24,474-grt, 620-passenger* ***ms Sagafjord*** *and the 24,492-grt, 732-passenger* ***ms Vistafjord*** *(Cunard), both with the same classic, rounded lines, provide top-class service with the real flair of yesteryear.*
**Rating:** ★★★★★+

**Top:** *The 4,260-grt, 116-passenger* ***ms Sea Goddess I*** *and* ***ms Sea Goddess II*** *(Cunard) are the ultimate small boutique ships, offering the height of personal service.*
**Rating:** ★★★★★+

**Above:** *The 9,975-grt, 212-passenger* ***ms Royal Viking Queen*** *(Royal Viking Line) is a small cruise ship which delivers the ultimate in luxury destination-intensive cruises.*
**Rating:** ★★★★★+

**Top:** *The 69,053-grt, 1,870-passenger* ***tsmv Queen Elizabeth 2*** *(Cunard)—with the unmistakable profile of a floating legend—is a city for all seasons, and beyond compare on the North Atlantic.*
**Rating:** ★★★★★+ to ★★★★

**Above:** *The 9,975-grt, 204-passenger* ***ms Seabourn Pride*** *and* ***ms Seabourn Sprit****, right, (Seabourn Cruise Line) are identical in grt to the ms Royal Viking Queen, larger than the Sea Goddesses, and offer a commendable mini-cruise ship experience.*
**Rating:** ★★★★★+

**Left:** *The 70,367-grt, 2,634-passenger* ***ms Fantasy*** *(Carnival Cruise Lines) specializes in three- and four-day Bahamas cruises from Port Canaveral.*
**Rating:** ★★★★

**Below:** *The 73,941-grt, 2,744-passenger* ***ms Majesty of the Seas*** *(Royal Caribbean Cruise Line). Sister ships are* ***ms Monarch of the Seas*** *and* ***ms Sovereign of the Seas****, both of which are in the same size and class.*
**Rating:** ★★★★+

**Below:** *The 67,000-grt, 1,975-passenger **ms Oriana** (P&O Cruises) debuts in 1995. She promises to be an outstanding vessel. (Not yet rated.)*

**Bottom:** *The 70,000-grt, 1,910-passenger **ms Crown Princess** and **ms Regal Princess** (Princess Cruises) are almost identical, featuring the dolphin-like enclosed design forward, and stark upright funnel cluster aft.*
**Rating:** ★★★★+

**Top:** *The 55,451-grt, 1,627-passenger* ***ms Maasdam*** *(Holland America Line) combines old-world charm and service with contemporary facilities.*
**Rating:** ★★★★+

**Above:** *The 48,563-grt, 2,020-passenger* ***ms Nordic Empress*** *(Royal Caribbean Cruise Line) offers three- and four-day Bahamas cruises from Miami all year.*
**Rating:** ★★★★

**Top:** *The 46,811-grt, 1,660-passenger* ***mv Horizon*** *and the 47,255-grt, 1,796-passenger* ***ms Zenith*** *(Celebrity Cruises) are both immaculate ships with service to match.*
**Rating:** ★★★★★

**Above:** *The 44,807-grt, 1,641-passenger* ***tes Canberra*** *(P&O Cruises). Dubbed the "Great White Whale," she is extremely popular amongst cruise passengers from the U.K.*
**Rating:** ★★★+

# Before You Go

## Baggage

There is usually no limit to the amount of personal baggage allowed on your cruise ship, but closet space is limited, so only take things you will use. Allow extra space for purchases. Towels, soap, and shower caps are provided on board.

It is important that all baggage be properly tagged with the owner's name, ship, cabin number, sailing date, and port of embarkation. Tags will be provided by the cruise line along with your ticket. Baggage transfers from airport to ship are generally smooth and problem-free when handled by the cruise line.

Liability for loss or damage to baggage is contained in the passenger contract. If you are not adequately covered, it is advisable to take out insurance for this. The policy should extend from the date of departure until two or three days after your return home. Coverage can be obtained from your cruise/travel agent.

## Clothing

If you think you might not wear it, don't take it: closet space on most ships is at a premium. Unless you are on an extended cruise, keep luggage to a minimum. Most airlines have a limit of two suitcases at check-in (44lb or 20kg) per person, plus a tote bag or carry-all for small items.

For cruises to tropical areas, where the weather is warm to hot with high humidity, casual wear should include plenty of light-weight cottons and other natural fibers. Any synthetic materials do not "breathe" as well and often retain heat. They should, however, be as opaque as possible to counteract the ultraviolet rays of the sun. Also, take a lightweight cotton sweater or two for the evenings, when the air-conditioning will seem even more powerful after a day in the sun.

The same is true for cruises to the Mediterranean, Greek Isles, or North Africa, although there will be little or no humidity most of the year. Certain areas may be dusty as well as dry. In these latitudes, the weather can be changeable and cool in the evenings from October to March, so take extra sweaters.

On cruises to Alaska, the North Cape or the Norwegian fjords, take warm comfortable clothing, plus a raincoat or parka for the northernmost port calls. Cruises to Alaska and the Land of the Midnight Sun only run during the peak summer months, when temperatures are pleasant and the weather is less likely to be inclement. Unless you are going to northern ports such as St. Petersburg during winter, you won't need thermal underwear. However, you will need it—and overcoats, too—if you are taking an adventure cruise to the Antarctic Peninsula or through the Northwest Passage.

In the Far East, clothing will depend on the time of year. The information package that accompanies your tickets will give recommendations. For cruises that start in the depths of winter from a northern port (New York or Southampton, for example) and cruise south to find the sun, take lightweight cottons plus a few sweaters.

Rainstorms in the tropics are infrequent and don't last long, but can give you a good soaking, so take inexpensive, lightweight rain wear for excursions.

At destinations with a strong religious tradition, like Venezuela, Haiti, Dominican Republic, Colombia, and countries in the Far East, shorts or bare shoulders may cause offense.

Aboard ship, dress rules are relaxed during the day, but evening wear is tasteful. Men should take a blazer or sports jacket and ties for the dining room and for "informal" occasions. Transatlantic cruises are normally elegant affairs.

If you are athletic, pack sports clothes for the gymnasium. The ladies should take a leotard and tights for aerobics.

For formal nights (usually two out of every seven), ladies should wear their best long evening gown, elegant cocktail dress, or smart pants suit. Gentlemen are expected to wear either a tuxedo or dark business suit. These "rules" are less rigid on short and moderately priced cruises.

There is normally a masquerade night on each cruise, so you may wish to take a costume. Or you can create something on board out of supplied materials. One of the staff may help, and there may be photographs of past entries. Prizes are given for the most creative costume.

No matter where in the world you are, comfortable low- or flat-heeled shoes are a *must* for women, except for formal nights. Light, airy walking shoes are best. If you are in the South Pacific or Caribbean and are not used to heat and humidity, your ankles may swell—tight shoes are not recommended. Rubber soles are best on deck.

• *Formal*
Tuxedo (alternatively a dark suit) for men; evening gown or other appropriate formal attire for women.

• *Informal*
Jacket and tie for men; cocktail dress, dressy pant suit, or the like for women.

• *Casual*
Slacks and jacket over sweater or open shirt for men; a blouse with skirt, slacks or similar comfortable attire for women.

On a typical 7-night cruise, this is what you might expect for the dress code:

| | |
|---|---|
| *Sat* | Casual |
| *Sun* | Formal (Captain's Welcome Aboard Cocktail Party) |
| *Mon* | Informal |
| *Tue* | Informal |
| *Wed* | Informal |
| *Thu* | Formal (Captain's Farewell Cocktail Party) |
| *Fri* | Casual |

## Documents

A passport is the most practical proof of citizenship and identification. Although it is not required on all cruises, take it along, if you have one. Voter's registration cards and driver's licenses are normally acceptable but are not considered valid proof of citizenship.

If you are a non-U.S. citizen taking a cruise from an American port, you must have a valid B-2 multiple-entry visitor's visa stamped in your passport in order to return to the United States.

If you are cruising to areas other than the Bahamas, Bermuda, the Caribbean, Alaska, Hawaii or Canada, and most of Europe, you may need a tourist visa. Your cruise/travel agent will advise you.

On cruises to the Orient particularly, but also to the Middle East and Africa, you may have to hand in your passport to the purser prior to landing. This enables customs and immigration officials to "clear" the ship more quickly, and is standard. Your passport will be returned when the ship departs, or prior to arrival in the port of disembarkation.

## Flying

For many people, flying to get to a port of embarkation has become the norm. Most cruise lines now include "free air" as part of the cruise ticket. The effects of rampant discounting, however, have resulted in cruise lines negotiating contracts with airlines that mean passengers sometimes have to travel on flights with absurd connections, even where direct flights are available. In the United States, the introduction of deregulation has resulted in most airlines operating on a "hub and spoke" system, with flights feeding into major centers to connect with other flights. It is now more difficult to find non-stop coast-to-coast flights, as airlines prefer passengers to go through the system to ensure full domestic flights. This is not so prevalent in Europe, but distances are comparatively shorter given the size of each country.

## Flying and Air Quality

If you are joining a ship in a far off port and your flight is over six hours duration, you might want to consider paying a little more to move further forward into Business Class or First Class, rather than Economy Class at the back of the plane. The reason for this recommendation is simply that the quality of fresh air is better at the front of the plane than it is at the back. Flying on certain types of aircraft can also dramatically affect the quality of the air in the plane.

It is not easy to change cabin air frequently, for, at 40,000 ft., the external air can be minus 75 degrees Fahrenheit, and almost completely dry. This air must then be heated to 175 degrees Fahrenheit, and moisture must be added before it is pumped into the cabin. This all uses fuel. The latest Boeing and Airbus aircraft have tried to cut down on waste by *recycling* some of the warm and somewhat moist cabin air. The air is filtered using a mesh to catch bacteria, but this adds to the time taken to change the air completely. The worst offenders are the Boeing 747-400 (long-haul) and Airbus A320. What to do if the air is bad? Tell the Senior Flight Purser, who will ask the engineer to increase the circulation.

Whilst on the subject of air quality, smokers should know that in some countries, smoking is banned on some flights. U.S. carriers forbid smoking on all domestic flights. British Airways has banned smoking on all domestic flights since 1988; SAS bans smoking on flights within Scandinavia; Air Canada prohibits smoking on all flights, domestic and international. Air France forbids smoking on flights of under two hours. Lufthansa, on the other hand, allows smoking on all flights, as do many Asian and south European carriers. This information was correct at the time of press, but do check with your travel advisor.

## Flying and Jet Lag

If you are flying a long distance to embark on your cruise or to fly home again, you should know that modern air travel is fast, safe, efficient, and comfortable (for the most part). Even experienced travelers, however, may occasionally find that the stresses of international travel hang on long after the flight is over. Eastbound flights seem to cause more pronounced jetlag than westbound flights. And while jet aircraft are pressurized, they generally are done so only to some 8,000 ft (2,400 meters) in altitude, causing discomfort in the ears and the stomach, and swollen feet. The air of the aircraft cabin is also slightly dry. A few precautions should reduce the less pleasant effects of flying around the world.

First, plan as well in advance of cruise as possible. It is best to take a daytime flight, in order to arrive at, or close to, bedtime. Be as quiet as possible for the 24 hours prior to flying, and allow for another five hours of rest after any flight which crosses more than five time zones.

Enjoy the food and liquor offered during the flight—but in moderation. The best beverages are those that are nonalcoholic and nonsparkling. Smokers may wish to smoke less, for the reduced pressure (and reduced oxygen) means the effect of carbon monoxide is greater, often resulting in a feeling of depression.

Babies and small children feel the least effects of time changes due to their shorter sleeping and waking cycles. Adults generally need more time to adjust.

## Medications

If planning a cruise that takes you away from your home country, make sure and take any medicines that you need, plus spare eyeglasses or contact lenses. In many countries it may be difficult to find certain medications. Others may be sold under different names. Those going on long cruises should ask their doctor for names of alternatives, in case the medicine they are taking is not available.

The pharmacy aboard ship will stock certain standard remedies, but again, don't expect a supply of unusual or obscure medicines. Remember to take along a doctor's prescription for any medications, especially when flying into foreign countries to join a ship, as customs may be difficult without documentation, particularly in the Far East.

Also, be advised that if you run out of your medications and need to obtain a supply aboard ship, even if you have a prescription, most ships will require that you see the doctor. There is a minimum charge of $15 for the visit, plus the cost of the medication.

Diabetic passengers should let spouses/companions carry a supply of insulin and syringes, as well as a quick source of glucose. Make sure you carry a sufficient supply with you, and don't pack it in any luggage to be checked in when flying.

## Money Matters

Most cruise ships deal primarily in U.S. dollars but some take British pounds, German marks, Greek drachmas, or Australian dollars, depending on ship. For on-board transactions, major credit cards and traveler's checks are widely accepted. Few lines take personal checks.

One new idea is the use of cruise line affinity credit cards that allow you to earn up to 3% of monthly net credit card purchases towards the cost of a cruise. To date, Carnival Cruise Lines (VISA), Dolphin Cruise Line and Majesty Cruise Line (MASTERCARD) are doing this.

Many ships now allow passengers to sign for drinks and assorted other services. On some ships a convenient way to settle expenses is to set up a shipboard credit on embarkation. This is especially useful on long voyages. Many lines now operate a "cashless" cruising policy, in which you pay for all on-board expenses by presigned credit card.

## Pets

Pets are simply not carried by cruise ships, with two exceptions. One is on the regular scheduled transatlantic services of *QE2*, which has 16 air-conditioned kennels (and even a genuine British lamp post), cat containers, plus several special cages for birds. The second is on the regular scheduled South Atlantic service from England to Cape Town and the Ascension Islands aboard the *St. Helena*. Quarantine and vaccination regulations should be obtained from the consulates of the country of intended entry.

## Photography

It is hard to find any situation more ideal for photography than a cruise. Through your photographs you can share your memories with others at home.

Consider your destination when buying film. It is best to use low-speed film in tropical areas such as the Caribbean or South Pacific, as high-speed film is easily damaged by heat. Take plenty of film with you; standard sizes are available in the ship's shop, but the selection is limited. If you purchase film on a port visit, try to buy from an air-conditioned store, and check the expiry date.

Keep your film as cool as possible, as the latent image on exposed film is fragile and easily affected by heat. There will be professional photographers on board who may develop film for you—for a fee.

When taking photographs at the various ports of call, respect the wishes of the local inhabitants. Ask permission to photograph someone close-up. Most will smile and tell you to go ahead. But some people are superstitious or truly afraid of having their picture taken and will shy away from you. Don't press the point.

## Work

If you need to work while on board, secretarial help and limited office facilities, including credit-card operated satellite-linked telephone and faxes, and computers, may be available, together with recording equipment, blackboards, slide projectors and screens. Advance notice is advisable, or talk with the hotel manager or purser when you board.

# Life Aboard

## Air-Conditioning

On all modern cruise ships, cabin temperature is regulated by individually controlled thermostats, so you can adjust it to suit you. The temperature in the public rooms is controlled automatically. On board, the air-conditioning is normally kept much cooler than you may be used to, so don't forget a sweater or scarf.

## Baby-sitting

On many ships, stewards, stewardesses, and other staff may be available as sitters for an hourly charge. Make arrangements at the purser's office.

## Beauty Salon/Barber Shop

It is advisable to make any appointments for the beauty salon or barber shop as soon after boarding as possible, especially on short cruises. Appointment times fill up rapidly, particularly before social events such as the captain's cocktail party. Charges are comparable to those ashore. The hours of opening will be posted at the salon, and also listed in the *Daily Program.*

## Bridge Visits

Check the *Daily Program* for announcements of visits to the bridge, for which appointment cards can be obtained from the purser's office or cruise staff office. On some ships, bridge visits are not allowed for reasons of security. On others, although personal visits are forbidden, a *Behind the Scenes* video may be shown on the in-cabin television system.

## Cashless Cruising

It is now quite common to cruise cash-free and settle your account with one easy payment. Often this is arranged by making an imprint of a credit card prior to departure, permitting you to sign for everything. Or you can pay by cash at the end of the cruise.

On many ships, it is no longer possible to pay using cash at the bar, in the beauty salon, or shops—a fact bemoaned by older passengers, many of whom often do not use or possess credit cards.

If your cruise ship includes a "private island" on its Bahamas/Caribbean itinerary, you will be asked to pay cash for all beverages, watersports/scuba diving gear and other items purchased ashore.

Before the end of the cruise, a detailed statement will be delivered to your cabin. Avoid lines by using a credit card for express check out. Some companies that use a "cashless" system may discontinue its use for the last day of the cruise, which can be most irritating.

## Casino

A large number of vessels feature a "full" casino, where blackjack, roulette, craps, and baccarat can be played. Chips and change are available.

Children under 18 are not allowed in the casino. The casino is closed in port due to international customs regulations, and taking photographs in the casino is forbidden. Note that German or Japanese registered ships are not permitted to operate casinos that give cash prizes.

## Comment Cards

On the last day of the cruise you are asked to fill out a company "comment card." Some cruise lines offer "incentives" such as a bottle of champagne or even a free short cruise. Be honest when you fill out this important form, for it can serve as communication between company and passenger. Be warned, however, that on many ships, dining room stewards present "sob" stories of how they will lose their station or section, or even their job, if you don't write "excellent" when you fill out your comment card. Some companies, such as Princess Cruises, provide information on filling out the comment cards, inviting nothing short of an "excellent" rating.

If there *have* been problems with the service, don't write or mark "excellent." Instead, be realistic and mark "good," "fair," or "poor" as the case may be. Otherwise, the cruise line will never know that there are problems and that the service needs improving.

## Communications

Each ship has been designated an internationally recognized call sign, which is made up of a combination of several letters and digits and can be obtained from the cruise line. For each of the ships listed in Part Two of this book, the radio call sign is given (except for those ships which are not yet in service). To receive a call during your cruise, simply give the call sign and name of the ship to those concerned before you leave.

When the ship is at sea, you can call from your cabin (or the ship's radio room) to anywhere in the world:

- by radio-telephone (a slight/moderate background noise might be noticed);
- by satellite (which will be as clear as your own home phone).

Direct dial satellite calls, a service started in 1986, are more expensive, but they are usually completed without delay. Many ships now also have credit card telephones located in public areas aboard ship, which connect instantly at any time of the day or night, via satellite. Satellite calls can still be made when the ship is in port, but radio-telephone calls cannot. You could, however, use the local telephones (often at the local post office).

Satellite telephone calls cost between $5 and $15 per minute, depending on the type of communications equipment the ship carries (the latest system, called Inmarsat-M, is digital and offers lower-priced calls). Cellular telephone calls, such as those operated by Florida-based CruisePhone, typically range from $5.95 to $9.00 per minute. On ships equipped with CruisePhone, payment is made by a major credit card when you make your call. It is more difficult to pay cash for a satellite or cellular telephone call. (Cruise lines should note that many older passengers do not own credit cards.)

It's also good to know that you can be contacted during your cruise through shore-to-ship calling. Your relatives and friends can reach you by calling the *High Seas Operator* in almost any country (in the United States, dial 1-800-SEA-CALL). Vessels equipped with satellite telephone links can be reached via the *Inmarsat* system, by calling any local operator and asking for the Inmarsat Operator. When connected, the name of the ship should be given, together with the ocean code (Atlantic is 871; Pacific is 872; Indian Ocean is 873).

Telegrams, telexes, and faxes are all accepted at the purser's office or radio room for transmission when the ship is at sea. Your in-cabin phone can also be used to call any other part of the ship.

### Customs Regulations

All countries vary in the allowances granted by their own Customs Service, but you will be informed aboard your cruise ship of the allowable amounts for your nationality and residency.

### Daily Program

The *Daily Program* contains a list of the day's activities, entertainment and social events, and is normally delivered to your cabin the evening before the day which it covers. It is important to read it carefully, so that you know what, when, and where things are happening. If you lose your copy, you can obtain another from the purser's office or your cabin steward.

### Deck Chairs

Deck chairs and cushions are available from the duty deck steward, free of charge on most ships. Specific locations cannot normally be reserved, except on the few ships where a charge is made, or by arrangement with the deck steward.

### Departure Tax

If you are disembarking in a foreign port, and flying home, be advised that there may well be a departure tax to pay at the airport. Cruise lines often neglect to advise passengers of this, with embarrassing results, especially when you are normally required to pay the departure tax in a local currency.

### Disembarkation

During the final part of your cruise, the cruise director will give an informal talk on customs, immigration, and disembarkation (sometimes called "debarkation") procedures. At least one member of each family should attend this important talk. This will help simplify and speed up the procedure and avoid confusion at arrival time.

The night before your ship reaches its final destination (in most cases this will be a return to the port you sailed from) you will be given a customs form to fill out. Any duty-free items bought from the shop on board must be included in your allowance, so save the receipts in case a customs officer wishes to see them.

The night before arrival, your main baggage should be packed and placed outside your cabin on retiring or before 4a.m. It will be collected, put in a central baggage area and off-loaded on arrival. Remember to leave out any fragile items and liquor, together with the clothes you intend to wear for disembarkation and onward travel (it's amazing just how many people have packed *everything*, only to find themselves in an embarrassing position on disembarkation day). Anything left in your cabin at this point will be considered hand baggage and has to be hand-carried off when you leave.

On disembarkation day, if you are on a two-sitting ship, be aware that breakfast is usually brought forward by one hour. This means that first-sitting breakfast is often as early as 6:15a.m.! If you are flying home that same day, it's going to turn into a very long day. It might be better to miss breakfast and sleep later, providing announcements on the ship's public address system don't wake you (it's possible on many ships to turn off such announcements).

Even worse than the early breakfast is the fact that you'll be told (requested, if you're lucky) to leave your cabin early, only to wait for hours in crowded public rooms. To add insult to injury, your cabin steward (after he's received his tip, of course) will knock on the door, saying he needs the sheets off the bed so the cabin can be made up for the incoming passengers. Cruise on a small "upscale" ship and this won't happen.

Before leaving the ship, remember to claim any items you have placed in the ship's safety deposit boxes and leave your cabin key in your cabin. Passengers cannot go ashore until all baggage has been off-loaded, and customs and/or immigration inspections or pre-inspections have been carried out on board.

In most ports, this takes two to three hours after arrival. Therefore, do not ask people to meet you at arrival time. They will not be allowed to board, and you can't get off until all formalities have been completed. Also, leave at least three hours from the time of arrival to catch a connecting flight or other transportation.

Listen for announcements about disembarkation procedures and try not to crowd the main disembarkation gangway or lobby areas. Once off the ship, you must identify your baggage at the pierside before going through any further customs (delays are usually minimal). Porters will be there to assist you.

### Drugstore

On some ships, there may be a separate drugstore in which a fairly extensive range of standard items will be available, while on others the drugstore will be a small section of the ship's main gift shop. Opening hours will be posted at the store and given in the *Daily Program.*

### Electric Current

Most ships operating in U.S. waters have standard American 110 AC current and sockets. Newer and refurbished ships have 110- and 220-volt AC (alternating current) outlets. A few older vessels have 220-volt DC (direct current) outlets, but transformers/converters are available.

In general, electrical appliances may only be used if they operate on AC. Check with your cabin steward or stewardess before plugging in anything more powerful than an electric razor (such as a high-wattage hair dryer), just to make sure that the cabin's circuitry can handle the load.

### Engine Room

On virtually all passenger ships, the engine room is off-limits to passengers, and visits are not allowed, for insurance and security reasons. On some ships, a technical information leaflet may be available from the purser's office. On others, a *Behind the Scenes* video may be shown on the in-cabin television system. For more specific or detailed information, contact a member of the ship's engineering staff via the purser's office.

## Gift Shops

The gift shop/ boutique/drugstore will offer a selection of souvenirs, gifts, toiletries, and duty-free items, as well as a basic stock of essentials. You'll find duty-free items, such as perfumes, watches, and so on, very competitively priced, and buying on board ship may save you the hassle of shopping ashore. Opening hours will be posted at the store and given in the *Daily Program*.

## Health and Fitness Facilities

Depending on the size of the ship, health and fitness facilities may include one or more of the following: gymnasium, weight room, sauna, solarium, exercise classes, jogging track, parcours, massage, swimming pool(s), whirlpool baths, nutrition lectures, herbal body wraps and scuba and snorkel instruction. For information, check with your cruise/travel agent, or, when on board, contact the Cruise Director or Purser's Office. Some ships now have elaborate spas where (for an extra fee, such as on the *Norway*), whole days of treatments are available.

## Launch (Tender) Services

Enclosed motor launches (called "tenders") are used on those occasions when your cruise ship is unable to berth at a port or island. In such cases, a regular launch service operates between ship and shore for the duration of the port call. Details of the launch service will be given in the Daily Program and announced over the ship's P.A. system. When stepping on or off a tender, remember to extend "forearm to forearm" to the person assisting you. Don't grip their hands because this simply has the effect of immobilizing the helper.

## Launderette

Some ships have self-service launderettes, equipped with washers, dryers and ironing facilities, all at no charge. Full time supervisory staff may be available to assist you, as on the *Queen Elizabeth 2*. (See the profile information for each individual ship in Part Two).

## Laundry and Dry Cleaning

Most ships offer a full laundry and pressing service. Some ships may also offer dry-cleaning facilities. A detailed list of services (and prices) should be in your cabin. Your steward will collect and deliver your laundry or dry-cleaning.

## Library

Most cruise ships have a library offering a large selection of books, reference material and periodicals. A small deposit (refundable on return of the book) is sometimes required should you wish to borrow a book from the library. Note that on the small luxury ships, the library is open 24 hours a day, and no deposit is required. On the larger ships, you'll probably find the library is open only a couple of hours each day, with the exception of those noted below.

Ships with the best libraries?

| | |
|---|---|
| *World Explorer* | 12,000 books |
| *Queen Elizabeth 2* | 6,000 books |
| *Majesty of the Seas*<br>*Monarch of the Seas*<br>*Sovereign of the Seas* | 2,000 books |
| *Crystal Harmony* | 1,500 books |

Cunard's *Queen Elizabeth 2* is, at present, the *only* ship with a full-time, fully-qualified *real* librarian—June Applebee—a real treasure.

Sadly, some of the Carnival Cruise Lines ships have superb library rooms and luscious, overstuffed armchairs, but, alas, no books! On many ships, the library is also where you request games like Scrabble, backgammon and chess.

## Lifeboat Drill

Safety at sea is the number one consideration of all members of the ship's crew. Standards are set by the Safety of Life at Sea (SOLAS) convention of the International Maritime Organization (IMO). For any evacuation procedure to be totally effective and efficient, passengers must know precisely where to go in the unlikely event that an emergency arises. For this reason, and to acquaint passengers with general safety procedures, a lifeboat drill is held during the cruise. According to international maritime law, this must take place within 24 hours of embarkation. Some ships sensibly program the passenger lifeboat drill prior to sailing, so as not to take time away from passengers during the cruise.

There have been few recent incidents requiring the evacuation of passengers, although three cruise ships have been totally lost following collisions (*Jupiter*, *Oceanos*, and *Royal Pacific*). Travel by ship, however, remains one of the safest means of transportation. Even so, it cannot be stressed enough that attendance at lifeboat drill is not only required by the captain, but also makes sense; participation is mandatory. You must, at the very least, know your boat station, and how to get to it, in the event of an emergency requiring evacuation.

If others are lighthearted about the drill, don't let it affect your seriousness of purpose. Note your exit and escape pathways and learn how to put on your lifejacket correctly. The 15 minutes the drill takes is a good investment in playing safe. (The *Royal Pacific* sank in 16 minutes in 1992 following a collision.)

Lifejackets are found in your cabin. Instructions of how to get to your boat station are on the back of the cabin door.

## Lost Property

Contact the purser's office immediately if you lose or find something on the ship. Notices regarding lost and found property may be posted on the bulletin boards.

## Mail

You can buy stamps and post letters on most ships. Some ships use the postal privileges and stamps of their flag of registration, and others buy local stamps at the next port of call. Mail is usually taken ashore by the ship's port agent just before the ship sails for the next port.

If you are sailing on an extended voyage (around the world, for example), the cruise line will send a list of all its agents and mailing addresses, along with your tickets and documents, before the cruise.

## Massage

Make any appointments for massage as soon as possible after boarding, in order to get a time and day of your choice. Larger ships have more staff, and offer more flexibility in appointment times.

The cost averages $1.00 per minute. On some ships, a massage service is available in your cabin, if it is large enough to accommodate a portable massage table.

## Medical Services

A doctor and nursing staff are aboard ship at all times. Usually there is a reasonably equipped hospital in miniature, although the standard of medical practice and of the physicians themselves varies greatly from line to line. Most shipboard doctors are generalists, and not cardiologists or neurosurgeons.

Unfortunately, many lines place a low priority on medical services (exceptions: *Europa* and *QE2*, whose medical facilities are outstanding, and whose doctors are highly skilled professionals). Most shipboard physicians are not certified in trauma treatment or medical evacuation procedures, for example. Most ships that cater to North American passengers tend to carry doctors licensed in the United States, Canada, or Britain, but on other ships, doctors come from a variety of countries and disciplines. Medical organizations, such as the American College of Emergency Physicians, have created a special division for cruise medicine.

Aboard ship, standard fees are charged for treatment, including for seasickness shots. Any existing health problems that will require treatment on board must be reported at the time of booking.

## Movies

On most cruise ships, a movie theater is an essential part of the ship's public-room facilities. The movies are recent, often selected by the cruise director or company entertainment director from a special film- or video-leasing service.

Some recently built or modified ships have replaced or supplemented the movie theater with television sets in each cabin. News and events filmed on board are shown as well as video movie features.

## News and Sports Bulletins

The news and sports results are reported in the ship's newspaper or placed on the bulletin board—normally located near the purser's office or in the library. For sports results not listed, ask at the purser's office, which may be able to obtain the results for you.

## Passenger Lists

All ships of yesteryear provided passenger lists with each passenger's name and home town. Few companies carry on the tradition (perhaps some passengers are traveling with someone they shouldn't!). Among the companies that still produce a passenger list are: Crystal Cruises, Cunard, Pearl Cruises (Ocean Cruise Lines), Royal Cruise Line, Royal Viking Line, Seabourn Cruise Line, Silversea Cruises, and Sun Line Cruises.

## Photographs

Professional photographers are on board to take pictures of passengers throughout the cruise, including their arrival on board. They also cover all main events and social functions, such as the captain's cocktail party.

All photographs can be viewed without any obligation to purchase (the price is likely to be in excess of $5.00 for a postcard-sized color photograph). They will be displayed on photo boards either in the main foyer, or in a separate photo gallery. The color and quality of these pictures are usually excellent. Duplicates may be obtained even after your cruise, from the shore-based headquarters of the photographic concessionaire.

### Postcards and Writing Paper

These are available from the writing room, library, purser's office, or your room steward. On many ships, they are available for a modest sum.

### Purser's Office

Also called the Reception Office, Guest Relations Desk, or Information Desk. Centrally located, this is the nerve center of the ship for general on-board information and problems. Opening hours are posted outside the office and given in the *Daily Program*. On some ships, the Purser's Office is open 24 hours a day.

### Religious Services

Interdenominational services are conducted on board, usually by the captain or staff captain. A few older ships (and the new ships of Costa Cruise Lines) have a small private chapel. Sometimes denominational services are also offered by specially invited or fellow-passenger members of the clergy.

### Room Service

Beverages and snacks are available at most hours. Liquor is normally limited to the hours when the ship's bars are open. Your room steward will advise you of the services that are offered. There is no charge for this service.

### Safety Aboard

Passenger safety is a high priority for all cruise lines. Crew members attend frequent emergency drills, lifeboat equipment is regularly tested, and fire-detecting devices, alarm and fire-fighting systems are checked throughout the ship. If you spot fire or smoke, use the nearest fire alarm box, alert a member of staff, or contact the bridge. Cruise lines should insist on a common language for all crew members, but this is far from reality.

Be aware that slipping, tripping and falling are the major sources of shipboard injury. This does not mean that ships are unsafe, but there are things you can do to minimize the chance of injury.

#### In your cabin

- Note that on many ships, particularly older vessels, there are raised lips separating bathroom from sleeping area.
- Do not use the fire sprinkler heads on most cabin ceilings as a resting place for hangers, however light they are.
- On older ships, it is wise to note how the door lock works—some require a key on the inside in order to unlock the door. Leave the key in the lock, so that in the event of a real emergency, you do not have to hunt for the key.

#### On deck

- On older ships, look out for raised lips in doorways leading to open deck areas. Be alert and step, don't trip, over them.
- Wear sensible shoes such as those with rubber soles (not crepe) when walking on deck or going to pool and lido areas. Do not wear high heels.

- Walk with caution when outer decks have been washed, or if it has rained—this is especially true of metal decks. There's nothing worse than falling onto a solid steel deck.
- Don't throw lighted cigarette or cigar ends, or knock out your pipe, over the ship's side. The sea might seem like a safe place to throw such items, but they can easily be sucked into an opening in the ship's side or onto an aft open deck area, only to cause a fire.

### How to Survive a Shipboard Fire

Shipboard fires generate heat, smoke, and often panic. In the unlikely event that you are in one, try to remain calm and think logically and clearly.

When you board the ship and get to your cabin, check the way from there to the emergency exits fore and aft. Count the number of cabin doorways and other distinguishing features to the exit in case you have to escape without the benefit of lighting, or in case the passageway is filled with smoke.

On many new ships, exit signs are located just above floor level, but on older vessels, exit signs may be above your head—virtually useless, as smoke and flames always rise.

You should also note the nearest fire alarm location and know how to use it in case of dense smoke and/or no lighting. Indeed, all cabins should have pull-out flashlights, but as yet most do not.

If you are in your cabin and there is fire in the passageway outside, first put on your lifejacket and feel the cabin door. If the door handle is hot, get a wet towel before trying to leave your cabin.

Check the passageway. If everything is clear, walk to the nearest emergency exit or stairway. If there is smoke in the passageway, crawl to the nearest exit. If the exit is blocked, then use an alternate one.

It may take considerable effort to open a fire door to the exit, as they are very heavy. Never use the elevators, as they may stop at a deck that is on fire or full of smoke, and when the door opens, you may not be able to escape.

In the event of a fire beginning in your cabin, report it immediately by telephone. Then try to leave your cabin and close the door behind you to prevent any smoke or flames from entering the passageway. Finally, sound the alarm and alert your neighbors.

## Sailing Time

In each port of call, the ship's sailing and all-aboard times will be posted at the gangway. The all-aboard time is usually half an hour before sailing (ships cannot wait for individual passengers who are delayed). On some ships, you will be given an identification card to be handed in at the gangway when you return from your visit ashore.

## Sauna

Many ships offer a sauna, which is usually small and compact, and occasionally unisex. Sometimes there is a small charge for its use, especially when combined with a massage. Towels are available at the sauna and there is also a small changing area. Opening times will be posted at the sauna and in the information material in your cabin. Reservations are not normally necessary.

## Seasickness

Seasickness is rare these days, even in rough weather. Ships have stabilizers—large underwater "fins" on each side of the hull—to counteract any rolling motion. Nevertheless, you could develop symptoms—anything from slight nausea to actual vomiting. What do you do?

Seasickness is more than a state of mind. It has real physical causes, specifically an imbalance of a mechanism in the inner ear. The mind and brain are accustomed to our walking or riding on a non-moving surface. If the surface itself moves in another direction, a signal is sent to the brain that something's wrong.

Both old-time sailors and modern physicians have their own remedies, and you can take your choice or try them all:

1. When the first movement of the ship is noticed, go out on deck and walk back and forth. The knees, which are our own form of stabilizer, will start getting their feel of balance and counteraction. In other words, you'll be "getting your sea legs."
2. When on deck, focus on a steady point, such as the horizon.
3. Get the breeze into your face, and if nauseous, suck an orange or lemon.
4. Eat lightly. Don't make the mistake of thinking a heavy meal will keep your stomach well anchored. It won't.
5. A recommended preventive for seasickness is ginger in powder form. (Half a teaspoon, mixed in a glass of warm water or milk. Drink before sailing.) It is said to settle any stomach for a period of up to eight hours.
6. "Sea Bands" (called "Aquastraps" in the U.K.) are a drug-free method of controlling motion sickness. These are slim bands (often in varying colors) that are wrapped around the wrist, with a circular "button" that presses against an acupressure point (*Nei Kuan*) on the lower arm. They should be attached a few minutes before you step aboard and be worn on both wrists throughout the cruise.
7. On board, Dramamine will be available in tablet form.
8. Now used by many is "the patch". This is called Transderm Scop, or Transderm V, available by prescription. It's like a small sticking plaster you put behind your ear, almost out of sight. For 72 hours it releases a minute quantity of a drug into the system which counteracts seasickness and nausea. Any side effects are relatively harmless, but check with your physician or ship's doctor. Unpredictable effects which have been observed include acute glaucoma, disorientation, dizziness, intense agitation, and hallucination. After removing the patch, it takes about 12 hours for the reaction to subside.
9. If you are in distress, the ship's doctor has an injection certain to cure all discomfort. It may make you drowsy as well, but the last thing on your mind will be staying awake at the movie.

All of this being said, bear in mind that in addition to the stabilizers on the hull, most cruises are in warm, calm waters and most cruise ships spend much time along the coast or pull into port regularly. The odds are all in your favour.

## Security

Following the *Achille Lauro* hijacking incident in 1985, the United States House of Representatives Committee on the Security of Ports and Vessels, and the United Nations, have suggested ways by which those traveling by cruise ship could expect to receive the same level of protection as those traveling by air. It is satisfying to report that we have seen the progressive formulation of a recognized standard of passenger ship protection. Cruise lines have reached this recognized standard as a result of several factors: a moral obligation which, like safety, is inherent in the industry; the expectation of passengers; and now the firmer and more formal pressures being applied throughout the world by governmental and coast guard authorities.

But in spite of these pressures it is still true that the "recognized" standard can be interpreted widely by different companies and ports. The most conscientious cruise lines, ferry operators, and ports follow the standards laid down by International Maritime Security (IMS), an English company that is the acknowledged world leader in cruise ship, ferry, and port security.

Increasingly, passengers find that at embarkation, as well as at way ports, they are required to go through metal detection devices at the gangway, and baggage will be subject to more stringent inspection procedures. The question of security is now being taken into account during the final ratings and evaluation of the ships in Part Two.

All cabins are provided with keys, and it is recommended that you keep your cabin locked at all times when you are not there. Some keys are normal, metal ones, and operate a mechanical lock, while newer and refurbished ships may have plastic "key cards," which operate electronically coded locks. Cruise lines are not responsible for money or valuables left in cabins and suggest you use a safety deposit box at the purser's office.

You will be issued a personal boarding pass when you embark. This serves as identification and must be shown at the gangway each time you board. If you misplace or lose it, let the purser's office know immediately. The system of boarding passes is one of many ways in which cruise lines ensure passenger safety.

## Shipboard Etiquette

Cruise lines want you to have a good vacation, but there are some rules that must be observed.

In public rooms, smoking and non-smoking sections are available. In the dining room, however, cigar and pipe smoking are not permitted at all.

If you take a video camera with you, note that, due to international copyright infringement regulations, taping of the professional entertainment shows and cabarets is strictly prohibited.

It's all right to be casual when on vacation, but not to enter a ship's dining room in just bathing suits. Bare feet, likewise, are not permitted.

## Sports Facilities

Depending on their size, ships offer a variety of sports facilities. These include some of the following: badminton, basketball practice area, golf driving cage, horseshoes, jogging track, miniature putting green, paddle tennis, quoits, ring toss, shuffleboard, skeet shooting, squash (rarely), table tennis, volleyball. Tournaments are arranged by the sports director or cruise staff. Check the *Daily Program* for times of events.

## Sun

If your cruise takes you to the sun, remember that the closer you get to the equator, the more potent and penetrating are the rays. The rays are most harmful between noon and 2p.m., when the sun is directly overhead.

If you are taking a short cruise to the Bahamas, Caribbean, or Mexico, be wary of trying to get the best possible tan in a short space of time. Use a protective sun cream (15–30 factor range), and reapply it every time you go for a swim or soak in the pool or ocean. Start with just 15 minutes' exposure and gradually work your way up to an hour or so. It is better to go home with a suntan than sunburn. If you overdo it, seek immediate help from the ship's doctor.

## Swimming Pools

Depending on the ship, it will have indoor or outdoor swimming pools. They may be closed in port due to local health regulations and/or cleaning. Hours of opening will be listed in the *Daily Program*. Diving is not normally allowed, since pools are shallow. Parents should note that pools on most ships are not supervised. Be aware that some ships use excessive chlorine or bleaching agents for cleanliness, which could cause colors to run on your bathing attire.

## Television

On most new and recently refurbished ships, in-cabin television is standard. Programing may be obtained by a mixture of satellite and video channels. Some ships can "lock-on" to live international news programs (such as *CNN*), or to *text-only* news services (like *Oceansat News*), for which cruise lines pay a subscription fee per cabin per month. Satellite television reception is often poor, however, due to the fact that ships at sea constantly move out of an extremely narrow beam being downloaded from the satellite and cannot "track" the signal as accurately as a land-based facility. Some ships in the Caribbean can pick up only the Spanish-language Pan-Am satellite.

## Tipping (Gratuities)

Many people find the whole question of tipping awkward and embarrassing. Use the information given here as a guideline, and add your own good judgment.

On some ships, suggestions regarding tips are subtly given, while on others, cruise directors, under the direction of the hotel manager, get carried away and are far too dictatorial. Ships such as those of Princess Cruises offer hints on tipping via the in-cabin video system.

Some brochures, like those of Holland America Line, state that "tipping is not required." Not required, maybe, but "expected" yes. The industry standard for cruises is roughly as follows:

- Dining room waiter: $3.00 per person per day;
- Busboy: $1.50–2.00 per day;
- Cabin steward/stewardess: $3.00 per person per day.

Suite and penthouse passengers should tip $5.00 per person per day to each of the dining room waiters and suite stewards/ stewardesses, as well as to the butler, if there is one.

Any other gratuities should be given according to services rendered, just as you would tip in any first-class restaurant or hotel. For example to the maitre d', wine waiter, and barman. On some ships (those that belong to Cunard, Norwegian Cruise Line, and Royal Caribbean Cruise Line, for example), the tip for the barman or bar waiter is automatically added to your bar check.

Gratuities are usually given on the last evening of a cruise of up to 14 days duration. For longer cruises, you normally extend half of the tip half way through and the rest on your last evening.

Note: On some *Greek* ships, gratuities are given to the *chief steward*, who shares them out at the end of each cruise. If you're on a river cruise, you may be asked to tip the Cruise Director (who is actually more of a cruise manager).

Envelopes for tipping are available from the purser's office, where you can also ask for advice on tipping.

On some of the best-rated ships, such as those listed below, gratuities can be prepaid, so that you do not have to tip at all on board. The ship's staff receive your tips direct from the company. Tipping is all very neat and tidy on: *QE2*, *Royal Viking Sun*, *Sagafjord*, and *Vistafjord.*

Tips are included in the cruise fare on the following ships, on which no extra tipping is permitted: *Club Med I*, *Club Med II*, *Sea Goddess I*, *Sea Goddess II*, *Seabourn Pride*, *Seabourn Spirit.*

### Origin of the Word "Tips"

Before the introduction of postage stamps, coachmen who carried passengers were often asked to carry a letter or other package. A small recompense was given for this service, called a "tip"—which stands for "to insure personal service." Hence, when in future some special service was provided, particularly in the hospitality industry, tips became an accepted way of saying thank you for services rendered.

## Twenty-Four-Hour Clock

On many European-based ships, the 24-hour clock is the standard way of referring to time, in keeping with the practicality of its use in international travel. In spite of the initial strangeness of this system of time-telling, you will soon find it not only simple to use, but far less likely to lead to confusion.

Up to midday, the hours are shown as 0100 to 1200. Thereafter they go from 1300 to 2400. Thus, 1400 is 2p.m.; 1520 is 3:20p.m.; and so on.

## Valuables

A small number of ships have a lock box built into each cabin. However, items of special value should be kept in a safety deposit box in the purser's office. Access to your valuables during the cruise is convenient and uncomplicated.

## Visitors

Passes for visitors to see you on board your ship must always be arranged in advance, preferably at the time of booking. Announcements will be made when it is time for all visitors to go ashore.

## Watersports

Some small vessels, such as *Black Prince*, *Club Med I* and *II*, *Sea Goddess I* and *II*, *Seabourn Pride*, *Seabourn Spirit*, *Wind Song*, *Wind Spirit*, and *Wind Star*, have a watersports platform that is lowered from the ship's stern. These ships carry windsurfers, waterski boats, jet skis, water-skis, and scuba and snorkel equipment, usually at no extra charge. *Seabourn Pride* and *Seabourn Spirit* also feature an enclosed swimming "cage", which is good for areas of the world where nasty fish might be lurking.

## Wine and Liquor

The cost of drinks on board is generally lower than on land, since ships have access to duty-free liquor. Drinks may be ordered in the dining room, at any of the ship's bars or from room service.

In the dining room, you can order wine with your meals from an extensive and reasonably priced wine list. If you like wine with your dinner, try to place your order at lunch time, as waiters are always busiest at the evening meal.

On some ships, a duty-free sales point will allow you to purchase wine and liquor for personal consumption in your cabin. Passengers are not normally permitted to bring this into the dining room or other public rooms, nor indeed any duty-free wine or liquor purchased in port. These regulations are naturally made to protect bar sales, which are a substantial source of on-board revenue for the cruise line.

Indeed, some lines have introduced a "corkage" fee as part of their policy to deter you from bringing your own wines into the dining room.

# Entertainment

After food, the most subjective (and talked-about) part of any *mainstream* cruise experience is the entertainment program. Menus always present a choice of several foods, whereas the same is not often possible in the field of cruise ship entertainment, which must be diversified and innovative, but never controversial. Ask 1,000 people what they would like to see as part of any evening entertainment program, and 1,000 different answers will ensue. It's all a matter of personal taste and choice. Whatever one expects, gone are the days when waiters doubled as singers to entertain passengers, although a few bar waiters are known to perform tray-spinning effects to boost their tips!

Many people expect top notch entertainment, "headline" marquee name cabaret artists, i.e. the world's most "popular" singers, and dazzling shows with slick special effects, just as one would find in the best venues in Las Vegas, London, or Paris. But there are many reasons why it's not exactly like that. Internationally known acts invariably have an entourage that must accompany them to any venue: their personal manager, musical director (often a pianist or conductor), a rhythm section (bass player and drummer), even their hairdresser. On land, one-night shows are possible, whereas on ships, an artist cannot always disembark after one night, especially when carrying equipment, costumes, and baggage. They can also lose valuable money-making bookings, and telephone contact. Although they can be contacted at sea, it *is* more difficult, and the telephone number is not their own. This makes the whole matter logistically and financially unattractive for all but the very largest ships on fixed itineraries, where a marquee name act might be considered a marketing draw.

When at home you can literally bring the world's top talent into your home via television. Cruise ships are a different entity altogether. Most entertainers do not like to be away from their "home base" for long periods, as they rely on the telephone for their work. Most do not like the long contracts that the majority of ships must offer in order to amortize the cost over several weeks.

Entertainers on ships must also *live* with their audiences for several days (sometimes weeks), something unheard of on land, as well as work on stages seldom designed for real live performances.

Many older (pre-1970) ships have very limited entertainment spaces, and few ships provide proper dressing rooms and backstage facilities for the storage of costumes, props, or effects, not to mention the extensive sound and lighting equipment most live "name" artists demand or need. Indeed, only the latest ships provide the extensive facilities needed for presenting the kind of high-tech shows one would find in Las Vegas, London, or New York, for example, with elaborate electronic backdrops, multislide projection, huge stageside video screens, pyrotechnic capabilities, and the latest light-mover and laser technology. Even the latest ships often lack enough dressing rooms and hanging space for the 150 costumes required in a typical ship production show.

Entertainment on today's large mainstream ships is market-driven. In other words, it is directed toward that segment of the industry that the cruise line's marketing department decrees it is targeting (discounting notwithstanding). This is mostly a family audience, so the entertainment must appeal to as broad an age range as possible—a tall order for any cruise line's director of entertainment.

A cruise line with several ships will normally have an entertainment department made up of an entertainment director and several assistants, and most cruise lines have contracts with one or more entertainment agencies who specialize in entertainment for cruise ships.

It is no use, for example, a company's booking a juggler who needs a floor-to-ceiling height of 12 ft., only to find that the ship has a show lounge with a height of just 7 ft. ("Couldn't he juggle sideways?" I've heard one cruise company executive ask!); or an acrobatic knife-throwing act (on a moving ship?); or a concert pianist when the ship only has an upright honky-tonk piano; or a singer who sings only in English if the passengers are German-speaking, and so on.

Indeed, the hardest audience to cater to is one of mixed nationalities (for example, German-speaking, English-speaking, Spanish-speaking passengers, each of whom expects entertainers to cater exclusively to their own linguistic group). With cruise lines now marketing to more international audiences in order to fill ships (and to avoid the rampant discounting in the North American marketplace), the problem of finding the right entertainment is far more acute.

Upscale cruise lines offer more classical music, even some light opera, fine lecturers and world-renowned authors than the seven-day package cruises heading for warm-weather destinations.

One area of entertainment that has become part of the experience, and is expected—particularly on the larger, mainstream cruise ships—is that of the glamorous "production show." This is the kind of show one would expect to see in any good Las Vegas show palace, with a team of singers and dancers, a production manager, lavish backdrops, extravagant sets, grand lighting, special effects, and custom-designed costumes.

Passengers booking back-to-back 7-day cruises (on alternating eastern and western Caribbean itineraries, for example) should be aware that entertainment is generally geared to 7-day cruises. Thus, you will usually find the same two or three production shows, and the same acts on the second week of your cruise. The way to avoid seeing everything twice is to pace yourself by just going to some events during the first week, and saving the rest for the second week.

## Show Biz at Sea

In today's high-tech world, putting together a lavish 50-60 minute production show takes the concerted efforts of a number of experienced people from the world of show business, and a cost of $1 million per show is not unheard of. Weekly running costs (performers' salaries; costume cleaning and repair; royalties; replacement audio and video tapes and so on) all add up to an expensive package for what is often a largely unappreciative and critical audience.

## Who's Who

Although production companies differ in their approach, the following list gives an idea of the various people involved behind the scenes.

### Executive Producer

His/her job is to transfer the show's concept from design to reality. First, the brief from the cruise line's director of entertainments might be for one new production show (the average being two major shows per seven-day cruise). They must first plan the show. After deciding an initial concept, they may call in the choreographer, vocal coach, and musical arranger for several lengthy meetings, so everyone agrees on the flow of the show.

### Choreographer

The choreographer is responsible for auditioning dancers, and for the creation, selection and teaching of all dance routines. He/she normally works in conjunction with the executive producer.

### Musical Director

His/her job is to coordinate all musical scores and arrangements. He/she may also train the singers in voice and microphone techniques, projection, accenting, phrasing, memory and general presentation, and oversee all session singers and musicians for the recording sessions, click-track tapes, and so on.

### Musical Arranger

After the music has been selected, musical arrangements must be made. For just one song, this can come to a cost of as much as $2,000 for a single arrangement for a 12-piece orchestra.

### Costume Designer

He/she must provide creative original designs for a minimum of seven costume changes in one show lasting 45 minutes. Costumes must also be practical, as they will be used repeatedly.

### Costume Maker

He/she must purchase all materials, and be able to produce all costumes required by the costume designer, in the time frame allotted.

### Graphic Designer

His/her job is to provide all the set designs, whether they are physical one- two- or three-dimensional sets for the stage, or photographic images created on slide film, video, laser disk or other electronic media. Increasingly, digital computer technology plays an important part in creating the images to be transferred via an electronic medium.

### Lighting Designer

His/her job is to create the lighting patterns and effects for a production show. Sequences and action on stage must be carefully lit to the best advantage. He/she will also present the completed lighting plot to a software company that will etch the plot into computer-controlled disks to be used every time the show runs.

## Production Show Timing

A complete, new, large-scale production show, from conception to first performance, takes several months. Here is a breakdown for a hypothetical show.

### Month 1

- Production team create show concept.
- Write storybook and submit it to all concerned.
- Second and third meetings of the production team. The set designer provides sketches and graphics.
- Costume designer contracted to design costumes for seven scene changes. Different costumes are usually required for each lead singer (one male, one female), and dancers.
- Costume maker given order for 70 costumes to be delivered in April.

### Month 2

- Advertise for dancers and singers.
- Book a rehearsal theater (with wooden stage) for auditions for dancers.
- Auditions and call-backs for dancers.
- Book a rehearsal studio (with piano, microphones and amplifiers) for auditions for singers.
- Auditions and call-backs for singers.
- Select suitable talent, issue contracts on behalf of the cruise line (usually five or six months). Talent will go back to their existing jobs while the new show is put together, making sure that they will be available for rehearsals once started. Measurements are taken for the costume designer.

### Month 3

- Fine-tuning by production team; timing of scene and costume changes.
- Order sets, backdrops, color slides. Video footage to be made.
- Go into the recording studio.
- Lay down: principal tracks<br>backing tracks.<br>click (SMPTE timing) track.
- Mix down and edit tape.
- Produce "master" and "mother" tapes.
- Produce copies for use aboard ship, as well as backup copies.

### Month 4

- Costume fitting; first dress rehearsal.
- Second costume fitting.

### Month 5

- Final rehearsals for intensive two- or three-week period.
- Give details of ship's mailing address to all cast members, so that they can receive mail while working aboard .
- Obtain working visas for all cast.

## Month 6

- Crate and freight show costumes, sets, and backdrops.
- Provide the cruise line with details for booking flights and transportation.
- Provide the company's port agents with a name and flight list so they can meet and transfer the cast to the ship.
- Take the show on the high seas.
- After boarding and getting to know the layout of the ship, there will usually be one week of intensive rehearsals, often from midnight to about 5a.m., while the cast that is coming off the ship (for vacation, or end of contract) will still be doing a regular cruise.

## Month 7

- The opening night for the new show will probably be on the first formal night of the cruise. No doubt all the ship's senior officers will be in attendance to "judge" the show.

## Bands/Musicians

Before the big production shows and artists can be booked, bands and musicians must be hired, often for long contracts. Polish musicians are favored for a ship's showband, as they are excellent music readers (necessary for all visiting cabaret artists, not to mention the big production shows).

American and British musicians are found on increasingly few ships, for cruise lines have experienced too many problems with drugs, drink, and unions. Most musicians work contracts of about six months. Entertaining lounge duos and solo pianists or singer/pianists are generally hired through an entertainment agency specializing in cruise ships.

Steel bands are recruited from the Caribbean, while other specialist bands (such as Country & Western) may come aboard for special occasions or charters.

## Other Entertainment

Most cruise ships organize acts that, while perhaps not nationally recognized "names," can provide two or three different shows during a seven-day cruise. These will be male/female singers, illusionists, puppeteers, hypnotists, and even circus acts, with wide age range appeal.

Comedians, comediennes and comedy duos who do "clean" material can find employment year-round on what is now known as the "cruise ship circuit." These comics enjoy good accommodations, are stars while on board, and often go from ship to ship on a standard rotation every few days. Raunchy, late-night "adults only" comedy is also found on some of the ships with younger, "hip" audiences, but few seem to have enough material for two different shows.

The larger a ship, the larger will be the entertainment program. On some ships, the cruise director may "double" as an act, but most companies prefer him/her to be strictly an administrative and social director, allowing more time to be with passengers. Whichever ship and cruise you choose, you'll find that being entertained "live" is far superior to sitting in front of a television, with its clinical presentation. That's show business!

# Nautical Notes

The world of ships is a world of its own, and associated with it is a whole language and culture which can sometimes be confusing—but always fascinating—to the newcomer. Here are a few tidbits of nautical information which may contribute to the pleasure of your cruise.

## Rules of the Road

Ships are subject to stringent international regulations. They must keep to the right in shipping lanes, and pass on the right (with certain exceptions). When circumstances are in doubt or shipping lanes are crowded, ships often use their whistles, in the same way an automobile driver uses directional signals to show which way he will turn. When one ship passes another, a single blast on the whistle means he is turning to starboard (right). Two blasts means a turn to port (left). The other vessel acknowledges by repeating the same signal.

Ships also carry navigational running lights at night—green for starboard, red for port. In addition, two white lights are carried on the masts, the forward one lower than the aft.

Flags and pennants form another part of a ship's communication facilities and are displayed for identification purposes. Each time a country is visited, its national flag is shown. While entering and leaving a port, the ship flies a blue and vertical stripes to request a pilot, while a half red, half white flag (divided vertically) indicates that a pilot is on board. Cruise lines and other passenger shipping lines also display their own "house" flag, proudly fluttering from the main mast.

In the shipping industry, a ship's funnel or smokestack is another means of identification, each line having its own funnel design and color scheme. The size, height, and number of funnels were points worth advertising at the turn of the century. Most ocean liners of the time had four funnels and were known as "four-stackers."

In today's cruise industry, perhaps the most distinctive funnel design belongs to the gleaming white ships in the Royal Caribbean Cruise Line fleet, whose four vessels each have a nightclub or lounge perched partway up the stack itself, making the ships instantly identifiable. The view from one of these is quite spectacular, although in bad weather, it's the room that will move most.

There are numerous customs at sea, many of them older than any maritime law. Superstition has always been an important element, as in the following example quoted in the British Admiralty Manual of Seamanship:

"The custom of breaking a bottle of wine over the stem of a ship when being launched originates from the old practice of toasting prosperity to a ship in a silver goblet of wine, which was then cast into the sea in order to prevent a toast of ill intent being drunk from the same cup. This practice proved too expensive and so was replaced in 1690 by the breaking of a bottle of wine over the stem."

## On The Watch

A ship's working day is composed of six four-hour time periods called "watches." In theory, a complement of officers and crew work the same watch round the clock: four hours on followed by eight hours off during any 24-hour period.

To avoid working identical hours day after day, one of the four-hour periods is split further into first and second "dog watches" of two hours each, as follows:

| | |
|---|---|
| 0000-0400 hours | midwatch |
| 0400-0800 hours | morning watch |
| 0800-1200 hours | forenoon watch |
| 1200-1600 hours | afternoon watch |
| 1600-1800 hours | first dog watch |
| 1800-2000 hours | second dog watch |
| 2000-2400 hours | evening watch |

On board ship, time is traditionally recorded by the striking of bells to indicate the state of the watch. Each bell represents a half hour of time on watch and the duty is ended when eight bells sound at midnight, 0400, 0800, 1200, etc.

## Wind Speeds

A navigational announcement to passengers is normally made once or twice a day giving the ship's position, temperature and weather information.

Wind velocity is measured on the Beaufort Scale, a method devised in 1805 by Commodore Francis Beaufort, later Admiral and Knight Commander of the Bath, for measuring the force of wind at sea. Originally, it measured the effect of the wind on a fully rigged man-of-war. It became official in 1874, when it was adopted by the International Meteorological Committee.

You might be confused by the numbering system for wind velocity. The 12 velocities, known as "force" on the Beaufort Scale, are as follows:

| Force | Speed (mph) | Description/Ocean Surface |
|---|---|---|
| 0 | 0-1 | Calm; glassy (like a mirror) |
| 1 | 1-3 | Light wind; rippled surface |
| 2 | 4-7 | Light breeze; small wavelets |
| 3 | 8-12 | Gentle breeze; large wavelets, scattered white-caps |
| 4 | 13-18 | Moderate breeze; small waves, frequent white-caps |
| 5 | 19-24 | Fresh breeze; moderate waves, numerous white-caps |
| 6 | 25-31 | Strong breeze; large waves, white foam crests |
| 7 | 32-38 | Moderate gale; streaky white foam |
| 8 | 39-46 | Fresh gale; moderately high waves |
| 9 | 47-54 | Strong gale; high waves |
| 10 | 55-63 | Whole gale, very high waves, curling crests |
| 11 | 64-73 | Storm; extremely high waves, froth and foam, poor visibility |
| 12 | 73+ | Hurricane; huge waves, thundering white spray, nil visibility |

## Knots and Logs

A knot is a unit of speed measuring one nautical mile per hour. (A nautical mile is equal to one sixtieth of a degree of the earth's circumference and measures exactly 6,080.2 ft. It is about 800 ft.—or one seventh—longer than a land mile.

Thus, when a ship is traveling at a speed of 20 knots (note: never referred to as 20 knots per hour), she is traveling at 20 nautical miles per hour.

This unit of measurement has its origin in the days prior to the advent of modern aids. At that time, sailors used a log and a length of rope in order to measure the distance which their boat had covered, as well as the speed at which it was advancing.

A 1574 tract by one William Bourne, entitled *A Regiment for the Sea*, records the method by which this was achieved. The log was weighted down at one end while the other end was affixed to a rope. The weighted end, when thrown over the stern, had the effect of making the log stand upright, thus being visible.

Sailors believed that the log remained stationary at the spot where it had been cast into the water, while the rope unravelled. By measuring the length of rope used, they could ascertain how far the ship had traveled, and were thus able to calculate its speed.

They first tied knots at regular intervals (eventually fixed at 47 ft. 3 in.) along the rope, and counted how many knots had passed through their hands in a specified time (later established as 28 seconds), measured by the amount of sand that had run out of an hour glass.

Simple multiplication followed, and the number of knots per hour their boat was traveling was clearly established.

The data thus obtained were put into a record—called a logbook. Today, a logbook contains day-to-day details of the life of a ship and its crew, as well as other pertinent information.

## Latitude and Longitude

Latitude signifies distance north or south of the equator, while longitude signifies distance east or west of the 0 degree at Greenwich, London. Both are recorded in degrees, minutes, and seconds. At the equator, one minute of longitude is equal to one nautical mile, but as the meridians converge after leaving the equator, meeting at the poles, the size of a degree becomes smaller.

## Prefixes

**ib** = ice-breaker (diesel- or nuclear-powered)
**ms** = motor ship (diesel power)
**mts** = motor twin screw (diesel power), *or* motor turbine ship (steam turbine power)
**mv** = motor vessel (diesel power)
**RMS** = Royal Mail Ship
**ss** = steamship
**ssc** = semi-submersible craft (swath)
**sts** = sail training ship
**tes** = turbo-electric ship (steam turbine power)
**ts** = turbine steamer (steam turbine power), *or* twin screw vessel
**tsmv** = twin screw motor vessel
**ys** = yacht ship

## Plimsoll Mark

The safety of ships at sea and all aboard them owes a great deal to a 19th-century British Member of Parliament called Samuel Plimsoll.

He was concerned about the frequent loss of ships due to overloading. In those days certain shipowners would load their vessels down to the gunwales in order to squeeze every ounce of revenue out of them. They gambled on good weather, good fortune and good seamanship to bring them safely into port. Consequently, many ships went to the bottom as a result of their buoyancy being seriously impaired by overloading.

Samuel Plimsoll helped enact legislation known as the Merchant Shipping Act of 1875, which required shipowners to mark their vessels with a circular disc bisected with a line which would be observed as a measure of their maximum draft, i.e. the depth to which a ship's hull could safely be immersed at sea. However, the Merchant Shipping Act of 1890 was even stricter, and required the Plimsoll Mark to be placed on the sides of vessels in accordance with tables prepared by competent authorities. The Plimsoll Mark is now found on the ships of every nation.

The Plimsoll Mark indicates three different depths: the depth to which a ship can be loaded in fresh water, which is less buoyant than salt water; the depth in summer, when seas are generally calmer; and the depth in winter, when seas can be much rougher.

## The Challenge of the Blue Riband

No award has inspired as much rivalry between shipping lines as the coveted Blue Riband, given to the liner making the fastest transatlantic crossing. Indeed, possession of the Blue Riband became—and still is—a source of national pride.

Already in the late 1800s references to the award were recorded, but the first real mention was on August 1, 1900, when the *Illustrated London News* reported that the Blue Riband had been won by the Hamburg America Line passenger ship *Deutschland.*

Although the great passenger liners of the North Atlantic raced to beat the speed record, there was no material award until 1935, when the late Harold K. Hales (1888–1942), a member of the British Parliament, offered a huge silver challenge trophy to the steamship line that established claim to the Blue Riband. So important did speed become, that newspapers carried daily records of distance steamed by major ships, as well as the duration of each crossing. Average speeds, although not revealed, could be calculated from the figures provided.

Naturally the distance covered can vary with each crossing of the Atlantic. Since 1900 the shortest distance recorded for Blue Riband purposes was 2,807 nautical miles, between Sandy Hook, New Jersey, and Queenstown (now Cobh) in Ireland, while the longest distance was 3,199 nautical miles, between Ambrose Light, New Jersey, and Cherbourg. Twelve ships have held the record westbound, and ten eastbound.

Some of the most illustrious passenger ships are listed among the holders of this prestigious award. For 22 years the Blue Riband was held by Cunard Line's *Mauretania*, passing briefly in 1929 to Germany's *Bremen* and in 1930 to that country's *Europa.*

In 1933 the Italian *Rex* took over, only to lose it two years later to France's

*Normandie*. Then came the *Queen Mary* to vie with the *Normandie*. Both kept the award for a year each, in 1936 and 1937 respectively, until in 1938 Cunard firmly retrieved it with the *Queen Mary*. In 1952, the prize was taken by the new liner, the *United States*.

The *United States* has the distinction of being the fastest *real* liner ever to win the Blue Riband. Between July 3 and 7, 1952, during an eastbound crossing from Ambrose to Bishop Rock, an average speed of 35.59 knots was recorded, although it is claimed that in achieving such a speed, mechanical damage was caused to the extent that any attempt to repeat the performance was virtually out of the question.

No major passenger ship has been built since the early 1950s to challenge the ss *United States*' record, although with the re-engining of Cunard's *QE2*, it is conceivable that she could attempt a Blue Riband crossing, having achieved over 36 knots during her sea trials.

On June 22, 1990, a 243-ft.-long, twin-hulled Sea Cat (catamaran-type) passenger ferry (and not a cruise ship) called *Hoverspeed Great Britain*, made a successful, though somewhat unsporting, bid for the Blue Riband. The vessel, commissioned by Hoverspeed of England to bolster the company's fleet of hovercraft in anticipation of impending competition from the Channel Tunnel, carried only one passenger, and had to refuel three times in mid-ocean, something no genuine ocean-going passenger liner has ever had to do. The trophy was awarded, however, and is now back in England, where it first started.

## Ship Talk

Ships and the sea have their own special vocabulary. This list may be of use.

**Abeam**—off the side of the ship, at a right angle to its length

**Aft**—near, toward or in the rear of the ship

**Ahead**—something that is ahead of the ship's bow

**Alleyway**—a passageway or corridor

**Alongside**—said of a ship when it is beside a pier or another vessel

**Amidships**—in or toward the middle of the ship; the longitudinal center portion of the ship

**Anchor Ball**—black ball hoisted above the bow to show that the vessel is anchored

**Astern**—at or toward the stern (back) of the ship

**Backwash**—motion in the water caused by the propeller(s) moving in a reverse (astern) direction

**Bar**—sandbar, usually caused by tidal or current conditions near the shore

**Beam**—width of the ship between its two sides at the widest point

**Bearing**—compass direction, expressed in degrees, from the ship to a particular objective or destination

**Below**—anything beneath the main deck

**Berth**—dock, pier, or quay. Also means bed on board ship

**Bilge**—lowermost spaces of the infrastructure of a ship

**Boat Stations**—allotted space for each person during lifeboat drill or any other emergency when lifeboats are lowered

**Bow**—the forwardmost part of the vessel

**Bridge**—navigational and command control center

**Bulkhead**—upright partition (wall) dividing the ship into compartments

**Bunkers**—the space where fuel is stored; "bunkering" means taking on fuel

**Cable Length**—a measured length equaling 100 fathoms or 600 feet

**Chart**—a nautical map used for navigating

**Colors**—refers to the national flag or emblem flown by the ship

**Companionway**—interior stairway

**Course**—direction in which the ship is headed, in degrees

**Davit**—a device for raising and lowering lifeboats

**Deadlight**—a ventilated porthole cover to prevent light from entering

**Disembark** (also Debark)—to leave a ship

**Dock**—berth, pier or quay

**Draft** (or Draught)—measurement in feet from the ship's waterline to the lowest point of its keel

**Embark**—to join a ship

**Fantail**—the rear or overhang of the ship

**Fathom**—distance equal to six feet

**Flagstaff**—a pole at the stern of a ship where the flag of the ship's country of registry is flown

**Free Port**—port or place that is free of customs duty and regulations

**Funnel**—chimney from which the ship's combustion gases are propelled into the atmosphere

**Galley**—the ship's kitchen

**Gangway**—the stairway or ramp link between ship and shore

**Gross Registered Tonnage (grt)**—not the weight of the ship but the total of all permanently enclosed spaces above and below decks, with certain exceptions, such as the bridge, radio room, galleys, washing facilities, and other specified areas. It is the basis for harbor dues. New international regulations introduced in 1982 require shipowners to re-measure the grt of their vessels (1 GRT = 100 cubic feet of enclosed space/2.83$m^3$) and not its weight

**Helm**—the apparatus for steering a ship

**House Flag**—the flag denoting the company to which a ship belongs

**Hull**—the frame and body of the ship exclusive of masts or superstructure

**Leeward**—the side which is sheltered from the wind

**Manifest**—a list of the ship's passengers, crew, and cargo

**Nautical Mile**—one sixtieth of a degree of the circumference of the earth, equal to 6,080.2 ft. It is about 800 ft. (or one seventh) longer than a land mile

**Pilot**—a person licensed to navigate ships into or out of a harbor or through difficult waters, and to advise the captain on handling the ship during these procedures

**Pitch**—the rise and fall of a ship's bow that may occur when the ship is under way

**Port**—the left side of a ship when facing forward

**Quay**—berth, dock, or pier

**Rudder**—a finlike device astern and below the waterline, for steering the vessel

**Screw**—a ship's propeller

**Stabilizer**—a gyroscopically operated retractable "fin" extending from either or both sides of the ship below the waterline to provide a more stable ride

**Starboard**—the right side of the ship when facing forward

**Stern**—the aftmost part of the ship which is opposite the bow

**Tender**—a smaller vessel, often a lifeboat, which is used to transport passengers between the ship and shore when the vessel is at anchor

**Wake**—the track of agitated water left behind a ship when in motion

**Waterline**—the line along the side of a ship's hull which corresponds to the surface of the water

**Windward**—the side toward which the wind blows

**Yaw**—the erratic deviation from the ship's set course, usually caused by a heavy sea

## The Bridge

A ship's navigation bridge is manned at all times, both at sea and in port. Besides the captain, who is master of the vessel, other senior officers take "watch" turns for four or eight hour periods. In addition, junior officers are continually honing their skills as experienced navigators, awaiting the day when they will be promoted to master of a luxury cruise ship.

Besides the ship's captain, there is a qualified officer on duty at all times—even when the ship is docked in port. The captain is always in command at times of high risk, such as when the ship is entering or leaving a port, when the density of traffic is particularly high, or when visibility is severely restricted by poor weather.

Navigation has come a long way since the days of the ancient mariners, who used only the sun and the stars to calculate their course across the oceans. The Space-Age development of sophisticated navigation equipment has enabled us to make giant strides from the less reliable techniques used long ago. Navigation satellites have allowed us to eliminate the guesswork of early navigation (the first global mobile satellite system came into being in 1979).

Today's navigators can establish their location accurately in any weather and at any time. There follows a description of some of the navigation instruments which will help you understand the complexities of seamanship today.

## System Control

The most sophisticated state of the art machinery and navigation systems are such technical marvels that sailors of yesteryear could not even conceive of their invention. The latest navigation and command system, known as "Electronic Chart Precise Integrated Navigation System" (ECPINS) now combines the electronics of the latest satellite positioning methods (Global Positioning System), with automatic course plotting, video map displays of the oceans, gyrocompass, echo sounders, sonar doppler log, wind speed, and the various sensors to provide, in one compact computer unit, a comprehensive at-a-glance display of the ship in relation to the rest of the world, all in one "real-time" position on a single monitor's electronic chart.

## The Compass

A compass is the instrument by which a ship may be steered on a pre-selected course, and by which bearings of *visible* objects can be taken in order to fix a ship's position on a navigation chart. There are two kinds of compass. The magnetic compass uses the inherent magnetic forces within and around the Earth; the gyro compass, a relatively recent invention, uses the properties of gyroscopic inertia and precession—ideally to align itself to true north–south.

## Steering

There are two different methods that can be used to steer a ship:

- Electro-Hydraulic steering uses automatic (telemotor-type) transmission from the wheel itself to the steering gear aft. This is generally used in conditions of heavy traffic, during maneuvers into and out of ports, or when there is poor visibility.
- Automatic steering (gyropilot) which is used only in the open sea. This system does not require anyone at the wheel. However, on all ships, a quartermaster is always at the wheel, keeping an eye on the system for extra safety—and in case a need should arise to switch from one steering system to another. This changeover from one to the other takes only a few seconds.

**Below:** *The 44,348-grt, 1,275-passenger* ***mv Royal Princess*** *(Princess Cruises) features 600 all-outside cabins, many of which have private balconies.*
**Rating:** ★★★★+

**Bottom:** *The 42,276-grt, 1,798-passenger* ***ms Seaward*** *(Norwegian Cruise Line) shows good open deck space and functionality in design.*
**Rating:** ★★★★

**Below:** *The 22,785-grt, 760-passenger* ***mv Regent Sea*** *(Regency Cruises) is one of only a handful of two-funnel ships today. She offers cruising for the budget-minded.*
**Rating:** ★★★

**Bottom:** *The 20,295-grt, 354-passenger* ***ssc Radisson Diamond*** *(Diamond Cruises), a world first: twin-hulled, semi-submersible, with four stabilizing fins and an underwater viewing area.*
**Rating:** ★★★★★

**Top:** *The 15,065-grt, 644-passenger* ***ms Kareliya*** *(CTC Cruise Lines), a good ship for the budget-minded passenger.*
**Rating:** ★★+

**Above:** *The 56,800-grt, 1,782-passenger* ***mv CostaRomantica*** *(Costa Cruises), sister ship to the* ***mv CostaClassica****, is ideal for families.*
**Rating:** ★★★★+

**Top:** *The 8,378-grt, 200-passenger* ***ms Hanseatic*** *(Hanseatic Tours) is a small, luxury expedition-type ship which features unusual destination-intensive itineraries.*
**Rating:** ★★★★★

**Above:** *The 3,153-grt, 138-passenger* ***ms World Discoverer*** *(Clipper Adventure Cruises) is a small vessel constructed for in-depth expedition cruises.*
**Rating:** ★★★★+

**Left:** *The diminutive 3,990-grt, 111-passenger* ***ms Renaissance Two*** *(Renaissance Cruises) is a small boutique ship which features destination-intensive itineraries.*
**Rating:** ★★★★

**Below:** *The 3,025-grt, 182-passenger* ***sv Star Flyer*** *(Star Clippers), with all 16 sails flying, is a true clipper ship, but with all modern amenities. Her almost identical sister is* ***sv Star Clipper****.*
**Rating:** ★★★★+

**Below:** *The 5,703-grt, 159-passenger **mys Wind Song, mys Wind Spirit** and **mys Wind Star** (Windstar Cruises)—a fine contemporary cruise experience.*
**Rating:** ★★★★+

**Top:** *The floating watersports marina in the stern of* ***ms Royal Viking Queen*** *(Royal Viking Line),* ***ms Seabourn Pride*** *and* ***ms Seabourn Spirit*** *(Seabourn Cruise Line).*

**Above:** *Welcoming a new cruise ship in the Port of Miami—the 53,700-grt, 1,766-passenger* ***ms CostaClassica*** *(Costa Cruises) in January 1992.*

**Top:** *The Viking Crown Lounge, the distinctive trademark of all Royal Caribbean Cruise Line ships, is set midway on the ship's funnel, and provides dramatic views.*

**Above:** *The cast of* ***The Love Boat*** *television series, seen here with Commodore John Young (third from right), who was the real ship's captain (now retired).*

## Satellite Navigator

With this latest high-tech piece of equipment, officers can read, on a small television screen, the ship's position anywhere in the world, any time, in any weather with pinpoint accuracy (within plus or minus 600 feet) in the open ocean.

The satellite navigator uses the information transmitted by a constellation of up to six orbiting satellites. Each satellite is in a normal circular polar orbit at an altitude of 450 to 700 nautical miles, and orbits the Earth in roughly 108 minutes. Data broadcast from each gives its current orbital position every two minutes.

Apart from telling the ship where it is, it can continuously provide the distance from any given point, calculate the drift caused by currents and so on, and tell the ship when the next satellite will pass.

The basis of satellite navigation is the U.S. Navy Satellite System (NNSS). This first became operational in January 1964 as the precision guidance system for the Polaris submarine fleet, and was made available for commercial use in 1967.

The latest system (and more accurate) is the GPS (Global Positioning System), which is now fitted to an increasing number of ships. This uses 24 satellites (18 of which are on-line at any given time) which can provide an accuracy in ship positioning of plus or minus 6 feet (just under 2 meters). Another variation is the NACOS Navigational Command System. NACOS collects information from satellites, radar, gyroscopic compass, speed log, surface navigational systems, engines, thrusters, rudders and human input. It then displays relevant computations and information on one screen controlled by a single keyboard.

## Radar

Radar is one of the most important developments in navigational aids, providing on screen a picture of all solid objects in a range selected by the navigator—from half a mile to a 72-mile radius. Its greatest asset is possibly as an invaluable aid to collision avoidance with other ships, although it has proven of value in finding a position when navigational marks or charted coastlines are within its range. Some ships have two or three radar sets with inter-switch units.

## Engine Telegraph

These automatic signalling devices communicate orders between the bridge and engine room. There may be three—one on the bridge and on each bridgewing.

## Bow Thruster

This small two-way handle controls the bow-thrusters—powerful engines in the bow that push the ship away from the dockside without tugs. Some new ships may also have thrusters at the stern.

## Rudder Angle Indicator

This device is normally located in front of, and above, the quartermaster. It provides both the commanding officer and the quartermaster with a constant readout of the degrees of rudder angle, either to port (left) or starboard (right).

### VHF Radio

This is a radio receiver and transmitter, operating on VHF (Very High Frequencies) with a "Line-of-Sight" range. It is used for communicating with other ships, pilots, port authorities, and so on.

### Radio Direction Finder

This operates on radio waves, enabling its operator to take bearings of shore radio stations. By crossing two or more bearings, you find the ship's position.

### Depth Indicator

This equipment (an echo-sounder) provides a constant digital monitor readout, together with a printed chart.

### Course Recorder

This records and prints all courses followed by the ship at all times.

### Clearview Screen

A simple but effective use of centrifugal force, where instead of an automobile-type windshield wiper, circular screens actually rotate at high speed to clear rain or sea spray away, providing the best possible view in even the worst weather.

### Engine Speed Indicators

These provide a reading of the number of revolutions per minute of the engines. Each engine has a separate indicator, giving the speed in forward or reverse.

### Facsimile Recorder

This is a special radio apparatus that is designed to receive meteorological and oceanographic maps, satellite pictures, and other pertinent weather information transmitted by maritime broadcast stations located all over the world.

## Emergency Controls

Control boards, electric circuits, and other devices control flooding and fires.

### Fire Control

If anyone sounds the fire alarm, an alarm automatically rings on the bridge. A red panel light will be illuminated on a large plan of the ship, indicating the section of the ship to be checked so that the crew can take immediate action.

In the event of a fire, a ship is sectioned into several distinct zones, each of which can be tightly closed off. In addition, most cruise ships have a water-fed sprinkler system that can be activated at the touch of a button, or automatically activated when sprinkler vials are broken by fire-generated heat.

New electronic fire detection systems are installed to increase safety further.

### Emergency Ventilation Control

This is an automatic fire damper system, also with a manual switch that is activated to stop or control the flow of air (oxygen) to all areas of the ship, so reducing the fanning effect on flame and smoke via air-conditioning and fan systems.

### Watertight Doors Control

Watertight doors throughout the ship can be closed off, in order to contain the movement of water flooding. A master switch activates all the doors in seconds.

Each watertight door can be operated electrically and manually. This means that nobody can be trapped in a watertight compartment.

### Stabilizers Control

A ship's two stabilizing fins can be extended, housed or controlled. They normally operate under the command of a gyroscope in the engine control room.

## Quips and Quotes

Passengers cruising for the first time are the source of all the following questions:

*"Do the crew sleep on board?"*

*"How far above sea level are we?"*

*"Does this elevator go up as well as down?"*

*"Will this elevator take me to my cabin?"*

*"What time's the Midnight Buffet?"*

*"Are there two sittings at the midnight buffet?"*

*"Is dinner in the dining room?"*

*"How many fjords to the dollar?"*

*"When the ship's at anchor tomorrow, can we walk ashore?"*

*"Do we have to stay up until midnight to change our clocks?"*

*"What time's the 2 o'clock tour?"*

*"Where's the bus for the walking tour?"*

*"Are the entertainers paid?"*

*"Will the ship wait for the tour buses to get back?"*

*"Will I get wet if I go snorkeling?"*

*"Do the Chinese do the laundry by hand?"*

*"Is the mail brought on by plane?"*

*"Does the ship dock in the middle of town?"*

*"Who's driving the ship if the Captain is at the cocktail party?"*

*"Is the doctor qualified?"*

*"Is the island surrounded by water?"*

*"I'm married, but can I come to the Singles Party?"*

*"Should I put my luggage outside the cabin before or after I go to sleep?"*

**Overheard in the dining room:**

*"Waiter, this vichyssoise is cold."*

*"Was the fish caught this morning by the crew?"*

Overheard on a British islands cruise:

*"Windsor Castle is terrific. But why did they build it so close to the airport?"*

Overheard on a Greek islands cruise:

*"Why did the Greeks build so many ruins?"*

Overheard on a round-Japan cruise, in Kagoshima, with Mount Suribaya in the background:

*"Can you tell me what time the volcano will erupt—I want to be sure to take a photograph?"*

Then there's the cruise line brochure which describes cabin layout: "cabins with double bed can accommodate a third passenger!" (Premier Cruise Lines)

And what about the saying "He let the cat out of the bag?" On board a square-rigger 150 years ago, this would have sent shudders through one's spine—for it meant that a sailor had committed an offense serious enough to have the "cat o' nine tails" extracted from its bag. The "cat" was a whip made of nine lengths of cord, each being about 18 inches long with three knots at the end, all fixed to a rope handle. It could bring serious injuries, even death upon the victim. It is no longer carried on today's tall ships, having been outlawed by the U.S. Congress in 1850, and then by Britain's Royal Navy in 1879.

## The Cruiser's Prayer

"Heavenly Father, look down on us, Your humble, obedient cruise passengers who are doomed to travel the seas and waterways of this earth, taking photographs, mailing post cards, buying useless souvenirs and walking around in ill-fitting swim wear.

"We beseech You, oh Lord, to see that our plane is not hi-jacked, our luggage is not lost, and that our over-sized carry-ons go unnoticed.

"Protect us from surly and unscrupulous taxi drivers, avaricious porters and unlicensed, English-speaking guides in foreign places.

"Give us this day Divine guidance in the selection of our cruise ships and our travel agents—in order that we may find our bookings and dining room reservations honored, our cabins of generous proportions, that our luggage arrives before the first evening meal, and our beds be made up.

"We humbly ask that our shower curtains will not provoke us into meaningless frustration and destructive thoughts.

"We pray that our cabin telephones work, the operator (human or electrical) speaks our tongue and that there are no phone calls from our children forcing us to abandon our cruise early.

"Lead us, dear Lord, to good, inexpensive restaurants in the world ashore —where the food is superb, the waiters friendly and the wine included in the price of a meal.

"Please grant that you give us a Cruise Director who does not cause excessive "creaming" from the spoils of bingo or horse racing, or does not stress only those jewelry stores from which he accepts an offering.

"Grant us the strength to take shore excursions—to visit the museums, cathedrals, spice stalls and gift shops listed in the guidebooks.

"And if on our return journey by non air-conditioned buses we slip into slumber, have mercy on us for our flesh is weak, hot and tired.

"Give us the wisdom to tip correctly at the end of our voyage. Forgive us for under tipping out of ignorance, and over tipping out of fear. Please make the Chief Purser and ship's staff love us for what we are and not for what we can contribute to their worldly goods or company comment forms.

"Dear God, keep our wives from shopping sprees and protect them from bargains they do not need or cannot afford. Lead them not into temptation in St. Thomas or Hong Kong for they know not what they do.

"Almighty father, keep our husbands from looking at foreign women and comparing them to us. Save them from making fools of themselves in cafés and nightclubs. Above all, please do not forgive them their trespasses for they know exactly what they do.

"And when our voyage is over and we return home to our loved ones, grant us the favor of finding someone who will look at our home videos and listen to our stories, so our lives as tourists will not have been in vain. This we ask you in the name of our chosen cruise line, and in the name of American Express, Visa, Mastercard, and our banks. Amen."

## Did you know ...?

...that the average time for a ship to pass through the Panama Canal is 8 hours? The fastest transit time was set by the USS *Manley*, at 4 hours and 38 mintues.

...that the first passenger ship to be fitted with stabilizers was the 24,215-grt, 1949-built *Chusan* of the Peninsular & Oriental Steam Navigation Company (P&O)?

...that the first "en suite" rooms (with private bathroom in cabin) were on board Cunard Line's *Campania* of 1893?

...that the first ship-to-shore wireless telegraphy took place on an American passenger ship, the *St Paul* in 1899?

...that the first passenger ship to exceed 10,000 grt was the *City of New York* of 1888 (British)?

...that the first passenger ship to exceed 40,000 grt was the White Star Line's *Olympic* of 1911?

...that the first passenger ship to exceed 80,000 grt was the Compagnie Generale Transatlantique's *Normandie* of 1935 (built at 79,280, and later measured at 82,799 in 1936).

...that the last three-funnel passenger ship was the Cunard/White Line's *Queen Mary* (1939–1967).

...that the last four-funnel passenger ship was Cunard's *Aquitania* (1914–1949)?

# Who's Who on Board

Consider that a cruise ship is a highly structured floating hotel, in which each crew member fills a well-defined role. A look at the chart on pages 120-121 will clarify the hierarchy aboard ship. The highest authority is the captain, and the chain of command works down through the ranks.

All members of the ship's company wear a uniform by which their station and function are instantly identifiable. Rank is also designated by the colors and insignia worn on the sleeves and epaulets of the uniform itself, although the colors in conjunction with the gold braid can vary somewhat. For example, throughout most of the industry, red generally signifies the medical department, but on ships of Italian registry, red signifies the purser's department.

## Captain

The captain is the master of the ship and has absolute dictatorial rights and control over his vessel, officers, crew, and passengers. He is a seaman first, and manager of the ship second. He is also expected to be a generous and worthy host (the social aspect of a captain's job today requires an investment of about a quarter of his time spent with his passengers). When passenger ships are registered for insurance coverage (normally with Lloyd's of London), the captain's credentials and past record are reviewed, together with the seaworthiness of the vessel itself.

Although on the bridge there may be several officers with a master's certificate, the captain still maintains unquestioned authority. He wears four gold bars on his sleeves and epaulets.

Every ship has a log, a daily record in which are noted all navigational and pertinent nautical data, details of reports from various department heads and any relevant information on passengers or crew. Maritime law dictates that only the captain is allowed to make daily entries in the log, a necessary but time-consuming part of his job. If a ship were to be abandoned, the log is the only record of the ship's operation, prevailing conditions, weather information, and geographical locations that could be reviewed. The captain normally attends numerous social functions during the course of a cruise, hosts a table in the dining room, and is often seen during the day on walkabout inspection tours.

## Staff Captain

The staff captain is second in command and can take over at any time if needed. As the title suggests, the staff captain is concerned not only with the navigation bridge, but also concentrates on the day-to-day running of the ship, its staff and crew, and all discipline.

In some companies the staff captain takes over when the captain is on leave; in others there is a "floating" captain who takes all the relief commands. The staff captain also wears four gold bars.

The captain and staff captain work closely together, dividing the duties according to company policy and/or personal interest. At all times, one of the two must be on call, and most cruise lines insist that one or the other remains on board in any port of call.

Although the captain earns a top salary, the staff captain is on almost the same scale. As a matter of interest, despite equal expertise and responsibility for a passenger count often three times as great, a ship's captain earns roughly half the salary of a jumbo jet pilot.

The airline captain has the added advantage of switching on an automatic pilot to handle almost every navigational task once aloft, and homes in on a runway through computer assistance and radar. His seagoing counterpart must be able to navigate manually and negotiate hidden reefs, sandbars, sunken vessels, and marker buoys—even hazards not recorded on any chart.

The seagoing captain also has the awesome responsibility of docking, maneuvering, and anchoring his ship, often in unfamiliar territory and sometimes in difficult weather conditions.

## Bridge Officers

Besides the captain and staff captain, other bridge officers include the chief officer, first officer, second officer, and several junior officers. Their job is the navigation and safe conduct of the vessel at all times. The bridge is manned 24 hours a day, even in port.

Also on the bridge are the fire-detection systems and controls for the fire and watertight doors, which can be activated by "compartments" in the event of a problem on the ship.

## Chief Engineer

The chief engineer (almost always referred to as "Chief") has the ultimate responsibility for the mechanical well-being of a cruise ship. This includes overseeing not only the main and auxiliary engines, but also the generators, electrical systems, air-conditioning, heating, plumbing, ventilation, refrigeration, and water desalinization systems.

He is trained in a multiplicity of on-board systems, and is, in fact, the only person on board who talks to the captain as an equal. With regard to engineering, he is mechanical master. He wears four gold bars.

## Chief Radio Officer

The function of the chief radio officer is to keep the ship in constant touch with the outside world. The radio station is where all radio, telegraph, telex, and satellite communication equipment is found. The radio officer is also in charge of the automated telephone exchange, and, on a large cruise ship, has a staff of at least three.

## Principal Medical Officer

On the large cruise ships, the medical department can be extremely busy, with up to 2,700 passengers and 1,000 crew to attend to. Hopefully, you will meet the doctor socially, not professionally.

# The Ship's Company

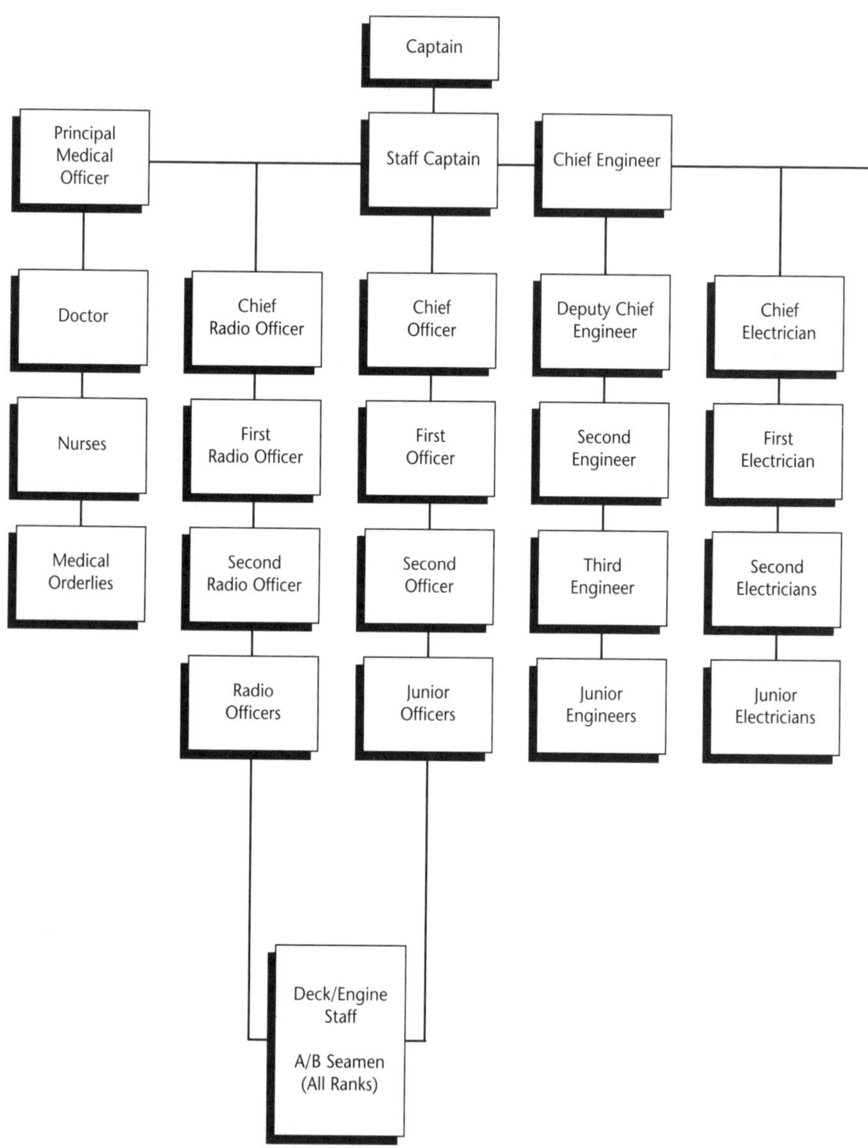

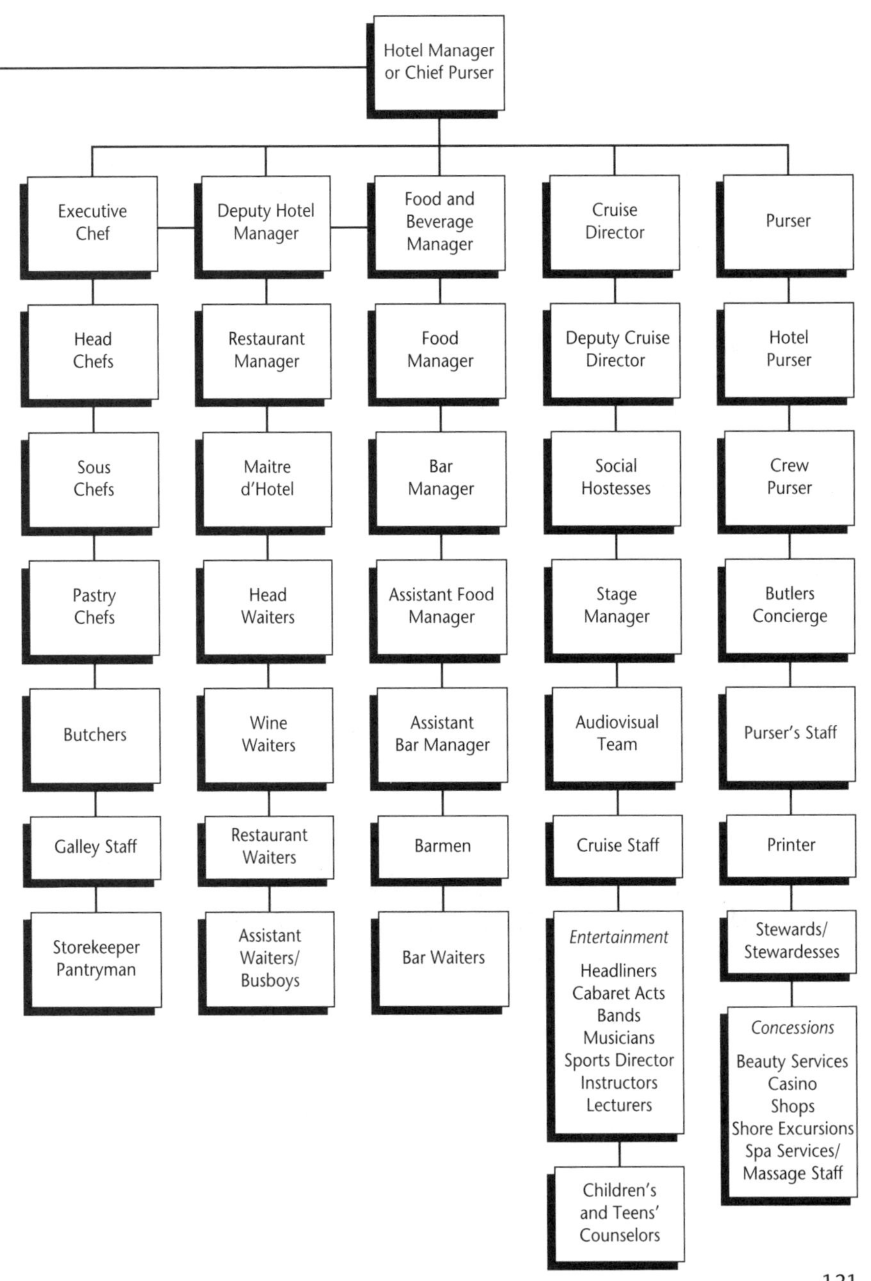
Hotel Manager or Chief Purser
Executive Chef
Head Chefs
Sous Chefs
Pastry Chefs
Butchers
Galley Staff
Storekeeper Pantryman
Deputy Hotel Manager
Restaurant Manager
Maitre d'Hotel
Head Waiters
Wine Waiters
Restaurant Waiters
Assistant Waiters/ Busboys
Food and Beverage Manager
Food Manager
Bar Manager
Assistant Food Manager
Assistant Bar Manager
Barmen
Bar Waiters
Cruise Director
Deputy Cruise Director
Social Hostesses
Stage Manager
Audiovisual Team
Cruise Staff
Entertainment
Headliners
Cabaret Acts
Bands
Musicians
Sports Director
Instructors
Lecturers
Children's and Teens' Counselors
Purser
Hotel Purser
Crew Purser
Butlers Concierge
Purser's Staff
Printer
Stewards/ Stewardesses
Concessions
Beauty Services
Casino
Shops
Shore Excursions
Spa Services/ Massage Staff

The hospital on many cruise ships is a miniature version of a hospital ashore, and may be equipped with an operating theater, an X-ray room, examination rooms, several beds, and an isolation unit. There is at least one fully qualified doctor on board every cruise ship that is carrying 50 or more passengers, plus a small nursing staff. There may also be a physiotherapist, medical orderlies who may be petty officers, and maybe even a dentist.

## Hotel Manager

As head of a "floating hotel" involving almost two-thirds of the entire crew, the hotel manager is in charge of overall passenger service, comfort, housekeeping, food, drink, and information services, plus entertainment—just as in any first-class hotel ashore.

There will also be several junior hotel officers and other staff to whom responsibility for the day-to-day running of various departments can be delegated.

The hotel manager's two most important associates and aides are the purser and the cruise director. At one time, the purser (called the chief purser on some ships) was responsible for the control of all passenger services. But due to the increasing emphasis placed on food, recreation, comfort, and entertainment, the new position of hotel manager has been developed.

On some ships, hotel managers are simply former chief pursers with a new title and added responsibilities.

If at any time during your cruise you have any unresolved problems or a request that has not been satisfied, contact the hotel manager or deputy hotel manager through the purser's office.

## Chief Purser

The chief purser's office is the financial, business, accommodations and information center of any ship and will be found in a convenient location in the main lobby area.

The purser's department handles all matters relating to money (including currency exchange), mail, telexes, telegrams, and telefaxes; it accepts valuables for safekeeping; and provides a complete information service, sometimes around the clock. The purser is also responsible for all passenger and crew accounts, purchasing and requisitioning of supplies, shipboard concessions, the on-board printing of items such as the *Daily Program* and menus, and manning the telephone switchboard, if the ship does not have an automatic system. The purser's domain also includes relations with customs and immigration officials in all ports of call.

The purser has two main assistants: the hotel purser and the crew purser. The hotel purser is in charge of all passenger business, including accommodations (often under the direction of a berthing officer), while the crew purser handles all matters relating to the ship's personnel and contracts.

If the ship is based in foreign waters, the crew purser also oversees crew changeovers and requests, and arranges flights, baggage, and any other incidental crew matters. Many larger ships have two complete crews, one of which will be on leave while the other works the ship. Often, this works on a continuous rotation basis.

## Deputy Hotel Manager

The deputy hotel manager can take over from the hotel manager at any time, while his special domain is the food and beverage operation. On some ships, this is run by a concessionaire, who supplies not only the food, but also the dining room and bar staff, in which case the deputy hotel manager's role is that of an aide to both the hotel manager and the chief purser.

## Concierge

On some luxury ships, such as those of Crystal Cruises and Royal Viking Line, the concierge acts as an invisible liaison officer between ship and passenger. The concierge's primary concern is the well-being and satisfaction of passengers, and duties may include setting up private parties, obtaining opera or theater tickets, arranging special transportation in ports of call, or simply obtaining items that passengers cannot find themselves.

## Cruise Director

Without a doubt, the most visible person on board, the cruise director, has the ultimate responsibility of planning and operating the passenger entertainment, activities and sports programs, and acting as the master of ceremonies for shipboard functions and events. The cruise director oversees every area of leisure and recreation. The position is thus highly demanding—and well paid.

Before each cruise, the cruise director sketches in all projected activities, entertainment, and movies on a huge chart, showing the program in time slots throughout each day.

He has a number of helpers under his command, including the cruise staff and social hosts, "headliner" and lesser entertainers, bands and musicians, lecturers, recreation, sports and health instructors, and others.

On some larger ships, there may be one or more assistant cruise directors or an entertainment manager, stage manager, and social director. Cruise lines label their staff positions in different ways.

A cruise director must plan entertainment, movies and special theme nights with dexterity, taking care not to offend anyone in the process.

On the first day of the cruise, the cruise director will usually invite all passengers to the main lounge and explain the entertainment program to them, at the same time urging passengers to take advantage of the many events planned for the cruise. He may also introduce his staff and give a brief ship orientation a short while after sailing.

At the start of each cruise, the cruise director usually gives a port lecture, often with audiovisual aids. In this, he will advise passengers what to do ashore, describe the excursions available, and even offer advice on where to shop. But beware the cruise director that oversells certain stores, for he could well be on a healthy commission!

The cruise director may be an officer (with two- or three-gold-stripe status), or he may be a "nonsailor" with a show biz background. Certainly one of the qualities required for the job is an ability to deal with difficult entertainers, crew and, of course, passengers!

The cruise director has an office, together with members of his cruise staff, through which he can be reached for anything relating to the entertainment, activities, and sports programs on board. In Part Two of this book, you'll find an evaluation of the cruise director and his staff for each ship rated.

Note that on some ships, notably those operated by German companies, the cruise director is more of a cruise manager, and also deals with matters such as immigration, port clearances, and travel arrangements for passengers. This position also occurs on Russian/ Ukrainian-registered ships chartered to German tour operators.

# Shore Excursions and Shopping

## Shore Excursions

For some people the idea of a cruise might simply be to get away from it all. Indeed, no matter how many ports the ship visits, some never go ashore, preferring instead to revel in the complete shipboard aspect of cruising. For these people, the ship is the ultimate destination, and they could just as well be on a cruise to nowhere.

For the vast majority, however, the ports offered on a cruise itinerary are important considerations, the ship providing the transportation—a means to link the destinations together. Shore excursions, both a challenge and a bane to cruise lines, are proving to be one of the most vital and attractive aspects of the total cruise experience. They are organized to be varied enough for everyone, from the young and active to the elderly and infirm.

Today you need not feel the least bit uncomfortable or hesitant in strange or unusual surroundings, or intimidated by languages other than your own. If you don't want to miss the major sightseeing attractions in each port, you'll find the organized shore excursions the perfect answer. Also, if you do not wish to be alone, they provide an ideal opportunity to get to know fellow passengers with similar interests.

Cruise lines generally plan and oversee shore excursions assuming that you have not seen a place. They aim to show you the most beautiful, striking, and fascinating aspects of a destination in a comfortable manner and at a reasonable price. Shore excursions are operated either by land, sea, or air, or sometimes a combination of all three. They are of varying duration: half-day sightseeing; full-day sightseeing, including lunch; evening outings, such as nightclub tours, including admission charges and one or more drinks; and overland excursions, often lasting several days and involving overnight stays in hotels.

On land, buses, rather than taxis or private cars, are often the principal choice of transportation. This cuts costs and allows the tour operator to narrow the selection of guides to only those most competent, knowledgeable, and fluent in English (or other languages), while providing some degree of security and control. In the case of air travel (often in small aircraft or by helicopter), operating companies and all equipment must be thoroughly inspected, as must their safety record.

If shore excursions include travel overland and meals, the quality of any food to be served is taken into account, as are the food preparation areas and hygiene standards of personnel.

Shore excursions come under the heading of "additional on-board expenses" for passengers, and are considered as sources of on-board revenue by the cruise lines. Yet most of the money generated by the sale of shore excursions never reaches the coffers of the cruise lines, but goes to third parties—the tour operators in the various ports of call. Only a handful of cruise products include shore excursions in the cruise fare, generally those lines specializing in "adventure" or "expedition" cruises to unusual and exotic destinations.

Interestingly, passengers often consider shore excursion prices as being high, unaware of the tremendous behind-the-scenes organization required, and the costs involved locally. A vast amount of time and money is spent by cruise lines setting up suitable shore excursion programs. The ship's shore excursion office is the last link in the chain of operation of a successful shore excursion program.

## Shore Excursion Director

In the head office of a cruise line is the shore excursion department, run by the director of shore excursions, who has the responsibility for setting up a successful program, sometimes worldwide. There may be several staff members involved in the department. Without doubt the finest shore excursions are provided by The Watters Group, of San Francisco. Others that are outstanding are, in order: Hapag-Lloyd Cruises, Crystal Cruises, and Cunard.

Directors who work for lines operating worldwide have the greatest challenge, since each cruise undertaken may have a completely different itinerary. Those employed by lines that offer seasonal itineraries, such as to Alaska, the Mexican Riviera, Caribbean, or Mediterranean, have fewer problems because the itinerary remains unchanged for a complete cruising season.

Perhaps the most challenging of all jobs is setting up a comprehensive shore excursion program for a world cruise or long exotic voyage, where organizing shore excursions often involves complex overland and flight arrangements and meetings with a number of government tourism officials.

One area that needs attention is in the description of shore excursions. Often, the language used can lead to disappointment and confusion. Ideally, all cruise lines should adopt the following definitions in their descriptive literature and for their lectures and presentations:

- The term "visit" should be taken to mean actually entering the place or building concerned.
- The term "see" should be taken to mean viewing from the outside (as from a bus, for example).

## Shore Excursion Operator

The shore excursion operator is the next link in the chain. Few lines run their own excursions, but instead contract a shore excursion operator for each port of call. They are responsible for providing the best means of transportation, local guides, food, entrance tickets to public buildings, gardens and nightclubs, and other attractions of the excursion.

Cruise lines and ground operators work together in planning or suggesting excursion itineraries, the operator offering the cruise line a "buying price per head" for the excursion or tour package. The margin between the buying price and the selling price to the cruise passenger can be as little as 50 cents or as much as 50 per cent. The average mark-up is about 20-25 per cent, an amount far lower than most cruisegoers imagine.

## Shore Excursion Manager

The ship's representative supervising the entire operation of the shore excursion program is the shore excursion manager. As the eyes and ears of the cruise line, the shore excursion manager can recommend to head office that any excursion be suspended if it is not to his satisfaction—which gives him a good deal of authority with local ground operators. Needless to say, some shore excursion managers can be bribed, to the detriment of passengers, with the result that some excursions are downright poor.

The shore excursion manager and staff will be on the dockside dispatching the excursions in each port. Any last minute problems or questions you have should be raised then.

## Shore Excursion Office

The shore excursion office is normally located in a central position on board, often close to the purser's office, in the main lobby area. This is where you should go for information about the ports of call or to purchase your shore excursion tickets, and where you will find the shore excursion manager and other members of the department. Please note that the staff cannot normally act as guides or interpreters.

At the shore excursion office you'll find details of the excursions and descriptive literature about the ports of call, with information on the history, language, population, currency, main sightseeing attractions, principal shopping areas, beaches and hotels, sports and watersports facilities, transportation, and principal eating establishments. For more specific information, see the shore excursion manager or visit the ship's library. On many ships, special full-color port booklets or cruise guides may be available. Shore excursion office opening times will be listed at the office, and in the *Daily Program.*

## Booking Excursions

Early booking of excursions is highly recommended, especially if they are listed as "limited participation." This means that there will be a restricted number of seats available, to be sold on a first come, first served basis. On some ships, where shore excursions can be booked prior to the sailing date, sellouts may occur. So, visit the shore excursion office as soon as you can after boarding and make your reservations early.

Payment is normally made via a ship's central billing system, by cash, traveler's check, or credit card. Note that on most ships, personal checks aren't accepted.

The shore excursion office usually attracts long lines shortly after the port lecture is given by the cruise director or shore excursion manager. You can avoid a wait by reading through the descriptive literature and making your reservations before that talk.

On some ships, prebooking forms for shore excursions will either be forwarded along with your cruise tickets and documents, or you may find them in your cabin on arrival. Prebooking means that you can reserve (and in some cases pay for) excursions before you board or before the shore excursion office is open for business.

For cancelations, most ships require a minimum of 24 hours' notice before the advertised shore excursion departure time. Refunds are at the discretion of the cruise line. Should you be unable to go on an excursion or change your mind, you will be able, in most cases, to sell your ticket to another passenger. Tickets do not normally have names or cabin numbers on them, except those which involve flights or overland arrangements. However, before attempting to resell any tickets, it is wise to check with the shore excursion manager.

## Choosing the Right Shore Excursion

As mentioned earlier, at the start of the cruise, the cruise director or shore excursion manager will give an informal audiovisual lecture on the ports of call on your cruise, together with a brief description of the excursions offered. Whether you are a novice or an experienced cruiser, make an effort to attend this talk. Remember to take a pencil and paper with you to jot down any important points and list the excursions that interest you most.

Look carefully at the shore excursion literature and circle those that appeal to you. Then go to the shore excursion office and ask any other questions you may have before you book.

Here are a few guidelines:

- Shore excursions are put together for general interest. If you want to see something that is not described in the excursion literature, don't take it. Go on your own or with friends.
- In the Caribbean, many sightseeing tours cover the same ground. Choose one and then do something different in the next port. (The same is true of the history/archaeology excursions operated in the Greek Isles.) It pays to avoid repeating a visit made already.
- If you are a history buff, remember that most excursions give very little in-depth history, and guides are often not acquainted with details beyond a superficial general knowledge. Pick up a pocket guidebook to the area or check the ship's library.
- City excursions are basically superficial. To get to know a city intimately, it is better to go it alone or with a small group of friends. Travel by taxi or bus directly to the places that are of most interest to you.
- If you enjoy diving or snorkeling, most Caribbean cruise ships operate dive-in excursions at a very reasonable price that includes flippers, mask, and snorkel. Instruction for novices is offered on board, and underwater cameras can often be rented, too.

## Helpful Hints

Shore excursions are timed to be most convenient for the greatest number of participants, taking into account the timing of meals on board. Where ships operate two dining room sittings, passengers on the second breakfast sitting may find themselves having to rush in order to participate in a morning excursion. Likewise, those on afternoon excursions may have to hurry to get to the first sitting at dinner on time.

Departure times are listed in the descriptive literature and in the *Daily Program*, and will be announced over the ship's public address system. Don't be late, or you may be too late. Note that there are absolutely no refunds if you miss the excursion.

If you are hearing impaired, make arrangements with the shore excursion manager to assist you in departing for your excursions at the correct times.

Only take along what is necessary; leave any valuables on the ship, together with any money and credit cards you don't plan to use. People in groups are often targets for pickpockets in major cities such as Barcelona, Caracas, and Rio de Janeiro. Also, beware of the excursion guide who gives you a colored disk to wear for "identification"—he may be marking you as a "rich" tourist for local shopkeepers. It is easier—and cheaper—to remember your guide's name and the bus number.

Lost or misplaced tickets should be reported immediately to the shore excursion manager. On most ships, excursion tickets, once sold, become the sole responsibility of the purchaser, and the cruise line is not generally able to issue replacements. If you place them on the dresser/vanity unit in the cabin, make sure they don't fall down the back, from where there may be no possibility of retrieval. Since tour tickets are not cheap, place them in a clearly-marked envelope right away, and put them in your wallet or purse.

In foreign ports, convert a little money into local currency for minor expenses during any tour, or take a supply of U.S. one-dollar bills—useful if you wish to buy a soft drink, for example, or wish to take a taxi to the ship, if you prefer to shop rather than go back on the bus.

## Going Independently

If you do not like to tour with groups of people, you can, of course, go ashore on your own, and in most places it's perfectly safe. In most areas of the world there are no restrictions on independent travel ashore, with the exception of the former countries of the Soviet Union, China, and areas of military importance, together with countries that stipulate restrictions on individual visas, such as Myanmar (formerly Burma).

Going ashore independently is ideal in the major cruise ports of Alaska, the Bahamas, Bermuda, the Caribbean, the Mexican Riviera, the Canary Islands, the Mediterranean, Aegean ports, and the islands of the South Pacific. In many South American ports, however, it is wise to go with a friend, especially if you are unfamiliar with the language.

Indeed, in countries where the language is unknown to you, you should always carry some identification (but not your passport), the name of your ship and the area in which it is docked. If the ship is anchored and you take a launch tender ashore, take note of exactly where the landing place is by observing nearby landmarks, as well as writing down the location. This will be invaluable if you get lost and need to take a taxi back to the launch.

On most ships you'll be given an identification tag or boarding pass at the purser's office or gangway. This must be handed in each time you return to the ship. Remember that ships have schedules (and sometimes tides) to meet, and that they will not wait for individual passengers who return late. If you are in a launch port in a tropical area and the weather changes for the worse, the ship's captain could well make a decision to depart early to avoid being hemmed in by an approaching storm—it has happened, especially in the Caribbean. If it does, locate the ship's agent in the port, who'll try to get you back (and the experience will provide dinner conversation for months).

If you are planning on going to a quiet, secluded beach to swim, first check with the cruise director or shore excursion manager, as certain beaches may be considered off-limits because of a dangerous undertow, drug pushers, or persistent hawkers. And, if you're thinking of going diving alone—don't! Not anywhere, even if you know the area well. Always go diving with at least one companion.

Naturally, going ashore independently does not have to mean going alone. You'll more than likely meet up with others on board ship who prefer their own group to the organized excursion and you can travel with them.

Of course, you don't have to go off the ship in ports at all. You are perfectly free to come and go from the ship as you please. Sometimes, after several days at sea, it will feel just wonderful to stay aboard to enjoy the peace and calm, while everyone else, it seems, has deserted the ship.

## Local Transport

In most ports, the same type of transportation is available for sightseeing. You can go by taxi, public bus, rental car, moped, motorcycle, or bicycle.

### Sightseeing by Taxi

If you decide to hire a taxi for sightseeing, be prepared to negotiate the price in advance, and don't pay until you get back to the ship or to your final destination. If you are with friends, hiring a taxi for a full- or half-day sightseeing trip can often work out far cheaper than renting a car, and you also avoid the hazards of driving. Naturally, prices vary according to where in the world you are, but if you can select a driver who speaks English, or whatever your national language is, and the taxi is comfortable, even air-conditioned, you're ahead.

Be wary of taxi drivers who wear a badge that claims, "I speak English," for it may be all the English they speak! To be certain, ask the driver a few questions, and make sure that the price you negotiate is clear to both of you. Better still, if your driver speaks only a little English, write down the agreed fare and show it to him. Make sure you know what currency the number represents.

### Traveling by Bus

Getting around by public bus can be an inexpensive method of sightseeing and of becoming immersed in the local life. In most countries, public transportation is very safe, but there are, of course, those places where it pays to keep an eye on your wallet or purse.

You will need a small amount of the local currency in order to travel on the bus system. This can usually be obtained on board your ship or at a local bank once at the port.

### Rental Car

If you are planning on renting a car for any specific ports of call, try to do so ahead of your cruise, through your travel agent. This will not only save you much precious time on your arrival in port, but it will go a long way to ensuring that there will be a rental car available when you arrive.

Before departing for your cruise, check to see if your driver's license is valid for the destination, as some countries may require you to obtain a local or visitor's license (for a fee) before allowing you to rent a car. Remember also to take along a major credit card, which you will need to make a deposit.

### Moped, Motorcycle, and Bicycle

Mopeds and motorcycles are available for hire in many ports. In places such as Bermuda, remember that roadside walls are of coral and limestone, and can give you a nasty rash if you scrape them.

Bicycles are a favorite way of getting around in many ports of the world, especially in the Orient. They are inexpensive to rent and you'll get some exercise as you pedal. One or two ships (and almost all canal barges) have bicycles on board for passenger use.

## The Shopping Scene

For many cruise passengers, shopping comes second only to eating. Indeed, one of the main joys of cruising is going ashore and shopping at leisure. Whether it's for local craftwork, handmade trinkets, articles of clothing, silk and cotton material, jewelry, or liquor, there's something special in store at each destination.

In some places, you will find shopping a bargain compared with home, depending on the exchange rate, and your local duty and taxation structure. The best ports for shopping are often those that are "duty free"—meaning that no customs duty is charged on goods bought.

The best duty-free shopping in the world is in Hong Kong and Singapore, but the Caribbean, situated on the "doorstep" of the United States, is also known for its good value shopping, with St. Thomas in the U.S. Virgin Islands the best known. Indeed, many people book a Caribbean cruise only if the itinerary includes St. Thomas.

Cruise lines are happy to go along with this. St. Thomas still offers prices that compare favorably with those on the mainland—particularly liquor at duty-free prices. But don't forget that you'll have to carry that liquor home (the airlines will not accept it as part of your baggage). Alcoholic beverages can't be mailed home, but many other items from St. Thomas or elsewhere can. Only send packages from a major island or port, where the postal service is reliable.

## General Hints for Shopping

A good general rule is: know in advance just what you are looking for, especially if your time is limited. But if time is no problem, browsing can be fun.

When shopping time is included in shore excursions, be careful of stores repeatedly recommended by the tour guides: the guides are likely to be receiving commissions from the merchants. Shop around and compare prices before you buy. Excellent shopping hints and recommendations are often given in the cruise director's port lecture at the start of your cruise. But if you notice cruise directors "pushing" certain stores, it is quite likely that they, too, are on commission. They do know, however, that the reputation of the cruise line is at stake if their suggestions are not in your best interests.

You should know that several cruise lines which operate in the Bahamas, Caribbean, and Mexican Riviera openly engage a company that provides the services of a "shopping lecturer" (Cunard, Holland America Line, Princess Cruises, Royal Caribbean Cruise Line, for example) aboard all or some of their ships. The shopping lecturer does nothing but promote selected shops, goods, and services heavily, fully authorized by the cruise line (which receives a commission from the same). This relieves the cruise director of any responsibilities, together with any question about his involvement, credibility, and financial remuneration.

Shopping maps, with "selected" stores highlighted, are placed in your cabin. Often, they come with a "guarantee" such as that offered by Princess Cruises: "Shop with confidence at each of the recommended stores. Each merchant listed on this map has been carefully selected on the basis of quality, fair dealing and value. These merchants have given Princess Cruises a guarantee of satisfaction valid for thirty (30) days after purchase, excluding passenger negligence and buyers' regret, and have paid a promotional fee for inclusion as a guaranteed store."

When shopping for local handicrafts, make sure they have indeed been made in the country. It can happen that the so-called local product has in fact been made in Taiwan, Hong Kong, or another Far Eastern country. It pays to check.

Also, be wary of "bargain-priced" name brands, such as Gucci bags and Rolex or Omega watches, as they may well be counterfeit and of dubious quality. For watches, check the guarantee.

If you have any specific questions, ask the cruise director, shore excursion manager, or one of the cruise staff. Some shopping information may be available in information literature about the port and this should be available at the ship's shore excursion office.

Keep in mind that the ship's shops are also duty free, and, for the most part, competitive in price. The shops on board are closed while in port, however, due to international customs regulations.

# Coastal Cruises

## Europe

Year-round coastal cruising along the shores of Norway to the Land of the Midnight Sun can be undertaken aboard the ships of the Hurtig-Ruten (Norwegian Coastal Express Line). The fleet of 11 ships (listed below) is comprised of three brand new 450-passenger vessels that could be cruise ships, together with a range of older vessels that are small, yet comfortable, working express, real coastal packet steamers. Their principal job is the delivery of mail, small packaged goods and foodstuffs, as well as passengers, to the communities which are spread along the shoreline, between the towns of Bergen and Kirkenes, on the route which is often called "Highway 1."

The 2,500-mile journey, half of which is north of the Arctic Circle, takes 11 days, but you can join it at any of the 35 ports of call and stay as long as you wish. Most seasoned travelers like to cruise for all 11 days. In 1993, the company carried some 286,000 passengers.

The service started over 100 years ago, in 1893, and the three companies that combine to run it have 11 ships. Each is of a different size, and, with between 69 and 230 cabins, can accommodate a maximum of between 144 and 488 passengers. Three new ships, each designed to carry 488 passengers, as well as 50 cars, were ordered in 1992. The first two, each of which has 230 cabins (209 outside/21 inside) debuted in 1993, the third debuted in 1994.

### Ships of the Hurtig-Ruten Fleet

| Name | Company | Berths | Built |
|---|---|---|---|
| ms *Harald Jarl* | 3 | 169 | 1960 (rebuilt 1984) |
| ms *Kong Harald* | 3 | 488 | 1993 |
| ms *Kong Olav* | 2 | 219 | 1964 (rebuilt 1986) |
| ms *Lofoten* | 1 | 228 | 1964 (rebuilt 1985) |
| ms *Midnatsol* | 3 | 322 | 1982 (rebuilt 1988) |
| ms *Narvik* | 2 | 308 | 1982 (rebuilt 1989) |
| ms *Nordlys* | 3 | 488 | 1994 |
| ms *Nordnorge* | 2 | 207 | 1964 (rebuilt 1986) |
| ms *Ragnvald Jarl* | 2 | 144 | 1956 (rebuilt 1985) |
| ms *Richard With* | 2 | 488 | 1993 |
| ms *Vesteralen* | 2 | 314 | 1983 (rebuilt 1988) |

**KEY** (1) FFR—Finnmark Fylkesrederi Og Ruteselskap
(2) OVDS—Ofotens Og Vesteraalens Dampskibisselskab
(3) TFDS—Troms Fylkes Dampskibisselskap

Archipelago hopping can be done on Sweden's east coast, too, by sailing in the daytime and staying overnight in one of the many small hotels on the way. One vessel sails from Norrtalje, north of Stockholm, to Oskarshamn, near the Baltic island of Öland, right through the spectacular Swedish archipelago. And you can now cruise from the Finnish city of Lappeenranta to the Estonian city of Viborg without even a visa, thanks to the positive effects of Perestroika.

Indeed, point-to-point coastal transportation between neighboring countries, major cities, and commercial centers is big business in northern Europe. Some of the larger cruise ferries could easily rival major cruise ships in other regions now. Designed to operate in all weather, their facilities are virtually the same, but with much smaller cabins and an emphasis on duty-free shopping.

Some would argue that ships such as the huge *Silja Serenade* and *Silja Symphony,* actually designed for cruising but used mainly as ferries, are constructed around their duty-free shopping centers. Be that as it may, these super-ferries are nothing short of fantastic as modes of transport and relaxation. It would take a separate book to list them all, along with their owning companies, as they tend to change hands rather frequently.

## Scotland

The fishing town of Oban, some two hours west of Glasgow by road, perhaps seems an unlikely point to start a cruise, but is home to one of the world's finest escape ships. The *Hebridean Princess*, a bathtub of a ship with Laura Ashley interiors, is a gem, and carries passengers around some of Scotland's magnificent coastline and islands.

## United States

In the United States, coastal vessels, flying the red, white, and blue flag, offer a change of style and pace from the big oceangoing liners. On these cruises, informality is the order of the day. Accommodating up to 160 passengers, the ships tend to be more like a private party or club—there's no pretentiousness. Unlike major cruise ships, these small vessels are rarely out of sight of land. The owners seek out lesser-known cruise areas, offering in-depth visits to destinations inaccessible to larger ships, both along the east coast, and in Alaska.

During the last few years, there has been little growth in this segment of the cruise market. If you prefer a small country inn to a larger resort, this type of cruise might appeal to you. The ships, each of which measures under 100 grt and is classified as a "D"-class vessel, are not subject to the bureaucratic regulations nor union rules that sounded the death knell for large U.S.-registered ships, and are restricted to cruising no more than 20 miles off shore.

You cruise in comfort at up to 12 knots. All public room facilities are limited, and because the vessels are of American registry, there's no casino on board. As far as entertainment goes, passengers are usually left to their own devices, although there may sometimes be a piano. Most of these vessels are in port during the evening, so you can go ashore for the local nightlife. Getting ashore is extremely easy; passengers can be off in a matter of minutes, with no waiting at the gangway.

Accommodations, though not elaborate, consist of all-outside cabins, each with its own large picture window and private bathroom. The cabins are small but quite cozy. Closet space is very limited, so take only what you absolutely need. The only drawback to all-outside cabins is that some open directly onto the deck—not convenient when it rains. Being closer to the engines, there is considerable noise throughout these vessels. The quietest cabins are at the bow, and most cruising is done during the day so that passengers will be able to sleep better at night. Tall passengers should note that the overall length of beds on most of these vessels is 6 ft. maximum.

The principal evening event on board is dinner in the dining room, which accommodates all passengers at once. This can be a family-style affair, with passengers at long tables, and the food passed around. The cuisine is decidedly American, with fresh local specialties.

There are usually three or four decks on these vessels, and no elevators. Stairs can be on the steep side, and are not recommended for people with walking difficulties. This kind of cruise is good for those who enjoy a family-type cruise experience in pleasant surroundings. The maxim "You just relax, we'll move the scenery" is very appropriate here.

Only three of the coastal and inland cruise vessels are featured in Part Two, since they are small and specialized with limited facilities. Five cruise lines (one of them, SeaSpirit Cruise Lines, is gay-owned and operated, for gay male passengers only) operate coastal cruises. Be aware that you may have a linen change only once or twice a week, and may not get a "turn-down" service.

## Coastal and Inland Cruises—United States

| **Cruise Line/Operator** | **Name** | **Passengers** |
|---|---|---|
| Alaska Sightseeing | *Spirit of Alaska* | 82 |
| Alaska Sightseeing | *Spirit of Columbia* | 72 |
| Alaska Sightseeing | *Spirit of Discovery* | 84 |
| Alaska Sightseeing | *Spirit of Glacier Bay* | 58 |
| American Canadian Caribbean Line | *Caribbean Prince* | 80 |
| American Canadian Caribbean Line | *Mayan Prince* | 90 |
| American Canadian Caribbean Line | *Niagara Prince* | 100 |
| Clipper Cruise Line | *Nantucket Clipper* | 120 |
| Clipper Cruise Line | *Yorktown Clipper* | 138 |
| SeaSpirit Cruise Lines | *SeaSpirit* | 122 |
| Wilderness Cruises | *Sea Lion* | 70 |

# River and Barge Cruises

Whether you want to cruise down the Nile, along the mighty Amazon, the stately Volga, the primal Sepik, the magnificent Rhine, the "blue" Danube or the "yellow" Yangtze—to say nothing of the Don and the Dnieper, or the Elbe—there's a cruise and vessel ready for you.

## Steamboating—U.S.A.

Most famous of all river cruises in the United States are those aboard the steamboats of the mighty Mississippi River. Mark Twain, an outspoken fan of Mississippi cruising, once said: "When man can go 700 miles an hour, he'll want to go seven again."

The grand traditions of the Steamboat era are carried on by the *Delta Queen* and *Mississippi Queen* (Delta Queen Steamboat Company), both of which are powered by steam engines that drive huge wooden paddlewheels at the stern.

The smaller of the two, the 180-passenger *Delta Queen*, was built on Scotland's Clydeside in 1926 and is on the U.S. National Register of Historic Places. She gained attention when President Carter spent a week aboard in 1979.

A half-century younger, the 400-passenger *Mississippi Queen* was built at a cost of some $27 million in Jefferson, Indiana, from where nearly 5,000 steamboats originated during the 19th century. (The *Mississippi Queen* was designed by James Gardner of London, creator of Cunard's *Queen Elizabeth* 2). Each steamboat features one of the rarest of musical instruments—a real "steam piano," driven by the boat's engine.

Aboard one of these steamboats, you'll find yourself stepping back in history and American folklore. Charm and old-world graciousness surround you, as do delightful woods, brass and flowing staircases. And once a year, the two boats rival each other in the Great Steamboat Race—a 10-day extravaganza in which the *Delta Queen* battles her larger sister, the *Mississippi Queen.*

Steamboat cruises last from two to 12 days, and during the year there are several theme cruises, with big bands and lively entertainment. The boats traverse the Mississippi and Ohio rivers.

A brand new American-built steamboat, called *American Queen* (Delta Queen Steamboat Company, who now also own American Hawaii Cruises), will debut in the summer of 1995. Built at a cost of $60 million by McDermott Shipyard, Morgan City, Louisiana, the riverboat features vintage tandem compound horizontal reciprocating steam engines (circa 1930) that originally drove a steam dredge called the *Kennedy*. The engines will be used to drive the 60-ton stern paddle wheel, made up of individual bucket boards (the paddles) of 30 feet long and 2 feet wide. The *American Queen* is the 30th steamboat built for the Delta Queen Steamboat Company.

It's a great life on the river, away from congested roads and airports. Also, there are no immigration or customs procedures in the heartland of America.

## European River Cruising

Cruising down one of Europe's great waterways is an experience in itself—quite different from sailing on an open sea, where motion has to be taken into consideration (rivers are always calm). These cruises provide a constant change of scenery, often passing through several countries, each with their own history and architecture, in a week-long journey. They are always close to land and offer the chance to visit cities and areas inaccessible to large ships. Indeed, watching the scenery slip past your floating hotel is one of the most refreshing ways to absorb the beauty that has inspired poets and artists over countless centuries. A cruise on the Danube, for example, will take you through four centuries.

In 1840–41, the Marquess of Londonderry, a member of the British aristocracy, crossed Europe using the Rhine and Danube rivers. Her experiences were published in a charming book entitled *A Steam Voyage to Constantinople*, which appeared in London in 1842. And who could forget the romance implied in Johann Strauss's famous waltz *On the Blue Danube*. The new Rhine-Main-Danube waterway is now open, at 2,175 miles the longest waterway in Europe. It connects 14 countries from Rotterdam on the North Sea to Sulina and Izmail on the Black Sea, and offers some of the most fascinating sights anywhere.

River vessels are long and low in the water, and their masts must fold down in order to negotiate the low bridges found along most of Europe's rivers. Although small when compared to oceangoing cruise ships, they do have a unique and friendly international atmosphere. The most modern vessels offer the discreet luxury of a floating hotel, and often have several public rooms, including a large dining room. They typically have three or four decks. Most are air-conditioned, and the newest will also feature an observation lounge, bar, heated swimming pool (even have a heated indoor pool), sauna, solarium, gymnasium, hairdresser, and shop kiosk.

Although the cabins may be small, with limited closet space, they will be mostly outside (facing the river), have a private bathroom, and will be very comfortable for a one-week journey. Cabins are largest on the *Mozart*, at 205 sq.ft., while most other river vessel cabins will be smaller. They are all generally clean and tidy, as well as functional. Many cabins on the most modern vessels feature a personal safe, mini-bar, television, and alarm clock/radio. In general, shore excursions *must* be booked at the same time as you book your cabin.

In Europe, river cruising has reached a highly sophisticated level, and you can be assured of good service and meals of a consistently high European standard. Dining is quite pleasant, although not quite a gourmet experience (with the exception of some vessels catered by Austrian and Swiss companies). A set menu is the norm, except for the most upscale vessels. Without doubt the best cuisine can be found aboard the *Danube Princess*, *Mozart* and *Prussian Princess*, although reasonably decent cuisine is served on many other river vessels.

Perhaps the best way to get to know

Russia is on a river cruise between Moscow and St. Petersburg. There are many vessels operating on the Don, Neva and Volga rivers, and many of these are chartered by foreign (non-Russian) cruise wholesalers and tour packagers. The vessels are well equipped, air-conditioned and almost always clean and tidy. Cruises include the services of a cruise manager and lecturers, and some companies also specialize in "home stays" before or after the cruise as part of an attractive cultural package. A Russian visa is required for all non-Russian visitors, which can be obtained for you by the cruise/tour company.

Typical rates for river cruises are from $800 to more than $3,000 per person for a one-week cruise (prices increase for the most popular periods), including meals, cabin with private facilities, side trips and airport/railway transfers. If you are already in Europe, many cruises can be bought "cruise-only" for greater flexibility. (See *Pick-a-Ship Chart*, page 164.)

TIP: It's best to go for an outside cabin on a deck that doesn't have a promenade deck walkway outside it. Normally, cabins on the lowest deck have a four-berth configuration. Informality is the order of the day, and, because rivers are calm by nature, you can't get seasick.

## The Nile

A journey on the Nile—the world's longest (and historically greatest) river—is a journey back in time, to over 4,000 years before the birth of Christ—when Pharaohs thought they were immortal. Although time proved them wrong, the people that lived along the river banks formed one of the greatest civilizations the world has known. The scenery has changed little in over 2,000 years, and the best way to see it is by river boat.

Many of the approximately 140 vessels that cruise the Nile offer excellent standards of comfort, food and service. Most have a swimming pool, lounge, piano bar and disco. A specialist lecturer in Ancient Egyptian history accompanies almost all sailings, which cruise the 140 miles between Aswan and Luxor in four or five days. Extended cruises, typically of seven or eight days, cover about 295 miles, visiting Dendera and Abydos. The longest cruises, of 10–12 days, cover 590 miles, and include visits to Sohag, El Amarna, Tuna El Gabal and Ashmuneim, ending in Cairo. In all, there are over 7,000 departures every year! If you're concerned about the recent spate of terrorist attacks on passengers, note that these have only occurred on the Cairo to Aswan section. But the best and most fascinating Nile cruising is between Aswan and Luxor, which is normally not touched by the terrorist groups.

Most Nile cruises include all sightseeing excursions, which are accompanied by experienced, trained guides who may be resident on board, or who may meet the boat at each call. Multi-lingual guides also accompany each cruise.

## Barge Cruising—Europe

Smaller than river vessels, and accurately called boats, "hotel barges" ply the inland waterways and canals of Europe from April to November, when the weather is generally good. Barge cruises are usually of 3, 6, or 13 days' duration, and offer a completely informal atmosphere, for up to a dozen passengers. The barges motor along slowly in the daytime, and moor early each evening, so that you can pay a visit to the local village, and get a restful night's sleep.

Hotel barges are more intimate still than river vessels, and offer a different experience. You go ashore on your own during the day and at night. Shopping opportunities are limited, and evening entertainment is always an impromptu affair. Most barges carry between eight and 24 passengers.

Hotel barges are beautifully fitted out with rich wood paneling, full carpeting, custom-built furniture and tastefully chosen fabrics. Each barge has a dining room/lounge-bar and is equipped with your total comfort in mind. Each barge captain takes pride in his vessel, often supplying rare memorabilia to be incorporated into the decor.

With locally grown fresh foods, usually purchased and prepared each day by a loving crew, you'll live well and be treated like a house guest. Most barges can also be chartered exclusively—just take your family and friends, for example.

The waterways of France, especially, offer beauty, tranquility and diverse interest, and barge cruising is an excellent way of exploring an area not previously visited. Most cruises include a visit to a famous vineyard and wine cellar, as well as side-trips to places of historic, architectural or scenic interests. You will be accompanied by a crew member familiar with the surrounding countryside. You can even go hot-air ballooning over the local countryside, and land to a welcome glass of champagne and a flight certificate. Although ballooning is an expensive extra, floating within earshot of chateaux, villages and over pastoral landscapes is a wonderful experience.

Depending on which barge and area you choose, dining aboard will range from home-style cooking to truly outstanding nouvelle cuisine, with all the trimmings. Hotel barges have English or English-speaking French crews.

Barging on the canals often means going through a constant succession of locks. Nowhere is this more enjoyable and entertaining than in the Burgundy region of France where, between Dijon and Macon, for example, a barge can negotiate as many as 54 locks in a six-day cruise. Interestingly, all lock-keepers in France are women!

Typical rates range from $600 to more than $3,000 per person for a six-day cruise. I don't recommend taking children. Rates include cabin with private facilities, all meals, excellent wine with lunch and dinner, other beverages, use of bicycles, side trips and airport/railway transfers. Some operators also provide a hotel night before or after the cruise. Clothing, by the way, is totally casual at all times, but at the beginning and end of the season, the weather can be unreliable, so take sweaters and rain gear, too.

# Expedition Cruises

"The risk one runs in exploring a coast in these unknown and icy seas is so very great that I can be so bold to say no man will ever venture farther than I have done and that the lands to the south will never be explored."

So wrote Captain James Cook in 1774. His voyage was a feat of great courage, for not only did he take the risk of entering an unknown sea, but his ship, the *Resolution*, was far too fragile a vessel (462 tons) to undertake such a trip. Yet there is no landscape quite so breathtaking and compelling as the polar regions of the south, and no experience so unforgettable as a visit there. Today's would-be Cooks have the curiosity and drive to move into adventure cruising.

With so many opportunities to cruise in Alaska and the Baltic, Caribbean, Mediterranean, and Mexican Riviera areas, you may be surprised to discover a small but growing group of enthusiasts heading out for strange and remote waters. But there are countless virtually untouched areas to be visited by the more adventurous.

On an expedition cruise, passengers take an active role in every aspect of the voyage, which is destination- and nature-intensive. Naturalists, historians, and lecturers are aboard each ship to provide background information and observations about wildlife. Each participant receives his or her personal *log book*—illustrated and written by the renowned wildlife artists and writers who accompany each cruise. Such a logbook documents the entire expedition and serves as a great source of information, as well as a complete "memoire" of the voyage. Expedition parka and waterproof boots are provided by all companies that offer these adventure cruises.

Imagine walking on pack ice in the Arctic Circle, exploring a penguin rookery on Antarctica or the Falkland Islands, searching for "lost" peoples in Melanesia, cruising close to the source of the Amazon, gazing at species of flora and fauna in the Galapagos Islands (Darwin's laboratory), or watching a genuine dragon (from a comfortable distance, of course). It's what expedition cruising is all about, and it's not really recommended for the novice cruisegoer.

Because of the briefings, lectures, and a laboratory at sea, there is a cultural and intellectual element to be found on expedition cruise vessels. There is no formal entertainment as such; passengers enjoy this type of cruise more for the camaraderie and learning experience. The ships themselves are designed and equipped to sail in ice-laden waters, and yet have a shallow enough draft to glide over coral reefs.

Expedition cruise vessels can, nevertheless, provide comfortable and even elegant surroundings for up to 200 passengers and a highly trained and knowledgeable staff, and offer first-class food and service. Without traditional cruise ports to stop at, the ship must be self-sufficient, capable of long-range cruising, as well as environmentally friendly.

Expedition cruising came about as a result of people wanting to find out more about this remarkable planet of ours—its incredible animal, bird, and marine life. It was pioneered in the late 1960s by Lars-Eric Lindblad, a Swedish-American who was determined to turn travel into adventure by opening up parts of the world tourists had never visited.

After chartering several vessels for adventure cruises to Antarctica, he organized the design and construction of a ship capable of going almost anywhere in comfort and safety. In 1969, the *Lindblad Explorer* was launched.

In the years that followed, the ship earned an enviable reputation in adventure travel. Lindblad's company sold the ship to Salen-Lindblad Cruising in 1982. They subsequently resold her to Society Expeditions, who renamed her the *Society Explorer*. She is now operated by Abercrombie & Kent as the *Explorer*.

Today there are but a handful of adventure/expedition cruise companies. They provide in-depth expertise and specially constructed vessels, usually with ice-hardened hulls that are capable of going into the vast reaches of the Arctic regions and Antarctica.

## Adventure Cruise Areas

Buddha was once asked to express verbally what life meant to him. He waited a moment—then, without speaking, held up a single rose. Several "destinations" on our planet cannot be adequately described by words—they have instead to be experienced, just as a single rose.

The principal adventure cruise areas of the world are: Alaska and the Aleutians, Amazona and the Orinoco, Antarctica, Australasia and the Great Barrier Reef, the Chilean fjords, the Galapagos Archipelago, Indonesia, Melanesia, the Northwest Passage, Polynesia and the South Pacific. Baha California and the Sea of Cortez, Greenland, the Red Sea, East Africa, the Réunion Islands and the Seychelles, West Africa and the Ivory Coast, and the South China Seas and China Coast are other adventure cruise destinations growing in popularity.

In order to put together their special cruise expeditions, the staff at the various companies turn to knowledgeable sources and advisors. Scientific institutions are consulted, experienced world explorers are questioned, and naturalists provide up-to-date reports on wildlife sightings, migrations and other natural phenomena. Although some days are scheduled for relaxation or preparing for the days ahead, participants are kept active both physically and mentally. And speaking of physical activity, it is unwise to consider such an adventure cruise if you are not completely ambulatory.

### Antarctica

Perhaps the most intriguing "destination" on earth is Antarctica, first sighted only in 1820 by the American sealer Nathaniel Palmer, British naval officer Edward Bransfield and Russian captain Fabian Bellingshausen. For most, it's nothing but a wind-swept frozen wasteland. For others, however, it represents the last pristine place on earth, empty of people, commerce and pollution, yet offering awesome scenery and a truly wonderful abundance of marine and bird life. There are no germs, and not a single tree. Over 6,000 people visited the continent in 1992—the first and only smoke-free continent on earth—yet the first human to come here did so within a generation of landing on the moon. There is not a single permanent inhabitant of the continent, whose ice is as much as two miles thick. Its total land mass equals more than all the rivers and lakes on earth and exceeds that of China and India combined. The continent has a raw beauty and ever-changing landscape. Once part of the ancient land mass known as Gondwanaland (which also included Africa, South America, India, Australasia and Madagascar), it is, perhaps, the closest thing on earth to another planet, and has an incredibly fragile ecosystem that needs protection.

Although visited by "soft" expedition cruise ships and even "normal"-sized cruise ships with ice-hardened hulls, you should know that the more remote "far side"—the Oates and Scott Coasts, McMurdo Sound and the famous Ross Ice Shelf—can only be visited by "real" ice-breaker expedition ships such as the *Kapitan Khlebnikov*, *Sovetskiy Soyuz*, *Yamal* and *World Discoverer*, as the winds can easily be 100m.p.h. or more.

## Galapagos

A word of advice about the Galapagos Islands: don't even think about taking a cruise with a "foreign-flag" expedition ship. The Ecuadoreans jealously guard their island, and prohibit the movement of almost all non-Ecuadorean-registered cruise vessels within its boundaries. Thus, the best way to see this place of Darwin's love is to fly to Quito and cruise on an Ecuadorean-registered vessel such as the *Isabella II* or *Santa Cruz*.

## Greenland

The world's largest island, Greenland, in the Northern Hemisphere's Arctic Circle, is technically a desert that is 82% covered with ice (actually compressed snow) which is up to 11,000 ft. thick. Greenland's rocks are among the world's oldest (the 3.8 billion-year-old Isukasia formations) and its ecosystem is one of the newest. Forget Alaska, the glacier at Jacobshavn (also known as Ilulissat) is the fastest moving in the world, and creates a new iceberg every five minutes. Greenland is said to have more dogs than people, and these provide the principal means of transport for the Greelanders.

## The Environment

Since the increase in environmental awareness, adventurers have banded together to protect the environment from further damage. In future, only those ships that are capable of meeting new "zero discharge" standards, like those introduced in the Arctic by the Canadian Coast Guard, will be allowed to proceed through environmentally sensitive areas.

The expedition companies are deeply concerned about the environment, and they spend much time and money in educating both crews and passengers about safe environmental procedures.

In the course of the past two years an "Antarctic traveler code" has been created, the rules of which are enforced by the expedition cruise companies, based on the Antarctic Conservation Act of 1978, and adopted by the U.S. Congress to protect and preserve the ecosystem, flora, and fauna of the Antarctic continent. By law, all U.S. citizens traveling to Antarctica must adhere to the Act.

Briefly, the Act makes it unlawful, unless authorized by regulation or permit issued under the Act, to take native animals or birds, to collect any special native plant or introduce species, to enter certain special areas (SPAs), or to discharge or dispose of any pollutants. To "take" means to remove, harass, molest, harm, pursue, hunt, shoot, kill, trap, capture, restrain, or tag any native mammal or bird, or to attempt to do as such.

Under the Act, violations are subject to civil penalties, including a fine of up to $10,000 and one year imprisonment for each violation. The Act is found in the library of each adventure/expedition ship which visits the continent.

## The Companies

### Abercrombie & Kent

This well-known company operates the older, but still highly suitable, *Explorer* (ex-*Society Explorer*).

### Clipper Cruise Lines

This company operates the more luxurious *World Discoverer*—a fine expedition cruise vessel with all creature comforts.

### Hanseatic Tours

This company operates the *Bremen* (ex-*Frontier Spirit*) and the *Hanseatic*, the latest high-tech, luxury expedition cruise vessels, and offers destination-intensive itineraries. The ships have luxurious fittings and are aimed at both English- and German-speaking passengers.

### Quark Expeditions

A new company, formed by the former president of Salen Lindblad Cruising (purchased by NYK of Japan in October 1991) and called Quark Expeditions, is the U.S. general sales agent for one or more Russian-owned nuclear- or diesel-powered ice-breakers. These offer some outstanding amenities and provide creature comforts for up to 100 passengers.

In the U.K., the company is represented by Noble Caledonia Ltd, of London.

### Special Expeditions

This operates the *Polaris*, a small, comfortable expedition vessel (see profile section for details). In addition, two small vessels, the *Sea Bird* and the *Sea Lion* (ex-Exploration Cruise Lines vessels), operate "soft" expedition cruises in protected coastal areas in the United States, including Alaska.

## The Northwest Passage

In 1984, Salen Lindblad Cruising made maritime history by successfully negotiating a westbound voyage through the Northwest Passage, a 41-day epic which started from St. John's, Newfoundland, and ended at Yokohama, Japan. The expedition cruise had taken two years of planning, and was sold out just days after it was announced.

The search for a Northwest Passage to the Orient attracted brave explorers for more than 400 years. Despite numerous attempts and loss of life, including Henry Hudson in 1610, a "white passage" to The East remained an elusive dream. Amundsen's 47-ton ship the *Gjoa* successfully navigated the route in 1906, taking three years to do so. It was not until 1943 that a Canadian ship, the *St. Roch*, became the first vessel in history to make the passage in a single season. The *Lindblad Explorer* became the 34th vessel, and the first cruise vessel, to complete The Northwest Passage.

## The Northeast Passage

In a spectacular 21-day voyage in July/August 1991, Quark Expeditions made maritime history with the Russian icebreaker *Sovetskiy Soyuz*, when they successfully negotiated a passage from Murmansk, in Russia, to Nome, Alaska, across the North Pole. The ship followed the trail which had been set by Admiral Peary in 1909, who crossed the North Pole with 56 Eskimos, leaving from Ellesmere Island by sled. Although the polar ice cap has been navigated by the U.S. nuclear submarines *Skate* and *Nautilus*—as well as by dirigible and airplane—this was the first passenger ship to make the hazardous crossing. The planning for this expedition took over two years.

# Sail-Cruise Ships

Thinking of a cruise but really want to sail? Been cruising on a conventional Caribbean cruise ship that is more like an endurance test? Whatever happened to the *romance* of sailing? Think no more, for the answer, to quote a movie title, is "back to the future."

If you're active, think about cruising under sail, with towering masts and washing-powder-white sails to power you along. There's simply nothing like the thrill of being aboard a multimasted tall ship, sailing under thousands of square feet of canvas through waters that mariners have sailed for centuries.

This is what cruising in the old traditional manner is all about, on board authentic sailing ships, on contemporary copies of clipper ships, or on the very latest high-tech cruise-sail ships. Even the most jaded cruise passengers will enjoy the exhilaration of being under sail.

Tall ships provide either a genuine sail-powered experience (such as *Sea Cloud*, *Sir Francis Drake*, *Star Clipper*, *Star Flyer*), or are contemporary vessels built to emulate sail-powered vessels, but which are actually *sail-assisted* vessels in an ultra-chic contemporary form (such as *Club Med I*, *Club Med II*, *Le Ponant*, *Wind Song*, *Wind Spirit*, *Wind Star*).

Whichever you choose, there are no rigid schedules, and life aboard equates to a totally unstructured lifestyle, apart from meal times. Weather conditions may often dictate whether a scheduled port visit will be made or not, but passengers sailing on these vessels are usually unconcerned with being ashore anywhere. They would rather savor the thrill of being one with nature, albeit in a comfortable, civilized setting, but without having to do the work themselves.

## Real Tall Ships

While we've all been dreaming of adventure, a pocketful of designers and yachtsmen have put pen to paper, hand in pocket and rigging to mast, and come up with a pot-pourri of stunning vessels to delight the eye and refresh the spirit.

The Star Clippers ships, *Star Clipper* and *Star Flyer*, are *working* four-masted barquentine clipper ships that rely on the wind about 80 per cent of the time. Their diesel engines are used only as backup in emergencies, for generating electrical power and for desalinating approximately 40 tons of seawater each day for shipboard needs. The crew perform almost every task on these ships, including hoisting, trimming, winching, and repairing the sails. The whole cruise experience evokes the feeling of sailing on some famous private yacht at the turn of the century. These two modern clipper ships were born of a real ship-loving owner, Mikaël Krafft.

When growing up, Krafft, himself a yachtsman (he sails a 128-foot schooner) in his native Sweden, was told tales of the four-masted barquentine-rigged clipper ships of yesteryear—the last one had been built 140 years ago. Krafft turned his boyhood dreams into reality in 1991, with the introduction of the tallest of the tall ships in the world, the Belgian-built *Star Flyer*. It has sails hoisted aloft on four masts, the tallest being 226 ft. high. One year later, the almost identical *Star Clipper* emerged from the same shipyard.

These are no ordinary clipper ships; they are built for passengers, who share in the experience of the trade winds of the Caribbean. With accommodations for up to 180 passengers, the new breed of clipper ships are the only ones to be fully certified under United States Coast Guard regulations. In addition, they also carry Lloyd's Register of Shipping's highest rating—a rating which has not been bestowed on any other sailing vessel since 1911.

*Star Flyer*, the first clipper sailing ship to be built for 140 years, became the first commercial sailing vessel to cross the North Atlantic in 90 years, and one of only a handful of sailing ships ever to be allowed into the Port of Miami under full sail. It is no exaggeration to say that to be aboard the *Star Clippers* is to have died and gone to yachtsman's heaven.

While rigging and sails above decks are totally traditional, accommodations below decks are very well equipped, though not as lavish as those on the Club Meds and Windstars. Spacious cabins are each equipped with twin beds that convert into a double bed, individually controlled air-conditioning, two-channel audio, color television (they didn't have those in 1840), personal safe, and private bathroom with shower, toilet, sink, and even a hairdryer (deluxe cabins also sport a bathtub and a refrigerator).

Take minimal clothing, for these ships are the ultimate in casual dress. No jacket and tie are needed in the dining room, which can accommodate all passengers at once in an open seating. Short-sleeved shirts and short trousers for the men, very casual shorts and tops for the ladies, are the order of the day (and night). The deck crew are real sailors, brought up with yachts and tall ships—and most wouldn't set foot on a cruise ship.

Passengers gather each morning for "captain's story-time." The captain also explains sailing maneuvers when changing the rigging or directing the ship as it sails into port. Passengers are encouraged to lend a hand, pulling on thick ropes to haul up the main sail. And they love it. At the end of the cruise, tipping (at a suggested $8 per passenger per day) is pooled and is distributed to all members of the crew.

Passengers are provided with many of the amenities of large modern cruise vessels, including air-conditioning, cashless cruising, occasional live music, a small shop, and swimming pools. There is no dress code, everything being as relaxed as you wish. At 9a.m. each day the captain, sometimes in two or three languages, gives a daily briefing of the important events of the day, such as what time he expects to enter port, the wind and sea conditions, and when passengers can help furl or unfurl the sails if they so wish.

The *Star Clippers* also carry a fine range of watersports craft for the use of passengers—at no extra charge (except scuba diving). The equipment includes a water-ski boat, sailfish, scuba diving, and snorkeling gear.

While cuisine aboard the *Star Clippers* is perhaps less than the advertised excellence (as far as presentation and choice are concerned), one has to take into account the tiny galley and preparation space provided. Seating in the dining room is awkward for "correct" service, and consists of six-seat tables set along the sides of the room. However, this *is* supposed to be a casual experience.

The above comments also apply in general to the beautiful, elegant *Sea Cloud*, an authentic 1930s three-masted barquentine whose masts are as high as a 20-story building. She was the largest private yacht ever built, when constructed in 1931 by E.F. Hutton for his wife, Marjorie Merriwether Post. Built for $1 million in the Krupp shipyard in Kiel, Germany, this steel-hulled yacht is incredibly impressive. The cuisine is quite superb, although choices are limited. This ship has some beautiful cabins, including two lavish owner's suites (both of which have fireplaces and French canopy bed) left over from her original days as a private yacht, and gorgeous hand-crafted interiors.

In addition to her retained and refurbished original suites and cabins, with their paneling, antiques and dressers, some newer, smaller cabins were also added when a consortium of German yachtsmen purchased the ship. The new owners spent $7.5 million refurbishing her. Many original oil paintings adorn her inner walls. Now owned and operated under charter, *Sea Cloud* sails in both Caribbean and Mediterranean waters and is a tribute to elegant times past. The wood-paneled dining room is splendid.

Another vintage ship, the *Sir Francis Drake*, also offers a real working tall ship experience, albeit in a much more casual setting than the *Star Clippers* or *Sea Cloud*. With carpeted cabins that each have a private bathroom, the ship caters to a more casual clientele than the *Star Clippers* or *Sea Cloud*. The cuisine is very basic, though not as basic as that encountered on the vessels of either Windjammer Barefoot Cruises or the Maine Windjammer Association.

## Contemporary Sail-Cruise Ships

At the other extreme, if you like sailing but want everything taken care of automatically (no energy needed), look no further than the *Club Med I* and *Club Med II* (Club Mediterranée)—with five masts the world's largest sail-cruise ships—and *Wind Song*, *Wind Spirit*, and *Wind Star* (Windstar Cruises), each with four masts. How so? Nary a hand touches the sails. It's all controlled by computer from an ultra-high-tech bridge.

Club Med ships are first and foremost cruise vessels with very impressive sails and tall aluminum masts, while Windstar Cruises' ships carry less than half the number of passengers of the Club Med ships (and fewer than the *Star Clippers*). From a yachtsman's point of view, the sail-to-power ratio is laughable. That's why these cruise ships with sails have engine power to get them into and out of port. (The *Star Clippers*, by contrast, do it by sail alone, except when there isn't any wind—which isn't often.) The Windstar ships were built first. You should be aware that on some itineraries, when there's little wind, you could well be under motor power for most of the cruise, with only a few hours spent under sail. The Windstar and Club Med ships would probably be under sail for no more than 40% of the time.

It was a Norwegian living in New York, Karl Andren, who first turned the concept of a cruise vessel with sails into reality. "Boyhood dream stuff," he said. The shipyard he chose, the Société Nouvelle des Ateliers et Chantiers du Havre (ACH, as it is known in Le Havre), enjoyed the challenge of building the most unusual vessels, being experts in the design and construction of cable-laying ships using the hydraulic power of servomechanisms—a concept that was transferred to the Windstar automatic computer-controlled sail rig. Gilbert Fournier, the president of the shipyard, and an expert computer programer, was fascinated with the project. Together, they delivered the three Windstar ships (a fourth was planned but never built), which carry mainly North American passengers. The Club Med vessels cater primarily to French-speaking passengers.

The Windstar and Club Med ships provide luxurious accommodations, outstanding full-service meals, and fine-tuned service, and the ships also feature entertainment (though the GOs—Gentils Organisateurs—on Club Med ships provide amateurish holiday-camp-style entertainment), and several public rooms,

## Sail-Cruise Ships

In terms of the quality of the overall sail-cruise experience, including being under sail, and the hotel and food product, here is a comparison chart, on a scale of 1-10:

| | **A** | **B** | **C** | **D** | **E** | **F** |
|---|---|---|---|---|---|---|
| Sail Experience: | 6 | 6 | 9 | 7 | 10 | 6 |
| Watersports: | 10 | 7 | 5 | 3 | 7 | 9 |
| Activities: | 9 | 6 | 5 | 3 | 6 | 8 |
| Accommodations: | 10 | 7 | 10 | 3 | 8 | 9 |
| Food Quality: | 8 | 7 | 8 | 4 | 6 | 8 |
| Menu Variety: | 8 | 6 | 6 | 3 | 7 | 7 |
| Food Service: | 7 | 8 | 7 | 4 | 6 | 8 |
| Bar Service: | 8 | 7 | 7 | 4 | 6 | 7 |
| Deck Service: | 7 | 6 | 6 | 4 | 3 | 7 |
| Value for Money: | 8 | 8 | 7 | 6 | 9 | 9 |

A = *Club Med I/II*
B = *Le Ponant*
C = *Sea Cloud*
D = *Sir Francis Drake*
E = *Star Clipper/Star Flyer*
F = *Wind Song/Wind Spirit/Wind Star*

all of which have contemporary sophisticated decor.

Another, slightly smaller but very chic, new entrant is the ultra-sleek *Le Ponant.* This three-masted ship caters to just 64 French-speaking passengers in elegant, yet casual, real high-tech surroundings, taking the original Windstar concept to the ultimate degree in 1990s technology.

Aboard the Club Meds, *Star Clippers*, Windstars and *Le Ponant*, watersports take over in the Caribbean when you're not ashore sampling the delights of smaller islands like St. Barthelemy, St. Eustatius,or Les Isles du Saintes, where the large "white-whale" cruise ships cannot go. The Club Meds, Windstars and *Le Ponant* feature an aft, fold-down watersports platform. On-board equipment includes scuba diving gear (you can take a full certification course), snorkeling equipment, water-ski boat, windsail boats and rubber Zodiacs to whisk you off to private, unspoiled beaches.

A separate section (pp.401–410) gives a comparison of these beautiful ships.

# World Cruises, Classic Voyages, and Crossings

## The World Cruise

The ultimate classic voyage for any experienced traveler is a world cruise. This is usually defined as the complete circumnavigation of the earth in a continuous one-way voyage that lasts approximately three months or longer. Ports of call are carefully thought out for interest and diversity, and the whole trip can last for as long as four months.

Voyages from cold to warm climates—almost always during January, February and March, when the weather in the Orient is at its best—bring crisp, clear days, sparkling nights, delicious food, tasteful entertainment, superb accommodations, delightful company, and unforgettable memories. It is for some the cultural, social, and travel experience of a lifetime, and for the few who can afford it, an annual event!

The concept of the world cruise first became popular in the 1920s, although it has existed since the 1880s. The first round-the-world voyage was made by Ferdinand Magellan in 1539.

A world cruise on today's ships means stabilized, air-conditioned comfort in luxury cabins, and extraordinary sightseeing and excursions ashore and overland. And on ships such as Cunard's venerable *Sagafjord*, every passenger will get to dine with the captain at least once.

A world cruise, which lasts between 80 and 110 days, gives you the opportunity to indulge yourself. Although at first the idea may sound totally extravagant, it need not be, and fares can be as low as $100 per day—to more than $3,000 per day. Alternatively, you can book just a segment of the cruise if you prefer.

How much a round-the-world voyage costs will depend on your choice of ship and accommodations. For 1995, double occupancy cruise fares will vary from about $8,000 to more than $100,000 per person. The *QE2*'s split-level penthouse suites, for example, can cost more than $360,000 each (based on two persons)! Gratuities alone would be over $2,000 for the full voyage! At the other end of the scale, a world cruise on a Russian/Ukrainian-registered ship is the least expensive method of going round the word by cruise ship. It almost pays not to stay home, at less than $10 per person per day—including gratuities!

## Planning and Preparation

Few enterprises can match the complexity of planning a world cruise. Over 675,000 main meals will be prepared in the galleys during the voyage. Several hundred professional entertainers, lecturers, bands, and musicians must all be booked about a year in advance. Airline tickets must be arranged for personnel flying in to join the ship—in the right port, and at the right time. Crew changeovers during the cruise must be organized. A ship the size of Cunard's *QE2* requires two major crew changes on the three-month-long voyage. This normally necessitates chartering a jumbo jet to and from the relevant port of call.

Because a modern world cruise ship has to be totally self-contained, a warehouse-full of spare parts (electrical, plumbing and engineering supplies, for example) must be anticipated, ordered, loaded, and stored somewhere aboard ship prior to sailing. For just about every shipboard department, the same fundamental consideration applies: once at sea, it will be impossible to pick up a replacement projector bulb, air-conditioning belt, table tennis ball, saxophone reed, or anything else that might run out.

The cruise director will have his hands full planning entertainment and social events for a long voyage—not like the "old days" when an occasional game of bingo, horse racing, or the daily tote would satisfy passengers.

Other preparations include reserving fuel at various ports on the itinerary. How much fuel does a cruise ship use? Well, that depends on the size of the ship. On the *Canberra*'s 90-day world cruise, for example, the 44,807-grt liner would steam 53 ft. per gallon of fuel, at a cruising speed of 20 knots.

A cruise line must give advance notice of the date and time that pilots will be needed, together with requirements for tugs, docking services, customs and immigration authorities, or meetings with local dignitaries and the press. Then there's the organization of dockside labor and stevedoring services at each port of call, plus planning and contracting of bus or transportation services for shore excursions.

The complexity of the preparations requires the concerted efforts of many departments and people on every continent to bring about, with exact timing, this ultimate cruising experience.

## Other Classic Voyages

Voyages to exotic destinations—China, the Orient, the South Pacific, around Africa and the Indian Ocean, or around South America—offer all the delights associated with a world cruise. The cruise can be shorter and hence less expensive, yet offer the same elegance and comfort, splendid food, delightful ambiance and interesting, well-traveled fellow passengers.

An exotic voyage can be a totally self-contained cruise to a specific destination, lasting anywhere from 30 days to more than 100. Or you can book a segment of a world cruise to begin at one of its ports of call, getting off at another port. "Segmenting" is ideal for those who wish to be a part of a world cruise but have neither the time nor the money for the prolonged extravagance of a three-to four-month vacation.

Segment cruising necessarily involves flying either to or from your cruise, or both. You can join your exotic cruise at such principal ports as Genoa, Rio de Janeiro, Acapulco, Honolulu, Sydney, Hong Kong, Singapore, Bangkok, Colombo, Bombay, Mombasa, or Athens, depending on ship and cruise.

Ships that already cruise worldwide during the year offer the most experienced world cruises or segments. Even though most of these accommodate a maximum of 750 passengers, they often operate at about 75 per cent capacity round the world, thus providing passengers with considerably more space than they would normally have.

## World Cruise Fleet

Although the best-known ships offering round-the-world or other extended cruises are luxury class (HI), some offer moderate (MOD), or even economy (LOW), prices. The following list includes ships which are currently scheduled for world cruises (or other extended voyages), and also gives others that have offered them in the past two years.

**LOW**—*Azerbaydzhan*
(Black SeaShipping/CTC Cruise Lines*)

**MOD**—*Canberra* (P&O Cruises)

**HI**—*Europa* (Hapag Lloyd Cruises)

**LOW**—*Kazakhstan*
(Black Sea Shipping/Delphin Seereisen*)

**MOD**—*Maxim Gorki* (Phoenix Seereisen)

**LOW**—*Odessa*
(Black Sea Shipping/Transocean Tours*)

**HI**—*Queen Elizabeth 2* (Cunard)

**MOD**—*Rotterdam* (Holland America Line)

**HI**—*Royal Viking Sun* (Royal Viking Line)

**HI**—*Sagafjord* (Cunard)

**MOD**—*Sea Princess* (P&O Cruises)

**MOD**—*Statendam* (Holland America Line)

** Chartered by/to this company*

### *Going Posh*

*This colloquialism for "grand" or "first rate" has its origin in the days of ocean steamship travel between England and India. Passengers would, at some cost, book their round trip passage as "Port Outward, Starboard Home." This would secure cabin bookings on the cooler side of the ship while crossing the unbearably hot Indian Ocean in the sun. Abbreviated as P.O.S.H., the expression soon came to be applied to first-class passengers who could afford that luxury.*

(Brewers Dictionary of Phrase & Fable, Cassell Ltd, 1981 Edition)

## Crossings

By "crossings," I mean crossings of the North Atlantic, over 3,000 miles of it, from the Old to the New World—or vice versa, although crossings might also include any other major ocean, such as the Pacific or the Indian ocean.

Crossing the North Atlantic by ship is an adventure, and a suspension of time—the most delicious way of enjoying shipboard life. It takes little more than a long weekend. After embarkation procedures have been completed, you will be shown to the gangway. Cross the gangway from pier to ship and you're in another world—a world that provides a complete antedote to the pressures of contemporary life ashore, and allows you to practice the fine art of doing nothing, if you so wish. After the exhilaration of a North Atlantic crossing, the anticipation among passengers of landfall throughout any ship is nothing short of electric.

Crossing the North Atlantic by passenger vessel should really be considered an art form. I have done it myself over 130 times, and always enjoy it immensely. As a former professional musician, I often consider crossings as rests in musical parlance, for both are "passages." Indeed, musicians often "hear" rests in between notes. So if ports of call are the musical notes of a voyage, then the rests are the days at sea—a temporary interlude, where indulgence of the person and psyche are of paramount importance.

Experienced mariners will tell you that a ship only behaves like a ship when it is on a crossing, for that's what a real ship is built for. Yet the days when ships were built specifically for crossings are almost gone. The only ship left that offers a regularly scheduled transatlantic service (a "crossing") is Cunard's famous *QE2*, the 69,053-grt ship which was superbly designed to hold well against the very worst weather Nature could offer on the North Atlantic. Indeed, captains work harder on an Atlantic crossing than on regular cruising schedules.

The most unpredictable weather in the world, together with fog off the Grand Banks of Newfoundland, can mean that the captain will spend torturous hours on the bridge, with little time for socializing. And when it's foggy, the crew of the *QE2* is often pestered by passengers wanting to know if the ship has yet approached latitude 41°46' north, longitude 50°14' west—where the *Titanic* struck an iceberg on that fateful April night in 1912.

There is something magical in "doing a crossing." It harkens back to the days when passengers turned up at the piers of the ports of New York, Southampton, Cherbourg, or Hamburg in droves, with chauffeurs and steamer trunks, jewels and finery ablaze in a show of what's best in life. Movie stars of the 1920s, 1930s and 1940s often traveled abroad on the largest liners of the day, to arrive refreshed, ready to dazzle European fans.

There's also the excitement and anticipation that precedes a crossing—the bustle of check-in, of being welcomed aboard and escorted to one's penthouse suite or cabin. Once the umbilical cord of the gangway is severed, bow and stern mooring lines are cast off, and with three long blasts on the ship's deep whistle the *QE2* is pried gently from her berth. She goes silently down the waterway, away from the world, as pretty as a picture, as serene as a Rolls-Royce and as sure as the Bank of England. Passengers on deck observe the foolhardy yachtsmen cutting under the raked bows of the *QE2*, while numerous motorboats try to keep up with the giant liner as she edges down the Hudson River, past Battery Park City, the Statue of Liberty, the restored Ellis Island, and then out toward the Verrazano-Narrows Bridge and the open sea. Coming the other way, arriving in New York by ship is one of the world's most thrilling travel experiences. After a five-day westbound crossing on the *QE2*, where days are 25 hours long (they are 23 hours long on an eastbound crossing), everything else is an anticlimax.

The *QE2* can accommodate up to 40 cars per crossing—just in case you really don't want to be parted from your wheels. It also provides kennels, so you can even take your pet, although when crossing eastbound to Southampton, remember that they will have to be quarantined for up to six months. The *QE2* is a distillation of over 150 years of transatlantic traditions, an oasis of creature comforts offered by no other ship.

Apart from the *QE2*'s regular crossings, a number of cruise lines today feature transatlantic crossings. Although little more than repositioning cruises—a way of moving ships which cruise the Mediterranean in summer to the Caribbean in winter, and vice versa—they do offer more chances to experience the romance and adventure of a crossing, usually in the Spring and Fall. Perhaps the most unusual transatlantic crossings—made twice a year—are aboard the sail-cruise vessel *Star Flyer*—a true four-masted barquentine vessel that can carry 180 passengers, totally under sail.

Most ships performing repositioning crossings actually cross using the "sunny southern route"—departing from southern ports such as Ft. Lauderdale, San Juan, or Barbados, and ending in Lisbon, Genoa, or Copenhagen via the Azores or the Canary Islands off the coast of northern Africa. In this way they avoid the more difficult weather that is often encountered on the North Atlantic. The crossings take longer, however, and last between eight and 12 days.

# Queen Elizabeth 2: Milestones Over the Years

*Queen Elizabeth 2* is a very special ship—part liner, part cruise ship—a real legend in her own lifetime, and the only ship offering regularly scheduled crossings all year. I worked aboard her in two roles: from December 1968 to October 1969 as leader of a jazz group; and from 1977 to 1980 as Shore Excursion Manager/Deputy Cruise Director.

Instead of allowing the ship to deteriorate, Cunard has spent a vast sum of money on constant refurbishments, the most recent being a $60 million refit in November/December 1994 that altered the actual passenger flow, and enhanced and increased her already considerable facilities and amenities.

During the ship's initial planning stages, naval architect Dan Wallace and director of engineering Tom Kameen were responsible for the ship's design, which was to be for a high speed, twin screw ship that would be capable of performing a five day transatlantic crossing. Cunard's chairman, Sir Basil Smallpiece, invited James Gardner and Dennis Lennon, well known industrial designers, to be general design co-ordinators. Gardner concentrated on the exterior aesthetics, while Lennon, in addition to designing the restaurant interiors—the basic shape of which had been determined by constructional and operational requirements—was also concerned with the introduction of a design signature that would be immediately apparent throughout the ship; for example, in staircases and corridors.The aim was that the interior design of *QE2* would emphasize the "classless" ship concept.

## 1955

Preparation work for a large liner such as *QE2* had already been underway for some time by 1955, and had included the introduction of an intensive weight-saving exercise in the design of Cunard's *Sylvania*, which was then under construction at the famous Clydebank shipyards in Glasgow. By agreement with the builders, John Brown's, parts of this vessel had various experimental features built in. Most of these were successful and provided many weight-saving devices which were to be adopted some 10 years later for the *QE2*. These included lightweight furniture, fiberglass shower units, new types of deck coverings and new construction and joinery methods.

In conjunction with British Steel's research section, a new type of girder was developed and tested. This girder had large holes for the various services (piping, wiring, etc.) cut in during fabrication, with the depth of the girder being slightly increased in order to compensate for the reduced tension. The result was a girder that was much lighter than the standard ones of the time, and which was used experimentally in *Sylvania*—a ship which was pioneering the way in terms of advanced construction techniques and materials usage.

## October 1963

Construction plans and financing were announced by Cunard Line in England.

## December 30, 1964

The contract to build was signed by Sir John Brocklebank, then chairman of Cunard, and Lord Aberconway, then chairman of Upper Clyde Shipbuilders (formerly John Brown's), a consortium of five major shipyards on the upper reaches of the River Clyde in Scotland. Some 300 British workers contributed to the building and furnishing of the ship. The contract price was UK£25.5 million, but this inevitably escalated as a result of increases in wage rates and costs of material during the building period. On completion, the total cost was approximately UK£30 million.

Coincidental with the building of *QE2* was the financial improvement of the Cunard Group, which meant that in 1968 the company was able to forgo part of a loan negotiated with the Board of Trade. This was in addition to the loan of UK£17,600,000 obtained in 1964 under the British Government's shipbuilding credit scheme. There was never any question of a direct constructional subsidy; Cunard was entirely responsible for meeting the full cost of *QE2*.

## July 4, 1965

On America's Independence Day—which also happened to be the 125th anniversary of the maiden voyage of Cunard's first ship, *Britannia*, in 1840—the first prefabricated section of the keel for hull number 736 of *QE2* was laid in the shipyard on Clydebank.

## September 20, 1967

"I name this ship Queen Elizabeth the Second. May God bless her and all who sail in her." With these historic words, Her Majesty Queen Elizabeth II named the new liner—not after herself, as some had claimed, but simply because this was the second ship to bear that name (the first *Queen Elizabeth* was still in operation at that time). Apparently it was an impulse decision on the part of Her Majesty to add the "second" to the name, which no one, not even at Cunard headquarters, had expected, for it had been secretly agreed that the ship would simply be called *Queen Elizabeth*. Ahead lay a year of fitting out; the new ship was to fill two roles—those of transatlantic express liner and leisure cruise ship.

On the transatlantic run, she was to be a two-class ship. It was decided that class distinction would be completely absent in the naming of public spaces, rooms and decks. Passengers occupying the best accommodations would simply have certain spaces and rooms reserved expressly for their use.

In addition, there was to be single sitting dining in the Grill Room and Columbia Restaurants, but two sittings in the Britannia Restaurant. However, the greater part of the accommodations would be open to all on board without restrictions. Passengers would then be allotted a restaurant according to which accommodations had been chosen.

## December 1968

*Queen Elizabeth 2* (or just *QE2* as she became affectionately known) sailed gracefully out of Gourock, Scotland, with 600 John Brown men aboard, still doing final fitting-out work. A brochure had advertised a Christmas Cruise, but passengers were informed it had been canceled when Cunard Line refused delivery of the ship as she was not completed. Instead, the workmen had a good Christmas (there was beer everywhere). The captain was Commodore William ("Bill") Warwick. The Cruise Director was Bryan Vickers. I was aboard.

## April 18, 1969

The *QE2* was commissioned.

## April 22, 1969

In a show of local support, coat hangers for the crew were donated by the District Spastics Association of Southampton, England—*QE2*'s home port. Cunard Line accepted delivery of the new ship from the builders and embarked on a "Preview Cruise" to the ports of Las Palmas, Tenerife and Lisbon. I was aboard with my own jazz trio, which performed each night in what was then the ship's most elegant nightclub (for First Class passengers only)—the Q4 Room (no longer in existence, although it was the "in" place to be in those days).

I remember well that the featured film was *2001: A Space Odyssey*, and that an English rock band called The Applejacks was playing. The ship actually had four "go-go" dancers who worked in the 736 Room (the discotheque of the day, which is now the exclusive "Queens Grill"—according to many, the finest restaurant afloat). Twice each day, passengers gathered for a classical concert staged in the Upper Deck Library.

## May 2, 1969, Maiden Voyage

*QE2* proudly sailed from Southampton on her maiden voyage. Her Majesty Queen Elizabeth II and her husband, the Duke of Edinburgh, paid an official visit to the ship prior to sailing. Five days later the ship arrived in New York to a tumultuous welcome. She was greeted there by Mayor John Lindsay.

## June 1970

*QE2* crosses from Southampton to New York in 3 days, 20 hours and 42 minutes, at an average speed of 30.36 knots. A casino is also added as U.S. gaming laws are relaxed.

## October 1970

*QE2*'s first long cruise gets underway—a 37-night voyage around North America, South America and Africa.

## January 9, 1971

In a dramatic rescue in the Grenadines, *QE2* takes on board 501 passengers and crew from the burning wreck of the 19,828-grt French Line cruise ship *Antilles*, and lands them at Barbados.

## January 1975, World Cruise

*QE2*'s first world cruise sets off. It is to be a successful voyage, and the ship is welcomed enthusiastically with celebrations and parties in all her ports of call. She proves herself newsworthy.

## May 1975

*QE2* meets "Operation Tall Ships" in Tenerife, Canary Islands.

## 1977, Refit

The Britannia Restaurant is converted into Tables of the World (later nicknamed "Stables of the World")—the largest of the ship's four restaurants. America also contributed to the changing face of the *QE2*, and in Bethlehem Steel Shipyard in Bayonne, New Jersey, two ultra-deluxe suites, appropriately called Queen Mary and Queen Elizabeth, were added.

The Grill Room became the Princess Grill and the 736 Club (formerly a discotheque) was transformed into the Queens Grill. At the same time, the under-used 24-hour Coffee Shop was divided and reworked into the galley (kitchen) space and the Queens Grill Lounge/Bar, one of the most elegant and prestigious spaces afloat.

The forward Lookout Bar on the Upper Deck was, sadly, changed into an enlarged galley for the Tables of the World. The London Gallery, an experimental art gallery with paintings for sale, was turned into the Reading Room—a restful space for first class passengers.

On Upper Deck amidships, the Portside Promenade and Library were transformed into a full casino christened The Players Club. Meanwhile, the Theatre Bar was changed into a discotheque for the younger crowd.

## 1978

National Geographic made a feature film about the great liners, featuring *QE2*.

## January 1979

*QE2* operated her tenth World Cruise. Included in the itinerary was a maiden transit of the Suez Canal, experienced by the greatest number of passengers ever.

## May 1982, the Falklands

*QE2* was requisitioned by Her Majesty's Government for service as a troop ship in the Falkland Islands. The requisition came as *QE2* was crossing from New York to Southampton after her inaugural visit to Philadelphia. I was aboard.

When *QE2* arrived in Southampton, it took only seven days to convert her into a troop ship, complete with helicopter landing pads. All furniture, artworks, slot machines, pianos and plants were off-loaded and placed into storage at Pickford's warehouse in Southampton.

## August 1982

*QE2* sets sail for engine trials following a nine-week-long refit to reconvert her to passenger service. The Golden Door Spa at Sea was added. The Q4 Room (the swinging nightclub room where I entertained passengers with a small jazz combo when the ship debuted in 1969) was converted into the Club Lido.

The ship's hull was painted pebble grey—not a pretty sight! *QE2* sailed on a transatlantic crossing for the first time since her Falklands service.

## April 1983

For the first time, *QE2* was paired for holiday packages with British Airways' supersonic aircraft, Concorde.

## May 1983

*QE2* honors New York's leading ladies with afternoon tea and a British fashion show during the "Britain Salutes New York" festivities. Guests of honor included city council woman Carol Bellamy.

## October 1983, Marathon

*QE2* enters a five-man team in the New York City Marathon. A collection is made for the National Lifeboat Association and Guide Dogs for the Blind charities. As a result, a guide dog, whose picture is aboard the ship, was subsequently christened Marathon.

## January 1984

A huge "magrodome" sliding glass roof was added to the Club Lido indoor/outdoor leisure center. The Reading Room was converted into a Computer Center, which fast became extremely popular. Later in the year, Cunard signed a $40 million contract with British Airways. More than 10,000 passengers now take a round-trip in completely unique style—one leisurely crossing on *QE2*, the other at supersonic speed on Concorde.

## June 1984

The first seagoing branch of Harrods was opened by Hermione Gingold.

## December 1984

Refurbishment of the Columbia Restaurant with softer colors and lighting.

## January 1985

American Express opened the first seagoing finance center aboard ship. It was located in the 2-Deck lobby.

## July 1985

Captain Robert ("Bob") Arnott, *QE2*'s longest serving captain, retires.

## January 1986

The first regular television programing at sea occurred, courtesy of NBC-TV. Passengers watched the Superbowl live in Lima, Peru, while on the ship's annual World Cruise.

## March 1986

The *International Herald Tribune* became the first newspaper to be printed on board ship, by means of its transmission to *QE2* via satellite.

## May 1986

A royal touch as Queen Elizabeth, the Queen Mother, visits *QE2* in Southampton for the Cunarder *Queen Mary*'s 50th anniversary celebrations.

## October 1986, Refit

*QE2* features her last voyage as a steam ship, prior to entering the Lloyd Werft shipyard in Bremerhaven, Germany for a six-month long, $160 million refit. Her steam engines and three boilers were exchanged for a nine-unit, diesel-electric propulsion system, and her two fixed-pitch six-bladed propellers were replaced by two skew-backed, controllable-pitch, five-bladed propellers weighing 42 tons each. A new and fatter funnel was constructed, designed to keep any soot off her expansive open decks. The refit took 179 days and a work force of men from 34 countries was involved.

## April 29, 1987

*QE2* undertakes her inaugural crossing from Southampton to New York under diesel-electric power. A flotilla of small craft led by Malcolm Forbes' famed yacht, the *Highlander*, escort the "new" *QE2* past the Statue of Liberty.

## May 8, 1994

*QE2* slides gracefully as a Rolls Royce away from her berth at Southampton Docks. There were no visible celebrations on deck, no champagne, no streamers, no cruise staff—in fact nothing to show that this was the Silver Anniversary of her maiden voyage from Southampton to New York some 25 years earlier. On the bridge for the historic moment were Commodore William ("Bill") Warwick (now retired, but then commodore of the Cunard fleet and captain of *QE2* on her maiden crossing in May 1969), his son, Ron Warwick, presently a Cunard captain, and the ship's present master, Captain John Burton-Hall. There were five passengers aboard who had been on the original crossing, of whom I was one.

The only sign of this special occasion was a large banner draped over a section of the Ocean Terminal, which said, quite simply, "Congratulations from ABP" (Associated British Ports). It was a celebration of another kind, however, with jazz music giants George Shearing, Gerry Mulligan, Ronnie Scott and others playing their way across the North Atlantic.

## November 1994, Refit

*QE2* is put into drydock for one month for an extensive refit. She undergoes a dramatic $60 million interior refurbishment, including numerous structural changes designed to facilitate better passenger flow and even more dining (and other facility) choices. All cabin bathrooms are replaced (a mammoth task), and several new suites are added, as well as an enlarged library and new book shop (an excellent idea) and Florist. The Club Lido magrodome-covered pool is replaced with a new, informal bistro-like dining area, complete with its own separate preparation galley. The Mauretania Restaurant becomes the Caronia Restaurant, together with a new Crystal Bar (which includes a 16-ft. long model of the *Caronia*, the former Cunard world cruise ship). In addition, the Columbia Restaurant becomes the Mauretania Restaurant, and a new Captain's Dining Area is added. The three Grill Rooms remain (but Queens Grill is completely refurbished, and banquette seating is replaced by individual seating). A new private "key club" has been established in the old Boardroom.

The showlounge balcony shopping area now features a large Card Room (port side) and a new Coffee Lounge (starboard side), while aft of the same area there is a new, aft-facing Observation Lounge and Bar. The shops are all being moved to where the lower level of the Theatre was located (a new, smaller, 130-seat Theatre is being created). A new Pub now occupies previously underutilized space on the starboard side, forward of the showlounge, which is being altered so that the stage and dressing rooms are aft rather than forward.

The Midships Bar (one of the only original rooms that was left) is being refurbished and possibly renamed, while the Yacht Club bar is being greatly enlarged, and a new nightclub created from space gained from an aft deck extension. A brand new Sports Deck is now atop ship, and a smaller one aft.

## The Future

During the past 25 years, *QE2* has become one of the most popular, and successful liners ever built. She has sailed more than three-and-a-half million nautical miles, catering to more than 1.5 million passengers. I hope her interiors will be changed into those reminiscent of the ocean liners of yesteryear, for that is what passengers expect of this ship. Until now, however, the interiors have been disappointing, built as she was in the late 1960s, when contemporary design and plastic laminates were all the rage (some 2 million square feet of Formica laminates were used in her original interiors).

When completed, the new enhancements will offer space, grace and pace.

PART TWO

# Cruise Ship Directory and Ratings

# Pick-a-Ship Chart

If you have only a vague idea of the kind of cruise you would like, this at-a-glance chart will help you compare cruise ships, river vessels, tall ships, and others, and select those that interest you most. You can then turn to the ratings and evaluations which follow for an in-depth look at each vessel. Some ships, such as small coastal vessels or Russian/Ukrainian ships, have not yet been evaluated.

## Key to Pick-a-Ship Chart

### Ship Name

Given in alphabetical order.

### Cruise Line/Operator

The owner, chartering company and/or operator.

### Product Identity Code (PIC)

This rating is the first serious attempt at worldwide product segmentation in the cruise industry. I have assigned a color-coding system for easy identification, rather than an alphabetical or numerical system. The descriptions are as accurate as possible, but exceptions may occur as cruise lines change their products.

### Pink

Not really a cruise—more a one-day gambling junket. For those who want the simplest taste of being on the water, surrounded by party-goers who like to gamble, drink and be merrily (make that loudly) entertained. Food will generally be buffet-style, and any à la carte menu items will be at extra cost. Day cabins may be available at extra cost, but there will be few of them. Entertainment will be of the very simplest, low-budget type, nothing more. Don't think of it as a cruise, please. It's really an attraction.

- *Expect plastic cutlery/plates for indoor/outdoor café use.*

### Green

These are short cruises of three, four, or five days. Good for first time cruisegoers of all ages who want to "get their feet wet" before taking the plunge and opting for a longer cruise—and for those who have only a limited time to spare. Expect full-service meals from an attentive, multi-national staff, and thriving casino action; almost non-stop activities and entertainment will be the norm on these ships. These are stimulating, rather than relaxing, cruises, on ships with a high Passenger Density Factor. (This translates to plenty of other passengers on board.)

- *Expect plastic cutlery/plates for indoor/outdoor café use.*
- *Two sittings for meals.*
- *Deck chairs do not have padded cushions.*
- *Gratuities not included.*
- *Port taxes not included.*
- *Passenger age range: 25–60.*

## Blue

Good for cruisegoers seeking an active, rather than a passive, first-time cruise experience for the standard seven days, at a modest rate. Food will be of an adequate (price-controlled) quality, little better than family-style food establishments ashore. Service from a multinational crew whose command of the English language may be mediocre at best. High Passenger Density Factor. Basic variety entertainment. Expect shows with lots of feathers, and loud, uncouth comedians.

- *Expect plastic cutlery/plates for indoor/outdoor café use.*
- *Two sittings for meals.*
- *Deck chairs do not have padded cushions.*
- *Gratuities not included.*
- *Port taxes not included.*
- *Passenger age range: 25 plus.*

## Orange

Comfortable cruise experience for first time and repeat cruisegoers who are seeking more than just the basics, and are not particularly looking for bargain basement rates. Better-than-basic cuisine, and service from a multi-national crew, with family-style entertainment. They are generally on older, refurbished, but comfortable, vessels with a fairly high Passenger Density Factor.

- *Expect plastic cutlery/plates for indoor/outdoor café use.*
- *Two sittings for meals.*
- *Deck chairs do not have padded cushions.*
- *Gratuities not included.*
- *Port taxes not included.*
- *Passenger age range: 40 plus.*

## Red

Ideal for families and single parents with children, who are seeking excellent entertainment and facilities and who want well organized activities for children, 'tweens and teens. Standard cuisine with an emphasis on family food—plenty of hamburgers and hot dogs, and a short wine list.

- *Expect plastic cutlery/plates for indoor/outdoor café use.*
- *Two sittings for meals.*
- *Deck chairs do not have padded cushions.*
- *Gratuities not included.*
- *Port taxes not included.*
- *Passenger age range: 0 plus.*

## Purple

This category is ideal for cruisegoers seeking a fine contemporary ship and cruise experience at a moderate rate. The food and service will be of a good to high standard, with a quality wine list. The Passenger Density Factor will be moderate, and entertainment will be of a decent quality.

- *Expect plastic cutlery/plates for indoor/outdoor café use.*
- *Two sittings for meals.*
- *Deck chairs do not have padded cushions.*
- *Gratuities not included.*
- *Port taxes not included.*
- *Passenger age range: 45 plus.*

## Bronze

For cruisegoers seeking a high standard of both ship and service. Ships in this category will offer old-world type hotel service. Very good (though not quite gourmet) food quality, presentation, and service, with a fine menu choice and an excellent wine list. Moderate to good Passenger Density Factor. Good quality entertainment—no smut.

- *May use real or plastic cutlery/plates, for indoor/outdoor café use.*
- *Two sittings for meals.*
- *Deck chairs may have padded cushions.*
- *Gratuities not included.*
- *Port taxes not included.*
- *Passenger age range: 45 plus.*

## Silver

For cruisegoers seeking an extremely high standard of ship and service. Fine food quality and a consistently high standard of presentation, as found in some of the best restaurants ashore. The wine list will be excellent, and will include several premium French vintages. The Passenger Density Factor will be reasonably low. Elegant entertainment, with little or no "plumage" in production shows. Cruise rates will be moderately high to high.

- *Only real (not plastic) cutlery/plates, for indoor/outdoor use.*
- *Single, or possibly two-sitting, dining, with at least two hours for the first sitting.*
- *Deck chairs should have padded cushions.*
- *Gratuities not included.*
- *Port taxes may or may not be included.*
- *Passenger age range: 35 plus.*

## Gold

This is the highest classification of ship, food and service—for cruisegoers who simply want the best, and are willing to pay for it. Gourmet food that is individually prepared, for the most part, and of a high international standard. Beluga or Sevruga caviar will be plentiful, and the wine list will be outstanding. Service will be by a superior, hand-picked European crew. Entertainment will be elegant—no dazzle and sizzle. Expect fine lecturers and writers for life enrichment programs. No hard sell anywhere on board. There will be open-sitting dining, or alternative restaurants, and, on smaller ships, no assigned tables.

- *Expect the finest attention to detail and only real (not plastic) cutlery/plates for indoor/outdoor use.*
- *Deck chairs have thick padded cushions.*
- *All gratuities included.*
- *Port taxes probably included.*
- *Passenger age range: 40 plus.*

## White

These ships feature specialist cruises for life enrichment and expedition cruisegoers. Standards will vary from reasonably comfortable to outstanding. Both food and service will be of a good to excellent quality, and service will be to a high standard from an international crew. The only entertainment on board will be lectures and life enrichment programs presented by specialists who are outstanding in their respective fields.

- *Gratuities not included.*
- *Port taxes may or may not be included.*
- *Passenger age range: 45 plus.*

### Grey

These ships will be out-of-the-ordinary vessels such as tall ships and wind sail ships that cater principally to adults, and are not generally recommended for families with children. The lifestyle will be almost totally unstructured, with little or no evening entertainment (perhaps a piano or a trio). Good watersports will be available, probably direct from a special platform at the stern. Dining will be an open-sitting arrangement, with food generally cooked in small batches, or made to order.

- *Gratuities not included.*
- *Port taxes not included.*
- *Passenger age range: 35 plus.*

### Black

These vessels are small (fewer than 150 passengers) and are a mixture of coastal and semi-expedition vessels that cannot be classified or licensed as true ocean-going vessels, for they cannot venture far from the shoreline. They may fly the American flag, and cater principally to adults seeking a small ship experience. There are few public rooms, and the choice of food will be somewhat limited in the dining room.

- *Gratuities not included.*
- *Port taxes not included.*
- *Passenger age range: 50 plus.*

## Price Guide

This is given to indicate what you can reasonably expect to pay per person per day, based on the minimum full published tariff rate available.

LOW = Low: up to $175 per person per day.

MOD = Moderate: $175 to $300 per person per day.

HI = High: over $300 per person per day.

## Dress Code/Lifestyle

CAS = Casual, very relaxed dress code.

INF = Informal, moderately conservative, resort attire suggested.

FOR = Formal, elegant, conservative attire requested.

ADV = Adventure clothing, heavy outdoor and cold weather wear.

## Cabin Insulation Rating

Cabins are rated on a scale of 1-10, with 10 being highest and most soundproof. Each rating takes into account the general noise level and the degree of insulation between cabins. This is a composite rating—taken from cabins on several decks.

## Health and Fitness Facilities

On a scale of 1-10, with 10 being the highest score. This rating is a guide to gymnasium/health and fitness facilities and equipment, instruction programs, and the degree of professionalism.

## Access Rating for the Physically Challenged

**A** = This ship is very accessible throughout, has specially equipped cabins for the physically challenged and excellent, ramped access to all decks and public areas, and is highly recommended.

**B** = This ship is very accessible throughout, has specially equipped cabins and good, ramped access to most, but not all, decks and public areas (gaining access to the swimming pool deck may present a minor problem).

**C** = This ship has generally good access to some, but not all, decks and public areas. Ramping could be better.

**D** = This ship has limited accessibility, and cannot be recommended for anyone who is severely mobility-limited or otherwise challenged.

**Z** = This ship should not be booked by *any* physically challenged passengers, especially those using a wheelchair. Not only are there no specially equipped cabins, but passageways and cabin doorways are too narrow, and "lips" prevent access to almost all areas.

## Junior Cruisers Rating

The cruise industry provides four basic categories of cruise products when it comes to children:

**A** = This ship welcomes children of all ages—'tweens and teens—with open arms, and provides a packed entertainment program, and plenty of specialized children's counselors.

**B** = This ship welcomes families with children, but may carry full-time counselors only during the summer and other holiday periods. There will be some children's programing, but generally only during the daytime while at sea.

**C** = This ship accepts bookings for families with children, but does not carry full-time counselors except during selected holidays. It has a limited program, and generally expects parents to entertain their youngsters.

**Z** = This ship is designed and operated principally for adults only; children are not provided for, and may only just be tolerated by other passengers if they are brought along.

# Pick-a-Ship Chart

## Index



## SHIPS

| Ship Name | GRT | Cruise Line/Operator | Product Identity Code | Price Guide | Dress Code/Lifestyle | Cabin Insul Rating | Health/Fitness Facilities | Access Rating | Junior Cruisers Rating |
|---|---|---|---|---|---|---|---|---|---|
| Achille Lauro | 23,862 | Starlauro Cruises | Blue | Low | Cas | 7 | 3 | D | C |
| Adriana | 4,590 | Jadrolinija/Seetours | Orange | Low | Inf | 7 | 3 | D | Z |
| Aegean Dolphin | 11,563 | Dolphin Hellas Shipping | Orange | Low | Cas | 4 | 3 | C | C |
| Akdeniz | 8,809 | Turkish Maritime Lines | Blue | Low | Cas | 3 | 1 | Z | Z |
| Albatros | 24,724 | Phoenix Seereisen | Orange | Mod | Inf | 8 | 5 | D | C |
| Alla Tarasova | 3,985 | Murmansk Shipping | Blue | Low | Cas | 4 | 1 | Z | Z |
| Ambasador I | 2,573 | Marco Polo Cruises | Blue | Low | Cas | 3 | 1 | Z | Z |
| American Adventure | 31,500 | American Family Cruises | Red | Low | Cas | 7 | 6 | C | A |
| Americana | 19,203 | Ivaran Lines | White | Mod | Inf | 7 | 1 | C | Z |
| Amerikanis | 19,904 | Fantasy Cruises | Orange/Red | Low | Cas | 6 | 4 | C | C |
| Andaman Princess | 4,898 | Siam Cruise Company | Blue | Low | Cas | 4 | 2 | Z | Z |
| Anna Karenina | 14,623 | Baltic Shipping | Blue | Low | Cas | 6 | 4 | D | C |
| Antonina Nezhdanova | 3,941 | Far Eastern Shipping | White | Low | Cas | 4 | 2 | Z | Z |
| Arcadia | 4,904 | Attika Shipping | Blue | Low | Cas | 4 | 2 | Z | Z |
| Argonaut | 4,007 | Epirotiki Lines | Orange | Low | Inf | 5 | 1 | Z | C |
| Arkona | 18,591 | Deutsche Seereederei | Bronze | Mod | Inf | 7 | 4 | C | Z |
| Astra | 5,635 | Neckermann Seereisen | Blue | Low | Cas | 3 | 1 | Z | Z |
| Asuka | 28,717 | NYK Cruises | Bronze | Hi | Inf | 8 | 5 | C | Z |
| Atalante | 13,113 | Paradise Cruises | Green | Low | Cas | 4 | 2 | C | C |
| Aurora I | 2,928 | Classical Cruises | Purple | Mod | Inf | 7 | 3 | Z | Z |
| Aurora II | 2,928 | Classical Cruises | Purple | Mod | Inf | 7 | 3 | Z | Z |
| Ausonia | 12,368 | Ausonia Cruises | Blue | Low | Cas | 6 | 4 | Z | C |
| Ayvasovskiy | 7,127 | Soviet Danube Shipping | Green | Low | Cas | 4 | 2 | Z | Z |

## SHIPS

| Ship Name | GRT | Cruise Line/Operator | Product Identity Code | Price Guide | Dress Code/Lifestyle | Cabin Insul Rating | Health/Fitness Facilities | Access Rating | Junior Cruisers Rating |
|---|---|---|---|---|---|---|---|---|---|
| Azerbaydzhan | 15,065 | CTC Cruises | Orange | Low | Cas | 5 | 4 | D | Z |
| Bali Sea Dancer | 3,852 | P&O Spice Island Cruises | Purple | Mod | Cas | 4 | 1 | Z | Z |
| Baltica | 9,436 | Baltic Line | Purple | Mod | Inf | 6 | 5 | Z | Z |
| Berlin | 9,570 | Deilmann Reederei | Bronze | Mod | Inf/For | 7 | 3 | C | Z |
| Black Prince | 11,209 | Fred Olsen Cruises | Orange | Low | Cas/Inf | 7 | 6 | D | Z |
| Bremen | 6,752 | Hanseatic/Hapag-Lloyd | White | Hi | Adv | 7 | 7 | C | Z |
| Britanis | 26,141 | Fantasy Cruises | Green/Red | Low | Cas | 7 | 5 | C | C |
| Caledonian Star | 3,095 | Noble Caledonia | White | Mod | Adv | 6 | 3 | D | Z |
| Canberra | 44,807 | P&O Cruises | Orange/Red | Low | Inf | 7 | 7 | C | A |
| Celebration | 47,262 | Carnival Cruise Lines | Blue/Red | Low | Cas | 8 | 7 | B | B |
| Century | 70,000 | Celebrity Cruises | Bronze | Mod | Inf | n/a | n/a | n/a | n/a |
| City of Rhodos | 6,497 | Cycladic Cruises | Green | Low | Cas | 2 | 1 | Z | Z |
| Columbus Caravelle | 7,560 | Odessa Cruise Company | White/Purple | Mod | Adv/Inf | 7 | 3 | C | Z |
| Constitution | 30,090 | American Hawaii Cruises | Blue | Mod | Cas | 6 | 5 | C | C |
| CostaAllegra | 28,430 | Costa Cruises | Blue | Low | Cas | 5 | 5 | C | C |
| CostaClassica | 53,700 | Costa Cruises | Blue | Mod | Inf | 6 | 7 | B | C |
| CostaMarina | 25,441 | Costa Cruises | Blue | Low | Cas | 5 | 5 | C | C |
| CostaRomantica | 56,800 | Costa Cruises | Blue | Mod | Inf | 6 | 7 | B | C |
| Crown Dynasty | 19,089 | Cunard Crown Cruises | Purple | Low | Cas/Inf | 8 | 6 | C | C |
| Crown Jewel | 19,046 | Cunard Crown Cruises | Purple | Low | Cas/Inf | 8 | 6 | C | C |
| Crown Monarch | 15,271 | Cunard Crown Cruises | Purple | Low | Cas/Inf | 7 | 6 | C | C |
| Crown Odyssey | 34,242 | Royal Cruise Line | Silver | Mod | Inf | 10 | 8 | A | Z |
| Crown Princess | 70,000 | Princess Cruises | Bronze | Mod | Inf | 9 | 9 | B | Z |
| Crystal Harmony | 48,621 | Crystal Cruises | Silver/Gold | Hi | Inf/For | 10 | 9 | A | Z |
| Crystal Symphony | 49,500 | Crystal Cruises | Silver/Gold | Hi | Inf/For | 10 | 9 | A | Z |
| Cunard Countess | 17,593 | Cunard Crown Cruises | Blue | Low | Cas | 5 | 4 | C | C |
| Cunard Princess | 17,495 | Cunard Crown Crusies | Blue | Low | Cas | 5 | 4 | C | C |
| Daphne | 9,436 | Costa Cruises | Purple | Low | Cas/Inf | 6 | 5 | C | Z |
| Delfin Star | 5,207 | Ocean Trade Chartering | Green | Mod | Inf | 7 | 3 | D | Z |
| Dmitriy Shostakovich | 10,303 | Black Sea Shipping | Blue | Low | Cas | 4 | 2 | D | C |
| Dolphin IV | 13,000 | Dolphin Cruise Line | Green | Low | Cas | 4 | 3 | D | C |
| Dreamward | 39,217 | Norwegian Cruise Line | Orange | Low | Cas | 8 | 8 | C | C |
| Ecstasy | 70,367 | Carnival Cruise Lines | Blue/Red | Low | Cas | 9 | 9 | B | B |
| Empress Katerina | 6,542 | Empress Cruise Lines | Blue | Low | Cas/Inf | 5 | 2 | Z | Z |
| Enchanted Seas | 23,879 | Commodore Cruise Lines | Blue | Low | Cas | 7 | 4 | C | C |

| Ship Name | GRT | Cruise Line/Operator | Product Identity Code | Price Guide | Dress Code/Lifestyle | Cabin Insul Rating | Health/Fitness Facilities | Access Rating | Junior Cruisers Rating |
|---|---|---|---|---|---|---|---|---|---|
| Enrico Costa | 16,495 | Costa Cruises | Blue | Low | Cas | 4 | 3 | Z | C |
| EugenioCosta | 32,753 | CostaCrociere | Blue | Low | Cas/Inf | 7 | 5 | Z | D |
| Europa | 37,012 | Hapag-Lloyd Line | Gold | Hi | For | 10 | 9 | A | Z |
| Excelsior Mercury | 4,180 | Excelsior Cruise Lines | Blue | Low | Cas | 5 | 1 | Z | Z |
| Excelsior Neptune | 4,195 | Excelsior Cruise Lines | Blue | Low | Cas | 5 | 1 | Z | Z |
| Explorer | 2,398 | Abercrombie & Kent | White | Hi | Cas | 3 | 1 | Z | Z |
| Fair Princess | 24,724 | Princess Cruises | Orange/Red | Mod | Inf | 8 | 5 | D | C |
| Fairstar | 23,764 | P&O Holidays | Blue/Red | Low | Cas | 6 | 5 | D | A |
| Fantasy | 70,367 | Carnival Cruise Lines | Green/Red | Low | Cas | 9 | 9 | B | B |
| Fascination | 70,367 | Carnival Cruise Lines | Green/Red | Low | Cas | 9 | 9 | B | B |
| Fedor Dostoyevsky | 20,158 | Black Sea Shipping | Purple | Low | Inf | 8 | 7 | B | Z |
| Fedor Shalyapin | 21,406 | Far Eastern Shipping | Blue | Low | Cas | 7 | 3 | Z | C |
| Festivale | 38,175 | Carnival Cruise Lines | Blue | Low | Cas | 7 | 6 | C | C |
| FiestaMarina | 27,250 | FiestaMarina Cruises | Green/Red | Low | Cas | 6 | 5 | C | B |
| Fuji Maru | 23,340 | Mitsui OSK Passenger Line | Purple/Bronze | Hi | Inf | 7 | 6 | C | Z |
| Funchal | 9,846 | Fritidskryss | Orange | Low | Cas | 6 | 3 | D | C |
| Georg Ots | 9,878 | Estonian Shipping | Blue | Low | Cas | 4 | 3 | D | Z |
| Golden Princess | 28,078 | Princess Cruises | Bronze | Mod | Inf | 9 | 8 | C | C |
| Gruziya | 15,402 | OdessAmerica Cruise Co. | Orange | Low | Cas | 5 | 4 | D | C |
| Hanseatic | 8,378 | Hanseatic Tours | White | Hi | Adv/Inf | 8 | 6 | D | Z |
| Hebridean Princess | 2,112 | Hebridean Island Cruises | Bronze | Hi | Cas/Inf | 8 | 1 | Z | Z |
| Holiday | 46,052 | Carnival Cruise Lines | Blue | Low | Cas | 7 | 7 | B | B |
| Horizon | 46,811 | Celebrity Cruises | Bronze | Mod | Inf | 9 | 9 | A | C |
| Ilich | 8,528 | Baltic Line | Green | Low | Cas | 4 | 2 | Z | C |
| Illiria | 3,852 | Classical Cruises | Purple | Mod | Cas | 4 | 1 | Z | Z |
| Imagination | 70,367 | Carnival Cruise Lines | Blue | Low | Cas | 9 | 9 | B | B |
| Independence | 30,090 | American Hawaii Cruises | Blue | Mod | Cas | 5 | 4 | C | C |
| Island Princess | 19,907 | Princess Cruises | Bronze | Mod | Inf | 8 | 6 | C | Z |
| Italia Prima | 15,000 | Nina Cruise Lines | Green | Low | Cas | 6 | 4 | C | Z |
| Ivan Franko | 20,064 | Black Sea Shipping | Blue | Low | Cas | 4 | 4 | C | C |
| Jason | 5,250 | Epirotiki Lines | Orange | Low | Cas | 4 | 2 | Z | C |
| Jin Jiang | 14,812 | Shanghai Shipping | Blue | Low | Cas | 5 | 2 | Z | Z |
| Jubilee | 47,262 | Carnival Cruise Lines | Blue | Low | Cas | 7 | 7 | B | B |
| Kapitan Dranitsyn | 12,288 | Murmansk Shipping | White | Hi | Cas/Adv | 7 | 7 | B | C |
| Kapitan Khlebnikov | 12,288 | Murmansk Shipping | White | Hi | Cas/Adv | 7 | 4 | Z | Z |

## SHIPS

| Ship Name | GRT | Cruise Line/Operator | Product Identity Code | Price Guide | Dress Code/Lifestyle | Cabin Insul Rating | Health/Fitness Facilities | Access Rating | Junior Cruisers Rating |
|---|---|---|---|---|---|---|---|---|---|
| Kareliya | 15,065 | CTC Cruises | Orange | Low | Cas | 5 | 4 | D | C |
| Kazakhstan | 15,410 | Black Sea Shipping | Orange | Low | Cas | 5 | 4 | D | C |
| Kazakhstan II | 16,600 | Delphin Seereisen | Orange | Low | Cas | 5 | 4 | D | C |
| Klavdiya Yelanskaya | 3,941 | Murmansk Shipping | Blue | Low | Cas | 4 | 1 | Z | Z |
| Konstantin Simonov | 9,885 | Baltic Line | Blue | Low | Cas | 3 | 2 | Z | Z |
| Kristina Regina | 3,878 | Kristina Cruises | Green | Mod | Cas | 5 | 2 | Z | Z |
| La Palma | 11,608 | Intercruise | Blue | Low | Cas | 5 | 3 | Z | C |
| Langkapuri Star Aquarius | 40,022 | Star Cruise | Orange/Red | Low | Cas/Inf | 6 | 8 | B | C |
| Legend of the Seas | 66,700 | Royal Caribbean Cruises | Purple | Mod | Cas | 8 | 8 | B | B |
| Leisure World | 16,254 | New Century Tours | Blue | Low | Cas | 5 | 4 | D | C |
| Leonid Sobinov | 21,846 | Black Sea Shipping | Blue | Low | Cas | 7 | 3 | Z | C |
| Lev Tolstoi | 12,600 | Black Sea Shipping | Blue | Low | Cas | 4 | 2 | Z | C |
| Maasdam | 55,451 | Holland America Line | Bronze | Mod | Inf | 7 | 8 | B | B |
| Majesty of the Seas | 73,941 | Royal Caribbean Cruises | Purple | Mod | Cas/Inf | 8 | 8 | B | B |
| Marco Polo | 20,502 | Orient Lines | White | Mod | Inf | 7 | 7 | D | C |
| Maxim Gorki | 24,981 | Phoenix Seereisen | Purple | Low | Cas | 7 | 5 | B | C |
| Meridian | 30,440 | Celebrity Cruises | Bronze | Mod | Inf | 8 | 9 | C | C |
| Mermoz | 13,691 | Paquet French Cruises | Orange | Mod | Cas/Inf | 6 | 4 | D | Z |
| Mikhail Sholokhov | 9,878 | Far Eastern Shipping | Blue | Low | Cas | 4 | 2 | Z | C |
| Monarch of the Seas | 73,941 | Royal Caribbean Cruises | Purple | Mod | Cas/Inf | 8 | 8 | B | B |
| Monterey | 21,051 | Starlauro Cruises | Orange | Low | Cas | 6 | 3 | D | C |
| Neptune | 4,000 | Epirotiki Lines | Blue | Low | Cas | 3 | 1 | Z | C |
| Nieuw Amsterdam | 33,930 | Holland America Line | Bronze | Mod | Inf | 9 | 8 | B | C |
| Nippon Maru | 21,903 | Mitsui OSK Passenger Line | Bronze | Hi | Inf | 7 | 6 | B | Z |
| Noordam | 33,930 | Holland America Line | Bronze | Mod | Inf | 9 | 8 | B | C |
| Nordic Empress | 48,563 | Royal Caribbean Cruises | Green | Mod | Cas/Inf | 8 | 8 | B | C |
| Nordic Prince | 23,200 | Royal Caribbean Cruises | Purple | Mod | Cas/Inf | 6 | 6 | D | C |
| Norway | 76,049 | Norwegian Cruise Line | Orange/Purple/Red | Mod | Cas | 9 | 10 | B | C |
| OceanBreeze | 21,486 | Dolphin Cruise Line | Blue | Low | Cas | 6 | 5 | D | C |
| Oceanic Grace | 5,218 | Oceanic Cruises | Silver | Hi | Inf/For | 7 | 6 | D | Z |
| Odessa | 13,252 | Black Sea Shipping | Orange | Low | Cas | 6 | 4 | D | Z |
| Odessa Song | 5,035 | Odessa Cruise Hellas | Orange | Low | Cas | 4 | 2 | Z | Z |
| Odessa Sun | 3,280 | Odessa Cruise Hellas | Orange | Low | Cas | 4 | 2 | Z | Z |
| Odysseus | 12,000 | Epirotiki Lines | Green | Low | Cas | 5 | 3 | D | C |
| Olympic | 12,800 | Epirotiki Lines | Green | Low | Cas | 3 | 3 | D | C |

| Ship Name | GRT | Cruise Line/Operator | Product Identity Code | Price Guide | Dress Code/Lifestyle | Cabin Insul Rating | Health/Fitness Facilities | Access Rating | Junior Cruisers Rating |
|---|---|---|---|---|---|---|---|---|---|
| Oriana | 67,000 | P&O Cruises | Purple | Mod | Inf | 9 | 8 | C | A |
| Orient Star | 3,941 | American Pacific Cruises | Blue | Low | Cas | 4 | 2 | Z | Z |
| Orient Venus | 21,884 | Nippon Cruise Kyakusen | Bronze | Hi | Inf | 7 | 5 | C | Z |
| Orpheus | 5,092 | Epirotiki Lines | White | Low | Cas | 5 | 1 | Z | C |
| Pacific Princess | 20,636 | Princess Cruises | Bronze | Mod | Inf | 8 | 6 | C | Z |
| Pallas Athena | 19,940 | Epirotiki Lines | Green | Low | Cas | 5 | 4 | D | C |
| Pearl | 12,475 | Pearl Cruises | Orange/Purple | Mod | Cas | 7 | 5 | C | Z |
| Polaris | 2,214 | Special Expeditions | White | Mod/Hi | Adv | 5 | 2 | Z | Z |
| Princesa Amorosa | 4,858 | Louis Cruise Lines | Green | Low | Cas | 4 | 2 | Z | C |
| Princesa Cypria | 7,896 | Louis Cruise Lines | Green | Low | Cas | 3 | 2 | Z | C |
| Princesa Marissa | 9,491 | Louis Cruise Lines | Green | Low | Cas | 3 | 2 | Z | C |
| Princesa Victoria | 14,917 | Louis Cruise Lines | Green | Low | Cas | 6 | 4 | D | C |
| Queen Elizabeth 2 | 69,053 | Cunard | Gold (a) | Hi | For | 10 | 10 | D | Z |
| | | | Bronze (b) | Mod/Hi | Inf/For | 9 | 10 | C | C |
| | | | Purple/Red (c) | Mod | Cas/Inf | 8 | 10 | B | A |
| Radisson Diamond | 20,295 | Diamond Cruise | Silver | Hi | Inf/For | 8 | 7 | D | Z |
| Regal Empress | 22,979 | Regal Cruises | Blue | Low | Cas | 5 | 4 | D | C |
| Regal Princess | 70,000 | Princess Cruises | Bronze | Mod | Inf | 9 | 9 | B | Z |
| Regent Jewel | 8,000 | Regency Cruises | Blue | Low | Cas | 6 | 2 | Z | C |
| Regent Rainbow | 24,851 | Regency Cruises | Blue/Orange | Low | Cas | 4 | 2 | Z | C |
| Regent Sea | 22,785 | Regency Cruises | Blue/Orange | Low | Cas | 8 | 4 | D | C |
| Regent Spirit | 12,433 | Regency Cruises | Blue | Low | Cas | 6 | 3 | D | C |
| Regent Star | 24,214 | Regency Cruises | Blue | Low | Cas | 7 | 4 | D | C |
| Regent Sun | 25,500 | Regency Cruises | Orange | Low | Cas | 8 | 6 | C | C |
| Renaissance One | 3,990 | Renaissance Cruises | Silver | Hi | Cas/Inf | 7 | 7 | D | Z |
| Renaissance Two | 3,990 | Renaissance Cruises | Silver | Hi | Cas/Inf | 7 | 7 | D | Z |
| Renaissance Three | 3,990 | Renaissance Cruises | Silver | Hi | Cas/Inf | 7 | 7 | D | Z |
| Renaissance Four | 3,990 | Renaissance Cruises | Silver | Hi | Cas/Inf | 7 | 7 | D | Z |
| Renaissance Five | 4,280 | Renaissance Cruises | Silver | Hi | Cas/Inf | 7 | 7 | D | Z |
| Renaissance Six | 4,280 | Renaissance Cruises | Silver | Hi | Cas/Inf | 7 | 7 | D | Z |
| Renaissance Seven | 4,280 | Renaissance Cruises | Silver | Hi | Cas/Inf | 7 | 7 | D | Z |
| Renaissance Eight | 4,280 | Renaissance Cruises | Silver | Hi | Cas/Inf | 7 | 7 | D | Z |
| Romantica | 7,537 | Ambassador Cruises | Green | Low | Cas | 4 | 1 | Z | C |
| Rotterdam | 38,645 | Holland America Line | Bronze | Mod | Inf | 9 | 7 | C | Z |

**a** = Grill Class **b** = First Class **c** = Transatlantic Class

## SHIPS

| Ship Name | GRT | Cruise Line/Operator | Product Identity Code | Price Guide | Dress Code/Lifestyle | Cabin Insul Rating | Health/Fitness Facilities | Access Rating | Junior Cruisers Rating |
|---|---|---|---|---|---|---|---|---|---|
| Royal Majesty | 32,396 | Majesty Cruise Line | Purple | Mod | Cas/Inf | 7 | 5 | B | C |
| Royal Odyssey | 28,078 | Royal Cruise Line | Silver | Mod | Inf | 9 | 7 | C | Z |
| Royal Princess | 44,348 | Princess Cruises | Silver | Mod | Inf | 9 | 7 | B | Z |
| Royal Star | 3,570 | Star Line | Orange | Mod | Cas | 5 | 1 | Z | Z |
| Royal Viking Queen | 9,975 | Royal Viking Line | Gold | Hi | For | 9 | 7 | C | Z |
| Royal Viking Sun | 37,845 | Royal Viking Line | Gold | Hi | For | 10 | 10 | A | Z |
| Russ | 12,798 | Far Eastern Shipping | Blue | Low | Cas | 4 | 2 | Z | Z |
| Ryndam | 55,451 | Holland America Line | Bronze | Mod | Inf | 7 | 8 | B | B |
| St. Helena | 6,767 | Curnow Shipping | Orange | Mod | Cas/Inf | 7 | 1 | Z | Z |
| Sagafjord | 24,474 | Cunard | Gold | Hi | For | 10 | 8 | B | Z |
| Sea Goddess I | 4,260 | Cunard | Gold | Hi | For | 9 | 5 | C | Z |
| Sea Goddess II | 4,260 | Cunard | Gold | Hi | For | 9 | 5 | C | Z |
| Sea Princess | 27,670 | P&O Cruises | Bronze | Mod | Inf | 9 | 5 | C | Z |
| Seabourn Pride | 9,975 | Seabourn Cruise Line | Gold | Hi | For | 10 | 7 | C | Z |
| Seabourn Spirit | 9,975 | Seabourn Cruise Line | Gold | Hi | For | 10 | 7 | C | Z |
| SeaBreeze I | 21,900 | Dolphin Cruise Line | Blue | Low | Cas | 6 | 5 | D | A |
| Seaward | 42,276 | Norwegian Cruise Line | Blue/Orange | Low | Cas | 8 | 8 | C | C |
| Seawind Crown | 24,568 | Seawind Cruise Line | Purple | Mod | Cas/Inf | 7 | 7 | C | D |
| Sensation | 70,367 | Carnival Cruise Lines | Green/Red | Low | Cas | 9 | 9 | B | B |
| Shota Rustaveli | 20,499 | Black Sea Shipping | Blue | Low | Cas | 5 | 4 | C | C |
| Silver Cloud | 16,800 | Silversea Cruises | Gold | Hi | Inf/For | 6 | 7 | Z | Z |
| Silver Wind | 16,800 | Silversea Cruises | Gold | Hi | Inf/For | 6 | 7 | C | Z |
| Sky Princess | 46,314 | Princess Cruises | Bronze | Mod | Inf | 7 | 8 | C | C |
| Song of America | 37,584 | Royal Caribbean Cruises | Purple | Mod | Cas/Inf | 8 | 7 | C | C |
| Song of Flower | 8,282 | Seven Seas Cruise Line | Silver | Hi | For | 8 | 6 | C | Z |
| Song of Norway | 23,005 | Royal Caribbean Cruises | Purple | Mod | Cas/Inf | 8 | 7 | D | C |
| Southward | 16,607 | Norwegian Cruise Line | Blue/Orange | Low | Cas | 5 | 5 | D | C |
| Sovereign of the Seas | 73,192 | Royal Caribbean Cruises | Purple | Mod | Cas/Inf | 8 | 8 | B | B |
| Sovetskiy Soyuz | 20,646 | Murmansk Shipping | White | Hi | Adv | 7 | 3 | Z | Z |
| Star Odyssey | 28,492 | Royal Cruise Line | Purple/Bronze | Mod | Cas/Inf | 9 | 8 | C | Z |
| Star Princess | 63,524 | Princess Cruises | Bronze/Red | Mod | Inf | 9 | 9 | B | A |
| Star/Ship Atlantic | 36,500 | Premier Cruise Lines | Blue/Red | Low | Cas | 7 | 7 | B | A |
| Star/Ship Majestic | 17,270 | Premier Cruise Lines | Blue/Red | Low | Cas | 5 | 4 | D | A |
| Star/Ship Oceanic | 39,241 | Premier Cruise Lines | Blue/Red | Low | Cas | 8 | 6 | C | A |
| Starward | 16,107 | Norwegian Cruise Line | Blue | Low | Cas | 5 | 5 | D | C |

| Ship Name | GRT | Cruise Line/Operator | Product Identity Code | Price Guide | Dress Code/Lifestyle | Cabin Insul Rating | Health/Fitness Facilities | Access Rating | Junior Cruisers Rating |
|---|---|---|---|---|---|---|---|---|---|
| Statendam | 55,451 | Holland America Line | Bronze | Mod | Inf | 7 | 8 | B | B |
| Stella Maris | 4,000 | Sun Line Cruises | Bronze | Mod | Inf | 4 | 1 | Z | Z |
| Stella Oceanis | 6,000 | Sun Line Cruises | Bronze | Mod | Inf | 5 | 2 | Z | Z |
| Stella Solaris | 17,832 | Sun Line Cruises | Bronze | Mod | Inf | 7 | 5 | C | Z |
| Sun Princess | 77,000 | Princess Cruises | Bronze | Mod | Inf | n/a | n/a | n/a | n/a |
| Sun Viking | 18,556 | Royal Caribbean Cruises | Purple | Mod | Cas/Inf | 7 | 4 | D | Z |
| Taras Shevchenko | 20,027 | Black Sea Shipping | Blue | Low | Cas | 5 | 4 | D | C |
| The Azur | 14,717 | Festival Cruises | Blue | Low | Cas | 6 | 7 | D | C |
| Triton | 14,155 | Epirotiki Lines | Green | Low | Cas | 6 | 5 | C | Z |
| Tropicale | 36,674 | Carnival Cruise Lines | Blue/Red | Low | Cas | 7 | 5 | C | C |
| Universe | 18,100 | World Explorer Cruises | White | Low | Adv | 7 | 3 | D | D |
| Viking Serenade | 40,132 | Royal Caribbean Cruises | Purple | Mod | Cas/Inf | 7 | 9 | C | C |
| Vistafjord | 24,492 | Cunard | Gold | Hi | For | 10 | 8 | B | Z |
| Vistamar | 7,478 | Mar Line | Purple | Mod | Cas/Inf | 6 | 6 | D | Z |
| Westerdam | 53,872 | Holland America Line | Bronze | Mod | Inf | 9 | 9 | B | Z |
| Windward | 39,217 | Norwegian Cruise Lines | Orange | Low | Cas | 8 | 8 | C | C |
| World Discoverer | 3,153 | Clipper Cruise Line | White | Hi | Adv | 6 | 2 | Z | Z |
| World Renaissance | 11,724 | Epirotiki Lines | Blue | Low | Cas | 7 | 4 | D | Z |
| Yamal | 20,646 | Murmansk Shipping | White | Hi | Adv | 7 | 3 | Z | Z |
| Zenith | 47,255 | Celebrity Cruises | Bronze | Mod | Inf | 9 | 9 | A | C |

## COASTAL CRUISE SHIPS

| Ship Name | Number of Cabins | Passenger Capacity | Cruise Line/Operator | Cruise Area | Year Built |
|---|---|---|---|---|---|
| Ambassador I | 45 | 90 | Galapagos Cruises | Galapagos | 1959 |
| Bucanero | 45 | 90 | Galapagos Cruises | Galapagos | 1950 |
| Caribbean Prince | 40 | 80 | American Canadian Caribbean Line | USA (East Coast) | 1983 |
| Isabella II | 20 | 34 | Metropolitan Touring | Galapagos | 1988 |

## COASTAL CRUISE SHIPS

| Ship Name | Number of Cabins | Passenger Capacity | Cruise Line/Operator | Cruise Area | Year Built |
|---|---|---|---|---|---|
| Mayan Prince | 45 | 90 | American Canadian Caribbean Line | USA/Mexico | 1992 |
| Nantucket Clipper | 60 | 120 | Clipper Cruise Line | USA (East Coast) | 1984 |
| New Shoreham II | 75 | 150 | American Canadian Caribbean Line | USA (East Coast) | 1979 |
| Reef Escape | 50 | 120 | Captain Cook Cruises | Australia (Great Barrier Reef) | 1992 |
| Santa Cruz | 43 | 90 | Metropolitan Touring | Galapagos | 1979 |
| Sea Bird | 35 | 70 | Special Expeditions | USA (West Coast) | 1982 |
| Sea Lion | 35 | 70 | Special Expeditions | USA (West Coast) | 1982 |
| Sea Spirit | 35 | 70 | SeaSpirit Cruise Lines | USA (East Coast) | 1983 |
| Spirit of Alaska | 39 | 82 | Alaska Sightseeing | Alaska | 1982 |
| Spirit of Discovery | 43 | 84 | Alaska Sightseeing | Alaska | 1981 |
| Spirit of Glacier Bay | 25 | 50 | Alaska Sightseeing | Alaska | 1971 |
| Temptress | 31 | 62 | Temptress Cruises | Australia | 1982 |
| Terra Australis | 51 | 126 | Cruceros Australis | Australia | 1983 |
| Yorktown Clipper | 65 | 138 | Clipper Cruise Line | USA/Caribbean | 1988 |

## ONE-DAY CRUISE SHIPS

| Ship Name | GRT | Cruise Line/Operator | Base Port | Caterer | Previous Name |
|---|---|---|---|---|---|
| Discovery I | 12,244 | Discovery Cruises | Ft. Lauderdale | Apollo | Blenheim |
| Scandinavian Dawn | 7,456 | SeaEscape | Ft. Lauderdale | Trident | Patra Express/St. George/ Scandinavian Sky II |
| Star of Texas | 27,250 | Gold Star Cruises | Galveston | Stellar Maritime | Olympic/Mardi Gras/ Empress of Canada |
| Viking Princess | 7,029 | Palm Beach Cruise Line | Palm Beach | Own | Ilmatar |

| Ship Name | Number of Cabins | Cruise Line/Operator | River |
|---|---|---|---|
| Abu Simbel | 12 | Hapi Travel | Nile |
| African Queen | 54 | 1990 VIP Travel | Nile |
| Ahmos | 40 | Cataract Tour | Nile |
| Aida I | 23 | Nile Valley Tours | Nile |
| Aida II | 92 | Nile Valley Tours | Nile |
| Akademik V.M. Glushkov | 166 | Minrechflot | Volga/Don |
| Akhnaton | 39 | Pyramids Nile Cruises | Nile |
| Al Salam | 42 | Ged Nile Cruises | Nile |
| Aleksei Surkov | 132 | Minrechflot | Neva/Sver |
| Alexander the Great | 62 | Jolley's Travel | Nile |
| Alexandr Pushkin | 75 | Minrechflot | Volga/Don |
| Altodouro | 40 | Sea Air Holidays | Duoro |
| Ambassador I | 25 | Nefer Nile Cruises | Nile |
| Ambassador II | 42 | Nefer Nile Cruises | Nile |
| American Queen | 206 | Delta Queen Steamboat | Mississippi |
| Amicitia | 62 | Sea-Air Holidays | Rhine/Mosel |
| Amoun Ra | 45 | Hapi Travel | Nile |
| Amur | 67 | Minrechflot | Danube |
| Andropov | 145 | Minrechflot | Neva |
| Anni Sheraton | 74 | Sheraton Nile Cruises | Nile |
| Anton Tschechov | 100 | Minrechtflot | Jenisej |
| Arabia | 38 | Middle East Floating Hotels | Nile |
| Arlene | 53 | KD River Cruises | Seine/Rhone |
| Atlas | 41 | Eastmar Travel | Nile |
| Aton Sheraton | 80 | Sheraton Nile Cruises | Nile |
| Aurora | 42 | Middle East Floating Hotels | Nile |
| Austria | 92 | KD River Cruises | Rhine/Moselle |
| Bashan | 37 | China Travel Service | Yangtse |
| Brisbane Explorer | 61 | Murray River Cruises | Murray |
| Britannia | 92 | KD River Cruises | Rhine/Moselle |
| Cairo | 72 | Shalakani Tours | Nile |
| Carpati | 60 | Navrom Shipping | Danube |
| Cheops | 80 | International Company | Nile |
| Cheops III | 67 | International Company | Nile |
| Chicherin | 145 | Minrechflot | Neva |

## RIVER VESSELS

| Ship Name | Number of Cabins | Cruise Line/Operator | River |
|---|---|---|---|
| China Glory | 56 | CITS | Yangtse |
| Clara Schumann | 62 | KD River Cruises | Elbe |
| Cleopatra | 46 | Nile Crusing Company | Nile |
| Columbia | 44 | Great Pacific Cruises | Snake |
| Coral One | 75 | Travcotels | Nile |
| Cybelle | 40 | Red Sea Cruises Hilton | Nile |
| Danube Princess | 86 | Peter Deilmann Shipping | Danube |
| Delta Queen | 88 | Delta Queen Steamboat | Mississippi |
| Delta Star | 80 | Rumanian Danube Shipping | Danube |
| Demjan Bjedny | 75 | Minrechflot | Lena |
| Deutschland | 92 | KD River Cruises | Rhine/Moselle |
| Diamond Boat | 75 | International Nile Cruises | Nile |
| Dimitriy Furmanov | 166 | Minrechflot | Volga/Don |
| Dnepr | 79 | First Danube Shipping | Dnepr |
| Donaustar | 80 | Navrom Shipping | Danube |
| Dresden | 62 | Peter Deilmann Reederei | Elbe |
| Dunaj | 67 | Minrechflot | Danube |
| Eman | 38 | Menf Tours | Nile |
| Embassy | 33 | Embassy Nile Cruises | Nile |
| Emei | 46 | China Travel Service | Yangtse |
| Esenin | 60 | Minrechflot | Upper Volga |
| Europa | 64 | KD River Cruises | Rhine/Moselle |
| Excelsior | 25 | Seti First Nile Cruises | Nile |
| Fedor Dostoyevsky | 166 | Minrechflot | Volga/Don |
| Flash I | 40 | Flash Tours | Nile |
| Flash II | 56 | Flash Tours | Nile |
| Fleur | 55 | International Cruises | Nile |
| Fleurette | 54 | Pullman International Hotels | Nile |
| Florenza | 81 | Garanah Tours | Nile |
| France | 96 | KD River Cruises | Rhine/Mosel |
| Gala | 40 | Red sea Cruises hilton | Nile |
| General Lavrinenkov | 143 | Minrechflot | Neva/Sver |
| General Valutin | 143 | Minrechflot | Dnepr |
| Gigi | 44 | Zamalek Nile Cruises | Nile |
| Giza | 58 | Shalakani Tours | Nile |

| Ship Name | Number of Cabins | Cruise Line/Operator | River |
|---|---|---|---|
| Glushkov | n/a | Richflot Ukrainy | Dnieper |
| Goddess | 29 | China Travel Service | Yangtse |
| Golden Boat | 50 | International Nile Cruises | Nile |
| Gondola | 28 | Garanah Tours | Nile |
| Hapi I | 33 | Hapi Travel | Nile |
| Hapi II | 33 | Hapi Travel | Nile |
| Hatshepsut | 36 | Pyramid Nile Cruise | Nile |
| Hawkesbury Explorer II | 61 | Murray River Cruises | Murray |
| Heinrich Hein | 51 | KD River Cruises | Danube |
| Helio | 52 | Heliopolis Tours | Nile |
| Helvetia | 82 | KD River Cruises | Rhine |
| Hoda | 33 | Hassan Sharaby | Nile |
| Horizon | 105 | First Cairo Cruises | Nile |
| Horus | 45 | Itta Tours | Nile |
| Hotp Sheraton | 74 | Sheraton Hotels | Nile |
| Ibis | 22 | Nile Navigation Company | Nile |
| Imperial | 37 | Travcotels | Nile |
| Isis Hilton | 48 | Hilton Nile Cruises | Nile |
| Italia | 92 | KD River Cruises | Rhine/Moselle |
| Jasmin | 62 | Jasmin Wings Cruises | Nile |
| Karnak | 21 | Pyramids Nile Cruises | Nile |
| Kasr El Nil | 51 | Movenpick Hotels | Nile |
| King Mina | 58 | Ged Nile Cruises | Nile |
| King Tut | 45 | Eastmar Travel | Nile |
| Kirov | 140 | Minrechflot | Neva/Volga |
| Konstantin Simonov | 145 | Minrechflot | Volga/Don |
| Kun Lun | 18 | China Travel Service | Yangtse |
| La Belle Epoque | 32 | Ark Travel | Nile |
| La Reine du Nil | 75 | Cataract Nile Cruises | Nile |
| Lady Diana | 60 | Zamzam Nile Cruise Co | Nile |
| Lady Hawkesbury | 60 | Captain Hook Cruises | Murray |
| Lady Ivy May | 80 | Rhine Cruises (GB) | Rhine/Moselle |
| Le Scribe | 44 | Rev Vacance Cruises | Nile |
| Lenin | 145 | Minrechflot | Neva |
| Lev Tolstoi | 116 | Minrechflot | Volga |

## RIVER VESSELS

| Ship Name | Number of Cabins | Cruise Line/Operator | River |
|---|---|---|---|
| Luxor City | 35 | Pyramids Nile Cruises | Nile |
| Marhaba | 40 | Club Mediteranée | Nile |
| Marshall Koshevoi | 140 | Minrechflot | Volga/Dnepr |
| Maxim Gorki | 85 | Minrechflot | Volga/Don |
| Melodie | 40 | VIP Company | Nile |
| Memphis | 20 | Eastmar Travel | Nile |
| Mikhail Lomonosov | 132 | Minrechtflot | Volga/Don |
| Mikhail Sholochov | 143 | Minrechflot | Volga/Don |
| Mikhail Svetlov | 75 | Minrechflot | Lena |
| Mississippi Queen | 204 | Delta Queen Steamboat | Mississippi |
| Moldavia | 80 | Soviet Danube Shipping | Danube |
| Montasser III | 80 | Montasser Nile Cruises | Nile |
| Moon River | 52 | Silver Moon Nile Cruises | Nile |
| Mozart | 113 | Peter Deilmann Reederei | Danube |
| Murray Princess | 55 | Murray River Cruises | Murray |
| Murray River Queen | 44 | Murray River Cruises | Murray |
| Nancy | 27 | Nefer Nile Cruises | Nile |
| Narkom Pakhamov | 135 | Minrechflot | Neva/Sver |
| Nederland | 96 | KD River Cruises | Rhine |
| Nefertari | 31 | Eastmar Travel | Nile |
| Nefertiti | 27 | Pyramids Nile Cruises | Nile |
| Nepthis Hilton | 65 | Hilton Nile Cruises | Nile |
| Neptune | 51 | Trans Egypt Travel | Nile |
| Nile Admiral | 20 | Presidential Nile Cruises | Nile |
| Nile Ambassador | 42 | Presidential Nile Cruises | Nile |
| Nile Ark | 28 | La Belle Epoque | Nile |
| Nile Beauty | 50 | Flotel Nile Cruises | Nile |
| Nile Bride | 62 | Nile Bride Cruises | Nile |
| Nile Crocodile | 60 | Nile Crocodile Cruises | Nile |
| Nile Delta | 17 | Hapi Travel | Nile |
| Nile Dream | 44 | Eastmar Travel | Nile |
| Nile Elegant | 65 | Memnon Nile Cruises | Nile |
| Nile Elite | 85 | Memnon Nile Cruises | Nile |
| Nile Emerald | 75 | Nile Sun Cruises | Nile |
| Nile Emperor | 75 | Presidential Nile Cruises | Nile |

| Ship Name | Number of Cabins | Cruise Line/Operator | River |
|---|---|---|---|
| Nile Empress | 30 | Travcotels | Nile |
| Nile Explorer | 20 | Gebsun Fluvial Tourism Co | Nile |
| Nile Fantasy | 20 | Travcotels | Nile |
| Nile Goddess | 68 | Sonesta Nile Cruises | Nile |
| Nile Jewel | 59 | Nile Sun Cruises | Nile |
| Nile Legend | 75 | Presidential Nile Cruises | Nile |
| Nile Majesty I | 105 | Mo Hotels Travel | Nile |
| Nile Majesty II | 97 | Mo Hotels Travel | Nile |
| Nile Monarch | 44 | Travcotels | Nile |
| Nile Pearl | 23 | Travcotels | Nile |
| Nile Plaza | 78 | Presidential Nile Cruises | Nile |
| Nile President | 68 | Presidential Nile Cruises | Nile |
| Nile Princess | 32 | Presidential Nile Cruises | Nile |
| Nile Queen | 60 | Sphynx Tours | Nile |
| Nile Rhapsody | 20 | Travcotels | Nile |
| Nile Ritz | 78 | Presidential Nile Cruises | Nile |
| Nile Romance | 75 | Flotel Nile Cruises | Nile |
| Nile Smart | 65 | Memnon Nile Cruises | Nile |
| Nile Smile | 65 | Memnon Nile Cruises | Nile |
| Nile Sovereign | 30 | Travcotels | Nile |
| Nile Sphynx | 64 | Sphynx Tours | Nile |
| Nile Splendor | 78 | Nile Splendor Cruises | Nile |
| Nile Star | 37 | Eastmar Travel | Nile |
| Nile Symphony | 75 | Presidential Nile Cruises | Nile |
| Nile Treasure | 46 | Master Cruises Co | Nile |
| Nora | 74 | Noratel Hotels & Tourism | Nile |
| Normandie | 53 | KD River Cruises | Seine/Rhone |
| Nour | 68 | Upper Egypt Tour | Nile |
| Novikov Priboy | 166 | Minrechflot | Volga/Don |
| Oberoi Sheherazad | 71 | Oberoi Nile Cruises | Nile |
| Oberoi Shehrayar | 71 | Oberoi Nile Cruises | Nile |
| Oltenita | 60 | Navrom Shipping | Danube |
| Olympia | 51 | Sea-Air Holidays | Rhine/Mosel |
| Orchid | 64 | Orchid Wings Cruises | Nile |
| Osiris Hilton | 48 | Hilton Nile Cruises | Nile |

## RIVER VESSELS

| Ship Name | Number of Cabins | Cruise Line/Operator | River |
|---|---|---|---|
| Papyrus | 50 | Rev Vacances | Nile |
| Poseidon | 45 | Swan Hellenic Rhine Cruises | Rhine |
| Prince Omar | 79 | Mohamed Osman | Nile |
| Princess Amira | 66 | Cataract Nile Cruises | Nile |
| Princess Eman | 42 | Hassan Sharab | Nile |
| Princess of the Nile | 58 | ASC | Nile |
| Princess of Provence | 75 | Peter Deilmann Shipping | Rhone |
| Princess of Prussia | 75 | Peter Deilmann Shipping | Elbe |
| Pyramids | 21 | Pyramids Nile Cruises | Nile |
| Queen Cleopatra | 18 | Pyramids Nile Cruises | Nile |
| Queen Isis | 49 | Isis Travel | Nile |
| Queen Nabila I | 62 | Nabila Nile Cruises | Nile |
| Queen Nabila III | 82 | Nabila Nile Cruises | Nile |
| Queen Nefer | 53 | Nefer Nile Cruises | Nile |
| Queen Nefertiti | 21 | Pyramids Nile Cruises | Nile |
| Queen of Sheba | 77 | Nabila Nile Cruises | Nile |
| Ra | 72 | Eastmar Travel | Nile |
| Ra II | 80 | Eastmar Travel | Nile |
| Radischtshev | 160 | Minrechflot | Danube/Volga |
| Ramses | 18 | Pyramid Nile Cruise | Nile |
| Ramses of Egypt | 39 | Nabila Nile Cruises | Nile |
| Ramses King of the Nile | 62 | Nabila Nile Cruises | Nile |
| Rembrandt Van Rhine | 50 | Feenstra Rhine Line | Rhine |
| Rev Vacances | 20 | Sphynx Tour | Nile |
| Rex Rheni | 78 | Sea-Air Holidays | Rhine/Mosel |
| Roland of England III | 72 | European Yacht Cruises | Rhine |
| Rosetta | 50 | Cataract Tour | Nile |
| Rossia | 163 | Minrechflot | Dnepr |
| Rousse | 98 | Bulgarian Danube Shipping | Danube |
| Royal Boat | 71 | A One Travel | Nile |
| Royale | 48 | Travcoatels | Nile |
| Russ | 155 | Minrechflot | Volga |
| Salacia | 56 | Trans Egypt Travel | Nile |
| Senouhe | 64 | Tanis Nile Cruises | Nile |
| Sergei Esenin | 60 | Minrechflot | Upper Volga |

| Ship Name | Number of Cabins | Cruise Line/Operator | River |
|---|---|---|---|
| Sergeij Kirov | 166 | Minrechflot | Neva |
| Seti I | 50 | Seti First Nile Cruises | Nile |
| Seti II | 33 | Seti First Nile Cruises | Nile |
| Seti III | 50 | Seti First Nile Cruises | Nile |
| Seti the Great | 71 | Seti First Nile Cruises | Nile |
| Sherry Boat | 61 | Sherry Nile Cruises | Nile |
| Silver Moon | 35 | Silver Moon Nile Cruises | Nile |
| Sinbad | 33 | Egyptian Nile Shipping | Nile |
| Sinouhe | 68 | Star Cruise | Nile |
| Sobek | 54 | Contact Tour | Nile |
| Sofia | 85 | Bulgarian Danube | Danube |
| Sonesta Nile Goddess | 70 | Sonesta Hotels | Nile |
| Song of Egypt | 79 | Song of Egypt Company | Nile |
| Spring I | 42 | Spring Tours | Nile |
| Star of Luxor | 66 | Star Line | Nile |
| Sun Boat I | 23 | Abercrombie & Kent | Nile |
| Sun Boat II | 32 | Abercrombie & Kent | Nile |
| Sun Boat III | 32 | Abercrombie & Kent | Nile |
| Swiss Pearl | 62 | Sea-Air Holidays | Main/Danube |
| Switzerland II | 53 | Sea-Air Holidays | Rhine/Mosel |
| Taras Shevchenko | 135 | Minrechflot | Neva/Sver |
| Tarot | 75 | Star Line | Nile |
| Telestar | 54 | Telestar Travel | Nile |
| Theodor Fontane | 62 | KD River Cruises | Elbe |
| Theodore Korner | 41 | First Danube Steamship Company | Danube |
| Tut Sheraton | 80 | Sheraton Hotels | Nile |
| Ukraina | 80 | Soviet Danube Shipping | Volga/Don |
| Ursula II | 50 | Sea-Air Holidays | Rhine/Mosel |
| Victoria Cruziana | 49 | Euro River Line | Rhine |
| Vissarion Belinski | 166 | Minrechflot | Neva |
| Volga | 79 | First Danube Shipping | Danube |
| Yangtse Paradise | 70 | China Travel Service | Yangtse |
| Yangtsejiang | 66 | China Travel Service | Yangtse |
| Yuri Andropov | 143 | Minrechflot | Volga/Don |
| Zonnebloem* | 35 | Zonnebloem Society | Rhine |

* = specially built for physically challenged passengers

## TALL SHIPS

| Ship Name | Passenger Capacity | Cruise Line/Operator | Cruise Area |
|---|---|---|---|
| Club Med I | 410 | Club Mediterranée | Carib/Medit |
| Club Med II | 410 | Club Mediterranée | Carib/Medit |
| Fantome | 126 | Windjammer Barefoot Cruises | Caribbean |
| Flying Cloud | 80 | Windjammer Barefoot Cruises | Caribbean |
| France II | 100 | Windjammer Barefoot Cruises | Bahamas |
| Le Ponant | 64 | Compagnie des Isles du Ponant | Caribbean |
| Lord Nelson* | 40 | Jubilee Trust | Caribbean |
| Mandalay | 72 | Windjammer Barefoot Cruises | Caribbean |
| Polynesia | 126 | Windjammer Barefoot Cruises | Caribbean |
| Sea Cloud | 69 | Sea Cloud Cruises | Caribbean |
| Sir Francis Drake | 34 | Tall Ship Adventures | Caribbean |
| Star Clipper | 180 | Star Clippers | Carib/Medit |
| Star Flyer | 180 | Star Clippers | Carib/Medit |
| Wind Song | 148 | Windstar Sail Cruises | Tahiti |
| Wind Spirit | 148 | Windstar Sail Cruises | Orient |
| Wind Star | 148 | Windstar Sail Cruises | Carib/Medit |
| Yankee Clipper | 65 | Windjammer Barefoot Cruises | Caribbean |

* = specially built for physically challenged passengers only

## MULTI-HULL VESSELS

| | | | |
|---|---|---|---|
| Island Explorer | 36 | P&O Spice Island Cruises | Indonesia |
| Melanesian Discoverer | 50 | Melanesian Tourist Services | New Guinea |
| Roylen Endeavour | 40 | Roylen Cruises | Australia |
| Spice Islander | 36 | P&O Spice Island Cruises | Indonesia |

# How a Ship is Evaluated

I have been evaluating and rating cruise ships and the cruise product professionally since 1980, and I have continually refined the rating and evaluation system. For this edition, the system has been altered dramatically in order to take into account the many changes in cruise product, delivery, and service standards, and the new features that have been built into the later ships.

Some sections of the former rating system have become almost obsolete, such as Shore Excursions. This is because most cruise operators are obliged to use the same shoreside tour operators, so there is little difference in this product between one cruise line and another.

I have also refined the system to take into account more of the passenger "software" (see page 188).

The star rating system remains, but the scoring system has been modified to reflect the changes in on-board facilities and standards of quality, presentation, and delivery.

This section includes 210 ocean-going cruise ships, expedition ships, and tall ships that were in service when this book was completed in May 1994. All except the 12 new, reconstructed, or specialized ships have been carefully evaluated, taking into account 300 separate inspection points based on personal sailings and visits to ships. For the sake of clarity, I have channeled the inspections into 15 sections. With a possible 10 points per section, the maximum possible score for any ship is 150 points.

The expedition cruise vessels and tall sail-cruise ships cannot be judged according to the same criteria as the "normal" cruise ships because they are purpose-built and many have unique features that reflect the type of expeditions they offer. I have adopted a weighting system for any exceptional cases.

I have also taken into consideration the fact that passengers of different nationalities expect different things from their cruise experiences. The passenger expectations on ships that operate in the Mediterranean with European passengers (particularly older vessels), for example, will vary considerably from those of North American passengers, who often want the latest in high-tech interiors, facilities, and features.

The stars beside the name of the ship at the top of each page relate directly to the Overall Rating. The highest number of stars awarded is five (★★★★★), the lowest is one. A plus (+) indicates that a ship deserves just that little bit more than the number of stars given.

| Overall Rating | Number of Stars |
|---|---|
| 135.1 and above | ★★★★★+ |
| 125.1-135 | ★★★★★ |
| 115.1-125 | ★★★★+ |
| 105.1-115 | ★★★★ |
| 100.1-105 | ★★★+ |
| 90.1-100 | ★★★ |
| 85.1-90 | ★★+ |
| 80.1-85 | ★★ |
| 80.1 or less | ★ |

Cruise lines are in the business of creating and selling cruise products and vacation packages of (perceived) excellence. Thus the common factor of all cruise ships is quality. Therefore, in appraising the cruise industry, it is inevitable that scores will be on the high side, and the difference in score from one ship to another may be very slight. This explains why of the 210 cruise vessels evaluated, 179 have achieved three stars or more.

## Comments

The smaller details and my personal comments on each ship may help you determine what is best for you. These have been separated into the following four parts:

**+** (positive features)
**–** (negative features)
**Dining** (cuisine, service, and the dining room experience)
**Other Comments**

Needless to say, there is no such thing as a "standard" cruise ship. They come in all sizes and shapes, with a wide variety of internal layouts, facilities, appointments, and levels of service—as do hotels on land. The one thing all ships do have in common is gross registered tonnage, often abbreviated to grt. This is an international measurement used for ship classification and insurance purposes.

Since size is often the key to the kind of facilities, level of comfort, and, of course, number of passengers on board, I have found it prudent to adopt a weighting system. It is not possible to evaluate a small ship such as the *Argonaut* or *Sea Goddess I* fairly against a large ship such as *Crystal Harmony* or *Horizon*, or a megaship such as the *Sovereign of the Seas* or *Ecstasy* using precisely the same criteria. The weighting system takes into account prices, food quality, and, in particular, the level of service from and the attitude of the crew (hospitality). The rating of expedition cruise vessels also includes garbage compacting and incineration, waste disposal, and compliance with the most recent environmental and safety regulations (MARPOL V).

The results, comments, and ratings are strictly personal, and are intended to guide you in formulating your own opinions and cruise plans. They are also intended to help travel agents to differentiate between the many cruise ships and cruise products on today's market.

## Changes in the Ratings

Cruise lines, ship owners, and operators should note that ratings, like stocks and shares, can go down as well as up, even when things have supposedly been improved. This is explained by increased competition, newer ships with better designed facilities, and other market- or passenger-driven factors. With an increasing number of ships in the marketplace, and the building of ships for niche operations, tougher evaluations have become necessary.

When discounting was introduced (to stimulate the demand for cruises), so too were cost-cutting measures. As a result, cruise cuisine and service standards have suffered from cut-backs in the past few years. The ratings now reflect this trend more accurately. It is encouraging that cruise lines are now playing "catch up" to those considered the best in their respective (unwritten) class.

**Ratings and evaluations cover four principal areas:**

1) The Ship
2) Accommodations
3) Cuisine/Service
4) Cruise Product

## 1) The Ship

### Ship: Condition/Cleanliness

Cleanliness and hygiene standards have become increasingly important in all aspects of everyday life, and even more so aboard a cruise ship, which is really a microcosm of modern society.

This score reflects the general condition of the ship, both internally and externally. It takes into account: the ship's age and maintenance requirements; the condition of the hull, exterior paint, decking materials, caulking, swimming pool surrounds, deck furniture, lifeboats, life rafts, and life-preserving equipment; interior cleanliness with regard to the public restrooms, elevators, floor coverings, carpeting, wall coverings, stairways, passageways, doorways, other access points, crew stairways, alleyways, accommodations, and galleys; food preparation, food storage rooms, and refrigeration units; and garbage handling, compacting, incineration, and waste disposal.

### Ship: Space/Flow/Comfort

This score reflects the use of common passenger spaces including: outside deck areas; sunbathing and sheltered deck space; swimming pools; outdoor and indoor promenades; interior spaces—density and passenger flow, and ceiling height; lobby areas, stairways and passageways, and public restrooms and facilities; signage, lighting, and air-conditioning/ventilation flow; the degree of comfort or crowding (passenger space ratio), passenger density, and crew to passenger ratio.

### Ship: Decor/Furnishings

This score reflects: the overall interior decor; the color scheme; hard and soft furnishings (including suitability and practicality); wood (and imitation wood) paneling, veneers, and use of glass and plastics; carpet material, tuft density, color and pattern practicality, and fit and finish (including seams and edging); chair comfort; ceiling treatments, bulkheads and treatments; reflective surfaces; artwork quality and suitability; and color definition and lighting.

### Ship: Fitness Facilities

This score reflects: the health spa, its location and its accessibility; the gymnasium, exercise room, and fitness, sports and games facilities; spa treatments and rejuvenation programs; swimming pools, whirlpools, grand baths, saunas, steam rooms, and massage rooms; and jogging and walking tracks.

## 2) Accommodations

### Cabins: Comfort/Facilities

This score reflects: the design and layout of cabins, balconies, beds/berths, furniture (its placement and practicality), and other fittings; closets and other hanging space, drawer space, and bedside tables; vanity unit, bathroom facilities, washbasin, cabinets, and toiletries storage; lighting, air-conditioning and ventilation; audio/visual facilities; quality and degree of luxuriousness; and bulkhead insulation, noise, and vibration levels.

### Cabins: Software

This score reflects the soft furnishings and details in cabins such as: the information manual (list of services), paper and postcards (including personalized stationery); telephone directory; laundry lists; tea- and coffee-making equipment; flowers (if any), fruit (if any); and bathroom amenities kits, bathrobes, slippers, and the size, thickness, quality and material content of towels.

## 3) Cuisine

This section is perhaps the most important, as food is often the main feature of today's cruise package. Cruise lines put maximum emphasis on telling passengers how good their food is, often to the point of being unable to deliver what is promised. Generally, however, the standard of food is good.

The rule of thumb is: if you were to eat out in a good restaurant, what would you expect? Does the ship meet your expectations? Would you come back again for the food?

There are perhaps as many different tastes as there are passengers. The "standard" market cruise lines cater for a wide range of tastes. Upscale cruise lines can offer food cooked individually to your taste. Generally, as in any good restaurant, you get what you pay for.

### Food: Dining Room/Cuisine

This score reflects: the main dining room's physical structure, window treatments, seating (alcoves and individual chairs, with/without armrests), lighting and ambiance, table set-ups, the quality and condition of linen, china, and cutlery, and table centerpieces (flowers); menus; food quality, presentation, food combinations, culinary creativity, variety, appeal, taste, palatability, freshness, color, balance, garnishes, and decorations; appetizers, soups, pastas, entrees, salads, desserts, breads, pastries, sandwiches, tableside cooking of pasta, flambeaus, and so on; fresh fruit and cakes; the wine list; and the price range.

### Food: Buffets/Informal Dining

This score reflects: the hardware (including sneeze guards, tongs, ice containers and ladles, and serving utensils); buffet displays, presentation, trays, and set-ups; food temperatures; breakfast, luncheon, deck buffets, midnight buffets, and latenight snacks; decorative elements such as ice carvings; and staff attitude, service, and communication skills.

### Food: Quality of Ingredients

This score reflects the overall quality of ingredients used, including: consistency and portion size; grades of meat, fish, and fowl; and the price paid by the cruise company for its food product per passenger per day. It is the quality of ingredients that most dictates the eventual presentation and quality of the finished product—as well as its taste.

## Service

### Service: Dining Room

This score reflects the professionalism of all restaurant staff: Maitre d' Hotel, dining room managers, head section waiters, and waiters and assistant waiters (busboys). It includes correct place settings and service, communication skills, attitude, flair, and finesse.

### Service: Bars/Lounges

This reflects: lighting and ambiance; service in bars and lounges; noise levels; communication skills (between bartenders, bar staff, and passengers in particular); staff attitude, personality, flair and finesse; and correct use of glasses.

### Service: Cabins

This score reflects: the cleaning and housekeeping staff, butlers, cabin stewards/stewardesses, and supervisory staff; attention to detail and cleanliness; in-cabin food service; linen changes; and language and communication skills.

## 4) Cruise Product

### Cruise: Entertainment

This score reflects the overall entertainment program and content as designed and targeted to specific passenger demographics. Cruise ship entertainment has to appeal to passengers of widely varying ages and types.

The rating includes: the physical plant (stage/bandstand); technical support, lighting, follow spotlight operation, and set and backdrop design; sound and light systems, recorded click-tracks and cues, and special effects; the variety and quality of large-scale production shows (including storyline/plot, content, cohesion, creativeness of costumes, relevancy, quality, choreography, and vocal content); cabaret; variety shows; singers; visual acts; bands; and solo musicians.

### Cruise: Activities Program

This score reflects the variety, quality and quantity of daytime activities and events. The rating includes: the cruise director and cruise staff (including their visibility, availability, ability, and professionalism); sports programs; participation games; special interest programs; and mind-enrichment lecturers.

### Cruise: Overall Hospitality

This score reflects the level of hospitality of the crew and their attention to detail and personal satisfaction. It includes: the professionalism of senior officers, middle management, supervisors, cruise staff, and general crew; social contact, appearance, and dress codes; atmosphere and ambiance; motivation; communication skills (most important); and the general ambiance.

### Watersports Facilities

This score reflects: the watersports equipment that is carried (including banana boat, jet skis, scuba tanks and snorkeling equipment); the waterski boat; windsurfers; instruction programs, overall staff supervision; the marina (usually located aft) or side-retractable watersports platforms; and the enclosed swimming area (if applicable).

## Notes

### Expedition Cruise Ships/ Tall Ships/Wind-Sail Ships

These are highly specialized vessels offering a particular kind of cruise experience. Consequently, they do not feature the same facilities as the majority of "standard" cruise ships, and their ratings are calculated in a different manner. The total score awarded is based on the cruise experience offered, the on-board facilities, the product itself, and the extent to which the company is concerned for the environment.

### Expedition Ships

These vessels are constructed for in-depth expedition cruising, with special ice-hardened hulls and the classification to operate legally in ecologically and environmentally sensitive areas. They are given a rating and a total score based on a number of relevant extra criteria. These include: classification of service; suitability for expeditions; cleanliness, hygiene, and sanitation; wet and dry garbage treatment and handling; concern for the environment; itineraries; shore expeditions; lecture facilities and lecturers; expedition leaders; medical facilities; evacuation provisions; operation of the inflatable zodiac landing craft; helicopter; air and ground transportation; ticketing and documentation; and the experience and reputation of the expedition company.

### Tall Ships/Sail-Cruise Ships

These ships are either specially constructed so as to provide a genuine sail powered experience (*Sea Cloud*, *Sir Francis Drake*, *Star Clipper*, *Star Flyer*), or they are contemporary vessels built to emulate sail-powered vessels but are really sail-assisted (*Club Med I*, *Club Med II*, *Le Ponant*, *Wind Song*, *Wind Spirit*, *Wind Star*).

They provide another dimension to the cruise experience, and, as with true expedition ships, cannot be evaluated in precisely the same way as other oceangoing cruise ships.

Their rating also includes a number of extra, relevant criteria. These include: onboard sail-cruise experience; relaxation facilities; provision of in-cabin entertainment facilities; open bridge policy; watersports facilities; lecturers and instructors; privacy and quiet spaces; destinations; and environmental policy.

## What Makes a Five-Star-Plus (★★★★★+) Ship

Ship-owners and cruise marketing directors often proudly describe their products as "luxury" and of a "five-star-plus" or "five-star" standard. However, in reality, very few ships deserve this designation. To merit it requires a combination of discreet sophistication and impeccable service; almost every need must be anticipated, and every amenity within the structural provisions of today's passenger ships must be provided. The cruise product should allow for a completely hassle-free vacation.

The training of crew to the highest levels of service is the responsibility of any ship owner competing for passengers willing to pay between $500 and $3,000 per person per day. Passengers want and demand what they perceive as "value for money"—no matter what amount is paid. Crew members that cannot communicate with passengers well, in their own language, cannot provide the same level of contact or service to them.

While rampant discounting has lowered the expectation level of many passengers, the level of service demanded by those paying top rates is quite justified.

### Hardware (The Ship Itself)

- The Passenger Space Ratio must be 35.0 or better (based on two per suite/cabin and obtained by dividing the gross register tonnage (GRT) by the number of passenger beds).
- The ship must be kept in pristine condition, with no signs of rusting.
- Safety must be of the utmost importance, with thoroughly trained fire crews, constant drills, and single-language communications for all emergency procedures.
- All lifeboat davits and safety equipment must be fully functional, and inspected by senior shipboard management once each week.
- Paintwork must be immaculate at all times (ships must be constantly painted, and a five-star-plus rating will not be considered for any ship that defers painting to dry dock).
- All exterior fittings must be in pristine condition. All faulty equipment must be replaced, and no wear and tear is acceptable.
- All gangways must be in immaculate condition, with non-slip stair treads.
- No light bulbs must be missing from the "string of lights" between the bow, mast, funnel, and stern.

### Software (Decor, Hospitality, and Service Standards)

### Accommodations

- "Suites" must have a day (lounge) area and a separate bedroom with a closable (and lockable) door. Cabins should not be described as "suites" if there is simply a curtain separating the sleeping area from the lounge area.
- Minimum cabin size must be 200 sq. ft. (18.5 sq. m.).
- Fresh flowers in all cabins.
- Personalized stationery in all suites (and in all cabins on any ship with fewer than 300 passengers).

- Leather-bound stationery/room service folder.
- 100% cotton towels (including hand towel, face towel, shower towel, and large bath towel). Bath towels are to be a minimum size of 48" by 30".
- 100% cotton bed linen, including pillowcases (points deducted for cotton/polyester mix). Bed linen should ideally feature the cruise line's logo .
- Thick, 100% cotton bathrobe, which must be changed daily.
- Special pillows for the "allergy-sensitive" available.
- Minimum of four storage drawers per passenger.
- Walk-in closets for all top-grade accommodations, and for "suites."
- Illuminated closets (preferably walk-in closets) with wooden (not plastic) hangers, tie rail, and shoe horn.
- Full- or half-tiled bathroom with bathtub and shower (bidet in suites).
- Refrigerator/mini-bar (fully stocked), with appropriate glassware, napkins, coasters, and cocktail stirrers.
- Separate make-up desk with mirror (could serve as a writing desk).
- Hairdryer (built-in or free-standing).
- Toiletries cabinet and storage space.
- Audio-visual entertainment center that includes a color television and VCR (preferably also a CD player), and enclosed in a cabinet where possible. One remote control for all units.
- Three audio channels, including one classical channel.
- Lunch and dinner menus delivered daily to all suites and upper grade cabins.
- Direct-dial satellite-linked telephone.
- Personal safe.
- No sharp edges.
- Course-by-course in-suite or in-cabin meal service, with individual chairs and adjustable-height dining table.
- Amenities kits to contain (minimum): shampoo, conditioner, body lotion, quality soap, and emery board .
- Minimum detectable inter-cabin noise.
- Wood (fire-retardant treated) rather than metal cabinetry and drawers.
- World news must be delivered to all cabins each day.
- "Butler service" should include pressing of clothes on embarkation, if needed, and canapés at 6 p.m. daily, correctly presented on a silver tray.
- Balcony furniture must have cushions or pads for seating, wiped down daily.
- Canvas (not plastic) laundry bags for personal self-service launderette use.
- Bottled water must be provided without charge and replaced daily.
- Umbrellas for all passengers (ships of up to 300 passengers).
- Umbrellas for all passengers in "suites" (ships of above 300 passengers), in-suite or at the gangway.

## Dining/Cuisine

- Waiters must recognize whether a passenger is right- or left-handed and set or change tableware accordingly.
- Place settings must include proper fish knives/forks.
- No "spotting" on cutlery.
- Hot linen/cloth towels must be provided before meals.
- Finger bowls must be provided for courses that include the use of fingers.

- Dining room meals must be placed on linen tablecloth with linen napkins, and changed for each meal.
- Finest quality glassware, and correct wine glasses must be used.
- Sugar bowls, containers, and sugar substitute packets are not to be placed on tables, but provided at point of service, unless requested by passengers.
- Special (off-menu) orders must be possible at any time in the dining room (with reasonable notice).
- Tableside cooking and presentation of whole fish, carved meats, poultry, pasta, and flambeau dessert items.
- Dessert trolley and cheese trolley (both with cover) should be used when possible. A minimum four types of biscuits/crackers should be offered.
- Beluga or Sevruga caviar in unlimited quantities, and at any time, served with the correct mother-of-pearl or bone (not metal) caviar spoons.
- A mix of silver service and plated meal service should be featured.
- Finest quality plateware.
- Meals individually cooked to order on ships of under 300 passengers.
- All sauces must be presented in correct sauce boats, and never in bottles.
- Bottled water must be provided, without charge, in all dining areas. Silver pitchers should be towel-wrapped to prevent condensation from dripping.
- Afternoon tea to have a minimum of six types of teas, plus herbal teas. No "super-market" varieties.
- Cappucino/espresso coffees available without charge in the dining room and at least two bars/lounges. A crystallized sugar stick must be provided.
- The wine list and stock must equal that of a one-star Michelin restaurant ashore, with a minimum of: three types of champagne; 30 white wines; 30 red wines; and five rosé or "blush" wines. Non- and low-alcoholic and organic wines should also be offered.
- Wine sommelier service with appropriate decanters, correct glassware, and leather-bound wine list.
- Course-by-course in-cabin dining at any time (in all cabins for ships of under 300 passengers; in "penthouse" or "suite" categories for ships of over 300 passengers).
- Bartenders that know your name and remember your favorite drinks.
- Dress codes must be enforced at all times in the dining room.
- Senior officers and social staff to host passenger tables each evening (preferably on a rotation basis).
- Nutritional information should be available to passengers who request it.

## General

- Meet and greet staff at airport to offer "refreshment packs" for passengers arriving on long-haul flights.
- All luggage must be transported as seamlessly as possible, without being handled by the passenger.
- White-gloved staff members must escort passengers to their suites/cabins upon embarkation.
- "No" should not be heard as an answer to any request.
- Ticket presentation box must include leather ticket/document wallet, and leather key card/boarding pass holder.

- Newspapers to be provided in ports of call wherever possible.
- Room service for simple items such as coffee, tea, croissants, etc., must take no more than five minutes.
- Room service for complete meals and complex orders must take no longer than 15 minutes.
- Full book and video library access 24 hours per day without charges of any kind (except on non-returned items).
- Complimentary self-service launderette.
- Concierge or similar to attend to details of personal comfort, arrangement of private cocktail parties, etc.
- Tender service that is continuous when in port, and not at designated times. Tenders must have cushioned seating areas, and tender stations ashore must have first-aid kits.
- Tour operators ashore must be told that each unit of transportation must have a practical first-aid kit suitable for most emergencies.
- Fresh flowers or pot-pourri in all public restrooms and cabin bathrooms.
- Flowers (not plastic) in shore tenders.
- Oriental rugs in lobby areas and public restrooms.
- Separate gangway for crew members.
- Cushions placed on seats and backs of all outdoor chairs (at the poolside and indoor/outdoor cafés, for example).
- The highest level of security, including passenger ID/charge cards.
- Baggage must be placed outside cabins upon retiring on the last night of the cruise (and no time specified before 3 a.m. on the morning of arrival).
- All port taxes and gratuities must be included.
- The crew must communicate in a single language (maritime tradition states "English") for all safety procedures.
- Crew alleyways to have individual steel garbage cans (not plastic) with separation of paper and plastic.

## Outdoor Decks/Leisure Areas

- Deck chaise longue chairs must be wood or stainless steel (not plastic).
- Padded cushions on all outdoor deck lounge chairs. Towels must be rolled up and placed on them each morning (weather permitting).
- A fresh supply of 100% cotton towels must be available at all times.
- Swimming pools and whirlpools available 24 hours, except due to cleaning, refilling, or other maintenance.
- Shower stalls must have wall-mounted dispensers for soap, shampoo, etc.
- Deck beverage service available on all open decks with seating areas, not just the principal deck.

## Not Acceptable on any Highly Rated Ship

- Paper or plastic cups for any drinks.
- Paper napkins for meals or buffets (they must be linen or cotton).
- Non-essential announcements.
- "Elevator" music playing continuously in passageways and on open decks.
- Accounts to be settled before the morning of disembarkation.
- Tinned fruits, except on request.

# The Ratings and Evaluations

## Ship Profiles
Technical and specific information on each ship is given, followed by a point by point evaluation and a summary that includes positive and negative points.

## Prefixes
The prefixes on the name of a ship are used to denote the type of propulsion system being used:

| | | |
|---|---|---|
| ib | = | ice-breaker (diesel/nuclear) |
| ms | = | motor ship (diesel) |
| mts | = | motor twin screw (diesel) *or* motor turbine ship (steam) |
| mv | = | motor vessel (diesel) |
| msy | = | motor sailing yacht |
| RMS | = | Royal Mail Ship |
| ss | = | steam ship |
| ssc | = | semi-submersible craft (swath) |
| sts | = | sail training ship |
| tes | = | turbo-electric ship (steam) |
| ts | = | turbine steamer (steam) *or* twin screw vessel |
| tsmv | = | twin screw motor vessel |
| ys | = | yacht ship |

## Principal Cruising Areas
Cruise length is given only for ships featuring year-round cruises to destinations such as the Bahamas or Caribbean.

## Cruise Line/Operator
The cruise line and operator will be different if the company that owns the vessel does not market and operate it.

## First Entered Service
Where two dates are given, the first is the ship's maiden passenger voyage, the second the date it began service for the present operator.

## Christened By
Where two names are given, the first is the person who christened the ship when first built, the second the person who christened it in its present incarnation.

## Engines/Propellers
The manufacturer and number of main engines is given, and the type of propeller, where known.

Propellers

| | | |
|---|---|---|
| CP | = | controllable pitch |
| DP | = | direct pitch |
| FP | = | fixed pitch |
| VP | = | variable pitch |

## Passenger Capacity
The number of passengers is based on: a) Two berths per cabin, plus all single cabins; b) All available berths filled.

## Passenger Space Ratio
Achieved by dividing the gross registered tonnage by the number of passengers.

## Cabin Size Range
From the smallest cabin to the largest suite, in square feet and square meters, rounded up to the nearest number.

# Index to Ships in this Section

**Daphne** (Costa Cruises)

**Delfin Star** (Effjohn International)

**Dimitriy Shostakovich** (Black Sea Shipping)

**Dolphin IV** (Dolphin Cruise Line)

**Dreamward** (Norwegian Cruise Line)

**Ecstasy** (Carnival Cruise Lines)

**Enchanted Seas** (Commodore Cruise Line)

**EnricoCosta** (Costa Cruises)

**EugenioCosta** (Costa Cruises)

**Europa** (Hapag-Lloyd Cruises)

**Explorer** (Abercrombie & Kent)

**Fair Princess** (Princess Cruises)

**Fairstar** (P&O Holidays)

**Fantasy** (Carnival Cruise Lines)

**Fascination** (Carnival Cruise Lines)

**Fedor Dostoyevsky** (Neckermann Seereisen)

**Fedor Shalyapin** (Black Sea Shipping)

**Festivale** (Carnival Cruise Lines)

**FiestaMarina** (FiestaMarina Cruises)

**Fuji Maru** (Mitsui OSK Passenger Line)

**Funchal** (Arcalia Shipping)

**Golden Princess** (Princess Cruises)

**Gruziya** (OdessaAmerica Cruise Company)

**Hanseatic** (Hanseatic Tours)

**Hebridean Princess** (Hebridean Island Cruises)

**Holiday** (Carnival Cruise Lines)

**Horizon** (Celebrity Cruises)

**Ilich** (Baltic Line)

**Illiria** (Classical Cruises)

**Imagination** (Carnival Cruise Lines)

**Independence** (American Hawaii Cruises)

**Island Princess** (Princess Cruises)

**Italia Prima** (Nina Cruises)

**Ivan Franko** (Black Sea Shipping)

**Jason** (Epirotiki Lines)

**Jubilee** (Carnival Cruise Lines)

**Kapitan Khlebnikov** (Quark Expeditions)

**Kareliya** (CTC Cruise Lines)

**Kazakhstan** (Black Sea Shipping)

**Kazakhstan II** (Delphin Seereisen)

**Klaudia Yelanskaya** (Murmansk Shipping)

**Konstantin Simonov** (Baltic Line)

**Kristina Regina** (Kristina Cruises)

**La Palma** (Intercruise)

**Langkapuri Star Aquarius** (Star Cruise)

**Legend of the Seas** (Royal Caribbean Cruises)

**Leisure World** (New Century Tours)

**Leonid Sobinov** (Baltic Shipping)

**Lev Tolstoi** (Transocean Tours)

**Maasdam** (Holland America Line)

**Majesty of the Seas** (Royal Caribbean Cruises)

**Marco Polo** (Orient Lines)

**Maxim Gorki** (Phoenix Seereisen)

**Meridian** (Celebrity Cruises)

**Mermoz** (Paquet French Cruises)

**Mikhail Sholokhov** (Far Eastern Shipping)

**Monarch of the Seas** (Royal Caribbean Cruises)

**Monterey** (Starlauro Cruises)

**Nantucket Clipper** (Clipper Cruise Line)

**Neptune** (Epirotiki Lines)

**Nieuw Amsterdam** (Holland America Line)

**Nippon Maru** (Mitsui OSK Passenger Line)

**Noordam** (Holland America Line)

**Nordic Empress** (Royal Caribbean Cruises)

**Nordic Prince** (Royal Caribbean Cruises)

**Norway** (Norwegian Cruise Line)

**OceanBreeze** (Dolphin Cruise Line)

**Oceanic Grace** (Oceanic Cruises)

**Odessa** (Transocean Cruise Lines)

**Odysseus** (Epirotiki Lines)

**Olympic** (Epirotiki Lines)

**Oriana** (P&O Cruises)

**Orient Star** (American Pacific Cruises)

**Orient Venus** (Japan Cruise Line)

**Orpheus** (Epirotiki Lines)

**Pacific Princess** (Princess Cruises)

**Pearl** (Pearl Cruises)

**Polaris** (Special Expeditions)

**Princesa Amorosa** (Louis Cruise Lines)

**Princesa Cypria** (Louis Cruise Lines)

**Princesa Marissa** (Louis Cruise Lines)

**Princesa Victoria** (Louis Cruise Lines)

**Queen Elizabeth 2** (Cunard)

**Radisson Diamond** (Diamond Cruises)

**Regal Empress** (Regal Cruises)

**Regal Princess** (Princess Cruises)

**Regent Jewel** (Regency Cruises)

**Regent Rainbow** (Regency Cruises)

**Regent Sea** (Regency Cruises)

**Regent Spirit** (Regency Cruises)

**Regent Star** (Regency Cruises)

**Regent Sun** (Regency Cruises)

**Renaissance One** (Renaissance Cruises)

**Renaissance Two** (Renaissance Cruises)

**Renaissance Three** (Renaissance Cruises)

**Renaissance Four** (Renaissance Cruises)

**Renaissance Five** (Renaissance Cruises)

**Renaissance Six** (Renaissance Cruises)

**Renaissance Seven** (Renaissance Cruises)

**Renaissance Eight** (Renaissance Cruises)

**Romantica** (Ambassador Cruises)

**Rotterdam** (Holland America Line)

**Royal Majesty** (Majesty Cruise Line)

**Royal Odyssey** (Royal Cruise Line)

**Royal Princess** (Princess Cruises)

**Royal Star** (Star Line Cruises)

**Royal Viking Queen** (Royal Viking Line)

**Royal Viking Sun** (Royal Viking Line)

**Ryndam** (Holland America Line)

**St. Helena** (Curnow Shipping)

**Sagafjord** (Cunard)

**Sea Goddess I** (Cunard)

**Sea Goddess II** (Cunard)

**Sea Princess** (P&O Cruises)

**Seabourn Pride** (Seabourn Cruise Line)

**Seabourn Spirit** (Seabourn Cruise Line)

**SeaBreeze I** (Dolphin Cruise Line)

**SeaSpirit** (Seaspirit Cruise Lines)

**Seaward** (Norwegian Cruise Line)

**Seawind Crown** (Seawind Cruise Line)

**Sensation** (Carnival Cruise Lines)

**Shota Rustaveli** (Black Sea Shipping)

**Silver Cloud** (Silversea Cruises)

**Silver Wind** (Silversea Cruises)

**Sky Princess** (Princess Cruises)

**Song of America** (Royal Caribbean Cruises)

**Song of Flower** (Seven Seas Cruise Line)

**Song of Norway** (Royal Caribbean Cruises)

**Southward** (Norwegian Cruise Line)

**Sovereign of the Seas** (Royal Caribbean Cruises)

**Sovetskiy Soyuz** (Murmansk Shipping)

**Star Odyssey** (Royal Cruise Line)

**Star Princess** (Princess Cruises)

**Star/Ship Atlantic** (Premier Cruise Lines)

**Star/Ship Majestic** (Premier Cruise Lines)

**Star/Ship Oceanic** (Premier Cruise Lines)

**Starward** (Norwegian Cruise Line)

**Statendam** (Holland America Line)

**Stella Maris** (Sun Line Cruises)

**Stella Oceanis** (Sun Line Cruises)

**Stella Solaris** (Sun Line Cruises)

**Sun Princess** (Princess Cruises)

**Sun Viking** (Royal Caribbean Cruises)

**Taras Shevchenko** (Black Sea Shipping)

**The Azur** (Festival Cruises)

**Triton** (Epirotiki Lines)

**Tropicale** (Carnival Cruise Lines)

**Universe** (World Explorer Cruises)

**Viking Serenade** (Royal Caribbean Cruises)

**Vistafjord** (Cunard)

**Vistamar** (Mar Line Shipping)

**Westerdam** (Holland America Line)

**Windward** (Norwegian Cruise Line)

**World Discoverer** (Clipper Cruise Line)

**World Renaissance** (Epirotiki Lines)

**Yamal** (Murmansk Shipping)

**Yorktown Clipper** (Clipper Cruise Line)

**Zenith** (Celebrity Cruises)

## SAIL-CRUISE SHIPS

**Club Med I** (Club Mediterranée)

**Club Med II** (Club Mediterranée)

**Le Ponant** (Compagnie des Isles du Ponant)

**Sea Cloud** (Sea Cloud Cruises)

**Sir Francis Drake** (Tall Ship Adventures)

**Star Clipper** (Star Clippers)

**Star Flyer** (Star Clippers)

**Wind Song** (Windstar Cruises)

**Wind Spirit** (Windstar Cruises)

**Wind Star** (Windstar Cruises)

# Index to Companies and Ships

# mv Achille Lauro ★★★

***Principal Cruising Area***
*Europe (7-11 nights)*
***Base Port:** Genoa*

| | | | |
|---|---|---|---|
| Cruise Line | | | *Starlauro Cruises* |
| Former Names | | | *Willem Ruys* |
| Gross Tonnage | | | *23,862* |
| Builder | | | *N.V. de Schelde (Holland)* |
| Original Cost | | | *n/a* |
| Christened By | | | *HRH Queen Wilhelmina* |
| First Entered Service | | | *Dec 2, 1947/Apr 13, 1966* |
| Interior Design | | | *Di Orio/Venezian* |
| Country of Registry | | | *Italy (IBHE)* |
| Tel No | *115-0152* | Fax No | *115-0152* |
| Length (ft/m) | | | *642.9/195.97* |
| Beam (ft/m) | | | *82.0/25.00* |
| Draft (ft/m) | | | *29.3/8.95* |
| Engines/Propellers | | | *8 Sulzer 8-cyl diesels/2* |
| Decks | *9* | Crew | *300* |
| Pass. Capacity (basis 2) | *752* | (all berths) | *1,372* |
| Pass. Space Ratio (basis 2) | *30.2* | (all berths) | *17.3* |
| Officers | *Italian* | Dining Staff | *European* |
| Total Cabins | | | *369* |
| Size (sq ft/m) | *n/a* | Door Width | *27"* |
| Outside Cabins | *204* | Inside Cabins | *151* |
| Single Cabins | *74* | Supplement | *Fixed rates* |
| Balcony Cabins | *19* | Wheelchair Cabins | *0* |
| Cabin Current | | | *220 AC/DC* |
| Refrigerator | | | *Category 11, 12 only* |
| Cabin TV | *No* | VCR | *No* |
| Dining Rooms | *1* | Sittings | *2* |
| Elevators | *5* | Door Width | *30"* |

| | | | |
|---|---|---|---|
| Casino | *Yes* | Slot Machines | *Yes* |
| Swimming Pools (outside) | *2* | (inside) | *0* |
| Whirlpools | *0* | Gymnasium | *Yes* |
| Sauna/Steam Rm | *Yes/No* | Massage | *Yes* |
| Self-Service Launderette | | | *Yes* |
| Movie Theater/Seats | | | *Yes/320* |
| Library | | | *No* |
| Children's Facilities | | | *Yes* |
| Watersports Facilities | | | *None* |
| Classification Society | | | *RINA* |

| **RATINGS** | **SCORE** |
|---|---|
| Ship: Condition/Cleanliness | 6.6 |
| Ship: Space/Flow/Comfort | 6.3 |
| Ship: Decor/Furnishings | 6.7 |
| Ship: Fitness Facilities | 5.2 |
| Cabins: Comfort/Facilities | 6.1 |
| Cabins: Software | 6.3 |
| Food: Dining Room/Cuisine | 6.6 |
| Food: Buffets/Informal Dining | 5.3 |
| Food: Quality of Ingredients | 6.0 |
| Service: Dining Room | 6.7 |
| Service: Bars/Lounges | 6.5 |
| Service: Cabins | 6.8 |
| Cruise: Entertainment | 6.3 |
| Cruise: Activities Program | 6.3 |
| Cruise: Hospitality Standard | 6.4 |
| OVERALL RATING | 94.1 |

**+** Distinctive vintage ocean liner styling with blue hull, long lines, and two impressive tall blue funnels. Expansive open deck and sunning space. Tennis court. Wooden decking and polished rails and brass trim are in excellent condition. Some recent refurbishing work has brightened the public rooms and made them much more attractive. Lovely balconied theater is reminiscent of old London theaters. Numerous public rooms to choose from, including a chapel. Wide variety of cabin grades. Spacious Lido Deck suites feature private balconies. Standard grade cabins are quite small, but homely, and moderately well equipped. However, closet space is really minimal.

**–** The mostly Italian passengers tend to be heavy smokers, and it is impossible to escape the smoke. Long lines for embarkation, disembarkation, buffets, and shore tenders.

**Dining** The dining room is attractive, but noisy. Very good pasta. Otherwise the food, and its quality and presentation, needs improvement. Menu choice is rather limited, and anything out of the ordinary, such as vegetarian or any of its derivatives, is a problem. Complimentary wine with lunch and dinner. The service is bubbly, but it lacks finesse and is hurried.

**Other Comments** An inexpensive cruise experience in the Mediterranean during the summer and the Indian Ocean during the winter, but lacking polish. Too many announcements. Geared to Italian-speaking passengers. Currency: lire. Insurance and gratuities are extra.

# mv Aegean Dolphin ★★★+

***Principal Cruising Area***
*Mediterranean (3-7 nights)*
***Base Port:*** *Piraeus*

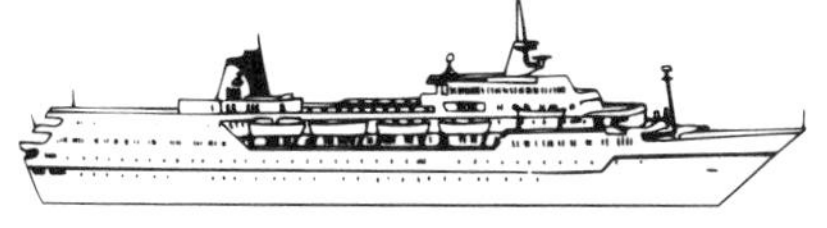

| | | | |
|---|---|---|---|
| Cruise Line | | | *Dolphin Hellas Shipping* |
| Former Names | | | *Narcis/Alkyon* |
| Gross Tonnage | | | *11,563* |
| Builder | | | *Santierul N. Galatz (Romania)* |
| Reconstruction | | | *Perama Shipyards (Greece)* |
| Original Cost | | | *n/a* |
| Christened By | | | *Captain A. Angelopoulos* |
| First Entered Service | | | *1974/May 1988* |
| Interior Design | | | *A&M Katzourakis* |
| Country of Registry | | | *Greece (SWEO)* |
| Tel No | *113-0627* | Fax No | *113-0627* |
| Length (ft/m) | | | *460.9/140.50* |
| Beam (ft/m) | | | *67.2/20.50* |
| Draft (ft/m) | | | *20.3/6.20* |
| Engines/Propellers | | | *2 Pielstick diesels/2 (CP)* |
| Decks | *8* | Crew | *190* |
| Pass. Capacity (basis 2) | *576* | (all berths) | *670* |
| Pass. Space Ratio (basis 2) | *20.0* | (all berths) | *17.2* |
| Officers | *Greek* | Dining Staff | *International* |
| Total Cabins | | | *288* |
| Size (sq ft/m) | *135-290/12.5-27* | Door Width | *24"* |
| Outside Cabins | *202* | Inside Cabins | *86* |
| Single Cabins | *0* | Supplement | *50%* |
| Balcony Cabins | *0* | Wheelchair Cabins | *Yes* |
| Cabin Current | *220 AC* | Refrigerator | *Yes* |
| Cabin TV | *Yes* | VCR | *No* |
| Dining Rooms | *1* | Sittings | *2* |
| Elevators | *2* | Door Width | *30"* |

| | | | |
|---|---|---|---|
| Casino | *Yes* | Slot Machines | *Yes* |
| Swimming Pools (outside) | *1* | (inside) | *0* |
| Whirlpools | *0* | Gymnasium | *Yes* |
| Sauna/Steam Rm | *Yes/No* | Massage | *Yes* |
| Self-Service Launderette | | | *Yes* |
| Movie Theater/Seats | | | *Yes/176* |
| Library | | | *Yes* |
| Children's Facilities | | | *No* |
| Watersports Facilities | | | *None* |
| Classification Society | | | *Lloyd's Register* |

| RATINGS | SCORE |
|---|---|
| Ship: Condition/Cleanliness | 7.3 |
| Ship: Space/Flow/Comfort | 7.3 |
| Ship: Decor/Furnishings | 7.4 |
| Ship: Fitness Facilities | 6.4 |
| Cabins: Comfort/Facilities | 7.6 |
| Cabins: Software | 7.4 |
| Food: Dining Room/Cuisine | 6.5 |
| Food: Buffets/Informal Dining | 6.2 |
| Food: Quality of Ingredients | 5.7 |
| Service: Dining Room | 6.8 |
| Service: Bars/Lounges | 6.7 |
| Service: Cabins | 7.1 |
| Cruise: Entertainment | 5.8 |
| Cruise: Activities Program | 6.1 |
| Cruise: Hospitality Standard | 6.0 |
| OVERALL RATING | 100.3 |

**+** The public rooms are tastefully decorated in contemporary colors, but with much use of mirrored surfaces. There's a good showroom, laid out amphitheater-style. The Belvedere Lounge, set high atop ship and forward, features a smart piano bar and good views. The mostly outside cabins are reasonably spacious for the ship's size, and have picture windows. Bathrobes provided. Dialysis station is a bonus. Service is quite attentive.

**–** Crowded open decks and limited sunning space when the ship is full. There's no library. Cabins do not have enough drawer or closet space for two. Bathrooms are small.

**Dining** The dining room, set low down, is bright and cheerful, but rather cramped, and has mostly large tables (no tables for two). Continental cuisine, with limited choice.

**Other Comments** This ship's profile looks quite smart, following an extensive $26m conversion/stretch in 1988, but is somewhat angular. Comfortable, but densely populated, surroundings, and a fairly decent price. Insurance and gratuities are extra.

# ts Albatros ★★★

***Principal Cruising Area***

*Europe (7 nights)*

***Base Port:*** *Bremerhaven*

| | | | |
|---|---|---|---|
| Cruise Line | *Phoenix Seereisen/V-Ships* | | |
| Former Names | *Dawn Princess/FairWind/Sylvania* | | |
| Gross Tonnage | *24,724* | | |
| Builder | *John Brown & Co. (UK)* | | |
| Original Cost | *n/a* | | |
| Christened By | *n/a* | | |
| First Entered Service | *Jun 5, 1957/Aug 18, 1993* | | |
| Interior Design | *Barbara Dorn* | | |
| Country of Registry | *Bahamas (C6LV3)* | | |
| Tel No | *130-6132* | Fax No | *130-6133* |
| Length (ft/m) | *608.2/185.40* | | |
| Beam (ft/m) | *80.3/24.49* | | |
| Draft (ft/m) | *29.3/8.94* | | |
| Engines/Propellers | *2/2 (FP)* | | |
| Decks | *11* | Crew | *330* |
| Pass. Capacity (basis 2) | *940* | (all berths) | *1100* |
| Pass. Space Ratio (basis 2) | *26.3* | (all berths) | *22.4* |
| Officers | *Italian* | Dining Staff | *International* |
| Total Cabins | *470* | | |
| Size (sq ft/m) | *90-241/8.3-22.3* | Door Width | *24"* |
| Outside Cabins | *239* | Inside Cabins | *231* |
| Single Cabins | *0* | Supplement | *Special brochure rates* |
| Balcony Cabins | *0* | Wheelchair Cabins | *0* |
| Cabin Current | 110 AC | | |
| Refrigerator | Cat. A | | |
| Cabin TV | *No* | VCR | *No* |
| Dining Rooms | *2* | Sittings | *1* |
| Elevators | *3* | Door Width | *36"* |

| | | | |
|---|---|---|---|
| Casino | *Yes* | Slot Machines | *Yes* |
| Swimming Pools (outside) | *3* | (inside) | *0* |
| Whirlpools | *0* | Gymnasium | *Yes* |
| Sauna/Steam Rm | *Yes/No* | Massage | *Yes* |
| Self-Service Launderette | *No* | | |
| Movie Theater/Seats | *No* | | |
| Library | *No* | | |
| Children's Facilities | *No* | | |
| Watersports Facilities | *None* | | |
| Classification Society | *Lloyds Register of Shipping* | | |

| RATINGS | SCORE |
|---|---|
| Ship: Condition/Cleanliness | 6.5 |
| Ship: Space/Flow/Comfort | 6.2 |
| Ship: Decor/Furnishings | 6.6 |
| Ship: Fitness Facilities | 5.0 |
| Cabins: Comfort/Facilities | 6.4 |
| Cabins: Software | 6.7 |
| Food: Dining Room/Cuisine | 6.8 |
| Food: Buffets/Informal Dining | 6.6 |
| Food: Quality of Ingredients | 6.7 |
| Service: Dining Room | 6.8 |
| Service: Bars/Lounges | 7.0 |
| Service: Cabins | 7.2 |
| Cruise: Entertainment | 7.3 |
| Cruise: Activities Program | 6.6 |
| Cruise: Hospitality Standard | 7.0 |
| OVERALL RATING | 99.4 |

**+** She is a sturdily constructed ship, stable at sea, and is quite well maintained. A second swimming pool, fitted into a former cargo hold, is for children. There is plenty of dark wood paneling and trim, with solid brass accents throughout. Fine library. Wide range of cabin sizes and configurations, all with heavy-duty furniture. Excellent and extensive itineraries. Young, willing Phoenix Seereisen staff.

**–** There's not much open deck and sunning space, especially when full. Public rooms are few, always crowded, and full of cigarette smoke.

**Dining** The two dining rooms are really quite charming, but the tables are close together. The menu is not very creative, and there is limited choice. Service is friendly and attentive, in true European style.

**Other Comments** This all-white ship was built in a vintage style, and has a large centrally-placed funnel. Furnishings consist of heavy, patterned fabrics that are very comfortable. This unpretentious ship does have an interesting old-world ambiance and charm that somehow help to make up for the lack of finesse. Principally for German-speaking passengers. Informal atmosphere. Insurance and gratuities are included.

# ss American Adventure ★★★★

***Principal Cruising Area***

*Caribbean (7 nights)*

***Base Port:** Miami*

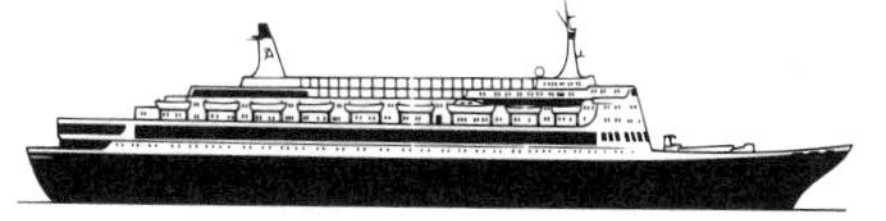

| | | | |
|---|---|---|---|
| Cruise Line | *American Family Cruises* | | |
| Former Names | *CostaRiviera/Guglielmo Marconi* | | |
| Gross Tonnage | *31,500* | | |
| Builder | *Cantieri Riuniti dell' Adriatico (Italy)* | | |
| Original Cost | *$33.7 million (reconstruction)* | | |
| Christened By | *Ms Connie Stevens/4 children* | | |
| First Entered Service | *Nov 18, 1963/Dec 18, 1993* | | |
| Interior Design | *Jeffrey Howard* | | |
| Country of Registry | *Italy (IBBG)* | | |
| Tel No | *115-0146* | Fax No | *115-0146* |
| Length (ft/m) | *700.9/213.65* | | |
| Beam (ft/m) | *94.1/28.71* | | |
| Draft (ft/m) | *28.3/8.65* | | |
| Engines/Propellers | *4 CRDA steam turbines/2* | | |
| Decks | *8* | Crew | *654* |
| Pass. Capacity (basis 2) | *924* | (all berths) | *1,500* |
| Pass. Space Ratio (basis 2) | *34.0* | (all berths) | *21.0* |
| Officers | *Italian* | Dining Staff | *International* |
| Total Cabins | *462* | | |
| Size (sq ft/m) | *150-210/14-19* | Door Width | *25"* |
| Outside Cabins | *286* | Inside Cabins | *176* |
| Single Cabins | *0* | Supplement | *100%* |
| Balcony Cabins | *0* | Wheelchair Cabins | *0* |
| Cabin Current | *110/220 AC* | | |
| Refrigerator | *No* | | |
| Cabin TV | *No* | VCR | *No* |
| Dining Rooms | *1* | Sittings | *2* |
| Elevators | *7* | Door Width | *26-36"* |

| | | | |
|---|---|---|---|
| Casino | *Yes* | Slot Machines | *Yes* |
| Swimming Pools (outside) | *3* | (inside) | *0* |
| Whirlpools | *3* | Gymnasium | *Yes* |
| Sauna/Steam Rm | *Yes/No* | Massage | *Yes* |
| Self-Service Launderette | *Yes* | | |
| Movie Theater/Seats | *Yes/186* | | |
| Library | *Yes* | | |
| Children's Facilities | *No* | | |
| Watersports Facilities | *None* | | |
| Classification Society | *RINA* | | |

| RATINGS | SCORE |
|---|---|
| Ship: Condition/Cleanliness | 8.0 |
| Ship: Space/Flow/Comfort | 7.6 |
| Ship: Decor/Furnishings | 7.6 |
| Ship: Fitness Facilities | 6.6 |
| Cabins: Comfort/Facilities | 7.3 |
| Cabins: Software | 7.5 |
| Food: Dining Room/Cuisine | 7.7 |
| Food: Buffets/Informal Dining | 7.5 |
| Food: Quality of Ingredients | 7.6 |
| Service: Dining Room | 7.8 |
| Service: Bars/Lounges | 7.7 |
| Service: Cabins | 7.8 |
| Cruise: Entertainment | 7.5 |
| Cruise: Activities Program | 7.7 |
| Cruise: Hospitality Standard | 7.7 |
| OVERALL RATING | 113.6 |

**+** Good amount of open deck and sunning space. Interior styling, colors, appointments, and everything else is geared to American families. Good array of public rooms, some for children only, with lots of nooks and crannies, and names like Fuzzy Wuzzy's Den, Rock-O-Saurus Club, Sea Haunt and Lucky Lindy's Bar. Excellent pizzeria and I.S.Y.S.W.A.S.F.I.C. (I Scream, You Scream, We All Scream For Ice Cream) parlor. Good sports program. American-registered pediatrician on all cruises.

**–** Cabin insulation is not good enough to drown out the noise of hundreds of kids. Bathrooms are small. Expect long lines for embarkation, disembarkation, buffets, and shore excursions. Incredibly noisy. Not for adults without kids, as there's nowhere to go to get away from them.

**Dining** The dining room is large and bubbly (noisy), but plain and unattractive, especially the ceiling. Good Continental food, with plentiful pasta, pizza, cookies, and buffets, and well thought out children's menus. Good service from an international staff comes with a smile.

**Other Comments** Former three-class ocean liner refurbished in 1993 in theme-park style for families and children. Some 56 cabins are for families of five or six, while 226 accommodate four. Very casual attire. Baby-sitting services available. Children's coaches. Comfortable family-filled surroundings for a modest price, and lots of fun. Insurance and gratuities are extra.

# mv Americana ★★★★+

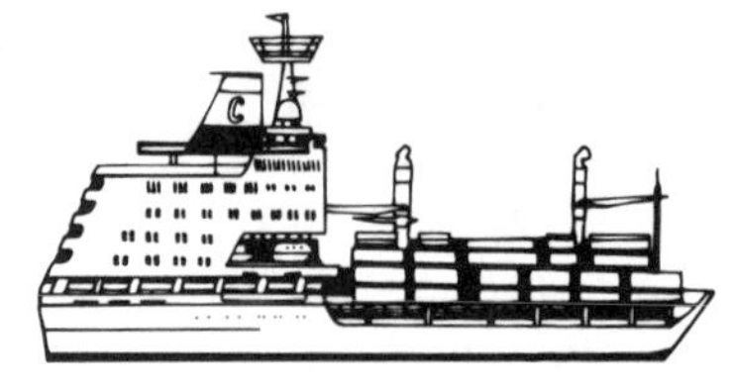

***Principal Cruising Area***

*South America (51/52 nights round-trip)*

***Base Port:** New Orleans*

| | | | |
|---|---|---|---|
| Cruise Line | | | *Ivaran Lines* |
| Former Names | | | *n/a* |
| Gross Tonnage | | | *19,203* |
| Builder | | | *Hyundai Heavy Industries (S.Korea)* |
| Original Cost | | | *$85 million* |
| Christened By | | | *Mrs Kari Holter-Sorensen* |
| First Entered Service | | | *5 Mar 1988* |
| Interior Design | | | *Platou Design* |
| Country of Registry | | | *Norway (LADX2)* |
| Tel No | *131-1131* | Fax No | *131-2714* |
| Length (ft/m) | | | *579.7/176.70* |
| Beam (ft/m) | | | *85.3/26.00* |
| Draft (ft/m) | | | *28.8/8.80* |
| Engines/Propellers | | | *1 MAN 7-cyl diesel/1 (CP)* |
| Decks | *6* | Crew | *44* |
| Pass. Capacity (basis 2) | *88* | (all berths) | *108* |
| Pass. Space Ratio (basis 2) | *218.2* | (all berths) | *177.8* |
| Officers | *Norwegian* | Dining Staff | *South American* |
| Total Cabins | | | *54* |
| Size (sq ft/m) | *134-500/12.5-46.5* | Door Width | *26"* |
| Outside Cabins | *42* | Inside Cabins | *12* |
| Single Cabins | 20 | Supplement | *None* |
| Balcony Cabins | *0* | Wheelchair Cabins | *0* |
| Cabin Current | | | *110/220 AC* |
| Refrigerator | | | *No* |
| Cabin TV | *No* | VCR | *No* |
| Dining Rooms | *1* | Sittings | *1* |
| Elevators | 2 | Door Width | *36"* |

| | | | |
|---|---|---|---|
| Casino | *Yes* | Slot Machines | *Yes* |
| Swimming Pools (outside) | *1* | (inside) | *0* |
| Whirlpools | *1* | Gymnasium | *Yes* |
| Sauna/Steam Rm | *Yes/No* | Massage | *Yes* |
| Self-Service Launderette | | | *Yes* |
| Movie Theater/Seats | | | *No* |
| Library | | | *Yes* |
| Children's Facilities | | | *No* |
| Watersports Facilities | | | *None* |
| Classification Society | | | *Det Norske Veritas* |

| RATINGS | SCORE |
|---|---|
| Ship: Condition/Cleanliness | 8.7 |
| Ship: Space/Flow/Comfort | 7.6 |
| Ship: Decor/Furnishings | 8.1 |
| Ship: Fitness Facilities | 7.8 |
| Cabins: Comfort/Facilities | 8.1 |
| Cabins: Software | 8.1 |
| Food: Dining Room/Cuisine | 8.0 |
| Food: Buffets/Informal Dining | 7.4 |
| Food: Quality of Ingredients | 7.8 |
| Service: Dining Room | 7.8 |
| Service: Bars/Lounges | 7.7 |
| Service: Cabins | 7.8 |
| Cruise: Entertainment | 6.6 |
| Cruise: Activities Program | 6.2 |
| Cruise: Hospitality Standard | 7.8 |
| OVERALL RATING | 115.5 |

**+** Incredible space ratio due to the fact that this is a well-designed freighter-cruise ship, with excellent passenger facilities placed astern of a 1,120-capacity container section. Elegant and beautifully finished interior, by the same designer as the *Sea Goddess* ships, among others. There are five cabin types. Two owners' suites are lavish, with separate bedroom and living room, and big picture windows. Other cabins are quite lovely, very well equipped, and with restful decor. Good number of single cabins. Many cabins have full bathtubs, and some have bidets. Generous sheltered and open sunning space. Well-stocked library. Gentlemen "hosts" on all cruises.

**–** No wrap-around promenade deck. No room service (except on doctor's orders). Steep gangway in ports.

**Dining** Elegant dining room has beautiful table settings, and overlooks the sea. Cuisine, while not elaborate, is appealing, well prepared, and features Norwegian and Continental fare. Breakfast and lunch are buffet-style. Elegant place settings and plateware.

**Other Comments** Needs a minimum of 50 passengers to be assured of priority berthing privileges in ports. Definitely for the older passenger with time to spare who enjoys privacy and the chance to explore places alone. The ultimate in contemporary freighter-cruise travel, with a fine itinerary. Port taxes included. Insurance and gratuities ($3 per day suggested) are extra.

# ss Amerikanis ★★★

***Principal Cruising Area***

*Europe (7 nights)*

***Base Port:*** *Amsterdam*

| | | | |
|---|---|---|---|
| Cruise Line | | | *Fantasy Cruises* |
| Former Names | | | *Kenya Castle* |
| Gross Tonnage | | | *19,904* |
| Builder | | | *Harland & Wolff (UK)* |
| Original Cost | | | *n/a* |
| Christened By | | | *n/a* |
| First Entered Service | | | *Apr 4, 1952/Aug 8, 1968* |
| Interior Design | | | *A&M Katzourakis* |
| Country of Registry | | | *Panama (3FIH2)* |
| Tel No | *113-1575* | Fax No | *113-1575* |
| Length (ft/m) | | | *576.5/175.72* |
| Beam (ft/m) | | | *74.3/22.66* |
| Draft (ft/m) | | | *26.6/8.13* |
| Engines/Propellers | | | *6 /2* |
| Decks | *8* | Crew | *400* |
| Pass. Capacity (basis 2) | *620* | (all berths) | *620* |
| Pass. Space Ratio (basis 2) | *32.1* | (all berths) | *32.1* |
| Officers | *Greek* | Dining Staff | *International* |
| Total Cabins | | | *310* |
| Size (sq ft/m) | *n/a* | Door Width | *28"* |
| Outside Cabins | *206* | Inside Cabins | *104* |
| Single Cabins | *3* | Supplement | *50%* |
| Balcony Cabins | *0* | Wheelchair Cabins | *0* |
| Cabin Current | | | *110/220 AC* |
| Refrigerator | | | *No* |
| Cabin TV | *Yes* | VCR | *No* |
| Dining Rooms | *2* | Sittings | *2* |
| Elevators | *2* | Door Width | *35"* |

| | | | |
|---|---|---|---|
| Casino | *Yes* | Slot Machines | *Yes* |
| Swimming Pools (outside) | *2* | (inside) | *0* |
| Whirlpools | *0* | Gymnasium | *Yes* |
| Sauna/Steam Rm | *Yes/No* | Massage | *Yes* |
| Self-Service Launderette | | | *No* |
| Movie Theater/Seats | | | *Yes/115* |
| Library | | | *Yes* |
| Children's Facilities | | | *Yes* |
| Watersports Facilities | | | *None* |
| Classification Society | | | *Lloyd's Register* |

| **RATINGS** | **SCORE** |
|---|---|
| Ship: Condition/Cleanliness | 6.2 |
| Ship: Space/Flow/Comfort | 6.0 |
| Ship: Decor/Furnishings | 6.8 |
| Ship: Fitness Facilities | 4.8 |
| Cabins: Comfort/Facilities | 6.8 |
| Cabins: Software | 7.8 |
| Food: Dining Room/Cuisine | 7.0 |
| Food: Buffets/Informal Dining | 6.4 |
| Food: Quality of Ingredients | 5.6 |
| Service: Dining Room | 6.8 |
| Service: Bars/Lounges | 6.4 |
| Service: Cabins | 7.0 |
| Cruise: Entertainment | 7.1 |
| Cruise: Activities Program | 6.3 |
| Cruise: Hospitality Standard | 6.7 |
| OVERALL RATING | 97.7 |

**+** Provides inexpensive, excellent value for money cruises at a very realistic price. Wide range of cabin sizes and styles. Some cabins have excellent closet and drawer space, heavy-duty fittings, and good soundproofing. Interesting artwork throughout. Well-planned destination-intensive itineraries. Good if you like older ships, with their wood and brass interiors and basic features.

**–** Often there are long lines for embarkation, disembarkation, and buffets. Dated fixtures, and slow, tired elevators. The service is almost friendly, basic, and has no finesse.

**Dining** A cramped dining room, with tables very close together (although there are tables for two) means it is difficult for waiters to provide decent service, but most passengers seem quite satisfied. The food is of a reasonable quality and presentation, but better quality ingredients would improve the dining experience. Poor selection of breads and fruits.

**Other Comments** This older ship with classic fifties liner styling and a long history of service to several passenger lines has been extremely well maintained. Her interior decor is now much lighter after a recent make-over, although she is, remember, over 40 years old, and it's time she was retired. Insurance and gratuities are extra.

# mv Andaman Princess ★★★

***Principal Cruising Areas***

*Andaman Sea/Thailand (7 nights)*

***Base Port:** Pattaya*

| | | | |
|---|---|---|---|
| Cruise Line | | | *Siam Cruise Company* |
| Former Names | | | *Apollo III/Svea Jarl* |
| Gross Tonnage | | | *4,898* |
| Builder | | | *Finnboda (Sweden)* |
| Original Cost | | | *$8 million* |
| Christened By | | | *Countess Estelle Bernadotte/ Mrs Prani Yasasindhu* |
| First Entered Service | | | *Apr 1962/1990* |
| Interior Design | | | *Kitti Sindhusek/ Chulalonggkoru University* |
| Country of Registry | | | *Thailand (HSJC)* |
| Tel No | *n/a* | Fax No | *n/a* |
| Length (ft/m) | | | *332.8/101.45* |
| Beam (ft/m) | | | *56.5/17.25* |
| Draft (ft/m) | | | *15.6/4.76* |
| Engines/Propellers | | | *2 MAN diesels/1* |
| Decks | *6* | Crew | *200* |
| Pass. Capacity (basis 2) | *276* | (all berths) | *350* |
| Pass. Space Ratio (basis 2) | *17.7* | (all berths) | *13.9* |
| Officers | *Thai* | Dining Staff | *Thai* |
| Total Cabins | | | *138* |
| Size (sq ft/m) | *54-344/5-32* | Door Width | *24"* |
| Outside Cabins | *86* | Inside Cabins | *52* |
| Single Cabins | *0* | Supplement | *200%* |
| Balcony Cabins | *0* | Wheelchair Cabins | *0* |
| Cabin Current | 220 AC | Refrigerator | No |
| Cabin TV | *No* | VCR | *No* |
| Dining Rooms | *2* | Sittings | *1* |

| | | | |
|---|---|---|---|
| Elevators | *2* | Door Width | *30"* |
| Casino | *Yes* | Slot Machines | *Yes* |
| Swimming Pools (outside) | *0* | (inside) | *0* |
| Whirlpools | *1 (large, indoor)* | Gymnasium | *Yes* |
| Sauna/Steam Rm | *Yes/No* | Massage | *Yes* |
| Self-Service Launderette | | | *No* |
| Movie Theater/Seats | | | *No* |
| Library | *No* | Children's Facilities | *Yes* |
| Watersports Facilities | | | *None* |
| Classification Society | | | *Lloyd's Register* |

| RATINGS | SCORE |
|---|---|
| Ship: Condition/Cleanliness | 6.1 |
| Ship: Space/Flow/Comfort | 6.0 |
| Ship: Decor/Furnishings | 6.3 |
| Ship: Fitness Facilities | 4.0 |
| Cabins: Comfort/Facilities | 6.2 |
| Cabins: Software | 6.4 |
| Food: Dining Room/Cuisine | 6.3 |
| Food: Buffets/Informal Dining | 6.0 |
| Food: Quality of Ingredients | 6.4 |
| Service: Dining Room | 7.0 |
| Service: Bars/Lounges | 6.6 |
| Service: Cabins | 6.7 |
| Cruise: Entertainment | 6.0 |
| Cruise: Activities Program | 6.1 |
| Cruise: Hospitality Standard | 7.3 |
| OVERALL RATING | 93.4 |

**+** Her original steam engines were exchanged for diesel propulsion in 1981. Lovely brass staircase. Lots of original wood paneling throughout. Snorkels and masks provided free, while underwater cameras can be rented. Fuji express photo lab for instant service. Good children's learning center teaches three alphabets. Except for 12 suites, most of which have lifeboat views, most cabins are small, cleanly equipped, and quite comfortable. All have been refurbished. Closet and storage space is limited.

**–** There's no outdoor deck space whatsoever.

**Dining** The two dining rooms are quite charming and have acres of lovely, original wood paneling. The food is of typically good quality Thai and Chinese, with attentive service from a very willing staff. There is also a 24-hour coffee shop for casual snacks.

**Other Comments** Charming ex-Swedish night ferry with aft-placed funnel. An extensive refurbishment has equipped the ship for specialized cruising, but the refurbishment didn't go far enough. More hardware maintenance needs to be done. This is the first attempt at operating a full-service cruise ship by Thai owners for Asian passengers, but it is not yet the luxury experience it claims to be. It is, however, an excellent way to experience cruising at modest rates in Thai waters, with their superb underwater life. Insurance and gratuities are extra.

# ms Antonina Nezhdanova ★★

***Principal Cruising Areas***

*Various (various)*

***Base Ports:** various*

| | | | |
|---|---|---|---|
| Cruise Line | | | *Far East Shipping* |
| Former Names | | | *n/a* |
| Gross Tonnage | | | *3,941* |
| Builder | | | *Brodgradiliste Uljanik (Yugoslavia)* |
| Original Cost | | | *n/a* |
| Christened By | | | *n/a* |
| First Entered Service | | | *1978* |
| Interior Design | | | *n/a* |
| Country of Registry | | | *Russia (ESWY)* |
| Tel No | *140-0371* | Fax No | *140-0371* |
| Length (ft/m) | | | *328.1/100.01* |
| Beam (ft/m) | | | *53.2/16.24* |
| Draft (ft/m) | | | *15.2/4.65* |
| Engines/Propellers | | | *2 Uljanik diesels/1* |
| Decks | *6* | Crew | *100* |
| Pass. Capacity (basis 2) | *96* | (all berths) | *188* |
| Pass. Space Ratio (basis 2) | *41.0* | (all berths) | *20.9* |
| Officers | *Russian* | Dining Staff | *Russian* |
| Total Cabins | | | *48* |
| Size (sq ft/m) | *n/a* | Door Width | *24"* |
| Outside Cabins | *48* | Inside Cabins | *0* |
| Single Cabins | *0* | Supplement | *100%* |
| Balcony Cabins | *0* | Wheelchair Cabins | *0* |
| Cabin Current | | | *220 AC* |
| Refrigerator | | | *No* |
| Cabin TV | *No* | VCR | *No* |
| Dining Rooms | *1* | Sittings | *1* |
| Elevators | *0* | Door Width | *n/a* |

| | | | |
|---|---|---|---|
| Casino | *No* | Slot Machines | *No* |
| Swimming Pools (outside) | *1* | (inside) | *No* |
| Whirlpools | *No* | Gymnasium | *No* |
| Sauna/Steam Rm | *Yes/No* | Massage | *No* |
| Self-Service Launderette | | | *No* |
| Movie Theater/Seats | | | *Yes/75* |
| Library | | | *Yes* |
| Children's Facilities | | | *No* |
| Watersports Facilities | | | *None* |
| Classification Society | | | *RS* |

| RATINGS | SCORE |
|---|---|
| Ship: Condition/Cleanliness | 5.3 |
| Ship: Space/Flow/Comfort | 5.5 |
| Ship: Decor/Furnishings | 6.1 |
| Ship: Fitness Facilities | 3.0 |
| Cabins: Comfort/Facilities | 5.7 |
| Cabins: Software | 6.0 |
| Food: Dining Room/Cuisine | 6.0 |
| Food: Buffets/Informal Dining | 5.4 |
| Food: Quality of Ingredients | 6.0 |
| Service: Dining Room | 6.2 |
| Service: Bars/Lounges | 6.4 |
| Service: Cabins | 6.5 |
| Cruise: Entertainment | 4.2 |
| Cruise: Activities Program | 4.6 |
| Cruise: Hospitality Standard | 6.1 |
| OVERALL RATING | 83.0 |

**+** Intimate, small ship with well-balanced profile is one of a series of eight identical sisters. Some have now been sold, while others are sometimes chartered to European operators. Has an ice-hardened hull suitable for some "soft" expedition cruising. Good open deck space for the size of the vessel. Outdoor observation deck and enclosed promenade deck for inclement weather. Charming forward music lounge has wooden dance floor. Rich, highly polished wood paneling throughout. Lovely, winding, brass-railed main staircase. Cabins are compact and spartan, but most can accommodate four persons, and stewardess service is basically sound.

**–** There's no indoor observation lounge. Poor lecture room with non-existent ventilation. Poor accounting system (no cashless cruising). Announcements are too loud and rather military in style. She is simply too small a ship for much open water cruising.

**Dining** The dining room is dark and unappealing, even though it has portholes. The food is an eclectic mixture, and certainly not memorable, with its heavy sauces and salt in everything. Very limited menu choice. Poor selection of cheeses and fruits. Willing waitress service.

**Other Comments** This ship is small, yet comfortable, and has plenty of character. Often chartered to Western operators for "soft" expedition-style cruises.

# mts Argonaut ★★★+

***Principal Cruising Area***

*Southern Europe (various)*

***Base Port:** Piraeus*

| | | | |
|---|---|---|---|
| Cruise Line | | | *Epirotiki Lines* |
| Former Names | | | *Orion/Vixen* |
| Gross Tonnage | | | *4,007* |
| Builder | | | *Frieder, Krupp Germaniawerft (Germany)* |
| Original Cost | | | *n/a* |
| Christened By | | | *n/a* |
| First Entered Service | | | *Sep 1929/1965* |
| Interior Design | | | *Maurice Bailey* |
| Country of Registry | | | *Greece (SWXZ)* |
| Tel No | *113-0507* | Fax No | *113-0507* |
| Length (ft/m) | | | *306.0/93.27* |
| Beam (ft/m) | | | *46.5/14.18* |
| Draft (ft/m) | | | *18.4/5.63* |
| Engines/Propellers | | | *2 Krupp diesels/2 (DP)* |
| Decks | *4* | Crew | *100* |
| Pass. Capacity (basis 2) | *174* | (all berths) | *183* |
| Pass. Space Ratio (basis 2) | *23.0* | (all berths) | *21.8* |
| Officers | *Greek* | Dining Staff | *Greek* |
| Total Cabins | | | *88* |
| Size (sq ft/m) | *n/a* | Door Width | *26"* |
| Outside Cabins | *82* | Inside Cabins | *6* |
| Single Cabins | *0* | Supplement | *50%* |
| Balcony Cabins | *0* | Wheelchair Cabins | *0* |
| Cabin Current | | | *110/220 AC* |
| Refrigerator | | | *No* |
| Cabin TV | *No* | VCR | *No* |
| Dining Rooms | *1* | Sittings | *1* |
| Elevators | *1* | Door Width | *30"* |

| | | | |
|---|---|---|---|
| Casino | *No* | Slot Machines | *No* |
| Swimming Pools (outside) | *1* | (inside) | *0* |
| Whirlpools | *0* | Gymnasium | *No* |
| Sauna/Steam Rm | *No/No* | Massage | *No* |
| Self-Service Launderette | | | *No* |
| Movie Theater/Seats | | | *No* |
| Library | | | *Yes* |
| Children's Facilities | | | *No* |
| Watersports Facilities | | | *None* |
| Classification Society | | | *Bureau Veritas* |

| RATINGS | SCORE |
|---|---|
| Ship: Condition/Cleanliness | 7.2 |
| Ship: Space/Flow/Comfort | 7.0 |
| Ship: Decor/Furnishings | 7.3 |
| Ship: Fitness Facilities | 4.0 |
| Cabins: Comfort/Facilities | 6.7 |
| Cabins: Software | 6.7 |
| Food: Dining Room/Cuisine | 7.1 |
| Food: Buffets/Informal Dining | 6.7 |
| Food: Quality of Ingredients | 6.7 |
| Service: Dining Room | 7.1 |
| Service: Bars/Lounges | 7.2 |
| Service: Cabins | 7.3 |
| Cruise: Entertainment | 6.0 |
| Cruise: Activities Program | 6.0 |
| Cruise: Hospitality Standard | 7.8 |
| OVERALL RATING | 100.8 |

**+** Extremely old, yet well-maintained, ship with a warm, intimate, and informal atmosphere. Gorgeous woods and trim used throughout. Comfortable decor in the limited public rooms. The winding center stairway is lovely. Extensive artworks of classical Greece throughout. This ship always features interesting itineraries, supplemented by guest lecturers and minimal entertainment. Cabins are adequate, no more.

**–** No observation lounge. Cabin bathrooms are small. The gangway is steep in ports.

**Dining** Large dining room features single sitting. Good Mediterranean-style food, but selection of breads, rolls, cheeses, and fruits should be improved. Attentive, friendly service, but without finesse.

**Other Comments** Charming, small, vintage ship built originally as a private yacht for the American wool magnate Carl Julius Forstmann. Often sails under long-term charter to special interest groups. This ship really provides a very comfortable, pleasing cruise experience for the discerning traveler who doesn't like large ships, crowds, or an impersonal environment.

# ms Arkona ★★★★

***Principal Cruising Area***

*Europe (various)*

***Base Port:*** *Bremerhaven*

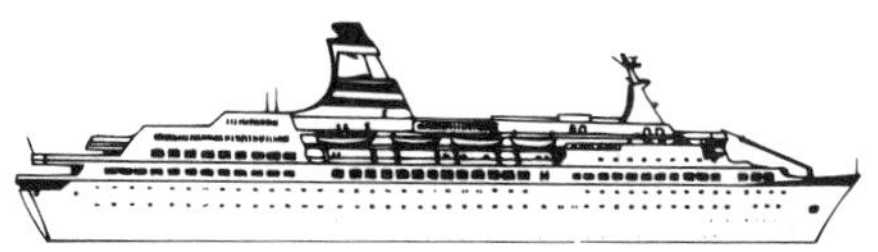

| | | | |
|---|---|---|---|
| Cruise Line | | | *Deutsche Seerederei* |
| Former Names | | | *Astor (I)/Berlin* |
| Gross Tonnage | | | *18,591* |
| Builder | | | *Howaldtswerke Deutsche Werft* |
| Original Cost | | | *$55 million* |
| Christened By | | | *Ms Lisa Weithuchter* |
| First Entered Service | | | *Dec 23, 1981/Oct 25, 1985* |
| Interior Design | | | *Hans Sebbart* |
| Country of Registry | | | *Germany (Y5CC)* |
| Tel No | *163-0103* | Fax No | *163-0103* |
| Length (ft/m) | | | *539.2/164.35* |
| Beam (ft/m) | | | *74.1/22.60* |
| Draft (ft/m) | | | *20.0/6.11* |
| Engines/Propellers | | | *4 MAN 6-cyl diesels/2 (CP)* |
| Decks | *8* | Crew | *243* |
| Pass. Capacity (basis 2) | *480* | (all berths) | *520* |
| Pass. Space Ratio (basis 2) | *38.7* | (all berths) | *35.7* |
| Officers | *German* | Dining Staff | *East European* |
| Total Cabins | | | *241* |
| Size (sq ft/m) | *n/a* | Door Width | *24"* |
| Outside Cabins | *159* | Inside Cabins | *82* |
| Single Cabins | *0* | Supplement | *40-75%* |
| Balcony Cabins | *0* | Wheelchair Cabins | *0* |
| Cabin Current | | | *220 AC* |
| Refrigerator | | | *No (suites have minibar)* |
| Cabin TV | *Yes* | VCR | |
| Dining Rooms | *1* | Sittings | *2* |
| Elevators | *6* | Door Width | *30"* |

| | | | |
|---|---|---|---|
| Casino | *No* | Slot Machines | *No* |
| Swimming Pools (outside) | *1* | (inside) | *1* |
| Whirlpools | *0* | Gymnasium | *Yes* |
| Sauna/Steam Rm | *Yes/No* | Massage | *Yes* |
| Self-Service Launderette | | | *No* |
| Movie Theater/Seats | | | *No* |
| Library | | | *Yes* |
| Children's Facilities | | | *No* |
| Watersports Facilities | | | *None* |
| Classification Society | | | *Germanischer Lloyd* |

| RATINGS | SCORE |
|---|---|
| Ship: Condition/Cleanliness | 8.1 |
| Ship: Space/Flow/Comfort | 8.0 |
| Ship: Decor/Furnishings | 7.9 |
| Ship: Fitness Facilities | 6.7 |
| Cabins: Comfort/Facilities | 7.8 |
| Cabins: Software | 7.8 |
| Food: Dining Room/Cuisine | 7.7 |
| Food: Buffets/Informal Dining | 7.6 |
| Food: Quality of Ingredients | 7.7 |
| Service: Dining Room | 6.8 |
| Service: Bars/Lounges | 6.7 |
| Service: Cabins | 6.8 |
| Cruise: Entertainment | 6.6 |
| Cruise: Activities Program | 6.5 |
| Cruise: Hospitality Standard | 7.3 |
| OVERALL RATING | 110.0 |

**+** Well constructed modern ship has a very handsome profile. Good open deck and sunning space, with gorgeous teakwood decking and rails. Beautifully-equipped interior fittings and decor, with much rosewood paneling and trim. Subdued lighting and soothing ambiance, highlighted by fine artwork throughout. Has good meetings facilities, a fine library, and, more importantly, an excellent pub with draught German beer. Excellent indoor spa and fitness center. Sophisticated hospital facilities include oxygen multi-step therapy and dialysis machines, and fully trained staff. Boat Deck suite rooms are simply lovely. Other cabins are well equipped and decorated. Bathrooms are compact but fully tiled, with good toiletry cabinets. Good traditional European hotel service.

**–** There's no wrap-around promenade deck. Starchy atmosphere. Too many smokers.

**Dining** The Arkona Restaurant, located high in the ship, has big picture windows and is quite elegant, with dark wood paneling and restful decor. The food is adequate to very good, though choice is somewhat limited. Occasional formal candlelight dinners are romantic. Limited cabin service menu.

**Other Comments** This ship cruises under long-term charter to German operators, and features good value for money cruising in contemporary comfort with German-speaking passengers who appreciate quality, fine surroundings, good food, and excellent destination-intensive itineraries.

# ms Astra ★★+

***Principal Cruising Area***
*Europe (various)*
***Base Port:*** *Bremerhaven*

| | | | |
|---|---|---|---|
| Cruise Line | | | *Caravella Shipping/ Neckermann Seereisen* |
| Former Names | | | *Istra* |
| Gross Tonnage | | | *5,635* |
| Builder | | | *Brodgradiliste (Yugoslavia)* |
| Original Cost | | | *n/a* |
| Christened By | | | *n/a* |
| First Entered Service | | | *1965/May 22, 1993* |
| Interior Design | | | *n/a* |
| Country of Registry | | | *Russia (UUKS)* |
| Tel No | *140-3475* | Fax No | *140-3475* |
| Length (ft/m) | | | *383.8/117.0m* |
| Beam (ft/m) | | | *54.1/16.5m* |
| Draft (ft/m) | | | *18.3/5.6m* |
| Engines/Propellers | | | *2 Sulzer diesels/2* |
| Decks | *5* | Crew | *120* |
| Pass. Capacity (basis 2) | *282* | (all berths) | *282* |
| Pass. Space Ratio (basis 2) | *19.9* | (all berths) | *19.9* |
| Officers | *Russian* | Dining Staff | *East European* |
| Total Cabins | | | *141* |
| Size (sq ft/m) | *n/a* | Door Width | *22"* |
| Outside Cabins | *83* | Inside Cabins | *58* |
| Single Cabins | *0* | Supplement | *Fixed brochure rate* |
| Balcony Cabins | *0* | Wheelchair Cabins | *0* |
| Cabin Current | *220 AC* | Refrigerator | *No* |
| Cabin TV | *No* | VCR | *No* |
| Dining Rooms | *1* | Sittings | *1* |
| Elevators | *0* | Door Width | *n/a* |

| | | | |
|---|---|---|---|
| Casino | *No* | Slot Machines | *No* |
| Swimming Pools (outside) | *1* | (inside) | *0* |
| Whirlpools | *0* | Gymnasium | *No* |
| Sauna/Steam Rm | *No/No* | Massage | *No* |
| Self-Service Launderette | | | *No* |
| Movie Theater/Seats | | | *No* |
| Library | | | *Yes* |
| Children's Facilities | | | *No* |
| Watersports Facilities | | | *None* |
| Classification Society | | | *Russian Survey* |

| RATINGS | SCORE |
|---|---|
| Ship: Condition/Cleanliness | 5.6 |
| Ship: Space/Flow/Comfort | 5.0 |
| Ship: Decor/Furnishings | 6.1 |
| Ship: Fitness Facilities | 4.0 |
| Cabins: Comfort/Facilities | 5.2 |
| Cabins: Software | 5.4 |
| Food: Dining Room/Cuisine | 6.5 |
| Food: Buffets/Informal Dining | 6.3 |
| Food: Quality of Ingredients | 6.1 |
| Service: Dining Room | 6.3 |
| Service: Bars/Lounges | 6.6 |
| Service: Cabins | 6.5 |
| Cruise: Entertainment | 5.0 |
| Cruise: Activities Program | 5.8 |
| Cruise: Hospitality Standard | 6.1 |
| OVERALL RATING | 88.5 |

**+** Small ship is good for "nooks and crannies" ports. Has an enclosed teak promenade deck. Interior decor is attractive in general. Features interesting itineraries. Two-deck-high Lido Bar is attractive. Very casual dress code and unpretentious, relaxed ambiance.

**–** There are few public rooms, and little open deck space. Maintenance needs more attention. Has narrow gangway in most ports. Public rooms are always crowded, and it's hard to get away from cigarette smokers.

**Dining** Although the dining room is quite warm and features attractive place settings (there are no tables for two), the food itself is limited in choice and variety. Poor selection of fresh fruits and breads. Ukrainian waitresses are quite charming, but there's little finesse.

**Other Comments** This small ship has a typical low-built, early sixties profile. At present under charter to Neckermann Seereisen, with Neckermann management on board, catering to German-speaking passengers.

# ms Asuka ★★★★★

***Principal Cruising Areas***

*Asia/Circle Japan/South Pacific (various)*

***Base Ports:*** *Tokyo/Yokohama*

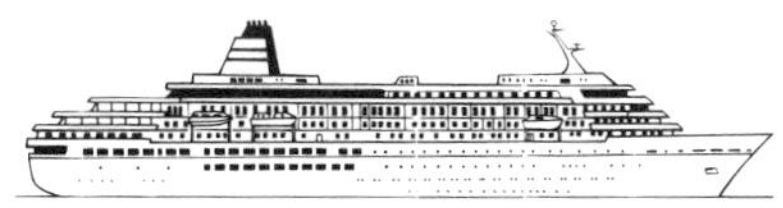

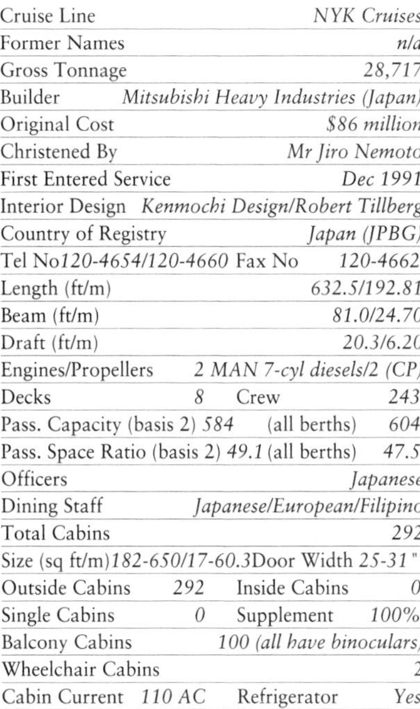

| | |
|---|---|
| Cruise Line | *NYK Cruises* |
| Former Names | *n/a* |
| Gross Tonnage | *28,717* |
| Builder | *Mitsubishi Heavy Industries (Japan)* |
| Original Cost | *$86 million* |
| Christened By | *Mr Jiro Nemoto* |
| First Entered Service | *Dec 1991* |
| Interior Design | *Kenmochi Design/Robert Tillberg* |
| Country of Registry | *Japan (JPBG)* |
| Tel No *120-4654/120-4660* Fax No | *120-4662* |
| Length (ft/m) | *632.5/192.81* |
| Beam (ft/m) | *81.0/24.70* |
| Draft (ft/m) | *20.3/6.20* |
| Engines/Propellers | *2 MAN 7-cyl diesels/2 (CP)* |
| Decks *8* Crew | *243* |
| Pass. Capacity (basis 2) *584* (all berths) | *604* |
| Pass. Space Ratio (basis 2) *49.1* (all berths) | *47.5* |
| Officers | *Japanese* |
| Dining Staff | *Japanese/European/Filipino* |
| Total Cabins | *292* |
| Size (sq ft/m) *182-650/17-60.3* Door Width | *25-31"* |
| Outside Cabins *292* Inside Cabins | *0* |
| Single Cabins *0* Supplement | *100%* |
| Balcony Cabins | *100 (all have binoculars)* |
| Wheelchair Cabins | 2 |
| Cabin Current *110 AC* Refrigerator | *Yes* |
| Cabin TV *Yes* VCR | *No* |
| Dining Rooms *1 (+ sushi rest)* Sittings | *2* |

| | |
|---|---|
| Elevators *5* Door Width | *31.5"* |
| Casino *Yes* Slot Machines | *Yes* |
| Swimming Pools (outside) *1* (inside) | *0* |
| Whirlpools *3* Gymnasium | *Yes* |
| Sauna/Steam Rm *Yes/Yes* Massage | *Yes* |
| Self-Service Launderette | *Yes* |
| Movie Theater/Seats | *Yes/97* |
| Library *Yes* Children's Facilities | *No* |
| Watersports Facilities | *None* |
| Classification Society | *Nippon Kaiji Kyokai* |

| RATINGS | SCORE |
|---|---|
| Ship: Condition/Cleanliness | 9.1 |
| Ship: Space/Flow/Comfort | 8.3 |
| Ship: Decor/Furnishings | 8.8 |
| Ship: Fitness Facilities | 8.6 |
| Cabins: Comfort/Facilities | 8.7 |
| Cabins: Software | 8.6 |
| Food: Dining Room/Cuisine | 8.8 |
| Food: Buffets/Informal Dining | 8.1 |
| Food: Quality of Ingredients | 8.7 |
| Service: Dining Room | 8.7 |
| Service: Bars/Lounges | 8.6 |
| Service: Cabins | 8.4 |
| Cruise: Entertainment | 8.6 |
| Cruise: Activities Program | 7.4 |
| Cruise: Hospitality Standard | 9.3 |
| OVERALL RATING | 128.7 |

**+** Handsome exterior styling, with good open deck space. Good meetings facilities, with high-tech audio-visual equipment. Wrap-around outdoor promenade deck. Excellent, spacious, Japanese grand bath facility. Intimate, small public rooms. Elegant interior decor and fine quality furnishings. Superb "club" suites. Excellent cabin insulation. Good closet and drawer space, including some lockable drawers. Tea-making units, bathrobes, slippers, and bathtubs in all cabins. "Watushi" tatami room. Sushi-making classes. Cellular pay telephones. Good entertainment.

**–** "Cake-layer" stacking of public rooms hampers passenger flow. Standard cabin bathrooms are small. No butler service in "club" suites. Massage room away from the grand bath area.

**Dining** The dining room has good space around tables and Western-style place settings (chopsticks available). Not enough tables for two. Japanese and Western food. Superb quality, excellent presentation. Traditional Japanese breakfast and luncheon, and international (Western-style) dinners. Good wines, but only one sake. Wedgwood china. The sushi bar is an outstanding à la carte room serving the very freshest foods, beautifully presented. The buffet area is too small.

**Other Comments** Looks like a smaller version of *Crystal Harmony*. Entertainment is a mix of Western productions (dubbed in Japanese) and traditional Japanese classical and contemporary cabaret styles. Children under 10 not allowed. Gratuities are neither expected nor allowed.

# ms Atalante ★★★

***Principal Cruising Areas***

*Egypt/Israel (3/4 nights)*

***Base Port:*** *Limassol*

| | | | |
|---|---|---|---|
| Cruise Line | | | *Paradise Cruises* |
| Former Names | | | *Tahitien* |
| Gross Tonnage | | | *13,113* |
| Builder | | | *Arsenal de la Marine National Francaise* |
| Original Cost | | | *n/a* |
| Christened By | | | *n/a* |
| First Entered Service | | | *May 4, 1953/Dec 18, 1992* |
| Interior Design | | | *n/a* |
| Country of Registry | | | *Cyprus (P3XW4)* |
| Tel No | *357-9-545600* | Fax No | *357-9-370298* |
| Length (ft/m) | | | *548.5/167.20* |
| Beam (ft/m) | | | *67.9/20.70* |
| Draft (ft/m) | | | *25.5/7.80* |
| Engines/Propellers | | | *2 B&W 10-cyl diesels/2* |
| Decks | *5* | Crew | *160* |
| Pass. Capacity (basis 2) | *484* | (all berths) | *635* |
| Pass. Space Ratio (basis 2) | *27.0* | (all berths) | *20.6* |
| Officers | *Greek* | Dining Staff | *International* |
| Total Cabins | | | *242* |
| Size (sq ft/m) | *n/a* | Door Width | *26"* |
| Outside Cabins | *188* | Inside Cabins | *54* |
| Single Cabins | *2* | Supplement | *50%* |
| Balcony Cabins | *0* | Wheelchair Cabins | *18* |
| Cabin Current | | | *220 AC/200 DC* |
| Refrigerator | | | *Top grade cabins only* |
| Cabin TV | *Yes* | VCR | *No* |
| Dining Rooms | *1* | Sittings | *2* |
| Elevators | *0* | Door Width | *26"* |

| | | | |
|---|---|---|---|
| Casino | *Yes* | Slot Machines | *Yes* |
| Swimming Pools (outside) | *2* | (inside) | *0* |
| Whirlpools | *0* | Gymnasium | *No* |
| Sauna/Steam Rm | *No/No* | Massage | *No* |
| Self-Service Launderette | | | *No* |
| Movie Theater/Seats | | | *No* |
| Library | | | *No* |
| Children's Facilities | | | *No* |
| Watersports Facilities | | | *None* |
| Classification Society | | | *Bureau Veritas* |

| RATINGS | SCORE |
|---|---|
| Ship: Condition/Cleanliness | 7.0 |
| Ship: Space/Flow/Comfort | 6.6 |
| Ship: Decor/Furnishings | 6.7 |
| Ship: Fitness Facilities | 5.0 |
| Cabins: Comfort/Facilities | 6.8 |
| Cabins: Software | 6.8 |
| Food: Dining Room/Cuisine | 6.8 |
| Food: Buffets/Informal Dining | 6.3 |
| Food: Quality of Ingredients | 6.0 |
| Service: Dining Room | 6.8 |
| Service: Bars/Lounges | 6.7 |
| Service: Cabins | 6.9 |
| Cruise: Entertainment | 5.6 |
| Cruise: Activities Program | 6.0 |
| Cruise: Hospitality Standard | 6.6 |
| OVERALL RATING | 96.6 |

**+** There is a generous amount of open deck and sunning space. Interior decor old and worn, yet adequate and comfortable. Cabins are small and rather spartan, although most have been recently redecorated in pastel shades. There is limited closet space, but you don't need much clothing for this casual cruise environment.

**–** The vessel has an awkward layout. Outdoor decking is worn in several places and needs attention. The nightlife is disco-loud. No finesse, although the staff are reasonably enthusiastic.

**Dining** The dining room is low down in the ship and musty. The food is fair, that's all—with little choice. Poor selection of breads, fruits, and cheeses. Buffets are minimal.

**Other Comments** This former passenger-car liner has a small, squat funnel amidships and a long fore deck. Limited public rooms, but recent decor changes are for the better. This ship is for the young, budget-minded cruiser wanting to party and travel without much service.

# ms Aurora I ★★★★+

***Principal Cruising Areas***
*Various (various)*
***Base Ports:*** *various*

| | | | |
|---|---|---|---|
| Cruise Line | | | *Classical Cruises* |
| Former Names | | | *Lady Diana* |
| Gross Tonnage | | | *2,928* |
| Builder | | | *Flender Werft (Germany)* |
| Original Cost | | | *$35 million* |
| Christened By | | | *Ms Carol Theodore* |
| First Entered Service | | | *Jan 5, 1992* |
| Interior Design | | | *Giorgio Vafiadis* |
| Country of Registry | | | *Bahamas (C6KP6)* |
| Tel No | *130-5141* | Fax No | *130-5144* |
| Length (ft/m) | | | *269.6/82.2* |
| Beam (ft/m) | | | *45.9/14.0* |
| Draft (ft/m) | | | *10.9/3.3* |
| Engines/Propellers | | | *2 KHD-MWM diesels/2* |
| Decks | *4* | Crew | *59* |
| Pass. Capacity (basis 2) | *80* | (all berths) | *80* |
| Pass. Space Ratio (basis 2) | *36.6* | (all berths) | *36.6* |
| Officers | *Greek* | Dining Staff | *International* |
| Total Cabins | | | *44* |
| Size (sq ft/m) | *250-430/23-40* | Door Width | *24"* |
| Outside Cabins | *44* | Inside Cabins | *0* |
| Single Cabins | 6 | Supplement | *Fixed brochure rates* |
| Balcony Cabins | *0* | Wheelchair Cabins | *0* |
| Cabin Current | | | *110/220 AC* |
| Refrigerator | | | *All cabins* |
| Cabin TV | *Yes* | VCR | *Yes* |
| Dining Rooms | *1* | Sittings | *Open* |
| Elevators | *0* | Door Width | *n/a* |

| | | | |
|---|---|---|---|
| Casino | *No* | Slot Machines | *No* |
| Swimming Pools (outside) | *1* | (inside) | *0* |
| Whirlpools | *0* | Gymnasium | *No* |
| Sauna/Steam Rm | *No/No* | Massage | *No* |
| Self-Service Launderette | | | *No* |
| Movie Theater/Seats | | | *No* |
| Library | | | *Yes* |
| Children's Facilities | | | *No* |
| Watersports Facilities | | | *None* |
| Classification Society | | | *Germanischer Lloyd* |

| RATINGS | SCORE |
|---|---|
| Ship: Condition/Cleanliness | 8.6 |
| Ship: Space/Flow/Comfort | 7.7 |
| Ship Facilities | 8.4 |
| Ship: Decor/Furnishings | 8.3 |
| Ship: Fitness/Watersports Facilities | 7.2 |
| Cabins: Comfort/Facilities | 8.1 |
| Cabins: Software | 8.1 |
| Food: Dining Room/Cuisine | 8.0 |
| Food: Buffets/Informal Dining | 7.7 |
| Food: Quality of Ingredients | 8.0 |
| Service: Dining Room | 7.7 |
| Service: Bars/Lounges | 7.7 |
| Service: Cabins | 7.9 |
| Cruise: Entertainment/Lecture Program | 8.1 |
| Cruise: Hospitality Standard | 8.0 |
| OVERALL RATING | 119.5 |

**+** Like an exclusive private club. This small ship is good for groups and alumni or business meetings. Features three teakwood decks for strolling, and real wooden "steamer" deck chairs. Warm friendly ambiance. Wood-accented trim and fine furnishings, plush chairs and couches, and fresh flowers always. Good library. Fax machine in each cabin. Large cabins for ship size, and most are very comfortable. Bathrooms have clean, crisp colors. All cabins have unobstructed views. Excellent lecture program (in English). Best for those traveling individually, seeking destination-oriented cruises in highly sophisticated surroundings, with a small number of fellow travelers and an emphasis on learning and education. Fascinating itineraries. No announcements.

**–** No wrap-around outdoor promenade deck. The swimming pool is tiny—it's really a "dip" pool. Public room space is limited. The ship, being small, rolls in heavy seas.

**Dining** The dining room is charming, intimate, and very comfortable, with smart contemporary decor. The cuisine is international in style, and food is well prepared and nicely presented, although there is not a great deal of menu choice. Fine china and flatware.

**Other Comments** Rather like having the privileges of a private yacht, without the burden of ownership, this ship travels off the beaten path to take you in style and comfort to learn about the more unusual parts of the planet. Port taxes are included. Gratuities are extra.

# ms Aurora II ★★★★ +

***Principal Cruising Areas***
*Various (various)*
***Base Ports:** various*

| | | | |
|---|---|---|---|
| Cruise Line | *Classical Cruises* | | |
| Former Names | *Lady Sarah* | | |
| Gross Tonnage | *2,928* | | |
| Builder | *Flender Werft (Germany)* | | |
| Original Cost | *$35 million* | | |
| Christened By | *Ms Jeanne Buiter* | | |
| First Entered Service | *Feb 27, 1992* | | |
| Interior Design | *Giorgio Vafiadis* | | |
| Country of Registry | *Bahamas (C6KP7)* | | |
| Tel No | *130-5151* | Fax No | *130-5154* |
| Length (ft/m) | *269.6/82.2* | | |
| Beam (ft/m) | *45.9/14.0* | | |
| Draft (ft/m) | *10.9/3.3* | | |
| Engines/Propellers | *2 KHD-MWM diesels/2* | | |
| Decks | *4* | Crew | *59* |
| Pass. Capacity (basis 2) | *80* | (all berths) | *80* |
| Pass. Space Ratio (basis 2) | *36.6* | (all berths) | *36.6* |
| Officers | *Greek* | Dining Staff | *International* |
| Total Cabins | *44* | | |
| Size (sq ft/m) | *250-430/23-40* | Door Width | *24"* |
| Outside Cabins | *44* | Inside Cabins | *0* |
| Single Cabins | 6 | Supplement | *Fixed brochure rates* |
| Balcony Cabins | *0* | Wheelchair Cabins | *0* |
| Cabin Current | *110/220 AC* | | |
| Refrigerator | *All cabins* | | |
| Cabin TV | *Yes* | VCR | *Yes* |
| Dining Rooms | *1* | Sittings | *Open* |
| Elevators | *0* | Door Width | *n/a* |

| | | | |
|---|---|---|---|
| Casino | *No* | Slot Machines | *No* |
| Swimming Pools (outside) | *1* | (inside) | *0* |
| Whirlpools | *0* | Gymnasium | *No* |
| Sauna/Steam Rm | *No/No* | Massage | *No* |
| Self-Service Launderette | *No* | | |
| Movie Theater/Seats | *No* | | |
| Library | *Yes* | | |
| Children's Facilities | *No* | | |
| Watersports Facilities | *None* | | |
| Classification Society | *Germanischer Lloyd* | | |

| RATINGS | SCORE |
|---|---|
| Ship: Condition/Cleanliness | 8.6 |
| Ship: Space/Flow/Comfort | 7.7 |
| Ship Facilities | 8.4 |
| Ship: Decor/Furnishings | 8.3 |
| Ship: Fitness/Watersports Facilities | 7.2 |
| Cabins: Comfort/Facilities | 8.1 |
| Cabins: Software | 7.9 |
| Food: Dining Room/Cuisine | 8.0 |
| Food: Buffets/Informal Dining | 7.7 |
| Food: Quality of Ingredients | 8.0 |
| Service: Dining Room | 7.7 |
| Service: Bars/Lounges | 7.7 |
| Service: Cabins | 8.1 |
| Cruise: Entertainment/Lecture Program | 8.1 |
| Cruise: Hospitality Standard | 8.0 |
| OVERALL RATING | 119.5 |

**+** Small, smart-looking ship has a low, sleek profile and royal blue hull, and is designed for destination-intensive cruising. Features teakwood outdoor decks and real wooden "steamer" deck chairs. Personal yacht-styling is reminiscent of a private country club. The cabins are large, and superbly equipped, with fine woods, a writing desk, and even a fax machine. All cabins have unobstructed views. Fascinating itineraries. Fortunately, no announcements are made, so this is a nice, quiet ship. Smaller even than the Renaissance Cruises vessels, they have limited public spaces, yet are good for those who seek a destination-oriented cruise in new and highly sophisticated surroundings, with a small number of fellow travelers, albeit at a high price.

**–** No wrap-around outdoor promenade deck. The swimming pool is tiny—it's really a "dip" pool. Public room space is limited. The ship, being small, rolls in heavy seas.

**Dining** The dining room is charming, intimate, and very comfortable, with smart, contemporary decor. The cuisine is international in style, and food is well prepared and nicely presented, although there is not a great deal of menu choice. Fine china and flatware.

**Other Comments** Rather like having the privileges of a private yacht, without the burden of ownership. Port taxes are included. Gratuities are extra.

# ts Ausonia ★★★

***Principal Cruising Area***
*Europe (6-11 nights)*
***Base Port:*** *Genoa*

| | | | |
|---|---|---|---|
| Cruise Line | | | *Ausonia Cruises* |
| Former Names | | | *n/a* |
| Gross Tonnage | | | *12,368* |
| Builder | | | *Cantieri Riuniti dell' Adriatico (Italy)* |
| Original Cost | | | *n/a* |
| Christened By | | | *n/a* |
| First Entered Service | | | *Sep 23, 1957* |
| Interior Design | | | *n/a* |
| Country of Registry | | | *Italy (IBAX)* |
| Tel No | *115-0673* | Fax No | *115-0673* |
| Length (ft/m) | | | *522.5/159.26* |
| Beam (ft/m) | | | *69.8/21.29* |
| Draft (ft/m) | | | *21.4/6.54* |
| Engines/Propellers | | | *4 steam turbines/2* |
| Decks | *8* | Crew | *210* |
| Pass. Capacity (basis 2) | *506* | (all berths) | *808* |
| Pass. Space Ratio (basis 2) | *24.4* | (all berths) | *15.3* |
| Officers | *Italian* | Dining Staff | *Italian* |
| Total Cabins | *253* | | |
| Size | *n/a* | Door Width | *26"* |
| Outside Cabins | *154* | Inside Cabins | *99* |
| Single Cabins | *8* | Supplement | *100%* |
| Balcony Cabins | *0* | Wheelchair Cabins | *0* |
| Cabin Current | | | *220 AC* |
| Refrigerator | | | *No* |
| Cabin TV | | | *upper grade* |
| VCR | | | *No* |
| Dining Rooms | *2* | Sittings | *2* |

| | | | |
|---|---|---|---|
| Elevators | *1* | Door Width | *30"* |
| Casino | *No* | Slot Machines | *No* |
| Swimming Pools (outside) | *1* | (inside) | *0* |
| Whirlpools | *1* | Gymnasium | *No* |
| Sauna/Steam Rm | *Yes/No* | Massage | *Yes* |
| Self-Service Launderette | | | *No* |
| Movie Theater/Seats | | | *Yes/125* |
| Library | *No* | Children's Facilities | *No* |
| Watersports Facilities | | | *None* |
| Classification Society | | | *Lloyd's Register* |

| RATINGS | SCORE |
|---|---|
| Ship: Condition/Cleanliness | 7.7 |
| Ship: Space/Flow/Comfort | 7.2 |
| Ship: Decor/Furnishings | 7.3 |
| Ship: Fitness Facilities | 5.0 |
| Cabins: Comfort/Facilities | 6.3 |
| Cabins: Software | 6.4 |
| Food: Dining Room/Cuisine | 6.7 |
| Food: Buffets/Informal Dining | 6.1 |
| Food: Quality of Ingredients | 6.2 |
| Service: Dining Room | 6.3 |
| Service: Bars/Lounges | 6.3 |
| Service: Cabins | 6.7 |
| Cruise: Entertainment | 5.5 |
| Cruise: Activities Program | 5.7 |
| Cruise: Hospitality Standard | 6.3 |
| OVERALL RATING | 95.7 |

**+** Well maintained ship with classic, swept-back lines and profile. Quite clean and tidy. Good open deck and sunning space. Ship underwent much mechanical and galley upgrading in late 1990. Upgraded public areas are light and spacious. Ballroom is pleasantly decorated in blues and creams. Small, compact, yet reasonably comfortable, cabins were refurbished in 1989-90. All have private facilities; uppermost cabin grades have full bathtub, others have showers, while two new suites feature whirlpool baths. There are several family cabins.

**–** Passengers are very heavy smokers, and it's almost impossible to get away from it. Steep gangway in most ports.

**Dining** The dining rooms are set high up and have good ocean views, but they are extremely noisy. Friendly, efficient, and bubbly Italian service throughout. Good Continental food, with some excellent pasta, although sauces are very heavy. Midnight pizza parties are very popular. Poor selection of fruits and cheeses.

**Other Comments** This ship operates in four languages (announcements are long, loud, and continual) and offers regular Mediterranean cruise service in very comfortable surroundings, with Italian flair, but no finesse in either food or service.

# ms Ayvasovskiy ★

***Principal Cruising Area***

*Black Sea/Mediterranean (7 nights)*

***Base Ports:*** *Trieste*

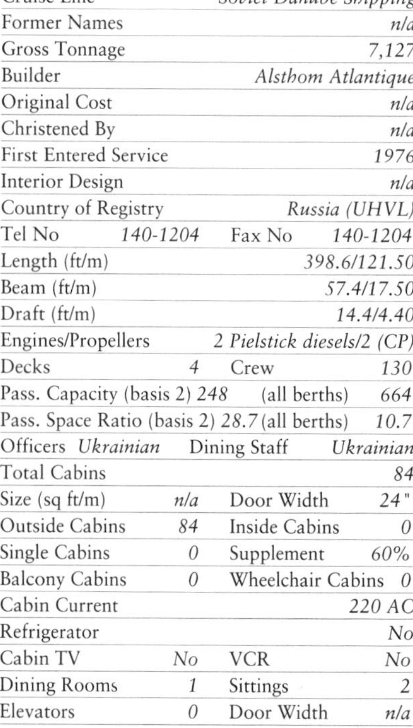

| | | | |
|---|---|---|---|
| Cruise Line | | | *Soviet Danube Shipping* |
| Former Names | | | *n/a* |
| Gross Tonnage | | | *7,127* |
| Builder | | | *Alsthom Atlantique* |
| Original Cost | | | *n/a* |
| Christened By | | | *n/a* |
| First Entered Service | | | *1976* |
| Interior Design | | | *n/a* |
| Country of Registry | | | *Russia (UHVL)* |
| Tel No | *140-1204* | Fax No | *140-1204* |
| Length (ft/m) | | | *398.6/121.50* |
| Beam (ft/m) | | | *57.4/17.50* |
| Draft (ft/m) | | | *14.4/4.40* |
| Engines/Propellers | | | *2 Pielstick diesels/2 (CP)* |
| Decks | *4* | Crew | *130* |
| Pass. Capacity (basis 2) | *248* | (all berths) | *664* |
| Pass. Space Ratio (basis 2) | *28.7* | (all berths) | *10.7* |
| Officers | *Ukrainian* | Dining Staff | *Ukrainian* |
| Total Cabins | | | *84* |
| Size (sq ft/m) | *n/a* | Door Width | *24"* |
| Outside Cabins | *84* | Inside Cabins | *0* |
| Single Cabins | *0* | Supplement | *60%* |
| Balcony Cabins | *0* | Wheelchair Cabins | *0* |
| Cabin Current | | | *220 AC* |
| Refrigerator | | | *No* |
| Cabin TV | *No* | VCR | *No* |
| Dining Rooms | *1* | Sittings | *2* |
| Elevators | *0* | Door Width | *n/a* |

| | | | |
|---|---|---|---|
| Casino | *No* | Slot Machines | *Yes* |
| Swimming Pools (outside) | *1* | (inside) | *1* |
| Whirlpools | *0* | Gymnasium | *No* |
| Sauna/Steam Rm | *Yes/No* | Massage | *No* |
| Self-Service Launderette | | | *No* |
| Movie Theater/Seats | | | *No* |
| Library | | | *No* |
| Children's Facilities | | | *No* |
| Watersports Facilities | | | *None* |
| Classification Society | | | *CIS* |

| RATINGS | SCORE |
|---|---|
| Ship: Condition/Cleanliness | 5.2 |
| Ship: Space/Flow/Comfort | 4.9 |
| Ship: Decor/Furnishings | 5.7 |
| Ship: Fitness Facilities | 4.0 |
| Cabins: Comfort/Facilities | 5.4 |
| Cabins: Software | 5.2 |
| Food: Dining Room/Cuisine | 5.2 |
| Food: Buffets/Informal Dining | 5.1 |
| Food: Quality of Ingredients | 5.3 |
| Service: Dining Room | 6.0 |
| Service: Bars/Lounges | 6.0 |
| Service: Cabins | 6.1 |
| Cruise: Entertainment | 4.2 |
| Cruise: Activities Program | 4.2 |
| Cruise: Hospitality Standard | 5.6 |
| OVERALL RATING | 78.1 |

**+** Attractive, well proportioned, small ship is purpose-built to provide two-day cruises between Izmail and Istanbul in conjunction with Danube river cruise on other specialized river vessels.

**–** Very small amount of open deck space. Only a limited amount of public room space. Steep gangway in most ports.

**Dining** Comfortable, almost attractive dining room has large picture windows. The food is barely adequate, with little choice. Poor bread, rolls, cheeses, and fruit selection. The service, however, is pleasant, but completely without finesse.

**Other Comments** Although the number of public rooms is limited, the ship provides a somewhat international ambiance, with passengers mainly from western and eastern European countries. If you don't expect elegance and finesse from this ship, you may be pleasantly surprised, especially for the time you spend aboard her. Chartered during the summer to UK-based Eurocruises for seven-night cruises. Port taxes, insurance, and gratuitites are extra.

# ms Azerbaydzhan ★★+

***Principal Cruising Areas***

*Various (various)*

***Base Ports:*** *London/Sydney*

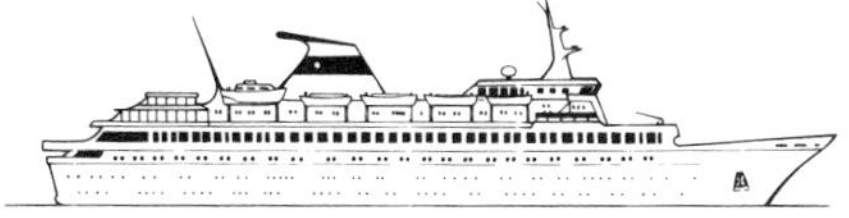

| | | | |
|---|---|---|---|
| Cruise Line | | | *CTC Cruise Lines* |
| Former Names | | | *n/a* |
| Gross Tonnage | | | *15,065* |
| Builder | | | *Wartsila (Finland)* |
| Original Cost | | | *$25 million* |
| Christened By | | | *n/a* |
| First Entered Service | | | *Jan 1976* |
| Interior Design | | | *Lloyd Werft* |
| Country of Registry | | | *Ukraine (UFZX)* |
| Tel No | *140-0740* | Fax No | *140-0740* |
| Length (ft/m) | | | *512.5/156.24* |
| Beam (ft/m) | | | *72.3/22.05* |
| Draft (ft/m) | | | *19.4/5.92* |
| Engines/Propellers | | | *2 Pielstick 18-cyl diesels/2 (CP)* |
| Decks | *8* | Crew | *240* |
| Pass. Capacity (basis 2) | *460* | (all berths) | *635* |
| Pass. Space Ratio (basis 2) | *32.7* | (all berths) | *23.7* |
| Officers | | | *Ukrainian* |
| Dining Staff | | | *European/Ukrainian* |
| Total Cabins | | | *230* |
| Size(sq ft/m) | *150-42/14-39.7* | Door Width | *25"* |
| Outside Cabins | *112* | Inside Cabins | *118* |
| Single Cabins | *0* | Supplement | *50%* |
| Balcony Cabins | *0* | Wheelchair Cabins | *0* |
| Cabin Current | | | *220 AC* |
| Refrigerator | | | *Boat deck cabins only* |
| Cabin TV | *Boat Deck only* | VCR | *No* |
| Dining Rooms | *2* | Sittings | *1* |

| | | | |
|---|---|---|---|
| Elevators | *1* | Door Width | *30"* |
| Casino | *Yes* | Slot Machines | *Yes* |
| Swimming Pools (outside) | *1* | (inside) | *0* |
| Whirlpools | *0* | Gymnasium | *Yes* |
| Sauna/Steam Rm | *Yes/No* | Massage | *Yes* |
| Self-Service Launderette | | | *Yes* |
| Movie Theater/Seats | | | *Yes/145* |
| Library | *Yes* | Children's Facilities | *Yes* |
| Watersports Facilities | | | *None* |
| Classification Society | | | *Ukraine Register of Shipping* |

| RATINGS | SCORE |
|---|---|
| Ship: Condition/Cleanliness | 6.0 |
| Ship: Space/Flow/Comfort | 6.1 |
| Ship: Decor/Furnishings | 6.0 |
| Ship: Fitness Facilities | 4.7 |
| Cabins: Comfort/Facilities | 6.1 |
| Cabins: Software | 6.3 |
| Food: Dining Room/Cuisine | 5.4 |
| Food: Buffets/Informal Dining | 5.0 |
| Food: Quality of Ingredients | 5.4 |
| Service: Dining Room | 6.5 |
| Service: Bars/Lounges | 7.1 |
| Service: Cabins | 7.2 |
| Cruise: Entertainment | 4.2 |
| Cruise: Activities Program | 5.6 |
| Cruise: Hospitality Standard | 6.5 |
| OVERALL RATING | 87.1 |

**+** Smart-looking ship with a squared funnel housing. Suites and deluxe cabins are large and very well furnished, with wood paneled walls and cabinetry. Other cabins are small, have clean lines, and are simply furnished, without much closet and drawer space. They are adequate and comfortable. Smart, but quite basic, the ship provides a civilized way to get to and from Australia (once each way each year). Good for the price-sensitive traveler. Good European itineraries.

**–** Many inside cabins. Has poor cabin insulation. Steep gangway in most ports. Inflexible staff need more hospitality training.

**Dining** Two rather plain, but cozy, dining rooms, (one is for smokers, the other for non-smokers). Attentive and friendly waitress service, but there's no real finesse. The cuisine is so-so, with limited choice, yet is well presented, and service comes with a smile.

**Other Comments** This ship has an informal, unpretentious ambiance. This ship, and CTC Cruises, will provide a good cruise experience for a modest price, principally for British and other European passengers. Has British (low-budget) entertainment, and Ukrainian crew show. Port taxes are included. Gratuities are extra.

# mv Berlin ★★★★+

***Principal Cruising Areas***

*Worldwide (various)*

***Base Port:*** *Bremerhaven*

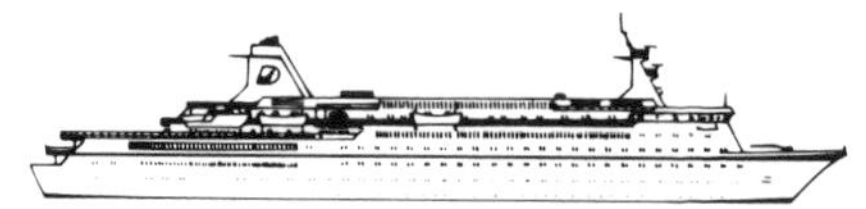

| | | | |
|---|---|---|---|
| Cruise Line | | | *Deilmann Reederei* |
| Former Names | | | *Princess Mahsuri* |
| Gross Tonnage | | | *9,570* |
| Builder | | | *Hawaldtswerke Deutsche Werft* |
| Original Cost | | | *n/a* |
| Christened By | | | *n/a* |
| First Entered Service | | | *Jun 9, 1980* |
| Interior Design | | | *HDW/Nobiskrug shipyard* |
| Country of Registry | | | *Germany (DLRC)* |
| Tel No | *112-0251* | Fax No | *112-0251* |
| Length (ft/m) | | | *457.0/139.30* |
| Beam (ft/m) | | | *57.5/17.52* |
| Draft (ft/m) | | | *15.7/4.80* |
| Engines/Propellers | | | *2 MAK 12-cyl diesels/2 (CP)* |
| Decks | *8* | Crew | *210* |
| Pass. Capacity (basis 2) | *422* | (all berths) | *448* |
| Pass. Space Ratio (basis 2) | *22.6* | (all berths) | *21.3* |
| Officers | *German* | Dining Staff | *German* |
| Total Cabins | | | *211* |
| Size (sq ft/m) | *93-192/8.6-17.8* | Door Width | *24"* |
| Outside Cabins | *158* | Inside Cabins | *53* |
| Single Cabins | *0* | Supplement | *Rates on request* |
| Balcony Cabins | *0* | Wheelchair Cabins | *0* |
| Cabin Current | | | *220 AC* |
| Refrigerator | | | *Promenade/Main Deck cabins only* |
| Cabin TV | *Yes* | VCR | *No* |
| Dining Rooms | *2* | Sittings | *2* |
| Elevators | *2* | Door Width | *30"* |

| | | | |
|---|---|---|---|
| Casino | *No* | Slot Machines | *No* |
| Swimming Pools (outside) | *1* | (inside) | *1* |
| Whirlpools | *0* | Gymnasium | *Yes* |
| Sauna/Steam Rm | *Yes/No* | Massage | *Yes* |
| Self-Service Launderette | | | *No* |
| Movie Theater/Seats | | | *Yes/330* |
| Library | | | *Yes* |
| Children's Facilities | | | *On request* |
| Watersports Facilities | | | *None* |
| Classification Society | | | *Germanischer Lloyd* |

| RATINGS | SCORE |
|---|---|
| Ship: Condition/Cleanliness | 8.2 |
| Ship: Space/Flow/Comfort | 7.9 |
| Ship: Decor/Furnishings | 8.0 |
| Ship: Fitness Facilities | 6.8 |
| Cabins: Comfort/Facilities | 7.8 |
| Cabins: Software | 7.8 |
| Food: Dining Room/Cuisine | 8.0 |
| Food: Buffets/Informal Dining | 8.1 |
| Food: Quality of Ingredients | 7.8 |
| Service: Dining Room | 7.9 |
| Service: Bars/Lounges | 7.8 |
| Service: Cabins | 7.7 |
| Cruise: Entertainment | 7.9 |
| Cruise: Activities Program | 7.8 |
| Cruise: Hospitality Standard | 8.1 |
| OVERALL RATING | 117.6 |

**+** Handsome contemporary ship, with crisp, clean, all-white lines and well balanced profile. Has an ice-strengthened hull. Star of the long-running German television show "Traumschiff" (Dream Ship). Very crisp and tidy throughout, she is luxuriously equipped with elegant, tasteful, though somewhat restful (dark), European decor and furnishings. Beautiful collection of original oil paintings from the personal collection of her owner, Peter Deilmann. Cabins are small, but very comfortable and well equipped, with just about everything you need. Bathrooms have shower units, no bathtubs. Intimate, highly personable atmosphere.

**–** Very small swimming pool.

**Dining** Lovely, comfortable dining room has big picture windows, and several tables for two. Attentive, professional, and correct European service with a smile. The food caters strictly to German tastes, with cream sauces accompanying entrees. Good selection of breads and cheeses.

**Other Comments** Continental passenger mix. Outstanding health spa treatments. This charming ship will provide a really deluxe, rather exclusive, destination-intensive cruise experience in elegant, intimate, and contemporary surroundings, for the discerning German-speaking passenger who doesn't need constant entertainment. Insurance and gratuities are included.

# ms Black Prince ★★★+

***Principal Cruising Areas***

*Canary Islands/Europe (14 nights)*

***Base Port:** Southampton*

| | | | |
|---|---|---|---|
| Cruise Line | | | *Fred Olsen Cruises* |
| Former Names | | | *n/a* |
| Gross Tonnage | | | *11,209* |
| Builder | | | *Fender Werft (Germany)* |
| Original Cost | | | *$20 million* |
| Christened By | | | *Lady Doris Denny* |
| First Entered Service | | | *1966* |
| Interior Design | | | *Platou Design* |
| Country of Registry | | | *Norway (LATE-2)* |
| Tel No | *131-3217* | Fax No | *131-3217* |
| Length (ft/m) | | | *470.4/143.40* |
| Beam (ft/m) | | | *66.6/20.30* |
| Draft (ft/m) | | | *20.0/6.10* |
| Engines/Propellers | | | *2 Pielstick 18-cyl diesels/2 (CP)* |
| Decks | *7* | Crew | *200* |
| Pass. Capacity (basis 2) | *446* | (all berths) | *517* |
| Pass. Space Ratio (basis 2) | *25.1* | (all berths) | *21.6* |
| Officers | *European* | Dining Staff | *Filipino/Thai* |
| Total Cabins | | | *238* |
| Size (sq ft/m) | *80-226/7.5-21* | Door Width | *26"* |
| Outside Cabins | *168* | Inside Cabins | *70* |
| Single Cabins | *30* | Supplement | *Fixed rates* |
| Balcony Cabins | *0* | Wheelchair Cabins | *2* |
| Cabin Current | | | *230 AC* |
| Refrigerator | | | *Selected cabins only* |
| Cabin TV | *No* | VCR | *No* |
| Dining Rooms | *2* | Sittings | *1* |
| Elevators | *2* | Door Width | *30"* |

| | | | |
|---|---|---|---|
| Casino | *Yes* | Slot Machines | *Yes* |
| Swimming Pools (outside) | *2* | (inside) | *0* |
| Whirlpools | *0* | Gymnasium | *Yes* |
| Sauna/Steam Rm | *Yes/No* | Massage | *Yes* |
| Self-Service Launderette | | | *No* |
| Movie Theater/Seats | | | *No* |
| Library | | | *Yes* |
| Children's Facilities | | | *No* |
| Watersports Facilities | | | *Aft marina pool* |
| Classification Society | | | *Det Norske Veritas* |

| RATINGS | SCORE |
|---|---|
| Ship: Condition/Cleanliness | 7.5 |
| Ship: Space/Flow/Comfort | 7.3 |
| Ship: Decor/Furnishings | 7.2 |
| Ship: Fitness Facilities | 6.0 |
| Cabins: Comfort/Facilities | 6.6 |
| Cabins: Software | 7.0 |
| Food: Dining Room/Cuisine | 7.0 |
| Food: Buffets/Informal Dining | 6.7 |
| Food: Quality of Ingredients | 7.0 |
| Service: Dining Room | 7.0 |
| Service: Bars/Lounges | 6.8 |
| Service: Cabins | 7.2 |
| Cruise: Entertainment | 7.3 |
| Cruise: Activities Program | 6.4 |
| Cruise: Hospitality Standard | 7.7 |
| OVERALL RATING | 104.7 |

**+** Well maintained, and run with family pride. Good indoor fitness center. Features a popular 60 ft. hydraulic "marina park" and free-float swimming pool surround that extends aft of the mother ship. Very homey ambiance, with much of the soft furnishings hand tailored on board. Outside suites are quite lovely. Other cabins are small, but well equipped, tastefully decorated, and quite comfortable. Large number of single cabins. Bi-level show lounge is pleasant.

**–** Two "sails" mounted topside serve no purpose and should be removed. It's hard to get away from smokers. Charge for room service.

**Dining** The two main dining rooms have big picture windows, and are very nicely decorated. There's also an informal, open-air buffet food area on the Marquee Deck. The food is generally of high quality, but there should be more menu choice, particularly at lunch, which is almost always buffet-style (every day is shrimp!). Good service, but communication with the Filipino waiters can prove frustrating.

**Other Comments** Solidly-built, white ship has a somewhat ungainly but likeable profile. This ship combines traditional Fred Olsen cruise values with a contemporary, yet intimate and friendly, ship, and lots of repeat passengers who wouldn't dream of trying another ship. Well suited to the informal British market. Currency: U.K. sterling (£). Gratuities are extra.

# ms Bremen ★★★★+

***Principal Cruising Areas***

*Worldwide expedition cruises (various)*

***Base Port:*** *Bremerhaven*

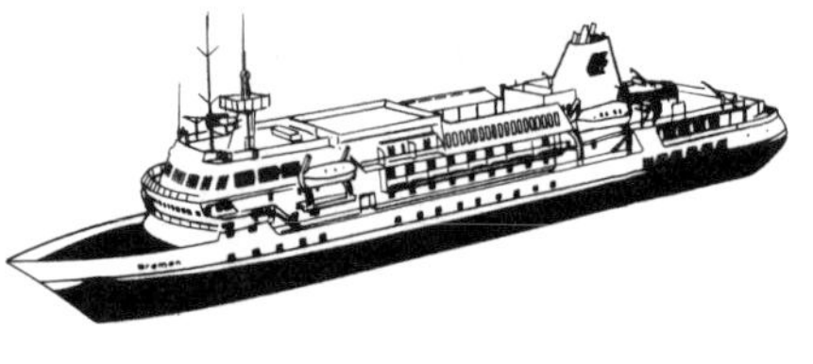

| | | | |
|---|---|---|---|
| Cruise Line | *Hapag-Lloyd Tours/Hanseatic Tours* | | |
| Former Names | *Frontier Spirit* | | |
| Gross Tonnage | *6,752* | | |
| Builder | *Mitsubishi Heavy Industries (Japan)* | | |
| Original Cost | *$42 million* | | |
| Christened By | *Kaoru Kanetaka/Mrs Wedemeier* | | |
| First Entered Service | *Nov 6, 1990/Nov 20, 1993* | | |
| Interior Design | *Wilfried Kohnemann* | | |
| Country of Registry | *Bahamas (C6JC3)* | | |
| Tel No | *110-3404* | Fax No | *110-3405* |
| Length (ft/m) | *365.8/111.51* | | |
| Beam (ft/m) | *55.7/17.00* | | |
| Draft (ft/m) | *15.7/4.80* | | |
| Engines/Propellers | *2 Mitsubishi 8-cyl diesels/2 (CP)* | | |
| Decks | *6* | Crew | *94* |
| Pass. Capacity (basis 2) | *164* | (all berths) | *184* |
| Pass. Space Ratio (basis 2) | *41.1* | (all berths) | *36.6* |
| Officers | *European* | Dining Staff | *Filipino* |
| Total Cabins | *82* | | |
| Size (sq ft/m) | *175-322/16.2-30* | Door Width | *26"* |
| Outside Cabins | *82* | Inside Cabins | *0* |
| Single Cabins | *0* | Supplement | *On request* |
| Balcony Cabins | *18* | Wheelchair Cabins | *2* |
| Cabin Current | *1* | | *10/220 AC* |
| Refrigerator | *No* | | |
| Cabin TV | *Yes* | VCR | *Yes* |
| Dining Room | *1 (open seating)* | | |
| Elevators | *2* | Door Width | *31"* |

| | | | |
|---|---|---|---|
| Casino | *No* | Slot Machines | *No* |
| Swimming Pools (outside) | *1* | (inside) | *0* |
| Whirlpools | *0* | Gymnasium | *Yes* |
| Sauna/Steam Rm | *Yes/No* | Massage | *No* |
| Self-Service Launderette | *Yes* | | |
| Lecture/Film Room | *Yes (seats 164)* | | |
| Library | *Yes* | | |
| Zodiacs | *12* | Helicopter Pad | *Yes* |
| Watersports Facilities | *None* | | |
| Classification Society | *Lloyd's Register* | | |

| RATINGS | SCORE |
|---|---|
| Ship: Condition/Cleanliness | 8.6 |
| Ship: Space/Flow/Comfort | 8.2 |
| Ship: Expedition Equipment | 8.5 |
| Ship: Decor/Furnishings | 8.3 |
| Cabins: Comfort/Facilities | 8.2 |
| Cabins: Software | 8.1 |
| Food: Dining Room/Cuisine | 8.1 |
| Food: Buffets/Informal Dining | 7.8 |
| Food: Quality of Ingredients | 8.0 |
| Service: Dining Room | 8.0 |
| Service: Bars/Lounges | 8.2 |
| Service: Cabins | 8.0 |
| Cruise: Itineraries/Operations | 8.5 |
| Cruise: Lecture Program | 8.4 |
| Cruise: Hospitality Standard | 8.2 |
| OVERALL RATING | 123.1 |

**+** This purpose-built expedition cruise vessel (ex-*Frontier Spirit*) has a handsome, contemporary profile and the latest high-tech equipment. Its wide beam provides great stability, and the long cruising range and ice-hardened hull gives access to the most remote destinations. Zero-discharge and highest ice classification. All equipment for in-depth marine and shore excursions provided. The all-outside cabins are spacious and very well equipped, each with a wall clock. Some also have a small balcony—a first on an expedition cruise vessel. Fine, well-planned destination-intensive itineraries, and good documentation and port information. Soft drinks in refrigerators are replenished daily, at no charge.

**–** Steep gangway. The sauna is tiny. Cabins don't have much drawer space.

**Dining** The dining room is quite charming, with elegant, sophisticated decor, and has big picture windows. The food is excellent, with high quality ingredients, although it is highly salted. Good choice of breads, pastries, cheeses, and fruits. The service is very good, with bi-lingual (German- and English-speaking) waiters and waitresses immaculately dressed.

**Other Comments** One of the most comfortable and practical expedition cruise vessels. It offers an outstanding learning and expedition experience (but not as luxurious as the *Hanseatic*). Catering principally to German speakers. Insurance, port taxes, and gratuities are included.

# ss Britanis ★★★

***Principal Cruising Area***
*Caribbean (7 nights)*
***Base Port:** Miami*

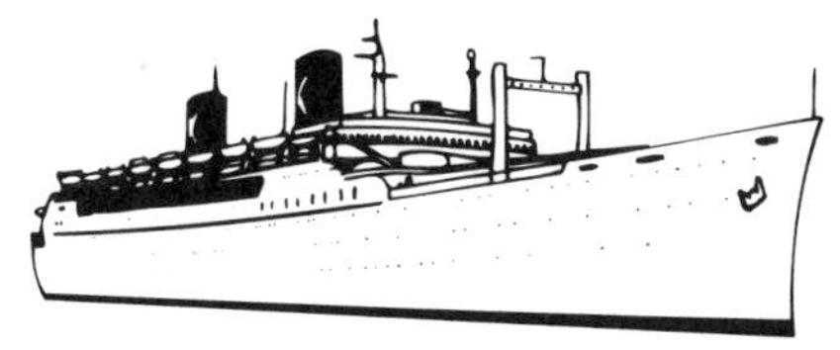

| | | | |
|---|---|---|---|
| Cruise Line | | | *Fantasy Cruises* |
| Former Names | | | *Monterey/Matsonia/Lurline* |
| Gross Tonnage | | | *26,141* |
| Builder | | | *Bethlehem Shipbuilders (USA)* |
| Original Cost | | | *$8 million* |
| Christened By | | | *n/a* |
| First Entered Service | | | *May 12, 1932/Feb 21, 1971* |
| Interior Design | | | *n/a* |
| Country of Registry | | | *Panama (HPEN)* |
| Tel No | *133-2531* | Fax No | *n/a* |
| Length (ft/m) | | | *641.7/195.60* |
| Beam (ft/m) | | | *79.3/24.19* |
| Draft (ft/m) | | | *28.2/8.60* |
| Engines | | | *4 Bethlehem steam turbines* |
| Propellers | | | *2 (FP)* |
| Passenger Decks | *8* | Number of Crew | *525* |
| Pass. Capacity (basis 2) | *926* | (all berths) | *960* |
| Pass. Space Ratio (basis 2) | *28.2* | (all berths) | *27.2* |
| Officers | *Greek* | Dining Staff | *International* |
| Total Cabins | | | *463* |
| Size (sq ft/m) | *n/a* | Door Width | *26-30"* |
| Outside Cabins | *159* | Inside Cabins | *304* |
| Single Cabins | *0* | Supplement | *50%* |
| Private Balcony Cabins | | | *0* |
| Wheelchair Accessible Cabin | | | *0* |
| Cabin Current | *110 AC/220 DC* | Refrigerator | *No* |
| Cabin TV | *No* | VCR | *No* |
| Dining Rooms | *2* | Seatings | *2* |

| | | | |
|---|---|---|---|
| Elevators | *3* | Door Width | *31"* |
| Casino | *Yes* | Slot Machines | *Yes* |
| Swimming Pools (outside) | *1* | (inside) | *0* |
| Whirlpools | *0* | Gymnasium | *Yes* |
| Sauna/Steam Rm | *Yes/No* | Massage | *Yes* |
| Self-Service Launderette | | | *No* |
| Cinema/Theater | *Yes/208* | Library | *Yes* |
| Children's Facilities/Playroom | | | *No* |
| Watersports Facilities | | | *None* |
| Classification Society | | | *American Bureau* |

| RATINGS | SCORE |
|---|---|
| Ship: Condition/Cleanliness | 6.4 |
| Ship: Space/Flow/Comfort | 6.6 |
| Ship: Decor/Furnishings | 6.5 |
| Ship: Fitness Facilities | 5.1 |
| Cabins: Comfort/Facilities | 6.2 |
| Cabins: Software | 6.3 |
| Food: Dining Room/Cuisine | 6.6 |
| Food: Buffets/Informal Dining | 6.1 |
| Food: Quality of Ingredients | 6.6 |
| Service: Dining Room | 7.1 |
| Service: Bars/Lounges | 6.8 |
| Service: Cabins | 6.9 |
| Cruise: Entertainment | 7.1 |
| Cruise: Activities Program | 6.7 |
| Cruise: Hospitality Standard | 7.1 |
| OVERALL RATING | 98.1 |

**+** Very solid, well-constructed ship that has tremendous charm and character. She is extremely well maintained, and, like a good wine, seems to get better with age. Lots of good woods and brass throughout. The public rooms have high ceilings, and are spacious, even a little majestic. Cabins are mostly inside, but are quite large and comfortable, even if everything doesn't work all the time (ships of this vintage always have plenty of idiosyncracies).

**–** She is now an old lady, and public rooms are always crowded when full. Interior stairways are quite dark and somber.

**Dining** The dining room is attractive, even though it is located on a lower deck. The food and menu choice are both far better than you might expect, and the buffet spreads are excellent, particularly considering the price. Limited selection of breads, pastries, cheeses, and fruits.

**Other Comments** This former vintage ocean liner celebrated an incredible 60th birthday in 1992. She has a classic profile, and is one of only a few ships today to feature two funnels. Attentive service from a staff who are eager to please, but there's no finesse. This ship offers tremendous value for money, and delivers far more than you would expect. A fine first cruise experience for those wanting to cruise on a limited budget in worn, yet tidy and welcoming, surroundings. I expect her to be retired by 1997.

# mv Caledonian Star ★★★+

***Principal Cruising Areas***

*Worldwide expedition cruises (various)*

***Base Port:*** *various*

| | | | |
|---|---|---|---|
| Cruise Line | *Noble Caledonia/Special Expeditions* | | |
| Former Names | *North Star/Marburg/Lindmar* | | |
| Gross Tonnage | *3,095* | | |
| Builder | *A.G. Weser Seebeckwerft (Germany)* | | |
| Original Cost | *n/a* | | |
| Christened By | *Ms Barbro Svensson* | | |
| First Entered Service | *1966/1984* | | |
| Interior Design | *Robert Tillberg* | | |
| Country of Registry | *Bahamas (C6BE4)* | | |
| Tel No | *110-4706* | Fax No | *110-4766* |
| Length (ft/m) | *292.6/89.20* | | |
| Beam (ft/m) | *45.9/14.00* | | |
| Draft (ft//m) | *20.3/6.20* | | |
| Engines/Propellers | *2 MAK 8-cyl diesels/1* | | |
| Decks | *6* | Crew | *59* |
| Pass. Capacity (basis 2) | *144* | (all berths) | *177* |
| Pass. Space Ratio (basis 2) | *21.4* | (all berths) | *17.4* |
| Officers | *Scandinavian* | Dining Staff | *International* |
| Total Cabins | *68* | | |
| Size (sq ft/m) | *192-269/17.8-25* | Door Width | *24"* |
| Outside Cabins | *68* | Inside Cabins | *0* |
| Single Cabins | *2* | Supplement | *On request* |
| Balcony Cabins | *0* | Wheelchair Cabins | *0* |
| Cabin Current | *110/220 AC* | Refrigerator | *All cabins* |
| Cabin TV | *Yes* | VCR | *No* |
| Dining Rooms | *1 (open sitting)* | | |
| Elevators | *0* | Door Width | *n/a* |
| Casino | *Yes* | Slot Machines | *Yes* |

| | | | |
|---|---|---|---|
| Swimming Pools (outside) | *1* | | |
| Whirlpools | *0* | Gymnasium | *No* |
| Sauna/Steam Rm | *No/No* | Massage | *No* |
| Self-Service Launderette | *No* | | |
| Lecture/Film Room | *No* | | |
| Library | *Yes* | | |
| Zodiacs | *4* | | |
| Helicopter Pad | *No* | | |
| Watersports Facilities | *None* | | |
| Classification Society | *Det Norske Veritas* | | |

| RATINGS | SCORE |
|---|---|
| Ship: Condition/Cleanliness | 7.2 |
| Ship: Space/Flow/Comfort | 5.6 |
| Ship: Expedition Equipment | 7.1 |
| Ship: Decor/Furnishings | 7.0 |
| Cabins: Comfort/Facilities | 5.8 |
| Cabins: Software | 6.0 |
| Food: Dining Room/Cuisine | 7.4 |
| Food: Buffets/Informal Dining | 6.7 |
| Food: Quality of Ingredients | 7.0 |
| Service: Dining Room | 7.4 |
| Service: Bars/Lounges | 7.5 |
| Service: Cabins | 7.6 |
| Cruise: Itineraries/Operations | 7.5 |
| Cruise: Lecture Program | 7.6 |
| Cruise: Hospitality Standard | 7.5 |
| OVERALL RATING | 104.9 |

**+** Reasonably handsome ship is extremely tidy and well maintained. Open bridge policy. Warm, intimate ambiance. Good range of public rooms for ship size. All-outside cabins are compact but comfortable, and have minibar-refrigerator, VCR (with educational videos), and good closet and drawer space. Homey and casual atmosphere. Comfortable and unpretentious throughout, with casual dress code. Carries several zodiac landing craft for in-depth excursions, as well as an enclosed, contemporary shore tender. Fine lecture room/library. Excellent lecturers on every cruise make this a real life-enrichment and learning experience, with an intellectual clientele and never a hint of participation or deck games.

**–** Interior stairways are a little steep. Exterior stairway to zodiac embarkation point is steep. Noise from the diesel engines is irksome.

**Dining** The dining room is small but quite charming, but the chairs are small. The cuisine is European in style (slanted towards British tastes), with high quality, very fresh ingredients, but not a lot of menu choice. Attentive, friendly service.

**Other Comments** This very casual, comfortable ship provides a well tuned destination-intensive, soft expedition cruise experience, at a very reasonable price, and attracts a lot of loyal repeat passengers, most of whom are British.

# tes Canberra ★★★+

***Principal Cruising Area***
*Europe (14 nights)*
***Base Port:*** *Southampton*

| | | | |
|---|---|---|---|
| Cruise Line | | | *P&O Cruises* |
| Former Names | | | *n/a* |
| Gross Tonnage | | | *44,807* |
| Builder | | | *Harland & Wolff (UK)* |
| Original Cost | | | *£17,021,000* |
| Christened By | | | *Dame Pattie Menzies, GBE* |
| First Entered Service | | | *Jun 2, 1961* |
| Interior Design | | | *Sir High Casson/ John Wright/Barbara Oakley* |
| Country of Registry | | | *Great Britain (GBVC)* |
| Tel No | *144-0205* | Fax No | *144-0205* |
| Length (ft/m) | | | *818.5/249.49* |
| Beam (ft/m) | | | *102.5/31.25* |
| Draft (ft/m) | | | *32.2/9.84* |
| Engines/Propellers | | | *2/2* |
| Decks | *10* | Crew | *860* |
| Pass. Capacity (basis 2) | *1,399* | (all berths) | *1,641* |
| Pass. Space Ratio (basis 2) | *32.0* | (all berths) | *27.3* |
| Officers | *British* | Dining Staff | *British/Goan* |
| Total Cabins | | | *780 (236 without facilities)* |
| Size (sq ft/m) | *63-525/5.8-48.7* | Door Width | *26"* |
| Outside Cabins | *462* | Inside Cabins | *318* |
| Single Cabins | *161* | Supplement | *Fixed rates* |
| Balcony Cabins | *0* | Wheelchair Cabins | *0* |
| Cabin Current | | | *230 AC* |
| Refrigerator | | | *Cat. AA/AB/AC/AD* |
| Cabin TV | *Yes (upper grade)* | VCR | *No* |
| Dining Rooms | *2* | Sittings | *2* |

| | | | |
|---|---|---|---|
| Elevators | *6* | Door Width | *40"* |
| Casino | *Yes* | Slot Machines | *Yes* |
| Swimming Pools (outside) | *3* | (inside) | *0* |
| Whirlpools | *0* | Gymnasium | *Yes* |
| Sauna/Steam Rm | *No/No* | Massage | *Yes* |
| Self-Service Launderette | | | *Yes* |
| Movie Theater/Seats | | | *Yes/460* |
| Library | *Yes* | Children's Facilities | *Yes* |
| Watersports Facilities | | | *None* |
| Classification Society | | | *Lloyd's Register* |

| RATINGS | SCORE |
|---|---|
| Ship: Condition/Cleanliness | 7.0 |
| Ship: Space/Flow/Comfort | 7.2 |
| Ship: Decor/Furnishings | 7.1 |
| Ship: Fitness Facilities | 6.5 |
| Cabins: Comfort/Facilities | 6.5 |
| Cabins: Software | 6.6 |
| Food: Dining Room/Cuisine | 6.6 |
| Food: Buffets/Informal Dining | 6.0 |
| Food: Quality of Ingredients | 6.6 |
| Service: Dining Room | 7.3 |
| Service: Bars/Lounges | 7.5 |
| Service: Cabins | 7.4 |
| Cruise: Entertainment | 7.6 |
| Cruise: Activities Program | 7.1 |
| Cruise: Hospitality Standard | 7.6 |
| OVERALL RATING | 104.6 |

**+** Well maintained ship has good open deck and sunning space, including expansive tiered open space around the forward swimming pool, and British-style canvas deck chairs. Popular favorites are the Crow's Nest Bar and Cricketer's Club. Lots of good wood paneling throughout. Luxury suites are superb. Wide range and variety of other cabins. An excellent ship for families. Good cabin soundproofing. Efficient, courteous service from Goan stewards.

**–** Expect long lines for shore tenders, buffets, and disembarkation. Some cabins share nearby bathroom facilities. Cabins on B Deck have obstructed views. Too many repetitive announcements and too many smokers.

**Dining** The two dining rooms (Atlantic is huge, Pacific smaller) provide excellent service by Goan waiters. Senior officers also host tables each night. The cuisine is decidedly British and "Colonial" in style: basic, but hearty; well cooked meats, excellent curries, plenty of fish, and desserts, but a lack of lobster, shrimp and pasta. Poor selection of breads. No midnight buffets.

**Other Comments** Often dubbed the "great white whale," the ship has good sea manners and sixties styling, with midships bridge and twin aft funnels. Probably due for retirement soon. Very comfortable, though not elegant, surroundings at an affordable price and with every stratum of society around you. Insurance and gratuities are extra.

# ms Celebration ★★★★

***Principal Cruising Area***

*Caribbean (7 nights year-round)*

***Base Port:*** *Miami (Saturday)*

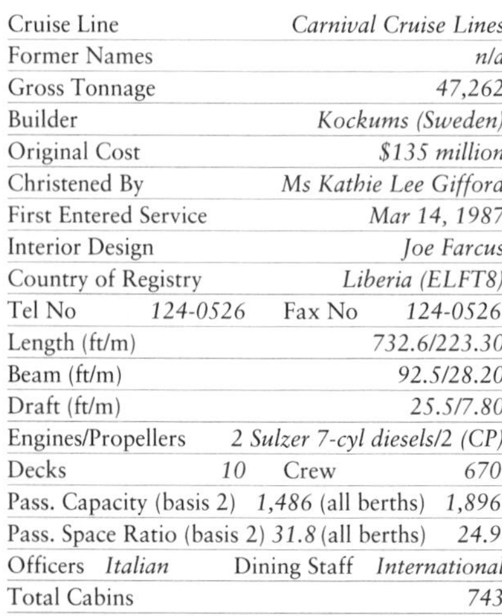

| | | | |
|---|---|---|---|
| Cruise Line | | | *Carnival Cruise Lines* |
| Former Names | | | *n/a* |
| Gross Tonnage | | | *47,262* |
| Builder | | | *Kockums (Sweden)* |
| Original Cost | | | *$135 million* |
| Christened By | | | *Ms Kathie Lee Gifford* |
| First Entered Service | | | *Mar 14, 1987* |
| Interior Design | | | *Joe Farcus* |
| Country of Registry | | | *Liberia (ELFT8)* |
| Tel No | *124-0526* | Fax No | *124-0526* |
| Length (ft/m) | | | *732.6/223.30* |
| Beam (ft/m) | | | *92.5/28.20* |
| Draft (ft/m) | | | *25.5/7.80* |
| Engines/Propellers | | | *2 Sulzer 7-cyl diesels/2 (CP)* |
| Decks | *10* | Crew | *670* |
| Pass. Capacity (basis 2) | *1,486* | (all berths) | *1,896* |
| Pass. Space Ratio (basis 2) | *31.8* | (all berths) | *24.9* |
| Officers | *Italian* | Dining Staff | *International* |
| Total Cabins | | | *743* |
| Size (sq ft/m) | *185/17.1* | Door Width | *30"* |
| Outside Cabins | *453* | Inside Cabins | *290* |
| Single Cabins | | | *0* |
| Supplement | | | *50/100%* |
| Balcony Cabins | *10* | Wheelchair Cabins | *14* |
| Cabin Current | | | *110 AC* |
| Refrigerator | | | *Category 12 only* |
| Cabin TV | *Yes* | VCR | *No* |
| Dining Rooms | *2* | Sittings | *2* |

| | | | |
|---|---|---|---|
| Elevators | *8* | Door Width | *36"* |
| Casino | *Yes* | Slot Machines | *Yes* |
| Swimming Pools (outside) | *3* | (inside) | *0* |
| Whirlpools | *2* | Gymnasium | *Yes* |
| Sauna/Steam Rm | *Yes/No* | Massage | *Yes* |
| Self-Service Launderette | | | *Yes* |
| Movie Theater/Seats | | | *No* |
| Library | *Yes* | Children's Facilities | *Yes* |
| Watersports Facilities | | | *None* |
| Classification Society | | | *Lloyd's Register* |

| RATINGS | SCORE |
|---|---|
| Ship: Condition/Cleanliness | 7.8 |
| Ship: Space/Flow/Comfort | 7.6 |
| Ship: Decor/Furnishings | 6.4 |
| Ship: Fitness Facilities | 7.8 |
| Cabins: Comfort/Facilities | 7.6 |
| Cabins: Software | 7.4 |
| Food: Dining Room/Cuisine | 6.7 |
| Food: Buffets/Informal Dining | 6.4 |
| Food: Quality of Ingredients | 5.3 |
| Service: Dining Room | 7.0 |
| Service: Bars/Lounges | 7.2 |
| Service: Cabins | 6.4 |
| Cruise: Entertainment | 8.0 |
| Cruise: Activities Program | 7.8 |
| Cruise: Hospitality Standard | 6.3 |
| OVERALL RATING | 105.7 |

**+** Busy, but good passenger flow. Double-width indoor promenades and good selection of public rooms. Superb nautically-themed decor in Wheelhouse Bar-Grill. There's even a brick sidewalk and New Orleans-themed decor throughout the public rooms. Cabins, most of which are identical, are of generous proportions, very comfortable, and well equipped. Especially good are ten suites with private balconies on Veranda Deck. Huge, active casino. Party atmosphere. Wide range of entertainment and activities. Excellent for families with children.

**–** The swimming pools are small. Expect long lines for embarkation, disembarkation, buffets, and shore tenders. Colorful, stimulating artworks. Dining rooms are cramped and noisy. Disappointing buffets. Nowhere to go for peace and quiet. Too many annoying announcements.

**Dining** The two dining rooms are very cramped when full, and extremely noisy. Don't even think about this ship if you like good food. The food is quantity, not quality, and the line doesn't spend much on its food product.

**Other Comments** Flamboyant interior decor in public rooms is stimulating, not restful, except for the beautiful (and unused) Admiral's Library, the only quiet room aboard. This ship offers dazzle and sizzle for the whole family, and provides a good choice for a first cruise, if you like lots of people, lots of noise, and lively action. Insurance and gratuities are extra.

# ms Century

***Principal Cruising Area***
*Caribbean (7 nights)*
***Base Port:*** *Ft. Lauderdale*

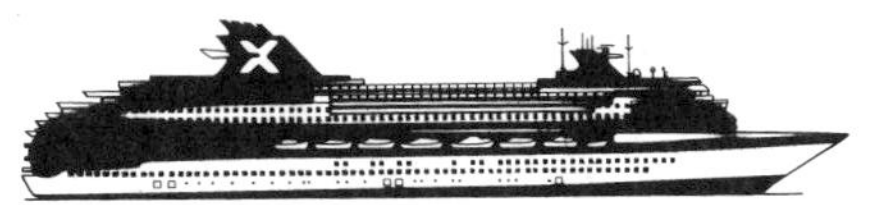

| | | | |
|---|---|---|---|
| Cruise Line | | | *Celebrity Cruises* |
| Former Names | | | *n/a* |
| Gross Tonnage | | | *70,000* |
| Builder | | | *Meyer Werft (Germany)* |
| Original Cost | | | *$320 million* |
| Christened By | | | *n/a* |
| First Entered Service | | | *Dec 1995* |
| Interior Design | | | *Katzourakis/McNeece* |
| Country of Registry | | | *Liberia* |
| Tel No | *n/a* | Fax No | *n/a* |
| Length (ft/m) | | | *807.1/246.00* |
| Beam (ft/m) | | | *105.6/32.20* |
| Draft (ft/m) | | | *24.6/7.50* |
| Engines/Propellers | | | *4 MAN-B&W diesels/2 (CP)* |
| Decks | *10* | Crew | *843* |
| Pass. Capacity (basis 2) | *1,750* | (all berths) | *1,750* |
| Pass. Space Ratio (basis 2) | *40.0* | (all berths) | *40.0* |
| Officers | *Greek* | Dining Staff | *International* |
| Total Cabins | | | *875* |
| Size (sq ft/m) | | | *170-1,200/15.7-111.5* |
| Door Width | | | *24"* |
| Outside Cabins | *571* | Inside Cabins | *304* |
| Single Cabins | *0* | Private Balcony Cabins | *61* |
| Wheelchair Cabins | | | *8* |
| Cabin TV | *Yes* | VCR | *Upper grades* |
| Dining Rooms | *2* | Sittings | *2* |
| Elevators | *9* | Door Width | *36"* |
| Cabin Current | | | *110/220 AC* |

| | | | |
|---|---|---|---|
| Casino | *Yes* | Slot Machines | *Yes* |
| Swimming Pools (outside) | *2* | (inside) | *1 hydropool (under a magrodome cover)* |
| Whirlpools | *4* | Gymnasium | *Yes* |
| Sauna/Steam Rm | *Yes/Yes* | Massage | *Yes* |
| Self-Service Launderette | | | *No* |
| Cinema/Theater | *Yes* | Library | *Yes* |
| Children's Facilities/Playroom | | | *Yes* |
| Watersports Facilities | | | *None* |
| Classification Society | | | *Lloyd's Register* |

| RATINGS | SCORE |
|---|---|
| Ship: Condition/Cleanliness | NYR |
| Ship: Space/Flow/Comfort | NYR |
| Ship: Decor/Furnishings | NYR |
| Ship: Fitness Facilities | NYR |
| Cabins: Comfort/Facilities | NYR |
| Cabins: Software | NYR |
| Food: Dining Room/Cuisine | NYR |
| Food: Buffets/Informal Dining | NYR |
| Food: Quality of Ingredients | NYR |
| Service: Dining Room | NYR |
| Service: Bars/Lounges | NYR |
| Service: Cabins | NYR |
| Cruise: Entertainment | NYR |
| Cruise: Activities Program | NYR |
| Cruise: Hospitality Standard | NYR |

*NYR = Not Yet Rated*

**+** This ship, looking like a larger version of *Horizon/Zenith*, is well balanced and has the distinctive Celebrity Cruises "X" funnel. Features a two-level, 1,000-seat showlounge/theater, three-deck-high main foyer, 4.5 acres of open deck space, and a stunning array of other public rooms. Outstanding health spa, set forward and high, has huge panoramic windows. Wide passageways provide plenty of indoor space. Wide variety of cabin types includes 18 family cabins. Has two finely decorated presidential suites of 1,200 sq. ft. located mid-ships in the most desirable position. All suites will feature butler service and in-cabin dining. All cabins have personal safe, mini-bar, refrigerator, and hairdryer, and are well equipped and decorated.

**–** Because she is a large ship, expect long lines for embarkation, disembarkation, shore excursions, and informal buffet meals, although *Celebrity* will do its best to minimize discomfort.

**Dining** Two-level dining room, each level with its own galley, as well as a bi-level lido cafe with well-designed serving lines. An in-suite dining alternative (for all meals, including dinner) will be featured for the two presidential and 48 century suites. Celebrity Cruises has established an enviable reputation for fine dining on its fleet, and this ship will continue the tradition.

**Other Comments** This latest and largest ship for Celebrity Cruises is expected to provide the best of features for its passengers. It will take over the itinerary of the *Zenith*.

# mts City of Rhodos ★

***Principal Cruising Area***

*Aegean (3/4 nights)*

***Base Port:** Piraeus (Fri/Mon)*

| | | | |
|---|---|---|---|
| Cruise Line | | | *Cycladic Cruises* |
| Former Names | | | *33 Orientales* |
| Gross Tonnage | | | *6,497* |
| Builder | | | *Society Espanola de Construciones Navale* |
| Original Cost | | | *n/a* |
| Christened By | | | *n/a* |
| First Entered Service | | | *1966* |
| Interior Design | | | *n/a* |
| Country of Registry | | | *Greece (SYXO)* |
| Tel No | *113-3131* | Fax No | *113-3131* |
| Length (ft/m) | | | *427.5/130.31* |
| Beam (ft/m) | | | *56.7/17.30* |
| Draft (ft/m) | | | *13.8/4.21* |
| Engines/Propellers | | | *2 B&W 10-cyl diesels/2 (FP)* |
| Decks | *5* | Crew | *160* |
| Pass. Capacity (basis 2) | *416* | (all berths) | *503* |
| Pass. Space Ratio (basis 2) | *15.6* | (all berths) | *12.9* |
| Officers | *Greek* | Dining Staff | *Greek* |
| Total Cabins | | | *208* |
| Size (sq ft/m) | *n/a* | Door Width | *22"* |
| Outside Cabins | *144* | Inside Cabins | *64* |
| Single Cabins | *0* | Supplement | *100%* |
| Balcony Cabins | *0* | Wheelchair Cabins | *0* |
| Cabin Current | | | *220 AC* |
| Refrigerator | | | *No* |
| Cabin TV | *No* | VCR | *No* |
| Dining Rooms | *1* | Sittings | *2* |
| Elevators | *0* | Door Width | *n/a* |

| | | | |
|---|---|---|---|
| Casino | *No* | Slot Machines | *No* |
| Swimming Pools (outside) | *1* | (inside) | *0* |
| Whirlpools | *0* | Gymnasium | *No* |
| Sauna/Steam Rm | *No/No* | Massage | *No* |
| Self-Service Launderette | | | *No* |
| Movie Theater/Seats | | | *No* |
| Library | | | *No* |
| Children's Facilities | | | *No* |
| Watersports Facilities | | | *None* |
| Classification Society | | | *American Bur. of Shipping* |

| RATINGS | SCORE |
|---|---|
| Ship: Condition/Cleanliness | 5.6 |
| Ship: Space/Flow/Comfort | 4.4 |
| Ship: Decor/Furnishings | 6.0 |
| Ship: Fitness Facilities | 3.0 |
| Cabins: Comfort/Facilities | 5.6 |
| Cabins: Software | 5.8 |
| Food: Dining Room/Cuisine | 5.8 |
| Food: Buffets/Informal Dining | 5.3 |
| Food: Quality of Ingredients | 5.6 |
| Service: Dining Room | 6.1 |
| Service: Bars/Lounges | 6.0 |
| Service: Cabins | 6.2 |
| Cruise: Entertainment | 4.6 |
| Cruise: Activities Program | 4.8 |
| Cruise: Hospitality Standard | 5.0 |
| OVERALL RATING | 79.8 |

**+** The public rooms are aft, away from the cabins, so noise in cabins is minimalized. Long, unattractive profile (this ship was rebuilt from former Argentinean coastal ferry), but it's alright for the passenger who wants a low-grade cruise experience.

**–** Very high-density vessel—cramped even when it's not full. Only two main public rooms plus a dining room. Small swimming pool, and not much open deck space for sunning. The ship's decor is well worn, unclean, and needs more attention. The cabins are small and barely adequate, except for the suites on Andros Deck. Too many announcements. Steep gangway in most ports.

**Dining** The dining room is mildly attractive, but has a low ceiling and is noisy. The cuisine is basic: low-budget food, unattractively presented, and with a poor selection of breads, cheeses, and fruits. Service is adequate, but there's not even a flicker of finesse.

**Other Comments** This ship caters to those who need to cruise the Aegean on a very limited budget, and who don't mind noise, crowded places, or really mediocre and unattractive food. Insurance and gratuities are extra.

# ms Columbus Caravelle ★★★★+

***Principal Cruising Areas***

*Worldwide (various)*

***Base Ports:*** *various*

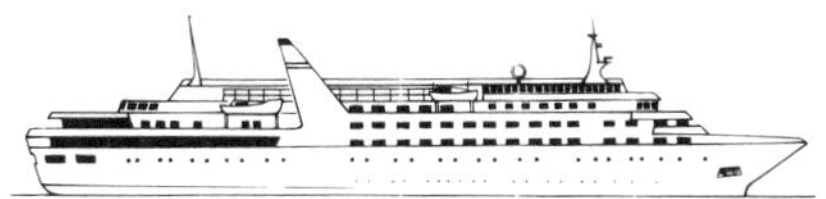

| | | | |
|---|---|---|---|
| Cruise Line | | | *MarQuest/Transocean Cruise Lines* |
| Former Names | | | *Sally Caravelle/Delfin Caravelle* |
| Gross Tonnage | | | *7,560* |
| Builder | | | *Rauma Yards (Finland)* |
| Original Cost | | | *$60 million* |
| Christened By | | | *Mrs Leena Matomaki* |
| First Entered Service | | | *Jul 1990/1991* |
| Interior Design | | | *Arto Kukkasiemi* |
| Country of Registry | | | *Bahamas (C6KP5)* |
| Tel No | *130-5133* | Fax No | *130-5133* |
| Length (ft/m) | | | *381.8/116.40* |
| Beam (ft/m) | | | *55.7/17.00* |
| Draft (ft/m) | | | *14.4/4.40* |
| Engines/Propellers | | | *2 VASA 8-cyl diesels/2* |
| Decks | *5* | Crew | *120* |
| Pass. Capacity (basis 2) | *250* | (all berths) | *303* |
| Pass. Space Ratio (basis 2) | *29.0* | (all berths) | *25.0* |
| Officers | | | *Ukrainian* |
| Dining Staff | | | *East/West European* |
| Total Cabins | | | *178* |
| Size (sq ft/m) | *78.5-243/7.2-22.5* | Door Width | *26"* |
| Outside Cabins | *98* | Inside Cabins | *80* |
| Single Cabins | *78* | Supplement | *None* |
| Balcony Cabins | *8* | Wheelchair Cabins | *2* |
| Cabin Current | | | *220 AC* |
| Refrigerator | | | *Yes* |
| Cabin TV | *Yes* | VCR | *Yes* |
| Dining Rooms | *1* | Sittings | *1* |

| | | | |
|---|---|---|---|
| Elevators | *2* | Door Width | *36"* |
| Casino | *No* | Slot Machines | *No* |
| Swimming Pools (outside) | *1* | (inside) | *0* |
| Whirlpools | *1* | Gymnasium | *No* |
| Sauna/Steam Rm | *2/No* | Massage | *Yes* |
| Self-Service Launderette | | | *No* |
| Lecture Room/Movie Theater/Seats | | | *Yes/156* |
| Library | | | *Yes* |
| Watersports Facilities | | | *None* |
| Classification Society | | | *American Bur. of Shipping* |

| RATINGS | SCORE |
|---|---|
| Ship: Condition/Cleanliness | 8.1 |
| Ship: Space/Flow/Comfort | 7.7 |
| Ship: Decor/Furnishings | 8.0 |
| Ship: Fitness Facilities | 6.6 |
| Cabins: Comfort/Facilities | 7.9 |
| Cabins: Software | 8.1 |
| Food: Dining Room/Cuisine | 7.9 |
| Food: Buffets/Informal Dining | 7.6 |
| Food: Quality of Ingredients | 7.7 |
| Service: Dining Room | 7.8 |
| Service: Bars/Lounges | 7.9 |
| Service: Cabins | 8.0 |
| Cruise: Entertainment | 7.2 |
| Cruise: Activities Program | 6.6 |
| Cruise: Hospitality Standard | 8.0 |
| OVERALL RATING | 115.1 |

**+** Twin, swept-back outboard funnels highlight the smart, though not overly handsome, exterior design of this small, delightful cruise ship, which has an ice-hardened hull and shallow draft, and carries rubber landing craft for flexible, in-depth, destination-oriented soft expedition cruise itineraries. Constructed to a high standard and quality of finish. All cabins are quiet, as they are located forward, with public rooms aft. Attractive wintergarden area. Handsome forward observation bar. Good outdoor observation decks. Well designed conference and lecture facilities. Contemporary Scandinavian interior design is tasteful; emerald green leather very prominent. Cabins are furnished to a high standard. Eight suites feature private balcony and whirlpool bathtub. Bathrobes for all. Large number of single cabins (no surcharge)—ideal vessel for solos.

**–** Limited public rooms, with few nooks and crannies. Limited closet and drawer space.

**Dining** Spacious dining room has light decor and good ambiance, and accommodates all passengers at one sitting. Service is by Russian and Ukrainian waitresses. The food is of good quality, but menu choice is rather limited.

**Other Comments** This ship will provide a very comfortable cruise experience for English- and German-speaking passengers, in extremely pleasant surroundings, at a realistic and attractive price. Maximum 170 passengers. All port charges are included. Gratuities are extra.

# ss Constitution ★★★

***Principal Cruising Area***

*Hawaii (7 nights year-round)*

***Base Port:** Honolulu (Saturday)*

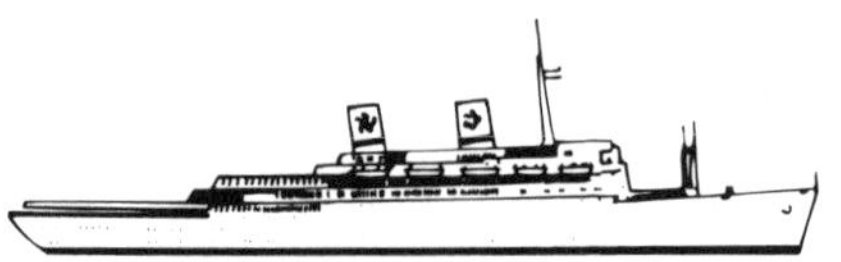

| | | | |
|---|---|---|---|
| Cruise Line | *American Hawaii Cruises* | | |
| Former Names | *Oceanic Constitution* | | |
| Gross Tonnage | *30,090* | | |
| Builder | *Bethlehem Shipbuilders (USA)* | | |
| Original Cost | *$20 million* | | |
| Christened By | *Mrs Charles Bey* | | |
| First Entered Service | *Jun 6, 1951/Jun 5, 1982* | | |
| Interior Design | *Henry Dreyfuss* | | |
| Country of Registry | *USA (KAEG)* | | |
| Tel No | *n/a* | Fax No | *n/a* |
| Length (ft/m) | *681.7/207.80* | | |
| Beam (ft/m) | *88.9/27.10* | | |
| Draft (ft/m) | *30.1/9.20* | | |
| Engines/Propellers | *4 Bethlehem steam turbines/2* | | |
| Decks | *9* | Crew | *315* |
| Pass. Capacity (basis 2) | *779* | (all berths) | *1000* |
| Pass. Space Ratio (basis 2) | *38.6* | (all berths) | *30.0* |
| Officers | *American* | Dining Staff | *American* |
| Total Cabins | *395* | | |
| Size (sq ft/m) | *75.3-410/7-38* | Door Width | *26"* |
| Outside Cabins | *176* | Inside Cabins | *219* |
| Single Cabins | *16* | Supplement | *60-100%* |
| Balcony Cabins | *0* | Wheelchair Cabins | *0* |
| Cabin Current | *110 AC* | | |
| Refrigerator | *Cat. 0/AA/A* | | |
| Cabin TV | *No* | VCR | *No* |
| Dining Rooms | *2* | Sittings | *2* |
| Elevators | *4* | Door Width | *31"* |

| | | | |
|---|---|---|---|
| Casino | *No* | Slot Machines | *No* |
| Swimming Pools (outside) | *2* | (inside) | *0* |
| Whirlpools | *0* | Gymnasium | *Yes* |
| Sauna/Steam Rm | *Yes/No* | Massage | *Yes* |
| Self-Service Launderette | *Yes* | | |
| Movie Theater/Seats | *Yes/144* | | |
| Library | *Yes* | | |
| Children's Facilities | *Yes* | | |
| Watersports Facilities | *None* | | |
| Classification Society | *American Bur. of Shipping* | | |

| RATINGS | SCORE |
|---|---|
| Ship: Condition/Cleanliness | 6.2 |
| Ship: Space/Flow/Comfort | 6.8 |
| Ship: Decor/Furnishings | 6.1 |
| Ship: Fitness Facilities | 5.8 |
| Cabins: Comfort/Facilities | 6.2 |
| Cabins: Software | 7.0 |
| Food: Dining Room/Cuisine | 6.3 |
| Food: Buffets/Informal Dining | 6.1 |
| Food: Quality of Ingredients | 6.4 |
| Service: Dining Room | 6.6 |
| Service: Bars/Lounges | 6.7 |
| Service: Cabins | 6.4 |
| Cruise: Entertainment | 6.0 |
| Cruise: Activities Program | 6.2 |
| Cruise: Hospitality Standard | 6.4 |
| OVERALL RATING | 95.2 |

**+** American built, registered, and crewed, this ship has good facilities for meetings. Expansive open deck space for sun-worshippers, set around two fresh-water swimming pools. There is a wrap-around outdoor promenade deck. Public areas are spacious and have high ceilings. Incredibly varied range of cabins (a carry-over from her nights as a three-class liner), mostly with ample room and decent closet and drawer space. Heavy-duty furniture and fittings are designed for unkind oceans, and some outside cabins have windows that open.

**–** Now over 40 years old and needs more than a facelift. Very awkward interior layout, with numerous dead-end passageways and poor signage. Room service is slow. The showlounge is not large enough and is always crowded.

**Dining** This ship has two dining rooms which are quite spacious and have cheerful decor and well spaced tables. The food is American-Polynesian in style, but presentation, quality of ingredients, and menu choice could be improved. Poor breads and bread rolls. Moderate wine list (most are from California). Service comes with a smile, but is slow. Don't expect finesse, nor European-style service. The first evening's dinner is buffet-style.

**Other Comments** Cruising in comfortable surroundings reminiscent of times past. Still has old public bathrooms. To be refurbished early in 1995. Insurance and gratuities are extra.

# mv CostaAllegra ★★★★

***Principal Cruising Areas***

*Mediterranean/Caribbean (7-13 nights)*

***Base Ports:*** *Venice/Miami*

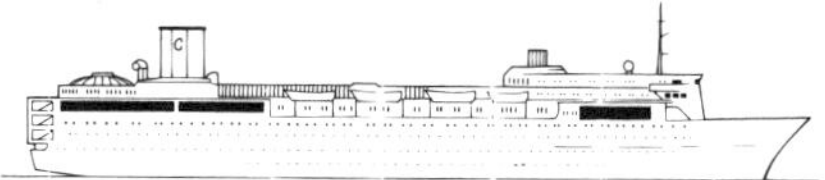

| | | | |
|---|---|---|---|
| Cruise Line | | | *Costa Cruises* |
| Former Names | | | *Annie Johnson* |
| Gross Tonnage | | | *28,430* |
| Builder | | | *Mariotti Shipyards (Italy)* |
| Original Cost | | | *$175 million* |
| Christened By | | | *Adrienne Greene, Nancy Lian, Dorothy Maitland, Cheryl Myerson, Bernice Rosmarin* |
| First Entered Service | | | *Dec 19, 1992* |
| Interior Design | | | *Guido Canali* |
| Country of Registry | | | *Italy (ICRA)* |
| Tel No | *115-1562* | Fax No | *115-1557* |
| Length (ft/m) | | | *616.7/187.94* |
| Beam (ft/m) | *84.6/25.75* | Draft (ft/m) | *27.1/8.22* |
| Engines/Propellers | | | *2 Wartsila 6-cyl diesels/2 (CP)* |
| Decks | *8* | Crew | *405* |
| Pass. Capacity (basis 2) | *810* | (all berths) | *1066* |
| Pass. Space Ratio (basis 2) | *35.1* | (all berths) | *26.6* |
| Officers | *Italian* | Dining Staff | *Italian/International* |
| Total Cabins | | | *405* |
| Size (sq ft/m) | *105-266/9.8-24.7* | Door Width | *24"* |
| Outside Cabins | *218* | Inside Cabins | *187* |
| Single Cabins | *0* | Supplement | *50%* |
| Balcony Cabins | *10* | Wheelchair Cabins | *8* |
| Cabin Current | | | *110 AC* |
| Refrigerator | | | *Grand suites* |
| Cabin TV | *Yes* | VCR | *No* |
| Dining Rooms | *1* | Sittings | *2* |

| | | | |
|---|---|---|---|
| Elevators | *4* | Door Width | *26-35'* |
| Casino | *Yes* | Slot Machines | *Yes* |
| Swimming Pools (outside) | *1* | (inside) | *0* |
| Whirlpools | *3* | Gymnasium | *Yes* |
| Sauna/Steam Rm | *Yes/Yes* | Massage | *No* |
| Self-Service Launderette | | | *No* |
| Movie Theater/Seats | | | *Yes/370* |
| Library | *Yes* | Children's Facilities | *Yes* |
| Watersports Facilities | | | *None* |
| Classification Society | | | *RINA* |

| RATINGS | SCORE |
|---|---|
| Ship: Condition/Cleanliness | 7.8 |
| Ship: Space/Flow/Comfort | 7.6 |
| Ship: Decor/Furnishings | 7.7 |
| Ship: Fitness Facilities | 6.6 |
| Cabins: Comfort/Facilities | 6.7 |
| Cabins: Software | 7.3 |
| Food: Dining Room/Cuisine | 7.0 |
| Food: Buffets/Informal Dining | 6.7 |
| Food: Quality of Ingredients | 6.6 |
| Service: Dining Room | 7.3 |
| Service: Bars/Lounges | 7.2 |
| Service: Cabins | 6.8 |
| Cruise: Entertainment | 6.6 |
| Cruise: Activities Program | 6.7 |
| Cruise: Hospitality Standard | 6.5 |
| OVERALL RATING | 105.1 |

**+** Slightly longer and larger than her sister ship, *CostaMarina*, the *CostaAllegra* enjoys better quality fit and finish. High glass-to-steel ratio, with numerous glass domes and walls admitting light. Good outdoor deck and sunning space. Cushioned pads provided for outdoor lounge chairs. Interesting glass-enclosed stern. Surprisingly fine interior decor with restful colors and soft furnishings. Decks are named after famous Italian painters.

**–** Angular-looking ship. Upright funnel. No forward observation lounge. Many small inside cabins. Poor cabin soundproofing. Expect long lines at buffets. Many pillars obstruct sightlines in showroom. Pompous attitude of officers.

**Dining** The dining room is quite spacious and has window views on three sides, but there are no tables for two. Dinner is later when the ship operates in Europe. The cuisine is mostly Continental, with many Italian dishes. Generally excellent service from a bubbly staff. Good fresh pasta dishes served daily. Fruit and cheese selection is poor.

**Other Comments** This ship will provide a good first cruise experience for young adults who enjoy European service and a real upbeat, elegant atmosphere with an Italian accent. Insurance and gratuities are extra.

# mv CostaClassica ★★★★

***Principal Cruising Areas***

*Caribbean/Europe (7 nights)*

***Base Ports:*** *San Juan/Venice*

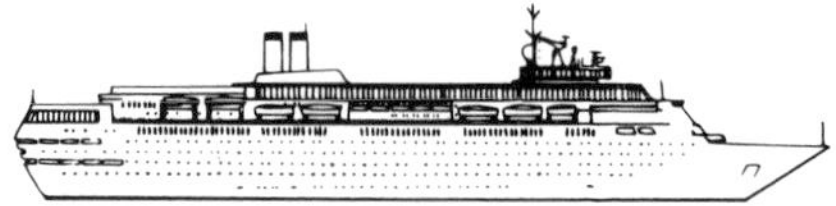

| | | | |
|---|---|---|---|
| Cruise Line | | | *Costa Cruises* |
| Former Names | | | *n/a* |
| Gross Tonnage | | | *53,700* |
| Builder | | | *Fincantieri (Italy)* |
| Original Cost | | | *$325 million* |
| Christened By | | | *Emilia Costa Viganego/ Angie Dickenson* |
| First Entered Service | | | *Jan 25, 1992* |
| Interior Design | | | *Gregotti Associates* |
| Country of Registry | | | *Italy (ICIC)* |
| Tel No | *115-1312* | Fax No | *115-1313* |
| Length (ft/m) | | | *718.5/220.61* |
| Beam (ft/m) | | | *98.4/30.8* |
| Draft (ft/m) | | | *25.0/7.60* |
| Engines/Propellers | | | *4 GMT-Sulzer diesels/2 (CP)* |
| Decks | *10* | Crew | *590* |
| Pass. Capacity (basis 2) | *1,308* | (all berths) | *1,766* |
| Pass. Space Ratio (basis 2) | *41.0* | (all berths) | *30.4* |
| Officers | *Italian* | Dining Staff | *Italian/International* |
| Total Cabins | | | *654* |
| Size (sq ft/m) | | | *185.1-430.5/17.2-40* |
| Door Width | | | *26-28"* |
| Outside Cabins | *438* | Inside Cabins | *216* |
| Single Cabins | *0* | Supplement | *50%* |
| Balcony Cabins | *10* | Wheelchair Cabins | *6* |
| Cabin Current | *110 AC* | Refrigerator | *Suites* |
| Cabin TV | *Yes* | VCR | *No* |
| Dining Rooms | *1* | Sittings | *2* |

| | | | |
|---|---|---|---|
| Elevators | *8* | Door Width | *35"* |
| Casino | *Yes* | Slot Machines | *Yes* |
| Swimming Pools (outside) | *2* | (inside) | *0* |
| Whirlpools | *4* | Gymnasium | *Yes* |
| Sauna/Steam Rm | *Yes/Yes* | Massage | *Yes* |
| Self-Service Launderette | | | *No* |
| Movie Theater/Seats | | | *Yes/577* |
| Library | *Yes* | Children's Facilities | *Yes* |
| Watersports Facilities | | | *None* |
| Classification Society | | | *RINA* |

| RATINGS | SCORE |
|---|---|
| Ship: Condition/Cleanliness | 8.0 |
| Ship: Space/Flow/Comfort | 8.0 |
| Ship: Decor/Furnishings | 8.1 |
| Ship: Fitness Facilities | 8.2 |
| Cabins: Comfort/Facilities | 8.2 |
| Cabins: Software | 8.0 |
| Food: Dining Room/Cuisine | 7.4 |
| Food: Buffets/Informal Dining | 6.4 |
| Food: Quality of Ingredients | 6.5 |
| Service: Dining Room | 7.7 |
| Service: Bars/Lounges | 7.6 |
| Service: Cabins | 7.8 |
| Cruise: Entertainment | 7.8 |
| Cruise: Activities Program | 7.6 |
| Cruise: Hospitality Standard | 7.4 |
| OVERALL RATING | 114.7 |

**+** Cushioned, outdoor deck lounge chairs. Excellent business and conference facilities. Six hermaphrodite statues in Piazza Navona are out of place in this otherwise typical contemporary version of a two-deck-high steamship lounge. Fine multi-tiered amphitheater-style showroom. Puccini Lounge is quite formal, and lovely. Cabins have cherrywood veneered cabinetry, and space-saving sliding doors to bathroom and closets. Good cabin soundproofing. Cabins for three or four are good for families with children. Dining room has good number of tables for two.

**–** Interior design doesn't quite work. Forward observation lounge/nightclub sits atop ship like a lump of cheese, and fails as a nightclub. Poor informal buffet area. Indifferent service. Clinical lobby. Uncarpeted, marble-covered staircases. Small cabin bathrooms. Long lines.

**Dining** The dining room has a lovely ceiling, but is very noisy. Electronically-controlled wall panels help create a European Renaissance atmosphere, but block off all windows. Reasonable Continental cuisine, with many Italian (very salty) dishes, but presentation, quality, and service need a lot more attention. The Alfresco Café is a real plus. Lounge afternoon tea is expensive. Breakfast and luncheon buffets are poor, and have long lines. Poor bread rolls and fruit.

**Other Comments** This ship has brought Costa into mainstream nineties cruising Italian-style, but I'm not sure about the toga parties. Insurance and gratuities are extra.

# mv CostaMarina ★★★+

## *Principal Cruising Areas*

*Mediterranean/South America (6-11/8-14 nights)*

***Base Ports:** Genoa/Buenos Aires/Rio de Janeiro*

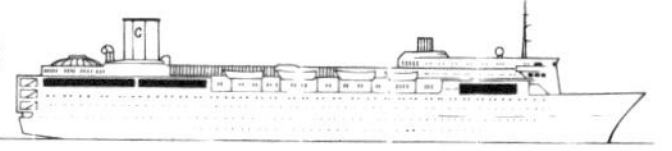

| | | | |
|---|---|---|---|
| Cruise Line | | | *Costa Cruises* |
| Former Names | | | *Axel Johnson* |
| Gross Tonnage | | | *25,441* |
| Builder | | | *Marriotti Shipyards (Italy)* |
| Original Cost | | | *$130 million* |
| Christened By | | | *Ersiliaa Bracaloni Pitorri/ Annette Funicello* |
| First Entered Service | | | *Jul 22, 1990* |
| Interior Design | | | *Guido Canali* |
| Country of Registry | | | *Italy (IBNC)* |
| Tel No | *115-0610* | Fax No | *115-0611* |
| Length (ft/m) | | | *571.8/174.25* |
| Beam (ft/m) | *84.6/25.75* | Draft (ft/m) | *26.1/8.20* |
| Engines/Propellers | | | *4 Pielstick diesels/2 (CP)* |
| Decks | *8* | Crew | *390* |
| Pass. Capacity (basis 2) | *772* | (all berths) | *1,025* |
| Pass. Space Ratio (basis 2) | | | *31.8* |
| Pass. Space Ratio (all berths) | | | *24.0* |
| Officers | *Italian* | Dining Staff | *Italian/International* |
| Total Cabins | | | *386* |
| Size (sq ft/m) | | | *104.4-258.3/9.7-24.6* |
| Door Width | | | *24"* |
| Outside Cabins | *183* | Inside Cabins | *203* |
| Single Cabins | *14* | Supplement | *50%* |
| Balcony Cabins | *0* | Wheelchair Cabins | *8 (inside)* |
| Cabin Current | *110 AC* | Refrigerator | *No* |
| Cabin TV | *Yes* | VCR | *No* |
| Dining Rooms | *1* | Sittings | *2* |

| | | | |
|---|---|---|---|
| Elevators | *4* | Door Width | *31"* |
| Casino | *Yes* | Slot Machines | *Yes* |
| Swimming Pools (outside) | 1 | (inside) | 0 |
| Whirlpools | *3* | Gymnasium | *Yes* |
| Sauna/Steam Rm | *Yes/Yes* | Massage | *Yes* |
| Self-Service Launderette | | | *No* |
| Movie Theater/Seats | | | *Yes (Main Lounge)/442* |
| Library | *Yes* | Children's Facilities | *Yes* |
| Watersports Facilities | | | *None* |
| Classification Society | | | *RINA* |

| RATINGS | SCORE |
|---|---|
| Ship: Condition/Cleanliness | 7.8 |
| Ship: Space/Flow/Comfort | 7.6 |
| Ship: Decor/Furnishings | 7.7 |
| Ship: Fitness Facilities | 6.6 |
| Cabins: Comfort/Facilities | 6.7 |
| Cabins: Software | 7.2 |
| Food: Dining Room/Cuisine | 6.8 |
| Food: Buffets/Informal Dining | 6.6 |
| Food: Quality of Ingredients | 6.6 |
| Service: Dining Room | 7.3 |
| Service: Bars/Lounges | 7.2 |
| Service: Cabins | 6.8 |
| Cruise: Entertainment | 6.6 |
| Cruise: Activities Program | 6.5 |
| Cruise: Hospitality Standard | 6.5 |
| OVERALL RATING | 104.5 |

**+** High glass-to-steel ratio, with numerous glass domes and walls. Good shopping boutiques. Outside cabins are quite comfortable. The illuminated cabin numbers are novel.

**–** Fit and finish is below the standard of competing ships in same price category. Very limited open deck and sunning space. There's no forward observation lounge. Tiny swimming pool. Simply too many inside cabins. Poor sightlines in showroom with too many (14) pillars. Poor library

**Dining** The dining room, located aft, has ocean views on three sides, is reasonably spacious, and is reached by escalator. Awful lime green color. There are only two tables for two. Table candle lights are poor quality. Good pasta, Continental cuisine, and bubbly service.

**Other Comments** Interesting, angular-looking, mid-sized ship. Has a cutaway stern virtually replaced by a glass wall, and a stark, upright funnel cluster. Most public rooms are located above accommodations decks. This very Italian ship will provide a good first cruise experience for young adults, and is best suited to European passengers. Insurance and gratuities are extra.

# mv CostaRomantica ★★★★+

*Principal Cruising Areas*

*Caribbean/Europe (7 nights)*

***Base Ports:** Miami/Genoa*

| | | | |
|---|---|---|---|
| Cruise Line | *Costa Cruises* | Elevators | *8* Door Width *35"* |
| Former Names | *n/a* | Casino | *Yes* Slot Machines *Yes* |
| Gross Tonnage | *56,800* | Swimming Pools (outside) | *2* (inside) *0* |
| Builder | *Fincantieri (Italy)* | Whirlpools | *4* Gymnasium *Yes* |
| Original Cost | *$325 million* | Sauna/Steam Rm | *Yes/No* Massage *Yes* |
| Christened By | *Maria Alessandra Fantoni Costa* | Self-Service Launderette | *No* |
| First Entered Service | *Nov 21, 1993* | Movie Theater/Seats | *Yes/626* |
| Interior Design | *Gregotti Associates* | Library *Yes* Children's Facilities | *Yes* |
| Country of Registry | *Italy (IBCR)* | Watersports Facilities | *None* |
| Tel No *115-1757* | Fax No *115-1760* | Classification Society | *RINA* |
| Length (ft/m) | *718.5/220.61* | | |
| Beam (ft/m) | *98.4/30.89* | **RATINGS** | **SCORE** |
| Draft (ft/m) | *25.0/7.60* | Ship: Condition/Cleanliness | 8.8 |
| Engines/Propellers | *4 GMT-Sulzer diesels/2 (CP)* | Ship: Space/Flow/Comfort | 8.6 |
| Decks *10* | Crew *600* | Ship: Decor/Furnishings | 9.0 |
| Pass. Capacity (basis 2) *1,356* | (all berths) *1,782* | Ship: Fitness Facilities | 8.2 |
| Pass. Space Ratio (basis 2) *41.8* | (all berths) *31.8* | Cabins: Comfort/Facilities | 8.2 |
| Officers *Italian* | Dining Staff *Italian/International* | Cabins: Software | 8.0 |
| Total Cabins | *678* | Food: Dining Room/Cuisine | 7.9 |
| Size (sq ft/m) | *185.1-430.5/17.2-40* | Food: Buffets/Informal Dining | 7.0 |
| Door Width | *26-28"* | Food: Quality of Ingredients | 6.8 |
| Outside Cabins *462* | Inside Cabins *216* | Service: Dining Room | 7.8 |
| Single Cabins *0* | Supplement *50%* | Service: Bars/Lounges | 7.6 |
| Balcony Cabins 10 | Wheelchair Cabins *6* | Service: Cabins | 7.9 |
| Cabin Current | *110 AC* | Cruise: Entertainment | 8.1 |
| Refrigerator | *Suites/Mini-suites* | Cruise: Activities Program | 7.6 |
| Cabin TV *Yes* | VCR *No* | Cruise: Hospitality Standard | 7.8 |
| Dining Rooms *1* | Sittings *2* | OVERALL RATING | 119.3 |

**+** Sister ship to *CostaClassica*, but with better interior design. Cushioned pads for outdoor deck lounge chairs. Excellent business and conference facilities. Tasteful decor. The multi-level atrium is open and spacious, with a revolving mobile sculpture. Amphitheater-style, two-deck high, multi-tiered showroom is good, with excellent audio-visual equipment. Fascinating artwork. Small chapel. Most cabins are a standard size, but have nicely-finished cherrywood cabinetry. Good soundproofing. Good number of triple and quad cabins, ideal for families with children.

**–** Layout and flow are somewhat disjointed. The showroom has stark, upright seating, and sightlines are interrupted by ten large pillars. Cabin bathrooms and showers are small. Expect long lines for embarkation, disembarkation, shore tenders, and buffets.

**Dining** The dining room is better designed and a little less noisy than on *CostaClassica*, and has many tables for two. Reasonable Continental cuisine, but presentation, quality, and service need more attention. Poor selection of bread rolls and fruits. However, pastas prepared by the head-waiters are excellent. Much improved and more practical buffet layout than on *CostaClassica*.

**Other Comments** Bold, contemporary, Italian-built ship with high sides and an upright funnel cluster. Inside, styling and colors blend contemporary Italian design and modern taste. Costa has returned to Italian-style cruising, something it does well. Insurance and gratuities are extra.

# ms Crown Dynasty ★★★★

***Principal Cruising Areas***

*Alaska/Caribbean (7 nights)*

***Base Ports:** Vancouver/Ft. Lauderdale*

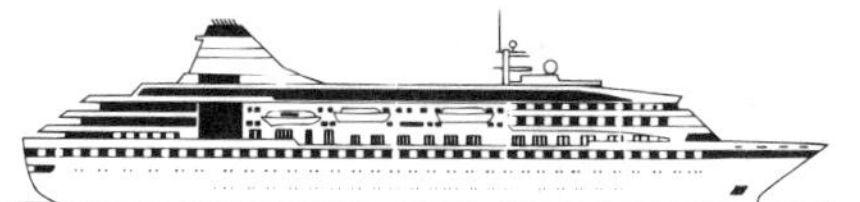

| | | | |
|---|---|---|---|
| Cruise Line | | | *Cunard Crown Cruises* |
| Former Names | | | *n/a* |
| Gross Tonnage | | | *19,089* |
| Builder | | | *Union Navale de Levante (Spain)* |
| Original Cost | | | *$100 million* |
| Christened By | | | *Mrs Betty Ford* |
| First Entered Service | | | *Jul 17, 1993* |
| Interior Design | | | *Yran & Storbraaten* |
| Country of Registry | | | *Panama (3FJX3)* |
| Tel No | *133-7757* | Fax No | *133-7761* |
| Length (ft/m) | | | *537.4/163.81* |
| Beam (ft/m) | *73.8/22.5* | Draft (ft/m) | *17.7/5.40* |
| Engines/Propellers | | | *2 Wartsila 8-cyl diesels/2 (CP)* |
| Decks | *7* | Crew | *330* |
| Pass. Capacity (basis 2) | *800* | (all berths) | *916* |
| Pass. Space Ratio (basis 2) | *23.8* | (all berths) | *20.8* |
| Officers | | | *European/Scandinavian* |
| Dining Staff | | | *Filipino* |
| Total Cabins | | | *401* |
| Size (sq ft/m) | *140-350 /13-32.5* | Door Width | *26.5"* |
| Outside Cabins | *277* | Inside Cabins | *124* |
| Single Cabins | *0* | Supplement | *50-100%* |
| Balcony Cabins | *10* | Wheelchair Cabins | *4* |
| Cabin Current | | | *110/220 AC* |
| Refrigerator | | | *Category 1* |
| Cabin TV | *Yes* | VCR | *No* |
| Dining Rooms | | | *1* |
| Sittings | | | *2 (open seating breakfast/lunch)* |

| | | | |
|---|---|---|---|
| Elevators | *4* | Door Width | *31"* |
| Casino | *Yes* | Slot Machines | *Yes* |
| Swimming Pools (outside) | *1* | (inside) | *0* |
| Whirlpools | *3* | Gymnasium | *Yes* |
| Sauna/Steam Rm | *Yes/No* | Massage | *Yes* |
| Self-Service Launderette | | | *No* |
| Movie Theater/Seats | | | *No* |
| Library | *No* | Children's Facilities | *No* |
| Watersports Facilities | | | *None* |
| Classification Society | | | *Det Norske Veritas* |

| RATINGS | SCORE |
|---|---|
| Ship: Condition/Cleanliness | 8.6 |
| Ship: Space/Flow/Comfort | 7.8 |
| Ship: Decor/Furnishings | 8.5 |
| Ship: Fitness Facilities | 8.2 |
| Cabins: Comfort/Facilities | 7.8 |
| Cabins: Software | 8.0 |
| Food: Dining Room/Cuisine | 7.9 |
| Food: Buffets/Informal Dining | 7.1 |
| Food: Quality of Ingredients | 6.7 |
| Service: Dining Room | 8.0 |
| Service: Bars/Lounges | 7.8 |
| Service: Cabins | 7.1 |
| Cruise: Entertainment | 7.8 |
| Cruise: Activities Program | 4.8 |
| Cruise: Hospitality Standard | 7.2 |
| OVERALL RATING | 113.3 |

**+** Nice exterior styling. Well designed five-deck-high, glass-walled atrium and off-center stairways. Clever interior design connects passengers with sea and light. Interior decor in public spaces is warm, with contemporary, but not brash, color combinations. Nicely furnished, wood-trimmed cabins feature large picture windows, vanity desk unit, good drawer space, curtained windows, and personal safe. Bathrooms are quite large, with generous toiletries cabinet. Very good value for money.

**–** Poor passenger flow. Poor cabin soundproofing. Tiny health spa. Showlounge is congested. Long lines for buffets and tenders. Staff, though friendly, lack finesse and flair.

**Dining** The dining room is quite cramped, with no tables for two, but it is attractive, and the ambiance is charming. The cuisine is disappointing, although it is improving. Against cruise price, however, it's reasonably good value, though lacking in quality and presentation. Varied menu, but food is invariably overcooked. Breakfast and midnight buffets are poor, and lunch buffets are unimaginative. Real cutlery is provided for the informal indoor/outdoor café.

**Other Comments** This sleek mid-sized sister ship to *Crown Jewel* is quite handsome. A welcome addition and a refreshing change for those that don't want to cruise on the crowded mega-ships. Great potential if managed and operated properly. Insurance and gratuities are extra.

# ms Crown Jewel ★★★★

***Principal Cruising Area***
*Caribbean (7 nights)*
***Base Port:** Ft. Lauderdale*

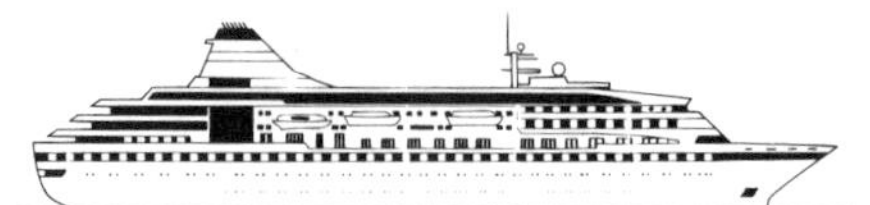

| | |
|---|---|
| Cruise Line | *Cunard Crown Cruises* |
| Former Names | *n/a* |
| Gross Tonnage | *19,046* |
| Builder | *Union Navale de Levante (Spain)* |
| Original Cost | *$100 million* |
| Christened By | *Isabel Cebrian de Viguerra* |
| First Entered Service | *Aug 10, 1992* |
| Interior Design | *Yran & Storbraaten* |
| Country of Registry | *Panama (3EW9)* |
| Tel No *133-6652* | Fax No *133-6653* |
| Length (ft/m) | *537.4/163.81* |
| Beam (ft/m) | *73.8/22.50* |
| Draft (ft/m) | *17.7/5.40* |
| Engines/Propellers | *2 Wartsila 8-cyl diesels/2 (CP)* |
| Decks *7* | Crew *330* |
| Pass. Capacity (basis 2) *820* | (all berths) *900* |
| Pass. Space Ratio (basis 2) *23.2* | (all berths) *21.1* |
| Officers | *European/Scandinavian* |
| Dining Staff *Filipino* | Total Cabins *410* |
| Size (sq ft/m) *140-350 /13-32.5* | Door Width *26.5"* |
| Outside Cabins *285* | Inside Cabins *125* |
| Single Cabins *0* | Supplement *50-100%* |
| Balcony Cabins *10* | Wheelchair Cabins *4* |
| Cabin Current | *110/220 AC* |
| Refrigerator | *Category 1* |
| Cabin TV *Yes* | VCR *No* |
| Dining Rooms | *1* |
| Sittings | *2 (open seating breakfast/lunch)* |

| | |
|---|---|
| Elevators *4* | Door Width *31"* |
| Casino *Yes* | Slot Machines *Yes* |
| Swimming Pools (outside) *1* | (inside) *0* |
| Whirlpools *3* | Gymnasium *Yes* |
| Sauna/Steam Rm *Yes/No* | Massage *Yes* |
| Self-Service Launderette | *No* |
| Movie Theater/Seats | *No* |
| Library *No* | Children's Facilities *No* |
| Watersports Facilities | *None* |
| Classification Society | *Det Norske Veritas* |

| RATINGS | SCORE |
|---|---|
| Ship: Condition/Cleanliness | 8.5 |
| Ship: Space/Flow/Comfort | 7.8 |
| Ship: Decor/Furnishings | 8.1 |
| Ship: Fitness Facilities | 8.1 |
| Cabins: Comfort/Facilities | 7.7 |
| Cabins: Software | 8.0 |
| Food: Dining Room/Cuisine | 7.8 |
| Food: Buffets/Informal Dining | 7.1 |
| Food: Quality of Ingredients | 6.7 |
| Service: Dining Room | 7.8 |
| Service: Bars/Lounges | 7.7 |
| Service: Cabins | 7.0 |
| Cruise: Entertainment | 7.8 |
| Cruise: Activities Program | 4.8 |
| Cruise: Hospitality Standard | 7.2 |
| OVERALL RATING | 112.1 |

**+** Traditional ship layout with good horizontal passenger flow. Large picture windows in most public rooms. Good open deck and sunning space. Well chosen decor, with contemporary color combinations. Nicely furnished and comfortable cabins with large picture windows. They are practical and well thought out. Bathrooms have large toiletries cabinet and one-person shower.

**–** Fit and finish is quite poor, particularly the quality of interior fabrics. The artwork is not aesthetically pleasing. Poor cabin soundproofing.

**Dining** The dining room is attractive, but quite cramped, and there are no tables for two. Charming ambiance. The cuisine is disappointing, although it is improving. Equating cuisine with cruise price, however, it's reasonably good value. A varied menu is provided, but food is invariably overcooked (a problem of distance from the galley). While not up to the standard of the small deluxe ships, creativity is generally good, but inconsistent. Service is average. Breakfast and midnight buffets are poor, and lunch buffets are unimaginative and unattractive.

**Other Comments** Handsome, mid-sized cruise ship with smart exterior styling. Features a five-deck-high, glass-walled atrium. A refreshing change for those that don't want to cruise on the megaships. Basically a sound product, and with fine-tuning in the hotel service areas, it will prove an admirable success story for Cunard Crown Cruises. Insurance and gratuities are extra.

# mv Crown Monarch ★★★★

***Principal Cruising Areas***

*Australia/South East Asia (various)*

***Base Port:*** *Sydney/Singapore*

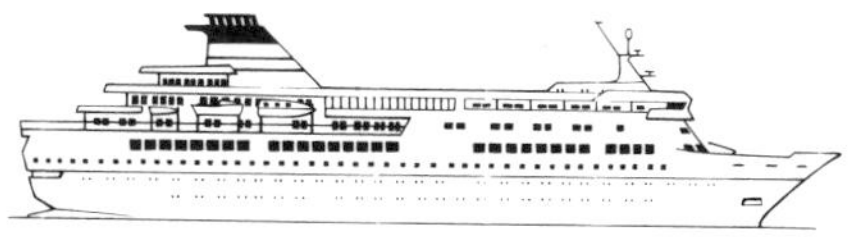

| | | | |
|---|---|---|---|
| Cruise Line | | | *Cunard Crown Cruises* |
| Former Names | | | *n/a* |
| Gross Tonnage | | | *15,271* |
| Builder | | | *Union Navale de Levante (Spain)* |
| Original Cost | | | *$95 million* |
| Christened By | | | *Mrs Gunvar "Gigi" Grundstad* |
| First Entered Service | | | *Dec 1, 1990* |
| Interior Design | | | *Oliver Design* |
| Country of Registry | | | *Panama (3EGA8)* |
| Tel No | *133-3627* | Fax No | *133-3630* |
| Length (ft/m) | | | *494.4/150.72* |
| Beam (ft/m) | | | *67.6/20.62* |
| Draft (ft/m) | | | *17.7/5.40* |
| Engines/Propellers | | | *2 Bergen diesels/2* |
| Decks | *7* | Crew | *215* |
| Pass. Capacity (basis 2) | *510* | (all berths) | *556* |
| Pass. Space Ratio (basis 2) | *29.9* | (all berths) | *27.4* |
| Officers | *Scandinavian* | Dining Staff | *Filipino* |
| Total Cabins | | | *255* |
| Size (sq ft/m) | | | *145-398.2/13.5-37* |
| Door Width | | | *32"* |
| Outside Cabins | *225* | Inside Cabins | *30* |
| Single Cabins | *0* | Supplement | *50-100%* |
| Balcony Cabins | *10* | Wheelchair Cabins | *5* |
| Cabin Current | | | *110 AC* |
| Refrigerator | | | *Category 1 only* |
| Cabin TV | *Yes* | VCR | *No* |
| Dining Rooms | *1* | Sittings | *2* |

| | | | |
|---|---|---|---|
| Elevators | *4* | Door Width | *31"* |
| Casino | *Yes* | Slot Machines | *Yes* |
| Swimming Pools (outside) | *1* | (inside) | *0* |
| Whirlpools | *2* | Gymnasium | *Yes* |
| Sauna/Steam Rm | *Yes/No* | Massage | *Yes* |
| Self-Service Launderette | | | *No* |
| Movie Theater/Seats | | | *No* |
| Library | *Yes* | Children's Facilities | *No* |
| Watersports Facilities | | | *None* |
| Classification Society | | | *Det Norske Veritas* |

| RATINGS | SCORE |
|---|---|
| Ship: Condition/Cleanliness | 7.6 |
| Ship: Space/Flow/Comfort | 7.7 |
| Ship: Decor/Furnishings | 8.0 |
| Ship: Fitness Facilities | 7.6 |
| Cabins: Comfort/Facilities | 7.7 |
| Cabins: Software | 8.0 |
| Food: Dining Room/Cuisine | 7.8 |
| Food: Buffets/Informal Dining | 7.1 |
| Food: Quality of Ingredients | 6.7 |
| Service: Dining Room | 7.6 |
| Service: Bars/Lounges | 7.5 |
| Service: Cabins | 7.8 |
| Cruise: Entertainment | 7.6 |
| Cruise: Activities Program | 6.4 |
| Cruise: Hospitality Standard | 7.6 |
| OVERALL RATING | 112.7 |

**+** This is a handsome, highly maneuverable, small ship with swept back funnel and fine, well balanced profile. Reasonably good open deck and sunning space. Lifeboats are well located to avoid obstructed views. Numerous public rooms to choose from, all tastefully decorated and very comfortable. Well designed interior has an excellent layout and good passenger flow. Suites with private balconies are excellent. All other cabins are nicely appointed and have elegant, pleasing decor and wood accents, and double-to-twin convertible beds with floral patterned bedspreads. Most cabins are large for the ship size.

**–** The indoor/outdoor café is poorly designed and has very limited seating and traffic flow. Poor cabin soundproofing. Disappointing cuisine needs attention and upgrading, as does the service.

**Dining** The dining room is quite charming, elegantly equipped, and has real wood chairs with arm rests, warm decor, and an informal atmosphere. The food is generally good, with generous portions, but choice is limited. Service is good to excellent, from a friendly and attentive staff.

**Other Comments** This ship will provide you with a decent quality, pleasant cruise experience in contemporary and extremely comfortable surroundings, at a modest price. Insurance and gratuities are extra.

# ms Crown Odyssey ★★★★+

***Principal Cruising Areas***

*Worldwide (various)*

***Base Ports:*** *various*

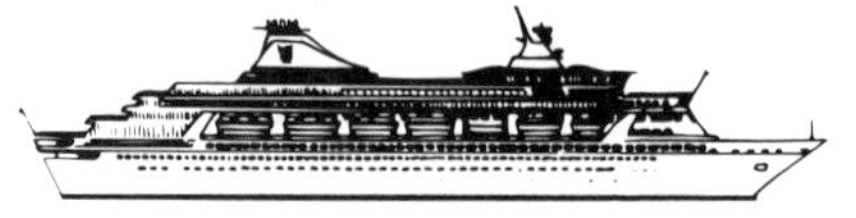

| | | | |
|---|---|---|---|
| Cruise Line | | | *Royal Cruise Line* |
| Former Names | | | *n/a* |
| Gross Tonnage | | | *34,242* |
| Builder | | | *Meyer Werft (Germany)* |
| Original Cost | | | *$178 million* |
| Christened By | | | *Ms Irene Panagopoulos* |
| First Entered Service | | | *Jun 7, 1988* |
| Interior Design | | | *Katzourakis/Terzoglou* |
| Country of Registry | | | *Bahamas (RCLB)* |
| Tel No | *110-4673* | Fax No | *110-4674* |
| Length (ft/m) | | | *615.9/187.75* |
| Beam (ft/m) | | | *92.5/28.20* |
| Draft (ft/m) | | | *23.8/7.26* |
| Engines/Propellers | | | *2 MAK 8-cyl diesels/2 (CP)* |
| Decks | *10* | Crew | *470* |
| Pass. Capacity (basis 2) | *1,052* | (all berths) | *1,221* |
| Pass. Space Ratio (basis 2) | *32.5* | (all berths) | *28.0* |
| Officers | *Greek* | Dining Staff | *Greek* |
| Total Cabins | | | *526* |
| Size (sq ft/m) | *154-615/14.3-57* | Door Width | *25"* |
| Outside Cabins | *412* | Inside Cabins | *114* |
| Single Cabins | *0* | Supplement | *100%* |
| Balcony Cabins | *16* | Wheelchair Cabins | *4* |
| Cabin Current | | | *110 AC* |
| Refrigerator | | | *Cat. AA/AB* |
| Cabin TV | *No* | VCR | *No* |
| Dining Rooms | *1* | Sittings | *2* |
| Elevators | *4* | Door Width | *36"* |

| | | | |
|---|---|---|---|
| Casino | *Yes* | Slot Machines | *Yes* |
| Swimming Pools (outside) | *1* | (inside) | *1* |
| Whirlpools | *4* | Gymnasium | *Yes* |
| Sauna/Steam Rm | *Yes/No* | Massage | *Yes* |
| Self-Service Launderette | | | *Yes* |
| Movie Theater/Seats | | | *Yes/215* |
| Library | | | *Yes* |
| Children's Facilities | | | *No* |
| Watersports Facilities | | | *None* |
| Classification Society | | | *Lloyd's Register* |

| RATINGS | SCORE |
|---|---|
| Ship: Condition/Cleanliness | 8.3 |
| Ship: Space/Flow/Comfort | 8.3 |
| Ship: Decor/Furnishings | 8.4 |
| Ship: Fitness Facilities | 7.8 |
| Cabins: Comfort/Facilities | 8.6 |
| Cabins: Software | 8.1 |
| Food: Dining Room/Cuisine | 7.8 |
| Food: Buffets/Informal Dining | 7.6 |
| Food: Quality of Ingredients | 7.0 |
| Service: Dining Room | 7.8 |
| Service: Bars/Lounges | 7.9 |
| Service: Cabins | 7.7 |
| Cruise: Entertainment | 7.5 |
| Cruise: Activities Program | 7.1 |
| Cruise: Hospitality Standard | 7.9 |
| OVERALL RATING | 117.8 |

**+** Well designed and built with a handsome profile, generally good passenger flow, ample space, and fine quality interiors. Well-planned itineraries. Good attention to detail, and quality evident everywhere. Spacious layout. Lavish public rooms. Generous warm woods and marble throughout. Good outdoor promenade deck. Stunning indoor spa and pool, with good facilities. Good theater-style showroom, though sightlines could be better. Outstanding suites. Most cabins are quite spacious, with good closet and drawer space. Some are very large. All come fully equipped and beautifully furnished. Good cabin soundproofing. Excellent staff.

**–** The Greek staff are often overly friendly, some passengers will not like the touching done by waiters. Long lines for tenders, embarkation, disembarkation (especially), elevators, and buffets. Cruise cuisine is moderately good, but needs upgrading.

**Dining** Classic, though noisy, dining room features a lovely stained-glass ceiling and comfortable seating. The cuisine is not gourmet in quality or presentation, but is more Continental in style. The waiters are excellent, and very attentive, though sometimes overly friendly.

**Other Comments** Excellent for the older passenger, this ship exudes quality, style, and charm, for a moderately decent price. Gentleman "host" program is excellent. You'll enjoy refined living at sea aboard this ship. Insurance and gratuities are extra.

# mv Crown Princess ★★★★+

***Principal Cruising Areas***

*Alaska/Caribbean (7 nights)*

***Base Ports:*** *Vancouver/Ft. Lauderdale*

| | | | |
|---|---|---|---|
| Cruise Line | | | *Princess Cruises* |
| Former Names | | | *n/a* |
| Gross Tonnage | | | *70,000* |
| Builder | | | *Fincantieri Navali (Italy)* |
| Original Cost | | | *$276.8 million* |
| Christened By | | | *Ms Sophia Loren* |
| First Entered Service | | | *Jul 8, 1990* |
| Interior Design | | | *H. Chambers Company* |
| Country of Registry | | | *Italy (ICBB)* |
| Tel No | *115-0543* | Fax No | *115-0544* |
| Length (ft/m) | | | *804.7/245.30* |
| Beam (ft/m) | | | *105.8/32.26* |
| Draft (ft/m) | | | *26.5/8.10* |
| Engines/Propellers | | | *4 MAN-B&W diesels/2* |
| Decks | *11* | Crew | *696* |
| Pass. Capacity (basis 2) | *1,590* | (all berths) | *1,910* |
| Pass. Space Ratio (basis 2) | *44.0* | (all berths) | *36.6* |
| Officers | *Italian* | Dining Staff | *International* |
| Total Cabins | | | *795* |
| Size (sq ft/m) | | | *190-575/17.6-53.4* |
| Door Width | | | *24"* |
| Outside Cabins | *624* | Inside Cabins | *171* |
| Single Cabins | *0* | Supplement | *40-100%* |
| Balcony Cabins | *184* | Wheelchair Cabins | *10* |
| Cabin Current | | | *110/220 AC* |
| Refrigerator | | | *Yes* |
| Cabin TV | *Yes* | VCR | *No* |
| Dining Rooms | *1* | Sittings | *2* |

| | | | |
|---|---|---|---|
| Elevators | *9* | Door Width | *46"* |
| Casino | *Yes* | Slot Machines | *Yes* |
| Swimming Pools (outside) | *2* | (inside) | *0* |
| Whirlpools | *4* | Gymnasium | *Yes* |
| Sauna/Steam Rm | *Yes/No* | Massage | *Yes* |
| Self-Service Launderette | | | *Yes* |
| Movie Theater/Seats | | | *Yes/169* |
| Library | *Yes* | Children's Facilities | *No* |
| Watersports Facilities | | | *None* |
| Classification Society | | | *Lloyd's Register* |

| RATINGS | SCORE |
|---|---|
| Ship: Condition/Cleanliness | 8.0 |
| Ship: Space/Flow/Comfort | 7.8 |
| Ship: Decor/Furnishings | 7.9 |
| Ship: Fitness Facilities | 8.0 |
| Cabins: Comfort/Facilities | 8.1 |
| Cabins: Software | 8.2 |
| Food: Dining Room/Cuisine | 7.4 |
| Food: Buffets/Informal Dining | 7.1 |
| Food: Quality of Ingredients | 7.1 |
| Service: Dining Room | 7.5 |
| Service: Bars/Lounges | 7.7 |
| Service: Cabins | 7.8 |
| Cruise: Entertainment | 8.1 |
| Cruise: Activities Program | 7.8 |
| Cruise: Hospitality Standard | 7.6 |
| OVERALL RATING | 116.1 |

**+** Innovative styling mixed with traditional features. Spacious interior layout. Good swimming pool deck. Good health spa. Strikingly elegant, three-deck-high atrium features grand staircase with bronze and granite fountain sculpture (real, stand-up cocktail parties are held here). Good cabin soundproofing. Interior space is excellent. Understated, soft pastels are highlighted by some very colorful artwork. Well designed cabins, 184 with private balconies. Large bathrooms. Walk-in closets, refrigerator, safe, and interactive video system. Twin beds convert to queen size in standard cabins. Characters Bar has wonderful drink concoctions and very unusual glasses. Kipling's has a fine "club" ambiance.

**–** No wrap-around outdoor promenade deck. Not enough outdoor space, and little connection with the outside. Internal layout is somewhat disjointed. Noise level (from slot machines) in the casino dome is high. Cabins for physically challenged have obstructed views. Long lines.

**Dining** The dining room is split into small sections, but there are no tables for two, and cuisine is very stodgy, with poor creativity and presentation, although it is being upgraded. Pasta dishes are quite good. Service is reasonable, but perfunctory. Excellent, but small, pizzeria.

**Other Comments** This ship provides a fine cruise environment in elegant and comfortable surroundings. Luke warm staff. Insurance and gratuities are extra.

# mv Crystal Harmony ★★★★★+

***Principal Cruising Areas***

*Worldwide (various)*

***Base Ports:** various*

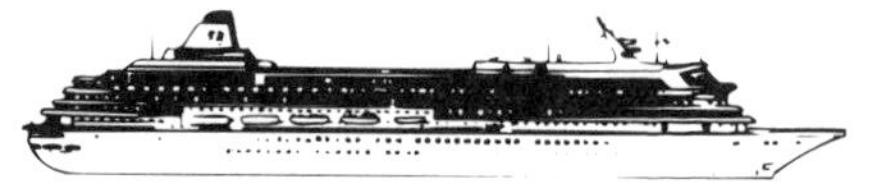

| | | | |
|---|---|---|---|
| Cruise Line | | | *Crystal Cruises* |
| Former Names | | | *n/a* |
| Gross Tonnage | | | *48,621* |
| Builder | | | *Mitsubishi Heavy Industries (Japan)* |
| Original Cost | | | *$240 million* |
| Christened By | | | *Ms Mary Tyler Moore* |
| First Entered Service | | | *Jul 24, 1990* |
| Interior Design | | | *Robert Tillberg* |
| Country of Registry | | | *Bahamas (C6IP2)* |
| Tel No | *110-3237* | Fax No | *110-3242* |
| Length (ft/m) | | | *790.5/240.96* |
| Beam (ft/m) | *97.1/29.60* | Draft (ft/m) | *24.6/7.50* |
| Engines/Propellers | | | *4 diesel-electrics/2 (CP)* |
| Decks | *8* | Crew | *545* |
| Pass. Capacity (basis 2) | *960* | (all berths) | *1,010* |
| Pass. Space Ratio (basis 2) | *50.6* | (all berths) | *48.9* |
| Officers | | | *Scandinavian/Japanese* |
| Dining Staff | | | *European/Filipino* |
| Total Cabins | | | *480* |
| Size (sq ft/m) | *183-948/17-88* | Door Width | *24-29"* |
| Outside Cabins | *461* | Inside Cabins | *19* |
| Single Cabins | *0* | Supplement | *20-100%* |
| Balcony Cabins | *260* | Wheelchair Cabins | *4* |
| Cabin Current | | | *115/220 AC* |
| Refrigerator | | | *All cabins* |
| Cabin TV | *Yes* | VCR | *Yes* |
| Dining Rooms | *3* | Sittings | *2* |
| Elevators | *8* | Door Width | *33-35"* |

| | | | |
|---|---|---|---|
| Casino | *Yes* | Slot Machines | *Yes* |
| Swimming Pools (outside) | 2 | (inside) | *0* |
| Whirlpools | 2 | Gymnasium | *Yes* |
| Sauna/Steam Rm | *Yes/Yes* | Massage | *Yes* |
| Self-Service Launderette | | | *Yes* |
| Movie Theater/Seats | | | *Yes/270* |
| Library | *Yes* | Children's Facilities | *Yes* |
| Watersports Facilities | | | *None* |
| Classification Society | | | *Lloyd's Register/ Nippon Kaiji Kyokai* |

| RATINGS | SCORE |
|---|---|
| Ship: Condition/Cleanliness | 9.2 |
| Ship: Space/Flow/Comfort | 9.5 |
| Ship: Decor/Furnishings | 9.2 |
| Ship: Fitness Facilities | 9.0 |
| Cabins: Comfort/Facilities | 8.8 |
| Cabins: Software | 9.0 |
| Food: Dining Room/Cuisine | 8.8 |
| Food: Buffets/Informal Dining | 8.8 |
| Food: Quality of Ingredients | 8.6 |
| Service: Dining Room | 9.1 |
| Service: Bars/Lounges | 9.0 |
| Service: Cabins | 9.0 |
| Cruise: Entertainment | 9.1 |
| Cruise: Activities Program | 8.7 |
| Cruise: Hospitality Standard | 9.5 |
| OVERALL RATING | 135.3 |

**+** Handsome, contemporary ship with raked clipper bow and well balanced, sleek, flowing lines. Excellent open deck, sunning space, and sports facilities. One of two outdoor swimming pools has a swim-up bar and can be covered by a magrodome. There's almost no sense of crowding anywhere, a superb example of comfort by design, quality construction, and engineering. Wrap-around teakwood deck for walking. Fine assortment of public entertainment lounges and small intimate rooms. Outstanding are the Vista (observation) Lounge and the supremely tranquil, elegant Palm Court, one of the nicest rooms afloat. A business center features laptop computer, printer, satellite fax, and telephone. Excellent book and video library. Theater features high definition video projection, and special headsets for the hearing-impaired. Useful self-service launderettes on each deck. Fine quality fabrics and soft furnishings, china, flatware, and silver. Together with the *Queen Elizabeth* 2, this ship has the best in-cabin television of any ship, and close-captioned videos for the hearing-impaired. Spacious, well designed accommodations, including four spectacular Crystal penthouses that feature a huge veranda and lounge, bedroom with queen sized bed and electric curtains, and a stunning ocean-view bathroom. Five butlers feature the best in personal service in the top category suites (Penthouse Deck 10), where all room service food arrives on sterling silver trays. More than half of all cabins have private verandas, and are supremely comfortable. Even in standard cabins, there's plenty of drawer space, some recently added to lower grade cabins, although closet hanging space is somewhat limited for long voyages. Excellent cabin soundproofing. Generously-sized Caswell-Massey personal bathroom amenities. Very friendly, well-trained, highly professional staff and excellent teamwork, under the direction of an all-European middle management. It is the attention to detail that makes a cruise on this ship so special (such as few announcements, and no background music anywhere).

**–** The main dining room features two sittings for dinner (the earlier sitting is too rushed). Entrances for the two alternative dining spots should be separated. Except for the penthouse suites, cabin bathrooms are somewhat compact and cramped. Some cabins (grades G and I), but no public rooms, have obstructed views.

**Dining** The dining room is elegant, with plenty of space around each table, well placed waiter service stations, and ample tables for two. Food is attractively presented and well served (silver service). It is of a very high standard, with fine quality ingredients used throughout. Mainly European dishes. Menus are extremely varied, and special orders are available, as is caviar and many other niceties. All in all, the food is most acceptable and, with the choice of the two alternative dining spots, provides consistently high ratings from passengers. Dinner in the main dining room is in two sittings, but with two alternative restaurants, off-menu choices, a fine hand-picked European staff, and impeccable service, dining is memorable. Pasta specialties are made each day on request to the head waiters. For those who enjoy caviar, it is available, but is Sevruga (Malossol) and not Beluga. The wine list is superb. Afternoon tea (and coffee) in the Palm Court is delightful, and refreshed constantly. Good choice of sandwiches, cakes, and pastries. Needless to say, service is generally excellent.

There are two alternative restaurants—Prego (superb pasta dishes) and Kyoto (with pseudo-Japanese specialties). There's no extra charge (but the recommended $5 waiter gratuity per meal should be included in the cruise fare). Both are intimate, have great views, and feature fine food.

**Other Comments** This ship has just about everything for the discerning, seasoned traveller who wants and is prepared to pay handsomely for fine style and the comfort and the facilities of a large vessel capable of extended voyages. This ship is without doubt an outstanding example of the latest style in contemporary grand hotels afloat, and provides choice and flexibility. With few design defects, *Crystal Harmony* is a standard setter in the cruise industry, and I have absolutely no hesitation in giving it my highest personal recommendation. You'll be surrounded by a cocoon of creative comfort and pampering to the highest degree. Insurance and gratuities are extra, but should be included.

# ms Crystal Symphony

***Principal Cruising Areas***

*Alaska/Australasia/South East Asia (various)*

***Base Ports:*** *various*

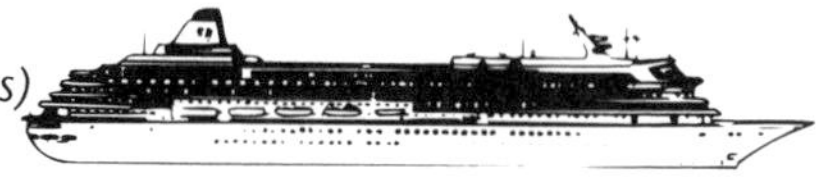

| | | | |
|---|---|---|---|
| Cruise Line | | | *Crystal Cruises* |
| Former Names | | | - |
| Gross Tonnage | | | *49,500* |
| Builder | | | *Kvaerner Masa-Yards (Finland)* |
| Original Cost | | | *$300 million* |
| Christened By | | | *n/a* |
| First Entered Service | | | *May 6, 1995* |
| Interior Design | | | *Robert Tillberg* |
| Country of Registry | | | *Bahamas* |
| Tel No | *n/a* | Fax No | *n/a* |
| Length (ft/m) | | | *779.0/238.0* |
| Beam (ft/m) | | | *98.5/30.02* |
| Draft (ft/m) | | | *24.9/7.60* |
| Engines/Propellers | | | *4 Sulzer diesel-electrics/2 (CP)* |
| Decks | *8* | Crew | *530* |
| Pass. Capacity (basis 2) | *960* | (all berths) | *1,010* |
| Pass. Space Ratio (basis 2) | *50.0* | (all berths) | *49.0* |
| Officers | *Norwegian* | Service Staff | *International* |
| Total Cabins | | | *480* |
| Size (sq ft/m) | | | *198-974/18.3-90.5* |
| Door Width | | | *24-29"* |
| Outside Cabins | *480* | Inside Cabins | *0* |
| Single Cabins | *0* | Supplement | *20-100%* |
| Balcony Cabins | *276* | Wheelchair Cabins | *8* |
| Cabin Current | | | *110/220 AC* |
| Refrigerator | | | *All* |
| Cabin TV | *Yes* | VCR | *Yes* |
| Dining Rooms | *3* | Sittings | *2 (dinner)* |

| | | | |
|---|---|---|---|
| Elevators | *8* | Door Width | *33-35"* |
| Casino | *Yes* | Slot Machines | *Yes* |
| Swimming Pools (outside) | 2 | (inside) | *0* |
| Whirlpools | 2 | Gymnasium | *Yes* |
| Sauna/Steam Rm | *Yes/Yes* | Massage | *Yes* |
| Self-Service Launderette | | | *Yes* |
| Movie Theater/Seats | | | *Yes/130* |
| Library | *Yes* | Children's Facilities | *Yes* |
| Watersports Facilities | | | *None* |
| Classification Society | | | *Lloyd's Registeri* |

| RATINGS | SCORE |
|---|---|
| Ship: Condition/Cleanliness | NYR |
| Ship: Space/Flow/Comfort | NYR |
| Ship: Decor/Furnishings | NYR |
| Ship: Fitness Facilities | NYR |
| Cabins: Comfort/Facilities | NYR |
| Cabins: Software | NYR |
| Food: Dining Room/Cuisine | NYR |
| Food: Buffets/Informal Dining | NYR |
| Food: Quality of Ingredients | NYR |
| Service: Dining Room | NYR |
| Service: Bars/Lounges | NYR |
| Service: Cabins | NYR |
| Cruise: Entertainment | NYR |
| Cruise: Activities Program | NYR |
| Cruise: Hospitality Standard | NYR |

*NYR = Not Yet Rated*

**+** Long-awaited second ship for this company has the same profile as *Crystal Harmony*, but has a slightly smaller funnel. Sophisticated machinery. Excellent passenger flow and feel of spaciousness. Fine outdoor wrap-around teakwood promenade deck. Has an expanded outdoor pool deck, with larger pools (plus one whirlpool at each swimming pool). Enlarged Palm Court is a beautiful, restful room, now with forward observation view. Nightclub layout is also enhanced. Standard cabins have a much improved layout, with more closet space and drawers. All bathrooms have two sinks, well-designed tub-shower units and better space utilization, but they are tight. The flow throughout the ship for handicapped persons is outstanding.

**–** None at press time, other than the fact that the dining room operates two sittings for dinner.

**Dining** The main dining room is quite elegant and well laid out. The two alternative dining rooms, one Italian, the other Chinese, are larger and set on a lower deck than on the sister ship, and each has a separate entrance.

**Other Comments** The comments for her sister ship, *Crystal Harmony*, generally apply, but some of the hardware improvements made on this ship will probably be retrofitted to *Crystal Harmony* soon.

# mv Cunard Countess ★★★+

***Principal Cruising Area***
*Caribbean (7/14 nights year-round)*
***Base Port:** San Juan (Saturday)*

| | | | |
|---|---|---|---|
| Cruise Line | | | *Cunard Crown Cruises* |
| Former Names | | | *n/a* |
| Gross Tonnage | | | *17,593* |
| Builder | | | *Burmeister & Wein (Denmark)* |
| Original Cost | | | *£12 million* |
| Christened By | | | *Mrs Janet Armstrong* |
| First Entered Service | | | *Aug 7, 1976* |
| Interior Design | | | *McNeece Design* |
| Country of Registry | | | *Bahamas (CBCF)* |
| Tel No | *110-4676* | Fax No | *110-4676* |
| Length (ft/m) | | | *536.6/163.56* |
| Beam (ft/m) | | | *74.9/22.84* |
| Draft (ft/m) | | | *19.0/5.82* |
| Engines/Propellers | | | *4 B&W 7-cyl diesels/2 (VP)* |
| Decks | *8* | Crew | *360* |
| Pass. Capacity (basis 2) | *790* | (all berths) | *956* |
| Pass. Space Ratio (basis 2) | *22.2* | (all berths) | *18.4* |
| Officers | *British* | Dining Staff | *International* |
| Total Cabins | | | *398* |
| Size (sq ft/m) | *88-265/8.1-24.6* | Door Width | *24"* |
| Outside Cabins | *249* | Inside Cabins | *149* |
| Single Cabins | *0* | Supplement | *50%* |
| Balcony Cabins | *0* | Wheelchair Cabins | *0* |
| Cabin Current | | | *110/220 AC* |
| Refrigerator | | | *Grades 1, 2* |
| Cabin TV | *No* | VCR | *No* |
| Dining Rooms | *1* | Sittings | *2* |
| Elevators | *2* | Door Width | *31"* |

| | | | |
|---|---|---|---|
| Casino | *Yes* | Slot Machines | *Yes* |
| Swimming Pools (outside) | *1* | (inside) | *0* |
| Whirlpools | *2* | Gymnasium | *Yes* |
| Sauna/Steam Rm | *Yes/No* | Massage | *No* |
| Self-Service Launderette | | | *No* |
| Movie Theater/Seats | | | *Yes/126* |
| Library | | | *Yes* |
| Children's Facilities | | | *No* |
| Watersports Facilities | | | *None* |
| Classification Society | | | *Lloyd's Register* |

| RATINGS | SCORE |
|---|---|
| Ship: Condition/Cleanliness | 6.1 |
| Ship: Space/Flow/Comfort | 6.3 |
| Ship: Decor/Furnishings | 6.6 |
| Ship: Fitness Facilities | 6.7 |
| Cabins: Comfort/Facilities | 5.8 |
| Cabins: Software | 7.7 |
| Food: Dining Room/Cuisine | 6.6 |
| Food: Buffets/Informal Dining | 6.1 |
| Food: Quality of Ingredients | 6.2 |
| Service: Dining Room | 7.0 |
| Service: Bars/Lounges | 6.8 |
| Service: Cabins | 7.2 |
| Cruise: Entertainment | 7.3 |
| Cruise: Activities Program | 7.1 |
| Cruise: Hospitality Standard | 7.6 |
| OVERALL RATING | 101.1 |

**+** This ship has a modern profile, with clean lines and a distinctive swept-back red funnel. Good selection of public rooms have attractive (now much lighter) colors and decor. Airy shopping arcade. Good nightclub that incorporates an aft open deck area. The cabins, mostly of a standard (small) size, are furnished with much lighter colors and better combinations, and are small, space-efficient units with metal fixtures and thin walls.

**–** Poor cabin insulation, which means you hear your neighbors brushing their hair. Cabins on the lowest deck (2 Deck) suffer from vibration and the odor of diesel fuel. Outside decks need attention. The cabin service snack menu should be upgraded.

**Dining** Pleasant dining room has large picture windows. Reasonable banquet food standard, tailored for U.K. tastes. Unusual requests are difficult. Poor fruit and cheese selection. Good, cheerful service from attentive staff, but lacking the finesse that Cunard was once known for.

**Other Comments** Passengers seeking a casual, destination-intensive cruise will probably like this, and come back for more. Good for a destination-oriented and fun-filled informal first Caribbean cruise experience for its mainly British passengers in comfortable, friendly, and informal surroundings, at a very realistic price. Not up to the standard found on the company's more deluxe, upscale ships. Port taxes included for U.K. passengers only.

# mv Cunard Princess ★★★+

***Principal Cruising Areas***

*Iberia/Mediterranean (7/10/11/14 nights)*

***Base Port:*** *Malaga*

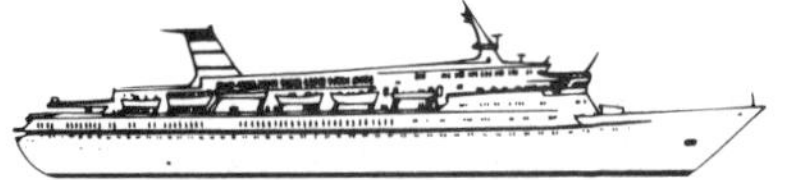

| | | | |
|---|---|---|---|
| Cruise Line | | | *Cunard Crown Cruises* |
| Former Names | | | *Cunard Conquest* |
| Gross Tonnage | | | *17,495* |
| Builder | | | *Burmeister & Wein (Denmark)* |
| Original Cost | | | *£12 million* |
| Christened By | | | *HRH Princess Grace of Monaco* |
| First Entered Service | | | *Mar 15, 1977* |
| Interior Design | | | *McNeece Design* |
| Country of Registry | | | *Bahamas (CPCG)* |
| Tel No | *110-4111* | Fax No | *110-4111* |
| Length (ft/m) | | | *536.6/163.56* |
| Beam (ft/m) | | | *74.9/22.84* |
| Draft (ft/m) | | | *19.0/5.82* |
| Engines/Propellers | | | *4 B&W 7-cyl diesels/2 (VP)* |
| Decks | *8* | Crew | *350* |
| Pass. Capacity (basis 2) | *804* | (all berths) | *959* |
| Pass. Space Ratio (basis 2) | *21.7* | (all berths) | *18.1* |
| Officers | *British* | Dining Staff | *International* |
| Total Cabins | | | *402* |
| Size (sq ft/m) | *88-265/8.1-24.6* | Door Width | *24"* |
| Outside Cabins | *266* | Inside Cabins | *136* |
| Single Cabins | *1* | Supplement | *50%* |
| Balcony Cabins | *0* | Wheelchair Cabins | *0* |
| Cabin Current | | | *110/220 AC* |
| Refrigerator | | | *Cat. 1/2* |
| Cabin TV | *No* | VCR | *No* |
| Dining Rooms | *1* | Sittings | *2* |
| Elevators | *2* | Door Width | *31"* |

| | | | |
|---|---|---|---|
| Casino | *Yes* | Slot Machines | *Yes* |
| Swimming Pools (outside) | *1* | (inside) | *0* |
| Whirlpools | *2* | Gymnasium | *Yes* |
| Sauna/Steam Rm | *Yes/No* | Massage | *No* |
| Self-Service Launderette | | | *No* |
| Movie Theater/Seats | | | *Yes/130* |
| Library | | | *Yes* |
| Children's Facilities | | | *No* |
| Watersports Facilities | | | *None* |
| Classification Society | | | *Lloyd's Register* |

| RATINGS | SCORE |
|---|---|
| Ship: Condition/Cleanliness | 6.8 |
| Ship: Space/Flow/Comfort | 6.3 |
| Ship: Decor/Furnishings | 6.6 |
| Ship: Fitness Facilities | 6.7 |
| Cabins: Comfort/Facilities | 5.8 |
| Cabins: Software | 7.7 |
| Food: Dining Room/Cuisine | 6.6 |
| Food: Buffets/Informal Dining | 6.1 |
| Food: Quality of Ingredients | 6.2 |
| Service: Dining Room | 7.0 |
| Service: Bars/Lounges | 6.8 |
| Service: Cabins | 7.2 |
| Cruise: Entertainment | 7.3 |
| Cruise: Activities Program | 7.1 |
| Cruise: Hospitality Standard | 7.6 |
| OVERALL RATING | 101.8 |

**+** Good open deck space for sun-worshippers. Plentiful public rooms with attractive decor, now in lighter colors. Excellent indoor-outdoor entertainment nightclub, which incorporates the occasional use of an aft open deck area. Pleasant dining room with sea views from big picture windows. Service is attentive and comes with a smile, but lacks finesse.

**–** Very poor cabin insulation. The cabins are small and compact, with tinny metal fixtures, very thin walls, and little closet space.

**Dining** Pleasant dining room has large picture windows. Reasonable banquet food standard, tailored for U.K. passengers. Out-of-the-ordinary requests become difficult. Good, cheerful service from an attentive staff, but it somehow lacks the finesse that Cunard was once known for. Poor cabin service menu should be upgraded.

**Other Comments** Almost identical to her sister ship, *Cunard Countess*, with the same contemporary profile and balanced looks. This ship will provide you with a very comfortable first cruise experience in a pleasing, very informal environment, at an excellent price, and to some well-chosen destinations. Cunard provides outstanding value for money, and that's why this ship is always popular. She is now marketed almost exclusively to British passengers, for whom port taxes are included.

# mts Daphne ★★★+

***Principal Cruising Areas***

*Europe/Mediterranean (12 nights)*

***Base Port:** Venice*

| | | | |
|---|---|---|---|
| Cruise Line | | | *Costa Cruises/Prestige Cruises* |
| Former Names | | | *Therisos Express/Port Sydney* |
| Gross Tonnage | | | *9,436* |
| Builder | | | *Swan, Hunter (UK)* |
| Original Cost | | | *n/a* |
| Christened By | | | *n/a* |
| First Entered Service | | | *Mar 1955/Jul 26, 1975* |
| Interior Design | | | *A&M Katzourakis* |
| Country of Registry | | | *Liberia (ELLU8)* |
| Tel No | *124-6505* | Fax No | *124-3127* |
| Length (ft/m) | | | *532.7/162.39* |
| Beam (ft/m) | | | *70.2/21.42* |
| Draft (ft/m) | | | *28.4/8.66* |
| Engines/Propellers | | | *2 Doxford 6-cyl diesels/2 (FP)* |
| Decks | *7* | Crew | *260* |
| Pass. Capacity (basis 2) | *412* | (all berths) | *508* |
| Pass. Space Ratio (basis 2) | *22.9* | (all berths) | *18.5* |
| Officers | *Italian* | Dining Staff | *Italian/Intl* |
| Total Cabins | | | *206* |
| Size (sq ft/m) | | | *150.6-349.8/14-32.5* |
| Door Width | | | *25"* |
| Outside Cabins | *189* | Inside Cabins | *17* |
| Single Cabins | *0* | Supplement | *50%* |
| Balcony Cabins | *6* | Wheelchair Cabins | *0* |
| Cabin Current | | | *220 DC* |
| Refrigerator | | | *Suites* |
| Cabin TV | *Suites* | VCR | *No* |
| Dining Rooms | *1* | Sittings | *1* |

| | | | |
|---|---|---|---|
| Elevators | *2* | Door Width | *22-31"* |
| Casino | *Yes* | Slot Machines | *Yes* |
| Swimming Pools (outside) | *1* | (inside) | *0* |
| Whirlpools | *2* | Gymnasium | *Yes* |
| Sauna/Steam Rm | *Yes/No* | Massage | *Yes* |
| Self-Service Launderette | | | *Yes* |
| Movie Theater/Seats | | | *Yes/200* |
| Library | *Yes* | Children's Facilities | *No* |
| Watersports Facilities | | | *None* |
| Classification Society | | | *RINA* |

| RATINGS | SCORE |
|---|---|
| Ship: Condition/Cleanliness | 7.1 |
| Ship: Space/Flow/Comfort | 7.2 |
| Ship: Decor/Furnishings | 7.2 |
| Ship: Fitness Facilities | 5.7 |
| Cabins: Comfort/Facilities | 7.0 |
| Cabins: Software | 7.2 |
| Food: Dining Room/Cuisine | 7.5 |
| Food: Buffets/Informal Dining | 6.9 |
| Food: Quality of Ingredients | 6.8 |
| Service: Dining Room | 7.2 |
| Service: Bars/Lounges | 7.0 |
| Service: Cabins | 7.1 |
| Cruise: Entertainment | 6.0 |
| Cruise: Activities Program | 6.0 |
| Cruise: Hospitality Standard | 7.0 |
| OVERALL RATING | 102.9 |

**+** Excellent outdoor deck and sunning space. Well maintained vessel. Good open deck and sunning space. Bright, contemporary colors in public rooms. Lovely theater, especially good for meetings. Spacious cabins with good, solid fittings and heavy-duty doors. There's plenty of closet and drawer space, and very good insulation between cabins. Bathrooms are of a generous size.

**–** There's no forward-looking observation lounge, and no wrap-around promenade deck.

**Dining** Charming dining room, with uncluttered seating. Friendly, attentive European service throughout. Food is very good, especially the pasta.

**Other Comments** Identical in outward appearance to sister *Danae* (no longer operating), and originally a general cargo vessel, her interior decor is quite different. This is a very comfortable ship, built to a high standard. She maintains an air of intimacy, has a fine range of public rooms, and represents good value when cruising on itineraries longer than a week.

# mv Delfin Star ★★★+

***Principal Cruising Area***

*Baltic (3/4 nights year-round)*

***Base Port:** Norrkoping*

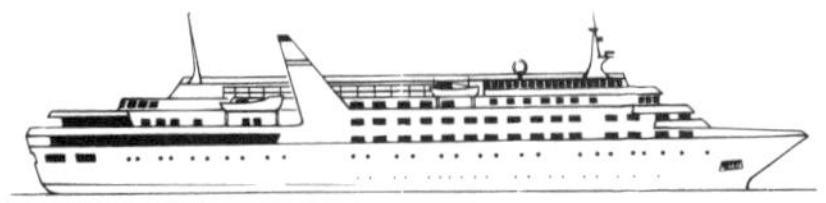

| | | | |
|---|---|---|---|
| Cruise Line | | | *Effjohn International/Baltic Line* |
| Former Names | | | *Baltic Clipper/Sally Clipper/ Delfin Clipper* |
| Gross Tonnage | | | *5,207* |
| Builder | | | *Rauma-Repola (Finland)* |
| Original Cost | | | *$50 million* |
| Christened By | | | *n/a* |
| First Entered Service | | | *Jul 1989* |
| Interior Design | | | *A&R Kukkasniemi* |
| Country of Registry | | | *Finland (OIZG)* |
| Tel No | *162-3147* | Fax No | *162-3147* |
| Length (ft/m) | | | *354.9/108.20* |
| Beam (ft/m) | | | *51.1/15.60* |
| Draft (ft/m) | | | *14.3/4.38* |
| Engines/Propellers | | | *2 VASA 6-cyl diesels/2 (CP)* |
| Decks | *5* | Crew | *70* |
| Pass. Capacity (basis 2) | *238* | (all berths) | *300* |
| Pass. Space Ratio (basis 2) | *23.9* | (all berths) | *19.0* |
| Officers | *Scandinavian* | Dining Staff | *Scandinavian* |
| Total Cabins | | | *119* |
| Size (sq ft/m) | *130/12* | Door Width | *24"* |
| Outside Cabins | *119* | Inside Cabins | *0* |
| Single Cabins | *0* | Supplement | *100%* |
| Balcony Cabins | *0* | Wheelchair Cabins | *0* |
| Cabin Current | | | *220 AC* |
| Refrigerator | | | *No* |
| Cabin TV | *Yes* | VCR | *No* |
| Dining Rooms | *1* | Sittings | *1* |

| | | | |
|---|---|---|---|
| Elevators | *2* | Door Width | *30"* |
| Casino | *Yes* | Slot Machines | *Yes* |
| Swimming Pools (outside) | *1* | (inside) | *0* |
| Whirlpools | *1* | Gymnasium | *Yes* |
| Sauna/Steam Rm | *Yes/No* | Massage | *Yes* |
| Self-Service Launderette | | | *No* |
| Movie Theater/Seats | | | *No* |
| Library | | | *No* |
| Children's Facilities | | | *Yes* |
| Classification Society | | | *Lloyd's Register* |

| **RATINGS** | **SCORE** |
|---|---|
| Ship: Condition/Cleanliness | 7.6 |
| Ship: Space/Flow/Comfort | 7.1 |
| Ship: Decor/Furnishings | 7.4 |
| Ship: Fitness Facilities | 4.1 |
| Cabins: Comfort/Facilities | 7.0 |
| Cabins: Software | 7.4 |
| Food: Dining Room/Cuisine | 6.4 |
| Food: Buffets/Informal Dining | 6.2 |
| Food: Quality of Ingredients | 6.7 |
| Service: Dining Room | 7.2 |
| Service: Bars/Lounges | 7.3 |
| Service: Cabins | 7.3 |
| Cruise: Entertainment | 6.0 |
| Cruise: Activities Program | 5.7 |
| Cruise: Hospitality Standard | 6.7 |
| OVERALL RATING | 100.3 |

**+** Built to a high standard of fit and finish. Cabins are located forward, public rooms aft. Tasteful, contemporary, Scandinavian interior design in the public areas. Cabins are fitted out to a high standard, with good closet and drawer space. Suites have whirlpool bathtubs and other nice touches.

**–** A little small for choppy open water.

**Dining** Spacious, pastel-colored dining room with good ambiance accommodates all passengers at one sitting. Good service by an attentive staff.

**Other Comments** Twin, swept-back outboard funnels highlight smart exterior design of small cruise ship with ice-hardened hull. This ship will be successful in a selected short cruise marketplace where it does not have to compete with larger ships. A very comfortable cruise in tasteful surroundings, at a moderate price, on a Baltic service, targeted to Scandinavian passengers.

# mv Dimitriy Shostakovich ★★

*Principal Cruising Area*
*Europe (14 nights)*
***Base Port:** Odessa*

| | | | |
|---|---|---|---|
| Cruise Line | | | *Black Sea Shipping* |
| Former Names | | | *n/a* |
| Gross Tonnage | | | *10,303* |
| Builder | | | *A. Warski (Poland)* |
| Original Cost | | | *n/a* |
| Christened By | | | *n/a* |
| First Entered Service | | | *1980* |
| Interior Design | | | *n/a* |
| Country of Registry | | | *Ukraine (UMYN)* |
| Tel No | *140-1336* | Fax No | *140-1336* |
| Length (ft/m) | | | *450.0/137.15* |
| Beam (ft/m) | | | *68.8/21.00* |
| Draft (ft/m) | | | *17.3/5.28* |
| Engines/Propellers | | | *2 Sulzer diesels/2* |
| Decks | *7* | Crew | *150* |
| Pass. Capacity (basis 2) | *278* | (all berths) | *494* |
| Pass. Space Ratio (basis 2) | *37.0* | (all berths) | *20.8* |
| Officers | | | *Russian/Ukrainian* |
| Dining Staff | | | *East European* |
| Total Cabins | | | *139* |
| Size (sq ft/m) | *100-320/9.3-29.7* | Door Width | *24"* |
| Outside Cabins | *66* | Inside Cabins | *73* |
| Single Cabins | *0* | Supplement | *100%* |
| Balcony Cabins | *0* | Wheelchair Cabins | *0* |
| Cabin Current | *220 AC* | Refrigerator | *No* |
| Cabin TV | *No* | VCR | *No* |
| Dining Rooms | *1* | Sittings | *1* |
| Elevators | *1* | Door Width | *30"* |

| | | | |
|---|---|---|---|
| Casino | *No* | Slot Machines | *No* |
| Swimming Pools (outside) | *1* | (inside) | *0* |
| Whirlpools | *0* | Gymnasium | *Yes* |
| Sauna/Steam Rm | *Yes/No* | Massage | *Yes* |
| Self-Service Launderette | | | *No* |
| Movie Theater/Seats | | | *No* |
| Library | | | *Yes* |
| Children's Facilities | | | *No* |
| Watersports Facilities | | | *None* |
| Classification Society | | | *RS* |

| RATINGS | SCORE |
|---|---|
| Ship: Condition/Cleanliness | 6.6 |
| Ship: Space/Flow/Comfort | 6.2 |
| Ship: Decor/Furnishings | 6.0 |
| Ship: Fitness Facilities | 5.6 |
| Cabins: Comfort/Facilities | 5.5 |
| Cabins: Software | 6.1 |
| Food: Dining Room/Cuisine | 5.3 |
| Food: Buffets/Informal Dining | 5.1 |
| Food: Quality of Ingredients | 5.1 |
| Service: Dining Room | 6.1 |
| Service: Bars/Lounges | 6.2 |
| Service: Cabins | 6.2 |
| Cruise: Entertainment | 4.3 |
| Cruise: Activities Program | 4.7 |
| Cruise: Hospitality Standard | 5.8 |
| OVERALL RATING | 84.8 |

**+** Fully-enclosed bridge, as well as an ice-hardened hull—good for cold-weather cruise areas. One of a series of five Polish-built vessels intended for all-weather line voyages.

**–** Limited open deck and sunning space. Tiny swimming pool. Limited choice of public rooms.

**Dining** The dining room is reasonably comfortable, and everyone dines in one sitting, with food served family-style. The food is pretty basic, no more, and menu choice is very limited, as is the selection of breads, cheeses and fruits.

**Other Comments** This ship has a square, angular profile with upright stern, stubby bow, and fat funnel. Interior decor is rather spartan, yet the ambiance is comfortable, improved by tropical plants. Cabins, some with upper pullman berths, are small and utilitarian in fittings and furnishings, but adequate. Bathrooms are small, however. This ship features a regular 14-day itinerary that provides a destination-oriented, basic cruise experience for an international clientele, at modest rates, nothing more. Insurance and gratuities are extra.

# ss Dolphin IV ★★★

***Principal Cruising Area***

*Bahamas (3/4 nights year-round)*

***Base Port:** Miami (Fri/Mon)*

| | | | |
|---|---|---|---|
| Cruise Line | | | *Dolphin Cruise Line* |
| Former Names | | | *Ithaca/Amelia De Melo/Zion* |
| Gross Tonnage | | | *13,000* |
| Builder | | | *Howaldtswerke Deutsche Werft* |
| Original Cost | | | *n/a* |
| Christened By | | | *n/a* |
| First Entered Service | | | *Mar 9, 1956/Jan 17, 1979* |
| Interior Design | | | *n/a* |
| Country of Registry | | | *Bahamas (HOOG)* |
| Tel No | *n/a* | Fax No | *n/a* |
| Length (ft/m) | | | *501.2/152.77* |
| Beam (ft/m) | | | *65.1/19.87* |
| Draft (ft/m) | | | *27.5/8.40* |
| Engines/Propellers | | | *2 DRG steam turbines/1* |
| Decks | *7* | Crew | *290* |
| Pass. Capacity (basis 2) | *588* | (all berths) | *684* |
| Pass. Space Ratio (basis 2) | *22.1* | (all berths) | *19.0* |
| Officers | *Greek* | Dining Staff | *International* |
| Total Cabins | | | *281* |
| Size (sq ft/m) | *73-258/6.7-24* | Door Width | *24"* |
| Outside Cabins | *206* | Inside Cabins | *75* |
| Single Cabins | *0* | Supplement | *50%* |
| Balcony Cabins | *0* | Wheelchair Cabins | *0* |
| Cabin Current | | | *110/220 AC* |
| Refrigerator | | | *No* |
| Cabin TV | *No* | VCR | *No* |
| Dining Rooms | *1* | Sittings | *2* |
| Elevators | *1* | Door Width | *27"* |

| | | | |
|---|---|---|---|
| Casino | *Yes* | Slot Machines | *Yes* |
| Swimming Pools (outside) | *1* | (inside) | *0* |
| Whirlpools | *1* | Gymnasium | *Yes* |
| Sauna/Steam Rm | *No/No* | Massage | *No* |
| Self-Service Launderette | | | *No* |
| Movie Theater/Seats | | | *No* |
| Library | | | *No* |
| Children's Facilities | | | *Yes* |
| Watersports Facilities | | | *None* |
| Classification Society | | | *Lloyd's Register* |

| RATINGS | SCORE |
|---|---|
| Ship: Condition/Cleanliness | 6.5 |
| Ship: Space/Flow/Comfort | 5.8 |
| Ship: Decor/Furnishings | 6.4 |
| Ship: Fitness Facilities | 4.5 |
| Cabins: Comfort/Facilities | 6.4 |
| Cabins: Software | 6.5 |
| Food: Dining Room/Cuisine | 7.0 |
| Food: Buffets/Informal Dining | 6.8 |
| Food: Quality of Ingredients | 6.6 |
| Service: Dining Room | 6.8 |
| Service: Bars/Lounges | 6.8 |
| Service: Cabins | 7.1 |
| Cruise: Entertainment | 6.8 |
| Cruise: Activities Program | 6.5 |
| Cruise: Hospitality Standard | 6.8 |
| OVERALL RATING | 97.3 |

**+** Attractive-looking older ship with pleasing lines, even with its noticeable "center sag." Public rooms are well decorated in clean, contemporary colors, with much use of reflective surfaces. Good shopping arcade. Revamped showroom is an improvement. The cabins are small, yet comfortable, and quite adequate for short cruises. Friendly staff and ambiance.

**–** Cramped open deck and sunning area due to high density. Very claustrophobic discotheque. Cabins on lower decks suffer from noise (and the smell of diesel) from the engine-room. Entertainment is rather weak and low budget.

**Dining** Charming dining room has warm ambiance, but is narrow and has a low ceiling. The food is reasonably good, even creative, but ingredients aren't the best. Service is moderately good, but is hurried and lacking in finesse, although the staff are friendly and try to please. Good buffet displays.

**Other Comments** This ship has a good, friendly, and lively ambiance, and is recommended for short, fun cruises for the young, active set, but I wonder how much longer she can compete with the bright new ships that offer more facilities, and indeed more of everything.

# ms Dreamward ★★★★+

***Principal Cruising Areas***

*Bermuda/Caribbean (7 nights)*

***Base Ports:** New York/Ft. Lauderdale*

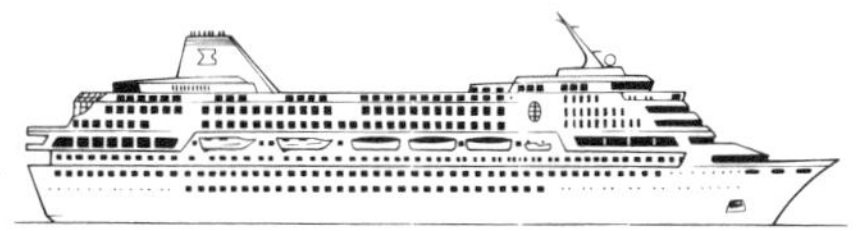

| | | | |
|---|---|---|---|
| Cruise Line | | | *Norwegian Cruise Line* |
| Former Names | | | *n/a* |
| Gross Tonnage | | | *39,217* |
| Builder | | | *Chantiers de l'Atlantique (France)* |
| Original Cost | | | *$240 million* |
| Christened By | | | *Diana Ross* |
| First Entered Service | | | *Dec 6, 1992* |
| Interior Design | | | *Yran & Storbraaten* |
| Country of Registry | | | *Bahamas (NCLG)* |
| Tel No | *130-5510* | Fax No | *130-5507* |
| Length (ft/m) | | | *623.3/190.00* |
| Beam (ft/m) | *93.5/28.50* | Draft (ft/m) | *22.3/6.80* |
| Engines/Propellers | | | *2 MAN 8-cyl diesels/2* |
| Decks | *11* | Crew | *483* |
| Pass. Capacity (basis 2) | *1,246* | (all berths) | *1,450* |
| Pass. Space Ratio (basis 2) | *32.9* | (all berths) | *28.2* |
| Officers | *Norwegian* | Dining Staff | *International* |
| Total Cabins | | | *623* |
| Size (sq ft/m) | *140-350/13-32.5* | Door Width | *26.5"* |
| Outside Cabins | *530* | Inside Cabins | *93* |
| Single Cabins | *0* | Supplement | *50-100%* |
| Balcony Cabins | | | *48* |
| Wheelchair Cabins | | | *6 (+30 for hearing-impaired)* |
| Cabin Current | | | *110 AC* |
| Refrigerator | | | *Cat. 1/2/3* |
| Cabin TV | *Yes* | VCR | *No* |
| Dining Rooms | *4* | Sittings | *2* |
| Elevators | *7* | Door Width | *31.5"* |

| | | | |
|---|---|---|---|
| Casino | *Yes* | Slot Machines | *Yes* |
| Swimming Pools (outside) | *1* | (inside) | *0* |
| Whirlpools | *2* | Gymnasium | *Yes* |
| Sauna/Steam Rm | *Yes/No* | Massage | *Yes* |
| Self-Service Launderette | | | *No* |
| Movie Theater/Seats | | | *No* |
| Library | | | *Yes* |
| Children's Facilities | | | *Yes* |
| Watersports Facilities | | | *None* |
| Classification Society | | | *Det Norske Veritas* |

| RATINGS | SCORE |
|---|---|
| Ship: Condition/Cleanliness | 8.7 |
| Ship: Space/Flow/Comfort | 7.9 |
| Ship: Decor/Furnishings | 8.1 |
| Ship: Fitness Facilities | 8.1 |
| Cabins: Comfort/Facilities | 7.8 |
| Cabins: Software | 8.0 |
| Food: Dining Room/Cuisine | 7.2 |
| Food: Buffets/Informal Dining | 6.3 |
| Food: Quality of Ingredients | 6.4 |
| Service: Dining Room | 7.7 |
| Service: Bars/Lounges | 7.6 |
| Service: Cabins | 7.6 |
| Cruise: Entertainment | 8.4 |
| Cruise: Activities Program | 7.8 |
| Cruise: Hospitality Standard | 7.7 |
| OVERALL RATING | 115.3 |

**+** Built first, this sister to *Windward* has a well-balanced profile, despite its large, square funnel housing. Much innovative design incorporated, with good passenger flow. The ship absorbs passengers well, and the ambiance is good. Tiered pool deck is innovative, and the aft sun terraces are a real plus. Pastel interior decor and color scheme is soothing and well applied. Cabins feature wood-trimmed cabinetry, and warm, restful decor. Hearing impaired cabins are innovative.

**–** The entrance lobby is uninviting. Even though carpeted, the steel interior stairwell steps are tinny. There's almost no drawer space in cabins, so take minimal clothing. Room service menu (choice) is poor. Casino is intimate, but very cramped at times. Snack bar is too crowded.

**Dining** There are four dining rooms (The Terraces is the best), all with the same menu, and a casual Sports Bar for breakfast, luncheon, and teatime buffets (poor). The cuisine is still a weak point, but is improving—best described as family diner food, with an emphasis on thick sauces and salad dressings. Service is perfunctory, at best, by waiters who speak little English and need more training. The wine list is quite good, with very moderate prices, and there are 19 types of beer. Standard cutlery, but no fish knives. Afternoon tea is not served anywhere.

**Other Comments** This ship is proving to be highly successful for NCL's sports-minded passengers. Insurance and gratuities are extra.

# ms Ecstasy ★★★★

***Principal Cruising Area***
*Caribbean (3/4 nights year-round)*
***Base Port:*** *Miami (Fri/Mon)*

| | | | |
|---|---|---|---|
| Cruise Line | | | *Carnival Cruise Lines* |
| Former Names | | | *n/a* |
| Gross Tonnage | | | *70,367* |
| Builder | | | *Kvaerner Masa-Yards (Finland)* |
| Original Cost | | | *$275 million* |
| Christened By | | | *Ms Kathie Lee Gifford* |
| First Entered Service | | | *Jun 2, 1991* |
| Interior Design | | | *Joe Farcus* |
| Country of Registry | | | *Liberia (ELNC5)* |
| Tel No | *124-4233* | Fax No | *124-4234* |
| Length (ft/m) | | | *855.8/260.60* |
| Beam (ft/m) | | | *104.0/31.40* |
| Draft (ft/m) | | | *25.9/7.89* |
| Engines/Propellers | | | *2 Sulzer 8-cyl diesels/2 (CP)* |
| Decks | *10* | Crew | *920* |
| Pass. Capacity (basis 2) | *2,040* | (all berths) | *2,594* |
| Pass. Space Ratio (basis 2) | *34.4* | (all berths) | *27.1* |
| Officers | *Italian* | Dining Staff | *International* |
| Total Cabins | | | *1,020* |
| Size (sq ft/m) | *185-421/17-39* | Door Width | *30"* |
| Outside Cabins | *618* | Inside Cabins | *402* |
| Single Cabins | *0* | Supplement | *50%/100%* |
| Balcony Cabins | *54* | Wheelchair Cabins | *20* |
| Cabin Current | | | *110 AC* |
| Refrigerator | | | *Cat. 11/12* |
| Cabin TV | *Yes* | VCR | *No* |
| Dining Rooms | *2* | Sittings | *2* |
| Elevators | *14* | Door Width | *36"* |

| | | | |
|---|---|---|---|
| Casino | *Yes* | Slot Machines | *Yes* |
| Swimming Pools (outside) | *3* | (inside) | *0* |
| Whirlpools | *6* | Gymnasium | *Yes* |
| Sauna/Steam Rm | *Yes/Yes* | Massage | *Yes* |
| Self-Service Launderette | | | *Yes* |
| Movie Theater/Seats | | | *No* |
| Library | | | *Yes* |
| Children's Facilities | | | *Yes* |
| Watersports Facilities | | | *None* |
| Classification Society | | | *Lloyd's Register* |

| RATINGS | SCORE |
|---|---|
| Ship: Condition/Cleanliness | 8.0 |
| Ship: Space/Flow/Comfort | 7.8 |
| Ship: Decor/Furnishings | 6.8 |
| Ship: Fitness Facilities | 7.8 |
| Cabins: Comfort/Facilities | 7.6 |
| Cabins: Software | 7.4 |
| Food: Dining Room/Cuisine | 6.7 |
| Food: Buffets/Informal Dining | 6.5 |
| Food: Quality of Ingredients | 5.3 |
| Service: Dining Room | 7.0 |
| Service: Bars/Lounges | 7.2 |
| Service: Cabins | 6.4 |
| Cruise: Entertainment | 7.9 |
| Cruise: Activities Program | 7.8 |
| Cruise: Hospitality Standard | 6.3 |
| OVERALL RATING | 106.5 |

**+** Good passenger flow throughout. Clever interior design. Vintage Rolls Royce on indoor promenade. Fine health spa. Stunning 7.2 ft.-high, "double helix," 10-ton sculpture graces marble and glass atrium that spans seven decks. Lovely library (but few books). Plain, but comfortable, cabins are roomy, with good storage space and practical bathrooms. Suites are very attractive. A great introduction to cruising for the novice passenger seeking an action-packed short cruise experience in contemporary surroundings, with the minimum of fuss, lots of enthusiasm, and good, noisy entertainment. Great for nightlife and silly games.

**–** Wild use of neon lighting in the interior decor. Color combinations are too wild and vivid. Poor food. Too many people, too many annoying announcements, and far too much hustling for drinks. Long lines for embarkation, disembarkation, and buffets.

**Dining** The two dining rooms have attractive decor and colors, but are large, crowded, and very noisy. The food is adequate, but there's little hint of quality, only quantity, despite being upgraded lately. Service is robotic, timed, and inflexible, although waiters are willing and friendly.

**Other Comments** Public rooms will transport you into a land of pure fantasy and escape, based on New York nightlife, and a kaleidoscope of colors. An enthusiastic staff will make sure you have fun, and that's what Carnival does best. Insurance and gratuities are extra.

# ss Enchanted Seas ★★★

***Principal Cruising Area***

*Mexico (7 nights year-round)*

***Base Port:*** *New Orleans*

| | | | |
|---|---|---|---|
| Cruise Line | | | *Commodore Cruise Line* |
| Former Names | | | *Queen of Bermuda/Canada Star/ Liberte/Island Sun/Volendam/Monarch Sun/Brazil* |
| Gross Tonnage | | | *23,879* |
| Builder | | | *Ingalls Shipbuilding (USA)* |
| Original Cost | | | *$26 million* |
| Christened By | | | *Mrs Emmett J. McCormack* |
| First Entered Service | | | *Sep 12, 1958/Nov 3, 1990* |
| Interior Design | | | *n/a* |
| Country of Registry | | | *Bahamas (3FMF2)* |
| Tel No | *113-1605* | Fax No | *133-1605* |
| Length (ft/m) | | | *617.4/188.20* |
| Beam (ft/m) | | | *84.3/25.70* |
| Draft (ft/m) | | | *27.2/8.30* |
| Engines/Propellers | | | *4 steam turbines/2* |
| Decks | *8* | Crew | *365* |
| Pass. Capacity (basis 2) | *740* | (all berths) | *846* |
| Pass. Space Ratio (basis 2) | *32.2* | (all berths) | *28.2* |
| Officers | *European* | Dining Staff | *International* |
| Total Cabins | | | *371* |
| Size (sq ft/m) | *104-293/9.6-27.2* | Door Width | *26"* |
| Outside Cabins | *290* | Inside Cabins | *79* |
| Single Cabins | *2* | Supplement | *50-100%* |
| Balcony Cabins | *0* | Wheelchair Cabins | *0* |
| Cabin Current | *110 AC* | Refrigerator | *No* |
| Cabin TV | *Yes* | VCR | *No* |
| Dining Rooms | *1* | Sittings | *2* |
| Elevators | *3* | Door Width | *30-33"* |

| | | | |
|---|---|---|---|
| Casino | *Yes* | Slot Machines | *Yes* |
| Swimming Pools (outside) | 2 | (inside) | *0* |
| Whirlpools | *0* | Gymnasium | *Yes* |
| Sauna/Steam Rm | *No/No* | Massage | *Yes* |
| Self-Service Launderette | | | *No* |
| Movie Theater/Seats | | | *Yes/200* |
| Library | | | *Yes* |
| Children's Facilities | | | *Yes* |
| Watersports Facilities | | | *None* |
| Classification Society | | | *American Bur. of Shipping* |

| RATINGS | SCORE |
|---|---|
| Ship: Condition/Cleanliness | 6.4 |
| Ship: Space/Flow/Comfort | 6.2 |
| Ship: Decor/Furnishings | 6.6 |
| Ship: Fitness Facilities | 4.5 |
| Cabins: Comfort/Facilities | 6.3 |
| Cabins: Software | 6.6 |
| Food: Dining Room/Cuisine | 6.3 |
| Food: Buffets/Informal Dining | 5.8 |
| Food: Quality of Ingredients | 6.0 |
| Service: Dining Room | 6.0 |
| Service: Bars/Lounges | 6.2 |
| Service: Cabins | 6.4 |
| Cruise: Entertainment | 6.0 |
| Cruise: Activities Program | 5.6 |
| Cruise: Hospitality Standard | 6.1 |
| OVERALL RATING | 91.0 |

**+** Somewhat traditional, ocean-liner profile. Extensively refurbished. Beautifully-finished outdoor teakwood decks. Being an older ship, she has spacious outdoor promenade areas. The public rooms are spacious and well equipped, with high ceilings, and pleasing decor and colors. The showroom is quite good, but cannot compare with those on larger, more modern ships. Large casino. Plenty of sheltered and open sunning space. Two outdoor pools are well used. Cabins are of a generous size, with nice, heavy-duty furniture and fittings.

**–** Expect long lines for casual buffet meals. Poor sightlines in showlounge.

**Dining** Charming dining room has large windows which provide light and a good ambiance. The menu choice is somewhat limited, but service is attentive and comes with a smile, even if it's without finesse. Poor selection of bread rolls, cheeses, and fruits.

**Other Comments** This ship offers an enjoyable first cruise experience in comfortable, old world style surroundings, at a very reasonable price. However, with all the discounting, service and product delivery standards have been lowered. Insurance and gratuities are extra.

# ts EnricoCosta ★★★

***Principal Cruising Areas***

*Europe/Mediterranean (6-11 nights)*

***Base Ports:** Amsterdam/Genoa*

| | | | |
|---|---|---|---|
| Cruise Line | | | *Costa Cruises* |
| Former Names | | | *Enrico C/Provence* |
| Gross Tonnage | | | *16,495* |
| Builder | | | *Swan, Hunter (UK)* |
| Original Cost | | | *n/a* |
| Christened By | | | *n/a* |
| First Entered Service | | | *Mar 30, 1951/February 1966* |
| Interior Design | | | *Architects Falletti/De Jorio* |
| Country of Registry | | | *Italy (ICEI)* |
| Tel No | *115-0561* | Fax No | *115-0561* |
| Length (ft/m) | | | *579.0/176.49* |
| Beam (ft/m) | | | *73.1/22.31* |
| Draft (ft/m) | | | *24.6/7.52* |
| Engines/Propellers | | | *2 Wartsila diesels/2 (FP)* |
| Decks | *7* | Crew | *330* |
| Pass. Capacity (basis 2) | *664* | (all berths) | *845* |
| Pass. Space Ratio (basis 2) | *24.8* | (all berths) | *19.5* |
| Officers | *Italian* | Dining Staff | *Italian/Intl* |
| Total Cabins | | | *332* |
| Size (sq ft/m) | *86.1-216.3/8-20.1* | Door Width | *26"* |
| Outside Cabins | *159* | Inside Cabins | *173* |
| Single Cabins | *0* | Supplement | *50%* |
| Balcony Cabins | *0* | Wheelchair Cabins | *0* |
| Cabin Current | | | *220 DC* |
| Refrigerator | | | *No* |
| Cabin TV | *No* | VCR | *No* |
| Dining Rooms | *1* | Sittings | *2* |
| Elevators | *2* | Door Width | *30"* |

| | | | |
|---|---|---|---|
| Casino | *No* | Slot Machines | *No* |
| Swimming Pools (outside) | *3* | (inside) | *0* |
| Whirlpools | *0* | Gymnasium | *No* |
| Sauna/Steam Rm | *No/No* | Massage | *No* |
| Self-Service Launderette | | | *Yes* |
| Movie Theater/Seats | | | *Yes/85* |
| Library | | | *No* |
| Children's Facilities | | | *Yes* |
| Watersports Facilities | | | *None* |
| Classification Society | | | *RINA* |

| RATINGS | SCORE |
|---|---|
| Ship: Condition/Cleanliness | 6.8 |
| Ship: Space/Flow/Comfort | 6.4 |
| Ship: Decor/Furnishings | 7.2 |
| Ship: Fitness Facilities | 4.6 |
| Cabins: Comfort/Facilities | 6.4 |
| Cabins: Software | 6.8 |
| Food: Dining Room/Cuisine | 6.7 |
| Food: Buffets/Informal Dining | 6.3 |
| Food: Quality of Ingredients | 6.7 |
| Service: Dining Room | 7.1 |
| Service: Bars/Lounges | 7.2 |
| Service: Cabins | 7.4 |
| Cruise: Entertainment | 6.4 |
| Cruise: Activities Program | 6.3 |
| Cruise: Hospitality Standard | 7.2 |
| OVERALL RATING | 99.5 |

**+** Solidly-built vessel which recently received an extensive refurbishment. Good open deck promenade areas. The newer facilities are fine, while others have been much upgraded. The public rooms feature "Belle Epoque" decor and are very smart, but crowded when full. Cabins are compact but comfortable, with tasteful, new pastel decor.

**–** Steep gangway. Ceilings are very plain and uninteresting. Entertainment is loud and poor.

**Dining** The dining room is comfortable, though rather noisy. Good, bubbly, Italian service and food, with excellent pasta, but other dishes lack quality.

**Other Comments** Traditional, ocean liner styling, reconstructed from her former life as a cargo-passenger liner. Large, single yellow funnel. Some 75 cabins are still without private facilities. Beautiful wood paneling and brass trim throughout adds warmth and old world elegance lacking in many new ships. This ship caters primarily to budget-minded European passengers looking for a Mediterranean cruise without the trimmings, and to many Italian passengers. Lots of loud announcements. Insurance and gratuities are extra.

# ts EugenioCosta ★★★+

***Principal Cruising Areas***

*Mediterranean/S. America (4,6,10/8-14 nights)*

***Base Ports:** Genoa/Buenos Aires/Rio*

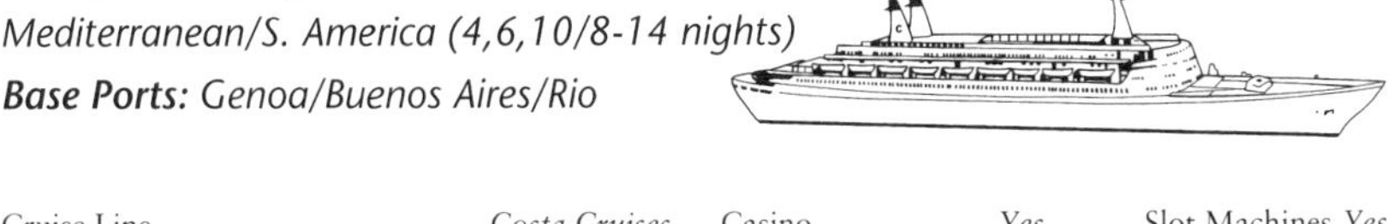

| | | | |
|---|---|---|---|
| Cruise Line | | | *Costa Cruises* |
| Former Names | | | *Eugenio C* |
| Gross Tonnage | | | *32,753* |
| Builder | | | *Cantieri Riuniti dell' Adriatico (Italy)* |
| Original Cost | | | *$24.5 million* |
| Christened By | | | *Pinuccia Costa Musso* |
| First Entered Service | | | *Aug 31, 1966/Dec 18, 1994* |
| Interior Design | | | *Architects Zoncada/De Jorio* |
| Country of Registry | | | *Italy (ICVV)* |
| Tel No | *115-0116* | Fax No | *115-0116* |
| Length (ft/m) | | | *713.2/217.39* |
| Beam (ft/m) | | | *96.1/29.39* |
| Draft (ft/m) | | | *28.3/8.63* |
| Engines/Propellers | | | *4 steam turbines/2 (FP)* |
| Decks | *10* | Crew | *480* |
| Pass. Capacity (basis 2) | *1,012* | (all berths) | *1,418* |
| Pass. Space Ratio (basis 2) | *32.3* | (all berths) | *23.0* |
| Officers | *Italian* | Dining Staff | *Italian/Intl* |
| Total Cabins | | | *506 (8 without facilities)* |
| Size (sq ft/m) | *93.6-236.8/8.7-22* | Door Width | *27"* |
| Outside Cabins | *271* | Inside Cabins | *235* |
| Single Cabins | *0* | Supplement | *50%* |
| Balcony Cabins | *0* | Wheelchair Cabins | *0* |
| Cabin Current | | | *127 AC* |
| Refrigerator | | | *No* |
| Cabin TV | *No* | VCR | *No* |
| Dining Rooms | *1* | Sittings | *2* |
| Elevators | *5* | Door Width | *29"* |

| | | | |
|---|---|---|---|
| Casino | *Yes* | Slot Machines | *Yes* |
| Swimming Pools (outside) | *2* | (inside) | *0* |
| Whirlpools | *1* | Gymnasium | *Yes* |
| Sauna/Steam Rm | *Yes/No* | Massage | *Yes* |
| Self-Service Launderette | | | *Yes* |
| Movie Theater/Seats | | | *Yes/230* |
| Library | | | *Yes* |
| Children's Facilities | | | *Yes* |
| Watersports Facilities | | | *None* |
| Classification Society | | | *RINA* |

| RATINGS | SCORE |
|---|---|
| Ship: Condition/Cleanliness | 7.1 |
| Ship: Space/Flow/Comfort | 7.3 |
| Ship: Decor/Furnishings | 7.6 |
| Ship: Fitness Facilities | 6.3 |
| Cabins: Comfort/Facilities | 7.3 |
| Cabins: Software | 7.4 |
| Food: Dining Room/Cuisine | 6.7 |
| Food: Buffets/Informal Dining | 6.3 |
| Food: Quality of Ingredients | 6.7 |
| Service: Dining Room | 7.3 |
| Service: Bars/Lounges | 7.3 |
| Service: Cabins | 7.6 |
| Cruise: Entertainment | 6.1 |
| Cruise: Activities Program | 6.4 |
| Cruise: Hospitality Standard | 7.1 |
| OVERALL RATING | 104.5 |

**+** Good, teakwood decking outdoors, and good open deck and sunning space. Spacious array of public rooms feature new, theme-park decor and colors. There's a good range of accommodations, with many different styles, sizes, and configurations of cabins. This ship is comfortable throughout, and provides good value cruising for families in a no-ties setting that is unashamedly an ultra-casual, high density, floating, all-year-round summer camp.

**–** Long lines for embarkation, disembarkation, buffets, and shore tenders. Many passengers smoke heavily, and it's almost impossible to get away from them. Nonsmokers should choose another ship.

**Dining** Pasta dishes are excellent, but other dishes can only be described as adequate, and certainly not memorable. Poor selection of breads, cheeses, and fruits.

**Other Comments** Well-proportioned ship with the graceful flowing lines of a sixties liner, and twin slender funnels aft. Provides good value cruises for its mainly Italian-speaking clientele.

# ms Europa ★★★★★+

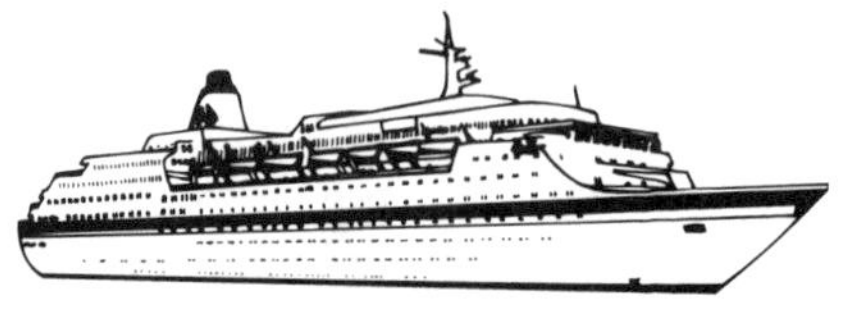

***Principal Cruising Areas***

*Worldwide (various)*

***Base Port:*** *Bremerhaven*

| | | | |
|---|---|---|---|
| Cruise Line | | | *Hapag-Lloyd Cruises* |
| Former Names | | | *n/a* |
| Gross Tonnage | | | *37,012* |
| Builder | | | *Bremer Vulkan (Germany)* |
| Original Cost | | | *$120 million* |
| Christened By | | | *Mrs Simone Veil* |
| First Entered Service | | | *Jan 8, 1982* |
| Interior Design | | | *Wilfried Kohnemann* |
| Country of Registry | | | *Germany (DLAL)* |
| Tel No | *112-0756* | Fax No | *112-0756* |
| Length (ft/m) | | | *654.9/199.63* |
| Beam (ft/m) | | | *93.8/28.60* |
| Draft (ft/m) | | | *27.6/8.42* |
| Engines/Propellers | | | *2 MAN 7-cyl diesels/2* |
| Decks | *10* | Crew | *300* |
| Pass. Capacity (basis 2) | *600* | (all berths) | *600* |
| Pass. Space Ratio (basis 2) | *61.6* | (all berths) | *61.6* |
| Officers | *German* | Dining Staff | *European* |
| Total Cabins | | | *316* |
| Size (sq ft/m) | *150-420/14-39* | Door Width | *27"* |
| Outside Cabins | *260* | Inside Cabins | *56* |
| Single Cabins | *32* | Supplement | *On request* |
| Balcony Cabins | *0* | Wheelchair Cabins | *1* |
| Cabin Current | | | *110/220 AC* |
| Refrigerator | | | *Yes* |
| Cabin TV | *Yes* | VCR | *Yes* |
| Dining Rooms | *1* | Sittings | *1* |
| Elevators | *4* | Door Width | *36"* |

| | | | |
|---|---|---|---|
| Casino | *No* | Slot Machines | *No* |
| Swimming Pools (outside) | *2* | (inside) | *1* |
| Whirlpools | *0* | Gymnasium | *Yes* |
| Sauna/Steam Rm | *Yes/Yes* | Massage | *Yes* |
| Self-Service Launderette | | | *Yes* |
| Movie Theater/Seats | | | *Yes/238* |
| Library | | | *Yes* |
| Children's Facilities | | | *No* |
| Watersports Facilities | | | *None* |
| Classification Society | | | *Germanischer Lloyd* |

| RATINGS | SCORE |
|---|---|
| Ship: Condition/Cleanliness | 9.4 |
| Ship: Space/Flow/Comfort | 9.5 |
| Ship: Decor/Furnishings | 9.2 |
| Ship: Fitness Facilities | 9.6 |
| Cabins: Comfort/Facilities | 9.3 |
| Cabins: Software | 9.0 |
| Food: Dining Room/Cuisine | 9.1 |
| Food: Buffets/Informal Dining | 8.9 |
| Food: Quality of Ingredients | 8.8 |
| Service: Dining Room | 8.8 |
| Service: Bars/Lounges | 8.6 |
| Service: Cabins | 9.0 |
| Cruise: Entertainment | 8.6 |
| Cruise: Activities Program | 8.5 |
| Cruise: Hospitality Standard | 9.0 |
| OVERALL RATING | 135.3 |

**+** Beautifully designed, handsome, contemporary ship presents a well-balanced, almost sleek profile. Stable and well behaved at sea. Immaculate maintenance. Outstanding outdoor deck and sunning space, including nudist deck. The Belvedere Lounge is one of the most elegant rooms afloat. Every cabin is superb. Elegance, space, and quality abound. Not a trace of gambling. Plenty of space per passenger. Dark, restful colors in public rooms and cabins, and subtle lighting throughout. Fine artwork. Outstanding health spa and rejuvenation facilities. All cabins feature mini-bar refrigerator with complimentary soft drinks, beer, and personal safe. Excellent cabin insulation. Impeccable staff and excellent service. Highest quality ship. No announcements.

**–** No wrap-around outdoor promenade deck. No Japanese-speaking hostesses.

**Dining** Spacious dining room. Fine silver service. Plenty of space between tables. Excellent ingredients and presentation. Geared to German tastes—carbohydrate-rich and heavy sauces.

**Other Comments** A most elegant cruise experience in supremely luxurious and quiet surroundings. A restful, restorative cruise, with fine quality European entertainment, outstanding itineraries, and superb food and service. Most crew members speak English, but the passengers are almost entirely German-speaking. It's just about the ultimate cruise experience, especially for long cruises. Port taxes and insurance are included. Gratuities are extra.

# mv Explorer ★★★

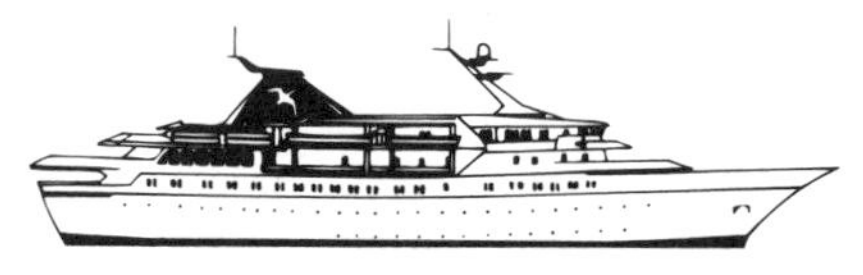

***Principal Cruising Areas***

*Worldwide expedition cruises (various)*

***Base Port:*** *various*

| | | | |
|---|---|---|---|
| Cruise Line | | | *Abercrombie & Kent* |
| Former Names | | | *Society Explorer/ Lindblad Explorer/World Explorer* |
| Gross Tonnage | | | *2,398* |
| Builder | | | *Nystad Varv Shipyard (Finland)* |
| Original Cost | | | *$2.5 million* |
| Christened By | | | *Mrs Sonja Lindblad* |
| First Entered Service | | | *1969/March 14, 1993* |
| Interior Design | | | *n/a* |
| Country of Registry | | | *Liberia (C6BA2)* |
| Tel No | *124-1223* | Fax No | *124-1223* |
| Length (ft/m) | | | *239.1/72.88* |
| Beam (ft/m) | *46.0/14.03* | Draft (ft/m) | *13.7/4.20* |
| Engines/Propellers | | | *1 MWM diesel/1* |
| Decks | *6* | Crew | *71* |
| Pass. Capacity (basis 2) | *100* | (all berths) | *114* |
| Pass. Space Ratio (basis 2) | *23.9* | (all berths) | *21.0* |
| Officers | | | *European* |
| Dining Staff | | | *European/Filipino* |
| Total Cabins | | | *50* |
| Size (sq ft/m) | *n/a* | Door Width | *30"* |
| Outside Cabins | *50* | Inside Cabins | *0* |
| Single Cabins | *8* | Supplement | *40-70% (all others)* |
| Balcony Cabins | *0* | Wheelchair Cabins | *0* |
| Cabin Current | *220 AC* | Refrigerator | *No* |
| Cabin TV | *No* | VCR | *No* |
| Dining Rooms | | | *1 (open seating)* |
| Elevators | *0* | Door Width | *n/a* |

| | | | |
|---|---|---|---|
| Casino | *No* | Slot Machines | *No* |
| Swimming Pools (outside) | *1* | (inside) | *0* |
| Whirlpools | *0* | Exercise Room | *Yes* |
| Sauna/Steam Rm | *Yes/No* | Massage | *Yes* |
| Self-Service Launderette | | | *No* |
| Lecture/Film Room | | | *Yes* |
| Library | | | *Yes* |
| Zodiacs | *Yes* | Helicopter Pad | *No* |
| Watersports Facilities | | | *None* |
| Classification Society | | | *Det Norske Veritas* |

| RATINGS | SCORE |
|---|---|
| Ship: Condition/Cleanliness | 6.0 |
| Ship: Space/Flow/Comfort | 5.6 |
| Ship: Expedition Equipment | 6.7 |
| Ship: Decor/Furnishings | 6.2 |
| Cabins: Comfort/Facilities | 5.5 |
| Cabins: Software | 5.4 |
| Food: Dining Room/Cuisine | 6.4 |
| Food: Buffets/Informal Dining | 6.1 |
| Food: Quality of Ingredients | 6.0 |
| Service: Dining Room | 7.0 |
| Service: Bars/Lounges | 6.6 |
| Service: Cabins | 7.0 |
| Cruise: Itineraries/Operations | 7.8 |
| Cruise: Lecture Program | 7.6 |
| Cruise: Hospitality Standard | 7.6 |
| OVERALL RATING | 97.5 |

**+** Well fitted out with all necessary equipment, including Zodiac rubber landing craft. Now aging and showing signs of wear and age. *National Geographic* maps presented in all cabins. Tasteful interior decor in public rooms. Large reference library. Outstanding lecturers and nature specialists on board.

**–** The cabins are extremely small and utilitarian, with little closet, drawer, and storage space. Even so they are just about adequate for an expedition. Bathrooms are really tiny, however.

**Dining** Intimate dining room is cheerful, though noisy, but seats all passengers at one sitting. Creatively presented food (but there's little choice) and wine list. Smiling, attentive, and genuinely friendly service, but it's quite casual.

**Other Comments** This specialist, unpretentious expedition cruise vessel with ice-hardened hull has a well-balanced profile and is extremely maneuverable, although she is looking tired, and maintenance could be improved. This is cruising for the serious adventurer who wants to explore the world yet have some of the comforts of home within reach. Port taxes and insurance are extra. Shore excursions and gratuities are included.

# tss Fair Princess ★★★

***Principal Cruising Areas***

*Alaska/Mexico (various/10 nights)*

***Base Ports:** Seward/Los Angeles*

| | | | |
|---|---|---|---|
| Cruise Line | | | *Princess Cruises* |
| Former Names | | | *Fairsea/Fairland/Carinthia* |
| Gross Tonnage | | | *24,724* |
| Builder | | | *John Brown & Co. (UK)* |
| Original Cost | | | *n/a* |
| Christened By | | | *HRH Princess Margaret* |
| First Entered Service | | | *Jun 27, 1956/Dec 1971* |
| Interior Design | | | *Barbara Dorn (1984 redesign)* |
| Country of Registry | | | *Liberia (ELMQ)* |
| Tel No | *124-0762* | Fax No | *124-0762* |
| Length (ft/m) | | | *608.2/185.40* |
| Beam (ft/m) | | | *80.3/24.49* |
| Draft (ft/m) | | | *28.5/8.71* |
| Engines/Propellers | | | *2 John Brown steam turbines/2* |
| Decks | *11* | Crew | *430* |
| Pass. Capacity (basis 2) | *890* | (all berths) | *1,100* |
| Pass. Space Ratio (basis 2) | *27.7* | (all berths) | *22.4* |
| Officers | *Italian* | Dining Staff | *European* |
| Total Cabins | | | *445* |
| Size (sq ft/m) | *90-241/8.3-22.3* | Door Width | *24"* |
| Outside Cabins | *228* | Inside Cabins | *217* |
| Single Cabins | *0* | Supplement | *40-100%* |
| Balcony Cabins | *0* | Wheelchair Cabins | *0* |
| Cabin Current | | | *110 AC* |
| Refrigerator | | | *Cat. A* |
| Cabin TV | *No* | VCR | *No* |
| Dining Rooms | *2* | Sittings | *2* |
| Elevators | *3* | Door Width | *36"* |

| | | | |
|---|---|---|---|
| Casino | *Yes* | Slot Machines | *Yes* |
| Swimming Pools (outside) | *3* | (inside) | *0* |
| Whirlpools | *0* | Gymnasium | *Yes* |
| Sauna/Steam Rm | *Yes/No* | Massage | *Yes* |
| Self-Service Launderette | | | *No* |
| Movie Theater/Seats | | | *Yes/330* |
| Library | | | *Yes* |
| Children's Facilities | | | *Yes* |
| Watersports Facilities | | | *None* |
| Classification Society | | | *Lloyd's Register* |

| RATINGS | SCORE |
|---|---|
| Ship: Condition/Cleanliness | 6.4 |
| Ship: Space/Flow/Comfort | 6.2 |
| Ship: Decor/Furnishings | 6.6 |
| Ship: Fitness Facilities | 5.0 |
| Cabins: Comfort/Facilities | 6.4 |
| Cabins: Software | 6.7 |
| Food: Dining Room/Cuisine | 6.8 |
| Food: Buffets/Informal Dining | 6.6 |
| Food: Quality of Ingredients | 6.7 |
| Service: Dining Room | 6.8 |
| Service: Bars/Lounges | 7.0 |
| Service: Cabins | 7.2 |
| Cruise: Entertainment | 7.4 |
| Cruise: Activities Program | 6.6 |
| Cruise: Hospitality Standard | 7.0 |
| OVERALL RATING | 99.4 |

**+** Open deck and sunning space is good, but becomes very crowded when the ship is full. Inside, the art-deco interiors on Promenade Deck are quite elegant. Good for families with children.

**–** Very crowded. Long lines for embarkation, disembarkation, and shore tenders. Very mundane interior decor and colors. Not much sophistication. The public rooms are reasonably comfortable, but barely adequate for the number of passengers, and it's difficult to get away from the many passengers who smoke. Popular pizzeria. Good facilities for families with children. Cabins are generally spacious, with heavy-duty furnishings and fittings, and bathrooms that are now a bit antiquated, with much exposed plumbing. Too many irritating announcements.

**Dining** The dining rooms, although crowded and noisy, have plenty of tables for two. Excellent pasta dishes, but not much else of quality. Fairly attentive, but tired, staff. The cuisine is low-budget banquet food—quantity, not quality. There is an excellent, and always busy pizzeria, especially popular with children.

**Other Comments** Solidly-constructed former ocean liner has classic, but now dated, lines and profile. This high-density ship represents moderately good cruising value, but the ship is now very tired and cannot compete with the newer breed of cruise ships in the company's fleet. Insurance and gratuities are extra.

# tss Fairstar ★★★

***Principal Cruising Areas***
*Asia/South Pacific (14 nights)*
***Base Port:** Sydney*

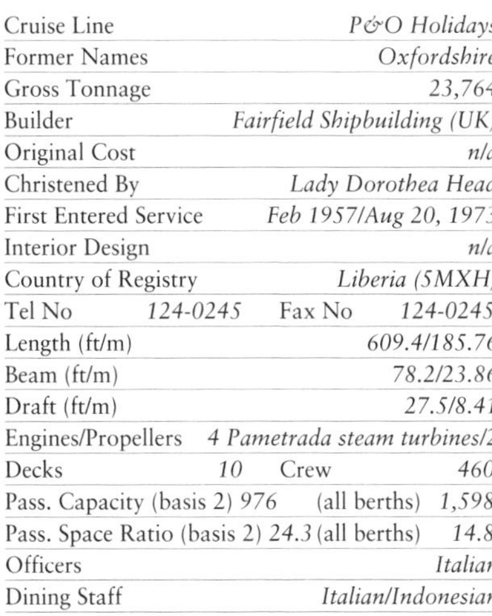

| | | | |
|---|---|---|---|
| Cruise Line | | | *P&O Holidays* |
| Former Names | | | *Oxfordshire* |
| Gross Tonnage | | | *23,764* |
| Builder | | | *Fairfield Shipbuilding (UK)* |
| Original Cost | | | *n/a* |
| Christened By | | | *Lady Dorothea Head* |
| First Entered Service | | | *Feb 1957/Aug 20, 1973* |
| Interior Design | | | *n/a* |
| Country of Registry | | | *Liberia (5MXH)* |
| Tel No | *124-0245* | Fax No | *124-0245* |
| Length (ft/m) | | | *609.4/185.76* |
| Beam (ft/m) | | | *78.2/23.86* |
| Draft (ft/m) | | | *27.5/8.41* |
| Engines/Propellers | | | *4 Pametrada steam turbines/2* |
| Decks | *10* | Crew | *460* |
| Pass. Capacity (basis 2) | *976* | (all berths) | *1,598* |
| Pass. Space Ratio (basis 2) | *24.3* | (all berths) | *14.8* |
| Officers | | | *Italian* |
| Dining Staff | | | *Italian/Indonesian* |
| Total Cabins | | | *488 (68 without facilities)* |
| Size (sq ft/m) | *86-301/8-28* | Door Width | *24"* |
| Outside Cabins | *169* | Inside Cabins | *319* |
| Single Cabins | *0* | Supplement | *On request* |
| Balcony Cabins | *0* | Wheelchair Cabins | *0* |
| Cabin Current | *115 AC* | Refrigerator | *No* |
| Cabin TV | *No* | VCR | *No* |
| Dining Rooms | *2* | Sittings | *2* |
| Elevators | *4* | Door Width | *26"* |

| | | | |
|---|---|---|---|
| Casino | *Yes* | Slot Machines | *Yes* |
| Swimming Pools (outside) | *1* | (inside) | *0* |
| Whirlpools | *0* | Gymnasium | *Yes* |
| Sauna/Steam Rm | *No/No* | Massage | *No* |
| Self-Service Launderette | | | *No* |
| Movie Theater/Seats | | | *Yes/360* |
| Library | | | *No* |
| Children's Facilities | | | *Yes* |
| Watersports Facilities | | | *None* |
| Classification Society | | | *Lloyd's Register* |

| RATINGS | SCORE |
|---|---|
| Ship: Condition/Cleanliness | 6.1 |
| Ship: Space/Flow/Comfort | 5.1 |
| Ship: Decor/Furnishings | 6.6 |
| Ship: Fitness Facilities | 4.7 |
| Cabins: Comfort/Facilities | 5.3 |
| Cabins: Software | 6.2 |
| Food: Dining Room/Cuisine | 6.7 |
| Food: Buffets/Informal Dining | 6.5 |
| Food: Quality of Ingredients | 5.7 |
| Service: Dining Room | 7.0 |
| Service: Bars/Lounges | 6.7 |
| Service: Cabins | 6.6 |
| Cruise: Entertainment | 6.1 |
| Cruise: Activities Program | 6.1 |
| Cruise: Hospitality Standard | 6.0 |
| OVERALL RATING | 91.4 |

**+** Well constructed older ship has classic lines and profile. Well maintained. New late-night Brasserie Delfino is popular. Sail-cloth shade around swimming pool. New arcade shopping area. Good for families with children—plenty of noisy activities. Other cabins fine for two, crowded with more. There is a curfew for children at night.

**–** Limited open deck and sunning space. Long lines for embarkation, disembarkation, and shore tenders. No sophistication. Public rooms are reasonably comfortable, but barely adequate for the number of passengers carried, and it's difficult to get away from the many passengers who smoke. Too many duty-free shops, and lines. No library. Really small cabin bathrooms, many with exposed plumbing. Too many irritating and repetitive announcements.

**Dining** The dining rooms, although crowded and noisy, have plenty of tables for two. The cuisine is low-budget banquet food, and is strictly quantity, not quality, although it's adequate, and there's always plenty of good pasta. There is an excellent and always busy pizzeria, especially popular with children.

**Other Comments** Lacks any sort of glamour, but makes up for it in spirit and a boisterous cruise atmosphere. Excellent value for money cruise product for younger "down-under" passengers who want a lively, active, noisy, fun-filled cruise. Insurance and gratuities are extra.

# ms Fantasy ★★★★

***Principal Cruising Area***
*Bahamas (3/4 nights year-round)*
***Base Port:*** *Port Canaveral (Thu/Sun)*

| | | | |
|---|---|---|---|
| Cruise Line | | | *Carnival Cruise Lines* |
| Former Names | | | *n/a* |
| Gross Tonnage | | | *70,367* |
| Builder | | | *Kvaerner Masa-Yards (Finland)* |
| Original Cost | | | *$225 million* |
| Christened By | | | *Mrs Tellervo Koivisto* |
| First Entered Service | | | *Mar 2, 1990* |
| Interior Design | | | *Joe Farcus* |
| Country of Registry | | | *Liberia (ELKI6)* |
| Tel No | *124-2660* | Fax No | *124-2661* |
| Length (ft/m) | | | *855.8/263.60* |
| Beam (ft/m) | | | *104.0/31.40* |
| Draft (ft/m) | | | *25.9/7.90* |
| Engines/Propellers | | | *2 /2 (CP)* |
| Decks | *10* | Crew | *920* |
| Pass. Capacity (basis 2) | *2,044* | (all berths) | *2,634* |
| Pass. Space Ratio (basis 2) | *34.4* | (all berths) | *26.7* |
| Officers | *Italian* | Dining Staff | *International* |
| Total Cabins | | | *1,022* |
| Size (sq ft/m) | *185-421/17-39* | Door Width | *30"* |
| Outside Cabins | *620* | Inside Cabins | *402* |
| Single Cabins | *0* | Supplement | *50%/100%* |
| Balcony Cabins | *54* | Wheelchair Cabins | *20* |
| Cabin Current | | | *110 AC* |
| Refrigerator | | | *Cat. 11/12* |
| Cabin TV | *Yes* | VCR | *No* |
| Dining Rooms | *2* | Sittings | *2* |
| Elevators | *14* | Door Width | *36"* |

| | | | |
|---|---|---|---|
| Casino | *Yes* | Slot Machines | *Yes* |
| Swimming Pools (outside) | *3* | (inside) | *0* |
| Whirlpools | *6* | Gymnasium | *Yes* |
| Sauna/Steam Rm | *Yes/Yes* | Massage | *Yes* |
| Self-Service Launderette | | | *Yes* |
| Movie Theater/Seats | | | *No* |
| Library | | | *Yes* |
| Children's Facilities | | | *Yes* |
| Watersports Facilities | | | *None* |
| Classification Society | | | *Lloyd's Register* |

| RATINGS | SCORE |
|---|---|
| Ship: Condition/Cleanliness | 8.0 |
| Ship: Space/Flow/Comfort | 7.8 |
| Ship: Decor/Furnishings | 6.8 |
| Ship: Fitness Facilities | 7.8 |
| Cabins: Comfort/Facilities | 7.6 |
| Cabins: Software | 7.4 |
| Food: Dining Room/Cuisine | 6.7 |
| Food: Buffets/Informal Dining | 6.5 |
| Food: Quality of Ingredients | 5.3 |
| Service: Dining Room | 7.0 |
| Service: Bars/Lounges | 7.2 |
| Service: Cabins | 6.4 |
| Cruise: Entertainment | 7.9 |
| Cruise: Activities Program | 7.8 |
| Cruise: Hospitality Standard | 6.3 |
| OVERALL RATING | 106.5 |

**+** Although somewhat ungainly, this Carnival megaship reflects the amazingly creative interior design work of Joe Farcus, with vibrant colors and extensive use of neon lighting. Almost vibration-free service from diesel electric propulsion system. Dramatic six-deck-high atrium, topped by the largest glass dome afloat. Expansive open deck areas. 28 outside suites have whirlpool tubs. Public entertainment lounges, bars, and clubs galore. Delightful library and quiet reading room, but few books. Handsome public rooms connected by wide indoor boulevards. Lavish, multi-tiered showroom and razzle-dazzle shows. Dramatic three-deck-high glass enclosed health spa. Banked jogging track. Gigantic casino has non-stop action.

**–** Expect long lines for embarkation, disembarkation, shore excursions, and buffets. Too many unnecessary announcements. Aggressive hustling for drinks. Large shop, poor merchandise.

**Dining** The two large dining rooms are noisy, but the decor is attractive. The food is very disappointing, even though it has been upgraded. The service is basic and pushy, with no finesse.

**Other Comments** The real fun begins at sundown, when *Carnival* excels in sound, lights, and razzle-dazzle shows. From the futuristic Electricity Discotheque to the ancient Cleopatra's Bar, this ship will entertain you in timely fashion. You'll never be bored, but you may forget to get off in port, unless it's to eat well. Insurance and gratuities are extra.

# ms Fascination ★★★★

***Principal Cruising Area***
*Caribbean (7 nights year-round)*
***Base Port:*** *San Juan*

| | | | |
|---|---|---|---|
| Cruise Line | | | *Carnival Cruise Lines* |
| Former Names | | | *n/a* |
| Gross Tonnage | | | *70,367* |
| Builder | | | *Kvaerner Masa-Yards (Finland)* |
| Original Cost | | | *$315 million* |
| Christened By | | | *n/a* |
| First Entered Service | | | *Jul 29, 1994* |
| Interior Design | | | *Joe Farcus* |
| Country of Registry | | | *Liberia (3EWK9)* |
| Tel No | *n/a* | Fax No | *n/a* |
| Length (ft/m) | | | *855.0/260.60* |
| Beam (ft/m) | | | *104.9/31.69* |
| Draft (ft/m) | | | *25.7/7.86* |
| Engines/Propellers | | | *2/2 (CP)* |
| Decks | *10* | Crew | *920* |
| Pass. Capacity (basis 2) | *2,040* | (all berths) | *2,594* |
| Pass. Space Ratio (basis 2) | *34.4* | (all berths) | *26.7* |
| Officers | *Italian* | Dining Staff | *International* |
| Total Cabins | | | *1,020* |
| Size (sq ft/m) | *185-421/17-39* | Door Width | *30"* |
| Outside Cabins | *618* | Inside Cabins | *402* |
| Single Cabins | *20* | Supplement | *50/100%* |
| Balcony Cabins | *26* | Wheelchair Cabins | *0* |
| Cabin Current | | | *110 AC* |
| Refrigerator | | | *Cat. 11/12* |
| Cabin TV | *Yes* | VCR | *No* |
| Dining Rooms | *2* | Sittings | *2* |
| Elevators | *14* | Door Width | *36"* |

| | | | |
|---|---|---|---|
| Casino | *Yes* | Slot Machines | *Yes* |
| Swimming Pools (outside) | *3* | (inside) | *0* |
| Whirlpools | *6* | Gymnasium | *Yes* |
| Sauna/Steam Rm | *Yes/Yes* | Massage | *Yes* |
| Self-Service Launderette | | | *Yes* |
| Movie Theater/Seats | | | *No* |
| Library | | | *Yes* |
| Children's Facilities | | | *Yes* |
| Watersports Facilities | | | *None* |
| Classification Society | | | *Lloyd's Register* |

| RATINGS | SCORE |
|---|---|
| Ship: Condition/Cleanliness | 8.5 |
| Ship: Space/Flow/Comfort | 7.8 |
| Ship: Decor/Furnishings | 8.7 |
| Ship: Fitness Facilities | 7.8 |
| Cabins: Comfort/Facilities | 7.6 |
| Cabins: Software | 7.4 |
| Food: Dining Room/Cuisine | 6.7 |
| Food: Buffets/Informal Dining | 6.5 |
| Food: Quality of Ingredients | 5.3 |
| Service: Dining Room | 7.1 |
| Service: Bars/Lounges | 7.2 |
| Service: Cabins | 6.5 |
| Cruise: Entertainment | 8.2 |
| Cruise: Activities Program | 7.8 |
| Cruise: Hospitality Standard | 6.4 |
| OVERALL RATING | 109.5 |

**+** This third in a series of five megaships for Carnival further reflects the fine creative interior design work of Joe Farcus. Almost vibration-free service from diesel electric propulsion system. Dramatic six-deck-high atrium, with cool marble and hot neon, topped by the largest glass dome afloat, features a spectacular artistic centerpiece. Expansive open deck areas, but never enough when the ship is full. 28 outside suites have whirlpool tubs and elegant decor. Public entertainment lounges, bars, and clubs galore, with something for everyone. Sophisticated Hollywood design theme in handsome public rooms connected by wide indoor boulevards, with 20 life-size film star sculptures positioned along Hollywood Boulevard (good photo opportunities!). Lavish, multi-tiered showroom and razzle-dazzle shows. Dramatic three-deck-high glass enclosed health spa. Banked jogging track. Huge casino has non-stop action. Large shop, poor but targeted merchandise.

**–** Expect long lines for embarkation, disembarkation, shore excursions and buffets.

**Dining** Two huge, noisy dining rooms with efficient service. Improved cuisine is still so-so.

**Other Comments** The real fun begins at sundown, when Carnival excels. The brochure is accurate—this ship delivers fun, albeit highly programed. With such a great ship to play on, you'll never be bored, but you may forget to get off in port! Insurance and gratuities are extra.

# ms Fedor Dostoyevsky ★★★★+

***Principal Cruising Areas***

*Worldwide (various)*

***Base Port:*** *Bremerhaven*

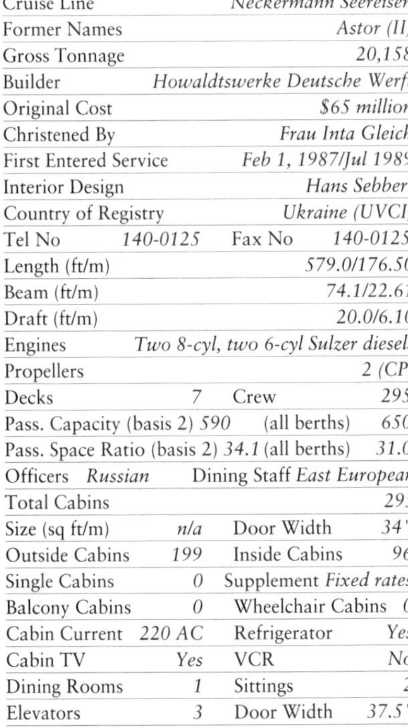

| | |
|---|---|
| Cruise Line | *Neckermann Seereisen* |
| Former Names | *Astor (II)* |
| Gross Tonnage | *20,158* |
| Builder | *Howaldtswerke Deutsche Werft* |
| Original Cost | *$65 million* |
| Christened By | *Frau Inta Gleich* |
| First Entered Service | *Feb 1, 1987/Jul 1989* |
| Interior Design | *Hans Sebbert* |
| Country of Registry | *Ukraine (UVCI)* |
| Tel No *140-0125* | Fax No *140-0125* |
| Length (ft/m) | *579.0/176.50* |
| Beam (ft/m) | *74.1/22.61* |
| Draft (ft/m) | *20.0/6.10* |
| Engines | *Two 8-cyl, two 6-cyl Sulzer diesels* |
| Propellers | *2 (CP)* |
| Decks *7* | Crew *295* |
| Pass. Capacity (basis 2) *590* | (all berths) *650* |
| Pass. Space Ratio (basis 2) *34.1* | (all berths) *31.0* |
| Officers *Russian* | Dining Staff *East European* |
| Total Cabins | *295* |
| Size (sq ft/m) *n/a* | Door Width *34"* |
| Outside Cabins *199* | Inside Cabins *96* |
| Single Cabins *0* | Supplement *Fixed rates* |
| Balcony Cabins *0* | Wheelchair Cabins *0* |
| Cabin Current *220 AC* | Refrigerator *Yes* |
| Cabin TV *Yes* | VCR *No* |
| Dining Rooms *1* | Sittings *2* |
| Elevators *3* | Door Width *37.5"* |

| | |
|---|---|
| Casino *No* | Slot Machines *No* |
| Swimming Pools (outside) *1* | (inside) *1* |
| Whirlpools *0* | Gymnasium *Yes* |
| Sauna/Steam Rm *Yes/No* | Massage *Yes* |
| Self-Service Launderette | *Yes* |
| Movie Theater/Seats | *No* |
| Library | *Yes* |
| Children's Facilities | *Yes* |
| Watersports Facilities | *None* |
| Classification Society | *RS* |

| RATINGS | SCORE |
|---|---|
| Ship: Condition/Cleanliness | 8.1 |
| Ship: Space/Flow/Comfort | 8.4 |
| Ship: Decor/Furnishings | 8.6 |
| Ship: Fitness Facilities | 7.8 |
| Cabins: Comfort/Facilities | 8.0 |
| Cabins: Software | 8.2 |
| Food: Dining Room/Cuisine | 8.0 |
| Food: Buffets/Informal Dining | 7.8 |
| Food: Quality of Ingredients | 7.6 |
| Service: Dining Room | 8.0 |
| Service: Bars/Lounges | 8.1 |
| Service: Cabins | 8.1 |
| Cruise: Entertainment | 7.9 |
| Cruise: Activities Program | 7.8 |
| Cruise: Hospitality Standard | 8.0 |
| OVERALL RATING | 120.4 |

**+** Very attractive ship with raked, squarish funnel. Finest ship in the Russian/Ukrainian-owned fleet. Built in the best German tradition. Almost everything is absolutely top quality. Fine teakwood decking and rails, and polished wood everywhere. Excellent worldwide itineraries. Basketball court. Supremely comfortable and varied public rooms and conference facilities. Wood-paneled tavern with German beer on draught is a fine retreat. Fine mix of traditional and contemporary styling. Well-designed interior fitness center and pool. Even has several dialysis machines and trained technician. Dark wood accented cabins are superbly equipped and tastefully decorated in fresh pastel colors. There is plenty of closet and drawer space. Good bathrooms, with toiletries cabinet.

**–** Deck service could be better. Poor cabin service menu.

**Dining** Exquisite dining room is one of the nicest afloat. Service is friendly, although food quality needs more attention, with presentation and choice below the standard of the rest of the product. Buffets are limited.

**Other Comments** Continental atmosphere. Mostly German-speaking passengers. This ship provides style, comfort, and elegance, and a fine leisurely cruise experience. Port taxes, insurance, and gratuities are included.

# ts Fedor Shalyapin ★★+

***Principal Cruising Area***
*Europe (various)*
***Base Ports:*** *various*

| | | | |
|---|---|---|---|
| Cruise Line | | | *Black Sea Shipping* |
| Former Names | | | *Franconia/Ivernia* |
| Gross Tonnage | | | *21,406* |
| Builder | | | *John Brown & Co. (UK)* |
| Original Cost | | | *n/a* |
| Christened By | | | *Mrs C.D. Howe* |
| First Entered Service | | | *Jul 1, 1955/Nov 20, 1973* |
| Interior Design | | | *n/a* |
| Country of Registry | | | *Ukraine (UZLA)* |
| Tel No | *n/a* | Fax No | *n/a* |
| Length (ft/m) | | | *607.9/185.30* |
| Beam (ft/m) | | | *79.7/24.30* |
| Draft (ft/m) | | | *28.8/8.80* |
| Engines | | | *4 John Brown Pametrada steam turbines* |
| Propellers | | | *2* |
| Decks | *7* | Crew | *380* |
| Pass. Capacity (basis 2) | *576* | (all berths) | *800* |
| Pass. Space Ratio (basis 2) | *37.1* | (all berths) | *26.7* |
| Officers | *Russian* | Dining Staff | *East European* |
| Total Cabins | | | *292* |
| Size (sq ft/m) | *90-241/8.3-22.3* | Door Width | *27"* |
| Outside Cabins | *159* | Inside Cabins | *133* |
| Single Cabins | *0* | Supplement | *100%* |
| Balcony Cabins | *0* | Wheelchair Cabins | *0* |
| Cabin Current | *110/220 AC* | Refrigerator | *No* |
| Cabin TV | *No* | VCR | *No* |
| Dining Rooms | *2* | Sittings | *2* |
| Elevators | *3* | Door Width | *36"* |

| | | | |
|---|---|---|---|
| Casino | *No* | Slot Machines | *No* |
| Swimming Pools (outside) | *1* | (inside) | *0* |
| Whirlpools | *0* | Gymnasium | *Yes* |
| Sauna/Steam Rm | *Yes/No* | Massage | *No* |
| Self-Service Launderette | | | *No* |
| Movie Theater/Seats | | | *Yes/260* |
| Library | | | *Yes* |
| Children's Facilities | | | *Yes* |
| Watersports Facilities | | | *None* |
| Classification Society | | | *Bureau Veritas/RS* |

| RATINGS | SCORE |
|---|---|
| Ship: Condition/Cleanliness | 5.8 |
| Ship: Space/Flow/Comfort | 6.8 |
| Ship: Decor/Furnishings | 6.4 |
| Ship: Fitness Facilities | 4.4 |
| Cabins: Comfort/Facilities | 6.0 |
| Cabins: Software | 6.2 |
| Food: Dining Room/Cuisine | 5.7 |
| Food: Buffets/Informal Dining | 5.5 |
| Food: Quality of Ingredients | 5.4 |
| Service: Dining Room | 6.0 |
| Service: Bars/Lounges | 6.1 |
| Service: Cabins | 6.2 |
| Cruise: Entertainment | 5.8 |
| Cruise: Activities Program | 5.9 |
| Cruise: Hospitality Standard | 6.0 |
| OVERALL RATING | 88.2 |

**+** Well-built, older, former transatlantic ship with classic steamship profile and single, large funnel looks good on the outside. Features two good indoor promenades. There are many cabin configurations to choose from. Some (former first class) cabins are quite large and have solid, heavy-duty furniture.

**–** Her interiors are now looking quite tired. They could also be cleaner. The furniture and fittings are quite worn and in need of extensive refurbishing. There are too many announcements.

**Dining** The unappetizing, somber dining room is located on a lower deck. The food, of which there is little choice, needs better presentation. The staff are quite friendly and attentive, but need better direction and supervision.

**Other Comments** Public rooms are rather poor, with the exception of the Music Salon and Theater. Cabins are reasonable, with heavy-duty fittings, but the decor is rather dated. This ship will appeal mainly to low-budget, Continental European passengers. Although the price may be right, this ship provides nothing more than a mediocre cruise experience, and would be better retired or used as a floating hotel. Gratuities are not included.

# tss Festivale ★★★+

***Principal Cruising Area***
*Caribbean (7 nights year-round)*
***Base Port:** San Juan (Sunday)*

| | | | |
|---|---|---|---|
| Cruise Line | | | *Carnival Cruise Lines* |
| Former Names | | | *TransVaal Castle/S.A. Vaal* |
| Gross Tonnage | | | *38,175* |
| Builder | | | *John Brown & Co. (UK)* |
| Original Cost | | | *n/a* |
| Christened By | | | *Mrs Clara Zonis* |
| First Entered Service | | | *Jan 18, 1962/Oct 28, 1978* |
| Interior Design | | | *Joe Farcus* |
| Country of Registry | | | *Bahamas (C6KP)* |
| Tel No | *110-3150* | Fax No | *110-3150* |
| Length (ft/m) | | | *760.1/231.70* |
| Beam (ft/m) | | | *90.1/27.49* |
| Draft (ft/m) | | | *31.9/9.75* |
| Engines/Propellers | | | *4 Parsons steam turbines/2* |
| Decks | *9* | Crew | *580* |
| Pass. Capacity (basis 2) | *1,146* | (all berths) | *1,400* |
| Pass. Space Ratio (basis 2) | *33.3* | (all berths) | *27.2* |
| Officers | *Italian* | Dining Staff | *International* |
| Total Cabins | | | *580* |
| Size (sq ft/m) | *50-167/4.6-15.5* | Door Width | *30"* |
| Outside Cabins | *272* | Inside Cabins | *308* |
| Single Cabins | *14* | Supplement | *50%/100%* |
| Balcony Cabins | *10* | Wheelchair Cabins | *0* |
| Cabin Current | | | *110 AC* |
| Refrigerator | | | *No* |
| Cabin TV | *No* | VCR | *No* |
| Dining Rooms | *1* | Sittings | *2* |
| Elevators | *4* | Door Width | *36"* |

| | | | |
|---|---|---|---|
| Casino | *Yes* | Slot Machines | *Yes* |
| Swimming Pools (outside) | *3* | (inside) | *0* |
| Whirlpools | *0* | Gymnasium | *Yes* |
| Sauna/Steam Rm | *Yes/No* | Massage | *Yes* |
| Self-Service Launderette | | | *No (has ironing room)* |
| Movie Theater/Seats | | | *Yes/202* |
| Library | | | *Yes* |
| Children's Facilities | | | *Yes* |
| Watersports Facilities | | | *None* |
| Classification Society | | | *Lloyd's Register* |

| RATINGS | SCORE |
|---|---|
| Ship: Condition/Cleanliness | 7.6 |
| Ship: Space/Flow/Comfort | 7.5 |
| Ship: Decor/Furnishings | 6.4 |
| Ship: Fitness Facilities | 7.1 |
| Cabins: Comfort/Facilities | 7.5 |
| Cabins: Software | 7.4 |
| Food: Dining Room/Cuisine | 6.4 |
| Food: Buffets/Informal Dining | 6.5 |
| Food: Quality of Ingredients | 5.3 |
| Service: Dining Room | 7.0 |
| Service: Bars/Lounges | 6.7 |
| Service: Cabins | 6.4 |
| Cruise: Entertainment | 8.0 |
| Cruise: Activities Program | 7.4 |
| Cruise: Hospitality Standard | 6.1 |
| OVERALL RATING | 103.3 |

**+** Classic former ocean liner styling with well-balanced profile and long bow. Looks like a real ship. Superb refurbishment has left much of the original wood and brass interior intact. Well maintained and reasonably clean throughout. Has a good array of public rooms. Fascinating, steel art deco staircase. Cabins are spacious, with plenty of closet and drawer space. Some large cabins are especially good for those with children. Good itinerary.

**–** Contemporary colors blend well, but are perhaps a little too bold. Outside cabins on Veranda Deck have obstructed views. The staff are not overly friendly, and hustle for drinks, and English is a problem for some. Expect long lines for embarkation, disembarkation, shore tenders, and buffets. Too many repetitive announcements.

**Dining** The dining room, located low down, is bright and cheerful, but noisy. There are no tables for two. The food, and its quality, are a real let-down. Service is fair, but is hurried and lacks polish.

**Other Comments** Underwent a $30 million reconstruction before starting as a CCL ship. This is a real fun ship experience, with lively casino action, for singles and the young at heart, who want a stimulating, not relaxing, vacation. Moderate rates and good value for money. Insurance and gratuities are extra.

# tss FiestaMarina ★★★

*Principal Cruising Area*

*Caribbean (3/4/7 nights year-round)*

*Base Ports: La Guaira/San Juan*

| | | | |
|---|---|---|---|
| Cruise Line | | | *FiestaMarina Cruises* |
| Former Names | | | *Carnivale/ Empress of Britain/Queen Anna Maria* |
| Gross Tonnage | | | *27,250* |
| Builder | | | *Fairfield Shipbuilding (UK)* |
| Original Cost | | | *£7,500,000* |
| Christened By | | | *H.M. Queen Elizabeth II/ Ms Dayanara Torres* |
| First Entered Service | | | *Apr 20, 1956/Oct 18, 1993* |
| Interior Design | | | *Joe Farcus* |
| Country of Registry | | | *Bahamas (C6KD6)* |
| Tel No | *n/a* | Fax No | *n/a* |
| Length (ft/m) | | | *640.0/195.08* |
| Beam (ft/m) | *87.0/26.51* | Draft (ft/m) | *29.0/8.84* |
| Engines/Propellers | | | *2 GT-Fairfield steam turbines/2* |
| Decks | *9* | Crew | *550* |
| Pass. Capacity (basis 2) | *950* | (all berths) | *1350* |
| Pass. Space Ratio (basis 2) | *28.6* | (all berths) | *20.1* |
| Officers | | | *Italian* |
| Dining Staff | | | *Latin American* |
| Total Cabins | | | *482* |
| Size (sq ft/m) | *n/a* | Door Width | *30"* |
| Outside Cabins | *217* | Inside Cabins | *265* |
| Single Cabins | *13* | Supplement | *50/100%* |
| Balcony Cabins | *0* | Wheelchair Cabins | *0* |
| Cabin Current | *110 AC* | Refrigerator | *No* |
| Cabin TV | *No* | VCR | *No* |
| Dining Rooms | *1* | Sittings | *2* |

| | | | |
|---|---|---|---|
| Elevators | *4* | Door Width | *36"* |
| Casino | *Yes* | Slot Machines | *Yes* |
| Swimming Pools (outside) | *2* | (inside) | *1* |
| Whirlpools | *1* | Gymnasium | *Yes* |
| Sauna/Steam Rm | *Yes/No* | Massage | *Yes* |
| Self-Service Launderette | | | *No (has ironing room)* |
| Movie Theater/Seats | | | *Yes/180* |
| Library | *No* | Children's Facilities | *Yes* |
| Watersports Facilities | | | *None* |
| Classification Society | | | *Lloyd's Register* |

| RATINGS | SCORE |
|---|---|
| Ship: Condition/Cleanliness | 6.4 |
| Ship: Space/Flow/Comfort | 6.2 |
| Ship: Decor/Furnishings | 6.7 |
| Ship: Fitness Facilities | 5.3 |
| Cabins: Comfort/Facilities | 6.2 |
| Cabins: Software | 6.5 |
| Food: Dining Room/Cuisine | 7.1 |
| Food: Buffets/Informal Dining | 6.6 |
| Food: Quality of Ingredients | 6.2 |
| Service: Dining Room | 7.1 |
| Service: Bars/Lounges | 7.2 |
| Service: Cabins | 7.3 |
| Cruise: Entertainment | 7.5 |
| Cruise: Activities Program | 6.5 |
| Cruise: Hospitality Standard | 7.0 |
| OVERALL RATING | 99.7 |

**+** Solidly-built former ocean liner, with midships funnel in distinctive Carnival colors. Extensive recent refurbishment. Delightful original woods and polished brass throughout. Teak outdoor and glass-enclosed indoor promenade decks encircle the ship. Large whirlpool added, and new, colorful, tiled outdoor deck. Improved decor in public rooms is jazzy.

**–** This ship could be cleaner. Many smokers aboard. Expect lines for embarkation, disembarkation and buffets. High-volume entertainment.

**Dining** The dining room is crowded, and noisy, but nicely redecorated. Features later dining times (7p.m./9.30p.m.) than most ships. The food is not for gourmets. Also features a tapas cantina.

**Other Comments** Rather stimulating interior colors and decor. Wide range of cabins, most of them large, some with rich wood furniture, all redecorated. Bathrooms are small. Action packed, noisy, but fun, casino. Beverage staff hustle a lot. This ship features lively party cruises specifically tailored for the Latin American market. Spanish-language ship and cruise line. Now owned by Epirotiki Lines and chartered to FiestaMarina Cruises. Non-stop action in an unsophisticated and very casual setting. An upbeat cruise at a decent price. Insurance and gratuities are extra.

# mv Fuji Maru ★★★★

***Principal Cruising Areas***

*Japan/South East Asia (various)*

***Base Port:*** *Tokyo*

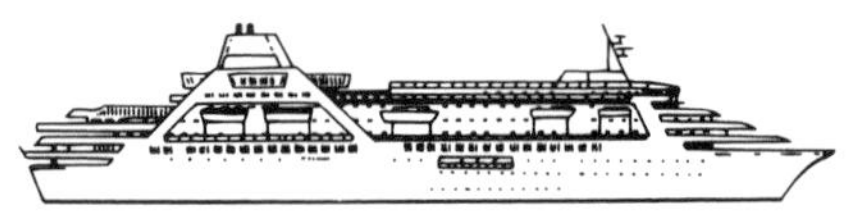

| | | | |
|---|---|---|---|
| Cruise Line | *Mitsui OSK Passenger Line* | | |
| Former Names | *n/a* | | |
| Gross Tonnage | *23,340* | | |
| Builder | *Mitsubishi (Japan)* | | |
| Original Cost | *$55 million* | | |
| Christened By | *Mr Shintaro Ishiwara* | | |
| First Entered Service | *Apr 29, 1989* | | |
| Interior Design | *Osamu Higuchi/Mikiya Murakami* | | |
| Country of Registry | *Japan (JBTQ)* | | |
| Tel No | *120-0467* | Fax No | *120-0470* |
| Length (ft/m) | *547.9/167.00* | | |
| Beam (ft/m) | *78.7/24.00* | Draft (ft/m) | *21.4/6.55* |
| Engines/Propellers | *2 Mitsubishi 8-cyl diesels/2 (CP)* | | |
| Decks | *8* | Crew | *190* |
| Pass. Capacity (basis 2) | *328* | (all berths) | *603* |
| Pass. Space Ratio (basis 2) | *71.1* | (all berths) | *38.7* |
| Officers | *Japanese* | | |
| Dining Staff | *Japanese/Filipino* | | |
| Total Cabins | *164* | | |
| Size (sq ft/m) | *182-376/17-35* | Door Width | *26"* |
| Outside Cabins | *164* | Inside Cabins | *0* |
| Single Cabins | *0* | Supplement | *25-60%* |
| Balcony Cabins | *0* | Wheelchair Cabins | *2* |
| Cabin Current | *100 AC* | | |
| Refrigerator | *Suites/deluxe cabins* | | |
| Cabin TV | *Yes* | VCR | *No* |
| Dining Rooms | *1* | Sittings | *1* |
| Elevators | *5* | Door Width | *28"* |

| | | | |
|---|---|---|---|
| Casino | *Yes (H)* | Slot Machines | *No* |
| Swimming Pools (outside) | *1* | (inside) | *0* |
| Whirlpools | *0(4 Japanese Baths)* | Gymnasium | *Yes* |
| Sauna/Steam Rm | *Yes/No* | Massage | *Yes (H)* |
| Self-Service Launderette | *Yes* | | |
| Movie Theater/Seats | *Yes/142* | | |
| Library | *Yes* | Children's Facilities | *Yes(H)* |
| Watersports Facilities | *None* | | |
| Classification Society | *Nippon Kaiji Kyokai* | | |

*(H) = On leisure cruises only*

| RATINGS | SCORE |
|---|---|
| Ship: Condition/Cleanliness | 7.3 |
| Ship: Space/Flow/Comfort | 7.8 |
| Ship: Decor/Furnishings | 7.5 |
| Ship: Fitness Facilities | 6.3 |
| Cabins: Comfort/Facilities | 6.7 |
| Cabins: Software | 7.1 |
| Food: Dining Room/Cuisine | 7.3 |
| Food: Buffets/Informal Dining | 6.6 |
| Food: Quality of Ingredients | 7.0 |
| Service: Dining Room | 7.3 |
| Service: Bars/Lounges | 7.4 |
| Service: Cabins | 6.8 |
| Cruise: Entertainment | 6.7 |
| Cruise: Activities Program | 6.7 |
| Cruise: Hospitality Standard | 8.2 |
| OVERALL RATING | 106.7 |

**+** Contemporary exterior has good profile and squat funnel. Well thought out, flexible, multi-functional design, principally for incentives, conventions, seminars, and training. Extensive lecture and conference rooms. The largest is two decks high, seats 600, and converts into a sports stadium or hall for industrial product introductions. Elegant lobby and two-level atrium. Classic wood-paneled library. Two Japanese-style grand baths. Traditional Japanese "Washitsu" tatami mat room. "Hanaguruma" owner's room is elegant for small formal functions. Sakura Salon (tea only) is soothing. Kohaku Bar with rich deep wood laminates and fine decor and taste. High-tech media and television system throughout. Two suites are quite lovely, and deluxe cabins are of a high standard and feature full bathtubs. Cabin insulation reasonable.

**–** Some outdoor upper decks are becoming shoddy. Outdoor decks are spartan.

**Dining** Dining room is attractive but overly bright. Cuisine is principally Japanese, with some Western dishes. One sitting for leisure cruises and two sittings for ship charter cruises. The food is of a good standard, but menus are repetitive.

**Other Comments** Bilingual multiplex TVs even in crew cabins. Good artwork throughout the plain and somewhat clinical interior. Fascinating exhibition, training, and educational charter cruise ship, although not ideal for individual passengers. No tipping allowed.

# ms Funchal ★★★

***Principal Cruising Area***

*Europe (various)*

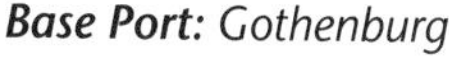

***Base Port:*** *Gothenburg*

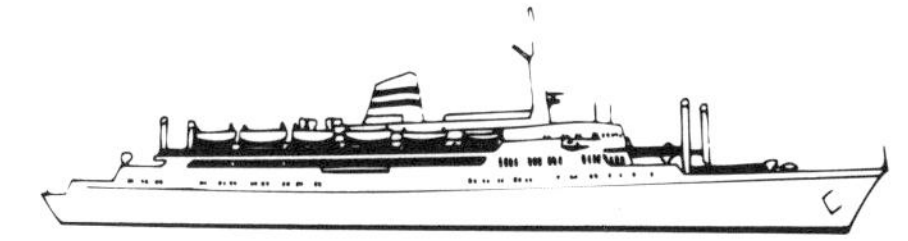

| | | | |
|---|---|---|---|
| Cruise Line | | | *Arcalia Shipping* |
| Former Names | | | *n/a* |
| Gross Tonnage | | | *9,846* |
| Builder | | | *Helsingor Skibsvog (Denmark)* |
| Original Cost | | | *n/a* |
| Christened By | | | *n/a* |
| First Entered Service | | | *Oct 31, 1961/May 1976* |
| Interior Design | | | *George Potamianos* |
| Country of Registry | | | *Panama (3EHK4)* |
| Tel No | *133-0320* | Fax No | *133-6716* |
| Length (ft/m) | | | *518.3/158.00* |
| Beam (ft/m) | | | *62.5/19.08* |
| Draft (ft/m) | | | *21.4/6.53* |
| Engines/Propellers | | | *2 9-cyl diesels/2 (FP)* |
| Decks | *6* | Crew | *155* |
| Pass. Capacity (basis 2) | *406* | (all berths) | *460* |
| Pass. Space Ratio (basis 2) | *24.2* | (all berths) | *21.4* |
| Officers | *European* | Dining Staff | *European* |
| Total Cabins | | | *222* |
| Size (sq ft/m) | *n/a* | Door Width | *24"* |
| Outside Cabins | *134* | Inside Cabins | *88* |
| Single Cabins | *38* | Supplement | *Fixed rates* |
| Balcony Cabins | *0* | Wheelchair Cabins | *0* |
| Cabin Current | | | *220 AC* |
| Refrigerator | | | *No* |
| Cabin TV | *No* | VCR | *No* |
| Dining Rooms | *1* | Sittings | *1* |
| Elevators | *2* | Door Width | *24"* |

| | | | |
|---|---|---|---|
| Casino | *Yes* | Slot Machines | *Yes* |
| Swimming Pools (outside) | *1* | (inside) | *0* |
| Whirlpools | *0* | Gymnasium | *Yes* |
| Sauna/Steam Rm | *Yes/No* | Massage | *No* |
| Self-Service Launderette | | | *No* |
| Movie Theater/Seats | | | *No* |
| Library | | | *Yes* |
| Children's Facilities | | | *No* |
| Watersports Facilities | | | *None* |
| Classification Society | | | *Lloyd's Register* |

| RATINGS | SCORE |
|---|---|
| Ship: Condition/Cleanliness | 6.8 |
| Ship: Space/Flow/Comfort | 6.8 |
| Ship: Decor/Furnishings | 7.0 |
| Ship: Fitness Facilities | 4.3 |
| Cabins: Comfort/Facilities | 6.2 |
| Cabins: Software | 6.5 |
| Food: Dining Room/Cuisine | 6.8 |
| Food: Buffets/Informal Dining | 6.5 |
| Food: Quality of Ingredients | 6.4 |
| Service: Dining Room | 7.1 |
| Service: Bars/Lounges | 7.0 |
| Service: Cabins | 7.2 |
| Cruise: Entertainment | 6.7 |
| Cruise: Activities Program | 6.5 |
| Cruise: Hospitality Standard | 7.4 |
| OVERALL RATING | 99.2 |

**+** This tidy-looking ship has a classic, well-balanced, but now dated profile. Very warm and attentive staff. Although showing her age, she has twin, sheltered promenade decks for those who enjoy strolling. The refurbished public rooms are well laid out, with plenty of wood paneling and wood trim. The cabins are very compact, yet quite well equipped, with just enough closet and drawer space, and decorated in pleasing colors.

**–** Cabin bathrooms, however, are small. Some cabins share bathrooms.

**Dining** The dining room is very tastefully decorated, and has a cozy, old-world atmosphere. The food, which is Scandinavian in style, is surprisingly good, as is the service.

**Other Comments** Very popular with northern Europeans, this ship offers a destination-oriented cruise experience in comfortable surroundings, ideally suited to singles and couples seeking good value for money. Insurance and gratuities are extra.

# ms Golden Princess ★★★★+

***Principal Cruising Areas***

*Alaska/Mexican Riviera (10/7 nights)*

***Base Ports:*** *San Francisco/Los Angeles*

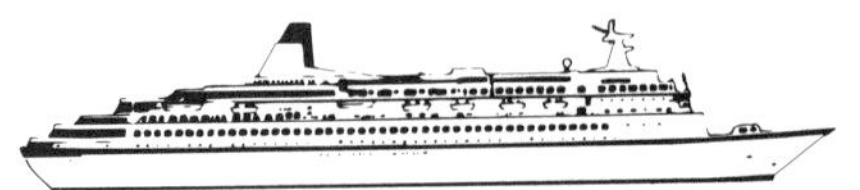

| | | | |
|---|---|---|---|
| Cruise Line | | | *Princess Cruises* |
| Former Names | | | *Sunward/Birka Queen/ Royal Viking Sky* |
| Gross Tonnage | | | *28,078* |
| Builder | | | *Wartsila (Finland)* |
| Original Cost | | | *$22.5 million* |
| Christened By | | | *Mrs Vesla Darre Hirsch* |
| First Entered Service | | | *Jun 13, 1973/Jun 3, 1993* |
| Interior Design | | | *Njal Eide* |
| Country of Registry | | | *Bahamas (C6CN3)* |
| Tel No | *110-4505* | Fax No | *110-4506* |
| Length (ft/m) | | | *674.1/205.47* |
| Beam (ft/m) | *82.6/25.20* | Draft (ft/m) | *24.7/7.55* |
| Engines/Propellers | | | *4 Sulzer 9-cyl diesels/2 (CP)* |
| Decks | *8* | Crew | *435* |
| Pass. Capacity (basis 2) | *804* | (all berths) | *867* |
| Pass. Space Ratio (basis 2) | *34.9* | (all berths) | *32.3* |
| Officers | *Scandinavian* | Dining Staff | *International* |
| Total Cabins | | | *402* |
| Size (sq ft/m) | *136-580/12.6-53.8* | Door Width | *24"* |
| Outside Cabins | *351* | Inside Cabins | *51* |
| Single Cabins | *38* | Supplement | *25-100%* |
| Balcony Cabins | *9* | Wheelchair Cabins | *0* |
| Cabin Current | | | *110/220 AC* |
| Refrigerator | | | *Cat. 1/2/3/4/5/6* |
| Cabin TV | *Yes* | VCR | *No* |
| Dining Rooms | *1* | Sittings | *2* |
| Elevators | *5* | Door Width | *35"* |

| | | | |
|---|---|---|---|
| Casino | *Yes* | Slot Machines | *Yes* |
| Swimming Pools (outside) | 2 | (inside) | *0* |
| Whirlpools | *0* | Gymnasium | *Yes* |
| Sauna/Steam Rm | *Yes/Yes* | Massage | *Yes* |
| Self-Service Launderette | | | *Yes* |
| Movie Theater/Seats | | | *Yes/156* |
| Library | | | *Yes* |
| Children's Facilities | | | *Yes* |
| Watersports Facilities | | | *None* |
| Classification Society | | | *Det Norske Veritas* |

| RATINGS | SCORE |
|---|---|
| Ship: Condition/Cleanliness | 8.4 |
| Ship: Space/Flow/Comfort | 8.2 |
| Ship: Decor/Furnishings | 8.3 |
| Ship: Fitness Facilities | 8.3 |
| Cabins: Comfort/Facilities | 8.3 |
| Cabins: Software | 8.2 |
| Food: Dining Room/Cuisine | 7.6 |
| Food: Buffets/Informal Dining | 7.3 |
| Food: Quality of Ingredients | 7.0 |
| Service: Dining Room | 7.7 |
| Service: Bars/Lounges | 7.6 |
| Service: Cabins | 7.8 |
| Cruise: Entertainment | 8.1 |
| Cruise: Activities Program | 7.9 |
| Cruise: Hospitality Standard | 8.4 |
| OVERALL RATING | 119.1 |

**+** Sleek, handsome outer styling and looks for this ex-Royal Viking Line ship. Beautifully balanced, and with sharply raked bow. Plenty of open deck and sunning space; in fact, there's plenty of space everywhere. Fine, outdoor wrap-around promenade deck. Lively casino action. Excellent fitness and sports facilities. Tasteful decor and colors following extensive refurbishment. Suites are very spacious and luxuriously equipped. All cabins are extremely well equipped and have good closet, drawer, and storage space. Most bathrooms are good, although some have awkward access. Cabin service is generally good.

**–** Maintenance is inconsistent. Cabins have tinny metal drawers.

**Dining** The spacious dining room has a high ceiling, a low noise level, and it provides an elegant setting for cuisine that is now seen to be improving. The line uses reasonable (not high) quality ingredients, but presentation should be better. Quality is in line with that of similarly priced ships, and the company is introducing upgraded menus. Pasta dishes are always a highlight aboard Princess ships. Vegetables are presented silver service style, not always coordinated with entree service. Poor bread rolls, pastries, and fruits. The wine list contains nearly 80 selections.

**Other Comments** A fine addition to the Princess Cruises fleet, and an excellent cruise experience in spacious, well furnished surroundings. Insurance and gratuities are extra.

# ms Gruziya ★★+

***Principal Cruising Areas***

*Mexibbean/Canada/New England (7 nights)*

***Base Ports:*** *Tampa/Montreal*

| | | | |
|---|---|---|---|
| Cruise Line | | | *OdessAmerica Cruise Company* |
| Former Names | | | *n/a* |
| Gross Tonnage | | | *15,402* |
| Builder | | | *Wartsila (Finland)* |
| Original Cost | | | *$25 million* |
| Christened By | | | *n/a* |
| First Entered Service | | | *Jun 30, 1975/Jun 5, 1992* |
| Interior Design | | | *n/a* |
| Country of Registry | | | *Ukraine (UUFC)* |
| Tel No | *140-0162* | Fax No | *140-0162* |
| Length (ft/m) | | | *512.6/156.27* |
| Beam (ft/m) | | | *72.3/22.05* |
| Draft (ft/m) | | | *19.4/5.92* |
| Engines/Propellers | | | *2 Pielstick 18-cyl diesels/2 (CP)* |
| Decks | *8* | Crew | *250* |
| Pass. Capacity (basis 2) | *432* | (all berths) | *640* |
| Pass. Space Ratio (basis 2) | *35.6* | (all berths) | *24.0* |
| Officers | *Ukrainian* | Dining Staff | *Ukrainian* |
| Total Cabins | | | *226* |
| Size (sq ft/m) | *150-428 /14-39.7* | Door Width | *25"* |
| Outside Cabins | *116* | Inside Cabins | *110* |
| Single Cabins | *0* | Supplement | *50%* |
| Balcony Cabins | *0* | Wheelchair Cabins | *0* |
| Cabin Current | | | *220 AC* |
| Refrigerator | | | *No* |
| Cabin TV | *No* | VCR | *No* |
| Dining Rooms | *2* | Sittings | *1* |
| Elevators | *2* | Door Width | *30"* |

| | | | |
|---|---|---|---|
| Casino | *Yes* | Slot Machines | *Yes* |
| Swimming Pools (outside) | *1* | (inside) | *0* |
| Whirlpools | *0* | Gymnasium | *Yes* |
| Sauna/Steam Rm | *Yes/No* | Massage | *Yes* |
| Self-Service Launderette | | | *Yes* |
| Movie Theater/Seats | | | *Yes/143* |
| Library | | | *Yes* |
| Children's Facilities | | | *No* |
| Watersports Facilities | | | *None* |
| Classification Society | | | *RS* |

| RATINGS | SCORE |
|---|---|
| Ship: Condition/Cleanliness | 6.0 |
| Ship: Space/Flow/Comfort | 6.1 |
| Ship: Decor/Furnishings | 6.0 |
| Ship: Fitness Facilities | 4.7 |
| Cabins: Comfort/Facilities | 6.1 |
| Cabins: Software | 6.3 |
| Food: Dining Room/Cuisine | 5.7 |
| Food: Buffets/Informal Dining | 5.2 |
| Food: Quality of Ingredients | 5.5 |
| Service: Dining Room | 6.5 |
| Service: Bars/Lounges | 7.1 |
| Service: Cabins | 7.2 |
| Cruise: Entertainment | 4.5 |
| Cruise: Activities Program | 5.7 |
| Cruise: Hospitality Standard | 6.7 |
| OVERALL RATING | 88.3 |

**+** Smart-looking, contemporary profile with swept-back, squarish funnel. An extensive refurbishment program added a new nightclub, high-ceilinged cinema, and new cabins. Tiered aft decks provide well protected, outdoor seating. Unusually deep swimming pool is a welcome change from those on most ships. Smart interior decor, but uninteresting ceilings. Top-grade suites are very spacious and welcoming. Other cabins are compact, yet quite comfortable, but more color would provide a more homey ambiance.

**–** Open deck and sunning space crowded when ship is full.

**Dining** The two dining rooms (one is nonsmoking), although plain, have light decor, big picture windows, and comfortable seating. Food is quite attractive, but choice is rather limited and could be upgraded. Family-style service is good, but lacks finesse. Although hotel staff are now more eager to please, language and communication is sometimes frustrating.

**Other Comments** This ship caters particularly to Canadians in the summer months, and Americans in the winter, and means you can get a little taste of Russia and Russian customs without having to visit the country itself. The ship carries a doctor, surgeon, and, surprisingly, a dentist. Insurance and gratuities are extra.

# ms Hanseatic ★★★★★

***Principal Cruising Areas***

*Worldwide expedition cruises (various)*

***Base Ports:*** *various*

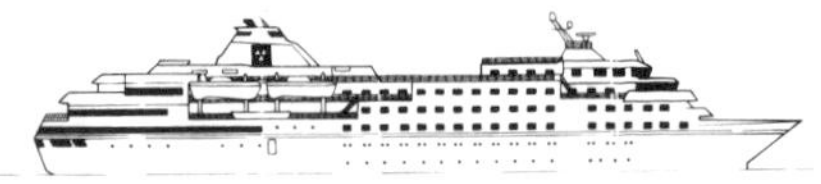

| | |
|---|---|
| Cruise Line | *Hanseatic Tours* |
| Former Names | *n/a* |
| Gross Tonnage | *8,378* |
| Builder | *Rauma Yards (Finland)* |
| Original Cost | *$68 million* |
| Christened By | *Ms Dagmar Berghoff* |
| First Entered Service | *Mar 27, 1993* |
| Interior Design | *Wilfried Koehnemann* |
| Country of Registry | *Bahamas (C6KA9)* |
| Tel No *110-3726* | Fax No *110-3727* |
| Length (ft/m) | *402.6/122.74* |
| Beam (ft/m) | *59.0/18.00* |
| Draft (ft/m) | *15.4/4.70* |
| Engines/Propellers | *2 MAK 8-cyl diesels/2 (CP)* |
| Decks *6* | Crew *125* |
| Pass. Capacity (basis 2) *160* | (all berths) *200* |
| Pass. Space Ratio (basis 2) *52.3* | (all berths) *41.8* |
| Officers *German* | Dining Staff *European/Filipino* |
| Total Cabins | *94* |
| Size (sq ft/m) *232-471/21.5-43.7* | Door Width *29"* |
| Outside Cabins *94* | Inside Cabins *0* |
| Single Cabins *0* | Supplement *on request* |
| Balcony Cabins *0* | Wheelchair Cabins *2* |
| Cabin Current | *220 AC* |
| Refrigerator | *Yes* |
| Cabin TV *Yes* | VCR *No* |
| Dining Rooms *1* | Sittings *open seating* |
| Elevators *2* | Door Width *32"* |

| | |
|---|---|
| Swimming Pools (outside) *1* | (inside) *0* |
| Whirlpools *1* | Exercise Room *Yes* |
| Sauna/Steam Rm *Yes/No* | Massage *Yes* |
| Self-Service Launderette | *No* |
| Lecture/Film Room | *Yes (seats 160)* |
| Library | *Yes* |
| Zodiacs *14* | Helicopter Pad *Yes* |
| Watersports Facilities | Yes *(banana boat, glass bottom boat)* |
| Classification Society | *Det Norske Veritas* |

| RATINGS | SCORE |
|---|---|
| Ship: Condition/Cleanliness | 9.2 |
| Ship: Space/Flow/Comfort | 9.0 |
| Ship: Expedition Equipment | 9.2 |
| Ship: Decor/Furnishings | 9.1 |
| Cabins: Comfort/Facilities | 9.1 |
| Cabins: Software | 9.0 |
| Food: Dining Room/Cuisine | 8.7 |
| Food: Buffets/Informal Dining | 8.6 |
| Food: Quality of Ingredients | 8.6 |
| Service: Dining Room | 8.7 |
| Service: Bars/Lounges | 8.7 |
| Service: Cabins | 8.7 |
| Cruise: Itineraries/Operations | 9.1 |
| Cruise: Lecture Program | 8.8 |
| Cruise: Hospitality Standard | 9.0 |
| OVERALL RATING | 133.5 |

**+** Fine, luxury ship. Has a fully enclosed bridge, an ice-hardened hull with highest super ice classification, the latest in high-tech navigation equipment, and an open bridge policy. Rubber boots, parkas, and boot/shoe washing room provided. Elegant public rooms. The all-outside cabins are large and very well equipped, with a separate lounge area, picture window, mini-bar, television, and locking drawers. All bathrooms have bathtub and bathrobe. Bridge Deck suites and cabins have butler service and full in-cabin dining privileges. Soft drinks in refrigerator, replenished daily, at no charge. Outstanding, well-planned itineraries. Very relaxing. Excellent documentation and ports of call information, and outstanding lecturers and naturalists.

**–** Principally for German-speaking and English-speaking passengers.

**Dining** The dining room is very elegant, warm, and welcoming, with fine Rosenthal china and silverware. Cuisine and service are first rate. Excellent selection of breads, cheeses, and fruits.

**Other Comments** Zodiacs for shore landings, and a glass bottom boat for coral reef viewing. Staff are very helpful. Destination-intensive, nature and life-enrichment cruises and expeditions in luxurious, comfortable, and elegant surroundings, to some of the world's most fascinating destinations, at a suitable price. All port taxes, insurance, gratuities, zodiac trips, and most shore excursions are included (except for cruises in Europe).

# mv Hebridean Princess ★★★★+

***Principal Cruising Area***
*Scottish Coast (UK) (7 nights)*
***Base Port:** Oban*

| | | | |
|---|---|---|---|
| Cruise Line | | | *Hebridean Islands Cruises* |
| Former Names | | | *Columba* |
| Gross Tonnage | | | *2,112* |
| Builder | | | *Hall Russell (Scotland)* |
| Original Cost | | | *n/a* |
| Christened By | | | *HRH the Duchess of York* |
| First Entered Service | | | *1964/Apr 26, 1989* |
| Interior Design | | | *Susan Binns* |
| Country of Registry | | | *Scotland (GNHV)* |
| Tel No | *144-0772* | Fax No | *144-0772* |
| Length (ft/m) | | | *235.0/71.6* |
| Beam (ft/m) | | | *46.0/14.0* |
| Draft (ft/m) | | | *10.0/3.0* |
| Engines/Propellers | | | *2 Crossley 8-cyl diesels/2 (FP)* |
| Decks | *5* | Crew | *35* |
| Pass. Capacity (basis 2) | *48* | (all berths) | *55* |
| Pass. Space Ratio (basis 2) | *44.0* | (all berths) | *38.4* |
| Officers | *British* | Dining Staff | *British* |
| Total Cabins | | | *29* |
| Size (sq ft/m) | *112-367/10.4-34* | Door Width | *24"* |
| Outside Cabins | *4* | Inside Cabins | *0* |
| Single Cabins | *10* | Supplement | *None* |
| Balcony Cabins | *4* | Wheelchair Cabins | *0* |
| Cabin Current | | | *240 AC* |
| Refrigerator | | | *Yes* |
| Cabin TV | *Yes* | VCR | *Some cabins* |
| Dining Rooms | *1* | Sittings | *1* |
| Elevators | *0* | Door Width | *n/a* |

| | | | |
|---|---|---|---|
| Casino | *No* | Slot Machines | *No* |
| Swimming Pools (outside) | *0* | (inside) | *0* |
| Whirlpools | *0* | Gymnasium | *No* |
| Sauna/Steam Rm | *No/No* | Massage | *No* |
| Self-Service Launderette | | | *No* |
| Movie Theater/Seats | | | *No* |
| Library | | | *Yes* |
| Children's Facilities | | | *No* |
| Watersports Facilities | | | *None* |
| Classification Society | | | *Lloyd's Register* |

| RATINGS | SCORE |
|---|---|
| Ship: Condition/Cleanliness | 8.5 |
| Ship: Space/Flow/Comfort | 8.4 |
| Ship: Facilities | 9.0 |
| Ship: Expedition Equipment | 8.0 |
| Ship: Fitness/Watersports Facilities | 5.7 |
| Cabins: Comfort/Facilities | 8.2 |
| Cabins: Software | 8.7 |
| Food: Dining Room/Cuisine | 9.1 |
| Food: Buffets/Informal Dining | 8.8 |
| Food: Quality of Ingredients | 8.2 |
| Service: Dining Room | 8.6 |
| Service: Bars/Lounges | 8.5 |
| Service: Cabins | 8.2 |
| Cruise: Entertainment/Lecture Program | 7.1 |
| Cruise: Hospitality Standard | 9.2 |
| OVERALL RATING | 124.2 |

**+** A charming little ship with stately service and a country cottage ambiance. Cabins are individually designed (with sweeping Laura Ashley-style drapes) and named (no numbers). All except three have private bathroom with bath or shower; some have gold-plated bathroom fittings. Brass cabin portholes open. Use of the ship's small boats, speedboat, bicycles, and fishing gear is included in the price, as are entrance fees to gardens, castles, and other attractions.

**–** This 30-year-old ship is strong, but has structural limitations and noisy diesel engines (however, the engines don't run at night, and the ship anchors well before bedtime).

**Dining** Totally nonsmoking dining room. Outstanding cuisine is about the same quality and presentation as the *Sea Goddess* ships. Fresh produce purchased locally. Waiter service for most things, and a delightful buffet table. Freshly-squeezed orange juice is always available. Extensive and moderately priced wine list, 18 types of whisky, and some fine premium and vintage cognac. Very personal and attentive service throughout.

**Other Comments** A pleasure to cruise on and a fine way to see some of the most beautiful scenery in the world—the Scottish highlands and islands. You are met at the rail station or airport in Glasgow and taken to Oban to join the ship. Direct bookings accepted. The only cruise vessel in the world with an all-British crew. Gratuities and insurance are extra.

# ms Holiday ★★★★

***Principal Cruising Area***
*Caribbean (7 nights year-round)*
***Base Port:*** *Miami (Saturday)*

| | | | |
|---|---|---|---|
| Cruise Line | | | *Carnival Cruise Lines* |
| Former Names | | | *n/a* |
| Gross Tonnage | | | *46,052* |
| Builder | | | *Aalborg Vaerft (Denmark)* |
| Original Cost | | | *$170 million* |
| Christened By | | | *Mrs Lin Arison* |
| First Entered Service | | | *Jul 13, 1985* |
| Interior Design | | | *Joe Farcus* |
| Country of Registry | | | *Bahamas (C6KM)* |
| Tel No | *110-3216* | Fax No | *110-3216* |
| Length (ft/m) | | | *726.9/221.57* |
| Beam (ft/m) | | | *92.4/28.17* |
| Draft (ft/m) | | | *25.5/7.77* |
| Engines/Propellers | | | *2 Sulzer 7-cyl diesels/2 (CP)* |
| Decks | *9* | Crew | *660* |
| Pass. Capacity (basis 2) | *1,452* | (all berths) | *1,800* |
| Pass. Space Ratio (basis 2) | *31.7* | (all berths) | *25.5* |
| Officers | *Italian* | Dining Staff | *International* |
| Total Cabins | | | *726* |
| Size (sq ft/m) | *185-190/17-17.6* | Door Width | *30"* |
| Outside Cabins | *447* | Inside Cabins | *279* |
| Single Cabins | *0* | Supplement | *50/100%* |
| Balcony Cabins | *10* | Wheelchair Cabins | *15* |
| Cabin Current | | | *110 AC* |
| Refrigerator | | | *Category 12 only* |
| Cabin TV | *Yes* | VCR | *No* |
| Dining Rooms | *2* | Sittings | *2* |
| Elevators | *8* | Door Width | *36"* |

| | | | |
|---|---|---|---|
| Casino | *Yes* | Slot Machines | *Yes* |
| Swimming Pools (outside) | *3* | (inside) | *0* |
| Whirlpools | *2* | Gymnasium | *Yes* |
| Sauna/Steam Rm | *Yes/No* | Massage | *Yes* |
| Self-Service Launderette | | | *Yes* |
| Movie Theater/Seats | | | *No* |
| Library | | | *Yes* |
| Children's Facilities | | | *Yes* |
| Watersports Facilities | | | *None* |
| Classification Society | | | *Lloyd's Register* |

| RATINGS | SCORE |
|---|---|
| Ship: Condition/Cleanliness | 7.8 |
| Ship: Space/Flow/Comfort | 7.6 |
| Ship: Decor/Furnishings | 6.4 |
| Ship: Fitness Facilities | 7.8 |
| Cabins: Comfort/Facilities | 7.6 |
| Cabins: Software | 7.4 |
| Food: Dining Room/Cuisine | 6.7 |
| Food: Buffets/Informal Dining | 6.4 |
| Food: Quality of Ingredients | 5.3 |
| Service: Dining Room | 7.0 |
| Service: Bars/Lounges | 7.2 |
| Service: Cabins | 6.4 |
| Cruise: Entertainment | 8.0 |
| Cruise: Activities Program | 7.6 |
| Cruise: Hospitality Standard | 6.3 |
| OVERALL RATING | 105.5 |

**+** Has distinctive, swept-back, red, white, and blue wing-tipped funnel. Numerous public rooms on two entertainment decks, with Broadway-themed interior decor. Good passenger flow. Double-wide indoor promenade, with real bus used as cafe. Stunning multi-tiered Americana Lounge showroom. Excellent casino. Plenty of dazzle and sizzle entertainment. Cabins are quite spacious, and attractively decorated. Especially nice are ten large suites with private balconies on Veranda Deck. All outside cabins have large picture windows instead of portholes.

**–** Bold, slab-sided, contemporary ship with short, rakish bow and stubby stern—typical of new buildings today. Long lines for embarkation, disembarkation, shore tenders, and buffets. Constant hustling for drinks, but at least it's done with a knowing smile.

**Dining** The two dining rooms have low ceilings, making the raised center sections seem rather crowded and very noisy. Food is quantity, not quality. Service is average, and hurried. Buffets are very basic, as is the selection of breads, rolls, and fruit.

**Other Comments** Bright colors in all public rooms except for elegant Carnegie Library (which has no books). Ideal for a first cruise experience in very comfortable, lively surroundings, and for the active set who enjoy constant stimulation and a fun-filled atmosphere, at an attractive price. Carnival does it well, but once is enough. Insurance and gratuities are extra.

# mv Horizon ★★★★★

***Principal Cruising Areas***

*Bermuda/Caribbean (7 nights)*

***Base Ports:** New York/San Juan*

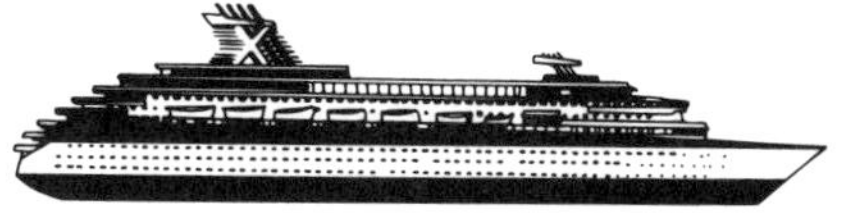

| | | | |
|---|---|---|---|
| Cruise Line | | | *Celebrity Cruises* |
| Former Names | | | *n/a* |
| Gross Tonnage | | | *46,811* |
| Builder | | | *Meyer Werft (Germany)* |
| Original Cost | | | *$185 million* |
| Christened By | | | *Mrs D. J. Chandris* |
| First Entered Service | | | *May 26, 1990* |
| Interior Design | | | *Katzourakis/McNeece* |
| Country of Registry | | | *Liberia (ELNG6)* |
| Tel No | *124-3527* | Fax No | *124-3532* |
| Length (ft/m) | | | *680.7/207.49* |
| Beam (ft/m) | | | *95.1/29.00* |
| Draft (ft/m) | | | *23.6/7.20* |
| Engines | | | *2 MAN-B&W 9-cyl diesels* |
| Propellers | | | *2 (CP)* |
| Decks | *9* | Crew | *645* |
| Pass. Capacity (basis 2) | *1,354* | (all berths) | *1,660* |
| Pass. Space Ratio (basis 2) | *34.5* | (all berths) | *28.1* |
| Officers | *Greek* | Dining Staff | *International* |
| Total Cabins | | | *677* |
| Size (sq ft/m) | *185-334/17-31* | Door Width | *24"* |
| Outside Cabins | *529* | Inside Cabins | *148* |
| Single Cabins | *0* | Supplement | *50%* |
| Balcony Cabins | *0* | Wheelchair Cabins | *4* |
| Cabin Current | *110 AC* | Refrigerator | *No* |
| Cabin TV | *Yes* | VCR | *No* |
| Dining Rooms | *1* | Sittings | *2* |
| Elevators | *7* | Door Width | *35.5"* |

| | | | |
|---|---|---|---|
| Casino | *Yes* | Slot Machines | *Yes* |
| Swimming Pools (outside) | *2* | (inside) | *0* |
| Whirlpools | *3* | Gymnasium | *Yes* |
| Sauna/Steam Rm | *Yes/No* | Massage | *Yes* |
| Self-Service Launderette | | | *No* |
| Movie Theater/Seats | | | *Yes/850* |
| Library | | | *Yes* |
| Children's Facilities | | | *Yes* |
| Watersports Facilities | | | *None* |
| Classification Society | | | *Lloyd's Register* |

| RATINGS | SCORE |
|---|---|
| Ship: Condition/Cleanliness | 9.0 |
| Ship: Space/Flow/Comfort | 8.7 |
| Ship: Decor/Furnishings | 8.6 |
| Ship: Fitness Facilities | 8.3 |
| Cabins: Comfort/Facilities | 8.2 |
| Cabins: Software | 8.1 |
| Food: Dining Room/Cuisine | 8.6 |
| Food: Buffets/Informal Dining | 8.2 |
| Food: Quality of Ingredients | 8.1 |
| Service: Dining Room | 8.3 |
| Service: Bars/Lounges | 8.1 |
| Service: Cabins | 8.2 |
| Cruise: Entertainment | 8.8 |
| Cruise: Activities Program | 8.3 |
| Cruise: Hospitality Standard | 8.6 |
| OVERALL RATING | 126.1 |

**+** Stunning, handsome contemporary ship has sleek lines. Spacious public rooms, with excellent passenger flow. Fine, elegant furnishings and appointments throughout. Soothing pastel colors everywhere. Two-level showroom is outstanding. There's nothing brash or glitzy about this ship anywhere. Cabins have fine quality fittings, are tastefully decorated, and are well above average size. Hairdryers in all cabins. Excellent closet and drawer space as well as good insulation. Suites are spacious, and have fine butler service. Elegant entertainment, with some of the best production shows afloat, and a good cruise staff.

**–** No self-service launderette. No balcony suites. Too many announcements. No cushioned pads for deck lounge chairs.

**Dining** The menu is excellent, with a wide variety of dishes with a French accent. Celebrity Cruises at present provides the best food on any two-sitting ship except *Crystal Harmony*. The dining room is large, yet feels small and very elegant, and there are a number of tables for two. Incredibly varied selection of food. Menus created by world famous master chef Michel Roux. Pastries and croissants are excellent. Very professional service. Midnight buffets are excellent.

**Other Comments** A superb cruise experience at a most modest price. It won't remain one of the industry's best kept secrets for long. Insurance and gratuities are extra.

# ms Ilich ★★★

***Principal Cruising Area***

*Baltic (2/5 nights year-round)*

***Base Port:*** *Stockholm*

| | | | |
|---|---|---|---|
| Cruise Line | | | *Baltic Line* |
| Former Names | | | *Skandia/Bore I* |
| Gross Tonnage | | | *8,528* |
| Builder | | | *Wartsila (Finland)* |
| Original Cost | | | *n/a* |
| Christened By | | | *n/a* |
| First Entered Service | | | *1973* |
| Interior Design | | | *n/a* |
| Country of Registry | | | *Russia (UPWX)* |
| Tel No | *140-0777* | Fax No | *140-0777* |
| Length (ft/m) | | | *419.9/128.00* |
| Beam (ft/m) | | | *72.1/22.00* |
| Draft (ft/m) | | | *19.3/5.90* |
| Engines/Propellers | | | *2 Sulzer diesels/2* |
| Decks | *5* | Crew | *160* |
| Pass. Capacity (basis 2) | *350* | (all berths) | *380* |
| Pass. Space Ratio (basis 2) | *24.3* | (all berths) | *22.4* |
| Officers | | | *Russian* |
| Dining Staff | | | *Ukrainian/Scandinavian* |
| Total Cabins | | | *175* |
| Size (sq ft/m) | *86-130/8-12* | Door Width | *22"* |
| Outside Cabins | *92* | Inside Cabins | *83* |
| Single Cabins | *0* | Supplement | *100%* |
| Balcony Cabins | *0* | Wheelchair Cabins | *0* |
| Cabin Current | *220 AC* | Refrigerator | *No* |
| Cabin TV | *No* | VCR | *No* |
| Dining Rooms | *2* | Sittings | *2* |
| Elevators | *0* | Door Width | *n/a* |

| | | | |
|---|---|---|---|
| Casino | *Yes* | Slot Machines | *Yes* |
| Swimming Pools (outside) | *0* | (inside) | *1* |
| Whirlpools | *0* | Gymnasium | *No* |
| Sauna/Steam Rm | *Yes/No* | Massage | *No* |
| Self-Service Launderette | | | *No* |
| Movie Theater/Seats | | | *No* |
| Library | | | *No* |
| Children's Facilities | | | *Yes* |
| Watersports Facilities | | | *None* |
| Classification Society | | | *Lloyd's Register* |

| RATINGS | SCORE |
|---|---|
| Ship: Condition/Cleanliness | 6.7 |
| Ship: Space/Flow/Comfort | 6.3 |
| Ship: Decor/Furnishings | 6.8 |
| Ship: Fitness Facilities | 4.2 |
| Cabins: Comfort/Facilities | 5.2 |
| Cabins: Software | 5.6 |
| Food: Dining Room/Cuisine | 6.7 |
| Food: Buffets/Informal Dining | 6.5 |
| Food: Quality of Ingredients | 6.4 |
| Service: Dining Room | 6.7 |
| Service: Bars/Lounges | 6.8 |
| Service: Cabins | 7.0 |
| Cruise: Entertainment | 6.0 |
| Cruise: Activities Program | 5.8 |
| Cruise: Hospitality Standard | 6.4 |
| OVERALL RATING | 93.1 |

**+** This conventional-looking, small former ferry is an ideal size for Baltic cruising. Features short cruises between Stockholm, St. Petersburg, and Riga (two full nights in St. Petersburg). Has six small, but well utilized, conference rooms. Entertainment is limited, but the crew show is good. Good facilities for families with children. Has a small indoor pool and numerous saunas.

**–** Very limited outdoor deck and sunning space, but it's not really needed as the weather is often on the chilly side. Cabins are very small, with spartan furnishings, and closet and drawer space is extremely limited. Cabin bathrooms are really tiny. A few cabins do not have private facilities.

**Dining** There are two restaurants (one à la carte) which are quite comfortable, and several lounges. The food is quite adequate, though don't expect gourmet presentation or selection. Good service from a friendly, multi-lingual staff.

**Other Comments** This tidy little ship provides a comfortable cruise experience, but in a densely populated environment. Gratuities are extra.

# mv Illiria ★★★+

***Principal Cruising Areas***
*Worldwide (various)*
***Base Ports:** various*

| | | | |
|---|---|---|---|
| Cruise Line | | | *Classical Cruises* |
| Former Names | | | *n/a* |
| Gross Tonnage | | | *3,852* |
| Builder | | | *Cantieri Navale Pellegrino (Italy)* |
| Original Cost | | | *n/a* |
| Christened By | | | *n/a* |
| First Entered Service | | | *1962* |
| Interior Design | | | *n/a* |
| Country of Registry | | | *Greece (SWAE)* |
| Tel No | *124-1440* | Fax No | *124-1441* |
| Length (ft/m) | | | *332.6/101.40* |
| Beam (ft/m) | | | *48.0/14.66* |
| Draft (ft/m) | | | *16.4/5.02* |
| Engines/Propellers | | | *2 GMT diesels/2* |
| Decks | *4* | Crew | *90* |
| Pass. Capacity (basis 2) | *143* | (all berths) | *148* |
| Pass. Space Ratio (basis 2) | *26.9* | (all berths) | *26.0* |
| Officers | *Greek* | Dining Staff | *Greek* |
| Total Cabins | | | *74* |
| Size (sq ft/m) | *n/a* | Door Width | *24"* |
| Outside Cabins | *64* | Inside Cabins | *10* |
| Single Cabins | *9* | Supplement | *Fixed rates* |
| Balcony Cabins | *0* | Wheelchair Cabins | *0* |
| Cabin Current | | | *220 AC* |
| Refrigerator | | | *No* |
| Cabin TV | *No* | VCR | *No* |
| Dining Rooms | *1* | Sittings | *Open* |
| Elevators | *0* | Door Width | *n/a* |

| | | | |
|---|---|---|---|
| Casino | *No* | Slot Machines | *No* |
| Swimming Pools (outside) | *1* | (inside) | *0* |
| Whirlpools | *0* | Gymnasium | *No* |
| Sauna/Steam Rm | *No/No* | Massage | *No* |
| Self-Service Launderette | | | *No* |
| Movie Theater/Seats | | | *No* |
| Library | | | *Yes* |
| Children's Facilities | | | *No* |
| Watersports Facilities | | | *None* |
| Classification Society | | | *American Bur. of Shipping* |

| RATINGS | SCORE |
|---|---|
| Ship: Condition/Cleanliness | 7.4 |
| Ship: Space/Flow/Comfort | 7.1 |
| Ship: Decor/Furnishings | 7.6 |
| Ship: Fitness Facilities | 4.0 |
| Cabins: Comfort/Facilities | 7.1 |
| Cabins: Software | 7.2 |
| Food: Dining Room/Cuisine | 7.4 |
| Food: Buffets/Informal Dining | 7.1 |
| Food: Quality of Ingredients | 7.3 |
| Service: Dining Room | 7.3 |
| Service: Bars/Lounges | 7.2 |
| Service: Cabins | 7.3 |
| Cruise: Lecture Program | 7.0 |
| Cruise: Activities Program | 5.0 |
| Cruise: Hospitality Standard | 7.4 |
| OVERALL RATING | 103.4 |

**+** A real gem of a ship. Small and compact. Very clean throughout and impeccably maintained, despite her age. Specializes in educational and expedition-style cruises under charter to various organizations and tour packagers. Well equipped, and the limited number of public rooms have pleasing decor and fabrics, all recently refurbished. Nice main lounge has fluted columns. Well-stocked reference library. Fine artworks throughout. Excellent lecture program. The cabins are reasonably spacious for the size of the ship, and have wood trim. All have private bathroom with shower, except two deluxe cabins which have full bathtub. Fine, attentive, yet unobtrusive, service from the all-Greek crew.

**–** Does not have an ice-hardened hull, despite its "expedition" style brochures. Cabins have little closet and drawer space, and bathrooms are small.

**Dining** Charming dining room is reminiscent of classical Greece. The cuisine is Continental. Open seating dining (sit where and with whom you like). Menu choice (American and Continental cuisine) is good, but not gourmet, and the selection of breads, cheeses, and fruits is limited.

**Other Comments** A very comfortable destination-oriented expedition cruise experience for those who want to get close to the natural world. Insurance and gratuities are extra.

# ms Imagination

***Principal Cruising Area***

*Caribbean (7 nights year-round)*

***Base Port:*** *Miami (Sunday)*

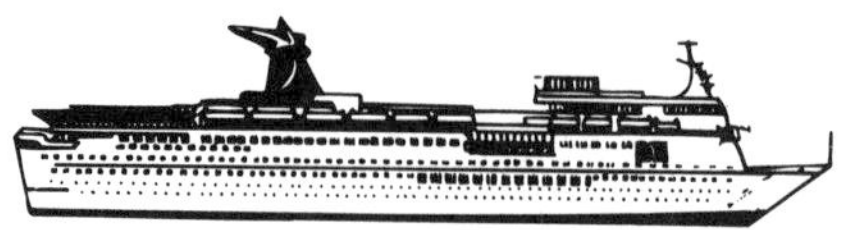

| | | | |
|---|---|---|---|
| Cruise Line | | | *Carnival Cruise Lines* |
| Former Names | | | *n/a* |
| Gross Tonnage | | | *70,367* |
| Builder | | | *Kvaerner Masa-Yards (Finland)* |
| Original Cost | | | *$330 million* |
| Christened By | | | *n/a* |
| First Entered Service | | | *July 8, 1995* |
| Interior Design | | | *Joe Farcus* |
| Country of Registry | | | *Liberia* |
| Tel No | *n/a* | Fax No | *n/a* |
| Length (ft/m) | | | *855.0/260.60* |
| Beam (ft/m) | | | *104.0/31.40* |
| Draft (ft/m) | | | *25.9/7.90* |
| Engines/Propellers | | | *28-cyl diesel-electrics/2 (CP)* |
| Decks | *10* | Crew | *920* |
| Pass. Capacity (basis 2) | *2,040* | (all berths) | *2,594* |
| Pass. Space Ratio (basis 2) | *34.4* | (all berths) | *26.7* |
| Officers | *Italian* | Dining Staff | *International* |
| Total Cabins | | | *1020* |
| Size (sq ft/m) | *185-421/17-39* | Door Width | *30"* |
| Outside Cabins | *620* | Inside Cabins | *402* |
| Single Cabins | *0* | Supplement | *50/100%* |
| Balcony Cabins | *54* | Wheelchair Cabins | *20* |
| Cabin Current | | | *110 AC* |
| Refrigerator | | | *Cat. 11/12* |
| Cabin TV | *Yes* | VCR | *No* |
| Dining Rooms | *2* | Sittings | *2* |
| Elevators | *14* | Door Width | *36"* |

| | | | |
|---|---|---|---|
| Casino | *Yes* | Slot Machines | *Yes* |
| Swimming Pools (outside) | *3* | (inside) | *0* |
| Whirlpools | *6* | Gymnasium | *Yes* |
| Sauna/Steam Rm | *Yes/Yes* | Massage | *Yes* |
| Self-Service Launderette | | | *Yes* |
| Movie Theater/Seats | | | *No* |
| Library | | | *Yes* |
| Children's Facilities | | | *Yes* |
| Watersports Facilities | | | *None* |
| Classification Society | | | *Lloyd's Register* |

| RATINGS | SCORE |
|---|---|
| Ship: Condition/Cleanliness | NYR |
| Ship: Space/Flow/Comfort | NYR |
| Ship: Decor/Furnishings | NYR |
| Ship: Fitness Facilities | NYR |
| Cabins: Comfort/Facilities | NYR |
| Cabins: Software | NYR |
| Food: Dining Room/Cuisine | NYR |
| Food: Buffets/Informal Dining | NYR |
| Food: Quality of Ingredients | NYR |
| Service: Dining Room | NYR |
| Service: Bars/Lounges | NYR |
| Service: Cabins | NYR |
| Cruise: Entertainment | NYR |
| Cruise: Activities Program | NYR |
| Cruise: Hospitality Standard | NYR |

NYR = Not Yet Rated

**+** Almost vibration-free service from diesel-electric propulsion system. Dramatic six-deck-high atrium, with cool marble and hot neon, topped by the largest glass dome afloat. Expansive open deck areas and excellent health spa. Whirlpool tubs in 28 outside suites. Public entertainment lounges, bars, and clubs galore. Dazzling colors and design themes in handsome public rooms connected by wide indoor boulevards. $1 million art collection. Lovely library, but almost no books. Lavish, yet elegant, multi-tiered showroom, and high energy razzle-dazzle shows. Three-deck-high glass-enclosed health spa. Banked jogging track. Gigantic casino for non-stop action.

**–** Sensory overkill. Large shop, poor merchandise. Too many announcements. Expect long lines for embarkation and disembarkation. Aggressive hustling for drinks.

**Dining** Two huge, noisy dining rooms with usual efficient, assertive service. Improved cuisine is so-so, but it's not *Carnival*'s strong point. Service is attentive, but fast and inflexible.

**Other Comments** Has a forthright, angular appearance, typical of today's designs. This fourth in a series of five megaships for Carnival reflects the amazingly creative and dazzling interior design work of Joe Farcus. Poor food, but the real fun begins at sundown, when Carnival excels. This ship will entertain and stimulate you in timely fashion. You'll never be bored, but you may forget to get off in port! Insurance and gratuities are extra.

# ss Independence ★★★

***Principal Cruising Area***

*Hawaii (7 nights)*

***Base Port:** Honolulu (Saturday)*

| | | | |
|---|---|---|---|
| Cruise Line | | | *American Hawaii Cruises* |
| Former Names | | | *Oceanic Independence/Sea Luck I* |
| Gross Tonnage | | | *30,090* |
| Builder | | | *Bethlehem Shipbuilders (USA)* |
| Original Cost | | | *$20 million* |
| Christened By | | | *Mrs John Slater* |
| First Entered Service | | | *Feb 10, 1951/Jun 15, 1980* |
| Interior Design | | | *Henry Dreyfuss* |
| Country of Registry | | | *USA (KPHI)* |
| Tel No | *808-847-3172* | Fax No | *808-848-0406* |
| Length (ft/m) | | | *682.4/208.01* |
| Beam (ft/m) | | | *89.1/27.18* |
| Draft (ft/m) | | | *30.1/9.19* |
| Engines/Propellers | | | *4 Bethlehem steam turbines/2* |
| Decks | *9* | Crew | *315* |
| Pass. Capacity (basis 2) | *747* | (all berths) | *1,000* |
| Pass. Space Ratio (basis 2) | *40.2* | (all berths) | *30.0* |
| Officers | *American* | Dining Staff | *American* |
| Total Cabins | | | *383* |
| Size (sq ft/m) | *75-410/7-38* | Door Width | *26"* |
| Outside Cabins | *165* | Inside Cabins | *218* |
| Single Cabins | *19* | Supplement | *60-100%* |
| Balcony Cabins | *0* | Wheelchair Cabins | *0* |
| Cabin Current | | | *110 AC* |
| Refrigerator | | | *Cat. O/AA/A* |
| Cabin TV | *No* | VCR | *No* |
| Dining Rooms | *1* | Sittings | *2* |
| Elevators | *4* | Door Width | *31"* |

| | | | |
|---|---|---|---|
| Casino | *No* | Slot Machines | *No* |
| Swimming Pools (outside) | *2* | (inside) | *0* |
| Whirlpools | *0* | Gymnasium | *Yes* |
| Sauna/Steam Rm | *Yes/No* | Massage | *Yes* |
| Self-Service Launderette | | | *Yes* |
| Movie Theater/Seats | | | *Yes/144* |
| Library | | | *Yes* |
| Children's Facilities | | | *Yes* |
| Watersports Facilities | | | *None* |
| Classification Society | | | *American Bur. of Shipping* |

| RATINGS | SCORE |
|---|---|
| Ship: Condition/Cleanliness | 6.2 |
| Ship: Space/Flow/Comfort | 6.8 |
| Ship: Decor/Furnishings | 6.1 |
| Ship: Fitness Facilities | 5.8 |
| Cabins: Comfort/Facilities | 6.2 |
| Cabins: Software | 7.0 |
| Food: Dining Room/Cuisine | 6.3 |
| Food: Buffets/Informal Dining | 6.1 |
| Food: Quality of Ingredients | 6.4 |
| Service: Dining Room | 6.6 |
| Service: Bars/Lounges | 6.7 |
| Service: Cabins | 6.4 |
| Cruise: Entertainment | 6.0 |
| Cruise: Activities Program | 6.2 |
| Cruise: Hospitality Standard | 6.4 |
| OVERALL RATING | 95.2 |

**+** Spacious public rooms with high ceilings. Sturdily-constructed older ship is one of only a handful of two-funnel ships still operating. Unusual cloud ceiling in lobby area. Good meetings facilities. Expansive open deck space, set around two fresh-water swimming pools. Wrap-around outdoor promenade deck. Inside, public areas are spacious. New Hawaii-themed decor is an improvement. Wide range of cabins types and configurations—all offer ample room plus decent closet and drawer space and fairly bright decor. Heavy-duty furniture and fittings, designed for unkind oceans. Local Hawaiian artists have their artwork on board. Dress is very casual.

**–** Now over 40 years old and needs more than a facelift. Slow room service. Showlounge is too small and is always crowded. Cabin bathrooms are small.

**Dining** Dining room is set low down, and without an ocean view, but it's fairly cheerful, and has tables for two, four, and six. The food is typically American-Polynesian in style, and could do with upgrading. Food presentation is poor, and inconsistent. Poor breads, bread rolls, and salads. Has mostly California wines. The first evening's dinner is buffet-style.

**Other Comments** Very casual atmosphere (better ambiance than sister ship *Constitution*). Moderately comfortable. With the ship in port every day but one, this is a destination-intensive cruise. Extensive refurbishment is planned for late 1994. Insurance and gratuities are extra.

# ms Island Princess ★★★★

***Principal Cruising Areas***

*Europe/Orient/South Pacific (various)*

***Base Ports:*** *various*

| | | | |
|---|---|---|---|
| Cruise Line | | | *Princess Cruises* |
| Former Names | | | *Island Venture* |
| Gross Tonnage | | | *19,907* |
| Builder | | | *Rheinstahl Nordseewerke (Germany)* |
| Original Cost | | | *$25 million* |
| Christened By | | | *n/a* |
| First Entered Service | | | *Feb 5, 1972/1974* |
| Interior Design | | | *Robert Tillberg* |
| Country of Registry | | | *Great Britain (GBBM)* |
| Tel No | *144-0214* | Fax No | *144-0214* |
| Length (ft/m) | | | *553.6/168.74* |
| Beam (ft/m) | *80.8/24.64* | Draft (ft/m) | *24.5/7.49* |
| Engines | | | *4 GMT-Fiat 10-cyl diesels* |
| Propellers | | | *2 (CP)* |
| Decks | *7* | Crew | *350* |
| Pass. Capacity (basis 2) | *610* | (all berths) | *717* |
| Pass. Space Ratio (basis 2) | *32.6* | (all berths) | *27.7* |
| Officers | *British* | Dining Staff | *International* |
| Total Cabins | | | *305* |
| Size (sq ft/m) | | | *126-443/11.7-41* |
| Door Width | | | *22-33"* |
| Outside Cabins | *238* | Inside Cabins | *67* |
| Single Cabins | *2* | Supplement | *40-100%* |
| Balcony Cabins | *0* | Wheelchair Cabins | *4* |
| Cabin Current | | | *110/220 AC* |
| Refrigerator | | | *A/B/C/D/DD* |
| Cabin TV | *Yes* | VCR | *No* |
| Dining Rooms | *1* | Sittings | *2* |

| | | | |
|---|---|---|---|
| Elevators | *4* | Door Width | *37"* |
| Casino | *Yes* | Slot Machines | *Yes* |
| Swimming Pools (outside) | *2* | (inside) | *0* |
| Whirlpools | *0* | Gymnasium | *Yes* |
| Sauna/Steam Rm | *Yes/No* | Massage | *Yes* |
| Self-Service Launderette | | | *No* |
| Movie Theater/Seats | | | *Yes/250* |
| Library | *Yes* | Children's Facilities | *No* |
| Watersports Facilities | | | *None* |
| Classification Society | | | *Lloyd's Register* |

| RATINGS | SCORE |
|---|---|
| Ship: Condition/Cleanliness | 7.7 |
| Ship: Space/Flow/Comfort | 7.6 |
| Ship: Decor/Furnishings | 8.0 |
| Ship: Fitness Facilities | 6.2 |
| Cabins: Comfort/Facilities | 7.5 |
| Cabins: Software | 7.6 |
| Food: Dining Room/Cuisine | 7.3 |
| Food: Buffets/Informal Dining | 7.0 |
| Food: Quality of Ingredients | 6.7 |
| Service: Dining Room | 7.9 |
| Service: Bars/Lounges | 8.0 |
| Service: Cabins | 7.8 |
| Cruise: Entertainment | 8.1 |
| Cruise: Activities Program | 7.8 |
| Cruise: Hospitality Standard | 8.0 |
| OVERALL RATING | 113.2 |

**+** Very attractive profile and exterior styling for this 22-year-old ship. Very pleasing lines. She recently underwent a dramatic facelift and refurbishment. Sharply-dressed officers and crew. Extremely spacious public areas, with wide passageways and high ceilings in public rooms. Elegant, spacious lobby. Very tasteful decor throughout, with pastel colors and fine artwork. The suites are quite large. Other cabins have ample room, and are well equipped, with plenty of closet and drawer space. Bathrobes and upgraded amenities in all cabins.

**–** No wrap-around outdoor promenade deck. Long lines for buffets. Teakwood decks are badly worn and need replacing.

**Dining** Features a lovely dining room, with decent service from an attentive staff. Food quality is basically good, if uncreative, and standards that slipped for a couple of years are now improving again. Very good pasta dishes. Poor bread rolls, pastries, and fruits.

**Other Comments** Quality prevails. This mid-sized ship is aging well, is quite elegant, and will provide passengers with an excellent cruise experience from start to finish, in very comfortable surroundings. For the older passenger who doesn't want to be part of the larger, more impersonal ships. Insurance and gratuities are extra.

# mv Italia Prima

***Principal Cruising Area***
*Europe (3/4/7 nights)*
***Base Port:*** *Civitavecchia (Rome)*

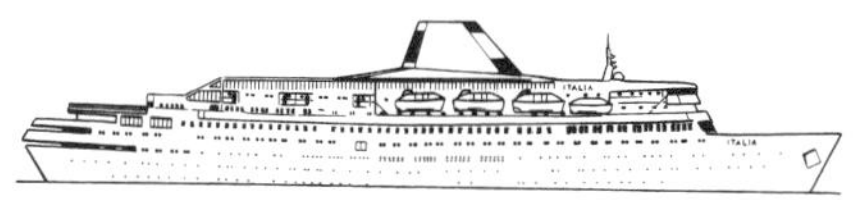

| | | | |
|---|---|---|---|
| Cruise Line/Operator | | | *Nina Cruises* |
| Former Names | | | *Volkerfreundschaft/ Stockholm/Fridtjof Nansen* |
| Gross Tonnage | | | *15,000* |
| Built | | | *Gotaverken (Sweden)* |
| Original Cost | | | *n/a* |
| Christened By | | | *n/a* |
| First Entered Service | | | *Feb 21, 1948/May 27, 1994* |
| Interior Design | | | *n/a* |
| Country of Registry | | | *Italy* |
| Tel No | *n/a* | Fax No | *n/a* |
| Length (ft/m) | | | *525.2/160.10* |
| Beam (ft/m) | | | *68.8/21.04* |
| Draft (ft/m) | | | *24.6/7.5* |
| Engines/Propellers | | | *2 Wartsila 16-cyl diesels/2 (CP)* |
| Decks | *7* | Crew | *260* |
| Pass. Capacity (basis 2) | *540* | (all berths) | *600* |
| Pass. Space Ratio (basis 2) | *27.7* | (all berths) | *25.0* |
| Officers | *Italian* | Dining Staff | *Italian* |
| Total Cabins | | | *260* |
| Size (sq ft/m) | *140-344/13-32* | Door Width | *24"* |
| Outside Cabins | *221* | Inside Cabins | *39* |
| Single Cabins | *0* | Supplement | *35%* |
| Balcony Cabins | *No* | Wheelchair Cabins | *No* |
| Cabin Current | | | *110 AC* |
| Refrigerator | | | *Yes* |
| Cabin TV | *Yes* | VCR | *No* |
| Dining Rooms | *1* | Sittings | *1* |

| | | | |
|---|---|---|---|
| Elevators | *2* | Door Width | *36"* |
| Casino | *Yes* | Slot Machines | *Yes* |
| Swimming Pools (outside) | *1* | (inside) | *0* |
| Whirlpools | *1* | Gymnasium | *Yes* |
| Sauna | *Yes* | Massage | *Yes* |
| Self-Service Launderette | | | *No* |
| Movie Theater/Seats | | | *Yes/400* |
| Library | *Yes* | Children's Facilities | *No* |
| Watersports Facilities | | | *None* |
| Classification Society | | | *RINA* |

| RATINGS | SCORE |
|---|---|
| Ship: Condition/Cleanliness | NYR |
| Ship: Space/Flow/Comfort | NYR |
| Ship: Decor/Furnishings | NYR |
| Ship: Fitness Facilities | NYR |
| Cabins: Comfort/Facilities | NYR |
| Cabins: Software | NYR |
| Food: Dining Room/Cuisine | NYR |
| Food: Buffets/Informal Dining | NYR |
| Food: Quality of Ingredients | NYR |
| Service: Dining Room | NYR |
| Service: Bars/Lounges | NYR |
| Service: Cabins | NYR |
| Cruise: Entertainment | NYR |
| Cruise: Activities Program | NYR |
| Cruise: Hospitality Standard | NYR |

NYR = Not Yet Rated

**+** Has a wrap-around outdoor promenade deck. Good selection of public rooms, including a good auditorium for meetings (holds 400). Contemporary decor with good choice of artwork. All cabins have bathtubs and mini-bars. The 38 suites feature jacuzzi bathtubs. Features both cruise- and land-based programs to the classic Italian destinations and Malta.

**–** Old hull. No forward observation lounge. Steep gangway in many ports.

**Dining** The large dining room is attractive and has tables for two, four, six, and eight. Distinctive Italian cuisine, with excellent pasta, and lots of it. Good selection of Italian wines. Also has a pizzeria. Limited selection of breads, fruits, and cheeses. Limited room service menu.

**Other Comments** This ex-ocean liner became famous when she rammed and sank the Andrea Doria. Now being reconstructed specifically as a cruise ship, she will cater to a European clientele. Insurance is included. Port taxes and gratuities are not included.

# ms Ivan Franko ★★★

***Principal Cruising Area***
*Europe (various)*
***Base Ports:** various*

| | | | |
|---|---|---|---|
| Cruise Line | | | *Black Sea Shipping* |
| Former Names | | | *n/a* |
| Gross Tonnage | | | *20,064* |
| Builder | | | *VEB Mathias Thesen (Germany)* |
| Original Cost | | | *n/a* |
| Christened By | | | *n/a* |
| First Entered Service | | | *Nov 14, 1964* |
| Interior Design | | | *n/a* |
| Country of Registry | | | *Ukraine (USLI)* |
| Tel No | *140-0233* | Fax No | *140-0233* |
| Length (ft/m) | | | *577.4/176.00* |
| Beam (ft/m) | | | *77.4/23.60* |
| Draft (ft/m) | | | *26.8/8.17* |
| Engines | | | *2 Sulzer-Werkspoor 7-cyl diesels* |
| Propellers | | | *2 (CP)* |
| Decks | *8* | Crew | *340* |
| Pass. Capacity (basis 2) | *580* | (all berths) | *714* |
| Pass. Space Ratio (basis 2) | *34.5* | (all berths) | *28.1* |
| Officers | *Russian* | Dining Staff | *Ukrainian* |
| Total Cabins | | | *290* |
| Size (sq ft/m) | *n/a* | Door Width | *26"* |
| Outside Cabins | *287* | Inside Cabins | *3* |
| Single Cabins | *0* | Supplement | *100%* |
| Balcony Cabins | *3* | Wheelchair Cabins | *0* |
| Cabin Current | *220 AC* | Refrigerator | *No* |
| Cabin TV | *No* | VCR | *No* |
| Dining Rooms | *2* | Sittings | *2* |
| Elevators | *3* | Door Width | *32"* |

| | | | |
|---|---|---|---|
| Casino | *No* | Slot Machines | *No* |
| Swimming Pools (outside) | *1* | (inside) | *1* |
| Whirlpools | *0* | Gymnasium | *Yes* |
| Sauna/Steam Rm | *Yes/No* | Massage | *Yes* |
| Self-Service Launderette | | | *No* |
| Movie Theater/Seats | | | *Yes/130* |
| Library | | | *Yes* |
| Children's Facilities | | | *No* |
| Watersports Facilities | | | *None* |
| Classification Society | | | *RS* |

| RATINGS | SCORE |
|---|---|
| Ship: Condition/Cleanliness | 6.2 |
| Ship: Space/Flow/Comfort | 6.6 |
| Ship: Decor/Furnishings | 6.2 |
| Ship: Fitness Facilities | 5.5 |
| Cabins: Comfort/Facilities | 6.1 |
| Cabins: Software | 6.4 |
| Food: Dining Room/Cuisine | 6.4 |
| Food: Buffets/Informal Dining | 6.3 |
| Food: Quality of Ingredients | 6.5 |
| Service: Dining Room | 6.6 |
| Service: Bars/Lounges | 6.9 |
| Service: Cabins | 7.0 |
| Cruise: Entertainment | 6.0 |
| Cruise: Activities Program | 5.4 |
| Cruise: Hospitality Standard | 6.4 |
| OVERALL RATING | 94.5 |

**+** Classic lines and traditional ship profile, with strong, ice-hardened hull. Interior decor also looks tired and worn, but wood paneling does add a degree of warmth.

**–** Black hull with white superstructure now looks tired and well worn. The ship needs better maintenance and cleaning. The stairwells are uncarpeted and very institutional. Cabins are almost all outside, but are simply and skimpily furnished, and some have no private facilities. There is little closet and drawer space, and bathrooms are small.

**Dining** The dining room is operated more like a cafeteria than a restaurant. Food is heavy, salty, and poorly presented, and choice is limited. Poor selection of breads, cheeses, and fruits. Service is unrefined, and there is much room for improvement.

**Other Comments** The staff are willing, but need more direction from management. This ship is in need of a major refurbishment and upgrading. Good for families on a low budget, but there's no finesse anywhere.

# mts Jason ★★★

*Principal Cruising Area*

*Europe (3/4/7 nights)*

***Base Port:** Piraeus*

| | | | |
|---|---|---|---|
| Cruise Line | | | *Epirotiki Lines* |
| Former Names | | | *Eros* |
| Gross Tonnage | | | *5,250* |
| Builder | | | *Cantieri Riuniti dell' Adriatico (Italy)* |
| Original Cost | | | *n/a* |
| Christened By | | | *n/a* |
| First Entered Service | | | *Apr 1967* |
| Interior Design | | | *Arminio Lozzi* |
| Country of Registry | | | *Greece (SZLZ)* |
| Tel No | *113-0175* | Fax No | *113-0175* |
| Length (ft/m) | | | *333.0/101.5* |
| Beam (ft/m) | | | *52.6/16.06* |
| Draft (ft/m) | | | *17.5/5.34* |
| Engines/Propellers | | | *2 Sulzer 7-cyl diesels/2* |
| Decks | *6* | Crew | *139* |
| Pass. Capacity (basis 2) | *268* | (all berths) | *310* |
| Pass. Space Ratio (basis 2) | *19.5* | (all berths) | *16.9* |
| Officers | *Greek* | Dining Staff | *Greek* |
| Total Cabins | | | *139* |
| Size (sq ft/m) | *73-182/6.7-17* | Door Width | *24"* |
| Outside Cabins | *103* | Inside Cabins | *36* |
| Single Cabins | *0* | Supplement | *50%* |
| Balcony Cabins | *0* | Wheelchair Cabins | *0* |
| Cabin Current | | | *220 AC* |
| Refrigerator | | | *No* |
| Cabin TV | *No* | VCR | *No* |
| Dining Rooms | *1* | Sittings | *2* |
| Elevators | *1* | Door Width | *30"* |

| | | | |
|---|---|---|---|
| Casino | *Yes* | Slot Machines | *Yes* |
| Swimming Pools (outside) | *1* | (inside) | *0* |
| Whirlpools | *0* | Gymnasium | *No* |
| Sauna/Steam Rm | *No/No* | Massage | *No* |
| Self-Service Launderette | | | *No* |
| Movie Theater/Seats | | | *No* |
| Library | | | *Yes* |
| Children's Facilities | | | *No* |
| Watersports Facilities | | | *None* |
| Classification Society | | | *Lloyd's Register* |

| RATINGS | SCORE |
|---|---|
| Ship: Condition/Cleanliness | 6.6 |
| Ship: Space/Flow/Comfort | 6.1 |
| Ship: Decor/Furnishings | 6.4 |
| Ship: Fitness Facilities | 3.0 |
| Cabins: Comfort/Facilities | 6.4 |
| Cabins: Software | 6.8 |
| Food: Dining Room/Cuisine | 6.5 |
| Food: Buffets/Informal Dining | 6.3 |
| Food: Quality of Ingredients | 6.0 |
| Service: Dining Room | 6.8 |
| Service: Bars/Lounges | 6.8 |
| Service: Cabins | 7.1 |
| Cruise: Entertainment | 5.0 |
| Cruise: Activities Program | 5.4 |
| Cruise: Hospitality Standard | 7.2 |
| OVERALL RATING | 92.4 |

**+** This charming little ship has a traditional, rather low profile. Simple layout provides good outdoor deck and sunning space. Warm ambiance filters from officers and crew to passengers. Tasteful interior decor reflects warmth and intimacy. There is a small fortune in artworks aboard this vessel, as well as a well-stocked library.

**–** Narrow gangway. Cabins are small, yet cozy and inviting, with a sofa bed that converts to a daytime sitting area. Bathrooms are small, but manageable.

**Dining** Lovely dining room has big picture windows, comfortable seating, and some precious tapestries. The cuisine is Continental, with some excellent Greek dishes.

**Other Comments** Service is friendly and quite attentive throughout, but lacks finesse. This ship will provide a most pleasant and intimate cruise experience in comfort and classical style, without the crowds, at a very fair price. Often under charter to various tour operators. Insurance and gratuities are extra.

# ms Jubilee ★★★★

***Principal Cruising Area***

*Mexican Riviera (7 nights year-round)*

***Base Port:*** *Los Angeles (Sunday)*

| | | | |
|---|---|---|---|
| Cruise Line | | | *Carnival Cruise Lines* |
| Former Names | | | *n/a* |
| Gross Tonnage | | | *47,262* |
| Builder | | | *Kockums (Sweden)* |
| Original Cost | | | *$135 million* |
| Christened By | | | *Mrs Yvonne Ryding* |
| First Entered Service | | | *Jul 6, 1986* |
| Interior Design | | | *Joe Farcus* |
| Country of Registry | | | *Liberia (ELFK6)* |
| Tel No | *124-0503* | Fax No | *124-0503* |
| Length (ft/m) | | | *733.0/223.40* |
| Beam (ft/m) | | | *92.5/28.20* |
| Draft (ft/m) | | | *24.9/7.60* |
| Engines/Propellers | | | *2 Sulzer 7-cyl diesels/2 (CP)* |
| Decks | *10* | Crew | *670* |
| Pass. Capacity (basis 2) | *1,486* | (all berths) | *1,896* |
| Pass. Space Ratio (basis 2) | *31.8* | (all berths) | *24.9* |
| Officers | *Italian* | Dining Staff | *International* |
| Total Cabins | | | *743* |
| Size (sq ft/m) | *185-420/17-39* | Door Width | *30"* |
| Outside Cabins | *453* | Inside Cabins | *290* |
| Single Cabins | *0* | Supplement | *50/100%* |
| Balcony Cabins | *10* | Wheelchair Cabins | *14* |
| Cabin Current | | | *110 AC* |
| Refrigerator | | | *Category 12 only* |
| Cabin TV | *Yes* | VCR | *No* |
| Dining Rooms | *2* | Sittings | *2* |
| Elevators | *8* | Door Width | *36"* |

| | | | |
|---|---|---|---|
| Casino | *Yes* | Slot Machines | *Yes* |
| Swimming Pools (outside) | *3* | (inside) | *0* |
| Whirlpools | *2* | Gymnasium | *Yes* |
| Sauna/Steam Rm | *Yes/No* | Massage | *Yes* |
| Self-Service Launderette | | | *Yes* |
| Movie Theater/Seats | | | *No* |
| Library | | | *Yes* |
| Children's Facilities | | | *Yes* |
| Watersports Facilities | | | *None* |
| Classification Society | | | *Lloyd's Register* |

| RATINGS | SCORE |
|---|---|
| Ship: Condition/Cleanliness | 7.6 |
| Ship: Space/Flow/Comfort | 7.6 |
| Ship: Decor/Furnishings | 6.4 |
| Ship: Fitness Facilities | 7.8 |
| Cabins: Comfort/Facilities | 7.6 |
| Cabins: Software | 7.4 |
| Food: Dining Room/Cuisine | 6.7 |
| Food: Buffets/Informal Dining | 6.4 |
| Food: Quality of Ingredients | 5.3 |
| Service: Dining Room | 7.0 |
| Service: Bars/Lounges | 7.1 |
| Service: Cabins | 6.4 |
| Cruise: Entertainment | 8.0 |
| Cruise: Activities Program | 7.6 |
| Cruise: Hospitality Standard | 6.3 |
| OVERALL RATING | 105.2 |

**+** Bold, rather shoebox-like, yet attractive, large ship with short, rakish bow. Distinctive, swept-back wing-tipped funnel. Flamboyant, vivid colors in all public rooms except for the elegant Churchill's Library, which has almost no books. Huge casino has almost round-the-clock action. Cabins are quite spacious, neatly equipped, and have attractive decor. Especially nice are ten large suites on Veranda Deck. Outside cabins feature large picture windows. Numerous public rooms spread throughout two entertainment decks. Excellent double-wide promenade deck. Stimulating, multi-tiered Atlantis Lounge showroom. Constant entertainment and activities.

**–** Has rather glitzy decor that is designed to stimulate, not relax you. Expect long lines for embarkation, disembarkation, shore tenders, and buffets. Too many annoying and unnecessary announcements. Constant hustling for drinks.

**Dining** The two dining rooms are very attractive, but have low ceilings, and the raised center section is cramped. The food, although upgraded, is still very much a low-budget affair. Poor selection of breads, rolls, and fruit. Service is hurried and without finesse.

**Other Comments** This ship provides novice cruisers with an excellent first cruise experience in very comfortable surroundings. Fun-filled and stimulating. Excellent for families with children, and good for singles who want lots of life. Very good value. Insurance and gratuities are extra.

# mv Kapitan Khlebnikov ★★★

***Principal Cruising Areas***

*Antarctica/Trans-polar expeditions (various)*

***Base Port:*** *Provideniya*

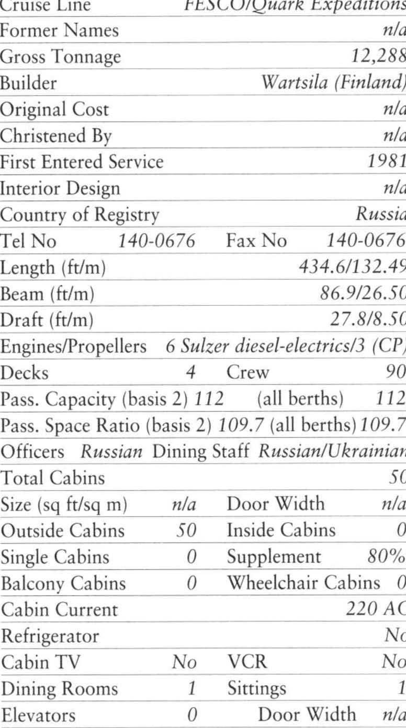

| Cruise Line | | | *FESCO/Quark Expeditions* |
|---|---|---|---|
| Former Names | | | *n/a* |
| Gross Tonnage | | | *12,288* |
| Builder | | | *Wartsila (Finland)* |
| Original Cost | | | *n/a* |
| Christened By | | | *n/a* |
| First Entered Service | | | *1981* |
| Interior Design | | | *n/a* |
| Country of Registry | | | *Russia* |
| Tel No | *140-0676* | Fax No | *140-0676* |
| Length (ft/m) | | | *434.6/132.49* |
| Beam (ft/m) | | | *86.9/26.50* |
| Draft (ft/m) | | | *27.8/8.50* |
| Engines/Propellers | | | *6 Sulzer diesel-electrics/3 (CP)* |
| Decks | *4* | Crew | *90* |
| Pass. Capacity (basis 2) | *112* | (all berths) | *112* |
| Pass. Space Ratio (basis 2) | *109.7* | (all berths) | *109.7* |
| Officers | *Russian* | Dining Staff | *Russian/Ukrainian* |
| Total Cabins | | | *50* |
| Size (sq ft/sq m) | *n/a* | Door Width | *n/a* |
| Outside Cabins | *50* | Inside Cabins | *0* |
| Single Cabins | *0* | Supplement | *80%* |
| Balcony Cabins | *0* | Wheelchair Cabins | *0* |
| Cabin Current | | | *220 AC* |
| Refrigerator | | | *No* |
| Cabin TV | *No* | VCR | *No* |
| Dining Rooms | *1* | Sittings | *1* |
| Elevators | *0* | Door Width | *n/a* |

| Casino | *No* | Slot Machines | *No* |
|---|---|---|---|
| Swimming Pools (outside) | *0* | (inside) | *1* |
| Whirlpools | *0* | Gymnasium | *Yes* |
| Sauna/Steam Rm | *2/No* | Massage | *No* |
| Self-Service Launderette | | | *No* |
| Lecture/Film Room | *No* | Library | *Yes* |
| Zodiacs | | | *4* |
| Helicopter Pad | | | *Yes (1 helicopter)* |
| Watersports Facilities | | | *None* |
| Classification Society | | | *RS* |

| RATINGS | SCORE |
|---|---|
| Ship: Condition/Cleanliness | 7.0 |
| Ship: Space/Flow/Comfort | 6.0 |
| Ship: Expedition Equipment | 8.7 |
| Ship: Decor/Furnishings | 5.4 |
| Cabins: Comfort/Facilities | 5.6 |
| Cabins: Software | 5.8 |
| Food: Dining Room/Cuisine | 6.7 |
| Food: Buffets/Informal Dining | 6.1 |
| Food: Quality of Ingredients | 6.5 |
| Service: Dining Room | 6.4 |
| Service: Bars/Lounges | 6.3 |
| Service: Cabins | 6.6 |
| Cruise: Itineraries/Operations | 7.7 |
| Cruise: Lecture Program | 7.6 |
| Cruise: Hospitality Standard | 7.4 |
| OVERALL RATING | 99.6 |

**+** This real, working icebreaker, one of a fleet of ten, has an incredibly thick hull, forthright profile and a bow like an inverted whale head. The funnel is placed amidships and the accommodations block is forwards. Cabins are spread over four decks, and all have private facilities and plenty of storage space. This vessel is particularly good for expedition cruises to Antarctica and the Arctic, and will provide comfortable surroundings, a friendly, very experienced and dedicated crew, and excellent value for money. Excellent naturalists and lecturers aboard. Heavy parkas and boots are provided for passengers. "Hands-on" expedition cruising.

**–** Basic amenities and rather spartan, but practical, decor.

**Dining** Hearty food and generous portions, with an emphasis on fish, served by hearty waitresses in a dining room that is comfortable and practical without being the slightest bit pretentious. The food production and presentation is supervised by Scandinavian advisors, who import Western foods specifically for these chartered voyages. Under Quark Expeditions, extra care and attention is given to Japanese passengers, and Japanese foods are specially provided.

**Other Comments** Diesel-electric engines produce 22,000 horesepower, and allow her to plough through ice several meters thick. Plenty of open deck and observation space. Another vessel in the same configuration and series is *Kapitan Dranitsyn.*

# ms Kareliya ★★+

***Principal Cruising Area***
*Europe (7 nights)*
***Base Port:*** *London (Tilbury)*

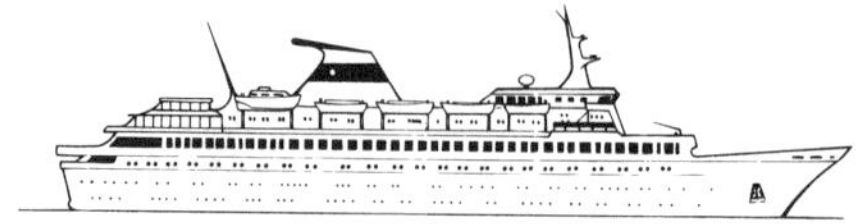

| | | | |
|---|---|---|---|
| Cruise Line | | | *CTC Cruise Lines* |
| Former Names | | | *Leonid Brezhnev* |
| Gross Tonnage | | | *15,065* |
| Builder | | | *Wartsila (Finland)* |
| Original Cost | | | *$25 million* |
| Christened By | | | *Mrs Landeman* |
| First Entered Service | | | *Dec 19, 1976/Mar 13, 1981* |
| Interior Design | | | *Wartsila/Lloyd Werft* |
| Country of Registry | | | *Ukraine (URRN)* |
| Tel No | *140-0261* | Fax No | *140-0261* |
| Length (ft/m) | | | *512.6/156.27* |
| Beam (ft/m) | *71.8/21.90* | Draft (ft/m) | *19.4/5.92* |
| Engines/Propellers | | | *2 Pielstick 18-cyl diesels/2 (CP)* |
| Decks | *8* | Crew | *250* |
| Pass. Capacity (basis 2) | *472* | (all berths) | *644* |
| Pass. Space Ratio (basis 2) | *31.1* | (all berths) | *23.3* |
| Officers | | | *Ukrainian* |
| Dining Staff | | | *British/Ukrainian* |
| Total Cabins | | | *236* |
| Size (sq ft/m) | *90.5-428/8.4-38* | Door Width | *25"* |
| Outside Cabins | *110* | Inside Cabins | *126* |
| Single Cabins | *0* | Supplement | *50%* |
| Balcony Cabins | *0* | Wheelchair Cabins | *0* |
| Cabin Current | | | *220 AC* |
| Refrigerator | | | *Boat Deck* |
| Cabin TV | *Boat Deck* | VCR | *No* |
| Dining Rooms | *2* | Sittings | *1* |
| Elevators | *2* | Door Width | *30"* |

| | | | |
|---|---|---|---|
| Casino | *Yes* | Slot Machines | *Yes* |
| Swimming Pools (outside) | *1* | (inside) | *0* |
| Whirlpools | *0* | Gymnasium | *Yes* |
| Sauna/Steam Rm | *Yes/No* | Massage | *Yes* |
| Self-Service Launderette | | | *Yes* |
| Movie Theater/Seats | | | *Yes/140* |
| Library | | | *Yes* |
| Children's Facilities | | | *Yes* |
| Watersports Facilities | | | *None* |
| Classification Society | | | *Ukraine Register of Shipping* |

| RATINGS | SCORE |
|---|---|
| Ship: Condition/Cleanliness | 6.3 |
| Ship: Space/Flow/Comfort | 6.2 |
| Ship: Decor/Furnishings | 6.1 |
| Ship: Fitness Facilities | 4.7 |
| Cabins: Comfort/Facilities | 6.1 |
| Cabins: Software | 6.3 |
| Food: Dining Room/Cuisine | 5.4 |
| Food: Buffets/Informal Dining | 5.0 |
| Food: Quality of Ingredients | 5.4 |
| Service: Dining Room | 6.5 |
| Service: Bars/Lounges | 7.0 |
| Service: Cabins | 7.3 |
| Cruise: Entertainment | 4.1 |
| Cruise: Activities Program | 5.6 |
| Cruise: Hospitality Standard | 6.7 |
| OVERALL RATING | 87.7 |

**+** Quite a smart-looking vessel, with a large, squarish funnel. Pleasing interior (but uncoordinated) decor. Her newer facilities provide more public rooms for passengers. The library and book selection have improved. The 12 suites on the Boat Deck are very large and well equipped. Other cabins are on the small side, but adequate, although bathrooms are small and utilitarian. Wide range of interesting and popular itineraries.

**–** Some inner cabins share bathrooms. Little drawer space in most cabins—not good for long voyages. Steep gangway in many ports. Interior colors are quite uncoordinated. No cabin service menu. Sadly, there are no fresh flowers anywhere.

**Dining** The two dining rooms (one for smokers, one for nonsmokers) are quite attractive, but noisy. Waitresses try hard, but there's no real finesse. The menu choice is very limited, and the quality needs improving. Poor selection of breads, fruits, and cheeses.

**Other Comments** This ship provides comfortable, reasonably warm, and friendly surroundings. Charming, but unsophisticated, crew. Caters primarily to British passengers wishing a destination-intensive cruise experience in comfortable surroundings, at a modest price. Amateurish entertainment. It is understood that this ship will go into dry dock for an extensive refit. Port taxes are included. Gratuities are not compulsory, but expected.

# ms Kazakhstan ★★+

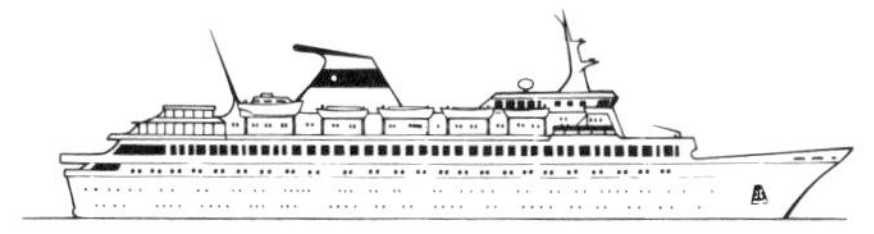

***Principal Cruising Area***
*Europe (various)*
***Base Port:*** *Bremerhaven*

| | | | |
|---|---|---|---|
| Cruise Line | | | *Black Sea Shipping* |
| Former Names | | | *n/a* |
| Gross Tonnage | | | *15,410* |
| Builder | | | *Wartsila (Finland)* |
| Original Cost | | | *$25 million* |
| Christened By | | | *n/a* |
| First Entered Service | | | *Jul 1, 1975* |
| Interior Design | | | *n/a* |
| Country of Registry | | | *Ukraine (ULSB)* |
| Tel No | *140-0772* | Fax No | *140-0772* |
| Length (ft/m) | | | *512.6/156.27* |
| Beam (ft/m) | | | *72.3/22.05* |
| Draft (ft/m) | | | *19.4/5.92* |
| Engines/Propellers | | | *2 Pielstick 18-cyl diesels/2 (CP)* |
| Decks | *7* | Crew | *250* |
| Pass. Capacity (basis 2) | *470* | (all berths) | *640* |
| Pass. Space Ratio (basis 2) | *32.7* | (all berths) | *24.0* |
| Officers | | | *Russian/Ukrainian* |
| Dining Staff | | | *Russian/Ukrainian* |
| Total Cabins | | | *235* |
| Size (sq ft/m) | *90.5-492/8.4-45.7* | Door Width | *25"* |
| Outside Cabins | *117* | Inside Cabins | *118* |
| Single Cabins | *0* | Supplement | *Fixed rates* |
| Balcony Cabins | *0* | Wheelchair Cabins | *0* |
| Cabin Current | *220 AC* | Refrigerator | *No* |
| Cabin TV | *No* | VCR | *No* |
| Dining Rooms | *2* | Sittings | *1* |
| Elevators | *1* | Door Width | *30"* |

| | | | |
|---|---|---|---|
| Casino | *No* | Slot Machines | *No* |
| Swimming Pools (outside) | *1* | (inside) | *0* |
| Whirlpools | *0* | Gymnasium | *Yes* |
| Sauna/Steam Rm | *Yes/No* | Massage | *Yes* |
| Self-Service Launderette | | | *Yes* |
| Movie Theater/Seats | | | *Yes/143* |
| Library | | | *Yes* |
| Children's Facilities | | | *No* |
| Watersports Facilities | | | *None* |
| Classification Society | | | *Ukraine Register of Shipping* |

| RATINGS | SCORE |
|---|---|
| Ship: Condition/Cleanliness | 6.1 |
| Ship: Space/Flow/Comfort | 6.1 |
| Ship: Decor/Furnishings | 6.0 |
| Ship: Fitness Facilities | 4.7 |
| Cabins: Comfort/Facilities | 6.0 |
| Cabins: Software | 6.1 |
| Food: Dining Room/Cuisine | 5.4 |
| Food: Buffets/Informal Dining | 5.0 |
| Food: Quality of Ingredients | 5.4 |
| Service: Dining Room | 6.5 |
| Service: Bars/Lounges | 7.0 |
| Service: Cabins | 7.1 |
| Cruise: Entertainment | 4.1 |
| Cruise: Activities Program | 5.6 |
| Cruise: Hospitality Standard | 6.5 |
| OVERALL RATING | 86.6 |

**+** Recent refurbishment added a cinema, a new nightclub, a foyer, Troika Bar, and more cabins. Eight suites on Boat Deck are quite spacious, and have full bathtubs, good closet and drawer space, and artwork. Other cabins are small and sparingly furnished, but adequate.

**–** Most cabins have little drawer space, and the insulation is poor. Communication with staff is frustrating, even though the staff are friendly.

**Dining** Two dining rooms are decorated nicely, and are quite comfortable. One for smokers, the other for nonsmokers, but there are no tables for two. One wall features a multi-color, multi-image contemporary glass mural.

**Other Comments** Sleek-looking ship with contemporary profile and smart, square funnel. Service is somewhat perfunctory, but the staff try hard. The itineraries are excellent and well planned. The ship itself provides a good cruise experience at a modest price, but there's little finesse. Rated when under charter to a German operator, but presently being used for the domestic cruise market in Ukraine. Insurance and gratuities are extra.

# ms Kazakhstan II ★★★+

***Principal Cruising Areas***

*Worldwide (various)*

***Base Ports:*** *various*

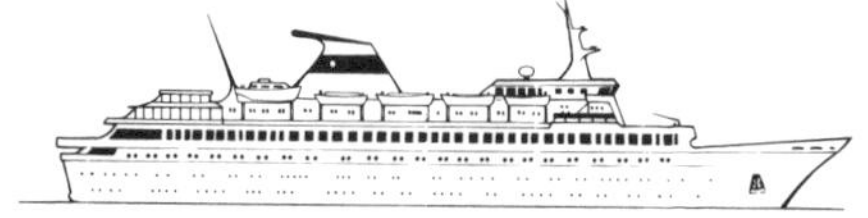

| | | | |
|---|---|---|---|
| Cruise Line | | | *Delphin Seereisen* |
| Former Names | | | *Belorussiya* |
| Gross Tonnage | | | *16,600* |
| Builder | | | *Wartsila (Finland)* |
| Original Cost | | | *$25 million* |
| Christened By | | | *Mrs Stepanova* |
| First Entered Service | | | *Jan 15, 1975/Dec 22, 1993* |
| Interior Design | | | *Lloyd Werft* |
| Country of Registry | | | *Ukraine (UUDP)* |
| Tel No | *140-0204* | Fax No | *140-0204* |
| Length (ft/m) | | | *512.5/156.24* |
| Beam (ft/m) | | | *71.8/21.90* |
| Draft (ft/(m) | | | *19.4/5.92* |
| Engines/Propellers | | | *2 Pielstick 18-cyl diesels/2 (CP)* |
| Decks | *8* | Crew | *250* |
| Pass. Capacity (basis 2) | *474* | (all berths) | *640* |
| Pass. Space Ratio (basis 2) | *35.02* | (all berths) | *25.9* |
| Officers | *Ukrainian* | Dining Staff | *Ukrainian* |
| Total Cabins | | | *237* |
| Size (sq ft/m) | *150-492/14-45.7* | Door Width | *25"* |
| Outside Cabins | *129* | Inside Cabins | *108* |
| Single Cabins | *0* | Supplement | *50%* |
| Balcony Cabins | *0* | Wheelchair Cabins | *0* |
| Cabin Current | | | *220 AC* |
| Refrigerator | | | *Boat deck* |
| Cabin TV | *Boat deck* | VCR | *No* |
| Dining Rooms | *1* | Sittings | *1* |
| Elevators | *1* | Door Width | *30"* |

| | | | |
|---|---|---|---|
| Casino | *Yes* | Slot Machines | *Yes* |
| Swimming Pools (outside) | *1* | (inside) | *0* |
| Whirlpools | *0* | Gymnasium | *Yes* |
| Sauna/Steam Rm | *Yes/No* | Massage | *Yes* |
| Self-Service Launderette | | | *Yes* |
| Movie Theater/Seats | | | *Yes/143* |
| Library | | | *Yes* |
| Children's Facilities | | | *No* |
| Watersports Facilities | | | *None* |
| Classification Society | | | *Ukraine Register of Shipping* |

| RATINGS | SCORE |
|---|---|
| Ship: Condition/Cleanliness | 7.7 |
| Ship: Space/Flow/Comfort | 6.6 |
| Ship: Decor/Furnishings | 7.4 |
| Ship: Fitness Facilities | 6.5 |
| Cabins: Comfort/Facilities | 6.7 |
| Cabins: Software | 7.2 |
| Food: Dining Room/Cuisine | 6.2 |
| Food: Buffets/Informal Dining | 6.1 |
| Food: Quality of Ingredients | 6.0 |
| Service: Dining Room | 7.3 |
| Service: Bars/Lounges | 7.4 |
| Service: Cabins | 7.3 |
| Cruise: Entertainment | 6.4 |
| Cruise: Activities Program | 6.2 |
| Cruise: Hospitality Standard | 6.7 |
| OVERALL RATING | 101.7 |

**+** New facilities added in an extensive refit and refurbishment program which improved all public areas with lighter, brighter, very attractive decor and smart furnishings. New facilities include a Lido Bar (with white rattan furniture), Delphin Lounge, health/fitness facilities and a single, large dining room. Boat Deck suites are very large and well equipped. Other cabins are less so, but very comfortable, although bathrooms are small. Dialysis Station is an excellent addition, as are the electric shoe polishers in the gents toilets. Low drinks prices. Superb itineraries.

**–** Poor cabin insulation and not much closet and drawer space, particularly for long voyages. Service has little finesse, and communication is often frustrating.

**Dining** Delightful large new dining room with picture windows. Italian catering is quite good, but presentation could be better. Limited choice of breads, cheeses, and fruits; buffets are basic.

**Other Comments** Smart-looking ship has a square funnel, and has been refurbished well following a shipyard roll-over incident. She provides a very comfortable cruise experience for a German-speaking clientele seeking a cruise where casual dress is the norm, to a fine array of destinations, at a very affordable price. It doesn't pretend to be a luxury product, but it offers more than one would think. Delphin Seereisen, the charterers, do a splendid job. Port taxes, insurance, and gratuities are included.

# ms Klaudia Yelanskaya ★

***Principal Cruising Area***

*Arctic (various)*

***Base Ports:*** *Murmansk/Tromso*

| | | | |
|---|---|---|---|
| Cruise Line | | | *Murmansk Shipping* |
| Former Names | | | *n/a* |
| Gross Tonnage | | | *3,941* |
| Builder | | | *Brodgradiliste Uljanik (Yugoslavia)* |
| Original Cost | | | *n/a* |
| Christened By | | | *n/a* |
| First Entered Service | | | *1976* |
| Interior Design | | | *n/a* |
| Country of Registry | | | *Russia* |
| Tel No | *140-1764* | Fax No | *140-1764* |
| Length (ft/m) | | | *328.1/100.01* |
| Beam (ft/m) | | | *53.2/16.24* |
| Draft (ft/m) | | | *15.2/4.65* |
| Engines/Propellers | | | *2 Uljanik diesels/1* |
| Decks | *6* | Crew | *80* |
| Pass. Capacity (basis 2) | *104* | (all berths) | *186* |
| Pass. Space Ratio (basis 2) | *37.8* | (all berths) | *21.1* |
| Officers | *Russian* | Dining Staff | *Russian/Ukrainian* |
| Total Cabins | | | *52* |
| Size (sq ft/m) | *n/a* | Door Width | *24"* |
| Outside Cabins | *52* | Inside Cabins | *0* |
| Single Cabins | *0* | Supplement | *100%* |
| Balcony Cabins | *0* | Wheelchair Cabins | *0* |
| Cabin Current | | | *220 AC* |
| Refrigerator | | | *No* |
| Cabin TV | *No* | VCR | *No* |
| Dining Rooms | *1* | Sittings | *1* |
| Elevators | *0* | Door Width | *n/a* |

| | | | |
|---|---|---|---|
| Casino | *No* | Slot Machines | *No* |
| Swimming Pools (outside) | *1* | (inside) | *No* |
| Whirlpools | *No* | Gymnasium | *No* |
| Sauna/Steam Rm | *Yes/No* | Massage | *No* |
| Self-Service Launderette | | | *No* |
| Movie Theater/Seats | | | *Yes/75* |
| Library | | | *Yes* |
| Children's Facilities | | | *No* |
| Watersports Facilities | | | *None* |
| Classification Society | | | *RS* |

| RATINGS | SCORE |
|---|---|
| Ship: Condition/Cleanliness | 5.6 |
| Ship: Space/Flow/Comfort | 4.8 |
| Ship: Decor/Furnishings | 6.0 |
| Ship: Fitness Facilities | 3.0 |
| Cabins: Comfort/Facilities | 5.5 |
| Cabins: Software | 5.7 |
| Food: Dining Room/Cuisine | 5.3 |
| Food: Buffets/Informal Dining | 5.0 |
| Food: Quality of Ingredients | 4.6 |
| Service: Dining Room | 6.0 |
| Service: Bars/Lounges | 6.2 |
| Service: Cabins | 6.4 |
| Cruise: Entertainment | 5.0 |
| Cruise: Activities Program | 4.4 |
| Cruise: Hospitality Standard | 5.7 |
| OVERALL RATING | 79.2 |

**+** Intimate, small ship with well-balanced profile is one of a series of eight identical sisters often chartered to European operators. Has an ice-hardened hull suitable for "soft" expedition cruising. Good open deck spaces for ship size. Recently underwent extensive refurbishment. Outdoor observation deck and enclosed promenade deck for inclement weather. Charming forward music lounge has wooden dance floor. Rich, highly polished wood paneling throughout, and winding brass-railed main staircase. Good cinema/lecture room.

**–** Cabins are compact and spartan, and most can accommodate four persons, but space really is tight, and there's little closet and drawer space.

**Dining** Comfortable dining room has ocean views, but no tables for two. Limited choice of food, but it is hearty. Friendly, attentive service. Poor selection of breads, fruits, and cheeses.

**Other Comments** This ship is small, and while not glamorous, comfortable and has plenty of character. Often chartered to Western tour operators for part of a year for soft expedition-style cruises, where all shore excursions and visas are normally included, and rated accordingly.

# mv Konstantin Simonov ★★

***Principal Cruising Area***
*Baltic (3 nights year-round)*
***Base Port:*** *Helsinki (Mon/Thu)*

| | | | |
|---|---|---|---|
| Cruise Line | | | *Baltic Line* |
| Former Names | | | *n/a* |
| Gross Tonnage | | | *9,885* |
| Builder | | | *Szszecin (Poland)* |
| Original Cost | | | *n/a* |
| Christened By | | | *n/a* |
| First Entered Service | | | *1982* |
| Interior Design | | | *n/a* |
| Country of Registry | | | *Russia* |
| Tel No | *n/a* | Fax No | *n/a* |
| Length (ft/m) | | | *441.2/134.50* |
| Beam (ft/m) | | | *68.8/21.00* |
| Draft (ft/m) | | | *17.3/5.28* |
| Engines/Propellers | | | *2 Sulzer diesels/2* |
| Decks | *6* | Crew | *160* |
| Pass. Capacity (basis 2) | *278* | (all berths) | *492* |
| Pass. Space Ratio (basis 2) | *35.5* | (all berths) | *20.0* |
| Officers | *Russian* | Dining Staff | *Russian* |
| Total Cabins | | | *139* |
| Size (sq ft/m) | *100-320/9.2-29.7* | Door Width | *24"* |
| Outside Cabins | *50* | Inside Cabins | *89* |
| Single Cabins | *0* | Supplement | *100%* |
| Balcony Cabins | *0* | Wheelchair Cabins | *0* |
| Cabin Current | | | *220 AC* |
| Refrigerator | | | *Suites and deluxe cabins* |
| Cabin TV | *Suites* | VCR | *No* |
| Dining Rooms | *2* | Sittings | *1* |
| Elevators | *1* | Door Width | *30"* |

| | | | |
|---|---|---|---|
| Casino | *No* | Slot Machines | *Yes* |
| Swimming Pools (outside) | *1* | (inside) | *0* |
| Whirlpools | *0* | Gymnasium | *No* |
| Sauna/Steam Rm | *Yes/No* | Massage | *Yes* |
| Self-Service Launderette | | | *No* |
| Movie Theater/Seats | | | *No* |
| Library | | | *Yes* |
| Children's Facilities | | | *No* |
| Watersports Facilities | | | *None* |
| Classification Society | | | *RS* |

| RATINGS | SCORE |
|---|---|
| Ship: Condition/Cleanliness | 6.6 |
| Ship: Space/Flow/Comfort | 6.2 |
| Ship: Decor/Furnishings | 6.0 |
| Ship: Fitness Facilities | 5.6 |
| Cabins: Comfort/Facilities | 5.5 |
| Cabins: Software | 6.1 |
| Food: Dining Room/Cuisine | 5.3 |
| Food: Buffets/Informal Dining | 5.1 |
| Food: Quality of Ingredients | 5.1 |
| Service: Dining Room | 6.1 |
| Service: Bars/Lounges | 6.2 |
| Service: Cabins | 6.2 |
| Cruise: Entertainment | 4.3 |
| Cruise: Activities Program | 4.7 |
| Cruise: Hospitality Standard | 5.8 |
| OVERALL RATING | 84.8 |

**+** Has a fully-enclosed bridge for all-weather operation. One of a series of five vessels intended for line voyages and short cruises. Interior decor is rather spartan and totally void of glitz. The ambiance is reasonably friendly. Suites are large and well equipped. Standard cabins are small and some are fitted with upper pullman berths. Most are utilitarian in fittings and furnishings, but quite adequate.

**–** Very limited open deck and sunning space, and tiny swimming pool. Both public room and cabin soft furnishings could be better.

**Dining** There are several dining rooms and cafeterias. Food quality varies depending on dining area chosen, but is quite adequate, no more. Menu choice is very limited.

**Other Comments** This ship has a square, angular profile with a square stern, stubby bow, and a fat, squat funnel. Wide choice of cabins. Choice of several bars. Service lacks training and finesse. Provides a basic, low-cost cruise experience for an international clientele wanting to visit St. Petersburg, at modest rates, nothing more. Her passenger capacity will be increased after the addition of some 100 beds in a refit expected to take place in late 1994.

# ms Kristina Regina ★★★

***Principal Cruising Area***

*Baltic (10/11/14 nights)*

***Base Ports:*** *Copenhagen/Helsinki*

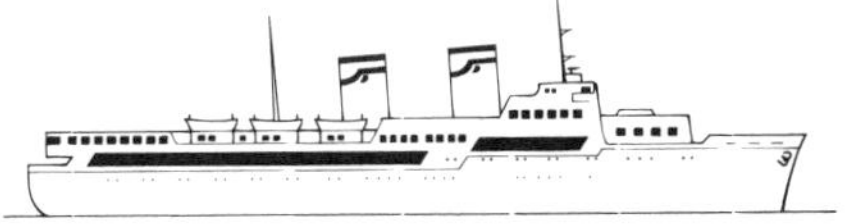

| | | | |
|---|---|---|---|
| Cruise Line | | | *Kristina Cruises* |
| Former Names | | | *Borea/Bore* |
| Gross Tonnage | | | *3,878* |
| Builder | | | *Oskarshamn Shipyard (Sweden)* |
| Original Cost | | | *n/a* |
| Christened By | | | *Mrs Maila Partanen* |
| First Entered Service | | | *1960/April 5, 1988* |
| Interior Design | | | *n/a* |
| Country of Registry | | | *Finland (OGBF)* |
| Tel No | *162-3154* | Fax No | *162-3154* |
| Length (ft/m) | | | *327.4/99.80* |
| Beam (ft/m) | | | *50.1/15.30* |
| Draft (ft/m) | | | *17.3/5.30* |
| Engines/Propellers | | | *2 Wartsila diesels/2* |
| Decks | *6* | Crew | *55* |
| Pass. Capacity (basis 2) | *276* | (all berths) | *350* |
| Pass. Space Ratio (basis 2) | *14.0* | (all berths) | *11.0* |
| Officers | *Finnish* | Dining Staff | *Finnish* |
| Total Cabins | | | *141* |
| Size (sq ft/m) | 65-125/6-11.6 | Door Width | *25.5"* |
| Outside Cabins | *108* | Inside Cabins | *33* |
| Single Cabins | *0* | Supplement | *100%* |
| Balcony Cabins | *0* | Wheelchair Cabins | *0* |
| Cabin Current | | | *220 AC* |
| Refrigerator | | | *No* |
| Cabin TV | *Deluxe cabins* | VCR | *No* |
| Dining Rooms | *2* | Sittings | *1* |
| Elevators | *0* | Door Width | *n/a* |

| | | | |
|---|---|---|---|
| Casino | *No* | Slot Machines | *No* |
| Swimming Pools (outside) | *0* | (inside) | *0* |
| Whirlpools | *0* | Gymnasium | *No* |
| Sauna/Steam Rm | *Yes/No* | Massage | *No* |
| Self-Service Launderette | | | *No* |
| Movie Theater/Seats | | | *No* |
| Library | | | *Yes* |
| Children's Facilities | | | *Yes* |
| Watersports Facilities | | | *None* |
| Classification Society | | | *Lloyd's Register* |

| RATINGS | SCORE |
|---|---|
| Ship: Condition/Cleanliness | 6.6 |
| Ship: Space/Flow/Comfort | 5.4 |
| Ship: Decor/Furnishings | 6.7 |
| Ship: Fitness Facilities | 3.7 |
| Cabins: Comfort/Facilities | 5.7 |
| Cabins: Software | 6.3 |
| Food: Dining Room/Cuisine | 6.4 |
| Food: Buffets/Informal Dining | 6.0 |
| Food: Quality of Ingredients | 6.3 |
| Service: Dining Room | 7.1 |
| Service: Bars/Lounges | 7.4 |
| Service: Cabins | 7.3 |
| Cruise: Entertainment | 3.5 |
| Cruise: Activities Program | 4.8 |
| Cruise: Hospitality Standard | 7.8 |
| OVERALL RATING | 91.0 |

**+** Wrap-around wooden promenade deck. Beautiful woods and lots of brass feature in the interior decor, and the Scandinavian artwork is fascinating. The main lounge doubles as a well designed auditorium/movie theater. All cabins have shower and toilet, radio, and telephone, but not much else, and they are really tiny, as are the bathrooms. Five allergy-free cabins.

**–** A high density ship—there's not much room to move about inside when full. Cabins have little closet and drawer space, so take only what's necessary.

**Dining** The dining room is charming, and features Continental cuisine, with a distinct accent on fish, seafood, and fresh berries. Good, hearty, and friendly service with a smile.

**Other Comments** This lovely old-world ship, built specifically for close-in northern European coastal and archipelago cruises, was extensively refurbished in 1990. Currency: U.S. dollars or Finnish marks. Gratuities are extra.

# ms La Palma ★★★

***Principal Cruising Area***
*Europe (7/11 nights)*
***Base Port:** Venice (Saturday)*

| | | | |
|---|---|---|---|
| Cruise Line | | | *Intercruise* |
| Former Names | | | *Delphi/La Perla/ Ferdinand De Lesseps* |
| Gross Tonnage | | | *11,608* |
| Builder | | | *Forges et Chantiers de la Gironde (France)* |
| Original Cost | | | *n/a* |
| Christened By | | | *George D. Louris* |
| First Entered Service | | | *Oct 3, 1952/Apr 1978* |
| Interior Design | | | *George D. Louris* |
| Country of Registry | | | *Greece (SXBS)* |
| Tel No | *113-0506* | Fax No | *113-0506* |
| Length (ft/m) | | | *492.4/150.09* |
| Beam (ft/m) | | | *62.6/19.10* |
| Draft (ft/m) | | | *22.0/6.72* |
| Engines/Propellers | | | *2 B&W 10-cyl diesels/2* |
| Decks | *7* | Crew | *230* |
| Pass. Capacity (basis 2) | *648* | (all berths) | *832* |
| Pass. Space Ratio (basis 2) | *17.9* | (all berths) | *13.9* |
| Officers | *Greek* | Dining Staff | *Greek* |
| Total Cabins | | | *324* |
| Size (sq ft/m) | *105-215/9.7-20* | Door Width | *24"* |
| Outside Cabins | *176* | Inside Cabins | *148* |
| Single Cabins | *5* | Supplement | *Fixed rates* |
| Balcony Cabins | *0* | Wheelchair Cabins | *0* |
| Cabin Current | | | *110/220 AC* |
| Refrigerator | | | *Cat. AS/A* |
| Cabin TV | *Deluxe* | VCR | *No* |
| Dining Rooms | *1* | Sittings | *2* |

| | | | |
|---|---|---|---|
| Elevators | *0* | Door Width | *n/a* |
| Casino | *Yes* | Slot Machines | *Yes* |
| Swimming Pools (outside) | *1* | (inside) | *0* |
| Whirlpools | *0* | Gymnasium | *No* |
| Sauna/Steam Rm | *No/No* | Massage | *No* |
| Self-Service Launderette | | | *No* |
| Movie Theater/Seats | | | *No* |
| Library | *Yes* | Children's Facilities | *No* |
| Watersports Facilities | | | *None* |
| Classification Society | | | *Grecian Lloyd* |

| RATINGS | SCORE |
|---|---|
| Ship: Condition/Cleanliness | 6.4 |
| Ship: Space/Flow/Comfort | 6.8 |
| Ship: Decor/Furnishings | 6.7 |
| Ship: Fitness Facilities | 4.2 |
| Cabins: Comfort/Facilities | 6.2 |
| Cabins: Software | 6.4 |
| Food: Dining Room/Cuisine | 6.4 |
| Food: Buffets/Informal Dining | 6.2 |
| Food: Quality of Ingredients | 6.3 |
| Service: Dining Room | 6.7 |
| Service: Bars/Lounges | 6.4 |
| Service: Cabins | 6.5 |
| Cruise: Entertainment | 5.4 |
| Cruise: Activities Program | 5.6 |
| Cruise: Hospitality Standard | 6.3 |
| OVERALL RATING | 92.5 |

**+** Basically a well maintained vessel. Plenty of open deck and sunning space except when ship is full. Water slide into swimming pool for children. This is one of only two ships to feature an isolated nudist sunbathing deck (the other being Hapag-Lloyd's *Europa*). Popular Bavarian beer garden on deck. Cheerful interior decor, with plenty of wood and wood trim throughout. Ten suites are very spacious and nicely furnished, while other cabins are moderately so. All have private facilities, and all have been refurbished.

**–** Steep gangway. Beverages are extremely expensive.

**Dining** Dining room is set low down, but is quite cozy. Continental cuisine is adequate, but there is little choice, especially for non-meat eaters. Poor selection of breads, cheeses, and fruits. Service comes with a smile.

**Other Comments** Traditional older styling, with low funnel profile. Passageways have floor-to-ceiling carpeting, which is difficult to keep clean, but provides good insulation. This is a high-density ship that caters best to young couples, families, and active singles on a modest budget. Flexible scheduling means passengers can embark and disembark at almost every port and take a full or part cruise. Mostly multi-national European passengers, and multi-lingual staff. Cruise rate is moderate. Insurance and gratuities are extra.

# mv Langkapuri Star Aquarius ★★★★

***Principal Cruising Area***
*South East Asia (2/3 nights)*
***Base Port:** Singapore*

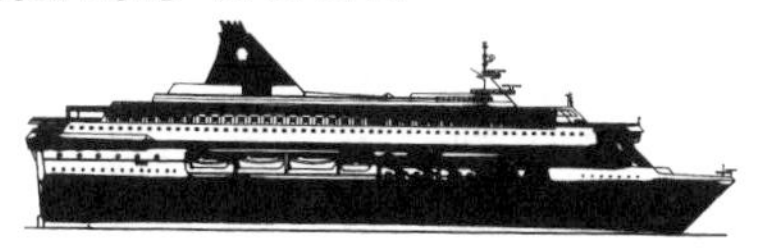

| | |
|---|---|
| Cruise Line/Operator | *Star Cruise* |
| Former Names | *Athena* |
| Gross Tonnage | *40,022* |
| Builder | *Wartsila (Finland)* |
| Original Cost | *SEK650 million* |
| Christened By | *Ms Marianne Myrsten* |
| First Entered Service | *April 1989/Dec 23, 1993* |
| Interior Design | *Robert Tillberg/PM design* |
| Country of Registry | *Panama (3FRG)* |
| Tel No | *02-011-719543* |
| Fax No | *02-011-719514* |
| Length (ft/m) | *579.3/176.6* |
| Beam (ft/m) | *97.1/29.6* |
| Draft (ft/m) | *20.3/6.2* |
| Engines/Propellers | *4 Sulzer diesels/2 (CP)* |
| Decks *12* | Crew *750* |
| Pass. Capacity (basis 2) *1,530* | (all berths) *1,900* |
| Pass. Space Ratio (basis 2) *26.1* | (all berths) *21.0* |
| Officers *Scandinavian* | Service Staff *Filipino* |
| Total Cabins | *718* |
| Size (sq ft/m) *67.8-145.3/6.3-13.5* | Door Width 24" |
| Outside Cabins *303* | Inside Cabins *415* |
| Single Cabins *42* | Supplement *Fixed rates* |
| Balcony Cabins *0* | Wheelchair Cabins *6* |
| Cabin Current | *220 AC* |
| Refrigerator | *No* |
| Cabin TV *Yes* | VCR *No* |
| Dining Rooms *4* | Sittings *1* |

| | |
|---|---|
| Elevators *5* | Door Width *40"* |
| Casino *Yes* | Slot Machines *Yes* |
| Swimming Pools (outside) *1* | (inside) *1* |
| Whirlpools *6* | Gymnasium *Yes* |
| Sauna/Steam Rm *Yes/Yes* | Massage *Yes* |
| Self-Service Launderette | *No* |
| Movie Theater/Seats | *Yes (2)/210 each* |
| Library *Yes* | Children's Facilities *Yes* |
| Watersports Facilities | *None* |
| Classification Society | *Det Norske Veritas* |

| RATINGS | SCORE |
|---|---|
| Ship: Condition/Cleanliness | 7.8 |
| Ship: Space/Flow/Comfort | 7.7 |
| Ship: Decor/Furnishings | 7.8 |
| Ship: Fitness Facilities | 6.9 |
| Cabins: Comfort/Facilities | 5.5 |
| Cabins: Software | 5.7 |
| Food: Dining Room/Cuisine | 7.7 |
| Food: Buffets/Informal Dining | 7.4 |
| Food: Quality of Ingredients | 8.1 |
| Service: Dining Room | 7.4 |
| Service: Bars/Lounges | 7.1 |
| Service: Cabins | 7.0 |
| Cruise: Entertainment | 6.6 |
| Cruise: Activities Program | 6.9 |
| Cruise: Hospitality Standard | 7.8 |
| OVERALL RATING | 107.4 |

**+** Scandinavian design combined with a touch of the Orient. Helipad. Outstanding new family facilities for children and teens. Huge, duty-free shopping center and supermarket. Newly added is a very imperial, regal looking casino for VIPs. Superb health club for men. Also has 11 meeting rooms, two conference auditoriums, and a business center. Free ice cream for kids.

**–** High density ship means crowded places, and long lines for shore visits, embarkation, and disembarkation. Except for some very imperial suites, the cabins are very small, with basic facilities and tiny bathrooms. Machines in the huge children's entertainment center cost money.

**Dining** With seven restaurants, there's a wide choice of cuisine and dining styles. This ship has a real Chinese restaurant (Cantonese and Sichuan) with a Hong Kong chef, and live fish tanks from which to select your seafood. There is also Japanese (including sushi bar, and private tatami room), Italian (candlelight dining), the Spice Island buffet (for laksa, satay and hawker delights), and three other snack cafés.

**Other Comments** This ex-Viking Line ferry has been skillfully converted into a cruise vessel for the Asian family market, with a reduction in berths from 2,200 to 1,900. Low ticket price, but everything costs extra, so a family cruise can end up being quite expensive. One bag and one carry-on per passenger. Handling charge and insurance not included. Gratuities are discouraged.

# ms Legend of the Seas

***Principal Cruising Areas***
*Alaska/Panama Canal (7 nights)*
***Base Port:** Vancouver*

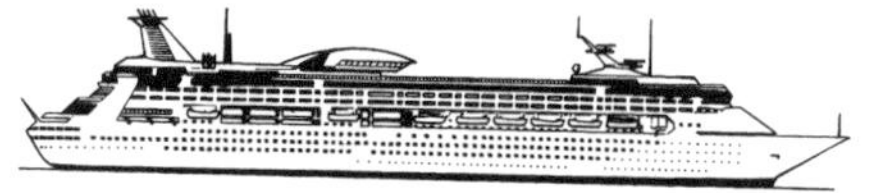

| | | | |
|---|---|---|---|
| Cruise Line | | | *Royal Caribbean Cruises* |
| Former Names | | | *n/a* |
| Gross Tonnage | | | *66,700* |
| Builder | | | *Chantiers de l'Atlantique (France)* |
| Original Cost | | | *$325 million* |
| Christened By | | | *n/a* |
| First Entered Service | | | *May 1995* |
| Interior Design | | | *Njal Eide, Howard Snoweiss, Mike Bidnell, Per Hoydahl, Lars Iwdal, Petter Yran, B. Wilday* |
| Country of Registry | | | *Norway* |
| Tel No | *n/a* | Fax No | *n/a* |
| Length (ft/m) | | | *867.0/264.20* |
| Beam (ft/m) | | | *105.0/32.00* |
| Draft (ft/m) | | | *24.5/7.46* |
| Engines/Propellers | | | *5 Wartsila 12-cyl diesels/2 (CP)* |
| Decks | *11* | Crew | *732* |
| Pass. Capacity (basis 2) | *1,808* | (all berths) | *2,068* |
| Pass. Space Ratio (basis 2) | *36.8* | (all berths) | *32.2* |
| Officers | *International* | Dining Staff | *International* |
| Total Cabins | | | *902* |
| Size (sq ft/m) | | | *138.1-148/12.8-106.6* |
| Door Width | | | *31"* |
| Outside Cabins | *575* | Inside Cabins | *327* |
| Single Cabins | 0 | Supplement | *50%* |
| Balcony Cabins | *231* | Wheelchair Cabins | *17* |
| Cabin Current | | | *110/220 AC* |
| Cabin TV | *Yes* | VCR | *Suites* |

| | | | |
|---|---|---|---|
| Dining Rooms | 1 | Sittings | 2 |
| Elevators | 11 | Door Width | 43" |
| Casino | *Yes* | Slot Machines | *Yes* |
| Swimming Pools (outside) | 2 | (inside) | *0* |
| Whirlpools | *4* | Gymnasium | *Yes* |
| Sauna/Steam Rm | *Yes/Yes* | Massage | *Yes* |
| Movie Theater/Seats | | | *n/a* |
| Library | *Yes* | Children's Facilities | *Yes* |
| Watersports Facilities | | | *None* |
| Classification Society | | | *Det Norske Veritas* |

| RATINGS | SCORE |
|---|---|
| Ship: Condition/Cleanliness | NYR |
| Ship: Space/Flow/Comfort | NYR |
| Ship: Decor/Furnishings | NYR |
| Ship: Fitness Facilities | NYR |
| Cabins: Comfort/Facilities | NYR |
| Cabins: Software | NYR |
| Food: Dining Room/Cuisine | NYR |
| Food: Buffets/Informal Dining | NYR |
| Food: Quality of Ingredients | NYR |
| Service: Dining Room | NYR |
| Service: Bars/Lounges | NYR |
| Service: Cabins | NYR |
| Cruise: Entertainment | NYR |
| Cruise: Activities Program | NYR |
| Cruise: Hospitality Standard | NYR |

NYR = Not Yet Rated

**+** Highest speed RCCL ship (at 24 knots) for distance cruises. Pool deck overhangs hull to provide a very wide deck, while still allowing the ship to navigate the Panama Canal. Outside light is brought into the inside in many places, with an extensive glass area that provides constant contact with sea and air. Features an innovative, single-level sliding glass roof (not a magrodome) over one of two swimming pools, providing a multi-activity, all-weather indoor-outdoor area. Tiered and balconied showlounge has excellent sightlines. Cabins are larger than on all previous RCCL ships, and include some outstanding large suites. Some cabins on Deck 8 also have a larger door for wheelchair access—in addition to the 17 cabins for the physically challenged.

**–** None known at press time, although as with any large ship, you should expect long lines for embarkation, disembarkation, buffets, and shore excursions.

**Dining** The two-deck-high dining room has dramatic glass walls, so passengers upstairs and downstairs can see one another. Cavernous indoor-outdoor café and good-sized snack area add to choices. Same consistent RCCL food and service expected.

**Other Comments** Few other details for this ship were available at press time, but this promises to be an outstanding cruise vessel for RCCL passengers who appreciate the company's consistency and fine-tuned product.

# ms Leisure World ★★★

***Principal Cruising Area***
*South East Asia (1-4 nights)*
***Base Port:** Singapore*

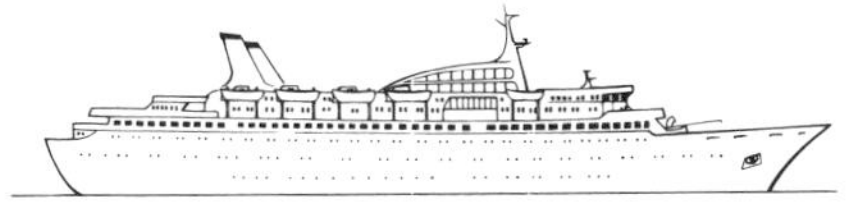

| | | | |
|---|---|---|---|
| Cruise Line | | | *New Century Tours* |
| Former Names | | | *Fantasy World/Asean World/ Shangri-La World/Skyward* |
| Gross Tonnage | | | *16,254* |
| Builder | | | *Seebeckwerft (Germany)* |
| Original Cost | | | *n/a* |
| Christened By | | | *n/a* |
| First Entered Service | | | *Dec 21, 1969/1990* |
| Interior Design | | | *Tage Wandborg* |
| Country of Registry | | | *BVI (C6CM5)* |
| Tel No | *110-4164* | Fax No | *110-4164* |
| Length (ft/m) | | | *525.3/160.13* |
| Beam (ft/m) | | | *74.9/22.84* |
| Draft (ft/m) | | | *20.6/6.29* |
| Engines/Propellers | | | *2 MAN 16-cyl diesels/2 (CP)* |
| Decks | *8* | Crew | *250* |
| Pass. Capacity (basis 2) | *730* | (all berths) | *1,071* |
| Pass. Space Ratio (basis 2) | *22.2* | (all berths) | *15.1* |
| Officers | *International* | Dining Staff | *International* |
| Total Cabins | | | *365* |
| Size (sq ft/m) | *90-330/8.3-30.5* | Door Width | *23"* |
| Outside Cabins | *219* | Inside Cabins | *145* |
| Single Cabins | *0* | Supplement | *100%* |
| Balcony Cabins | *0* | Wheelchair Cabins | *0* |
| Cabin Current | *110/220 AC* | Refrigerator | *No* |
| Cabin TV | *No* | VCR | *No* |
| Dining Rooms | *1* | Sittings | *2* |
| Elevators | *4* | Door Width | *29"* |

| | | | |
|---|---|---|---|
| Casino | *Yes* | Slot Machines | *Yes* |
| Swimming Pools (outside) | *1* | (inside) | *0* |
| Whirlpools | *0* | Gymnasium | *Yes* |
| Sauna/Steam Rm | *Yes/No* | Massage | *Yes* |
| Self-Service Launderette | | | *No* |
| Movie Theater/Seats | | | *Yes/180* |
| Library | | | *Yes* |
| Children's Facilities | | | *Yes* |
| Watersports Facilities | | | *None* |
| Classification Society | | | *Det Norske Veritas* |

| RATINGS | SCORE |
|---|---|
| Ship: Condition/Cleanliness | 6.2 |
| Ship: Space/Flow/Comfort | 6.4 |
| Ship: Decor/Furnishings | 6.5 |
| Ship: Fitness Facilities | 6.1 |
| Cabins: Comfort/Facilities | 6.1 |
| Cabins: Software | 6.7 |
| Food: Dining Room/Cuisine | 6.2 |
| Food: Buffets/Informal Dining | 6.0 |
| Food: Quality of Ingredients | 5.6 |
| Service: Dining Room | 6.1 |
| Service: Bars/Lounges | 6.1 |
| Service: Cabins | 6.2 |
| Cruise: Entertainment | 5.7 |
| Cruise: Activities Program | 5.9 |
| Cruise: Hospitality Standard | 6.3 |
| OVERALL RATING | 92.1 |

**+** Attractive, modern, yet somewhat dated-looking, ship from the seventies has a distinctive daytime sun lounge set high and forward against the ship's mast. Refurbished interior features light, airy decor in clean, crisp colors. Lounge and bar atop ship has plenty of light. Pleasant balconied theater. Good karaoke lounge for those inevitable sing-alongs.

**–** Very high density ship means crowded public areas and long lines for buffets and elevators. Except for ten suites, cabins are small, with very limited closet and drawer space, tinny metal furniture, and poor cabin soundproofing. The staff lack finesse. Despite what the brochures proclaim, this is not a luxury ship by any stretch of the imagination. Attracts many gamblers.

**Dining** The dining room, although attractive, is cramped and extremely noisy, and food service is fast and without finesse. Choice of à la carte menu or Asian/Western buffet. There's a mixture of Asian and Western dishes. Food quality is so-so, but the price is reasonably low.

**Other Comments** Adequate for short cruises. Cheerful, but rather hurried service. Wine service is poor. This ship is fine for active passengers wanting an upbeat cruise experience at a fair price, in comfortable, friendly, but not elegant, surroundings.

# ss Leonid Sobinov ★★

***Principal Cruising Area***
*Europe (14 nights)*
***Base Port:*** *Toulouse*

| | | | |
|---|---|---|---|
| Cruise Line | | | *Baltic Shipping* |
| Former Names | | | *Carmania/Saxonia* |
| Gross Tonnage | | | *21,846* |
| Builder | | | *John Brown Shipyard (Scotland)* |
| Original Cost | | | *n/a* |
| Christened By | | | *Lady Winston Churchill* |
| First Entered Service | | | *Sep 2, 1954/Feb 25, 1974* |
| Interior Design | | | *n/a* |
| Country of Registry | | | *Malta* |
| Tel No | *125-6223* | Fax No | *125-6223* |
| Length (ft/m) | | | *604/184.00* |
| Beam (ft/m) | | | *80.0/24.40* |
| Draft (ft/m) | | | *26.2/8.00* |
| Engines/Propellers | | | *4 John Brown steam turbines/2* |
| Decks | *7* | Crew | *400* |
| Pass. Capacity (basis 2) | *700* | (all berths) | *925* |
| Pass. Space Ratio (basis 2) | *31.2* | (all berths) | *23.6* |
| Officers | | | *Russian/Ukrainian* |
| Dining Staff | | | *Russian/Ukrainian* |
| Total Cabins | | | *288* |
| Size (sq ft/m) | *90-241/8.3-22.3* | Door Width | *24"* |
| Outside Cabins | *158* | Inside Cabins | *130* |
| Single Cabins | *0* | Supplement | *100%* |
| Balcony Cabins | *0* | Wheelchair Cabins | *0* |
| Cabin Current | *110/220 AC* | Refrigerator | *No* |
| Cabin TV | *No* | VCR | *No* |
| Dining Rooms | *1* | Sittings | *2* |
| Elevators | *3* | Door Width | *30"* |

| | | | |
|---|---|---|---|
| Casino | *No* | Slot Machines | *No* |
| Swimming Pools (outside) | *1* | (inside) | *0* |
| Whirlpools | *0* | Gymnasium | *No* |
| Sauna/Steam Rm | *No/No* | Massage | *No* |
| Self-Service Launderette | | | *No* |
| Movie Theater/Seats | | | *Yes/260* |
| Library | | | *Yes* |
| Children's Facilities | | | *Yes* |
| Watersports Facilities | | | *None* |
| Classification Society | | | *RS* |

| RATINGS | SCORE |
|---|---|
| Ship: Condition/Cleanliness | 4.1 |
| Ship: Space/Flow/Comfort | 5.3 |
| Ship: Decor/Furnishings | 5.3 |
| Ship: Fitness Facilities | 4.1 |
| Cabins: Comfort/Facilities | 5.3 |
| Cabins: Software | 5.6 |
| Food: Dining Room/Cuisine | 5.4 |
| Food: Buffets/Informal Dining | 5.1 |
| Food: Quality of Ingredients | 5.2 |
| Service: Dining Room | 6.5 |
| Service: Bars/Lounges | 6.4 |
| Service: Cabins | 6.6 |
| Cruise: Entertainment | 5.3 |
| Cruise: Activities Program | 5.4 |
| Cruise: Hospitality Standard | 6.1 |
| OVERALL RATING | 81.7 |

**+** This former Cunard ocean liner has classic lines and a deep-draft, go-anywhere hull shape. Now re-named after a famous operatic singer. Solidly built—they don't build ships like this any more. Good wrap-around outdoor promenade deck as one would expect from a former transatlantic ship, a kidney-shaped swimming pool, and, on the port side, an interesting Steak Bar. Good array of public rooms, bars, and lounges. Acres of good wood paneling, and much brass-trimmed furniture throughout. The cabins are reasonably spacious and have heavy-duty fittings and furnishings, but they are well worn, and a major refurbishment now would prove expensive.

**–** In her heyday, she had nice interior decor, but she is now becoming a little neglected. Outside, there are areas of major rust showing, and the wood decking could be better.

**Dining** The dining room is reasonably practical, but the decor and lighting are now very dated. The cuisine is very basic, with a very poor selection of breads, fruits, and cheeses.

**Other Comments** This is cheap and cheerful cruising for a European-based passenger mix, but it's time the old girl was retired.

# mv Lev Tolstoi ★★

*Principal Cruising Area*

*Europe (various)*

***Base Ports:*** *Bremerhaven/Savona*

| | | | |
|---|---|---|---|
| Cruise Line | | | *Transocean Tours* |
| Former Names | | | *n/a* |
| Gross Tonnage | | | *12,600* |
| Builder | | | *Szszecin (Poland)* |
| Original Cost | | | *n/a* |
| Christened By | | | *n/a* |
| First Entered Service | | | *1982* |
| Interior Design | | | *n/a* |
| Country of Registry | | | *Ukraine (UWSU)* |
| Tel No | *140-1354* | Fax No | *140-1354* |
| Length (ft/m) | | | *441.2/134.50* |
| Beam (ft/m) | | | *68.8/21.00* |
| Draft (ft/m) | | | *17.3/5.28* |
| Engines/Propellers | | | *2 Sulzer diesels/2* |
| Decks | *6* | Crew | *150* |
| Pass. Capacity (basis 2) | *264* | (all berths) | *290* |
| Pass. Space Ratio (basis 2) | *47.7* | (all berths) | *43.4* |
| Officers | *Ukrainian* | Dining Staff | *Russian/Ukrainian* |
| Total Cabins | | | *132* |
| Size (sq ft/m) | *100-320 /9.2-29.7* | Door Width | *24"* |
| Outside Cabins | *58* | Inside Cabins | *74* |
| Single Cabins | *0* | Supplement | *100%* |
| Balcony Cabins | *0* | Wheelchair Cabins | *0* |
| Cabin Current | | | *220 AC* |
| Refrigerator | | | *No* |
| Cabin TV | *2 deluxe cabins* | VCR | *No* |
| Dining Rooms | *1* | Sittings | *1* |
| Elevators | *1* | Door Width | *30"* |

| | | | |
|---|---|---|---|
| Casino | *Yes* | Slot Machines | *Yes* |
| Swimming Pools (outside) | *1* | (inside) | *0* |
| Whirlpools | *0* | Gymnasium | *Yes* |
| Sauna/Steam Rm | *Yes/No* | Massage | *Yes* |
| Self-Service Launderette | | | *No* |
| Movie Theater/Seats | | | *No* |
| Library | | | *Yes* |
| Children's Facilities | | | *No* |
| Watersports Facilities | | | *None* |
| Classification Society | | | *RS* |

| RATINGS | SCORE |
|---|---|
| Ship: Condition/Cleanliness | 6.6 |
| Ship: Space/Flow/Comfort | 6.2 |
| Ship: Decor/Furnishings | 6.0 |
| Ship: Fitness Facilities | 5.6 |
| Cabins: Comfort/Facilities | 5.5 |
| Cabins: Software | 6.1 |
| Food: Dining Room/Cuisine | 5.3 |
| Food: Buffets/Informal Dining | 5.1 |
| Food: Quality of Ingredients | 5.1 |
| Service: Dining Room | 6.1 |
| Service: Bars/Lounges | 6.2 |
| Service: Cabins | 6.2 |
| Cruise: Entertainment | 4.3 |
| Cruise: Activities Program | 4.7 |
| Cruise: Hospitality Standard | 5.8 |
| OVERALL RATING | 84.8 |

**+** This ship has a square, angular profile with boxy stern, stubby bow, and a fat funnel—otherwise she's handsome! Fully-enclosed bridge for all-weather operation. One of a series of five Polish-built vessels intended for line voyages but now used as a cruise ship. Attractive itineraries. The interior decor is quite smart, with soft pastel colors, and the ambiance is friendly and comfortable. Some cabins are fitted with upper pullman berths. Apart from seven large cabins, all are small and somewhat spartan in fittings and furnishings, and there's little drawer space.

**–** Limited amount of open deck and sunning space, and tiny swimming pool.

**Dining** The dining room is plain, yet attractive, and has large picture windows with white chiffon curtains. The cuisine is "meat and potatoes basic"—adequate, but highly salted. Service is provided by charming Ukrainian waitresses.

**Other Comments** Service is somewhat perfunctory, but getting better. Now under charter to Transocean Tours, whose staff are excellent. This ship provides a basic, inexpensive cruise experience for a mostly German-speaking clientele, at modest rates, but don't expect too much.

# ms Maasdam ★★★★+

***Principal Cruising Areas***
*Alaska/Caribbean (7 nights)*
***Base Ports:*** *Vancouver/Ft. Lauderdale*

| | | | |
|---|---|---|---|
| Cruise Line | | | *Holland America Line* |
| Former Names | | | *n/a* |
| Gross Tonnage | | | *55,451* |
| Builder | | | *Fincantieri (Italy)* |
| Original Cost | | | *$215 million* |
| Christened By | | | *Ms June Allyson* |
| First Entered Service | | | *Dec 3, 1993* |
| Interior Design | | | *VFD Interiors/Joe Farcus* |
| Country of Registry | | | *Bahamas (C6VF)* |
| Tel No | *130-6156* | Fax No | *130-6157* |
| Length (ft/m) | | | *719.3/219.30* |
| Beam (ft/m) | *101.0/30.80* | Draft (ft/m) | *24.6/7.50* |
| Engines/Propellers | | | *2 Sulzer V12-cyl diesels/2 (VP)* |
| Decks | *10* | Crew | *588* |
| Pass. Capacity (basis 2) | *1,264* | (all berths) | *1,627* |
| Pass. Space Ratio (basis 2) | *43.8* | (all berths) | *34.0* |
| Officers | | | *Dutch* |
| Dining Staff | | | *Filipino/Indonesian* |
| Total Cabins | | | *632* |
| Size (sq ft/m) | | | *187-1,126/17.3-104.5* |
| Door Width | | | *26"* |
| Outside Cabins | *501* | Inside Cabins | *131* |
| Single Cabins | *0* | Supplement | *50-100%* |
| Balcony Cabins | *150* | Wheelchair Cabins | *6* |
| Cabin Current | | | *110/220 AC* |
| Refrigerator | | | *Category PS/S/A/B* |
| Cabin TV | *Yes* | VCR | *No* |
| Dining Rooms | *1* | Sittings | *2* |

| | | | |
|---|---|---|---|
| Elevators | *12* | Door Width | *40"* |
| Casino | *Yes* | Slot Machines | *Yes* |
| Swimming Pools (outside) | *1* | (inside) | *1* |
| Whirlpools | *2* | Gymnasium | *Yes* |
| Sauna/Steam Rm | *Yes/No* | Massage | *Yes* |
| Self-Service Launderette | | | *Yes* |
| Movie Theater/Seats | | | *Yes/249* |
| Library | *Yes* | Children's Facilities | *No* |
| Watersports Facilities | | | *None* |
| Classification Society | | | *Lloyd's Register* |

| RATINGS | SCORE |
|---|---|
| Ship: Condition/Cleanliness | 8.7 |
| Ship: Space/Flow/Comfort | 8.2 |
| Ship: Decor/Furnishings | 8.5 |
| Ship: Fitness Facilities | 7.7 |
| Cabins: Comfort/Facilities | 8.1 |
| Cabins: Software | 8.0 |
| Food: Dining Room/Cuisine | 7.8 |
| Food: Buffets/Informal Dining | 7.6 |
| Food: Quality of Ingredients | 7.2 |
| Service: Dining Room | 7.7 |
| Service: Bars/Lounges | 7.6 |
| Service: Cabins | 8.1 |
| Cruise: Entertainment | 7.0 |
| Cruise: Activities Program | 7.2 |
| Cruise: Hospitality Standard | 8.2 |
| OVERALL RATING | 117.6 |

**+** The decor is softer and more sophisticated than on sister ship *Statendam*. Antiques and artwork are stunning. Fine flower arrangements in public areas. Good passenger flow. Mid-level, inboard lifeboats. Dramatic three-deck-high atrium foyer. A magrodome roof covers the large indoor-outdoor swimming pool/whirlpools and central lido. The two-deck-high showroom is well thought out. Lovely reference library (no fiction). In-suite dining in 28 suites (for four). Cabins are spacious, tastefully decorated, and well laid out.

**–** Long lines. Cabin closet space is tight. Narrow escalators. Communication with staff is often frustrating. No division of smoking and nonsmoking areas at the outdoor Lido Café.

**Dining** Two-level dining room, located at the stern, is quite dramatic, with a grand staircase, panoramic views, a canopy of Murano glass, and a music balcony. Open seating for breakfast and lunch, two seatings for dinner. Food and service are very plain, basic American cuisine, but nicely presented. Spa Cuisine menu is a useful addition. The Rosenthal china is lovely. Service is friendly and attentive, but robotic. The Lido buffet is good, but the line should upgrade its choice of bread rolls, pastries, and teas. Canned fruits are used.

**Other Comments** A well-built, quality ship, but without the charm of the line's older *Rotterdam*. Port taxes, insurance, and gratuities (not "required," but expected) are extra.

# ms Majesty of the Seas ★★★★+

***Principal Cruising Area***

*Caribbean (7 nights year-round)*

***Base Port:*** *Miami (Sunday)*

| | | | |
|---|---|---|---|
| Cruise Line | | | *Royal Caribbean Cruises* |
| Former Names | | | *n/a* |
| Gross Tonnage | | | *73,941* |
| Builder | | | *Chantiers de l'Atlantique* |
| Original Cost | | | *$300 million* |
| Christened By | | | *H.M. Queen Sonja of Norway* |
| First Entered Service | | | *Apr 26, 1992* |
| Interior Design | | | *Njal Eide* |
| Country of Registry | | | *Norway (LAOI4)* |
| Tel No | *131-3370* | Fax No | *131-3370* |
| Length (ft/m) | | | *873.6/266.30* |
| Beam (ft/m) | | | *105.9/32.30* |
| Draft (ft/m) | | | *24.9/7.60* |
| Engines/Propellers | | | *4 Pielstick 9-cyl diesels/2 (VP)* |
| Decks | *12* | Crew | *822* |
| Pass. Capacity (basis 2) | *2,354* | (all berths) | *2,744* |
| Pass. Space Ratio (basis 2) | *31.4* | (all berths) | *26.9* |
| Officers | *Norwegian* | Dining Staff | *International* |
| Total Cabins | | | *1,177* |
| Size (sq ft/m) | *120-446/11-41.5* | Door Width | *23"* |
| Outside Cabins | *732* | Inside Cabins | *445* |
| Single Cabins | *0* | Supplement | *50%* |
| Balcony Cabins | *62* | Wheelchair Cabins | *4* |
| Cabin Current | | | *110 AC* |
| Refrigerator | | | *Cat. R/A* |
| Cabin TV | *Yes* | VCR | *No* |
| Dining Rooms | *2* | Sittings | *2* |
| Elevators | *18* | Door Width | *39"* |

| | | | |
|---|---|---|---|
| Casino | *Yes* | Slot Machines | *Yes* |
| Swimming Pools (outside) | *2* | (inside) | *0* |
| Whirlpools | *2* | Gymnasium | *Yes* |
| Sauna/Steam Rm | *Yes/No* | Massage | *Yes* |
| Self-Service Launderette | | | *No* |
| Movie Theater/Seats | | | *Yes/200* |
| Library | | | *Yes* |
| Children's Facilities | | | *Yes* |
| Watersports Facilities | | | *None* |
| Classification Society | | | *Det Norske Veritas* |

| RATINGS | SCORE |
|---|---|
| Ship: Condition/Cleanliness | 8.0 |
| Ship: Space/Flow/Comfort | 8.0 |
| Ship: Decor/Furnishings | 7.9 |
| Ship: Fitness Facilities | 7.6 |
| Cabins: Comfort/Facilities | 7.6 |
| Cabins: Software | 7.7 |
| Food: Dining Room/Cuisine | 7.9 |
| Food: Buffets/Informal Dining | 7.6 |
| Food: Quality of Ingredients | 7.1 |
| Service: Dining Room | 7.7 |
| Service: Bars/Lounges | 7.6 |
| Service: Cabins | 7.6 |
| Cruise: Entertainment | 8.2 |
| Cruise: Activities Program | 7.9 |
| Cruise: Hospitality Standard | 8.0 |
| OVERALL RATING | 116.4 |

**+** Spacious, well-designed interior, with excellent signage. Viking Crown Lounge and bar surrounds funnel and provides a stunning view. Beautiful, well stocked and well used library. Most cabins are small, but comfortable and attractive. Family suites sleep four. Excellent cabaret. Good children's/teens' programs and counselors. Japanese-speaking staff at the purser's desk.

**–** Deck space very cramped when full. Too many announcements. Long wait for aft elevators. Expect long lines for embarkation, disembarkation, buffets, and shore tenders.

**Dining** The two musical-themed dining rooms are large and colorful, without excessive noise. The dining room is well organised, with emphasis on highly programed (robotic) service, and without finesse. Menu choices are varied. Quality is well above average for a mass-market product. French, Oriental, Italian, Caribbean, and American theme nights and waiters/busboys in costume. Dining is an enjoyable, but casual, experience. The wine list is quite extensive. Free sodas and non-alcoholic coffees during meals upon request. Staff are overly friendly, even intrusive.

**Other Comments** You'll be overwhelmed by the public spaces, and underwhelmed by the size of cabins. This is a well run, fine-tuned, highly-programed cruise product geared to North American passengers seeking an action-packed cruise vacation in seven nights, at a moderately good price, with around 2,500 fellow passengers. Insurance and gratuities are extra.

# mv Marco Polo ★★★★

***Principal Cruising Areas***

*Orient/Pacific/Indian Ocean (various)*

***Base Ports:*** *various*

| | | | |
|---|---|---|---|
| Cruise Line | | | *Orient Lines* |
| Former Names | | | *Aleksandr Pushkin* |
| Gross Tonnage | | | *20,502* |
| Builder | | | *VEB Mathias Thesen (Germany)* |
| Original Cost | | | *n/a* |
| Christened By | | | *Patricia Herrod* |
| First Entered Service | | | *Apr 13, 1966/Oct 30, 1993* |
| Interior Design | | | *A&M Katzourakis* |
| Country of Registry | | | *Bahamas (C6JZ7)* |
| Tel No | *630-869310/1/2/3* | Fax No | *130-6216* |
| Length (ft/m) | | | *578.4/176.28* |
| Beam (ft/m) | *77.4/23.60* | Draft (ft/m) | *26.8/8.17* |
| Engines/Propellers | | | *2 Sulzer 7-cyl diesels/2 (CP)* |
| Decks | *8* | Crew | *356* |
| Pass. Capacity (basis 2) | *848* | (all berths) | *915* |
| Pass. Space Ratio (basis 2) | *24.1* | (all berths) | *22.4* |
| Officers | European | *Dining Staff* | Filipino |
| Total Cabins | | | *425* |
| Size (sq ft/m) | *120-480 /11-44.5* | Door Width | *24"* |
| Outside Cabins | *294* | Inside Cabins | *131* |
| Single Cabins | *0* | Supplement | *25%* |
| Balcony Cabins | *0* | Wheelchair Cabins | *2* |
| Cabin Current | | | *110/220 AC* |
| Refrigerator | | | *Suites/Jr. suites* |
| Cabin TV | *Yes* | VCR | *No* |
| Dining Rooms | *2* | Sittings | *2* |
| Elevators | *4* | Door Width | *31"* |
| Casino | *Yes* | Slot Machines | *Yes* |

| | | | |
|---|---|---|---|
| Swimming Pools (outside) | *1* | (inside) | *0* |
| Whirlpools | *3* | Gymnasium | *Yes* |
| Sauna/Steam Rm | *Yes/No* | Massage | *Yes* |
| Self-Service Launderette | | | *No* |
| Movie Theater/Seats | | | *No* |
| Library | | | *Yes* |
| Children's Facilities | | | *No* |
| Zodiacs | *10* | Helipad | *Yes* |
| Watersports Facilities | | | *None* |
| Classification Society | | | *Bureau Veritas* |

| RATINGS | SCORE |
|---|---|
| Ship: Condition/Cleanliness | 8.0 |
| Ship: Space/Flow/Comfort | 7.7 |
| Ship: Decor/Furnishings | 8.0 |
| Ship: Fitness Facilities | 7.6 |
| Cabins: Comfort/Facilities | 7.7 |
| Cabins: Software | 7.7 |
| Food: Dining Room/Cuisine | 8.3 |
| Food: Buffets/Informal Dining | 8.1 |
| Food: Quality of Ingredients | 7.8 |
| Service: Dining Room | 7.7 |
| Service: Bars/Lounges | 7.5 |
| Service: Cabins | 7.7 |
| Cruise: Entertainment | 5.8 |
| Cruise: Activities Program | 6.8 |
| Cruise: Hospitality Standard | 7.7 |
| OVERALL RATING | 114.1 |

**+** Still recognizable as the former Soviet cruise ship *Aleksandr Pushkin*, she has a good profile, a strong ice-strengthened hull, and huge storage spaces for long voyages. Refitted and refurbished, she now features destination-intensive cruises at realistic prices. Fitted with the latest navigational aids and biological waste treatment center. Helipad. Very tasteful interior decor, with careful use of mirrored surfaces, and colors that do not clash. Comfortable throughout and rides well.

**–** Some Upper Deck and Sky Deck cabins have lifeboat-obstructed views. Cabin software and detail is not the high point. Too few elevators. Expect long lines for zodiac shore tenders.

**Dining** The main dining room is nicely decorated, practical in design, and functions well. There are tables for two, four, six, eight, or ten. Fine place settings and china. The food itself is of a very high standard, with much attention to detail and good presentation, although, at these prices, it's not gourmet food. The wine list is limited, but reasonably priced.

**Other Comments** This ship has a classic sixties profile. Expedition pioneer Lars-Eric Lindblad leads some cruises, while other cruises will have a program of fine lecturers and specialists. Excellent and well-planned destination-intensive itineraries are for the older passenger who wants to see parts of the world, in comfort, at a very affordable price. Gratuities are not included. Port taxes, insurance, and gratuities are extra (port taxes included for E.U. passengers).

# ts Maxim Gorki ★★★★

***Principal Cruising Area***

*Europe (various)*

***Base Port:*** *Bremerhaven*

| | | | |
|---|---|---|---|
| Cruise Line | | | *Phoenix Seereisen* |
| Former Names | | | *Hanseatic/Hamburg* |
| Gross Tonnage | | | *24,981* |
| Builder | | | *Howaldtswerke Deutsche Werft* |
| Original Cost | | | *£5.6 million* |
| Christened By | | | *n/a* |
| First Entered Service | | | *Mar 28, 1969/Jan 1974* |
| Interior Design | | | *n/a* |
| Country of Registry | | | *Bahamas (C6IQ5)* |
| Tel No | *130-5670* | Fax No | *130-5670* |
| Length (ft/m) | | | *638.8/194.72* |
| Beam (ft/m) | *87.3/26.62* | Draft (ft/m) | *27.0/8.25* |
| Engines/Propellers | | | *4 AEG steam turbines/2* |
| Decks | *10* | Crew | *340* |
| Pass. Capacity (basis 2) | *650* | (all berths) | *788* |
| Pass. Space Ratio (basis 2) | *38.4* | (all berths) | *31.7* |
| Officers | | | *Russian/Ukrainian* |
| Dining Staff | | | *Russian/Ukrainian* |
| Total Cabins | | | *326* |
| Size (sq ft/m) | *n/a* | Door Width | *27"* |
| Outside Cabins | *210* | Inside Cabins | *116* |
| Single Cabins | *2* | Supplement | *20-50%* |
| Balcony Cabins | *0* | Wheelchair Cabins | *0* |
| Cabin Current | | | *220 AC* |
| Refrigerator | | | *Suites only* |
| Cabin TV | *Yes* | VCR | *No* |
| Dining Rooms | *3* | Sittings | *1* |
| Elevators | *4* | Door Width | *27"* |

| | | | |
|---|---|---|---|
| Casino | *No* | Slot Machines | *No* |
| Swimming Pools (outside) | *1* | (inside) | *1* |
| Whirlpools | *0* | Gymnasium | *Yes* |
| Sauna/Steam Rm | *Yes/No* | Massage | *Yes* |
| Self-Service Launderette | | | *Yes* |
| Movie Theater/Seats | | | *Yes/290* |
| Library | | | *Yes* |
| Children's Facilities | | | *No* |
| Watersports Facilities | | | *None* |
| Classification Society | | | *Det Norske Veritas* |

| RATINGS | SCORE |
|---|---|
| Ship: Condition/Cleanliness | 7.8 |
| Ship: Space/Flow/Comfort | 8.0 |
| Ship: Decor/Furnishings | 7.9 |
| Ship: Fitness Facilities | 6.8 |
| Cabins: Comfort/Facilities | 6.5 |
| Cabins: Software | 6.9 |
| Food: Dining Room/Cuisine | 7.1 |
| Food: Buffets/Informal Dining | 6.7 |
| Food: Quality of Ingredients | 6.8 |
| Service: Dining Room | 7.4 |
| Service: Bars/Lounges | 7.5 |
| Service: Cabins | 7.6 |
| Cruise: Entertainment | 7.4 |
| Cruise: Activities Program | 6.8 |
| Cruise: Hospitality Standard | 7.2 |
| OVERALL RATING | 108.4 |

**+** White ship with long, pleasing lines and outer styling, easily identified by its odd-looking, platform-topped funnel. Generally well maintained, with newly added facilities. Good open deck and sunning space. Well-designed public rooms. Good wood paneling throughout. Fine Russian crew show. Spacious cabins, many with wood paneling and trim. Large bathrooms feature full bathtub in all except 20 cabins. Superb deluxe cabins are fully equipped, and have huge picture windows, while others have portholes. In-cabin Russian and German satellite TV programs.

**–** Now 25 years old, the ship needs refurbishing extensively, especially the wood paneling. Old-fashioned entertainment facilities. The decor, while restful, is dark and dull.

**Dining** The three restaurants are set low down, but are cheerfully decorated. Excellent lager on draught, and water fountains on all accommodations decks. Moderately good food, and wine at lunch and dinner is included, but more choice and better presentation would be welcome. Attentive, courteous service from a well-meaning staff.

**Other Comments** This ship provides an excellent cruise experience in very comfortable, almost elegant, surroundings, at a modest price. Particularly targeted to German-speaking passengers who appreciate good value. Port taxes, insurance, and gratuities are all included.

# ss Meridian ★★★★+

***Principal Cruising Areas***

*Bermuda/Caribbean (7 nights/10/11 nights)*

***Base Ports:*** *New York/Ft. Lauderdale*

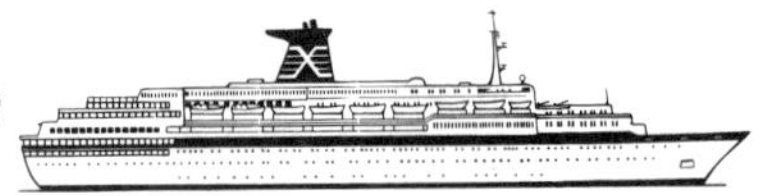

| | | | |
|---|---|---|---|
| Cruise Line | | | *Celebrity Cruises* |
| Former Names | | | *Galileo/Galileo Galilei* |
| Gross Tonnage | | | *30,440* |
| Builder | | | *Cantieri Riuniti dell' Adriatico (Italy)* |
| Original Cost | | | *n/a* |
| Christened By | | | *Mrs Jeanne Chandris* |
| First Entered Service | | | *Apr 22, 1963/Feb 1990* |
| Interior Design | | | *A&M Katzourakis* |
| Country of Registry | | | *Panama (3FIP2)* |
| Tel No | *110-3143* | Fax No | *110-3145* |
| Length (ft/m) | | | *700.9/213.65* |
| Beam (ft/m) | | | *94.1/28.71* |
| Draft (ft/m) | | | *28.3/8.64* |
| Engines/Propellers | | | *4 De Laval steam turbines/2* |
| Decks | *8* | Crew | *580* |
| Pass. Capacity (basis 2) | *1,106* | (all berths) | *1,398* |
| Pass. Space Ratio (basis 2) | *27.5* | (all berths) | *21.7* |
| Officers | *Greek* | Dining Staff | *International* |
| Total Cabins | | | *553* |
| Size (sq ft/m) | *n/a* | Door Width | *26"* |
| Outside Cabins | *295* | Inside Cabins | *258* |
| Single Cabins | *0* | Supplement | *50%* |
| Balcony Cabins | *0* | Wheelchair Cabins | *2* |
| Cabin Current | | | *110/220 AC* |
| Refrigerator | | | *Suites* |
| Cabin TV | *No* | VCR | *No* |
| Dining Rooms | *1* | Sittings | *2* |
| Elevators | *3* | Door Width | *26"* |

| | | | |
|---|---|---|---|
| Casino | *Yes* | Slot Machines | *Yes* |
| Swimming Pools (outside) | *1* | (inside) | *0* |
| Whirlpools | *3* | Gymnasium | *Yes* |
| Sauna/Steam Rm | *Yes/No* | Massage | *Yes* |
| Self-Service Launderette | | | *No* |
| Movie Theater/Seats | | | *Yes/218* |
| Library | | | *Yes* |
| Children's Facilities | | | *Yes* |
| Watersports Facilities | | | *None* |
| Classification Society | | | *Lloyd's Register* |

| RATINGS | SCORE |
|---|---|
| Ship: Condition/Cleanliness | 8.0 |
| Ship: Space/Flow/Comfort | 7.6 |
| Ship: Decor/Furnishings | 7.9 |
| Ship: Fitness Facilities | 7.6 |
| Cabins: Comfort/Facilities | 7.8 |
| Cabins: Software | 8.0 |
| Food: Dining Room/Cuisine | 8.4 |
| Food: Buffets/Informal Dining | 8.0 |
| Food: Quality of Ingredients | 8.1 |
| Service: Dining Room | 8.0 |
| Service: Bars/Lounges | 7.7 |
| Service: Cabins | 7.8 |
| Cruise: Entertainment | 7.7 |
| Cruise: Activities Program | 7.5 |
| Cruise: Hospitality Standard | 7.8 |
| OVERALL RATING | 117.9 |

**+** Well-balanced, classic ship profile, with rakish bow, rounded stern, and new funnel—they don't build ships this strong or this stable any more. Expansive sheltered deck areas and open deck sunning space. Wide selection of cabin sizes and configurations, all well equipped. Captain's Deck suites have skylights, and are large, comfortable, and well equipped. Public rooms have high ceilings and soft, elegant pastel decor, with good use of mirrored surfaces. Large casino. Charming twin garden lounges for quiet reading. Very warm inviting ship with an attentive staff.

**–** Long lines for embarkation, disembarkation, shore tenders, and buffets, especially during the summer Bermuda season. Bathrooms are fairly small. No cushioned pads for deck lounge chairs.

**Dining** The dining room is warm and inviting, with tables laid with full service cutlery. Outstanding, French-influenced cuisine with varied menus created by three-star Michelin master chef Michel Roux. Fine quality ingredients and presentation. Fine selection of pastries and dessert items. Service is friendly, attentive, and polished. Attractive, well presented buffets.

**Other Comments** Fine $70m reconstruction in 1990, although her aft profile has changed somewhat. This ship delivers an excellent, friendly cruise experience, with fine service and outstanding value for money at very realistic rates. Very highly recommended and especially suited to the longer 10- and 11-day cruises, which are outstanding. Insurance and gratuities are extra.

# ms Mermoz ★★★

***Principal Cruising Areas***

*Caribbean/Europe (14 nights)*

***Base Port:** Toulouse/Toulouse*

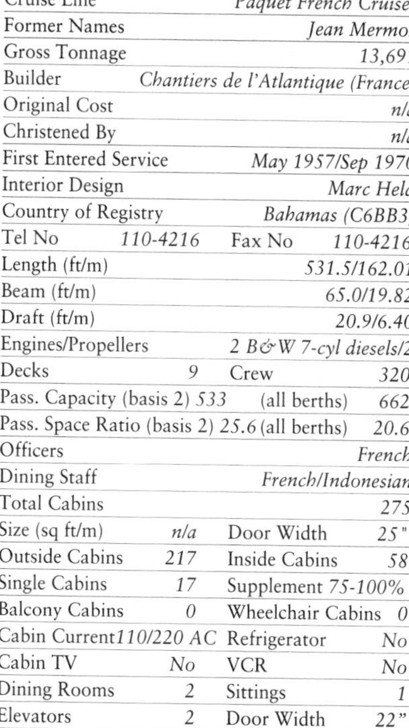

| | | | |
|---|---|---|---|
| Cruise Line | | | *Paquet French Cruises* |
| Former Names | | | *Jean Mermoz* |
| Gross Tonnage | | | *13,691* |
| Builder | | | *Chantiers de l'Atlantique (France)* |
| Original Cost | | | *n/a* |
| Christened By | | | *n/a* |
| First Entered Service | | | *May 1957/Sep 1970* |
| Interior Design | | | *Marc Held* |
| Country of Registry | | | *Bahamas (C6BB3)* |
| Tel No | *110-4216* | Fax No | *110-4216* |
| Length (ft/m) | | | *531.5/162.01* |
| Beam (ft/m) | | | *65.0/19.82* |
| Draft (ft/m) | | | *20.9/6.40* |
| Engines/Propellers | | | *2 B&W 7-cyl diesels/2* |
| Decks | *9* | Crew | *320* |
| Pass. Capacity (basis 2) | *533* | (all berths) | *662* |
| Pass. Space Ratio (basis 2) | *25.6* | (all berths) | *20.6* |
| Officers | | | *French* |
| Dining Staff | | | *French/Indonesian* |
| Total Cabins | | | *275* |
| Size (sq ft/m) | *n/a* | Door Width | *25"* |
| Outside Cabins | *217* | Inside Cabins | *58* |
| Single Cabins | *17* | Supplement | *75-100%* |
| Balcony Cabins | *0* | Wheelchair Cabins | *0* |
| Cabin Current | *110/220 AC* | Refrigerator | *No* |
| Cabin TV | *No* | VCR | *No* |
| Dining Rooms | *2* | Sittings | *1* |
| Elevators | *2* | Door Width | *22"* |

| | | | |
|---|---|---|---|
| Casino | *Yes* | Slot Machines | *Yes* |
| Swimming Pools (outside) | *2* | (inside) | *0* |
| Whirlpools | *Yes* | Gymnasium | *No* |
| Sauna/Steam Rm | *Yes/No* | Massage | *Yes* |
| Self-Service Launderette | | | *No* |
| Movie Theater/Seats | | | *Yes/240* |
| Library | | | *Yes* |
| Children's Facilities | | | *No* |
| Watersports Facilities | | | *None* |
| Classification Society | | | *Bureau Veritas* |

| RATINGS | SCORE |
|---|---|
| Ship: Condition/Cleanliness | 5.5 |
| Ship: Space/Flow/Comfort | 5.7 |
| Ship: Decor/Furnishings | 6.2 |
| Ship: Fitness Facilities | 4.7 |
| Cabins: Comfort/Facilities | 4.8 |
| Cabins: Software | 6.0 |
| Food: Dining Room/Cuisine | 7.8 |
| Food: Buffets/Informal Dining | 7.4 |
| Food: Quality of Ingredients | 7.7 |
| Service: Dining Room | 7.4 |
| Service: Bars/Lounges | 7.5 |
| Service: Cabins | 7.6 |
| Cruise: Entertainment | 6.4 |
| Cruise: Activities Program | 5.6 |
| Cruise: Hospitality Standard | 6.7 |
| OVERALL RATING | 97.0 |

**+** Delightful, chic, art deco interior decor, with earth tone color scheme throughout and a real "colonial" ambiance. Quaint and typically French in atmosphere and service. Spa and solarium are good, with emphasis on hydrotherapy. The annual Classical Music Festival cruise is a real cultural delight. Much artwork and models are of interest to ship lovers. Cabins are not large, and only basically equipped, but they are tastefully furnished, cozy, and comfortable, with solid fixtures and lots of wood. Good closet and drawer space. Bathrobes provided for everyone.

**–** Cabin bathrooms are very small. Steep gangway in some ports.

**Dining** Outstanding cuisine that is extremely creative, especially during special theme cruises. Fine grill room and food. There is also a 65,000-bottle wine cellar, and wine is complimentary with dinner.

**Other Comments** Traditional older ship with good lines, but a rather dated profile. This ship is for those who enjoy being with French-speaking passengers and who wish to cruise at a moderate price. Insurance and gratuities are extra.

# ms Mikhail Sholokhov ★★

***Principal Cruising Areas***

*Indonesia/South Pacific (various)*

***Base Ports:*** *various*

| | | | |
|---|---|---|---|
| Cruise Line | | | *Far Eastern Shipping* |
| Former Names | | | *n/a* |
| Gross Tonnage | | | *9,878* |
| Builder | | | *Adolf Warski Werft (Poland)* |
| Original Cost | | | *n/a* |
| Christened By | | | *n/a* |
| First Entered Service | | | *1986* |
| Interior Design | | | *n/a* |
| Country of Registry | | | *Russia (UKSK)* |
| Tel No | *140-0360* | Fax No | *140-0360* |
| Length (ft/m) | | | *441.0/134.40* |
| Beam (ft/m) | | | *68.8/21.00* |
| Draft (ft/m) | | | *18.3/5.60* |
| Engines/Propellers | | | *2 Sulzer diesels/2* |
| Decks | *7* | Crew | *168* |
| Pass. Capacity (basis 2) | *234* | (all berths) | *412* |
| Pass. Space Ratio (basis 2) | *42.2* | (all berths) | *23.9* |
| Officers | | | *Russian/Ukrainian* |
| Dining Staff | | | *East European* |
| Total Cabins | | | *117* |
| Size (sq ft/m) | *100-320/9.2-29.7* | Door Width | *24"* |
| Outside Cabins | *71* | Inside Cabins | *46* |
| Single Cabins | *0* | Supplement | *100%* |
| Balcony Cabins | *0* | Wheelchair Cabins | *0* |
| Cabin Current | *220 AC* | Refrigerator | *No* |
| Cabin TV | *No* | VCR | *No* |
| Dining Rooms | *1* | Sittings | *1* |
| Elevators | *1* | Door Width | *30"* |

| | | | |
|---|---|---|---|
| Casino | *No* | Slot Machines | *No* |
| Swimming Pools (outside) | *1* | (inside) | *0* |
| Whirlpools | *0* | Gymnasium | *Yes* |
| Sauna/Steam Rm | *Yes/No* | Massage | *Yes* |
| Self-Service Launderette | | | *No* |
| Movie Theater/Seats | | | *No* |
| Library | | | *Yes* |
| Children's Facilities | | | *No* |
| Watersports Facilities | | | *None* |
| Classification Society | | | *RS* |

| RATINGS | SCORE |
|---|---|
| Ship: Condition/Cleanliness | 6.6 |
| Ship: Space/Flow/Comfort | 6.2 |
| Ship: Decor/Furnishings | 6.0 |
| Ship: Fitness Facilities | 5.6 |
| Cabins: Comfort/Facilities | 5.5 |
| Cabins: Software | 6.1 |
| Food: Dining Room/Cuisine | 5.3 |
| Food: Buffets/Informal Dining | 5.1 |
| Food: Quality of Ingredients | 5.1 |
| Service: Dining Room | 6.1 |
| Service: Bars/Lounges | 6.2 |
| Service: Cabins | 6.2 |
| Cruise: Entertainment | 4.3 |
| Cruise: Activities Program | 4.7 |
| Cruise: Hospitality Standard | 5.8 |
| OVERALL RATING | 84.8 |

**+** This ship has an ice-hardened hull and fully-enclosed bridge for all-weather operations. One of a new series of five built in Poland. Attractive, though dated, decor in the limited number of public rooms.

**–** This is a somewhat boxy looking vessel with a stubby bow and huge, square funnel. Reasonably good open deck and sunning space, but the swimming pool is very small. Limited number of public rooms. No cashless cruising.

**Dining** The dining room is cheerful, and dining is family-style. Food and menu choice are reasonable, no more. Service is perfunctory, but the staff do try hard.

**Other Comments** Interior decor is reasonably pleasant, but somewhat spartan. Cabins are small, space-efficient units that have little warmth. Operates mainly in the Indonesian islands and the South Pacific. This ship provides a reasonable cruise experience that is definitely for the budget-conscious. Don't expect any finesse. Insurance, port taxes, and gratuitites are extra.

# ms Monarch of the Seas ★★★★+

***Principal Cruising Area***
*Caribbean (7 nights year-round)*
***Base Port:*** *San Juan (Sunday)*

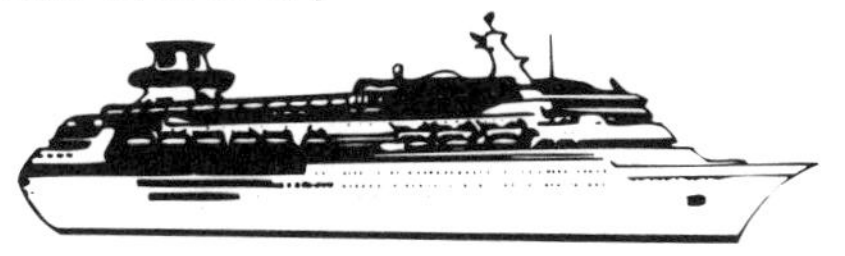

| | | | |
|---|---|---|---|
| Cruise Line | | | *Royal Caribbean Cruises* |
| Former Names | | | *n/a* |
| Gross Tonnage | | | *73,941* |
| Builder | | | *Chantiers de l'Atlantique* |
| Original Cost | | | *$300 million* |
| Christened By | | | *Ms Lauren Bacall* |
| First Entered Service | | | *Nov 17, 1991* |
| Interior Design | | | *Njal Eide* |
| Country of Registry | | | *Norway (LAMU4)* |
| Tel No | *131-2764* | Fax No | *131-2764* |
| Length (ft/m) | | | *873.6/266.30* |
| Beam (ft/m) | | | *105.9/32.30* |
| Draft (ft/m) | | | *24.9/7.60* |
| Engines/Propellers | | | *4 Pielstick 9-cyl diesels/2 (VP)* |
| Decks | *12* | Crew | *822* |
| Pass. Capacity (basis 2) | *2,354* | (all berths) | *2,744* |
| Pass. Space Ratio (basis 2) | *31.0* | (all berths) | *26.9* |
| Officers | *Norwegian* | Dining Staff | *International* |
| Total Cabins | | | *1,177* |
| Size (sq ft/m) | *120-446/11-41.5* | Door Width | *23"* |
| Outside Cabins | *732* | Inside Cabins | *445* |
| Single Cabins | *0* | Supplement | *50-100%* |
| Balcony Cabins | *62* | Wheelchair Cabins | *4* |
| Cabin Current | | | *110 AC* |
| Refrigerator | | | *Cat. R/A* |
| Cabin TV | *Yes* | VCR | *No* |
| Dining Rooms | *2* | Sittings | *2* |
| Elevators | *18* | Door Width | *39"* |

| | | | |
|---|---|---|---|
| Casino | *Yes* | Slot Machines | *Yes* |
| Swimming Pools (outside) | *2* | (inside) | *0* |
| Whirlpools | *2* | Gymnasium | *Yes* |
| Sauna/Steam Rm | *Yes/No* | Massage | *Yes* |
| Self-Service Launderette | | | *No* |
| Movie Theater/Seats | | | *Yes-2/146 each* |
| Library | | | *Yes* |
| Children's Facilities | | | *Yes* |
| Watersports Facilities | | | *None* |
| Classification Society | | | *Det Norske Veritas* |

| RATINGS | SCORE |
|---|---|
| Ship: Condition/Cleanliness | 8.0 |
| Ship: Space/Flow/Comfort | 8.0 |
| Ship: Decor/Furnishings | 7.9 |
| Ship: Fitness Facilities | 7.6 |
| Cabins: Comfort/Facilities | 7.6 |
| Cabins: Software | 7.7 |
| Food: Dining Room/Cuisine | 7.9 |
| Food: Buffets/Informal Dining | 7.6 |
| Food: Quality of Ingredients | 7.1 |
| Service: Dining Room | 7.7 |
| Service: Bars/Lounges | 7.6 |
| Service: Cabins | 7.8 |
| Cruise: Entertainment | 8.2 |
| Cruise: Activities Program | 7.9 |
| Cruise: Hospitality Standard | 8.0 |
| OVERALL RATING | 116.6 |

**+** Stable and smooth sailing. Fine array of public rooms, some with good dance floor space. Exceptional library. Cabins, though small, are comfortable and attractively decorated. Special "family suites" sleep four. Good children's and teens' programs and counselors. Japanese-speaking staff at the purser's desk.

**–** Crowded open deck space. Small cabins, but you probably won't spend much time there anyway. Long wait for aft elevators. Poor room service menu. Too many announcements. Expect long lines for disembarkation, buffets, and shore tenders.

**Dining** The two musical-themed dining rooms are large (no tables for two). Attentive, consistently good service (but no flair). Presentation has suffered lately. Reasonable noise level. Dining room operation is well orchestrated. Menu choices are good. Quality is above average. Most nights are themed (French, Oriental, Italian, Caribbean, American), with waiters and busboys in costumes. The wine list is quite extensive, and sodas and non-alcoholic coffees are provided free upon request during meals. The staff are overly friendly, even intrusive.

**Other Comments** Delightful Viking Crown Lounge around funnel stack, but without a bar (*Sovereign of the Seas* has one). Excellent facilities. Consistently good, well operated, and highly programed service from a somewhat robotic staff. Insurance and gratuities are extra.

# ss Monterey ★★★+

***Principal Cruising Area***
*Europe (4-11 nights)*
***Base Port:*** *Venice*

| | | | |
|---|---|---|---|
| Cruise Line | | | *Starlauro Cruises* |
| Former Names | | | *Free State Mariner* |
| Gross Tonnage | | | *21,051* |
| Builder | | | *Bethlehem Steel Corp. (USA)* |
| Original Cost | | | *n/a* |
| Christened By | | | *n/a* |
| First Entered Service | | | *Dec 18, 1952/Aug 27, 1988* |
| Interior Design | | | *Platou Design* |
| Country of Registry | | | *Panama (KFCN)* |
| Tel No | *133-3517* | Fax No | *133-3517* |
| Length (ft/m) | | | *563.6/171.81* |
| Beam (ft/m) | | | *76.3/23.27* |
| Draft (ft/m) | | | *29.3/8.95* |
| Engines/Propellers | | | *2 Bethlehem steam turbines/1* |
| Decks | *4* | Crew | *280* |
| Pass. Capacity (basis 2) | *600* | (all berths) | *638* |
| Pass. Space Ratio (basis 2) | *35.0* | (all berths) | *32.9* |
| Officers | *Italian* | Dining Staff | *International* |
| Total Cabins | | | *300* |
| Size (sq ft/m) | *n/a* | Door Width | *26"* |
| Outside Cabins | *171* | Inside Cabins | *129* |
| Single Cabins | *0* | Supplement | *Fixed rates* |
| Balcony Cabins | *0* | Wheelchair Cabins | *0* |
| Cabin Current | | | *110 AC* |
| Refrigerator | | | *Cat. 13, 14* |
| Cabin TV | *13, 14* | VCR | *No* |
| Dining Rooms | *1* | Sittings | *2* |
| Elevators | *2* | Door Width | *30"* |

| | | | |
|---|---|---|---|
| Casino | *Yes* | Slot Machines | *Yes* |
| Swimming Pools (outside) | *1* | (inside) | *0* |
| Whirlpools | *2* | Gymnasium | *Yes* |
| Sauna/Steam Rm | *Yes/No* | Massage | *Yes* |
| Self-Service Launderette | | | *No* |
| Movie Theater/Seats | | | *Yes/107* |
| Library | | | *Yes* |
| Children's Facilities | | | *No* |
| Watersports Facilities | | | *None* |
| Classification Society | | | *American Bur. of Shipping* |

| RATINGS | SCORE |
|---|---|
| Ship: Condition/Cleanliness | 6.4 |
| Ship: Space/Flow/Comfort | 6.6 |
| Ship: Decor/Furnishings | 6.6 |
| Ship: Fitness Facilities | 5.3 |
| Cabins: Comfort/Facilities | 6.8 |
| Cabins: Software | 7.2 |
| Food: Dining Room/Cuisine | 7.3 |
| Food: Buffets/Informal Dining | 6.7 |
| Food: Quality of Ingredients | 7.0 |
| Service: Dining Room | 7.4 |
| Service: Bars/Lounges | 7.2 |
| Service: Cabins | 7.6 |
| Cruise: Entertainment | 6.6 |
| Cruise: Activities Program | 6.0 |
| Cruise: Hospitality Standard | 7.6 |
| OVERALL RATING | 102.3 |

**+** Traditional fifties liner profile, and a stable sea ship with an almost vertical bow and an overhanging, aircraft-carrier-like stern that is not at all handsome. Was refurbished in moderate art deco style, when a new sports deck was added. Good sheltered and open deck space. Friendly crew and atmosphere. There is a wide choice of cabin sizes and configurations—but only the top three categories have full bathtubs. Extremely spacious suites; other cabins are very roomy, well-equipped units. Bathrobes are provided.

**–** Too much cold steel and not enough warmth in the interior decoration. Cabins forward on Boat Deck have lifeboat obstructed views.

**Dining** Charming, two-tier dining room is set low down, and decorated in soft earth tones, so the ambiance is elegant. Continental cuisine, with some excellent pasta. Poor selection of breads, cheeses, and fruits. Service is friendly and attentive, but somewhat hurried.

**Other Comments** This ship will cruise you in reasonably elegant style and surroundings, with mainly European, and particularly Italian-speaking, passengers. Currency: lire. Port taxes are included. Insurance and gratuities are extra.

# Nantucket Clipper ★★★

***Principal Cruising Areas***

*U.S./Canada Coast/Virgin Islands (7/7-14 nights)*

***Base Ports:** various*

| | | | |
|---|---|---|---|
| Cruise Line | | | *Clipper Cruise Line* |
| Former Names | | | *n/a* |
| Gross Tonnage | | | *1,471* |
| Builder | | | *Jeffboat (USA)* |
| Original Cost | | | *$9 million* |
| Christened By | | | *n/a* |
| First Entered Service | | | *Dec 23, 1984* |
| Interior Design | | | *n/a* |
| Country of Registry | | | *USA (WSQ8373)* |
| Tel No | *n/a* | Fax No | *n/a* |
| Length (ft/m) | | | *207.0/63.00* |
| Beam (ft/m) | | | *37.0/11.20* |
| Draft (ft/m) | | | *8.0/2.40* |
| Engines/Propellers | | | *2 Detroit diesels/2* |
| Decks | *4* | Crew | *37* |
| Pass. Capacity (basis 2) | *102* | (all berths) | *102* |
| Pass. Space Ratio (basis 2) | *14.4* | (all berths) | *14.4* |
| Officers | *American* | Dining Staff | *American* |
| Total Cabins | | | *51* |
| Size (sq ft/m) | *121-138/11.2-12.8* | Door Width | *24"* |
| Outside Cabins | *51* | Inside Cabins | *0* |
| Single Cabins | *0* | Supplement | *Fixed rates* |
| Balcony Cabins | *0* | Wheelchair Cabins | *0* |
| Cabin Current | | | *110 AC* |
| Refrigerator | | | *No* |
| Cabin TV | *No* | VCR | *No* |
| Dining Rooms | *1* | Sittings | *1* |
| Elevators | *0* | Door Width | *n/a* |

| | | | |
|---|---|---|---|
| Casino | *No* | Slot Machines | *No* |
| Swimming Pools (outside) | *0* | (inside) | *0* |
| Whirlpools | *0* | Gymnasium | *No* |
| Sauna/Steam Rm | *No/No* | Massage | *No* |
| Self-Service Launderette | | | *No* |
| Movie Theater/Seats | | | *No* |
| Library | | | *Yes* |
| Children's Facilities | | | *No* |
| Watersports Facilities | | | *None* |
| Classification Society | | | *American Bur. of Shipping* |

| RATINGS | SCORE |
|---|---|
| Ship: Condition/Cleanliness | 6.4 |
| Ship: Space/Flow/Comfort | 4.0 |
| Ship: Decor/Furnishings | 6.8 |
| Ship: Fitness Facilities | 3.0 |
| Cabins: Comfort/Facilities | 6.1 |
| Cabins: Software | 6.5 |
| Food: Dining Room/Cuisine | 7.1 |
| Food: Buffets/Informal Dining | 6.2 |
| Food: Quality of Ingredients | 7.0 |
| Service: Dining Room | 7.1 |
| Service: Bars/Lounges | 7.0 |
| Service: Cabins | 7.3 |
| Cruise: Entertainment | 4.0 |
| Cruise: Activities Program | 5.6 |
| Cruise: Hospitality Standard | 7.3 |
| OVERALL RATING | 91.4 |

**+** This small, shallow draft vessel is specially built for coastal and inland cruises and is very maneuverable. Well maintained. Extremely high density ship has only two public rooms—the dining room and an observation lounge. Wrap-around open walking deck. Passengers can visit the bridge at any time. The all-outside cabins (in four categories) are very small, but somehow comfortable and tastefully furnished, with wood-accented trim and good sound insulation.

**–** Very small cabins. High engine noise level when underway. The per diem price is high for what you get, and airfare is extra.

**Dining** The dining room is warm and inviting, and has large picture windows. There are table assignments only for dinner, which is at a single sitting. There are no tables for two. Features simple and plain cuisine, with limited menu choice and small portions.

**Other Comments** Service is by young, friendly, all-American, college-age types. This is most definitely an "Americana" experience for those seeking to learn more about the coastal ports around the U.S.A. Casual and unstructured lifestyle, rather like a small, but not luxurious, country club afloat, with much attention to detail. Not to be compared with big ship ocean cruising. No mindless activities or corny games. Insurance and gratuities are extra.

# mv Neptune ★★★

***Principal Cruising Area***
*Aegean (3/4 nights)*
***Base Port:*** *Piraeus*

| | | | |
|---|---|---|---|
| Cruise Line | | | *Epirotiki Lines* |
| Former Names | | | *Meteor/Zephiros* |
| Gross Tonnage | | | *4,000* |
| Builder | | | *Aalborg Vaerft (Denmark)* |
| Original Cost | | | *n/a* |
| Christened By | | | *n/a* |
| First Entered Service | | | *1955/1972* |
| Interior Design | | | *Arminio Lozzi* |
| Country of Registry | | | *Greece (SXOS)* |
| Tel No | *113-0653* | Fax No | *113-0653* |
| Length (ft/m) | | | *301.8/92.00* |
| Beam (ft/m) | *45.1/13.75* | Draft (ft/m) | *18.5/5.64* |
| Engines | | | *2 B&W 9-cylinder diesels* |
| Propellers | | | *1 (CP)* |
| Decks | *5* | Crew | *105* |
| Pass. Capacity (basis 2) | *186* | (all berths) | *208* |
| Pass. Space Ratio (basis 2) | *21.5* | (all berths) | *19.2* |
| Officers | *Greek* | Dining Staff | *Greek* |
| Total Cabins | | | *93* |
| Size (sq ft/m) | *60-235/5.5-21.8* | Door Width | *22"* |
| Outside Cabins | *70* | Inside Cabins | *23* |
| Single Cabins | *5* | Supplement | *50%* |
| Balcony Cabins | *0* | Wheelchair Cabins | *0* |
| Cabin Current | | | *220 AC/220 DC* |
| Refrigerator | | | *No* |
| Cabin TV | *No* | VCR | *No* |
| Dining Rooms | *1* | Sittings | *1* |
| Elevators | *0* | Door Width | *n/a* |

| | | | |
|---|---|---|---|
| Casino | *Yes* | Slot Machines | *No* |
| Swimming Pools (outside) | *1* | (inside) | *0* |
| Whirlpools | *0* | Gymnasium | *No* |
| Sauna/Steam Rm | *No/No* | Massage | *No* |
| Self-Service Launderette | | | *No* |
| Movie Theater/Seats | | | *No (TV/video viewing room)* |
| Library | | | *Yes* |
| Children's Facilities | | | *No* |
| Watersports Facilities | | | *None* |
| Classification Society | | | *Lloyd's Register* |

| RATINGS | SCORE |
|---|---|
| Ship: Condition/Cleanliness | 5.8 |
| Ship: Space/Flow/Comfort | 5.9 |
| Ship: Decor/Furnishings | 6.8 |
| Ship: Fitness Facilities | 3.2 |
| Cabins: Comfort/Facilities | 5.8 |
| Cabins: Software | 6.5 |
| Food: Dining Room/Cuisine | 6.7 |
| Food: Buffets/Informal Dining | 6.3 |
| Food: Quality of Ingredients | 6.0 |
| Service: Dining Room | 7.2 |
| Service: Bars/Lounges | 7.3 |
| Service: Cabins | 7.3 |
| Cruise: Entertainment | 5.0 |
| Cruise: Activities Program | 5.8 |
| Cruise: Hospitality Standard | 7.0 |
| OVERALL RATING | 92.6 |

**+** Charming little ship, with traditional ship profile, clean, tidy lines, and a rather large funnel. Warm, intimate, and friendly atmosphere in a casual setting. Good sunning space for ship size, with real wooden deck lounge chairs. The limited number of public rooms have pleasing colors and decor, and feature some interesting works of art. Especially noteworthy is the poolside mosaic. Well-stocked library. Apart from three large suite rooms that feature a full bathtub, cabins are compact but quite comfortable.

**–** Cabins have very limited closet and drawer space. Steep gangway in many ports.

**Dining** The dining room is located high up and has large picture windows. Typically Mediterranean cuisine that is inconsistent. Limited selection of breads, cheeses, and fruits. Friendly, but rather hurried, service comes with a smile. Poor room service menu.

**Other Comments** This ship, which is often chartered to various operators, will provide an intimate, highly personalized cruise experience in comfortable, though not elegant, surroundings, at a very fair price, and is ideally suited to European passengers. Port taxes, insurance, and gratuities are extra (except when under charter).

# ms Nieuw Amsterdam ★★★★+

***Principal Cruising Areas***

*Alaska/Caribbean (7 nights)*

***Base Ports:** Vancouver/Tampa*

| | | | |
|---|---|---|---|
| Cruise Line | | | *Holland America Line* |
| Former Names | | | *n/a* |
| Gross Tonnage | | | *33,930* |
| Builder | | | *Chantiers de l'Atlantique (France)* |
| Original Cost | | | *$150 million* |
| Christened By | | | *HRH Princess Margriet* |
| First Entered Service | | | *Jul 9, 1983* |
| Interior Design | | | *VFD Interiors* |
| Country of Registry | | | *Netherlands Antilles (PJCH)* |
| Tel No | *115-0123* | Fax No | *114-0123* |
| Length (ft/m) | | | *704.2/214.66* |
| Beam (ft/m) | *89.4/27.26* | Draft (ft/m) | *24.6/7.52* |
| Engines/Propellers | | | *4 Sulzer 7-cyl diesels/2 (CP)* |
| Decks | *10* | Crew | *542* |
| Pass. Capacity (basis 2) | *1,210* | (all berths) | *1,350* |
| Pass. Space Ratio (basis 2) | *28.0* | (all berths) | *25.1* |
| Officers | | | *Dutch* |
| Dining Staff | | | *Filipino/Indonesian* |
| Total Cabins | | | *605* |
| Size (sq ft/m) | *152-295/14-27.5* | Door Width | *27"* |
| Outside Cabins | *411* | Inside Cabins | *194* |
| Single Cabins | *0* | Supplement | *50-100%* |
| Balcony Cabins | *0* | Wheelchair Cabins | *4* |
| Cabin Current | | | *110/220 AC* |
| Refrigerator | | | *Category A* |
| Cabin TV | *Yes* | VCR | *No* |
| Dining Rooms | *1* | Sittings | *2* |
| Elevators | *7* | Door Width | *30"* |

| | | | |
|---|---|---|---|
| Casino | *Yes* | Slot Machines | *Yes* |
| Swimming Pools (outside) | *2* | (inside) | *0* |
| Whirlpools | *1* | Gymnasium | *Yes* |
| Sauna/Steam Rm | *Yes/No* | Massage | *Yes* |
| Self-Service Launderette | | | *Yes* |
| Movie Theater/Seats | | | *Yes/230* |
| Library | | | *Yes* |
| Children's Facilities | | | *No* |
| Watersports Facilities | | | *None* |
| Classification Society | | | *Lloyd's Register* |

| RATINGS | SCORE |
|---|---|
| Ship: Condition/Cleanliness | 8.3 |
| Ship: Space/Flow/Comfort | 8.2 |
| Ship: Decor/Furnishings | 8.2 |
| Ship: Fitness Facilities | 7.5 |
| Cabins: Comfort/Facilities | 8.1 |
| Cabins: Software | 7.8 |
| Food: Dining Room/Cuisine | 7.7 |
| Food: Buffets/Informal Dining | 6.8 |
| Food: Quality of Ingredients | 7.1 |
| Service: Dining Room | 7.8 |
| Service: Bars/Lounges | 7.7 |
| Service: Cabins | 8.0 |
| Cruise: Entertainment | 6.6 |
| Cruise: Activities Program | 7.1 |
| Cruise: Hospitality Standard | 8.2 |
| OVERALL RATING | 115.1 |

**+** Nicely-raked bow. Plenty of open deck space. Traditional teakwood outdoor decks, including wrap-around promenade deck. Spacious interior design and layout, with pleasing colors. Much use of polished teak and rosewood paneling. Stunning antiques and artwork. Explorers' Lounge is relaxing for after-meal coffee and live chamber music. Balconied main lounge, reminiscent of former ocean liner era. Spacious, well equipped cabins with quality furniture and fittings, good counter and storage space, and good sized bathrooms. Top three categories have full bathtubs. Several cabins have king- or queen-sized beds. Cabin insulation is good. Well-trained staff.

**–** Long, squat, angular outer profile. Suffers from vibration at stern. Communicating with the Indonesian waiters can be frustrating. Some cabins have obstructed views. Expect long lines for buffets and shore tenders. Entertainment is poor (low-budget).

**Dining** Large, attractive dining room. Open seating for breakfast and lunch, two seatings for dinner. Attractively presented food, but not adventurous. Quality has deteriorated lately. Entrees are devoid of taste. Poor choice of breads, bread rolls, and fruits. Friendly service.

**Other Comments** Recommended for seasoned, senior-age travelers wanting a quality, traditional cruise experience in elegant surroundings at a realistic and moderate price level. Port taxes, insurance, and gratuities are extra (gratuities are "not required," but expected).

# ms Nippon Maru ★★★★

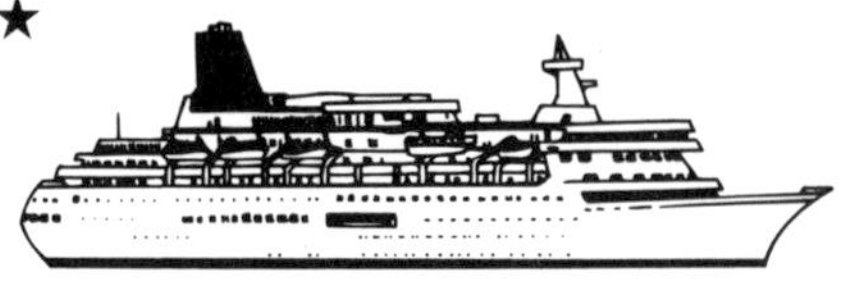

***Principal Cruising Areas***

*Japan/South East Asia (various)*

***Base Port:*** *Tokyo*

| | | | |
|---|---|---|---|
| Cruise Line | | | *Mitsui OSK Passenger Line* |
| Former Names | | | *n/a* |
| Gross Tonnage | | | *21,903* |
| Builder | | | *Mitsubishi Heavy Industries (Japan)* |
| Original Cost | | | *$59.4 million* |
| Christened By | | | *Mr Susumi Temporin* |
| First Entered Service | | | *Sep 27, 1990* |
| Interior Design | | | *Osamu Higuchi/Mikiya Murakami* |
| Country of Registry | | | *Japan (JNNU)* |
| Tel No | *120-0462* | Fax No | *120-0462* |
| Length (ft/m) | | | *546.7/166.65* |
| Beam (ft/m) | *78.7/24.00* | Draft (ft/m) | *21.4/6.55* |
| Engines/Propellers | | | *2 Mitsubishi 8-cyl diesels/2 (CP)* |
| Decks | *7* | Crew | *160* |
| Pass. Capacity (basis 2) | *408* | (all berths) | *607* |
| Pass. Space Ratio (basis 2) | *53.6* | (all berths) | *36.0* |
| Officers | *Japanese* | Dining Staff | *Japanese* |
| Total Cabins | | | *204* |
| Size (sq ft/m) | *150-430/14-40* | Door Width | *26"* |
| Outside Cabins | *189* | Inside Cabins | *15* |
| Single Cabins | *0* | Supplement | *25-60%* |
| Balcony Cabins | *0* | Wheelchair Cabins | *2* |
| Cabin Current | | | *100 AC* |
| Refrigerator | | | *Yes* |
| Cabin TV | *Yes* | VCR | *No* |
| Dining Rooms | *1* | Sittings | *1* |
| Elevators | *5* | Door Width | *28"* |
| Casino | *Yes (H)* | Slot Machines | *No* |

| | | | |
|---|---|---|---|
| Swimming Pools (outside) | *1* | (inside) | *0* |
| Whirlpools | *4 (Japanese baths)* | Gymnasium | *Yes* |
| Sauna/Steam Rm | *Yes/No* | Massage | *Yes (H)* |
| Self-Service Launderette | | | *Yes* |
| Movie Theater/Seats | | | *Yes/135* |
| Library | | | *Yes* |
| Children's Facilities | | | *Yes (H)* |
| Watersports Facilities | | | *None* |
| Classification Society | | | *Nippon Kaiji Kyokai* |

*(H) = On leisure cruises only*

| RATINGS | SCORE |
|---|---|
| Ship: Condition/Cleanliness | 8.0 |
| Ship: Space/Flow/Comfort | 7.7 |
| Ship: Decor/Furnishings | 8.1 |
| Ship: Fitness Facilities | 6.6 |
| Cabins: Comfort/Facilities | 7.3 |
| Cabins: Software | 7.2 |
| Food: Dining Room/Cuisine | 7.4 |
| Food: Buffets/Informal Dining | 6.7 |
| Food: Quality of Ingredients | 7.0 |
| Service: Dining Room | 7.5 |
| Service: Bars/Lounges | 7.4 |
| Service: Cabins | 7.0 |
| Cruise: Entertainment | 6.8 |
| Cruise: Activities Program | 6.8 |
| Cruise: Hospitality Standard | 7.8 |
| OVERALL RATING | 109.7 |

**+** Traditional profile and single funnel aft of midships. All public rooms have high ceilings. Elegant and dramatic six-deck-high atrium. Good ship, specially built and outfitted for the domestic Japanese seminar/lecture market and for individual passengers. Excellent teakwood decking. Well-designed public rooms, with high quality furnishings and soothing colors—typical in Japanese hotels. Features true Japanese baths, as well as a "Washitsu" tatami room.

**–** Outdoor maintenance could be better. No room service.

**Dining** The dining room is quite plain, with two special smaller private rooms. Both traditional Japanese cuisine and Western dishes. One sitting for leisure cruises (limit of 350 passengers) and two sittings for ship charter cruises. Food presentation is good but simplistic. Menu rotation could be improved. Service is generally good.

**Other Comments** Except for one accommodations deck, all cabins are located forward, with public rooms aft, in a cake-layer stacking. Small outdoor swimming pool with magrodome sliding glass roof, reminiscent of the Club Lido on *Queen Elizabeth 2*. Balconied main lounge. Tastefully decorated suites and deluxe cabins with good storage space, but standard cabins are rather spartan and quite small, yet adequate. Moderate rates. This ship is without the luxury one might expect in a top hotel. No tipping is allowed.

# ms Noordam ★★★★+

***Principal Cruising Areas***

*Alaska/Caribbean (7 nights)*

***Base Ports:*** *Vancouver/Ft. Lauderdale*

| | | | |
|---|---|---|---|
| Cruise Line | | | *Holland America Line* |
| Former Names | | | *n/a* |
| Gross Tonnage | | | *33,930* |
| Builder | | | *Chantiers de l'Atlantique (France)* |
| Original Cost | | | *$160 million* |
| Christened By | | | *Mrs Beatrijs van De Wallbake* |
| First Entered Service | | | *Apr 8, 1984* |
| Interior Design | | | *VFD Interiors* |
| Country of Registry | | | *Netherlands Antilles (PJCO)* |
| Tel No | *175-0105* | Fax No | *175-0110* |
| Length (ft/m) | | | *704.2/214.66* |
| Beam (ft/m) | | | *89.4/27.26* |
| Draft (ft/m) | | | *24.2/7.40* |
| Engines/Propellers | | | *2 Sulzer 7-cyl diesels/2 (CP)* |
| Decks | *10* | Crew | *530* |
| Pass. Capacity (basis 2) | *1,210* | (all berths) | *1,350* |
| Pass. Space Ratio (basis 2) | *28.0* | (all berths) | *25.1* |
| Officers | *Dutch* | Dining Staff | *Filipino/Indonesian* |
| Total Cabins | | | *605* |
| Size (sq ft/m) | *152-295/14-27.5* | Door Width | *27"* |
| Outside Cabins | *411* | Inside Cabins | *194* |
| Single Cabins | *0* | Supplement | *50-100%* |
| Balcony Cabins | *0* | Wheelchair Cabins | *4* |
| Cabin Current | | | *110/220 AC* |
| Refrigerator | | | *Cat. A* |
| Cabin TV | *Yes* | VCR | *No* |
| Dining Rooms | *1* | Sittings | *2* |
| Elevators | *7* | Door Width | *30"* |

| | | | |
|---|---|---|---|
| Casino | *Yes* | Slot Machines | *Yes* |
| Swimming Pools (outside) | *2* | (inside) | *0* |
| Whirlpools | *1* | Gymnasium | *Yes* |
| Sauna/Steam Rm | *Yes/No* | Massage | *Yes* |
| Self-Service Launderette | | | *Yes* |
| Movie Theater/Seats | | | *Yes/230* |
| Library | | | *Yes* |
| Children's Facilities | | | *No* |
| Watersports Facilities | | | *None* |
| Classification Society | | | *Lloyd's Register* |

| RATINGS | SCORE |
|---|---|
| Ship: Condition/Cleanliness | 8.3 |
| Ship: Space/Flow/Comfort | 8.2 |
| Ship: Decor/Furnishings | 8.2 |
| Ship: Fitness Facilities | 7.5 |
| Cabins: Comfort/Facilities | 8.1 |
| Cabins: Software | 7.8 |
| Food: Dining Room/Cuisine | 7.7 |
| Food: Buffets/Informal Dining | 6.8 |
| Food: Quality of Ingredients | 7.1 |
| Service: Dining Room | 7.8 |
| Service: Bars/Lounges | 7.7 |
| Service: Cabins | 8.0 |
| Cruise: Entertainment | 6.6 |
| Cruise: Activities Program | 7.1 |
| Cruise: Hospitality Standard | 8.2 |
| OVERALL RATING | 115.1 |

**+** Traditional teakwood outdoor decks, including wrap-around promenade deck. Outstanding 17th- and 18th-century artworks and collection of Dutch artifacts. Flower bouquets are lovely. Crow's Nest observation lounge is a favorite retreat. Explorers' Lounge is fine for after-dinner coffees with live chamber music. Good indoor/outdoor dining area. Spacious, well equipped, and practical cabins. Plenty of storage and decent bathrooms (top three categories have full bathtubs). Excellent in-cabin video programing. Good cabin insulation. Good, well-trained staff.

**–** Some cabins on Boat Deck and Navigation Deck have obstructed views. Expect long lines for buffets. Low-budget entertainment.

**Dining** Charming and spacious dining room. Open seating for breakfast and lunch, two seatings for dinner. Excellent service—always with a smile. International cuisine with an American flavor, but ingredients are not the best quality. Poor choice of breads, rolls, and fruits.

**Other Comments** Identical exterior to *Nieuw Amsterdam*, but different interior colors and decor. This ship will cruise you (leave the children at home, please, for they'll be out of place here) for a week in style, but at an affordable, realistic price. Port taxes, insurance, and gratuities are extra (gratuities are "not required," but they are expected by the staff).

# ms Nordic Empress ★★★★

***Principal Cruising Area***

*Bahamas (3/4 nights year-round)*

***Base Port:*** *Miami (Fri/Mon)*

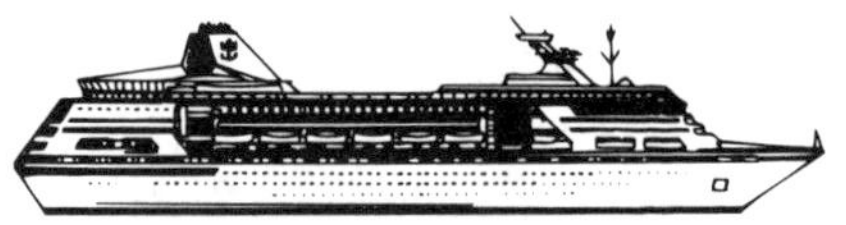

| | | | |
|---|---|---|---|
| Cruise Line | | | *Royal Caribbean Cruises* |
| Former Names | | | *n/a* |
| Gross Tonnage | | | *48,563* |
| Builder | | | *Chantiers de l'Atlantique (France)* |
| Original Cost | | | *$170 million* |
| Christened By | | | *Ms Gloria Estefan* |
| First Entered Service | | | *Jun 25, 1990* |
| Interior Design | | | *Njal Eide* |
| Country of Registry | | | *Liberia (ELJV7)* |
| Tel No | *124-3540* | Fax No | *124-3547* |
| Length (ft/m) | | | *692.2/211.00* |
| Beam (ft/m) | | | *100.7/30.70* |
| Draft (ft/m) | | | *23.2/7.10* |
| Engines/Propellers | | | *4 Pielstick diesels/2 (CP)* |
| Decks | *12* | Crew | *671* |
| Pass. Capacity (basis 2) | *1,600* | (all berths) | *2,020* |
| Pass. Space Ratio (basis 2) | *30.2* | (all berths) | *24.0* |
| Officers | *Scandinavian* | Dining Staff | *International* |
| Total Cabins | | | *800* |
| Size (sq ft/m) | *117-269/10.8-25* | Door Width | *23"* |
| Outside Cabins | *471* | Inside Cabins | *329* |
| Single Cabins | *0* | Supplement | *50-100%* |
| Balcony Cabins | *69* | Wheelchair Cabins | *4* |
| Cabin Current | | | *110 AC* |
| Refrigerator | | | *Category R/A* |
| Cabin TV | *Yes* | VCR | *No* |
| Dining Rooms | *1* | Sittings | *2* |
| Elevators | *7* | Door Width | *30"* |

| | | | |
|---|---|---|---|
| Casino | *Yes* | Slot Machines | *Yes-220* |
| Swimming Pools (outside) | *2* | (inside) | *0* |
| Whirlpools | *4* | Gymnasium | *Yes* |
| Sauna/Steam Rm | *Yes/No* | Massage | *Yes* |
| Self-Service Launderette | | | *No* |
| Movie Theater/Seats | | | *No* |
| Library | | | *No* |
| Children's Facilities | | | *Yes* |
| Watersports Facilities | | | *None* |
| Classification Society | | | *Det Norske Veritas* |

| RATINGS | SCORE |
|---|---|
| Ship: Condition/Cleanliness | 8.0 |
| Ship: Space/Flow/Comfort | 7.6 |
| Ship: Decor/Furnishings | 7.6 |
| Ship: Fitness Facilities | 7.3 |
| Cabins: Comfort/Facilities | 7.2 |
| Cabins: Software | 7.7 |
| Food: Dining Room/Cuisine | 7.8 |
| Food: Buffets/Informal Dining | 7.6 |
| Food: Quality of Ingredients | 7.1 |
| Service: Dining Room | 7.7 |
| Service: Bars/Lounges | 7.6 |
| Service: Cabins | 7.6 |
| Cruise: Entertainment | 8.2 |
| Cruise: Activities Program | 7.9 |
| Cruise: Hospitality Standard | 7.8 |
| OVERALL RATING | 114.7 |

**+** Contemporary ship with short bow and squared stern. Looks quite stunning. Designed for short cruises. Outdoor polished wood wrap-around promenade deck. Ingenious use of lighting throughout interior. Stunning tri-level casino. Popular electronic golf room. Superb outdoor pool deck. Viking Crown Lounge, aft of the funnel, is a bi-level nightclub-disco. Nine cabins have private balconies overlooking the stern. Conditioned, upbeat service.

**–** Expect long lines for embarkation, disembarkation, and buffets. Two-level showroom has extremely poor sightlines in balcony. Constant repetitive announcements are irritating.

**Dining** The two-level musical-themed dining room is delightful, though noisy (but not excessively so). Huge windows overlook the stern. Well orchestrated dining. Service is too hurried and lacks finesse. Consistently good food, but not memorable. Menu choices are varied. Quality is well above average. Most nights are themed (French, Oriental, Italian, Caribbean, American), with waiters and busboys in costumes. Dining is a most enjoyable, but rather casual, experience. The wine list is quite extensive. Sodas and non-alcoholic coffees are provided free during meals.

**Other Comments** Stunning nine-deck-high atrium is focal point—but no chairs, due to fire regulations. Suites and cabins are small, but quite comfortable for short cruises. Glamorous for short party atmosphere cruises, with high passenger density. Insurance and gratuities are extra.

# ms Nordic Prince ★★★+

***Principal Cruising Areas***

*Alaska/Caribbean (7/7-11 nights)*

***Base Ports:** Vancouver/Miami*

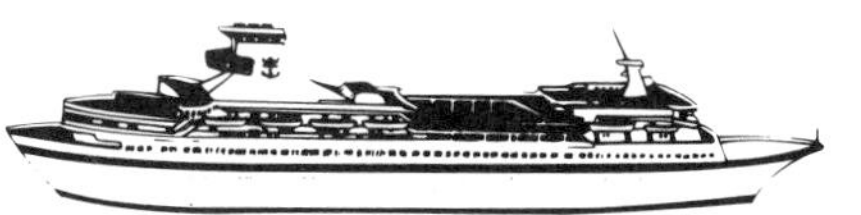

| | | | |
|---|---|---|---|
| Cruise Line | | | *Royal Caribbean Cruises* |
| Former Names | | | *n/a* |
| Gross Tonnage | | | *23,200* |
| Builder | | | *Wartsila (Finland)* |
| Original Cost | | | *$13.5 million* |
| Christened By | | | *Ms Ingrid Bergman* |
| First Entered Service | | | *Jul 31, 1971* |
| Interior Design | | | *Njal Eide* |
| Country of Registry | | | *Norway (LAPJ)* |
| Tel No | *131-0547* | Fax No | *131-0547* |
| Length (ft/m) | | | *637.5/194.32* |
| Beam (ft/m) | | | *78.8/24.03* |
| Draft (ft/m) | | | *21.9/6.70* |
| Engines/Propellers | | | *4 Sulzer 9-cyl diesels/2 (CP)* |
| Decks | *8* | Crew | *434* |
| Pass. Capacity (basis 2) | *1,012* | (all berths) | *1,127* |
| Pass. Space Ratio (basis 2) | *22.9* | (all berths) | *20.5* |
| Officers | *Norwegian* | Dining Staff | *International* |
| Total Cabins | | | *506* |
| Size (sq ft/m) | *120-483/11.1-44.8* | Door Width | *25"* |
| Outside Cabins | *324* | Inside Cabins | *182* |
| Single Cabins | *0* | Supplement | *50-100%* |
| Balcony Cabins | *0* | Wheelchair Cabins | *0* |
| Cabin Current | | | *110 AC* |
| Refrigerator | | | *Owner's suite only* |
| Cabin TV | *No* | VCR | *No* |
| Dining Rooms | *1* | Sittings | *2* |
| Elevators | *4* | Door Width | *35"* |

| | | | |
|---|---|---|---|
| Casino | *Yes* | Slot Machines | *Yes* |
| Swimming Pools (outside) | *1* | (inside) | *0* |
| Whirlpools | *0* | Gymnasium | *Yes* |
| Sauna/Steam Rm | *Yes/No* | Massage | *Yes* |
| Self-Service Launderette | | | |
| Movie Theater/Seats | | | *No* |
| Library | | | *No* |
| Children's Facilities | | | *No* |
| Watersports Facilities | | | *None* |
| Classification Society | | | *Det Norske Veritas* |

| RATINGS | SCORE |
|---|---|
| Ship: Condition/Cleanliness | 7.4 |
| Ship: Space/Flow/Comfort | 6.7 |
| Ship: Decor/Furnishings | 7.0 |
| Ship: Fitness Facilities | 6.6 |
| Cabins: Comfort/Facilities | 5.8 |
| Cabins: Software | 7.7 |
| Food: Dining Room/Cuisine | 6.8 |
| Food: Buffets/Informal Dining | 6.6 |
| Food: Quality of Ingredients | 7.1 |
| Service: Dining Room | 6.7 |
| Service: Bars/Lounges | 6.5 |
| Service: Cabins | 6.1 |
| Cruise: Entertainment | 7.8 |
| Cruise: Activities Program | 7.6 |
| Cruise: Hospitality Standard | 7.4 |
| OVERALL RATING | 103.8 |

**+** Contemporary seventies look with reasonably sleek lines, raked bow, and cantilevered Viking Crown Lounge high up on funnel. Stretched sister to *Song of Norway*. Has beautifully polished, outdoor, wrap-around promenade deck. Good interior layout and passenger flow. Good wooden paneling and trim throughout.

**–** High density ship means long lines for embarkation, disembarkation, buffets, shore tenders, and elevators. The open deck space for sunning is crowded and noisy, with too many lounge chairs and constant steel band and other music. Constant aroma of strong cleaning chemicals. Cabins are very small and compact, with mediocre closets and almost no storage space, yet somehow everyone seems to manage. Far too many announcements.

**Dining** Good general dining room operation and choice of food, although it all seems to taste the same, consistently. Attentive, polished, friendly, but hurried, dining room service, and strong pressure from the waiters for good passenger comments is annoying.

**Other Comments** Stretched in 1980. Scandinavian decor is clean and bright, but now looks dated. This is a stimulating, not relaxing, cruise experience. This ship provides both novice and repeat passengers with well-programed flair, and a fine-tuned, activity-filled cruise product in noisy, busy, yet comfortable, surroundings. Insurance and gratuities are extra.

# ss Norway ★★★★

***Principal Cruising Areas***

*Bahamas/Caribbean (7 nights year-round)*

***Base Port:*** *Miami (Saturday)*

| | | | |
|---|---|---|---|
| Cruise Line | *Norwegian Cruise Line* | | |
| Former Names | *France* | | |
| Gross Tonnage | *76,049* | | |
| Builder | *Chantiers de l'Atlantique (France)* | | |
| Original Cost | *$80 million* | | |
| Christened By | *Madame Charles de Gaulle* | | |
| First Entered Service | *Feb 3, 1962/Jun 1, 1980* | | |
| Interior Design | *Tage Wandborg/Angelo Donghia* | | |
| Country of Registry | *Bahamas (C6CM7)* | | |
| Tel No | *110-4603* | Fax No | *110-4604* |
| Length (ft/m) | *1,035.1/315.50* | | |
| Beam (ft/m) | *109.9/33.50* | | |
| Draft (ft/m) | *35.4/10.80* | | |
| Engines | *4 CEM Parsons steam turbines* | | |
| Propellers | *4* | | |
| Decks | *12* | Crew | *875* |
| Pass. Capacity (basis 2) | *2,044* | (all berths) | *2,370* |
| Pass. Space Ratio (basis 2) | *37.2* | (all berths) | *32.8* |
| Officers | *Norwegian* | Dining Staff | *International* |
| Total Cabins | *1,013* | | |
| Size (sq ft/m) | *100-957/9.2-89* | Door Width | *28"* |
| Outside Cabins | *647* | Inside Cabins | *366* |
| Single Cabins | *20* | Supplement | *50-100%* |
| Balcony Cabins | *56* | Wheelchair Cabins | *10* |
| Cabin Current | *110 AC* | | |
| Refrigerator | *1/2/3/4/5/owner's suite* | | |
| Cabin TV | *Yes* | VCR | *No* |
| Dining Rooms | *2* | Sittings | *2* |
| Elevators | *13* | Door Width | *30-41"* |
| Casino | *Yes* | Slot Machines | *Yes* |
| Swimming Pools (outside) | *2* | (inside) | *1* |
| Whirlpools | *2* | Gymnasium | *Yes* |
| Sauna/Steam Rm | *Yes/No* | Massage | *Yes* |
| Self-Service Launderette | *Yes* | | |
| Movie Theater/Seats | *Yes/840* | | |
| Library | *Yes* | Children's Facilities | *Yes* |
| Watersports Facilities | *None* | | |
| Classification Society | *Bureau Veritas* | | |

| RATINGS | SCORE |
|---|---|
| Ship: Condition/Cleanliness | 7.7 |
| Ship: Space/Flow/Comfort | 7.5 |
| Ship: Decor/Furnishings | 7.3 |
| Ship: Fitness Facilities | 8.0 |
| Cabins: Comfort/Facilities | 7.8 |
| Cabins: Software | 6.7 |
| Food: Dining Room/Cuisine | 7.5 |
| Food: Buffets/Informal Dining | 7.2 |
| Food: Quality of Ingredients | 6.4 |
| Service: Dining Room | 7.2 |
| Service: Bars/Lounges | 7.1 |
| Service: Cabins | 7.5 |
| Cruise: Entertainment | 8.2 |
| Cruise: Activities Program | 7.6 |
| Cruise: Hospitality Standard | 7.3 |
| OVERALL RATING | 111.0 |

**+** Legendary, grand former classic ocean liner *France* is presently the world's largest cruise ship. New soft furnishings and much marble freshen the interior. Fast, efficient transportation ashore. Well varnished outdoor decks. Club Internationale is an elegant carryover from her former days. Excellent proscenium theater for dazzle and sizzle production shows. Large active casino. Very wide range of suites and cabins. All have high ceilings, long beds, good closet and drawer space, and full amenities. Owner's suites are extremely lavish.

**–** Long lines everywhere. Poor deck and sunning space. Doesn't dock anywhere because of its size. Roman Spa fitness facilities incur hefty extra charge. Too many announcements.

**Dining** Two large dining rooms. Few tables for two, and tables are close together. The food is not memorable and menus are disappointing. Poor bread, rolls, and fruit. Variable service. The new (extra charge) Le Bistro offers a taste of Italy in "South Miami Beach" style. American hotel banquet food. Good, moderately-priced wine list.

**Other Comments** Public rooms are pleasing. All suite occupants should have a private dining room. Recommended for active passengers and families with children of all ages. This ship will provide an action-packed, sun-filled cruise in comfortable, but overpopulated, surroundings, at a decent price. Insurance and gratuities are extra.

# ss OceanBreeze ★★★

***Principal Cruising Area***
*Caribbean (7 nights year-round)*
***Base Port:** Aruba (Saturday)*

| | | | |
|---|---|---|---|
| Cruise Line | | | *Dolphin Cruise Line* |
| Former Names | | | *Azure Seas/Calypso/ Monarch Star/Southern Cross* |
| Gross Tonnage | | | *21,486* |
| Builder | | | *Harland & Wolff (UK)* |
| Original Cost | | | *n/a* |
| Christened By | | | *HRH Queen Elizabeth II* |
| First Entered Service | | | *Mar 29, 1955/May 31, 1992* |
| Interior Design | | | *A&M Katzourakis* |
| Country of Registry | | | *Panama (H8MW)* |
| Tel No | *124-6254* | Fax No | *124-6254* |
| Length (ft/m) | | | *603.8/184.06* |
| Beam (ft/m) | 80.0/24.41 | Draft (ft/m) | 26.1/7.97 |
| Engines | | | *4 Harland & Wolff steam turbines* |
| Propellers | | | *2* |
| Decks | *9* | Crew | *380* |
| Pass. Capacity (basis 2) | *782* | (all berths) | *946* |
| Pass. Space Ratio (basis 2) | *27.4* | (all berths) | *22.7* |
| Officers | *International* | Dining Staff | *International* |
| Total Cabins | | | *391* |
| Size (sq ft/m) | *99-400/9-37* | Door Width | *23"* |
| Outside Cabins | *241* | Inside Cabins | *150* |
| Single Cabins | *0* | Supplement | *50%* |
| Balcony Cabins | *0* | Wheelchair Cabins | *0* |
| Cabin Current | *110/220 AC* | Refrigerator | No |
| Cabin TV | *No* | VCR | *No* |
| Dining Rooms | *1* | Sittings | *2* |
| Elevators | *2* | Door Width | *28"* |

| | | | |
|---|---|---|---|
| Casino | *Yes* | Slot Machines | *Yes* |
| Swimming Pools (outside) | *1* | (inside) | *0* |
| Whirlpools | *1* | Gymnasium | *Yes* |
| Sauna/Steam Rm | *Yes/No* | Massage | *No* |
| Self-Service Launderette | | | *No* |
| Movie Theater/Seats | | | *Yes/55* |
| Library | | | *Yes* |
| Children's Facilities | | | *No* |
| Watersports Facilities | | | *None* |
| Classification Society | | | *Bureau Veritas* |

| RATINGS | SCORE |
|---|---|
| Ship: Condition/Cleanliness | 6.5 |
| Ship: Space/Flow/Comfort | 5.9 |
| Ship: Decor/Furnishings | 6.5 |
| Ship: Fitness Facilities | 4.5 |
| Cabins: Comfort/Facilities | 6.3 |
| Cabins: Software | 6.5 |
| Food: Dining Room/Cuisine | 7.0 |
| Food: Buffets/Informal Dining | 6.8 |
| Food: Quality of Ingredients | 6.6 |
| Service: Dining Room | 6.8 |
| Service: Bars/Lounges | 6.9 |
| Service: Cabins | 7.1 |
| Cruise: Entertainment | 6.8 |
| Cruise: Activities Program | 6.6 |
| Cruise: Hospitality Standard | 6.8 |
| OVERALL RATING | 97.6 |

**+** Attractive older ship with long, low profile easily identified by its single funnel located astern. Well maintained, although showing her age in places. Very good open deck and sunning space. Much changed interior from the original. Two-level casino is beautifully decorated, in art deco style, and action-packed, in what used to be the cinema. Cabins are comfortable and nicely decorated in earth tones, and, though not large, well equipped, with heavy-duty fittings.

**–** Expect long lines for embarkation, disembarkation and buffets. Lots of smokers. Many crew members do not speak English well.

**Dining** The dining room is located low in the ship, but has a warm and cheerful ambiance. The food is generally good, and there's plenty of it, but it isn't gourmet. Service is quite reasonable and attentive, but there's no finesse.

**Other Comments** An action-filled ship, good for those wanting a decent cruise experience for a modest price, in very casual surroundings. At the start and end of the cruise you have to deal with the awful, crowded Aruba airport, so be prepared. Insurance and gratuities are extra.

# ms Oceanic Grace ★★★★+

***Principal Cruising Areas***

*Japan/South East Asia (various)*

***Base Port:*** *Yokohama*

| | | | |
|---|---|---|---|
| Cruise Line | | | *Oceanic Cruises/Showa Line* |
| Former Names | | | *n/a* |
| Gross Tonnage | | | *5,218* |
| Builder | | | *NKK Tsu Shipyard (Japan)* |
| Original Cost | | | *$40 million* |
| Christened By | | | *Ms Mineko Takamine* |
| First Entered Service | | | *Apr 22, 1989* |
| Interior Design | | | *Studio Acht* |
| Country of Registry | | | *Japan (JMIA)* |
| Tel No | *120-1634* | Fax No | *120-6134* |
| Length (ft/m) | | | *337.5/102.90* |
| Beam (ft/m) | | | *50.5/15.40* |
| Draft (ft/m) | | | *14.1/4.30* |
| Engines/Propellers | | | *2 Wartsila 16-cyl diesels/2 (CP)* |
| Decks | *4* | Crew | *70* |
| Pass. Capacity (basis 2) | *120* | (all berths) | *120* |
| Pass. Space Ratio (basis 2) | *43.4* | (all berths) | *43.4* |
| Officers | *Japanese* | Dining Staff | *International* |
| Total Cabins | | | *60* |
| Size (sq ft/m) | *196-260/18.2-24* | Door Width | *23.5"* |
| Outside Cabins | *60* | Inside Cabins | *0* |
| Single Cabins | *0* | Supplement | *$355 per day* |
| Balcony Cabins | | | *8* |
| Wheelchair Cabins | | | *1* |
| Cabin Current | *115 AC* | Refrigerator | *Yes* |
| Cabin TV | *Yes* | VCR | *Yes* |
| Dining Rooms | *1* | Sittings | *1* |
| Elevators | *1* | Door Width | *31.5"* |

| | | | |
|---|---|---|---|
| Casino | *No* | Slot Machines | *No* |
| Swimming Pools (outside) | *1* | (inside) | *0* |
| Whirlpools | *1* | Gymnasium | *Yes* |
| Sauna/Steam Rm | *Yes/Yes* | Massage | *Yes* |
| Self-Service Launderette | | | *No* |
| Movie Theater/Seats | | | *No* |
| Library | *Yes* | Children's Facilities | *No* |
| Watersports Facilities | | | *Aft platform/scuba/snorkel/water-ski/zodiacs* |
| Classification Society | | | *Nippon Kaiji Kyokai* |

| RATINGS | SCORE |
|---|---|
| Ship: Condition/Cleanliness | 8.4 |
| Ship: Space/Flow/Comfort | 8.1 |
| Ship: Decor/Furnishings | 8.0 |
| Ship: Fitness/Watersports | 8.0 |
| Cabins: Comfort/Facilities | 8.2 |
| Cabins: Software | 8.0 |
| Food: Dining Room/Cuisine | 8.3 |
| Food: Buffets/Informal Dining | 8.2 |
| Food: Quality of Ingredients | 8.3 |
| Service: Dining Room | 8.1 |
| Service: Bars/Lounges | 7.9 |
| Service: Cabins | 8.0 |
| Cruise: Entertainment | 7.1 |
| Cruise: Activities Program | 7.2 |
| Cruise: Hospitality Standard | 8.2 |
| OVERALL RATING | 120.0 |

**+** Elegant ship for discerning cruisers. Impressive contemporary looks, with twin outboard funnels. Decompression chamber for scuba divers. Plenty of open deck and sunning space. Teakwood jogging track. Integrated, balanced East-West interior design concept. Clean, sophisticated decor. Can be used for "membership club" cruising (members get the suites). Tastefully furnished all-outside cabins feature blond wood cabinetry, three-sided mirrors, personal safe, wooden hangars in closet, mini-bar/refrigerator, safe, tea-making unit, cotton bathrobes, slippers, shoe horn, clothes brush, and deep, full-sized bathtub. Small country club setting, with excellent, highly personalized service from a very willing and attentive staff.

**–** The small swimming pool is really a "dip" pool. Cabins with balconies have awkward balcony door handles. Cabin toilet seats are too high. Watersports equipment is not used on the short cruises around the Japan coast. Room service items are at extra charge.

**Dining** Warm and inviting dining room features the freshest of foods from local ports of call. Japanese cuisine. Chefs and hotel staff are provided by the superb Palace Hotel in Tokyo.

**Other Comments** This is an excellent ship for discerning watersports aficionados. Scuba equipment rental is extra. Port taxes are included. Gratuities are neither expected nor allowed.

# mv Odessa ★★★+

***Principal Cruising Areas***

*Worldwide (various)*

***Base Ports:*** *Bremerhaven/Savona*

| | | | |
|---|---|---|---|
| Cruise Line | | | *Transocean Cruise Lines* |
| Former Names | | | *Copenhagen* |
| Gross Tonnage | | | *13,252* |
| Builder | | | *Vickers Ltd (UK)* |
| Original Cost | | | *n/a* |
| Christened By | | | *n/a* |
| First Entered Service | | | *Jul 18, 1975* |
| Interior Design | | | *n/a* |
| Country of Registry | | | *Ukraine (EWBK)* |
| Tel No | *140-2777* | Fax No | *140-0223* |
| Length (ft/m) | | | *447.1/136.30* |
| Beam (ft/m) | | | *70.6/21.52* |
| Draft (ft/m) | | | *19.0/5.81* |
| Engines/Propellers | | | *2 Pielstick 16-cyl diesels/2 (CP)* |
| Decks | *5* | Crew | *250* |
| Pass. Capacity (basis 2) | *482* | (all berths) | *570* |
| Pass. Space Ratio (basis 2) | *27.4* | (all berths) | *23.2* |
| Officers | | | *Russian/Ukrainian* |
| Dining Staff | | | *Russian/Ukrainian* |
| Total Cabins | | | *241* |
| Size (sq ft/m) | *109-375/10-34.8* | Door Width | *26"* |
| Outside Cabins | *241* | Inside Cabins | *0* |
| Single Cabins | *0* | Supplement | *50-100%* |
| Balcony Cabins | *0* | Wheelchair Cabins | *0* |
| Cabin Current | *220 AC* | Refrigerator | *Suites* |
| Cabin TV | *Yes* | VCR | *No* |
| Dining Rooms | *1* | Sittings | *2* |
| Elevators | *4* | Door Width | *33"* |

| | | | |
|---|---|---|---|
| Casino | *No* | Slot Machines | *Yes* |
| Swimming Pools (outside) | *1* | (inside) | *0* |
| Whirlpools | *0* | Gymnasium | *Yes* |
| Sauna/Steam Rm | *Yes/No* | Massage | *Yes* |
| Self-Service Launderette | | | *No* |
| Movie Theater/Seats | | | *Yes/152* |
| Library | | | *Yes* |
| Children's Facilities | | | *No* |
| Watersports Facilities | | | *None* |
| Classification Society | | | *Lloyd's Register* |

| RATINGS | SCORE |
|---|---|
| Ship: Condition/Cleanliness | 7.1 |
| Ship: Space/Flow/Comfort | 7.0 |
| Ship: Decor/Furnishings | 7.7 |
| Ship: Fitness Facilities | 5.8 |
| Cabins: Comfort/Facilities | 7.0 |
| Cabins: Software | 7.6 |
| Food: Dining Room/Cuisine | 7.1 |
| Food: Buffets/Informal Dining | 6.6 |
| Food: Quality of Ingredients | 6.8 |
| Service: Dining Room | 6.9 |
| Service: Bars/Lounges | 6.8 |
| Service: Cabins | 7.1 |
| Cruise: Entertainment | 6.6 |
| Cruise: Activities Program | 6.3 |
| Cruise: Hospitality Standard | 7.4 |
| OVERALL RATING | 103.8 |

**+** Handsome ship with well-balanced traditional lines and profile. Looking spiffy following a major refit. Maintenance and cleanliness are good. Fine selection of public rooms, lounges, and bars, most with very tasteful decor. Neat, three-deck-high spiral staircase topped with glass skylight. Attractive balconied theater. All cabins are outside, completely new, somewhat small, but very tastefully furnished, with good closet and drawer space, and pastel colors. Artwork has been upgraded. Bathrobes provided in all cabins.

**–** Steep gangway in many ports.

**Dining** Charming Odessa restaurant is set high up in the ship and has intricate artwork on integral columns. Service is quite attentive from Russian waitresses. The food product has been upgraded recently, but there's a limited selection of breads, cheeses, and fruits.

**Other Comments** Transocean Cruise Lines' staff are really keen young professionals who do an excellent job with their passengers. This ship is highly recommended for German-speaking passengers who want to cruise in quite elegant, yet informal, surroundings, at a modest price. Port taxes and insurance are included. Gratuities are extra.

# mts Odysseus ★★★

***Principal Cruising Area***
*Southern Europe (3/4/7 nights)*
***Base Port:*** *Piraeus*

| | |
|---|---|
| Cruise Line | *Epirotiki Lines* |
| Former Names | *Aquamarine/Marco Polo/ Princesa Isabel* |
| Gross Tonnage | *12,000* |
| Builder | *Society Espanola Shipyard (Spain)* |
| Original Cost | *n/a* |
| Christened By | *n/a* |
| First Entered Service | *1962/Spring 1987* |
| Interior Design | *Arminio Lozzi* |
| Country of Registry | *Greece (J4GU)* |
| Tel No *113-0652* | Fax No *113-0652* |
| Length (ft/m) | *470.1/143.30* |
| Beam (ft/m) | *61.0/18.60* |
| Draft (ft/m) | *21.3/6.50* |
| Engines/Propellers | *2 B&W 8-cyl diesels/2* |
| Decks *7* | Crew *194* |
| Pass. Capacity (basis 2) *452* | (all berths) *486* |
| Pass. Space Ratio (basis 2) *26.5* | (all berths) *24.7* |
| Officers *Greek* | Dining Staff *Greek* |
| Total Cabins | *226* |
| Size (sq ft/m) *102-280/9.5-26* | Door Width *24"* |
| Outside Cabins *183* | Inside Cabins *43* |
| Single Cabins *0* | Supplement *50%* |
| Balcony Cabins *0* | Wheelchair Cabins *0* |
| Cabin Current *110 AC* | Refrigerator *No* |
| Cabin TV *No* | VCR *No* |
| Dining Rooms *2* | Sittings *2* |
| Elevators *1* | Door Width *30"* |

| | |
|---|---|
| Casino *Yes* | Slot Machines *Yes* |
| Swimming Pools (outside) *1* | (inside) *0* |
| Whirlpools *4* | Gymnasium *Yes* |
| Sauna/Steam Rm *Yes/No* | Massage *Yes* |
| Self-Service Launderette | *No* |
| Movie Theater/Seats | *Yes/145* |
| Library | *Yes* |
| Children's Facilities | *No* |
| Watersports Facilities | *None* |
| Classification Society | *Lloyd's Register* |

| RATINGS | SCORE |
|---|---|
| Ship: Condition/Cleanliness | 6.9 |
| Ship: Space/Flow/Comfort | 6.5 |
| Ship: Decor/Furnishings | 6.8 |
| Ship: Fitness Facilities | 3.7 |
| Cabins: Comfort/Facilities | 6.4 |
| Cabins: Software | 6.9 |
| Food: Dining Room/Cuisine | 6.6 |
| Food: Buffets/Informal Dining | 6.3 |
| Food: Quality of Ingredients | 6.0 |
| Service: Dining Room | 7.3 |
| Service: Bars/Lounges | 7.2 |
| Service: Cabins | 7.3 |
| Cruise: Entertainment | 5.4 |
| Cruise: Activities Program | 5.7 |
| Cruise: Hospitality Standard | 7.2 |
| OVERALL RATING | 96.2 |

**+** Attractive-looking vessel with a well-balanced profile. Acquired and completely reconstructed by Epirotiki in 1987. Ample open deck and sunning space. Twin teak-decked sheltered promenades. Good range of public rooms feature pleasing Mediterranean decor. The Taverna is especially popular with the younger set. Attractive, quite roomy, mostly outside cabins have convertible sofa-bed (a few have double beds), good closet and drawer space, and tasteful wood trim.

**–** Steep gangway in most ports. Cabin bathrooms are small.

**Dining** The dining room is quite charming. Food is typically Continental, and features several Greek dishes. Warm, attentive service in true Epirotiki style, but menu choice is limited. Selection of breads, cheeses, and fruits is poor.

**Other Comments** This ship is for those who want to cruise at a modest cost, in warm surroundings, on a very comfortable vessel. Often chartered by learning enrichment tour operators. Insurance and gratuities are extra.

# ms Olympic

***Principal Cruising Areas***

*Aegean/Mediterranean (7 nights)*

***Base Port:*** *Piraeus*

| | | | |
|---|---|---|---|
| Cruise Line | | | *Epirotiki Lines* |
| Former Names | | | *Ocean Majesty/Kypros Star* |
| Gross Registered Tonnage | | | *12,800* |
| Builder | | | *Astilleros Espanola (Spain)* |
| Original Cost | | | *$65 million* |
| Christened By | | | *Epirotiki Lines* |
| First Entered Service | | | *April 15, 1994* |
| Interior Design | | | *A&M Katzourakis* |
| Country of Registry | | | *Greece (SZWX)* |
| Tel No | *113-2141* | Fax No | *113-2142* |
| Length (ft/m) | | | *449.4/137.00* |
| Beam (ft/m) | | | *62.3/19.00* |
| Draft (ft/m) | | | *19.3/5.90* |
| Engines/Propellers | | | *diesels/2* |
| Passenger Decks | | | *7* |
| Number of Crew | | | *235* |
| Pass. Capacity (basis 2) | *526* | (all berths) | *621* |
| Pass. Space Ratio (basis 2) | *24.3* | (all berths) | *20.6* |
| Officers | *Greek* | Dining Staff | *Greek* |
| Total Cabins | | | *273* |
| Size (sq ft/m) | *39.3-52.4/3.7-4.9* | Door Width | *24"* |
| Outside Cabins | *186* | Inside Cabins | *87* |
| Single Cabins | *4* | Supplement | *50%* |
| Balcony Cabins | *8* | Wheelchair Cabins | *2* |
| Cabin Current | *110/220 AC* | Refrigerator | *No* |
| Cabin TV | *Yes* | VCR | *No* |
| Dining Rooms | *1* | Sittings | *2* |
| Elevators | *3* | Door Width | *36"* |

| | | | |
|---|---|---|---|
| Casino | *Yes* | Slot Machines | *Yes* |
| Swimming Pools (outside) | *1* | (inside) | *0* |
| Whirlpools | *1* | Gymnasium | *Yes* |
| Sauna/Steam Rm | *Yes/No* | Massage | *Yes* |
| Self-Service Launderette | | | *No* |
| Movie Theater/Seats | | | *No* |
| Library | | | *Yes* |
| Children's Facilities | | | *No* |
| Watersports Facilities | | | *None* |
| Classification Society | | | *American Bur. of Shipping* |

| RATINGS | SCORE |
|---|---|
| Ship: Condition/Cleanliness | NYR |
| Ship: Space/Flow/Comfort | NYR |
| Ship: Decor/Furnishings | NYR |
| Ship: Fitness Facilities | NYR |
| Cabins: Comfort/Facilities | NYR |
| Cabins: Software | NYR |
| Food: Dining Room/Cuisine | NYR |
| Food: Buffets/Informal Dining | NYR |
| Food: Quality of Ingredients | NYR |
| Service: Dining Room | NYR |
| Service: Bars/Lounges | NYR |
| Service: Cabins | NYR |
| Cruise: Entertainment | NYR |
| Cruise: Activities Program | NYR |
| Cruise: Hospitality Standard | NYR |

NYR = Not Yet Rated

**+** This ship has been chartered by Epirotiki Lines as a temporary, additional vessel for the busy summer season. She has been completely refurbished and remodeled as a cruise vessel, with the exception of hull, shaft, and propellers. There are several good public rooms, bars, and lounges.

**–** High density vessel, so expect long lines for embarkation, disembarkation, shore excursions, and buffets. Open deck and sunning space is rather limited. The cabins are extremely small and well below the size of cabins on other Epirotiki ships. Has a somewhat awkward interior layout and steep interior stairways.

**Dining** The dining room is set low down in the ship, but is quite attractive, but also quite noisy. This is Continental in style, with the emphasis on Greek preparation and presentation, but don't expect exotic dishes. Limited choice of breads, fruits, and cheeses.

**Other Comments** Well-balanced, almost handsome profile with aft-placed funnel and inboard lifeboats. This ship was a former Spanish ro-ro ship which has undergone an extensive transformation and is under charter to Epirotiki Lines.

# ms Oriana

***Principal Cruising Areas***
*Worldwide (12-90 days)*
***Base Port:** Southampton*

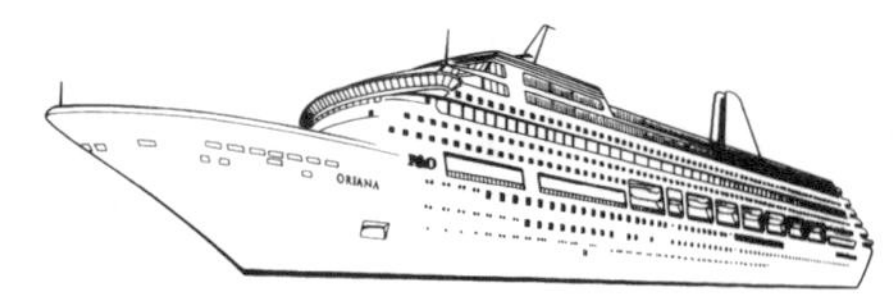

| | | | |
|---|---|---|---|
| Cruise Line/Operator | | | *P&O Cruises* |
| Former Names | | | *n/a* |
| Gross Tonnage | | | *67,000* |
| Builder | | | *Meyer Werft (Germany)* |
| Original Cost | | | *£200 million* |
| Christened By | | | *n/a* |
| First Entered Service | | | *Apr 1995* |
| Interior Design | | | *Tillberg/McNeece/Yran* |
| Country of Registry | | | *Great Britain* |
| Tel No | *n/a* | Fax No | *n/a* |
| Length (ft/m) | | | *850.0/260.0* |
| Beam (ft/m) | | | *105.6/32.2* |
| Draft (ft/m) | | | *26.0/7.9* |
| Engines | | | *2x9-cyl+2x6-cyl MAN diesels* |
| Propellers | | | *2 (CP)* |
| Decks | *10* | Crew | *760* |
| Pass. Capacity (basis 2) | *1,828* | (all berths) | *1,975* |
| Pass. Space Ratio (basis 2) | *36.7* | (all berths) | *33.9* |
| Officers | *British* | Dining Staff | *International* |
| Total Cabins | | | *914* |
| Size (sq ft/m) | *150-409/14-38* | Door Width | *24"* |
| Outside Cabins | *594* | Inside Cabins | *320* |
| Single Cabins | *112* | Supplement | - |
| Balcony Cabins | *118* | Wheelchair Cabins | *8* |
| Cabin Current | *110/220 AC* | Refrigerator | *Yes* |
| Cabin TV | *Yes* | VCR | *Suites* |
| Dining Rooms | *2* | Sittings | *2* |
| Elevators | *10* | Door Width | *44"* |

| | | | |
|---|---|---|---|
| Casino | *Yes* | Slot Machines | *Yes* |
| Swimming Pools (outside) | *3* | (inside) | *0* |
| Whirlpools | *5* | Gymnasium | *Yes* |
| Sauna/Steam Rm | *Yes/Yes* | Massage | *Yes* |
| Self-Service Launderette | | | *Yes* |
| Movie Theater/Seats | | | *Yes/658* |
| Library | | | *Yes* |
| Children's Facilities | | | *Yes* |
| Watersports Facilities | | | *None* |
| Classification Society | | | *Lloyd's Register* |

| RATINGS | SCORE |
|---|---|
| Ship: Condition/Cleanliness | NYR |
| Ship: Space/Flow/Comfort | NYR |
| Ship: Decor/Furnishings | NYR |
| Ship: Fitness Facilities | NYR |
| Cabins: Comfort/Facilities | NYR |
| Cabins: Software | NYR |
| Food: Dining Room/Cuisine | NYR |
| Food: Buffets/Informal Dining | NYR |
| Food: Quality of Ingredients | NYR |
| Service: Dining Room | NYR |
| Service: Bars/Lounges | NYR |
| Service: Cabins | NYR |
| Cruise: Entertainment | NYR |
| Cruise: Activities Program | NYR |
| Cruise: Hospitality Standard | NYR |

NYR = Not Yet Rated

**+** Well thought-out design, with spacious layout and horizontal passenger flow. Four-deck-high atrium. Splendid amount of open deck and sunning space, important for outdoors-loving British passengers. Inboard lifeboats. Large number of public entertainment rooms. Outstanding John Wyckham-designed real theater. Andersons's Lounge (named after the founder members of Peninsular Steam in the 1830s) has a series of 19th century marine paintings. Some outstanding sculptures. Wide range of well equipped cabin configurations and categories, with much emphasis on family cabins. Suites and cabins with balconies have an inter-connecting door, and include a trouser press and ironing board. Much use of rich, warm, limed oak or cherrywood.

**–** None known at press time.

**Dining** Two restaurants, Peninsular and Oriental, located midships and aft, are quite stunning.

**Other Comments** Conventional, rather than innovative, contemporary ship that follows Canberra as the next generation ship—and the first cruise ship specificically designed for the growing British market. This ship, while quite contemporary in design features and facilities, will please P&O traditionalists, and promises to provide an outstanding cruise experience.

# ms Orient Star

***Principal Cruising Area***
*South East Asia (various)*
***Base Ports:*** *various*

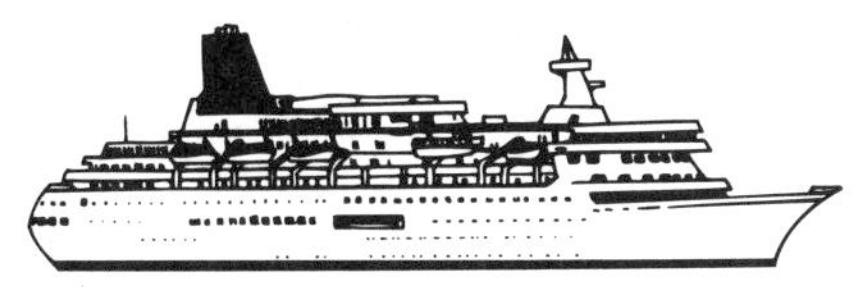

| | | | |
|---|---|---|---|
| Cruise Line | | | *American Pacific Cruises* |
| Former Names | | | *Olga Sadovskaya* |
| Gross Tonnage | | | *3,941* |
| Builder | | | *Brodgradiliste Uljanik (Yugoslavia)* |
| Original Cost | | | *n/a* |
| Christened By | | | *n/a* |
| First Entered Service | | | *1977/1994* |
| Interior Design | | | *n/a* |
| Country of Registry | | | *Russia (ESWY)* |
| Tel No | *140-0371* | Fax No | *140-0371* |
| Length (ft/m) | | | *328.1/100.01* |
| Beam (ft/m) | | | *53.2/16.24* |
| Draft (ft/m) | | | *15.2/4.65* |
| Engines/Propellers | | | *2 Uljanik diesels/1* |
| Decks | *6* | Crew | *100* |
| Pass. Capacity (basis 2) | *96* | (all berths) | *188* |
| Pass. Space Ratio (basis 2) | *41.0* | (all berths) | *20.9* |
| Officers | *Russian* | Dining Staff | *Russian/Ukrainian* |
| Total Cabins | | | *48* |
| Size (sq ft/m) | *n/a* | Door Width | *24"* |
| Outside Cabins | *48* | Inside Cabins | *0* |
| Single Cabins | *0* | Supplement | *100%* |
| Balcony Cabins | | | *0* |
| Wheelchair Cabins | | | *0* |
| Cabin Current | *220 AC* | Refrigerator | *No* |
| Cabin TV | *No* | VCR | *No* |
| Dining Rooms | *1* | Sittings | *1* |
| Elevators | *0* | Door Width | *n/a* |

| | | | |
|---|---|---|---|
| Casino | *No* | Slot Machines | *No* |
| Swimming Pools (outside) | *1* | (inside) | *No* |
| Whirlpools | *No* | Gymnasium | *No* |
| Sauna/Steam Rm | *Yes/No* | Massage | *No* |
| Self-Service Launderette | | | *No* |
| Movie Theater/Seats | | | *Yes/75* |
| Library | | | *Yes* |
| Children's Facilities | | | *No* |
| Watersports Facilities | | | *None* |
| Classification Society | | | *RS* |

| RATINGS | SCORE |
|---|---|
| Ship: Condition/Cleanliness | NYR |
| Ship: Space/Flow/Comfort | NYR |
| Ship: Decor/Furnishings | NYR |
| Ship: Fitness Facilities | NYR |
| Cabins: Comfort/Facilities | NYR |
| Cabins: Software | NYR |
| Food: Dining Room/Cuisine | NYR |
| Food: Buffets/Informal Dining | NYR |
| Food: Quality of Ingredients | NYR |
| Service: Dining Room | NYR |
| Service: Bars/Lounges | NYR |
| Service: Cabins | NYR |
| Cruise: Entertainment | NYR |
| Cruise: Activities Program | NYR |
| Cruise: Hospitality Standard | NYR |

NYR = Not Yet Rated

**+** Intimate, small ship has a well-balanced profile. Ice-hardened hull suitable for soft expedition cruising. Reasonable open deck space. Recently underwent extensive refurbishment. Outdoor observation deck and enclosed promenade deck for inclement weather. Charming forward music lounge has wooden dance floor. Rich, highly polished wood paneling throughout. Lovely, winding, brass-railed main staircase. Good cinema/lecture room.

**–** The cabins are very compact and spartan, but most can accommodate four persons. Steep, narrow gangway. Poor cabin insulation.

**Dining** Comfortable dining room has ocean views. Limited choice of food, but service is friendly and quite attentive. Poor selection of breads, fruits, and cheeses.

**Other Comments** This ship is small, yet comfortable, and has plenty of character, but don't expect much finesse.

# mv Orient Venus ★★★★

***Principal Cruising Areas***

*Japan/South East Asia (various)*

***Base Port:*** *Tokyo*

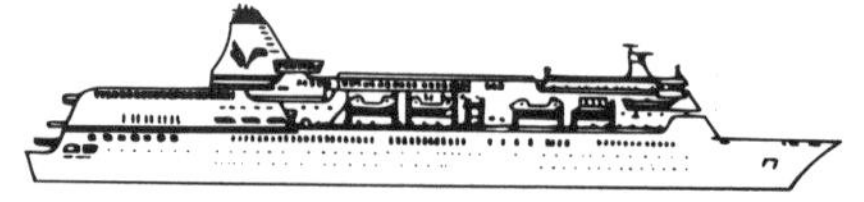

| | | | |
|---|---|---|---|
| Cruise Line | | | *Japan Cruise Line (Nippon Cruise Kyakusen)* |
| Former Names | | | *n/a* |
| Gross Tonnage | | | *21,884* |
| Builder | | | *Ishikawajima Heavy Industries (Japan)* |
| Original Cost | | | *$150 million* |
| Christened By | | | *Mr Yasuo Iritani* |
| First Entered Service | | | *July 1990* |
| Interior Design | | | *Daimaru Design & Engineering* |
| Country of Registry | | | *Japan (JFYU)* |
| Tel No | *120-1731* | Fax No | *120-1731* |
| Length (ft/m) | | | *570.8/174.00* |
| Beam (ft/m) | | | *78.7/24.00* |
| Draft (ft/m) | | | *21.3/6.52* |
| Engines/Propellers | | | *2 United diesels/2* |
| Decks | *8* | Crew | *120* |
| Pass. Capacity (basis 2) | *390* | (all berths) | *606* |
| Pass. Space Ratio (basis 2) | *56.1* | (all berths) | *36.1* |
| Officers | *Japanese* | Dining Staff | *Japanese/Asian* |
| Total Cabins | | | *195* |
| Size (sq ft/m) | *183-592/17-55* | Door Width | *26"* |
| Outside Cabins | *195* | Inside Cabins | *0* |
| Single Cabins | *0* | Supplement | *100%* |
| Balcony Cabins | *2* | Wheelchair Cabins | *0* |
| Cabin Current | | | *110 AC* |
| Refrigerator | | | *Yes* |
| Cabin TV | *Yes* | VCR | *No* |
| Dining Rooms | *2* | Sittings | *1* |

| | | | |
|---|---|---|---|
| Elevators | *3* | Door Width | *24"* |
| Casino | *No* | Slot Machines | *No* |
| Swimming Pools (outside) | *1* | (inside) | *0* |
| Whirlpools | *0* | Gymnasium | *Yes* |
| Sauna/Steam Rm | *No/No* | Massage | *No* |
| Self-Service Launderette | | | *Yes* |
| Movie Theater/Seats | | | *Yes/606* |
| Library | *Yes* | Children's Facilities | *No* |
| Watersports Facilities | | | *None* |
| Classification Society | | | *Nippon Kaiji Kyokai* |

| RATINGS | SCORE |
|---|---|
| Ship: Condition/Cleanliness | 8.1 |
| Ship: Space/Flow/Comfort | 8.0 |
| Ship: Decor/Furnishings | 8.0 |
| Ship: Fitness Facilities | 7.8 |
| Cabins: Comfort/Facilities | 7.8 |
| Cabins: Software | 7.5 |
| Food: Dining Room/Cuisine | 7.4 |
| Food: Buffets/Informal Dining | 7.2 |
| Food: Quality of Ingredients | 7.0 |
| Service: Dining Room | 7.7 |
| Service: Bars/Lounges | 7.8 |
| Service: Cabins | 7.6 |
| Cruise: Entertainment | 7.0 |
| Cruise: Activities Program | 7.2 |
| Cruise: Hospitality Standard | 7.9 |
| OVERALL RATING | 114.0 |

**+** New, conventional-shaped ship has a graceful profile. Night and Day lounge set at funnel base looking forward over swimming pool. Expansive open deck and sunning space. Windows of the Orient is a small, attractive, peaceful, forward observation lounge. Superb conference facilities. Fine array of public rooms. Horseshoe-shaped main lounge has fine sightlines to platform stage. Expansive open sunning deck aft of funnel. Four cabin grades provide variety of well-equipped, all-outside, Western-style cabins. Two suites are huge and have private verandas.

**–** Does not cater well to individual passengers. Rather plain decor in many public rooms.

**Dining** Very attractive main dining room. Romanesque Grill is unusual, with classic period decor and high, elegant ceiling. Features reasonably good, but rather commercial, Japanese cuisine exclusively.

**Other Comments** This Western-style ship will provide its mostly Japanese corporate passengers with extremely comfortable surroundings, and a superb cruise and seminar/learning environment and experience.

# mts Orpheus ★★★

***Principal Cruising Area***

*Southern Europe (14 nights)*

***Base Port:*** *Piraeus*

| | | | |
|---|---|---|---|
| Cruise Line | | | *Epirotiki Lines* |
| Former Names | | | *Thesus/Munster I/Munster* |
| Gross Tonnage | | | *5,092* |
| Builder | | | *Harland & Wolff (UK)* |
| Original Cost | | | *n/a* |
| Christened By | | | *n/a* |
| First Entered Service | | | *1952/1969* |
| Interior Design | | | *Arminio Lozzi* |
| Country of Registry | | | *Greece (SXUI)* |
| Tel No | *113-3165* | Fax No | *113-3165* |
| Length (ft/m) | | | *374.8/114.26* |
| Beam (ft/m) | | | *50.1/15.30* |
| Draft (ft/m) | | | *16.0/4.88* |
| Engines/Propellers | | | *2 B&W 10-cyl diesels/2* |
| Decks | *6* | Crew | *140* |
| Pass. Capacity (basis 2) | *304* | (all berths) | *318* |
| Pass. Space Ratio (basis 2) | *16.7* | (all berths) | *16.0* |
| Officers | *Greek* | Dining Staff | *Greek* |
| Total Cabins | | | *152* |
| Size (sq ft/m) | *n/a* | Door Width | *24"* |
| Outside Cabins | *117* | Inside Cabins | *35* |
| Single Cabins | *7* | Supplement | *50-90%* |
| Balcony Cabins | *0* | Wheelchair Cabins | *0* |
| Cabin Current | | | *220 AC* |
| Refrigerator | | | *No* |
| Cabin TV | *No* | VCR | *No* |
| Dining Rooms | *1* | Sittings | *Open* |
| Elevators | *0* | Door Width | *n/a* |

| | | | |
|---|---|---|---|
| Casino | *No* | Slot Machines | *No* |
| Swimming Pools (outside) | *1* | (inside) | *0* |
| Whirlpools | *0* | Gymnasium | *No* |
| Sauna/Steam Rm | *No/No* | Massage | *No* |
| Self-Service Launderette | | | *No* |
| Movie Theater/Seats | | | *No* |
| Library | | | *Yes* |
| Children's Facilities | | | *No* |
| Watersports Facilities | | | *None* |
| Classification Society | | | *Lloyd's Register* |

| RATINGS | SCORE |
|---|---|
| Ship: Condition/Cleanliness | 6.8 |
| Ship: Space/Flow/Comfort | 6.4 |
| Ship: Decor/Furnishings | 6.9 |
| Ship: Fitness Facilities | 3.9 |
| Cabins: Comfort/Facilities | 6.0 |
| Cabins: Software | 6.7 |
| Food: Dining Room/Cuisine | 6.7 |
| Food: Buffets/Informal Dining | 6.2 |
| Food: Quality of Ingredients | 6.0 |
| Service: Dining Room | 7.6 |
| Service: Bars/Lounges | 7.3 |
| Service: Cabins | 7.5 |
| Cruise: Entertainment | 6.9 |
| Cruise: Activities Program | 6.8 |
| Cruise: Hospitality Standard | 7.7 |
| OVERALL RATING | 99.4 |

**+** Traditional ship profile, with small, squat funnel. Charming and very well maintained. Ample open deck and sunning space for ship size. Very comfortable public rooms with Mediterranean decor, good patterned fabrics, and some fine artwork. The cabins are very compact, but nicely equipped and more than adequate.

**–** High density means that public rooms are always crowded when the ship is full. Limited amount of closet, drawer, and storage space.

**Dining** Pretty dining room features open seating policy. Attentive, friendly service.

**Other Comments** Homey ambiance. Operates on a long-term charter to Swan Hellenic for a program of outstanding, in-depth, life-enrichment cruises, with excellent guest lecturers and informed, yet informal, presentations. This ship will provide a very comfortable two-week cruise in an informal style at a very modest price. Insurance and gratuities are extra.

# mv Pacific Princess ★★★★

***Principal Cruising Areas***

*Worldwide (various)*

***Base Ports:*** *various*

| | | | |
|---|---|---|---|
| Cruise Line | | | *Princess Cruises* |
| Former Names | | | *Sea Venture* |
| Gross Tonnage | | | *20,636* |
| Builder | | | *Rheinstahl Nordseewerke (Germany)* |
| Original Cost | | | *$25 million* |
| Christened By | | | *n/a* |
| First Entered Service | | | *May 14, 1971/Jun 1971* |
| Interior Design | | | *Robert Tillberg* |
| Country of Registry | | | *Great Britain (GBCF)* |
| Tel No | *144-0212* | Fax No | *144-0212* |
| Length (ft/m) | | | *553.6/168.74* |
| Beam (ft/m) | *80.8/24.64* | Draft (ft/m) | *25.2/7.70* |
| Engines | | | *4 GMT-Fiat 10-cyl diesels* |
| Propellers | | | *2 (CP)* |
| Decks | *7* | Crew | *350* |
| Pass. Capacity (basis 2) | *610* | (all berths) | *717* |
| Pass. Space Ratio (basis 2) | *33.8* | (all berths) | *28.7* |
| Officers | *British* | Dining Staff | *International* |
| Total Cabins | | | *305* |
| Size (sq ft/m) | | | *126-443/11.7-41* |
| Door Width | | | *22-33"* |
| Outside Cabins | *238* | Inside Cabins | *67* |
| Single Cabins | *2* | Supplement | *25-100%* |
| Balcony Cabins | *0* | Wheelchair Cabins | *4* |
| Cabin Current | | | *110/220 AC* |
| Refrigerator | | | *A/B/C/D/DD* |
| Cabin TV | *Yes* | VCR | *No* |
| Dining Rooms | *1* | Sittings | *2* |

| | | | |
|---|---|---|---|
| Elevators | *4* | Door Width | *37"* |
| Casino | *Yes* | Slot Machines | *Yes* |
| Swimming Pools (outside) | *2* | (inside) | *0* |
| Whirlpools | *0* | Gymnasium | *Yes* |
| Sauna/Steam Rm | *Yes/No* | Massage | *Yes* |
| Self-Service Launderette | | | *No* |
| Movie Theater/Seats | | | *Yes/250* |
| Library | *Yes* | Children's Facilities | *No* |
| Watersports Facilities | | | *None* |
| Classification Society | | | *Lloyd's Register* |

| RATINGS | SCORE |
|---|---|
| Ship: Condition/Cleanliness | 7.7 |
| Ship: Space/Flow/Comfort | 7.6 |
| Ship: Decor/Furnishings | 8.0 |
| Ship: Fitness Facilities | 6.2 |
| Cabins: Comfort/Facilities | 7.5 |
| Cabins: Software | 7.6 |
| Food: Dining Room/Cuisine | 7.3 |
| Food: Buffets/Informal Dining | 7.0 |
| Food: Quality of Ingredients | 6.7 |
| Service: Dining Room | 7.9 |
| Service: Bars/Lounges | 8.0 |
| Service: Cabins | 7.8 |
| Cruise: Entertainment | 8.1 |
| Cruise: Activities Program | 7.8 |
| Cruise: Hospitality Standard | 8.0 |
| OVERALL RATING | 113.2 |

**+** Well proportioned, handsome ship has high superstructure and quite graceful lines. Fine open deck and sunning areas. Extremely spacious public areas with wide passageways, looking sharp after a major cosmetic refurbishment project. One swimming pool has magrodome roof for use in inclement weather. Tasteful earth-toned decor throughout, with complementary artwork. Good movie theater. Suites and all other cabins are quite roomy and well appointed. Excellent production shows and general entertainment. Very smartly dressed officers and crew. Bathrobes for all passengers.

**–** No wrap-around outdoor promenade deck, and the present teak decking is badly worn in many places. The outdoor Lido Deck's buffet area is untidy. Plastic glasses are a turn-off.

**Dining** The dining room is located on a lower deck, but has pleasant, light decor and feels comfortable and spacious. Good service and fairly good food, although standards have been slipping, as a result of discounted fares.

**Other Comments** This ship is definitely for the older passenger. Quite elegant and moderately expensive, it will cruise you in very comfortable, elegant surroundings, in style. However, it is small compared to Princess Cruises' newer ships, and cannot offer the same range of facilities and services. Insurance and gratuities are extra.

# ms Pearl ★★★+

***Principal Cruising Area***
*South East Asia (various)*
***Base Port:*** *Singapore*

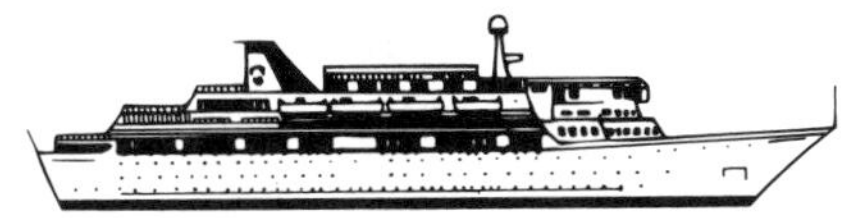

| | | | |
|---|---|---|---|
| Cruise Line | | | *Pearl Cruises* |
| Former Names | | | *Ocean Pearl/ Pearl of Scandinavia/Finnstar* |
| Gross Tonnage | | | *12,475* |
| Builder | | | *Wartsila (Finland)* |
| Original Cost | | | *n/a* |
| Christened By | | | *HRH Princess Galyani Vadhana* |
| First Entered Service | | | *May 25, 1967/Jun 1982* |
| Interior Design | | | *A&M Katzourakis* |
| Country of Registry | | | *Bahamas (C6DC)* |
| Tel No | *110-4105* | Fax No | *130-5352* |
| Length (ft/m) | | | *517.4/157.7* |
| Beam (ft/m) | | | *65.9/20.10* |
| Draft (ft/m) | | | *19.0/5.80* |
| Engines/Propellers | | | *4 Wartsila 9-cyl diesels/2 (CP)* |
| Decks | *9* | Crew | *232* |
| Pass. Capacity (basis 2) | *489* | (all berths) | *739* |
| Pass. Space Ratio (basis 2) | *25.5* | (all berths) | *16.8* |
| Officers | *British* | Dining Staff | *European/Filipino* |
| Total Cabins | | | *250* |
| Size (sq ft/m) | *n/a* | Door Width | *22"* |
| Outside Cabins | *188* | Inside Cabins | *62* |
| Single Cabins | *11* | Supplement | *75-100%* |
| Balcony Cabins | *0* | Wheelchair Cabins | *6* |
| Cabin Current | | | *110/220 AC* |
| Refrigerator | | | *No* |
| Cabin TV | *No* | VCR | *No* |
| Dining Rooms | *1* | Sittings | *2* |

| | | | |
|---|---|---|---|
| Elevators | *2* | Door Width | *31"* |
| Casino | *Yes* | Slot Machines | *Yes* |
| Swimming Pools (outside) | *1* | (inside) | *1* |
| Whirlpools | *0* | Gymnasium | *Yes* |
| Sauna/Steam Rm | *Yes/No* | Massage | *Yes* |
| Self-Service Launderette | | | *No* |
| Movie Theater/Seats | | | *Yes/62* |
| Library | *Yes* | Children's Facilities | *No* |
| Watersports Facilities | | | *None* |
| Classification Society | | | *Bureau Veritas* |

| RATINGS | SCORE |
|---|---|
| Ship: Condition/Cleanliness | 6.6 |
| Ship: Space/Flow/Comfort | 5.8 |
| Ship: Decor/Furnishings | 7.2 |
| Ship: Fitness Facilities | 6.1 |
| Cabins: Comfort/Facilities | 7.0 |
| Cabins: Software | 7.5 |
| Food: Dining Room/Cuisine | 7.6 |
| Food: Buffets/Informal Dining | 7.3 |
| Food: Quality of Ingredients | 6.9 |
| Service: Dining Room | 7.3 |
| Service: Bars/Lounges | 7.1 |
| Service: Cabins | 7.1 |
| Cruise: Entertainment | 6.7 |
| Cruise: Activities Program | 6.4 |
| Cruise: Hospitality Standard | 7.2 |
| OVERALL RATING | 103.8 |

**+** Almost-attractive profile after an extensive refit that included structural alterations, a more contemporary funnel, and a more rakish bow. Well-planned destination-intensive and fascinating itineraries. New layout provides better passenger flow. Tasteful decor includes many earth tones. Lovely woods throughout give much warmth. Marco Polo show lounge is a great improvement. Wonderful statues of Buddha. Indonesian and Filipino hotel staff provide personal service with a smile, although standards have declined noticeably. Explorer's suites are excellent, with lots of wood paneling, and have portholes that actually open. All cabins are quite spacious, and are well equipped, with lots of closet, drawer, and storage space. Bathrobes provided for all passengers. This company does China cruises very well.

**–** Lots of pushy passengers. Too many announcements. The ship is not as clean as it should be.

**Dining** The dining room is very attractive, set high in the ship and located forward, with excellent ocean views. The food is very creative, and the presentation is consistently good, but bread rolls and pastry items are poor.

**Other Comments** This ship provides a fine way to see the Orient in comfort and style, and at a realistic price, although standards have been noted to decline recently, and the ship has taken on an Anglo-French ambiance. Insurance and gratuities are extra.

# ms Polaris ★★★★

***Principal Cruising Areas***

*Worldwide (various)*

***Base Ports:** various*

| | | | |
|---|---|---|---|
| Cruise Line | | | *Special Expeditions* |
| Former Names | | | *Lindblad Polaris/Oresund* |
| Gross Tonnage | | | *2,214* |
| Builder | | | *Aalborg Vaerft (Denmark)* |
| Original Cost | | | *n/a* |
| Christened By | | | *n/a* |
| First Entered Service | | | *1960/6 May 1987* |
| Interior Design | | | *G. Unnar Svensson* |
| Country of Registry | | | *Bahamas (C6CB8)* |
| Tel No | *110-4424* | Fax No | *110-3276* |
| Length (ft/m) | | | *236.6/72.12* |
| Beam (ft/m) | *42.7/13.03* | Draft (ft/m) | *13.7/4.30* |
| Engines/Propellers | | | *2 Nohab 6-cyl diesels/2 (VP)* |
| Decks | *4* | Crew | *43* |
| Pass. Capacity (basis 2) | *82* | (all berths) | *84* |
| Pass. Space Ratio (basis 2) | *27.0* | (all berths) | *26.3* |
| Officers | *Swedish* | Dining Staff | *Filipino* |
| Total Cabins | | | *41* |
| Size (sq ft/m) | *100-230/9.2-21.3* | Door Width | *24"* |
| Outside Cabins | *41* | Inside Cabins | *0* |
| Single Cabins | *0* | Supplement | *50%* |
| Balcony Cabins | *0* | Wheelchair Cabins | *0* |
| Cabin Current | | | *220 AC* |
| Refrigerator | | | *No* |
| Cabin TV | *No* | VCR | *No* |
| Dining Rooms | | | *1* |
| Elevators | *0* | Door Width | *n/a* |
| Casino | No | Slot Machines | *No* |

| | | | |
|---|---|---|---|
| Swimming Pools (outside) | | | *0* |
| Whirlpools | | | *0* |
| Exercise Room | | | *No* |
| Sauna/Steam Rm | *Yes/No* | Massage | *No* |
| Self-Service Launderette | | | *No* |
| Lecture/Film Room | | | *No* |
| Library | *Yes* | Zodiacs | *8* |
| Helicopter Pad | | | *No* |
| Watersports Facilities | | | *None* |
| Classification Society | | | *Bureau Veritas* |

| RATINGS | SCORE |
|---|---|
| Ship: Condition/Cleanliness | 7.3 |
| Ship: Space/Flow/Comfort | 5.7 |
| Ship: Expedition Equipment | 7.6 |
| Ship: Decor/Furnishings | 7.4 |
| Cabins: Comfort/Facilities | 5.6 |
| Cabins: Software | 6.4 |
| Food: Dining Room/Cuisine | 7.6 |
| Food: Buffets/Informal Dining | 7.3 |
| Food: Quality of Ingredients | 6.9 |
| Service: Dining Room | 7.7 |
| Service: Bars/Lounges | 7.5 |
| Service: Cabins | 7.6 |
| Cruise: Itineraries/Operations | 8.0 |
| Cruise: Lecture Program | 7.8 |
| Cruise: Hospitality Standard | 8.1 |
| OVERALL RATING | 108.5 |

**+** Carries zodiacs for in-depth excursions and landings, as well as a glass bottom boat. Tidy Scandinavian interior furnishings and decor, with lots of wood trim. The cabins are quite roomy for the ship's size, and nicely equipped, but there's little drawer space. Some have been refurbished, and feature large (lower) beds with wooden headboards. Each has a hairdryer. Cabin keys are not used. Friendly, very intimate atmosphere on board. Excellent lecturers and nature observers, and a restful, well-stocked library.

**–** Few public rooms. No cabin service menu. Cabin bathrooms are really tiny.

**Dining** New dining room has big picture windows. Seating is at individual tables for improved access. Very good food, with major emphasis on fish and seafood dishes. There is also a fine wine list. Breakfast and lunch are buffet-style. Friendly service from a caring, attentive staff.

**Other Comments** This "soft" expedition cruise vessel of modest proportions has a dark blue hull and white superstructure. Nicely refurbished, it has a recently added fantail and much improved aft outdoor lounge area. No formal entertainment, but no-one needs it. This is a delightful vessel to choose for your next destination- and learning-intensive "soft" expedition cruise experience.

# mts Princesa Amorosa ★★

***Principal Cruising Area***

*Mediterranean (3/4 nights)*

***Base Port:** Limassol*

| | | | |
|---|---|---|---|
| Cruise Line | | | *Louis Cruise Lines* |
| Former Names | | | *Galaxias/Galaxy/Scottish Coast* |
| Gross Tonnage | | | *4,858* |
| Builder | | | *Harland & Wolff (UK)* |
| Original Cost | | | *n/a* |
| Christened By | | | *Mr C. Loizou* |
| First Entered Service | | | *1957/1990* |
| Interior Design | | | *P. Yapanis* |
| Country of Registry | | | *Cyprus (P3NE3)* |
| Tel No | *n/a* | Fax No | *n/a* |
| Length (ft/m) | | | *342.2/104.32* |
| Beam (ft/m) | | | *52.6/16.06* |
| Draft (ft/m) | | | *15.7/4.81* |
| Engines/Propellers | | | *2 B&W diesels/2* |
| Decks | *6* | Crew | *130* |
| Pass. Capacity (basis 2) | *272* | (all berths) | *308* |
| Pass. Space Ratio (basis 2) | *17.8* | (all berths) | *15.7* |
| Officers | *Cypriot/Greek* | Dining Staff | *International* |
| Total Cabins | | | *136* |
| Size (sq ft/m) | *n/a* | Door Width | *22"* |
| Outside Cabins | *111* | Inside Cabins | *25* |
| Single Cabins | *0* | Supplement | *50%* |
| Balcony Cabins | *0* | Wheelchair Cabins | *0* |
| Cabin Current | | | *220 AC* |
| Refrigerator | | | *No* |
| Cabin TV | *No* | VCR | *No* |
| Dining Rooms | *1* | Sittings | *2* |
| Elevators | *0* | Door Width | *n/a* |

| | | | |
|---|---|---|---|
| Casino | *Yes* | Slot Machines | *Yes* |
| Swimming Pools (outside) | *1* | (inside) | *0* |
| Whirlpools | *0* | Gymnasium | *No* |
| Sauna/Steam Rm | *No/No* | Massage | *No* |
| Self-Service Launderette | | | *No* |
| Movie Theater/Seats | | | *No* |
| Library | | | *Yes* |
| Children's Facilities | | | *No* |
| Watersports Facilities | | | *None* |
| Classification Society | | | *Lloyd's Register* |

| RATINGS | SCORE |
|---|---|
| Ship: Condition/Cleanliness | 5.3 |
| Ship: Space/Flow/Comfort | 5.1 |
| Ship: Decor/Furnishings | 6.0 |
| Ship: Fitness Facilities | 4.0 |
| Cabins: Comfort/Facilities | 5.8 |
| Cabins: Software | 6.1 |
| Food: Dining Room/Cuisine | 5.7 |
| Food: Buffets/Informal Dining | 5.6 |
| Food: Quality of Ingredients | 5.6 |
| Service: Dining Room | 6.1 |
| Service: Bars/Lounges | 6.2 |
| Service: Cabins | 6.3 |
| Cruise: Entertainment | 5.0 |
| Cruise: Activities Program | 5.1 |
| Cruise: Hospitality Standard | 5.5 |
| OVERALL RATING | 83.4 |

**+** Most cabins are outside and are quite comfortable, with crisp Mediterranean colors and some wood trim, but they are small, and bathrooms are really tiny.

**–** Limited public room and facilities make it confining for trips of more than a few nights. Steep, narrow gangway in many ports. Long lines for buffets.

**Dining** Dining room has portholes, and is quite cheerful. Food is decidedly Mediterranean, with limited choice. Service is barely adequate, no more, although the staff do try hard.

**Other Comments** This small white ship is old and shows poor maintenance. Barely adequate amount of deck space. Public rooms have been refurbished. Earth-tone colors used to good effect, creating a mild sense of spaciousness. Cabins located above disco are noisy. This ship is crowded when full, but offers a reasonably pleasant short cruise experience if your expectations are not high. Insurance and gratuities are extra.

# mv Princesa Cypria ★★

*Principal Cruising Area*
*Mediterranean (3/4 nights)*
***Base Port:** Limassol*

| | | | |
|---|---|---|---|
| Cruise Line | | | *Louis Cruise Lines* |
| Former Names | | | *Asia Angel/Lu Jiang/ Princesse Margrethe* |
| Gross Tonnage | | | *7,896* |
| Builder | | | *Cantieri del Terreno (Italy)* |
| Original Cost | | | *n/a* |
| Christened By | | | *Mr C. Loizou* |
| First Entered Service | | | *1968/1989* |
| Interior Design | | | *A. Lozzi/P. Yapanis* |
| Country of Registry | | | *Cyprus (P3CQ3)* |
| Tel No | *n/a* | Fax No | *n/a* |
| Length (ft/m) | | | *409.9/124.95* |
| Beam (ft/m) | | | *63.3/19.31* |
| Draft (ft/m) | | | *17.8/5.43* |
| Engines/Propellers | | | *2 B&W diesels/2* |
| Decks | *6* | Crew | *210* |
| Pass. Capacity (basis 2) | *542* | (all berths) | *610* |
| Pass. Space Ratio (basis 2) | *14.5* | (all berths) | *12.9* |
| Officers | *Greek/Cypriot* | Dining Staff | *International* |
| Total Cabins | | | *271* |
| Size (sq ft/m) | *n/a* | Door Width | *24"* |
| Outside Cabins | *142* | Inside Cabins | *129* |
| Single Cabins | *0* | Supplement | *50%* |
| Balcony Cabins | *0* | Wheelchair Cabins | *0* |
| Cabin Current | *220 AC* | Refrigerator | *No* |
| Cabin TV | *No* | VCR | *No* |
| Dining Rooms | *2* | Sittings | *Open (Buffets)* |
| Elevators | *2* | Door Width | *30"* |

| | | | |
|---|---|---|---|
| Casino | *Yes* | Slot Machines | *Yes* |
| Swimming Pools (outside) | *0* | (inside) | *0* |
| Whirlpools | *0* | Gymnasium | *No* |
| Sauna/Steam Rm | *No/No* | Massage | *No* |
| Self-Service Launderette | | | *No* |
| Movie Theater/Seats | | | *No* |
| Library | | | *No* |
| Children's Facilities | | | *No* |
| Watersports Facilities | | | *None* |
| Classification Society | | | *Det Norske Veritas* |

| RATINGS | SCORE |
|---|---|
| Ship: Condition/Cleanliness | 5.1 |
| Ship: Space/Flow/Comfort | 5.4 |
| Ship: Decor/Furnishings | 6.1 |
| Ship: Fitness Facilities | 4.1 |
| Cabins: Comfort/Facilities | 6.2 |
| Cabins: Software | 6.3 |
| Food: Dining Room/Cuisine | 5.8 |
| Food: Buffets/Informal Dining | 5.7 |
| Food: Quality of Ingredients | 5.6 |
| Service: Dining Room | 6.0 |
| Service: Bars/Lounges | 6.2 |
| Service: Cabins | 6.3 |
| Cruise: Entertainment | 5.2 |
| Cruise: Activities Program | 5.0 |
| Cruise: Hospitality Standard | 5.5 |
| OVERALL RATING | 84.5 |

**+** Offers a low-cost way to visit several ports.

**–** Open deck and sunning space are inadequate. Poor exterior maintenance (but improving slowly). Furniture is worn and needs upgrading. Extremely high density ship means public rooms are always crowded. Low ceilings and too many support pillars create a rather confined feeling. Very small and spartan cabins, with virtually no closet and drawer space, many without private facilities. Bathrooms are tiny. Long lines for buffets and shore excursions.

**Dining** The dining room is set high up and forward and has large picture windows, while the second is set amidships. The food is adequate, and basic, but no more, and service comes without finesse. In a word: disappointing.

**Other Comments** Low foredeck is typical of this former ferry, whose profile is stubby and poorly balanced. Carries both cars and passengers on short voyages. This vessel is for cruisegoers looking for really low fares, and completely unpretentious surroundings, in a cruise that goes to the Holy Land. The company's slogan—"the ultimate in cruising"— is pure myth, although standards are improving. Port taxes, insurance, and gratuities are extra.

# mv Princesa Marissa ★★+

***Principal Cruising Area***
*Mediterranean (3/4 nights)*
***Base Port:*** *Limassol*

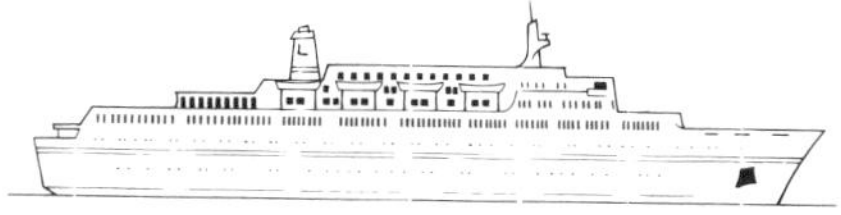

| | | | |
|---|---|---|---|
| Cruise Line | | | *Louis Cruise Lines* |
| Former Names | | | *Finnhansa/Princessan* |
| Gross Tonnage | | | *9,491* |
| Builder | | | *Wartsila (Finland)* |
| Original Cost | | | *n/a* |
| Christened By | | | *Mr C. Loizou* |
| First Entered Service | | | *1966/1990* |
| Interior Design | | | *G. Petrides/P. Yapanis* |
| Country of Registry | | | *Cyprus (P3HO2)* |
| Tel No | *n/a* | Fax No | *n/a* |
| Length (ft/m) | | | *441.0/134.42* |
| Beam (ft/m) | | | *65.3/19.92* |
| Draft (ft/m) | | | *17.7/5.40* |
| Engines/Propellers | | | *2 Sulzer diesels/2* |
| Decks | *9* | Crew | *230* |
| Pass. Capacity (basis 2) | *648* | (all berths) | *720* |
| Pass. Space Ratio (basis 2) | *14.6* | (all berths) | *13.1* |
| Officers | | | *Cypriot/Greek* |
| Dining Staff | | | *International* |
| Total Cabins | | | *324* |
| Size (sq ft/m) | *n/a* | Door Width | *22"* |
| Outside Cabins | *125* | Inside Cabins | *198* |
| Single Cabins | *0* | Supplement | *50%* |
| Balcony Cabins | *0* | Wheelchair Cabins | *0* |
| Cabin Current | *220 AC* | Refrigerator | *No* |
| Cabin TV | *No* | VCR | *No* |
| Dining Rooms | *2* | Sittings | *2* |
| Elevators | *1* | Door Width | *30"* |

| | | | |
|---|---|---|---|
| Casino | *Yes* | Slot Machines | *Yes* |
| Swimming Pools (outside) | *0* | (inside) | *0* |
| Whirlpools | *0* | Gymnasium | *No* |
| Sauna/Steam Rm | *Yes/No* | Massage | *No* |
| Self-Service Launderette | | | *No* |
| Movie Theater/Seats | | | *No* |
| Library | | | *No* |
| Children's Facilities | | | *Yes* |
| Watersports Facilities | | | *None* |
| Classification Society | | | *Det Norske Veritas* |

| RATINGS | SCORE |
|---|---|
| Ship: Condition/Cleanliness | 6.1 |
| Ship: Space/Flow/Comfort | 6.0 |
| Ship: Decor/Furnishings | 5.8 |
| Ship: Fitness Facilities | 5.6 |
| Cabins: Comfort/Facilities | 6.8 |
| Cabins: Software | 7.0 |
| Food: Dining Room/Cuisine | 5.8 |
| Food: Buffets/Informal Dining | 5.8 |
| Food: Quality of Ingredients | 5.3 |
| Service: Dining Room | 6.0 |
| Service: Bars/Lounges | 5.8 |
| Service: Cabins | 6.2 |
| Cruise: Entertainment | 5.1 |
| Cruise: Activities Program | 5.4 |
| Cruise: Hospitality Standard | 6.0 |
| OVERALL RATING | 88.7 |

**+** This former passenger-car ferry with square stern, twin funnels, and short, somewhat stubby bow also carries 95 cars. Public room decor is quite contemporary, with warm colors and extensive use of mirrored surfaces. Low-back chairs are uncomfortable.

**–** Very high passenger density—crowded at every turn, but especially when full. Low ceilings, typical of ferries. Very poor open deck and sunning space. Few crew for so many passengers. Cabins are the smallest on any cruise ship, and have virtually no closet, drawer, or storage space. Too many inside cabins, most without private facilities.

**Dining** Dining room is quite attractive, but service is basically buffet style. Dining room chairs are well worn.

**Other Comments** Features short Cyprus-Egypt-Israel cruises. This high density vessel has little to offer, other than basic transportation and low fares. Fine as a ferry, but not really a cruise ship. Insurance and gratuities are extra.

# mv Princesa Victoria ★★+

*Principal Cruising Areas*
*Egypt/Israel (2/3 nights)*
***Base Port:** Limassol*

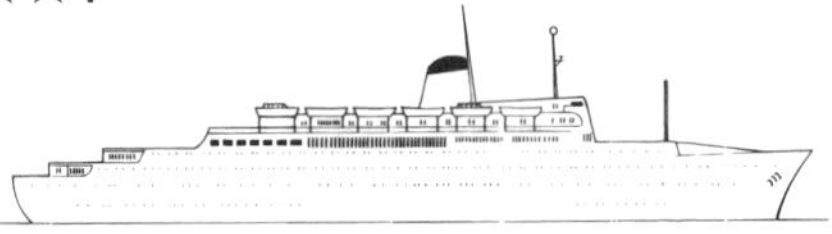

| | | | |
|---|---|---|---|
| Cruise Line | | | *Louis Cruise Lines* |
| Former Names | | | *The Victoria/Victoria/ Dunottar Castle* |
| Gross Tonnage | | | *14,917* |
| Builder | | | *Harland & Wolff (UK)* |
| Original Cost | | | *n/a* |
| Christened By | | | *n/a* |
| First Entered Service | | | *Jul 3, 1936/Feb 1993* |
| Interior Design | | | *A&M Katzourakis* |
| Country of Registry | | | *Cyprus (P3YG4)* |
| Tel No | *110-1627* | Fax No | *110-1630* |
| Length (ft/m) | | | *572.8/174.60* |
| Beam (ft/m) | | | *71.9/21.92* |
| Draft (ft/m) | | | *27.8/8.50* |
| Engines/Propellers | | | *2 GMT 7-cyl diesels/2* |
| Decks | *7* | Crew | *330* |
| Pass. Capacity (basis 2) | *564* | (all berths) | *650* |
| Pass. Space Ratio (basis 2) | *26.4* | (all berths) | *22.9* |
| Officers | *Cypriot/Greek* | Dining Staff | *International* |
| Total Cabins | | | *286* |
| Size (sq ft/m) | *n/a* | Door Width | *26"* |
| Outside Cabins | *216* | Inside Cabins | *70* |
| Single Cabins | *8* | Supplement | *50%* |
| Balcony Cabins | *0* | Wheelchair Cabins | *0* |
| Cabin Current | *115 AC* | Refrigerator | *No* |
| Cabin TV | *No* | VCR | *No* |
| Dining Rooms | *1* | Sittings | *2* |
| Elevators | *3* | Door Width | *26"* |

| | | | |
|---|---|---|---|
| Casino | *Yes* | Slot Machines | *Yes* |
| Swimming Pools (outside) | 2 | (inside) | *0* |
| Whirlpools | *0* | Gymnasium | *Yes* |
| Sauna/Steam Rm | *Yes/No* | Massage | *No* |
| Self-Service Launderette | | | *No* |
| Movie Theater/Seats | | | *Yes/250* |
| Library | | | *Yes* |
| Children's Facilities | | | *Yes* |
| Watersports Facilities | | | *None* |
| Classification Society | | | *Lloyd's Register* |

| RATINGS | SCORE |
|---|---|
| Ship: Condition/Cleanliness | 6.3 |
| Ship: Space/Flow/Comfort | 5.9 |
| Ship:Decor/Furnishings | 5.7 |
| Ship: Fitness Facilities | 5.6 |
| Cabins: Comfort/Facilities | 6.8 |
| Cabins: Software | 7.0 |
| Food: Dining Room/Cuisine | 5.8 |
| Food: Buffets/Informal Dining | 5.8 |
| Food: Quality of Ingredients | 5.3 |
| Service: Dining Room | 6.0 |
| Service: Bars/Lounges | 5.8 |
| Service: Cabins | 6.2 |
| Cruise: Entertainment | 5.6 |
| Cruise: Activities Program | 5.5 |
| Cruise: Hospitality Standard | 6.1 |
| OVERALL RATING | 89.4 |

**+** This ship has been well maintained, despite her age. The center stairway is real art deco style. Friendly ambiance. Cabins are quite spacious and feature heavy-duty furniture and fittings. Suite rooms are cavernous, and large bathrooms come with deep, full bathtubs. Attentive service.

**–** Public rooms are limited for a ship this size. Riviera Club is a contemporary room out of keeping with the rest of ship's public rooms, and colors are rather cold. Constant repetitive announcements are annoying. Poor separation of smokers and nonsmokers. Long lines for buffets.

**Dining** The dining room is set low down, but is extremely comfortable and has a fine two-deck-high center section, complete with music balcony. The standard of cuisine is simply adequate—quantity, not quality. Salads, pastries, and fruits are very poor.

**Other Comments** Solidly-constructed ship of vintage years with a classic liner profile. Good open deck space for sunning. Small, but well-patronized, casino. This ship provides a good cruise experience for first-time cruisers, in pleasant surroundings, and at a most realistic price. Offers good value cruising, and is the best ship in the fleet of this fledgling company. Insurance and gratuities are extra.

# tsmv Queen Elizabeth 2 ★★★★★+ to ★★★★

***Principal Cruising Areas***

*Transatlantic Service/Caribbean/Europe*

*(Transatlantic: 5-nights/cruises: various)*

***Base Ports:*** *New York/Southampton*

| | | | |
|---|---|---|---|
| Cruise Line | | | *Cunard* |
| Former Names | | | *n/a* |
| Gross Tonnage | | | *69,053* |
| Builder | | | *Upper Clyde Shipbuilders (UK)* |
| Original Cost | | | *£29,091,000* |
| Christened By | | | *H.M. Queen Elizabeth II* |
| First Entered Service | | | *May 2, 1969* |
| Interior Design | | | *Dennis Lennon & Partners* |
| Country of Registry | | | *Great Britain (GBTT)* |
| Tel No | *144-0412* | Fax No | *144-1331* |
| Length (ft/m) | | | *963.0/293.50* |
| Beam (ft/m) | *105.1/32.03* | Draft (ft/m) | *32.4/9.87* |
| Eng./Propellers | | | *9 MAN-B&W 9-cyl diesels/2 (CP)* |
| Decks | *13* | Crew | *1,015* |
| Pass. Capacity (basis 2) | *1,814* | (all berths) | *1,870* |
| Pass. Space Ratio (basis 2) | *38.0* | (all berths) | *36.9* |
| Officers | *British* | Dining Staff | *British/Intl* |
| Total Cabins | | | *957* |
| Size (sq ft/m) | *107-785/10-73* | Door Width | *26-31"* |
| Outside Cabins | *672* | Inside Cabins | *285* |
| Single Cabins | *110* | Supplement | *15-100%* |
| Balcony Cabins | *34* | Wheelchair Cabins | *2* |
| Cabin Current | | | *110/220 AC* |
| Refrigerator | | | *Signal/Sports/Boat Deck* |
| Cabin TV | *Yes* | VCR | *Yes* |
| Dining Rooms | *5* | Sittings | *1* |
| Elevators | *13* | Door Width | *36-50"* |
| Casino | *Yes* | Slot Machines | *Yes* |
| Swimming Pools (outside) | *2* | (inside) | *2* |
| Whirlpools | *4* | Gymnasium | *Yes* |
| Sauna/Steam Rm | *Yes/No* | Massage | *Yes* |
| Self-Service Launderette | | | *Yes* |
| Movie Theater/Seats | | | *Yes/531* |
| Library | | | *Yes* |
| Children's Facilities | | | *Yes* |
| Watersports Facilities | | | *None* |
| Classification Society | | | *Lloyd's Register* |
| Ratings: | | | Classes *(a)Grill (b)First (c)Transatlantic* |

| RATINGS SCORE | (a) | (b) | (c) |
|---|---|---|---|
| Ship: Condition/Cleanliness | 9.1 | 8.8 | 7.3 |
| Ship: Space/Flow/Comfort | 9.0 | 8.4 | 7.5 |
| Ship: Decor/Furnishings | 9.1 | 8.5 | 7.5 |
| Ship: Fitness Facilities | 9.0 | 9.0 | 9.0 |
| Cabins: Comfort/Facilities | 9.1 | 8.3 | 7.2 |
| Cabins: Software | 9.0 | 8.6 | 7.5 |
| Food: Dining Room/Cuisine | 9.6 | 7.7 | 6.2 |
| Food: Buffets/Informal Dining | 8.7 | 8.1 | 6.4 |
| Food: Quality of Ingredients | 9.3 | 8.1 | 6.6 |
| Service: Dining Room | 9.2 | 7.1 | 6.1 |
| Service: Bars/Lounges | 9.0 | 8.6 | 7.5 |
| Service: Cabins | 9.1 | 8.5 | 7.1 |
| Cruise: Entertainment | 8.5 | 8.5 | 8.6 |
| Cruise: Activities Program | 8.6 | 8.4 | 8.6 |
| Cruise: Hospitality Standard | 9.2 | 8.2 | 6.2 |
| OVERALL RATING | 135.5 | 124.8 | 109.3 |

**+** She is the only regularly scheduled transatlantic liner still in service, and still the fastest cruise ship in the world.

**–** Expect lines for embarkation, disembarkation, shore tenders, buffets, and (at peak times) elevators. Has two sittings in the Mauretania Restaurant. Baggage delivery could be improved.

**Dining** There are, at present, five restaurants (which include many tables for two), assigned according to the grade of cabin booked. The menus are always varied and well balanced.

**Other Comments** She is a special, dual-purpose superliner that performs a regular schedule of 26 transatlantic crossings as well as several cruises each year, together with an annual round-the-world cruise from January to April. Originally constructed as a steam turbine ship, in 1986, her turbines were extracted and exchanged for a diesel-electric propulsion system, resulting in greater speed, economy, and reliability. At the end of 1994, she is to undergo a $45 million interior refurbishment. All cabin bathrooms are to be replaced, and several new suites will be added. There will be an enlarged library, a new bookshop (an excellent idea), and a florist. The Club-Lido magrodome-covered pool will be replaced by a new, informal, bistro-like dining area. The Mauretania (Transatlantic Class) will move from Upper Deck to the Quarter Deck and a new Captain's Dining Area will be added. The Columbia restaurant (First Class) will be moved upstairs to become the Caronia. The Grill Rooms will remain, but a new, private "key club" will

be created. A new card room, observation lounge and bar, and a new pub are all planned, and a new sports deck will be created atop ship. When completed, the enhancements should add further space and grace to her pace.

**Transatlantic Crossings** At speeds over 30 knots some vibration is evident at the stern, as on any fast ship. She features the most extensive facilities of any passenger ship afloat and carries up to 40 cars. She is a city at sea, and, like any city, there are many parts of town. Although the brochure gives two classes for transatlantic travel (First Class and Transatlantic Class), there are in fact three: Grill Class, First Class, and Transatlantic Class. Grill Class accommodations consist of penthouse suites (with real butler service) and luxury outside cabins, with dining in one of three grill rooms—Queens Grill and Princess Grills I and II (five star). First Class accommodations consist of outside double cabins, and inside and outside single cabins, with dining in the Columbia Restaurant (four star). Transatlantic Class accommodations feature lower-priced cabin grades, with two-sitting dining in the Mauretania restaurant (three star). All other restaurants have single, open sitting dining. All passengers enjoy the use of all public rooms, except the Queens Grill Lounge, reserved for Grill Class passengers. The expanded Queens Grill (tables are very close together) has a separate galley, best waiters and service, a very formal atmosphere, and food that can be rated among the world's best when ordered off-menu. The Princess Grills and Columbia restaurant share a galley (Kosher food is available, from a Kosher chef), but service in the intimate Princess Grills is superior. The Mauretania restaurant has an improved menu and food but service lacks finesse. Grill Class and First Class passengers have separate deck space and assigned chairs, but sit with other passengers for major shows and other entertainment and functions. Grill Class is an elegant way to cross the Atlantic; First Class isn't what it used to be; Transatlantic Class is mass-market transportation, albeit in a fine setting. However, in the final analysis, this is the last of the transatlantic liners and a wonderful experience.

**Cruises** The penthouse suites are superb. The dramatic Grand Lounge has three tiers, a horseshoe-shaped staircase, and a high-tech sound and light system. The Teen Center, Adult Center, and Sporting Center are clustered together aft, close to the outdoor sports facilities. The shopping concourse is decorated in art deco style, and features a walk-through brand name open shopping area with European prices. An Executive Board Room is available. The Yacht Club is delightfully nautical. It has an extensive safety deposit center and passenger accounts office, and an automated telephone system. Midships Lobby now has one of the elegant pianos from the *Queen Mary*. The large computer center is a real bonus. Club Lido indoor-outdoor center is good for the young at heart. Elegant Midships Bar. Nicely refurbished theater. The superb professionally-run library (over 6,000 books, in five languages) should be extended into the former card room. Player's Club Casino has expanded dramatically, and now features fitting art deco decor. The new health spa is excellent. Synagogue. British officers and seamanship, but hotel staff have changed to an international mix, quite attentive and service-oriented, though many don't speak English well. Consistently fine quality entertainment and lecture programs. One class only for cruises. One sitting in all dining rooms except Mauretania. Improved cuisine. Luncheon and midnight buffets are improved, but long lines for both. Cashless cruising. Fine English nannies and children's facilities. Refined living at sea for those in upper grade accommodations; otherwise it's just a big ship with superb facilities. *Queen Elizabeth 2* is the most perfectly integrated ship afloat. Tender ports should be avoided, however. Newer staff need more training and direction. After a refit in 1994, the public rooms and passenger facilities and color-coordinations will have improved.

# ssc Radisson Diamond ★★★★★

***Principal Cruising Areas***

*Caribbean/Mediterranean (4/5/7 nights)*

***Base Ports:*** *San Juan/Nice*

| | | | |
|---|---|---|---|
| Cruise Line | | | *Diamond Cruises* |
| Former Names | | | *n/a* |
| Gross Tonnage | | | *20,295* |
| Builder | | | *Rauma Yards (Finland)* |
| Original Cost | | | *$125 million* |
| Christened By | | | *Dame Kiri Te Kanawa* |
| First Entered Service | | | *May 31, 1992* |
| Interior Design | | | *Vincent Kwok Interiors* |
| Country of Registry | | | *Finland (OJDO)* |
| Tel No | *162-3243* | Fax No | *162-3252* |
| Length (ft/m) | | | *423.2/129.00* |
| Beam (ft/m) | *104.9/32.00* | Draft (ft/m) | *26.2/8.00* |
| Engines | | | *2 Wartsila 8-cyl diesels* |
| Propellers | | | *2 nozzles* |
| Decks | *6* | Crew | *192* |
| Pass. Capacity (basis 2) | *354* | (all berths) | *354* |
| Pass. Space Ratio (basis 2) | *57.3* | (all berths) | *57.3* |
| Officers | | | *Finnish/American* |
| Dining Staff | | | *American/International* |
| Total Cabins | | | *177* |
| Size (sq ft/m) | *220/20.5* | Door Width | *27"* |
| Outside Cabins | *177* | Inside Cabins | *0* |
| Single Cabins | *0* | Supplement | *25-50%* |
| Balcony Cabins | *123* | Wheelchair Cabins | *2* |
| Cabin Current | *110/220 AC* | Refrigerator | *Yes* |
| Cabin TV | *Yes* | VCR | *Yes* |
| Dining Rooms | *1* | Sittings | *Open* |
| Elevators | *3* | Door Width | *38"* |

| | | | |
|---|---|---|---|
| Casino | *Yes* | Slot Machines | *Yes* |
| Swimming Pools (outside) | *1* | (inside) | *0* |
| Whirlpools | *1* | Gymnasium | *Yes* |
| Sauna/Steam Rm | *Yes/Yes* | Massage | *Yes* |
| Self-Service Launderette | | | *No* |
| Movie Theater/Seats | | | *No* |
| Library | *Yes* | Children's Facilities | *No* |
| Watersports Facilities | | | *Retractable aft marina, jet-ski, water-ski* |
| Classification Society | | | *Det Norske Veritas* |

| RATINGS | SCORE |
|---|---|
| Ship: Condition/Cleanliness | 9.1 |
| Ship: Space/Flow/Comfort | 8.6 |
| Ship: Decor/Furnishings | 8.4 |
| Ship: Fitness Facilities | 6.8 |
| Cabins: Comfort/Facilities | 9.2 |
| Cabins: Software | 8.8 |
| Food: Dining Room/Cuisine | 9.1 |
| Food: Buffets/Informal Dining | 9.0 |
| Food: Quality of Ingredients | 9.0 |
| Service: Dining Room | 8.8 |
| Service: Bars/Lounges | 8.1 |
| Service: Cabins | 9.2 |
| Cruise: Entertainment | 7.3 |
| Cruise: Activities Program | 6.7 |
| Cruise: Hospitality Standard | 8.2 |
| OVERALL RATING | 126.3 |

**+** Innovative design and sophisticated business center and facilities, ideal for small groups and conventions. Four stabilizing fins, so motion is theoretically minimized. Outstanding passenger space. Five-deck-high atrium with glass-enclosed elevators. Underwater viewing area. Outdoor jogging track. Beautifully designed, spacious, and well-equipped all-outside cabins, most with private balconies, are all furnished in blond woods, with marble bathroom vanities and full bathtub. Bay windows in 47 suites.

**–** Many public rooms are inside. Maximum speed of 12.5 knots is slow. Awkward contra-flow interior staircase. Multi-level entertainment room is awkward. Excellent health spa facilities, but they can't be reached by elevator. Very uncomfortable chairs in the main dining room.

**Dining** The two-deck-high dining room has a 270 degree view over the stern, and open seating. Cuisine quality and food presentation are European, and outstanding. Health foods and dietary specials. Excellent wine list. The Grill is an casual indoor/outdoor dining spot that features superb home-made pasta dishes. Dining is a pleasure on this ship.

**Other Comments** This semi-submersible twin-hulled cruise vessel is the first of its kind in the world. It offers high standards of service in sophisticated and personable, yet somewhat bland, surroundings. Insurance and gratuities are extra.

# ms Regal Empress ★★★

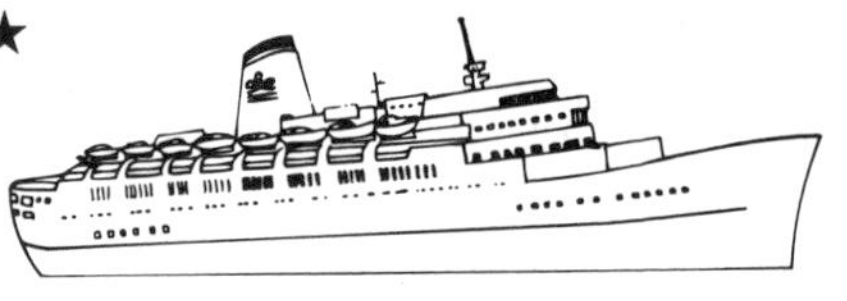

***Principal Cruising Areas***

*Bermuda/Caribbean (2-7 nights)*

***Base Ports:*** *New York/Tampa*

| | | | |
|---|---|---|---|
| Cruise Line | | | *Regal Cruises* |
| Former Names | | | *Caribe I/Olympia* |
| Gross Tonnage | | | *22,979* |
| Builder | | | *Alex Stephen & Son (UK)* |
| Original Cost | | | *n/a* |
| Christened By | | | *HRH Queen Frederica* |
| First Entered Service | | | *Oct 15, 1953/May 14, 1993* |
| Interior Design | | | *n/a* |
| Country of Registry | | | *Panama (3EIC2)* |
| Tel No | *n/a* | Fax No | *n/a* |
| Length (ft/m) | | | *611.8/186.50* |
| Beam (ft/m) | | | *79.0/24.10* |
| Draft (ft/m) | | | *28.2/8.60* |
| Engines/Propellers | | | *4 Deutz 12-cyl diesels/2* |
| Decks | *8* | Crew | *345* |
| Pass. Capacity (basis 2) | *875* | (all berths) | *1,160* |
| Pass. Space Ratio (basis 2) | *26.2* | (all berths) | *19.8* |
| Officers | *European* | Dining Staff | *International* |
| Total Cabins | | | *451* |
| Size (sq ft/m) | | | *105-295/9.7-27.5* |
| Door Width | | | *28-32"* |
| Outside Cabins | *226* | Inside Cabins | *225* |
| Single Cabins | *9* | Supplement | *100%* |
| Balcony Cabins | *0* | Wheelchair Cabins | *1* |
| Cabin Current | *110 AC* | Refrigerator | *No* |
| Cabin TV | *No* | VCR | *No* |
| Dining Rooms | *1* | Sittings | *2* |
| Elevators | *3* | Door Width | *36"* |

| | | | |
|---|---|---|---|
| Casino | *Yes* | Slot Machines | *Yes* |
| Swimming Pools (outside) | *1* | (inside) | *0* |
| Whirlpools | *2* | Gymnasium | *Yes* |
| Sauna/Steam Rm | *No/No* | Massage | *No* |
| Self-Service Launderette | | | *No* |
| Movie Theater/Seats | | | *Yes/166* |
| Library | | | *Yes* |
| Children's Facilities | | | *Yes* |
| Watersports Facilities | | | *None* |
| Classification Society | | | *Det Norske Veritas* |

| RATINGS | SCORE |
|---|---|
| Ship: Condition/Cleanliness | 5.7 |
| Ship: Space/Flow/Comfort | 5.9 |
| Ship: Decor/Furnishings | 6.5 |
| Ship: Fitness Facilities | 5.0 |
| Cabins: Comfort/Facilities | 6.5 |
| Cabins: Software | 6.3 |
| Food: Dining Room/Cuisine | 6.3 |
| Food: Buffets/Informal Dining | 5.8 |
| Food: Quality of Ingredients | 5.7 |
| Service: Dining Room | 6.3 |
| Service: Bars/Lounges | 6.2 |
| Service: Cabins | 6.6 |
| Cruise: Entertainment | 6.0 |
| Cruise: Activities Program | 5.8 |
| Cruise: Hospitality Standard | 6.4 |
| OVERALL RATING | 91.0 |

**+** This 40-year-old ship has a good traditional ocean liner profile, with a newer, yet more traditional, funnel than the initial effort. Good open deck space for sun-lovers, although very crowded when the ship is full. Good, polished teak decking. Enclosed promenade decks are popular. Fine satin woods and brass on the staircases. Superb library with untouched, original paneling.

**–** Steep, narrow gangway in some ports. No covered lifeboats/tenders. Expect long lines for embarkation, disembarkation, and buffets. Awkward layout.

**Dining** Lovely old-world dining room is a step back in time to a more gracious era, with its original oil paintings on burnished wood paneling, ornate lighting fixtures, etched glass panels, and original murals depicting New York and Rio. Most tables are for groups of six or more, with a few tables for four. Smoking and nonsmoking sections are provided on the starboard and port sides respectively. Food is plentiful, and to quite a good standard for the price, with the exception of the buffets, which are rough.

**Other Comments** Large, lively casino. Cabins are quite roomy, with good closet and reasonable drawer space, and heavy-duty fittings. Service is good, but there's absolutely no finesse. This ship will provide you with a cruise in comfortable, but not elegant, surroundings, at a modest price. Good for those seeking old world charm. Insurance and gratuities are extra.

# ms Regal Princess ★★★★+

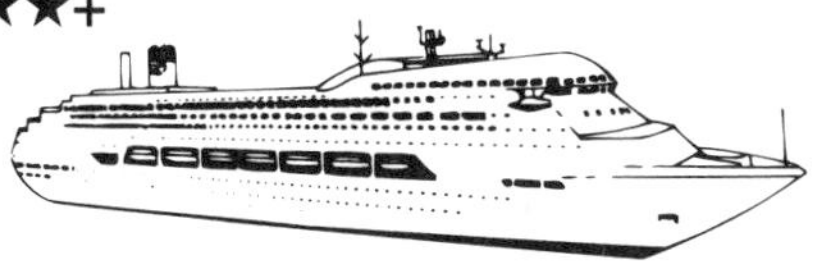

***Principal Cruising Areas***

*Alaska/Caribbean (7 nights)*

***Base Ports:*** *Vancouver/Ft. Lauderdale*

| | | | |
|---|---|---|---|
| Cruise Line | | | *Princess Cruises* |
| Former Names | | | *n/a* |
| Gross Tonnage | | | *70,000* |
| Builder | | | *Fincantieri Navali (Italy)* |
| Original Cost | | | *$276.8 million* |
| Christened By | | | *Mrs Margaret Thatcher* |
| First Entered Service | | | *Aug 17, 1991* |
| Interior Design | | | *H. Chambers Company* |
| Country of Registry | | | *Liberia (ICGP)* |
| Tel No | *124-5712* | Fax No | *124-5712* |
| Length (ft/m) | | | *803.8/245.00* |
| Beam (ft/m) | | | *105.6/32.20* |
| Draft (ft/m) | | | *25.5/7.80* |
| *Engines/Propellers* | | | *4 MAN-B&W diesels/2* |
| Decks | *12* | Crew | *696* |
| Pass. Capacity (basis 2) | *1,590* | (all berths) | *1,910* |
| Pass. Space Ratio (basis 2) | *44.0* | (all berths) | *36.6* |
| Officers | *Italian* | Dining Staff | *Intl* |
| Total Cabins | | | *795* |
| Size (sq ft/m) | *190-587/17.6-54.5* | Door Width | *24"* |
| Outside Cabins | *624* | Inside Cabins | *171* |
| Single Cabins | *0* | Supplement | *25-100%* |
| Balcony Cabins | *184* | Wheelchair Cabins | *10* |
| Cabin Current | | | *110/220 AC* |
| Refrigerator | | | *All cabins* |
| Cabin TV | *Yes* | VCR | *No* |
| Dining Rooms | *1* | Sittings | *2* |
| Elevators | *9* | Door Width | *46-53"* |

| | | | |
|---|---|---|---|
| Casino | *Yes* | Slot Machines | *Yes* |
| Swimming Pools (outside) | *2* | (inside) | *0* |
| Whirlpools | *4* | Gymnasium | *Yes* |
| Sauna/Steam Rm | *Yes/No* | Massage | *Yes* |
| Self-Service Launderette | | | *Yes* |
| Movie Theater/Seats | | | *Yes/169* |
| Library | | | *Yes* |
| Children's Facilities | | | *No* |
| Watersports Facilities | | | *None* |
| Classification Society | | | *Lloyd's Register* |

| RATINGS | SCORE |
|---|---|
| Ship: Condition/Cleanliness | 8.0 |
| Ship: Space/Flow/Comfort | 7.8 |
| Ship: Decor/Furnishings | 8.1 |
| Ship: Fitness Facilities | 8.0 |
| Cabins: Comfort/Facilities | 8.1 |
| Cabins: Software | 8.2 |
| Food: Dining Room/Cuisine | 7.4 |
| Food: Buffets/Informal Dining | 7.2 |
| Food: Quality of Ingredients | 7.0 |
| Service: Dining Room | 7.5 |
| Service: Bars/Lounges | 7.7 |
| Service: Cabins | 7.9 |
| Cruise: Entertainment | 8.1 |
| Cruise: Activities Program | 7.8 |
| Cruise: Hospitality Standard | 7.6 |
| OVERALL RATING | 116.4 |

**+** Innovative styling blended with traditional features. Bathrobes for all passengers. Superb, huge, dolphin-shaped observation dome houses the casino, but it doesn't work as a nightclub. The striking, elegant, three-deck-high atrium is practical, spacious, and well designed. Well co-ordinated colors and sumptuous carpeting. Flowers everywhere. Lovely artwork helps create an intimate atmosphere. Plenty of public rooms, but most have pillars obstructing flow and sight-lines. Well-designed accommodations, with ample drawer and hanging space, and excellent bath-rooms. Prompt, attentive room service. Good ticket documentation.

**–** Crowded outdoor sunning space. Disjointed layout. No wrap-around outdoor promenade deck. Poor ceiling insulation in suites and mini-suites. Cabins for the physically challenged have obstructed views. Long lines for embarkation, disembarkation, shore tenders, and buffets.

**Dining** This ship has a quieter dining hall than on the *Crown*, but is still noisy, and there are no tables for two. Unfortunately, the food quality is not as good as one would expect from this company, although improvements are expected soon. Poor bread and fruits.

**Other Comments** Sister ship to the *Crown Princess*, with the same appearance and upright funnel. Twin pools. Excellent drinks in the Characters Bar. Ideal for those who want a big ship around them, but there's little contact with the outside. Insurance and gratuities are extra.

# mv Regent Jewel

***Principal Cruising Areas***

*Europe/South East Asia (7,14/7 nights)*

***Base Ports:*** *Istanbul/Piraeus*

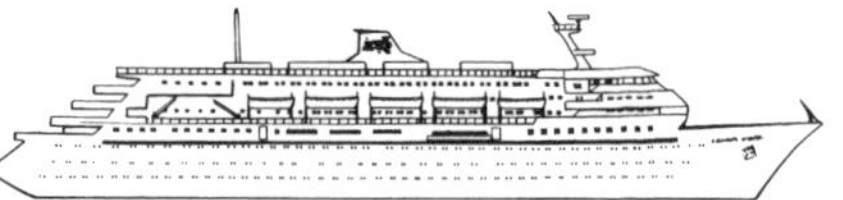

| | | | |
|---|---|---|---|
| Cruise Line | | | *Regency Cruises* |
| Former Names | | | *Sun Fiesta/Canguro Verde, Durr* |
| Gross Tonnage | | | *8,000* |
| Builder | | | *Fincantieri (Italy)* |
| Original Cost | | | *n/a* |
| Christened By | | | *n/a* |
| First Entered Service | | | *1968/Jun 26, 1994* |
| Interior Design | | | *A&M Katzourakis* |
| Country of Registry | | | *Bahamas* |
| Tel No | *n/a* | Fax No | *n/a* |
| Length (ft/m) | | | *425.0 ft/129.5* |
| Beam (ft/m) | | | *63.0/19.2* |
| Draft (ft/m) | | | *17.7/5.4* |
| Engines/Propellers | | | *2 GMT diesels/2 (CP)* |
| Decks | *8* | Crew | *240* |
| Pass. Capacity (basis 2) | *502* | (all berths) | *618* |
| Pass. Space Ratio (basis 2) | *15.9* | (all berths) | *12.9* |
| Officers | | | *Greek/European* |
| Dining Staff | | | *European/Intl* |
| Total Cabins | | | *251* |
| Size (sq ft/m) | *135-244/12.5-22.6* | Door Width | 24" |
| Outside Cabins | *158* | Inside Cabins | *93* |
| Single Cabins | *0* | Supplement | *40-100%* |
| Balcony Cabins | *0* | Wheelchair Cabins | *2* |
| Cabin Current | *110 AC* | Refrigerator | *No* |
| Cabin TV | *Yes* | VCR | *No* |
| Dining Rooms | *1* | Sittings | *2* |
| Elevators | *2* | Door Width | 30" |

| | | | |
|---|---|---|---|
| Casino | *Yes* | Slot Machines | *Yes* |
| Swimming Pools (outside) | *1* | (inside) | *0* |
| Whirlpools | *1* | Gymnasium | *Yes* |
| Sauna/Steam Rm | *No/No* | Massage | *Yes* |
| Self-Service Launderette | | | *No* |
| Movie Theater/Seats | | | *No* |
| Library | | | *Yes* |
| Children's Facilities | | | *No* |
| Watersports Facilities | | | *None* |
| Classification Society | | | |

| RATINGS | SCORE |
|---|---|
| Ship: Condition/Cleanliness | NYR |
| Ship: Space/Flow/Comfort | NYR |
| Ship: Decor/Furnishings | NYR |
| Ship: Fitness Facilities | NYR |
| Cabins: Comfort/Facilities | NYR |
| Cabins: Software | NYR |
| Food: Dining Room/Cuisine | NYR |
| Food: Buffets/Informal Dining | NYR |
| Food: Quality of Ingredients | NYR |
| Service: Dining Room | NYR |
| Service: Bars/Lounges | NYR |
| Service: Cabins | NYR |
| Cruise: Entertainment | NYR |
| Cruise: Activities Program | NYR |
| Cruise: Hospitality Standard | NYR |

NYR = Not Yet Rated

**+** Newly-constructed ship, featuring an enclosed promenade deck. Has a good number and range of public rooms for ship size. The mostly outside cabins are quite attractive, with pastel colours, but the fabrics and soft furnishings could be of better quality. Cabin bathrooms have showers. No cabins have bathtubs. Some 66 cabins have double beds, while others are twins, with many featuring third and fourth births.

**—** Very high density ship means it's really crowded when full, so expect long lines for embarkation, disembarkation, shore excursions, and buffets. Limited number of public rooms. Tiny outdoor pool. Cabins are quite small, and barely adequate.

**Dining** Same comments as other Regency Cruises ships. Poor selection of fruit in cabins, and limited room service menu.

**Other Comments** This former Strintzis Line ferry was refurbished in Greece, but her profile is not an attractive one. Regency Cruises has such a diverse fleet that it's hard to find consistency. Insurance and gratuitites are extra.

# ss Regent Rainbow ★★★

***Principal Cruising Areas***

*Mexican Caribbean/Alaska (4-7 nights)*

***Base Ports:*** *Tampa/Vancouver*

| | | | |
|---|---|---|---|
| Cruise Line | *Regency Cruises* | | |
| Former Names | *Diamond Island/ Santa Rosa/Samos Sky* | | |
| Gross Tonnage | *24,851* | | |
| Builder | *Newport News Shipbuilding (USA)* | | |
| Original Cost | *$25 million* | | |
| Christened By | *Mrs J. Peter Grace* | | |
| First Entered Service | *Jun 12, 1958/Jan 22, 1993* | | |
| Interior Design | *Polly Pahyanni* | | |
| Country of Registry | *Bahamas (C6HX6)* | | |
| Tel No | *130-5570/1/2* | Fax No | *130-5573* |
| Length (ft/m) | *599.0/182.57* | | |
| Beam (ft/m) | *84.0/25.6* | Draft (ft/m) | *27.5/8.38* |
| Engines | *2 General Electric steam turbines* | | |
| Propellers | *2* | | |
| Decks | *10* | Crew | *420* |
| Pass. Capacity (basis 2) | *956* | (all berths) | *1,168* |
| Pass. Space Ratio (basis 2) | *25.8* | (all berths) | *21.4* |
| Officers | *Greek/European* | Dining Staff | *Intl* |
| Total Cabins | *484* | | |
| Size (sq ft/m) | *125-305/11.6-28.3* | | |
| Door Width | *25-29"* | | |
| Outside Cabins | *329* | Inside Cabins | *155* |
| Single Cabins | *12* | Supplement | *40-100%* |
| Balcony Cabins | *0* | Wheelchair Cabins | *2* |
| Cabin Current | *110/220 AC* | Refrigerator | *Suites* |
| Cabin TV | *Yes* | VCR | *No* |
| Dining Rooms | *1* | Sittings | *2* |

| | | | |
|---|---|---|---|
| Elevators | *3* | Door Width | *31"* |
| Casino | *Yes* | Slot Machines | *Yes* |
| Swimming Pools (outside) | *1* | (inside) | *0* |
| Whirlpools | *2* | Gymnasium | *Yes (tiny)* |
| Sauna/Steam Rm | *Yes/No* | Massage | *Yes* |
| Self-Service Launderette | *No* | | |
| Movie Theater/Seats | *No* | | |
| Library | *Yes* | Children's Facilities | *Yes* |
| Watersports Facilities | *None* | | |
| Classification Society | *American Bur. of Shipping* | | |

| RATINGS | SCORE |
|---|---|
| Ship: Condition/Cleanliness | 6.4 |
| Ship: Space/Flow/Comfort | 6.3 |
| Ship: Decor/Furnishings | 6.8 |
| Ship: Fitness Facilities | 4.0 |
| Cabins: Comfort/Facilities | 6.3 |
| Cabins: Software | 6.6 |
| Food: Dining Room/Cuisine | 7.4 |
| Food: Buffets/Informal Dining | 6.8 |
| Food: Quality of Ingredients | 6.9 |
| Service: Dining Room | 7.0 |
| Service: Bars/Lounges | 7.0 |
| Service: Cabins | 6.2 |
| Cruise: Entertainment | 5.6 |
| Cruise: Activities Program | 6.0 |
| Cruise: Hospitality Standard | 6.0 |
| OVERALL RATING | 95.3 |

**+** Wrap-around outdoor promenade. Very pleasant, surprisingly comfortable, and warm interior decor that is contemporary without being brash, but the artwork is cheap. Original cabins are quite spacious, with good closet and drawer space.

**–** She's high sided, with a narrow beam, and rolls in poor weather. With new upper decks added, her new profile is not handsome. Very poor open deck and sunning space. High density ship means little room to move about in when full. Newly added cabins are smaller and have very poor insulation. Large casino with high ceiling, and adjacent poker room, are very lively.

**Dining** The dining room has large picture windows and a neat orchestra balcony (with an awful piano). Food quality and presentation are good for the budget provided. Service is friendly, yet somewhat perfunctory.

**Other Comments** Former American-built liner has had a great amount of reconstruction ($72 million) in 1992 in Greece, after being laid up for over ten years. Squat funnel is awkward, although the conversion was a practical one. Low-budget entertainment is generally of poor quality. For short cruises, however, the ship provides a range of public spaces that promotes a good party ambiance. Insurance and gratuities are extra.

# mv Regent Sea ★★★

***Principal Cruising Areas***

*Alaska/Caribbean (7 nights)*

**Base Ports:** Vancouver/Tampa

| | | | |
|---|---|---|---|
| Cruise Line | | | *Regency Cruises* |
| Former Names | | | *Samantha/San Paolo/ Navarino/Gripsholm* |
| Gross Tonnage | | | *22,785* |
| Builder | | | *Ansaldo Sestri-Ponente (Italy)* |
| Original Cost | | | *£7,000,000* |
| Christened By | | | *Princess Margarethe/Robert Stack* |
| First Entered Service | | | *May 14, 1957/Nov 17, 1985* |
| Interior Design | | | *Patricia Hayes & Associates* |
| Country of Registry | | | *Bahamas (C6117)* |
| Tel No | *110-3126* | Fax No | *110-3257* |
| Length (ft/m) | | | *631.2/192.41* |
| Beam (ft/m) | | | *81.8/24.95* |
| Draft (ft/m) | | | *27.8/8.49* |
| Engines/Propellers | | | *2 Gotaverken 9-cyl diesels/2* |
| Decks | *8* | Crew | *365* |
| Pass. Capacity (basis 2) | *715* | (all berths) | *760* |
| Pass. Space Ratio (basis 2) | *31.8* | (all berths) | *29.9* |
| Officers | *European* | Dining Staff | *Intl* |
| Total Cabins | | | *358* |
| Size (sq ft/m) | *172-280/16-26* | Door Width | *31"* |
| Outside Cabins | *335* | Inside Cabins | *25* |
| Single Cabins | *1* | Supplement | *30-100%* |
| Balcony Cabins | *0* | Wheelchair Cabins | *3* |
| Cabin Current | | | *110 AC* |
| Refrigerator | | | *Suites* |
| Cabin TV | *No* | VCR | *No* |
| Dining Rooms | *2* | Sittings | *2* |

| | | | |
|---|---|---|---|
| Elevators | *4* | Door Width | *26"* |
| Casino | *Yes* | Slot Machines | *Yes* |
| Swimming Pools (outside) | *1* | (inside) | *0* |
| Whirlpools | *2* | Gymnasium | *Yes* |
| Sauna/Steam Rm | *Yes/No* | Massage | *Yes* |
| Self-Service Launderette | | | *No* |
| Movie Theater/Seats | | | *Yes/218* |
| Library | *Yes* | Children's Facilities | *No* |
| Watersports Facilities | | | *None* |
| Classification Society | | | *Lloyd's Register* |

| RATINGS | SCORE |
|---|---|
| Ship: Condition/Cleanliness | 6.0 |
| Ship: Space/Flow/Comfort | 7.1 |
| Ship: Decor/Furnishings | 6.4 |
| Ship: Fitness Facilities | 5.3 |
| Cabins: Comfort/Facilities | 5.8 |
| Cabins: Software | 6.7 |
| Food: Dining Room/Cuisine | 7.4 |
| Food: Buffets/Informal Dining | 6.8 |
| Food: Quality of Ingredients | 6.9 |
| Service: Dining Room | 7.0 |
| Service: Bars/Lounges | 7.1 |
| Service: Cabins | 6.4 |
| Cruise: Entertainment | 5.6 |
| Cruise: Activities Program | 6.0 |
| Cruise: Hospitality Standard | 6.2 |
| OVERALL RATING | 96.7 |

**+** Well-constructed former ocean liner has classic lines and styling, and is one of only a handful of two-funnel ships. Generous open deck and sunning space, with good teakwood decking and railings. Rich, burnished wood trim in good condition. Public rooms are spacious and well equipped. Wide array of public rooms, including indoor garden palm courts. Good indoor pool and spa facilities. European flair is evident in the decor, furnishings, and colors. Nicely paneled library. The mostly outside cabins are of generous proportions, with ample drawer and closet space. Most beds parallel the ship's axis. Large cabins have heavy duty fittings. Friendly, comfortable ambiance throughout.

**–** Looks tired and shabby. Awkward layout and flow, due to conversion from former two-class liner. Stale cigarette smoke odor everywhere. Most Sun Deck cabins have lifeboat-obstructed views. Cabins need better cleaning. Long lines for buffets and shore tenders.

**Dining** Bright and cheerful dining room features portholes. Open seating for breakfast and lunch. Many improvements, and the cuisine is American-Continental, with a nice French accent, but the company only provides a low budget for its food.

**Other Comments** Reasonably attentive service. This ship will provide cruising in a good style, and at a modest price. Insurance and gratuities are extra.

# mv Regent Spirit ★★★

***Principal Cruising Areas***

*Caribbean/Mediterranean (7/7,14 nights)*

***Base Ports:*** *Cozumel/Nice*

| | | | |
|---|---|---|---|
| Cruise Line | | | *Regency Cruises* |
| Former Names | | | *Constellation/Danaos/Anna Nery* |
| Gross Tonnage | | | *12,433* |
| Builder | | | *Brod Uljanik (Yugoslavia)* |
| Original Cost | | | *n/a* |
| Christened By | | | *n/a* |
| First Entered Service | | | *Aug 27, 1962/Nov 20, 1993* |
| Interior Design | | | *A&M Katzourakis* |
| Country of Registry | | | *Bahamas* |
| Tel No | *130-5421* | Fax No | *130-5422* |
| Length (ft/m) | | | *492.1/150.00* |
| Beam (ft/m) | | | *62.3/19.00* |
| Draft (ft/m) | | | *18.3/5.60* |
| Engines/Propellers | | | *2 B&W 7-cyl diesels/2* |
| Decks | *8* | Crew | *230* |
| Pass. Capacity (basis 2) | *422* | (all berths) | *532* |
| Pass. Space Ratio (basis 2) | *29.4* | (all berths) | *23.3* |
| Officers | | | *Greek/European* |
| Dining Staff | | | *Greek/International* |
| Total Cabins | | | *211* |
| Size (sq ft/m) | *145-230/13.5-21.3* | Door Width | *24"* |
| Outside Cabins | *211* | Inside Cabins | *0* |
| Single Cabins | *0* | Supplement | *40-100%* |
| Balcony Cabins | *0* | Wheelchair Cabins | *5* |
| Cabin Current | | | *110/220 AC* |
| Refrigerator | | | *No* |
| Cabin TV | *No* | VCR | *No* |
| Dining Rooms | *1* | Sittings | *2* |

| | | | |
|---|---|---|---|
| Elevators | *2* | Door Width | *25"* |
| Casino | *Yes* | Slot Machines | *Yes* |
| Swimming Pools (outside) | *1* | (inside) | *0* |
| Whirlpools | *0* | Gymnasium | *Yes* |
| Sauna/Steam Rm | *Yes/No* | Massage | *Yes* |
| Self-Service Launderette | | | *No* |
| Movie Theater/Seats | | | *No* |
| Library | *Yes* | Children's Facilities | *No* |
| Watersports Facilities | | | *None* |
| Classification Society | | | *Lloyd's Register* |

| RATINGS | SCORE |
|---|---|
| Ship: Condition/Cleanliness | 6.3 |
| Ship: Space/Flow/Comfort | 5.7 |
| Ship: Decor/Furnishings | 6.8 |
| Ship: Fitness Facilities | 4.0 |
| Cabins: Comfort/Facilities | 6.3 |
| Cabins: Software | 6.6 |
| Food: Dining Room/Cuisine | 7.4 |
| Food: Buffets/Informal Dining | 6.8 |
| Food: Quality of Ingredients | 6.9 |
| Service: Dining Room | 7.0 |
| Service: Bars/Lounges | 7.0 |
| Service: Cabins | 6.2 |
| Cruise: Entertainment | 5.6 |
| Cruise: Activities Program | 6.0 |
| Cruise: Hospitality Standard | 6.1 |
| OVERALL RATING | 94.7 |

**+** This smart looking ship with a squat funnel was converted into a fine cruise ship in 1982, and greatly refurbished in 1983. Good enclosed deck promenade space. Wrap-around promenade deck. All-outside, "minimum decor" cabins that are comfortable and reasonably attractive, although soft furnishings could be improved. Bathrooms are very small except in the suites.

**–** Reasonable open deck and sunning space, but the single swimming pool is very small. There are too few public rooms for this number of passengers, particularly when the ship is full. Cabins have little closet and drawer space, particularly as most cabins accommodate a third (and sometimes a fourth) person.

**Dining** Menu descriptions make the food appear better than it is, although the choice is good. Limited selection of fruits, vegetables, breads, and garnishes. Quite simply put, you get what you pay for.

**Other Comments** Formerly operated by the Greek "K" Lines fleet, but has been laid up since 1985. There are few public rooms, but one of them is now an enlarged casino. Regency Cruises keeps changing the deployment of it ships, so do check the latest brochure. The ship is pleasant, but it is not a luxury ship or product by any means, so don't let the brochure fool you. Insurance, port taxes, and gratuities are extra.

# mv Regent Star ★★★

***Principal Cruising Areas***
*Alaska/Caribbean (7 nights)*
***Base Ports:** Vancouver/Montego Bay*

| | | | |
|---|---|---|---|
| Cruise Line | | | *Regency Cruises* |
| Former Names | | | *Statendam/Rhapsody* |
| Gross Tonnage | | | *24,214* |
| Builder | | | *Wilton-Fijenoord (Holland)* |
| Original Cost | | | *n/a* |
| Christened By | | | *HRH Crown Princess Beatrix* |
| First Entered Service | | | *Feb 6, 1957/Jul 26, 1987* |
| Interior Design | | | *Patricia Hayes & Associates* |
| Country of Registry | | | *Bahamas (C6DY)* |
| Tel No | *110-4137* | Fax No | *110-3646* |
| Length (ft/m) | | | *642.3/195.80* |
| Beam (ft/m) | | | *81.0/24.70* |
| Draft (ft/m) | | | *27.5/8.40* |
| Engines/Propellers | | | *2 SWD diesels/2* |
| Decks | *9* | Crew | *450* |
| Pass. Capacity (basis 2) | *944* | (all berths) | *1,000* |
| Pass. Space Ratio (basis 2) | *25.6* | (all berths) | *24.2* |
| Officers | *European/Greek* | Dining Staff | *Intl* |
| Total Cabins | | | *474* |
| Size (sq ft/m) | *86-260/8-24* | Door Width | *28"* |
| Outside Cabins | *291* | Inside Cabins | *183* |
| Single Cabins | *2* | Supplement | *30-100%* |
| Balcony Cabins | *0* | Wheelchair Cabins | *0* |
| Cabin Current | | | *110 AC* |
| Refrigerator | | | *No* |
| Cabin TV | *No* | VCR | *No* |
| Dining Rooms | *1* | Sittings | *2* |
| Elevators | *2* | Door Width | *28-31"* |

| | | | |
|---|---|---|---|
| Casino | *Yes* | Slot Machines | *Yes* |
| Swimming Pools (outside) | *1* | (inside) | *1* |
| Whirlpools | *2* | Gymnasium | *Yes* |
| Sauna/Steam Rm | *Yes/No* | Massage | *Yes* |
| Self-Service Launderette | | | *No* |
| Movie Theater/Seats | | | *Yes/294* |
| Library | | | *Yes* |
| Children's Facilities | | | *No* |
| Watersports Facilities | | | *None* |
| Classification Society | | | *Lloyd's Register* |

| RATINGS | SCORE |
|---|---|
| Ship: Condition/Cleanliness | 5.7 |
| Ship: Space/Flow/Comfort | 6.4 |
| Ship: Decor/Furnishings | 6.2 |
| Ship: Fitness Facilities | 5.3 |
| Cabins: Comfort/Facilities | 5.8 |
| Cabins: Software | 6.7 |
| Food: Dining Room/Cuisine | 7.4 |
| Food: Buffets/Informal Dining | 6.8 |
| Food: Quality of Ingredients | 6.9 |
| Service: Dining Room | 7.0 |
| Service: Bars/Lounges | 7.0 |
| Service: Cabins | 6.2 |
| Cruise: Entertainment | 5.6 |
| Cruise: Activities Program | 6.0 |
| Cruise: Hospitality Standard | 6.0 |
| OVERALL RATING | 95.0 |

**+** Well-constructed older vessel with classic former ocean liner profile. Now looking tired, however. Exterior maintenance is very shoddy, but a recent refurbishment has cosmetically upgraded interior spaces and public rooms. Reasonable amount of open deck and sunning space. Good array of public rooms, with tasteful decor and colors. Useful indoor fitness center. Quite roomy and nicely furnished outside cabins, many of which feature a full bathtub and have good closet and drawer space.

**—** Bridge Deck cabins have lifeboat-obstructed views. Lines for buffets and shore tenders. Stale smoke odor everywhere. Same size as *Regent Sea* but carries many more passengers, so always feels crowded. Inside cabins are very small.

**Dining** Food quality and choice could be improved, although most passengers seem satisfied.

**Other Comments** European-style service and Continental cuisine. The ship provides a reasonably good cruise experience at modest, always discounted rates, in reasonably comfortable surroundings, with a friendly staff. However, increased competition provides a much greater choice of alternative—and cleaner—ships. Insurance and gratuities are extra.

# ss Regent Sun ★★★

***Principal Cruising Areas***

*Caribbean/Canada/New England (7 nights)*

***Base Ports:*** *San Juan/New York/Montreal*

| | | | |
|---|---|---|---|
| Cruise Line | | | *Regency Cruises* |
| Former Names | | | *Royal Odyssey, Doric, Hanseatic, Shalom* |
| Gross Tonnage | | | *25,500* |
| Builder | | | *Chantiers de l'Atlantique (France)* |
| Original Cost | | | *£7,500,000* |
| Christened By | | | *Mrs Paula Ben Gurion* |
| First Entered Service | | | *Apr 17, 1964/Dec 9, 1988* |
| Interior Design | | | *A&M Katzourakis* |
| Country of Registry | | | *Bahamas (C6HB3)* |
| Tel No | *110-3762* | Fax No | *110-3763* |
| Length (ft/m) | | | *628.9/191.70* |
| Beam (ft/m) | | | *81.5/24.85* |
| Draft (ft/m) | | | *27.3/8.33* |
| Engines/Propellers | | | *4 Parsons steam turbines/2* |
| Decks | *9* | Crew | *410* |
| Pass. Capacity (basis 2) | *842* | (all berths) | *930* |
| Pass. Space Ratio (basis 2) | *30.2* | (all berths) | *27.4* |
| Officers | *Greek/European* | Dining Staff | *Intl* |
| Total Cabins | | | *420* |
| Size (sq ft/m) | *140-294/13-27.3* | Door Width | *27"* |
| Outside Cabins | *346* | Inside Cabins | *76* |
| Single Cabins | *2* | Supplement | *30-100%* |
| Balcony Cabins | *0* | Wheelchair Cabins | *2* |
| Cabin Current | *110 AC* | Refrigerator | *No* |
| Cabin TV | *No* | VCR | *No* |
| Dining Rooms | *1* | Sittings | *2* |
| Elevators | *5* | Door Width | *30"* |

| | | | |
|---|---|---|---|
| Casino | *Yes* | Slot Machines | *Yes* |
| Swimming Pools (outside) | *1* | (inside) | *1* |
| Whirlpools | *0* | Gymnasium | *Yes* |
| Sauna/Steam Rm | *Yes/No* | Massage | *Yes* |
| Self-Service Launderette | | | *No* |
| Movie Theater/Seats | | | *Yes/263* |
| Library | | | *Yes* |
| Children's Facilities | | | *No* |
| Watersports Facilities | | | *None* |
| Classification Society | | | *American Bur. of Shipping* |

| RATINGS | SCORE |
|---|---|
| Ship: Condition/Cleanliness | 6.6 |
| Ship: Space/Flow/Comfort | 6.8 |
| Ship: Decor/Furnishings | 6.7 |
| Ship: Fitness Facilities | 5.4 |
| Cabins: Comfort/Facilities | 6.3 |
| Cabins: Software | 6.7 |
| Food: Dining Room/Cuisine | 7.4 |
| Food: Buffets/Informal Dining | 6.8 |
| Food: Quality of Ingredients | 6.9 |
| Service: Dining Room | 7.3 |
| Service: Bars/Lounges | 7.1 |
| Service: Cabins | 6.5 |
| Cruise: Entertainment | 5.6 |
| Cruise: Activities Program | 6.0 |
| Cruise: Hospitality Standard | 6.1 |
| OVERALL RATING | 98.2 |

**+** Good-looking ship with classic profile and pleasing lines. Good, contemporary, yet elegant, decor and colors. Spacious, well equipped, and nicely furnished cabins have good amount of closet, drawer, and storage space. Spacious interior features two enclosed promenades and a good array of public rooms.

**–** Maintenance is shoddy and needs more attention and supervision. The odor of stale cigarette smoke throughout the ship is overbearing, and the poor air-conditioning doesn't help. Long lines for lido buffets, and the seats are very low. Officers rarely socialize. The casino is constantly full of smokers.

**Dining** Features Continental cuisine. Limited selection of vegetables. Dining room service is poor and uncoordinated.

**Other Comments** Cabins on top deck have lifeboat-obstructed views. Attractive dining room and seating. This ship is the nicest of the fleet of Regency's ships, and will cruise you in reasonably comfortable style and at a modest price, but those added cabins mean crowded spaces at times. Staff are reasonably friendly, but there's no real finesse. Insurance and gratuities are extra.

# ms Renaissance ★★★★ One/Two/Three/Four

***Principal Cruising Areas:*** *various (7 nights)*
***Base Ports:*** *various*

| | | | |
|---|---|---|---|
| Cruise Line | | | *Renaissance Cruises* |
| Former Names | *n/a* | Gross Tonnage | *3,990* |
| Builder | | | *Cantieri Navale Ferrari (Italy)* |
| Original Cost | | | *$20 million each* |
| Christened By | *(1) Ms C Astrup; (2) Mrs G Reggio; (3) Mrs Papagapitos; (4) Mrs F Paoletti* | | |
| First Entered Service | *(1) Dec 30, 1989; (2) Apr 21, 1990; (3) Aug 18, 1990; (4) Jan 7, 1991* | | |
| Interior Design | | | *Bertelotti/Yran & Storbraaten* |
| Country of Registry | *Liberia (1) ICEA; (2) ICGR; (3) ICTR; (4) ICDR* | | |
| Tel No | (1) *115-0510;* (2) *125-0164; (3) 125-0166; (4) 125-0171.* Fax No: *(1) 115-0565; (2) 125-0165; (3) 125-0167; (4) 125-0172* | | |
| Length *289.7ft* | Beam *50.2ft* | Draft *12.0ft* | |
| Engines/Propellers | | | *2 MAN-B&W diesels/2* |
| Decks | *5* | Crew | *72* |
| Pass. Capacity (basis 2) | *100* | (all berths) | *111* |
| Pass. Space Ratio (basis 2) | *39.9* | (all berths) | *35.9* |
| Officers | *Italian* | Dining Staff | *European/Filipino* |
| Total Cabins | | | *50* |
| Size (sq ft/m) | *231.5-282/21.5-26.2* | Door Width | *24"* |
| Outside Cabins | *50* | Inside Cabins | *0* |
| Single Cabins | *0* | Supplement | *30-65%* |
| Balcony Cabins | *4* | Wheelchair Cabins | *0* |
| Cabin Current | *110 AC* | Refrigerator | *Yes* |
| Cabin TV | *Yes* | VCR | *Yes* |
| Dining Rooms | *1* | Sittings | *1* |
| Elevators | *1* | Door Width | *30"* |
| Casino | *Yes* | Slot Machines | *Yes* |
| Swimming Pools (outside) | *1* | (inside) | *0* |
| Whirlpools | *1* | Gymnasium | *No* |
| Sauna/Steam Rm | *Yes/No* | Massage | *No* |
| Self-Service Launderette | *No* | Movie Theater | *No* |
| Library | *No* | Children's Facilities | *No* |
| Watersports Facilities | | | *Aft platform, sailfish, snorkel equipment, zodiacs* |
| Classification Society | | | *Det Norske Veritas* |

| RATINGS | SCORE |
|---|---|
| Ship: Condition/Cleanliness | 7.2 |
| Ship: Space/Flow/Comfort | 7.3 |
| Ship: Decor/Furnishings | 8.0 |
| Ship: Fitness Facilities | 7.5 |
| Cabins: Comfort/Facilities | 8.0 |
| Cabins: Software | 8.0 |
| Food: Dining Room/Cuisine | 8.0 |
| Food: Buffets/Informal Dining | 7.8 |
| Food: Quality of Ingredients | 7.8 |
| Service: Dining Room | 8.0 |
| Service: Bars/Lounges | 7.8 |
| Service: Cabins | 8.0 |
| Cruise: Entertainment | 6.0 |
| Cruise: Activities Program | 6.3 |
| Cruise: Hospitality Standard | 7.6 |
| OVERALL RATING | 113.3 |

**+** Contemporary mega-yacht looks and handsome styling throughout. Exquisite all-outside suites with lots of mirrors, handcrafted Italian furniture, and wet bar (pre-stocked at extra cost). Wooden outside promenade deck. Refined and attractive interior. Accommodations are located forward, public rooms aft. Cabins have queen-sized bed, a sitting area, and most things you need. Bathrooms have showers with fold-down seat, real teakwood floors, and marble vanities.

**–** This first series doesn't sail well in inclement weather. Tiny "dip" pool is not a swimming pool. Open deck and sunning space is quite cramped. Plastic woods (looks too perfect). Library book selection is poor. Cabin storage is very limited. Bathrooms are very compact. No bathtubs.

**Dining** Small, elegant dining room on the lowest deck, with portholes. Tables for two, four, six, and even eight. Sit where, with whom, and when you like. Self-service, buffet-style, cold foods for breakfast and lunch, with hot foods on the menu and served properly. The dining room works well. Food quality, choice, and presentation are excellent, and close to California "lean cuisine," but choice is limited, particularly entrees. 800 calorie menu . Good-to-excellent service.

**Other Comments** Four small, identical, and intimate cruise vessels out of a fleet of eight. Comfortable and inviting, but poorly maintained. Destination-intensive, refined, quiet, relaxed cruising without crowds, dressing up, scheduled activities, or entertainment.

# ms Renaissance ★★★★+
# Five/Six/Seven/Eight

***Principal Cruising Areas:*** *various (7 nights)*
***Base Ports:*** *various*

| | |
|---|---|
| Cruise Line | *Renaissance Cruises* |
| Former Names *n/a* | Gross Tonnage *4,280* |
| Builder | *Nuovi Cantieri Apuania (Italy)* |
| Original Cost | *$25 million each* |
| Christened By | *(5) Mrs Lyng-Olsen; (6) Blessed by shipyard priest; (7) n/a; (8) n/a* |
| First Entered Service | *(5) Mar 24, 1991; (6) Oct 5, 1991; (7) Dec 21, 1991; (8) May 30, 1992* |
| Interior Design | *Bertelotti/Yran & Storbraaten* |
| Country of Registry | *Liberia (5) ICLH; (6) ICSR (7) ICPG; (8) ICWR* |
| Tel No *(5) 125-0135; (6) 125-0142; (7) 115-1322; (8) 115-1375* | Fax No *(5) 125-0134; (6) 125-0141; (7) 125-0146; (8) 125-0145* |
| Length *297.2ft* Beam *50.2ft* | Draft *13.0ft* |
| Engines/Propellers | *2 MAN-B&W diesels/2* |
| Decks *5* | Crew *72* |
| Pass. Capacity (basis 2) *114* | (all berths) *114* |
| Pass. Space Ratio (basis 2) *37.5* | (all berths) *37.5* |
| Officers *Italian* | Dining Staff *European/Filipino* |
| Total Cabins | *50* |
| Size (sq ft/m)*215-312/20.0-29.0* | Door Width *24"* |
| Outside Cabins *50* | Inside Cabins *0* |
| Single Cabins *0* | Supplement *30-65%* |
| Balcony Cabins *4* | Wheelchair Cabins *0* |
| Cabin Current *110 AC* | Refrigerator *Yes* |
| Cabin TV *Yes* | VCR *Yes* |
| Dining Rooms *1* | Sittings *1* |

| | |
|---|---|
| Elevators *1* | Door Width *30"* |
| Casino *Yes* | Slot Machines *Yes* |
| Swimming Pools (outside) *1* | (inside) *0* |
| Whirlpools *1* | Gymnasium *No* |
| Sauna/Steam Rm *Yes/No* | Massage *Yes* |
| Self-Service Launderette *No* | Movie Theater *No* |
| Library *Yes* | Children's Facilities *No* |
| Watersports Facilities | *Aft platform, sailfish, snorkel equipment, zodiacs* |
| Classification Society | *Det Norske Veritas* |

| RATINGS | SCORE |
|---|---|
| Ship: Condition/Cleanliness | 8.0 |
| Ship: Space/Flow/Comfort | 7.8 |
| Ship: Decor/Furnishings | 8.2 |
| Ship: Fitness Facilities | 7.8 |
| Cabins: Comfort/Facilities | 8.1 |
| Cabins: Software | 8.0 |
| Food: Dining Room/Cuisine | 8.0 |
| Food: Buffets/Informal Dining | 7.8 |
| Food: Quality of Ingredients | 7.8 |
| Service: Dining Room | 8.0 |
| Service: Bars/Lounges | 8.0 |
| Service: Cabins | 8.0 |
| Cruise: Entertainment | 6.6 |
| Cruise: Activities Program | 6.4 |
| Cruise: Hospitality Standard | 7.8 |
| OVERALL RATING | 116.3 |

**+** Increased length, ducktail stern, and redesigned layout make these four vessels superior to the first four in the series, especially for stability and comfort. One outside promenade deck. Reasonable open deck and sunning space. Elegant interior design. Exquisite suites—lots of mirrors and handcrafted Italian furniture, walk-in closets, three-sided vanity mirrors, and refrigerator (pre-stocked when you book, at extra cost).

**–** Main lounge has six pillars which destroy sightlines to the small stage area.

**Dining** Open seating for all meals. Small, elegant dining room with several tables for two, four, six, and even eight. Sit where you like, with whom you like, and at what time you like. Meals are self-service, buffet-style, cold foods for breakfast and lunch, with hot foods on the table menu and served properly. Dining room operation works well. Staff are attentive, but many waiters wear dirty sneakers during the day. Quality, choice, and presentation are all excellent.

**Other Comments** Similar in design to the *Sea Goddess* vessels. Contemporary "mega-yacht" looks and handsome styling, with twin flared funnels. Small book and video library. Very comfortable and totally inviting, offering destination-intensive cruising for the cruisegoer who appreciates the finer things in life, and is prepared to pay for them. Not quite up to the standard of a *Sea Goddess* or *Seabourn* vessel; still a good cruise experience, but for less money.

# mv Romantica ★★

***Principal Cruising Areas***

*Egypt/Israel (3/4 nights year-round)*

***Base Port:** Limassol*

| | | | |
|---|---|---|---|
| Cruise Line | | | *Ambassador Cruises* |
| Former Names | | | *Romanza/Aurelia/ Beaverbrae/Huscaran* |
| Gross Tonnage | | | *7,537* |
| Builder | | | *Blohm & Voss (Germany)* |
| Original Cost | | | *n/a* |
| Christened By | | | *n/a* |
| First Entered Service | | | *Apr 1939/1991* |
| Interior Design | | | *n/a* |
| Country of Registry | | | *Cyprus (P3DW4)* |
| Tel No | *110-1113* | Fax No | *110-1113* |
| Length (ft/m) | | | *487.5/148.60* |
| Beam (ft/m) | | | *60.3/18.39* |
| Draft (ft/m) | | | *21.9/6.70* |
| Engines/Propellers | | | *3 MAN 7-cyl diesels/1* |
| Decks | *7* | Crew | *190* |
| Pass. Capacity (basis 2) | *568* | (all berths) | *727* |
| Pass. Space Ratio (basis 2) | *13.2* | (all berths) | *10.3* |
| Officers | *Greek* | Dining Staff | *International* |
| Total Cabins | | | *293* |
| Size (sq ft/m) | *n/a* | Door Width | *22"* |
| Outside Cabins | *152* | Inside Cabins | *141* |
| Single Cabins | *8* | Supplement | *100%* |
| Balcony Cabins | *0* | Wheelchair Cabins | *0* |
| Cabin Current | *220 AC* | Refrigerator | *No* |
| Cabin TV | *No* | VCR | *No* |
| Dining Rooms | *1* | Sittings | *2* |
| Elevators | *0* | Door Width | *n/a* |

| | | | |
|---|---|---|---|
| Casino | *No* | Slot Machines | *Yes* |
| Swimming Pools (outside) | *1* | (inside) | *0* |
| Whirlpools | *0* | Gymnasium | *No* |
| Sauna/Steam Rm | *No/No* | Massage | *No* |
| Self-Service Launderette | | | *No* |
| Movie Theater/Seats | | | *Yes/204* |
| Library | | | *No* |
| Children's Facilities | | | *No* |
| Watersports Facilities | | | *None* |
| Classification Society | | | *Lloyd's Register* |

| RATINGS | SCORE |
|---|---|
| Ship: Condition/Cleanliness | 4.6 |
| Ship: Space/Flow/Comfort | 4.7 |
| Ship: Decor/Furnishings | 5.9 |
| Ship: Fitness Facilities | 4.2 |
| Cabins: Comfort/Facilities | 5.7 |
| Cabins: Software | 5.9 |
| Food: Dining Room/Cuisine | 5.6 |
| Food: Buffets/Informal Dining | 5.4 |
| Food: Quality of Ingredients | 5.6 |
| Service: Dining Room | 6.4 |
| Service: Bars/Lounges | 6.2 |
| Service: Cabins | 6.5 |
| Cruise: Entertainment | 5.8 |
| Cruise: Activities Program | 5.7 |
| Cruise: Hospitality Standard | 6.1 |
| OVERALL RATING | 84.3 |

**+** Well-constructed ship, of vintage years but well maintained and still going strong.

**–** Open deck and sunning space is very limited, and crowded when full. Steep, narrow gangway in most ports. Narrow interior passageways. Cabins are very small indeed, and there's virtually no closet and storage space, except under beds. This high-density vessel is popular with European passengers, which means several different languages and constant, annoying announcements.

**Dining** Charming dining room. Reasonable food, but it seldom arrives hot. Poor selection of breads, fruits, and cheeses.

**Other Comments** Good choice of public rooms, but crowded when ship is full. Interior decor is typically Mediterranean. Service is friendly and attentive. This ship is ideal for those wanting to cruise in basic surroundings and modest comfort, at a modest price. Insurance and gratuities are not included.

# ss Rotterdam ★★★+

***Principal Cruising Areas***

*Alaska/Caribbean (various)*

***Base Ports:*** *Vancouver/Ft. Lauderdale*

| | | | |
|---|---|---|---|
| Cruise Line | | | *Holland America Line* |
| Former Names | | | *n/a* |
| Gross Tonnage | | | *38,645* |
| Builder | | | *Rotterdamsche Dry Dock (Holland)* |
| Original Cost | | | *$30 million* |
| Christened By | | | *HRH Queen Juliana* |
| First Entered Service | | | *Sep 3, 1959* |
| Interior Design | | | *Kym Anton/Julie Stanley* |
| Country of Registry | | | *Netherlands Antilles (PJSU)* |
| Tel No | *175-0101* | Fax No | *175-0124* |
| Length (ft/m) | | | *748.6/228.20* |
| Beam (ft/m) | | | *94.1/28.71* |
| Draft (ft/m) | | | *29.6/9.04* |
| Engines/Propellers | | | *6 Parsons steam turbines/2* |
| Decks | *10* | Crew | *603* |
| Pass. Capacity (basis 2) | *1,114* | (all berths) | *1,250* |
| Pass. Space Ratio (basis 2) | *34.6* | (all berths) | *30.9* |
| Officers | *Dutch* | Dining Staff | *Filipino/Indonesian* |
| Total Cabins | | | *575* |
| Size (sq ft/m) | | | *112-370/10.5-34.3* |
| Door Width | | | *25-27"* |
| Outside Cabins | *307* | Inside Cabins | *268* |
| Single Cabins | *32* | Supplement | *50-100%* |
| Balcony Cabins | *0* | Wheelchair Cabins | *0 (ramps available)* |
| Cabin Current | *110 AC* | Refrigerator | *Cat. A* |
| Cabin TV | *No* | VCR | *No* |
| Dining Rooms | *2* | Sittings | *2* |

| | | | |
|---|---|---|---|
| Elevators | *7* | Door Width | *31"* |
| Casino | *Yes* | Slot Machines | *Yes* |
| Swimming Pools (outside) | *1* | (inside) | *1* |
| Whirlpools | *0* | Gymnasium | *Yes* |
| Sauna/Steam Rm | *Yes/No* | Massage | *Yes* |
| Self-Service Launderette | | | *Yes* |
| Movie Theater/Seats | | | *Yes/620* |
| Library | *Yes* | Children's Facilities | *No* |
| Watersports Facilities | | | *None* |
| Classification Society | | | *Lloyd's Register* |

| RATINGS | SCORE |
|---|---|
| Ship: Condition/Cleanliness | 6.9 |
| Ship: Space/Flow/Comfort | 7.0 |
| Ship: Decor/Furnishings | 6.8 |
| Ship: Fitness Facilities | 6.6 |
| Cabins: Comfort/Facilities | 6.4 |
| Cabins: Software | 7.8 |
| Food: Dining Room/Cuisine | 6.6 |
| Food: Buffets/Informal Dining | 6.3 |
| Food: Quality of Ingredients | 7.2 |
| Service: Dining Room | 7.7 |
| Service: Bars/Lounges | 7.5 |
| Service: Cabins | 7.4 |
| Cruise: Entertainment | 6.4 |
| Cruise: Activities Program | 6.7 |
| Cruise: Hospitality Standard | 7.6 |
| OVERALL RATING | 104.9 |

**+** Sturdily built, handsome ship has beautiful rounded lines. Gracious, graceful, and well maintained. Expansive open deck and sunning space. Gorgeous flower displays everywhere. Acres of beautiful wood paneling and wood trim. Two-level Ritz Carlton is one of the most elegant art deco rooms afloat. Fine collection of artworks and antiques. Wide choice of cabins. All are comfortable and very well equipped. Lots of cabins for single cruisers—a welcome touch, especially for the extended voyages for which this ship is once again becoming known. Lovely theater.

**–** No wrap-around outdoor deck. Partly enclosed promenade deck. Numerous public rooms. Mismatch of color combinations. Expansive casino seems out of place. Smokers and nonsmokers are not separated on outdoor decks. Many cabin bathrooms have exposed plumbing. Low-budget entertainment. Long lines for embarkation, disembarkation, buffets, and shore tenders.

**Dining** Two high-ceilinged dining rooms. Refined dining, with excellent food and service, if you stick to the menu (communication with the Indonesian staff can be quite frustrating). Open seating for breakfast and lunch, two seatings for dinner. Attractively presented food, but meals are not memorable. Entrees are generally tasteless. Poor selection of bread rolls and fruit.

**Other Comments** A cruise on this stately ship fits comfortably—like a well-worn shoe—and the price is agreeable, too. Port taxes, insurance, and gratuities (expected) are extra.

# ms Royal Majesty ★★★★

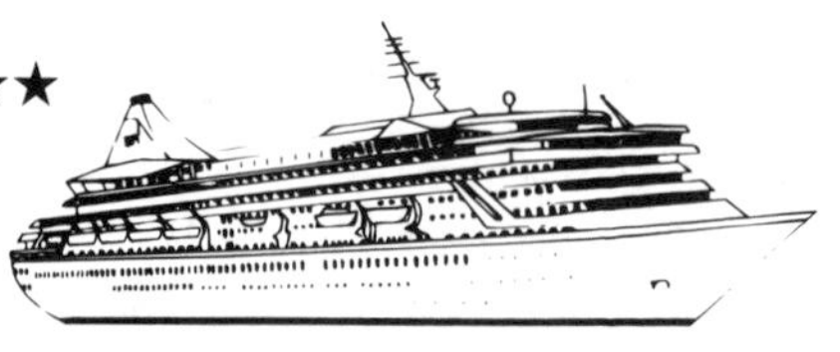

***Principal Cruising Areas***

*Bahamas/Bermuda (3,4/7 nights)*

***Base Ports:*** *Miami/Boston*

| | | | |
|---|---|---|---|
| Cruise Line | | | *Majesty Cruise Line* |
| Former Names | | | *n/a* |
| Gross Tonnage | | | *32,396* |
| Builder | | | *Kvaerner Masa Yards (Finland)* |
| Original Cost | | | *$229 million* |
| Christened By | | | *Ms Liza Minelli* |
| First Entered Service | | | *Sep 18, 1992* |
| Interior Design | | | *A&M Katzourakis* |
| Country of Registry | | | *Panama (3ETG9)* |
| Tel No | *133-6557* | Fax No | *133-6563* |
| Length (ft/m) | | | *567.9/173.10* |
| Beam (ft/m) | | | *90.5/27.60* |
| Draft (ft/m) | | | *20.3/6.20* |
| Engines/Propellers | | | *4 Wartsila 6-cyl diesels/2* |
| Decks | *9* | Crew | *525* |
| Pass. Capacity (basis 2) | *1,056* | (all berths) | *1,501* |
| Pass. Space Ratio (basis 2) | *31.3* | (all berths) | *21.5* |
| Officers | *Greek* | Dining Staff | *International* |
| Total Cabins | | | *528 (132 no-smoking)* |
| Size (sq ft/m) | *118-375/11-34.8* | Door Width | *28"* |
| Outside Cabins | *343* | Inside Cabins | *185* |
| Single Cabins | *0* | Supplement | *50%* |
| Balcony Cabins | *0* | Wheelchair Cabins | *4* |
| Cabin Current | | | *110/220 AC* |
| Refrigerator | | | *Suites* |
| Cabin TV | *Yes* | VCR | *Suites* |
| Dining Rooms | *1* | Sittings | *2* |
| Elevators | *4* | Door Width | *50"* |

| | | | |
|---|---|---|---|
| Casino | *Yes* | Slot Machines | *Yes* |
| Swimming Pools (outside) | *1* | (inside) | *0* |
| Whirlpools | *2* | Gymnasium | *Yes* |
| Sauna/Steam Rm | *Yes/No* | Massage | *Yes* |
| Self-Service Launderette | | | *No* |
| Movie Theater/Seats | | | *Yes/100* |
| Library | | | *Yes* |
| Children's Facilities | | | *Yes (also children's pool)* |
| Watersports Facilities | | | *none* |
| Classification Society | | | *Det Norske Veritas* |

| RATINGS | SCORE |
|---|---|
| Ship: Condition/Cleanliness | 8.6 |
| Ship: Space/Flow/Comfort | 8.4 |
| Ship: Decor/Furnishings | 8.6 |
| Ship: Fitness Facilities | 7.6 |
| Cabins: Comfort/Facilities | 7.8 |
| Cabins: Software | 7.0 |
| Food: Dining Room/Cuisine | 7.5 |
| Food: Buffets/Informal Dining | 7.2 |
| Food: Quality of Ingredients | 7.6 |
| Service: Dining Room | 6.0 |
| Service: Bars/Lounges | 7.4 |
| Service: Cabins | 7.7 |
| Cruise: Entertainment | 7.6 |
| Cruise: Activities Program | 6.7 |
| Cruise: Hospitality Standard | 7.1 |
| OVERALL RATING | 112.8 |

**+** Smart, attractive ship has a good profile. Tastefully equipped, with lots of teak and brass accents, discreet lighting, soothing colors, and no glitz. Wide passageways provide a feeling of inner spaciousness. Three good conference/meeting rooms. Suites feature butler service, and are well equipped, though not large. Most other cabins are on the small side, but very comfortable. 158 cabins are for nonsmokers. All cabins provided with ironing boards—strange for a short-cruise ship. Bathrobes provided for all passengers. Chic ship with a nice touch of elegance and open walking areas provide a fine feel to the ship.

**–** Open deck and sunning space is very limited. No cushioned pads for deck chairs. Many cabins on Queen's Deck have obstructed views. Showroom is poorly designed. Shows are weak. Too many announcements. Long lines for shore excursions, buffets, and pizza. Noisy dining room.

**Dining** The dining room is quite intimate, and totally nonsmoking, but the tables are rather close together. The food, menu, creativity, and service are good—best of all three- and four-day Bahamas cruise ships, but bread rolls and fruits could be better.

**Other Comments** In the Royal Observatory, models and plans of 19th century sailing ships provide a nautical ambiance. A very comfortable short cruise experience. Entertainment and passenger handling need more attention. Insurance and gratuities are extra.

# ms Royal Odyssey ★★★★+

*Principal Cruising Areas*

*Europe/South Pacific (various)*

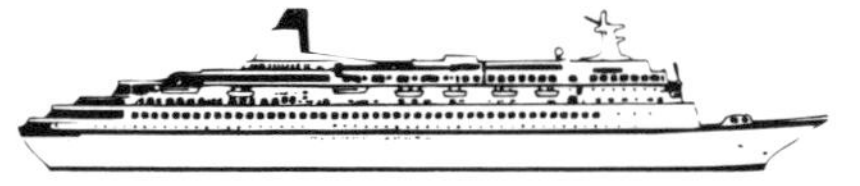

***Base Ports:** Piraeus/Singapore*

| | | | |
|---|---|---|---|
| Cruise Line | | | *Royal Cruise Line* |
| Former Names | | | *Royal Viking Sea* |
| Gross Tonnage | | | *28,078* |
| Builder | | | *Wartsila (Finland)* |
| Original Cost | | | *$22.5 million* |
| Christened By | | | *Mrs U Klaveness/Mrs E Golteus* |
| First Entered Service | | | *Nov 25, 1973/Dec 21, 1991* |
| Interior Design | | | *A&M Katzourakis* |
| Country of Registry | | | *Bahamas (C6CN4)* |
| Tel No | *110-4504* | Fax No | *110-4511* |
| Length (ft/m) | | | *674.2/205.50* |
| Beam (ft/m) | | | *83.6/25.50* |
| Draft (ft/m) | | | *23.6/7.20* |
| Engines/Propellers | | | *4 Sulzer 9-cyl diesels/2 (CP)* |
| Decks | *8* | Crew | *435* |
| Pass. Capacity (basis 2) | *765* | (all berths) | *820* |
| Pass. Space Ratio (basis 2) | *36.7* | (all berths) | *34.2* |
| Officers | *Greek* | Dining Staff | *Greek* |
| Total Cabins | | | *410* |
| Size (sq ft/m) | *136-580/12.6-53.8* | Door Width | *24"* |
| Outside Cabins | *357* | Inside Cabins | *53* |
| Single Cabins | *55* | Supplement | *100%* |
| Balcony Cabins | *9* | Wheelchair Cabins | *0* |
| Cabin Current | | | *110/220 AC* |
| Refrigerator | | | *Category A/B only* |
| Cabin TV | *Yes* | VCR | *No* |
| Dining Rooms | *1* | Sittings | *1* |
| Elevators | *5* | Door Width | *35"* |

| | | | |
|---|---|---|---|
| Casino | *Yes* | Slot Machines | *Yes* |
| Swimming Pools (outside) | *1* | (inside) | *0* |
| Whirlpools | *3* | Gymnasium | *Yes* |
| Sauna/Steam Rm | *Yes/No* | Massage | *Yes* |
| Self-Service Launderette | | | *No* |
| Movie Theater/Seats | | | *Yes/156* |
| Library | | | *Yes* |
| Children's Facilities | | | *No* |
| Watersports Facilities | | | *None* |
| Classification Society | | | *Det Norske Veritas* |

| RATINGS | SCORE |
|---|---|
| Ship: Condition/Cleanliness | 8.0 |
| Ship: Space/Flow/Comfort | 8.7 |
| Ship: Decor/Furnishings | 8.1 |
| Ship: Fitness Facilities | 7.6 |
| Cabins: Comfort/Facilities | 7.8 |
| Cabins: Software | 7.8 |
| Food: Dining Room/Cuisine | 7.8 |
| Food: Buffets/Informal Dining | 7.6 |
| Food: Quality of Ingredients | 7.0 |
| Service: Dining Room | 7.9 |
| Service: Bars/Lounges | 7.8 |
| Service: Cabins | 7.8 |
| Cruise: Entertainment | 6.8 |
| Cruise: Activities Program | 7.0 |
| Cruise: Hospitality Standard | 7.6 |
| OVERALL RATING | 115.3 |

**+** Contemporary profile, with well-balanced lines and beautifully raked bow. Well-maintained, with good open deck, sunning, and sports areas. Public rooms are quite elegant, with high ceilings. Good fitness facilities. All cabins are well-equipped with good closet, drawer, and storage space. Some cabins have whirlpool bathtubs. Bathrobes for all passengers. Excellent gentleman "host" program for older single female passengers.

**–** All inside decks are the same color—boring and cheap! Generally good service, but some passengers find stewards overly friendly. Some bathrooms have awkward access.

**Dining** The food is Continental in style. Fish and vegetables were overcooked and highly salted. Bland salads. Reduced salt, fat, cholesterol, and calorie meals available. Greek salad always available (but how do passengers know if it's not on the menu?). One pasta dish is usually included at each meal. Reasonable wine selection. Dining is single sitting, with assigned tables for two, four, six, or eight. Breakfast and luncheon can be taken outdoors by the pool. Too much canned fruit. Poor choice of bread rolls and fruits. Hot food choice is restricted.

**Other Comments** Attention to detail is apparent in most areas. Poor destination information. However, RCL's repeat passengers get a fine cruise experience at an appropriate price, but the entertainment is a little behind the times. Insurance and gratuities are extra.

# mv Royal Princess ★★★★+

*Principal Cruising Areas*

Various (various)

***Base Ports:*** various

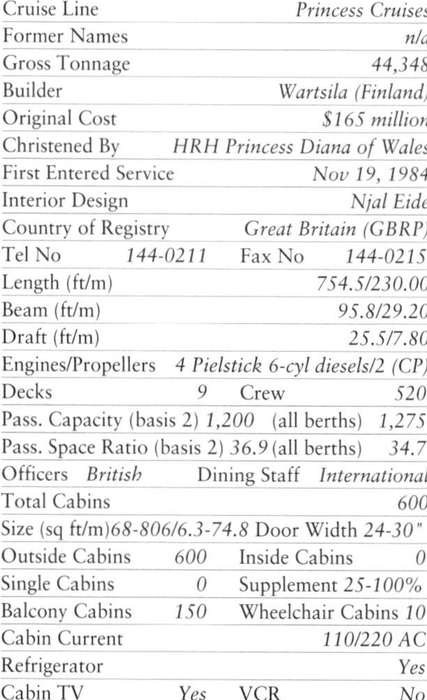

| | | | |
|---|---|---|---|
| Cruise Line | | | *Princess Cruises* |
| Former Names | | | *n/a* |
| Gross Tonnage | | | *44,348* |
| Builder | | | *Wartsila (Finland)* |
| Original Cost | | | *$165 million* |
| Christened By | | | *HRH Princess Diana of Wales* |
| First Entered Service | | | *Nov 19, 1984* |
| Interior Design | | | *Njal Eide* |
| Country of Registry | | | *Great Britain (GBRP)* |
| Tel No | *144-0211* | Fax No | *144-0215* |
| Length (ft/m) | | | *754.5/230.00* |
| Beam (ft/m) | | | *95.8/29.20* |
| Draft (ft/m) | | | *25.5/7.80* |
| Engines/Propellers | | | *4 Pielstick 6-cyl diesels/2 (CP)* |
| Decks | *9* | Crew | *520* |
| Pass. Capacity (basis 2) | *1,200* | (all berths) | *1,275* |
| Pass. Space Ratio (basis 2) | *36.9* | (all berths) | *34.7* |
| Officers | *British* | Dining Staff | *International* |
| Total Cabins | | | *600* |
| Size (sq ft/m) | *68-806/6.3-74.8* | Door Width | *24-30"* |
| Outside Cabins | *600* | Inside Cabins | *0* |
| Single Cabins | *0* | Supplement | *25-100%* |
| Balcony Cabins | *150* | Wheelchair Cabins | *10* |
| Cabin Current | | | *110/220 AC* |
| Refrigerator | | | *Yes* |
| Cabin TV | *Yes* | VCR | *No* |
| Dining Rooms | *1* | Sittings | *2* |
| Elevators | *6* | Door Width | *25-33"* |

| | | | |
|---|---|---|---|
| Casino | *Yes* | Slot Machines | *Yes* |
| Swimming Pools (outside) | *2 (+2 splash pools)* | (inside) | *0* |
| Whirlpools | *2* | Gymnasium | *Yes* |
| Sauna/Steam Rm | *Yes/No* | Massage | *Yes* |
| Self-Service Launderette | | | *Yes* |
| Movie Theater/Seats | | | *Yes/150* |
| Library | *Yes* | Children's Facilities | *No* |
| Watersports Facilities | | | *None* |
| Classification Society | | | *Lloyd's Register* |

| RATINGS | SCORE |
|---|---|
| Ship: Condition/Cleanliness | 8.8 |
| Ship: Space/Flow/Comfort | 8.9 |
| Ship: Decor/Furnishings | 8.8 |
| Ship: Fitness Facilities | 7.8 |
| Cabins: Comfort/Facilities | 8.6 |
| Cabins: Software | 8.2 |
| Food: Dining Room/Cuisine | 7.5 |
| Food: Buffets/Informal Dining | 7.2 |
| Food: Quality of Ingredients | 7.0 |
| Service: Dining Room | 7.5 |
| Service: Bars/Lounges | 7.7 |
| Service: Cabins | 7.8 |
| Cruise: Entertainment | 8.2 |
| Cruise: Activities Program | 8.0 |
| Cruise: Hospitality Standard | 8.3 |
| OVERALL RATING | 120.3 |

**+** Handsome, contemporary outer styling, with short, well raked bow. Excellent outdoor deck and sunning space. Wrap-around outdoor promenade deck. Very good, though unconventional, interior layout and passenger flow. Spacious passageways and delightful, imposing staircases. Decor increases the feeling of space and light. All-outside cabins (152 have private verandas) are well thought out and very comfortable. Suites are gorgeous. All have bathtub, shower, and three-sided mirrors. Bathrobes provided. Prompt, attentive room service.

**–** Lacks small, intimate public rooms. Poor library. Some cabins on Baja and Caribe decks have lifeboat-obstructed views. The Lido buffet area is too cramped and poorly designed. The room service menu should be upgraded. Staff dress could be improved. Signs are adequate only.

**Dining** The dining room is lovely. Disappointing cuisine. Most food is overcooked. Limited choice of vegetables. Poor quality fish, most covered with gravy-based sauces. Meat quality is very good, however. Pasta is always on the menu. Portions are generous, but presentation poor.

**Other Comments** The Horizon Lounge, set around the funnel base, has superb views, but should not be a discotheque. Standards of service, quality, and presentation of foods have declined. A fine cruise experience in spacious, elegant surroundings, at the appropriate, often discounted, price. Small details are forgotten, however. Insurance and gratuities are extra.

# mv Royal Star ★★★

***Principal Cruising Area***

*South Indian Ocean (4/8/12/15 nights)*

***Base Port:** Mombasa*

| | | | |
|---|---|---|---|
| Cruise Line | | | *Star Line Cruises* |
| Former Names | | | *Ocean Islander/San Giorgio/ City of Andros* |
| Gross Tonnage | | | *3,570* |
| Builder | | | *Cantieri Riuniti dell' Adriatico (Italy)* |
| Original Cost | | | *n/a* |
| Christened By | | | *Mrs Sandra Ruedin* |
| First Entered Service | | | *1956/Dec 15, 1990* |
| Interior Design | | | *A&M Katzourakis* |
| Country of Registry | | | *Bahamas (C6CF4)* |
| Tel No | *110-4407* | Fax No | *110-3460* |
| Length (ft/m) | | | *367.4/112.00* |
| Beam (ft/m) | *51.0/15.55* | Draft (ft/m) | *18.2/5.56* |
| Engines/Propellers | | | *2 Fiat 7-cyl diesels/2 (FP)* |
| Decks | *5* | Crew | *125* |
| Pass. Capacity (basis 2) | *216* | (all berths) | *250* |
| Pass. Space Ratio (basis 2) | *16.5* | (all berths) | *14.2* |
| Officers | *Greek* | Dining Staff | *European* |
| Total Cabins | | | *108* |
| Size (sq ft/m) | *107.6-398.2/10-37* | Door Width | *29"* |
| Outside Cabins | 97 | Inside Cabins | *11* |
| Single Cabins | 0 | Supplement | *Fixed rates* |
| Balcony Cabins | *1* | Wheelchair Cabins | *0* |
| Cabin Current | | | *110 AC* |
| Refrigerator | | | *Superior suites* |
| Cabin TV | *No* | VCR | *Superior suites* |
| Dining Rooms | *1* | Sittings | *2* |
| Elevators | *1* | Door Width | *25"* |

| | | | |
|---|---|---|---|
| Casino | *Yes* | Slot Machines | *Yes* |
| Swimming Pools (outside) | *1* | (inside) | *0* |
| Whirlpools | *0* | Gymnasium | *Yes* |
| Sauna/Steam Rm | *Yes/No* | Massage | *Yes* |
| Self-Service Launderette | | | *No* |
| Movie Theater/Seats | | | *No* |
| Library | | | *Yes* |
| Children's Facilities | | | *No* |
| Watersports Facilities | | | *None* |
| Classification Society | | | *American Bur. of Shipping* |

| RATINGS | SCORE |
|---|---|
| Ship: Condition/Cleanliness | 6.7 |
| Ship: Space/Flow/Comfort | 6.8 |
| Ship: Decor/Furnishings | 7.1 |
| Ship: Fitness Facilities | 4.3 |
| Cabins: Comfort/Facilities | 6.4 |
| Cabins: Software | 6.7 |
| Food: Dining Room/Cuisine | 7.0 |
| Food: Buffets/Informal Dining | 6.6 |
| Food: Quality of Ingredients | 6.8 |
| Service: Dining Room | 7.2 |
| Service: Bars/Lounges | 7.3 |
| Service: Cabins | 7.4 |
| Cruise: Entertainment | 5.2 |
| Cruise: Activities Program | 4.8 |
| Cruise: Hospitality Standard | 6.7 |
| OVERALL RATING | 97.0 |

**+** Charming little vessel, with well-balanced profile. Best suited for cruising in sheltered areas. Clean and tidy throughout. Warm, intimate, highly personable ambiance. Ample open deck space. Attractive, contemporary Scandinavian interior decor. The cabins, although not large, are pleasantly decorated, with good-quality furnishings and ample closet and drawer space.

**–** Steep, narrow gangway in most ports.

**Dining** Charming dining room, with good service and international cuisine, although standards are variable. Wines included with meals. Limited selection of breads, cheeses, and fruits. Limited cabin service menu. Poor afternoon tea.

**Other Comments** Well packaged and operated by the African Safari Club group of hotels, this ship will provide a most enjoyable cruise and safari experience in very comfortable, small-ship surroundings, at an extremely realistic price. Insurance and gratuities are extra.

# ms Royal Viking Queen ★★★★★+

***Principal Cruising Areas***

*Worldwide (7 nights)*

***Base Ports:** various*

| | | | |
|---|---|---|---|
| Cruise Line | | | *Royal Viking Line* |
| Former Names | | | *n/a* |
| Gross Tonnage | | | *9,975* |
| Builder | | | *Schichau Seebeckwerft (Germany)* |
| Original Cost | | | *$87 million* |
| Christened By | | | *Mrs Inger Kloster* |
| First Entered Service | | | *Mar 25, 1992* |
| Interior Design | | | *Yran & Storbraaten* |
| Country of Registry | | | *Bahamas (C6KO6)* |
| Tel No | *130-5227* | Fax No | *130-5232* |
| Length (ft/m) | | | *439.9/134.10* |
| Beam (ft/m) | *62.9/19.20* | Draft (ft/m) | *16.7/5.10* |
| Engines/Propellers | | | *2x12-cyl+2x8-cyl diesels/2 (CP)* |
| Decks | *6* | Crew | *135* |
| Pass. Capacity (basis 2) | *212* | (all berths) | *212* |
| Pass. Space Ratio (basis 2) | *47.0* | (all berths) | *47.0* |
| Officers | *Norwegian* | Dining Staff | *European* |
| Total Cabins | | | *106* |
| Size (sq ft/m) | | | *277-554/25.7-51.5* |
| Door Width | | | *25-31"* |
| Outside Cabins | *106* | Inside Cabins | *0* |
| Single Cabins | *0* | Supplement | *60-100%* |
| Balcony Cabins | *6* | Wheelchair Cabins | *4* |
| Cabin Current | *110/220 AC* | Refrigerator | *Yes* |
| Cabin TV | *Yes* | VCR | *Yes* |
| Dining Rooms | *1* | Sittings | *Open* |
| Elevators | *3* | Door Width | *39"* |
| Casino | *Yes* | Slot Machines | *Yes* |

| | | | |
|---|---|---|---|
| Swimming Pools (outside) | *1* | (inside) | *0* |
| Whirlpools | *3* | Gymnasium | *Yes* |
| Sauna/Steam Rm | *Yes/Yes* | Massage | *Yes* |
| Self-Service Launderette | | | *No* |
| Movie Theater/Seats | | | *No* |
| Library | | | *Yes* |
| Children's Facilities | | | *No* |
| Watersports Facilities | | | *Aft platform, marina pool, scuba, snorkel, windsurf, waterski, 2 zodiacs* |
| Classification Society | | | *Det Norske Veritas* |

| RATINGS | SCORE |
|---|---|
| Ship: Condition/Cleanliness | 9.6 |
| Ship: Space/Flow/Comfort | 9.3 |
| Ship Facilities | 9.0 |
| Ship: Decor/Furnishings | 9.5 |
| Ship: Fitness/Watersports | 9.1 |
| Cabins: Comfort/Facilities | 9.4 |
| Cabins: Software | 9.4 |
| Food: Dining Room/Cuisine | 9.2 |
| Food: Buffets/Informal Dining | 8.0 |
| Food: Quality of Ingredients | 8.5 |
| Service: Dining Room | 9.2 |
| Service: Bars | 9.0 |
| Service: Cabins | 9.1 |
| Cruise: Entertainment/Lecture Program | 8.6 |
| Cruise: Hospitality Standard | 9.2 |
| OVERALL RATING | 137.1 |

**+** Strikingly sleek ship with a handsome profile, almost identical to the two *Seabourn* vessels. Two fine mahogany water taxis. Aft watersports platform and marina. Sumptuous public areas. Wide central passageways. Fine quality interior fixtures and fittings. Elegant decor and artwork. Comfortably large and beautifully equipped suites. Large walk-in closet, 100% cotton towels and bathrobes, personalized stationery, and complimentary bar. Impeccable service from hand-picked European staff.

**–** No wrap-around outdoor promenade deck. Beverages should be included in the cruise fare.

**Dining** In-suite, course-by-course dining available at any time. Very elegant decor in the formal dining room (arguably nicer than the *Seabourns*). Fine, creative cuisine that is well presented, and cooked to order. The menu is never repeated, no matter how long the voyage. Special orders are available whenever you want them, and there's always plenty of caviar. Good choice of exotic fruits, and cheeses. The wine list is extensive, but prices are high.

**Other Comments** Almost all-inclusive price (you pay for bar drinks). Correct formal dress essential. This ship will provide the most discerning passengers with an outstanding level of personal service and cruise experience, and receives my highest praise and recommendations. Port taxes and gratuities are included.

# ms Royal Viking Sun ★★★★★+

***Principal Cruising Areas***

*Worldwide (various)*

***Base Ports:*** *various*

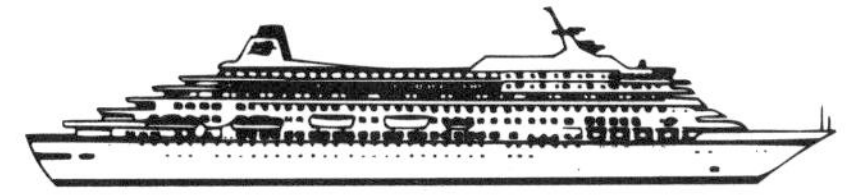

| | | | |
|---|---|---|---|
| Cruise Line | | | *Royal Viking Line* |
| Former Names | | | *n/a* |
| Gross Tonnage | | | *37,845* |
| Builder | | | *Wartsila (Finland)* |
| Original Cost | | | *$125 million* |
| Christened By | | | *Mr James Stewart* |
| First Entered Service | | | *Dec 16, 1988* |
| Interior Design | | | *Njal Eide* |
| Country of Registry | | | *Bahamas (C6DM3)* |
| Tel No | *110-4517* | Fax No | *110-4514* |
| Length (ft/m) | | | *674.2/205.50* |
| Beam (ft/m) | | | *91.8/28.00* |
| Draft (ft/m) | | | *23.6/7.20* |
| Engines/Propellers | | | *4 Sulzer 8-cyl diesels/2* |
| Decks | *8* | Crew | *460* |
| Pass. Capacity (basis 2) | *740* | (all berths) | *814* |
| Pass. Space Ratio (basis 2) | *51.1* | (all berths) | *46.4* |
| Officers | *Norwegian* | Dining Staff | *European* |
| Total Cabins | | | *370* |
| Size (sq ft/m) | *138-724/12.8-67.2* | Door Width | *31"* |
| Outside Cabins | *350* | Inside Cabins | *20* |
| Single Cabins | *2* | Supplement | *60-100%* |
| Balcony Cabins | *145* | Wheelchair Cabins | *4* |
| Cabin Current | | | *110 AC* |
| Refrigerator | | | *All cabins* |
| Cabin TV | *Yes* | VCR | *Yes* |
| Dining Rooms | *1* | Sittings | *1* |
| Elevators | *4* | Door Width | *40"* |

| | | | |
|---|---|---|---|
| Casino | *Yes* | Slot Machines | *Yes* |
| Swimming Pools (outside) | *2* | (inside) | *0* |
| Whirlpools | *2* | Gymnasium | *Yes* |
| Sauna/Steam Rm | *Yes/Yes* | Massage | *Yes* |
| Self-Service Launderette | | | *Yes* |
| Movie Theater/Seats | | | *Yes/101* |
| Library | | | *Yes* |
| Children's Facilities | | | *No* |
| Watersports Facilities | | | *None* |
| Classification Society | | | *Det Norske Veritas* |

| RATINGS | SCORE |
|---|---|
| Ship: Condition/Cleanliness | 9.5 |
| Ship: Space/Flow/Comfort | 9.5 |
| Ship: Decor/Furnishings | 9.5 |
| Ship: Fitness Facilities | 9.3 |
| Cabins: Comfort/Facilities | 9.2 |
| Cabins: Software | 9.1 |
| Food: Dining Room/Cuisine | 9.0 |
| Food: Buffets/Informal Dining | 9.0 |
| Food: Quality of Ingredients | 8.7 |
| Service: Dining Room | 9.2 |
| Service: Bars | 9.1 |
| Service: Cabins | 9.4 |
| Cruise: Entertainment | 8.6 |
| Cruise: Activities Program | 8.6 |
| Cruise: Hospitality Standard | 9.5 |
| OVERALL RATING | 137.2 |

**+** Ultra-contemporary ship has sleek, flowing lines, a sharply-raked bow and well-rounded profile, with lots of floor-to-ceiling glass. The ship's tenders are thoughtfully air-conditioned and even have radar and a toilet. Maintenance is excellent. Wide outdoor teakwood decks provide excellent walking areas, including a wrap-around promenade deck. (Even the ship's bridge has a wooden floor.) There are two glass-walled elevators. Separate baggage elevators mean passengers never have to wait for luggage. Incredibly spacious and well designed interior layout. Impressive public rooms and tasteful decor throughout. Two handrails, one wooden, one chrome, are provided on all stairways—a thoughtful extra touch. The Stella Polaris Lounge, the ship's forward observation lounge, is simply lovely, and one of the most elegant lounges at sea. Pebble Beach is the name of the ship's own golf club, complete with wet bar and electronic golf simulator. The Dickens Library is now a well organized delight. Distinguished male guest hosts are provided on all cruises. The Owner's Suite, at 723 sq. ft., is exquisite, and features two bathrooms, one of which has a large whirlpool bathtub with ocean views. Superb penthouse suites have large balconies and gracious butler service. Most cabins are of generous proportions, and are well equipped, with just about everything you would need. Over a third of cabins have a private balcony. All have walk-in closets, lockable drawers, full-length mirrors, hairdryers, and fluffy cotton bathrobes. Fine Scandinavian stewardesses provide excellent, unobtrusive service.

Four well equipped, L-shaped cabins for the physically challenged are well designed, quite large, and feature special wheel-in bathrooms with shower facilities and closet. First class air travel is provided to all passengers on long, exotic voyages. Gratuities are included.

**–** There's no way to get from the uppermost pool, which has a swim-up (sit-in) bar, to the second pool, located adjacent to the health spa and gymnasium, without first going inside the vessel. The carpeting quality in some areas is poor, with too many strips and joins, typical of shipyard subcontractors. The Oak Room features a marble fireplace, although it can't be used due to United States Coast Guard regulations.

**Dining** Excellent cuisine and fine European service are provided in an unhurried, caring atmosphere, with a menu that is never repeated, no matter how long the voyage. The food is creative and well presented, with good use of garnishes. Delightful, well-chosen wine list from distinguished vintners around the world. There is also a separate, but somewhat under-used, wine bar. In the dining room, mineral water, which should be included at these cruise prices, should be served for all meals, instead of the overly chlorinated water provided. There's an excellent and well utilized indoor-outdoor lido buffet area. A separate Grill Room is an elegant alternative dining spot, with a great view and an à la carte menu, but used only for special functions. Although the wine list is extensive, wine prices are very high.

**Other Comments** Presently the highest rated ship in the world, this delightful vessel is unmistakably Royal Viking Line, built for long-distance cruising (including an annual complete world cruise) in great comfort. Her beauty is the result of three designers—Njal R. Eide (ship design), Finn G. Nilsson (accommodations), and Frank Mingis (owner's suite, penthouse suites, and assisted in selecting the interior color scheme, china, glass and silverware). There are two outdoor swimming pools. The gymnasium and spa facilities are excellent.

Whether by intention or not, the ship has created a two-class feeling, with passengers in "upstairs" penthouse suites and "A" grade staterooms gravitating to the somewhat quieter Stella Polaris lounge, while others go to the main entertainment deck.

This ship has fine facilities, including a concierge, self-service launderettes, guest lecture program, 24-hour information office, and true 24-hour room service, for the discriminating passenger who demands the very finest in personal surroundings, food, and service, regardless of price. Absolutely first class, this Sun is set to shine for a long time.

Committed to the pursuit of excellence, she is one of the finest breed of grand hotels at sea, with a gracious ambiance, ably commanded by a well-loved and very proud Captain Ola Harsheim. The ship's direct competition is the *Crystal Harmony* (arguably a more elegant ship, but with two sittings for dinner) and the outstanding *Europa* (principally for German-speaking passengers). While this ship is not perfect (the perfect ship hasn't yet been delivered), the few design flaws that are evident (for example, poorly designed bar service counters; odd signage in the elevators), Royal Viking Line has a long tradition of excellence that should, without doubt, be maintained. A long cruise aboard *Royal Viking Sun* is arguably one of the world's finest travel experiences. Port taxes are included. Insurance and gratuities are extra.

# ms Ryndam ★★★★+

***Principal Cruising Areas***

*Caribbean/Europe (7 nights)*

***Base Port:*** *Ft. Lauderdale*

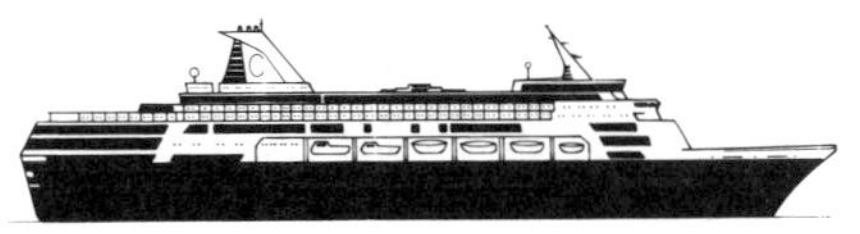

| | | | |
|---|---|---|---|
| Cruise Line | *Holland America Line* | | |
| Former Names | *n/a* | | |
| Gross Tonnage | *55,451* | | |
| Builder | *Fincantieri (Italy)* | | |
| Original Cost | *$215 million* | | |
| Christened By | *n/a* | | |
| First Entered Service | *Nov 9, 1994* | | |
| Interior Design | *VFD Interiors/Joe Farcus* | | |
| Country of Registry | *Bahamas* | | |
| Tel No | *n/a* | Fax No | *n/a* |
| Length (ft/m) | *719.3/219.30* | | |
| Beam (ft/m) | *101.0/30.80* | | |
| Draft (ft/m) | *24.6/7.50* | | |
| Engines/Propellers | *2 Sulzer V12-cyl diesels/2 (VP)* | | |
| Decks | *10* | Crew | *588* |
| Pass. Capacity (basis 2) | *1,264* | (all berths) | *1,627* |
| Pass. Space Ratio (basis 2) | *43.8* | (all berths) | *34.0* |
| Officers | *Dutch* | | |
| Dining Staff | *Filipino/Indonesian* | | |
| Total Cabins | *632* | | |
| Size (sq ft/m) | *187-1,126/17.3-104.5* | | |
| Door Width | *26"* | | |
| Outside Cabins | *501* | Inside Cabins | *131* |
| Single Cabins | *0* | Supplement | *50-100%* |
| Balcony Cabins | *150* | Wheelchair Cabins | *6* |
| Cabin Current | *110/220 AC* | Refrigerator | *PS/S/A/B* |
| Cabin TV | *Yes* | VCR | *No* |
| Dining Rooms | *1* | Sittings | *2* |

| | | | |
|---|---|---|---|
| Elevators | *12* | Door Width | *40"* |
| Casino | *Yes* | Slot Machines | *Yes* |
| Swimming Pools (outside) | *1* | (inside) | *1* |
| Whirlpools | *2* | Gymnasium | *Yes* |
| Sauna/Steam Rm | *Yes/No* | Massage | *Yes* |
| Self-Service Launderette | *Yes* | | |
| Movie Theater/Seats | *Yes/249* | | |
| Library | *Yes* | Children's Facilities | *No* |
| Watersports Facilities | *None* | | |
| Classification Society | *Lloyd's Register* | | |

| RATINGS | SCORE |
|---|---|
| Ship: Condition/Cleanliness | 8.8 |
| Ship: Space/Flow/Comfort | 8.2 |
| Ship: Decor/Furnishings | 8.6 |
| Ship: Fitness Facilities | 7.7 |
| Cabins: Comfort/Facilities | 8.1 |
| Cabins: Software | 8.0 |
| Food: Dining Room/Cuisine | 7.8 |
| Food: Buffets/Informal Dining | 7.6 |
| Food: Quality of Ingredients | 7.2 |
| Service: Dining Room | 7.7 |
| Service: Bars/Lounges | 7.6 |
| Service: Cabins | 8.1 |
| Cruise: Entertainment | 7.0 |
| Cruise: Activities Program | 7.2 |
| Cruise: Hospitality Standard | 8.2 |
| OVERALL RATING | 117.8 |

**+** Third of a three-ship group, this new sister ship to *Maasdam* and *Statendam* is certain to please HAL fans. Mid-level, inboard lifeboats. Excellent teakwood decking, and no astroturf anywhere. Asymmetrical interior layout. Three-deck-high atrium foyer is stunning. Magrodome roof covers indoor-outdoor pool and central lido area. Cabins are spacious, very tastefully decorated, and well laid out, although some are a little cramped for two. Superb Dutch antiques and outstanding art collection. Interior decor more subdued than on *Statendam*, and more tasteful.

**–** Two-deck-high showroom is well thought out, but the ceiling is low and sightlines are not as good as they could be. Expect lines for embarkation, disembarkation, the buffet, and shore tenders. The escalator is virtually useless. Communication with staff is sometimes frustrating.

**Dining** Two-deck-high dining room with dramatic grand staircase located at stern is very elegant, and has panoramic windows on three sides (lower level). Food and service are of typical HAL standards (disappointing), but there is much use of fine china. Twenty-eight suites, each of which can accommodate four, will feature an in-suite dining alternative.

**Other Comments** There's no doubt she is a well-built, quality ship, and takes over from *Rotterdam* as the new breed of contemporary, yet sophisticated, ship of the nineties for HAL, continuing the company's strong maritime traditions.

# RMS St. Helena

***Principal Cruising Areas***

*England/St. Helena/South Africa (27 nights)*

***Base Port:*** *Cardiff*

| | | | |
|---|---|---|---|
| Cruise Line | | | *Curnow Shipping* |
| Operator | | | *St. Helena Line* |
| Former Names | | | *n/a* |
| Gross Registered Tonnage | | | *6,767* |
| Builder | | | *A&P Appledore (Scotland)* |
| Original Cost | | | *£32 million* |
| Christened By | | | *HRH Prince Andrew* |
| First Entered Service | | | *Oct 1990* |
| Interior Design | | | *Ron Baxter* |
| Country of Registry | | | *England (MMHE5)* |
| Tel No | *144-1730* | Fax No | 144-1730 |
| Length (ft/m) | | | *344.4/105.00* |
| Beam (ft/m) | | | *62.9/19.20* |
| Draft (ft/m) | | | *19.6/6.00* |
| Engines | | | *Two 6-cyl Mirrlees Blackstone diesels* |
| Propellers | | | *2 (CP)* |
| Decks | *4* | Crew | *36* |
| Pass. Capacity (basis 2) | *96* | (all berths) | *128* |
| Pass. Space Ratio (basis 2) | *70.4* | (all berths) | *52.8* |
| Officers | | | *British/St. Helenian* |
| Dining Room | | | *British/St. Helenian* |
| Total Cabins | | | *49* |
| Size (sq ft/m) | *51.8-202/4.8-18.7* | Door Width | *24"* |
| Outside Cabins | *37* | Inside Cabins | *12* |
| Single Cabins | *0* | Supplement | *200%* |
| Balcony Cabins | *0* | Wheelchair Cabins | *1* |
| Cabin Current | *220 AC* | Refrigerator | *No* |
| Cabin TV | *No* | VCR | *No* |

| | | | |
|---|---|---|---|
| Dining Rooms | *1* | Sittings | *2* |
| Elevators | *1* | Door Width | *30"* |
| Casino | *No* | Slot Machines | *Yes* |
| Swimming Pools (outside) | *1* | (inside) | *0* |
| Whirlpools | *0* | Gymnasium | *No* |
| Sauna/Steam Rm | *No/No* | *Massage* | *No* |
| Self-Service Launderette | | | *Yes* |
| Cinema/Theater | | | *No* |
| Library | *Yes* | Children's Facilities | *Yes* |
| Classification Society | | | *Lloyd's Register* |

| RATINGS | SCORE |
|---|---|
| Ship: Condition/Cleanliness | NYR |
| Ship: Space/Flow/Comfort | NYR |
| Ship: Decor/Furnishings | NYR |
| Ship: Fitness Facilities | NYR |
| Cabins: Comfort/Facilities | NYR |
| Cabins: Software | NYR |
| Food: Dining Room/Cuisine | NYR |
| Food: Buffets/Informal Dining | NYR |
| Food: Quality of Ingredients | NYR |
| Service: Dining Room | NYR |
| Service: Bars/Lounges | NYR |
| Service: Cabins | NYR |
| Cruise: Entertainment | NYR |
| Cruise: Activities Program | NYR |
| Cruise: Hospitality Standard | NYR |

NYR = Not Yet Rated

**+** Has all modern conveniences, including stabilizers and air-conditioning. Operates just like a full-size cruise vessel, and has an open bridge policy. Passengers can even take their pets. Pleasant library/reading lounge. Free self-service laundry. Accommodations are in two-, three, or four-berth cabins, simply furnished, but many cabins are without private facilities. The brochure states that landing at Ascension is at times "a hazardous process" due to slippery and steep wharf steps—that's telling it like it is. The staff are welcoming and delightful to sail with.

**–** Two-sitting dining on such a small ship is a nuisance. There are several cabins without private facilities. Tiny swimming pool.

**Dining** The dining room is totally nonsmoking. The food is very British, with hearty breakfasts and a relatively simple menu, but the food is attractively presented on fine china. Afternoon tea, complete with freshly baked cakes, is a must.

**Other Comments** This amazing little combination cargo-passenger ship operates a regular Cardiff-Tenerife-St. Helena-Ascension Island-Tristan Da Cunha-Capetown line service which is like a mini-cruise, or long voyage, with lots of days at sea. There are six round-trip sailings a year. Insurance, port taxes, and gratutities are not included.

# ms Sagafjord ★★★★★+

***Principal Cruising Areas***
*Worldwide (various)*
***Base Ports:** various*

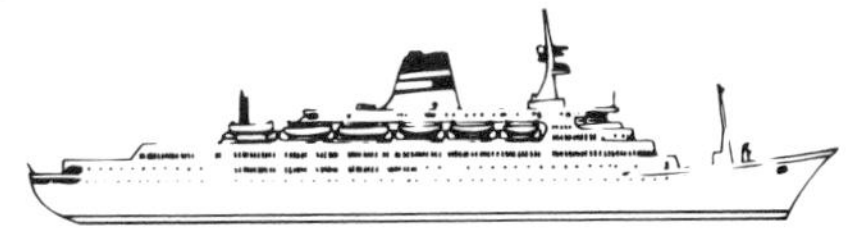

| | | | |
|---|---|---|---|
| Cruise Line | | | *Cunard* |
| Former Names | | | *n/a* |
| Gross Tonnage | | | *24,474* |
| Builder | | | *Forges et Chantiers de la Mediteranee* |
| Original Cost | | | *$30 million* |
| Christened By | | | *Mrs Leif Hoegh* |
| First Entered Service | | | *Oct 2, 1965/1983* |
| Interior Design | | | *Platou Design* |
| Country of Registry | | | *Bahamas (C6ZU)* |
| Tel No | *110-4115* | Fax No | *110-3564* |
| Length (ft/m) | | | *619.6/188.88* |
| Beam (ft/m) | | | *80.3/24.49* |
| Draft (ft/m) | | | *27.0/8.25* |
| Engines/Propellers | | | *2 Sulzer 9-cyl diesels/2* |
| Decks | *7* | Crew | *350* |
| Pass. Capacity (basis 2) | *589* | (all berths) | *620* |
| Pass. Space Ratio (basis 2) | *41.5* | (all berths) | *39.4* |
| Officers | *Norwegian* | Dining Staff | *European* |
| Total Cabins | | | *321* |
| Size (sq ft/m) | *97-387/9-36* | Door Width | *27"* |
| Outside Cabins | *298* | Inside Cabins | *23* |
| Single Cabins | *43* | Supplement | *75%* |
| Balcony Cabins | *26* | Wheelchair Cabins | *13* |
| Cabin Current | | | *110 AC* |
| Refrigerator | | | *Category I/II* |
| Cabin TV | *Yes* | VCR | *No* |
| Dining Rooms | *1* | Sittings | *1* |
| Elevators | *4* | Door Width | *28"* |

| | | | |
|---|---|---|---|
| Casino | *Yes* | Slot Machines | *Yes* |
| Swimming Pools (outside) | *1* | (inside) | *1* |
| Whirlpools | *1* | Gymnasium | *Yes* |
| Sauna/Steam Rm | *Yes/No* | Massage | *Yes* |
| Self-Service Launderette | | | *Yes* |
| Movie Theater/Seats | | | *Yes/181* |
| Library | | | *Yes* |
| Children's Facilities | | | *No* |
| Watersports Facilities | | | *None* |
| Classification Society | | | *Lloyd's Register* |

| RATINGS | SCORE |
|---|---|
| Ship: Condition/Cleanliness | 8.8 |
| Ship: Space/Flow/Comfort | 9.3 |
| Ship: Decor/Furnishings | 9.1 |
| Ship: Fitness Facilities | 8.8 |
| Cabins: Comfort/Facilities | 9.2 |
| Cabins: Software | 9.0 |
| Food: Dining Room/Cuisine | 9.3 |
| Food: Buffets/Informal Dining | 9.0 |
| Food: Quality of Ingredients | 9.1 |
| Service: Dining Room | 9.2 |
| Service: Bars/Lounges | 8.8 |
| Service: Cabins | 9.1 |
| Cruise: Entertainment | 8.7 |
| Cruise: Activities Program | 8.7 |
| Cruise: Hospitality Standard | 9.1 |
| OVERALL RATING | 135.2 |

**+** One of the most beautifully proportioned ships afloat. Built for long-distance cruising, she has a very spacious interior, with high-ceilinged public rooms and tasteful decor. Quiet as a fine watch. Wide, open decks. Well maintained. Fine quality furnishings and fittings. Superb cinema. Her main lounge is among the best afloat. Large, fairly spacious suites and cabins, with superb fittings and excellent insulation. Many single cabins. Generous storage. Gracious service.

**–** Some areas show signs of wear, and further facelifting and cosmetic upgrades are needed.

**Dining** Sumptuous dining room with its high central ceiling and grand entrance staircase is both a rarity and a real classic among ships today. Excellent plateware and flatware. Extremely creative cuisine. Fine quality ingredients. No menu is ever repeated. Special orders are well accommodated. Classic service (no bus boys). Artistically presented food, consistent with nouvelle cuisine. Pastries and desserts are of a very high standard. Outstanding variety of fruits. Espresso and capuccino are available at no charge in the dining room. Extensive wine list.

**Other Comments** As long as Cunard remains committed to maintaining the ship and keeping service standards high, she will attract passengers that appreciate quality and service. Designed for long-distance worldwide cruising, she excels in quiet, refined living at sea. Port taxes and insurance are extra. Gratuities are not included, but can be pre-paid.

# mv Sea Goddess I ★★★★★+

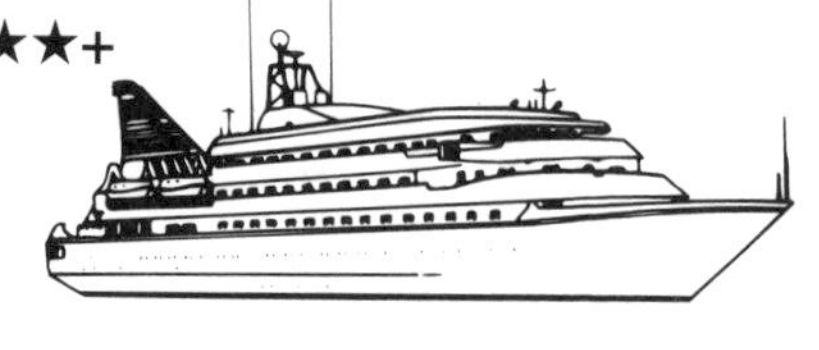

*Principal Cruising Areas*
*Caribbean/Europe (7-11 nights)*
***Base Ports:** St. Thomas/Nice*

| | | | |
|---|---|---|---|
| Cruise Line | | | *Cunard* |
| Former Names | | | *n/a* |
| Gross Tonnage | | | *4,260* |
| Builder | | | *Wartsila (Finland)* |
| Original Cost | | | *$34 million* |
| Christened By | | | *Mrs Nina Naarstad* |
| First Entered Service | | | *Apr 14, 1984* |
| Interior Design | | | *Yran & Storbraaten* |
| Country of Registry | | | *Norway (LMXP3)* |
| Tel No | *131-1225* | Fax No | *131-0645* |
| Length (ft/m) | | | *343.8/104.81* |
| Beam (ft/m) | | | *47.9/14.60* |
| Draft (ft/m) | | | *13.6/4.17* |
| Engines/Propellers | | | *2 VASA 12-cyl diesels/2 (CP)* |
| Decks | *5* | Crew | *90* |
| Pass. Capacity (basis 2) | *116* | (all berths) | *116* |
| Pass. Space Ratio (basis 2) | *36.7* | (all berths) | *36.7* |
| Officers | *Norwegian* | Dining Staff | *European* |
| Total Cabins | | | *58* |
| Size (sq ft/m) | *179.8-410/16.7-38* | Door Width | *24"* |
| Outside Cabins | 58 | Inside Cabins | 0 |
| Single Cabins | 0 | Supplement | *On request* |
| Balcony Cabins | *0* | Wheelchair Cabins | *0* |
| Cabin Current | *110/220 AC* | Refrigerator | *Yes* |
| Cabin TV | *Yes* | VCR | *Yes* |
| Dining Rooms | *1* | Sittings | *Open* |
| Elevators | *1* | Door Width | *31"* |
| Casino | *Yes* | Slot Machines | *Yes* |

| | | | |
|---|---|---|---|
| Swimming Pools (outside) | *1* | (inside) | *0* |
| Whirlpools | *1* | Gymnasium | *Yes* |
| Sauna/Steam Rm | *Yes/No* | Massage | *Yes* |
| Self-Service Launderette | | | *No* |
| Movie Theater/Seats | | | *No* |
| Library | | | *Yes* |
| Children's Facilities | | | *No* |
| Watersports Facilities | | | *Aft platform, scuba, snorkel, waterski, windsurf, zodiacs (2)* |
| Classification Society | | | *Lloyd's Register* |

| RATINGS | SCORE |
|---|---|
| Ship: Condition/Cleanliness | 9.0 |
| Ship: Space/Flow/Comfort | 9.1 |
| Ship Facilities | 9.2 |
| Ship: Decor/Furnishings | 9.2 |
| Ship: Fitness/Watersports Facilities | 9.1 |
| Cabins: Comfort/Facilities | 9.1 |
| Cabins: Software | 9.0 |
| Food: Dining Room/Cuisine | 9.5 |
| Food: Buffets/Informal Dining | 9.3 |
| Food: Quality of Ingredients | 9.2 |
| Service: Dining Room | 9.2 |
| Service: Bars/Lounges | 9.2 |
| Service: Cabins | 9.1 |
| Cruise: Entertainment/Lecture Program | 8.6 |
| Cruise: Hospitality Standard | 9.3 |
| OVERALL RATING | 137.1 |

**+** Small ship with an ultra-sleek profile and private club ambiance. Meticulously maintained. Watersports facilities at no extra charge. Lovely private club atmosphere. Flowers everywhere. Elegant, chic public rooms and decor. Cute gymnasium and spa classes by Golden Door staff. Oriental rugs in lobby. Finest quality furnishings and fabrics throughout, with marble and blond wood accents. Cabins are fully equipped all-outside suites with beds next to windows so you can entertain in the living area without going past the sleeping area. Cotton bathrobes and towels.

**–** Tenders are now outdated and should be replaced. Bathroom doors open inward.

**Dining** Very elegant, warm, and inviting dining salon, with supremely attentive, impeccable personalized European service. Plenty of space around tables. Tables for two, four, six, or eight are immaculately laid. Taped classical music is played for lunch, live piano music for dinner. Exquisite cuisine prepared to order. In-suite dining at any time. Á la carte 24 hours a day. There's plenty of Beluga caviar. Fine wines, special vintages, and premier crus (extra cost).

**Other Comments** Refined, unstructured, private living at sea is the hallmark of life on this vessel. I cannot recommended it highly enough for the experienced, independent traveller who doesn't like cruise ships. A floating culinary celebration—like having your own private island! Port taxes and insurance are extra. Gratuities are included, and no further tipping is allowed.

# mv Sea Goddess II ★★★★★+

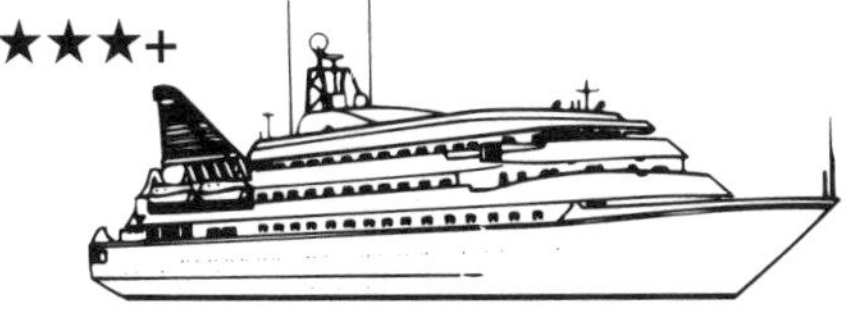

***Principal Cruising Areas***

*Europe/Orient (7-14 nights)*

***Base Ports:*** *Nice/Singapore*

| | | | |
|---|---|---|---|
| Cruise Line | | | *Cunard* |
| Former Names | | | *n/a* |
| Gross Tonnage | | | *4,260* |
| Builder | | | *Wartsila (Finland)* |
| Original Cost | | | *$34 million* |
| Christened By | | | *HRH Princess Caroline of Monaco* |
| First Entered Service | | | *May 11, 1985* |
| Interior Design | | | *Yran & Storbraaten* |
| Country of Registry | | | *Norway (LNQX3)* |
| Tel No | *131-1235* | Fax No | *131-0644* |
| Length (ft/m) | | | *343.8/104.81* |
| Beam (ft/m) | | | *47.9/14.60* |
| Draft (ft/m) | | | *13.6/4.17* |
| Engines/Propellers | | | *2 VASA 12-cyl diesels/2 (CP)* |
| Decks | *5* | Crew | *90* |
| Pass. Capacity (basis 2) | *115* | (all berths) | *115* |
| Pass. Space Ratio (basis 2) | *36.7* | (all berths) | *36.7* |
| Officers | *Norwegian* | Dining Staff | *Scandinavian* |
| Total Cabins | | | *58* |
| Size (sq ft/m) | *179.8-410/16.7-38* | Door Width | *24"* |
| Outside Cabins | *58* | Inside Cabins | *0* |
| Single Cabins | 1 | Supplement | *On request* |
| Balcony Cabins | *0* | Wheelchair Cabins | *0* |
| Cabin Current | *110/220 AC* | Refrigerator | *Yes* |
| Cabin TV | *Yes* | VCR | *Yes* |
| Dining Rooms | *1* | Sittings | *Open* |
| Elevators | *1* | Door Width | *31"* |
| Casino | *Yes* | Slot Machines | *Yes* |

| | | | |
|---|---|---|---|
| Swimming Pools (outside) | *1* | (inside) | *0* |
| Whirlpools | *1* | Gymnasium | *Yes* |
| Sauna/Steam Rm | *Yes/No* | Massage | *Yes* |
| Self-Service Launderette | | | *No* |
| Movie Theater/Seats | | | *No* |
| Library | | | *Yes* |
| Children's Facilities | | | *No* |
| Watersports Facilities | | | *Aft platform, banana boat, scuba, snorkel, waterski, windsurf, zodiacs (2)* |
| Classification Society | | | *Lloyd's Register* |

| RATINGS | SCORE |
|---|---|
| Ship: Condition/Cleanliness | 9.0 |
| Ship: Space/Flow/Comfort | 9.1 |
| Ship Facilities | 9.2 |
| Ship: Decor/Furnishings | 9.2 |
| Ship: Fitness/Watersports Facilities | 9.1 |
| Cabins: Comfort/Facilities | 9.1 |
| Cabins: Software | 9.0 |
| Food: Dining Room/Cuisine | 9.5 |
| Food: Buffets/Informal Dining | 9.3 |
| Food: Quality of Ingredients | 9.2 |
| Service: Dining Room | 9.2 |
| Service: Bars/Lounges | 9.2 |
| Service: Cabins | 9.1 |
| Cruise: Entertainment/Lecture Program | 8.6 |
| Cruise: Hospitality Standard | 9.3 |
| OVERALL RATING | 137.1 |

**+** Lovely vessel with an ultra-sleek, contemporary, and very handsome profile. Immaculately run and maintained. Her shallow draft allows access to small ports that mainstream ships cannot possibly enter. Delightful public rooms feature highest-quality furnishings and tasteful decor. There is a profusion of green plants, giving the ship a warm connection with nature.

**–** Pleasant waterfall at outdoor café, but it doesn't belong on a ship. The tenders need to be replaced or reconditioned. Bathroom doors open inward.

**Dining** Elegant dining salon is instantly inviting and warm. Open seating means you can dine wherever, whenever, and with whomever you want. Only the very freshest and finest ingredients are used. All meals are cooked individually to order. Special orders are welcomed. Fine European service. Dine in-suite at any time. Excellent outdoor buffets, but you never have to serve yourself.

**Other Comments** Lovely all-outside cabins. The bedroom is next to the window, unlike on the *Seabourn* ships. Hospitality and anticipation are art forms practised to the highest degree. For the discriminating person requiring an elegant, private environment in which to be pampered, in a highly personal, unstructured setting. I can't think of a more sophisticated way to go cruising, unless its on a longer *Sea Goddess* cruise. Dress is resort casual by day, dressy by night. The staff are simply wonderful. Port taxes and insurance are extra. Gratuities are included.

# mv Sea Princess ★★★★+

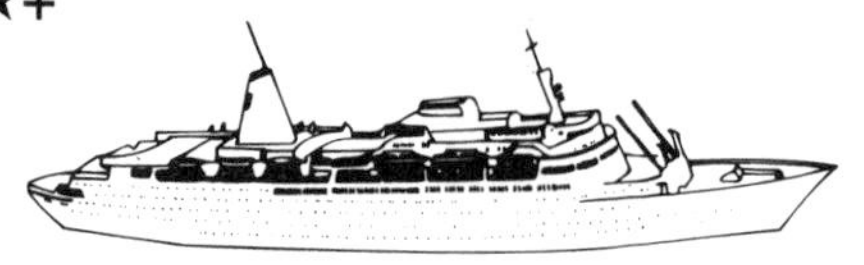

***Principal Cruising Area***
*Europe (14 nights)*
***Base Port:** Southampton*

| | |
|---|---|
| Cruise Line | *P&O Cruises* |
| Former Names | *Kungsholm* |
| Gross Tonnage | *27,670* |
| Builder | *John Brown & Co. (UK)* |
| Original Cost | *$22 million* |
| Christened By | *Mrs Dan Axel-Brostron* |
| First Entered Service | *Apr 22, 1966/Feb 16, 1979* |
| Interior Design | *Robert Tillberg* |
| Country of Registry | *Great Britain (GBBA)* |
| Tel No *144-0320* | Fax No *144-0320* |
| Length (ft/m) | *660.2/201.23* |
| Beam (ft/m) | *87.1/26.57* |
| Draft (ft/m) | *28.0/8.56* |
| Engines/Propellers | *2 Gotaverken 9-cyl diesels/2* |
| Decks *8* | Crew *380* |
| Pass. Capacity (basis 2) *714* | (all berths) *743* |
| Pass. Space Ratio (basis 2) *38.7* | (all berths) *37.2* |
| Officers *British* | Dining Staff *British/Goan* |
| Total Cabins | *365* |
| Size (sq ft/m) | *138-467/12.8-43.3* |
| Door Width | *25-27"* |
| Outside Cabins *295* | Inside Cabins *70* |
| Single Cabins 22 | Supplement *Fixed rates* |
| Balcony Cabins *0* | Wheelchair Cabins *10* |
| Cabin Current | *220 AC* |
| Refrigerator | *AA/BA/BD* |
| Cabin TV *Higher grade* | VCR *No* |
| Dining Rooms *1* | Sittings *2* |

| | |
|---|---|
| Elevators *4* | Door Width *32"* |
| Casino *Yes* | Slot Machines *Yes* |
| Swimming Pools (outside) 2 | (inside) *1* |
| Whirlpools *1* | Gymnasium *Yes* |
| Sauna/Steam Rm *Yes/No* | Massage *Yes* |
| Self-Service Launderette | *Yes* |
| Movie Theater/Seats | *Yes/289* |
| Library *Yes* | Children's Facilities *Yes* |
| Watersports Facilities | *None* |
| Classification Society | *Lloyd's Register* |

| RATINGS | SCORE |
|---|---|
| Ship: Condition/Cleanliness | 8.0 |
| Ship: Space/Flow/Comfort | 7.8 |
| Ship: Decor/Furnishings | 8.0 |
| Ship: Fitness Facilities | 7.4 |
| Cabins: Comfort/Facilities | 7.8 |
| Cabins: Software | 8.0 |
| Food: Dining Room/Cuisine | 7.6 |
| Food: Buffets/Informal Dining | 7.3 |
| Food: Quality of Ingredients | 6.7 |
| Service: Dining Room | 7.7 |
| Service: Bars/Lounges | 7.8 |
| Service: Cabins | 7.7 |
| Cruise: Entertainment | 7.7 |
| Cruise: Activities Program | 7.6 |
| Cruise: Hospitality Standard | 8.0 |
| OVERALL RATING | 115.1 |

**+** Handsome, solidly-built ex-ocean liner with flowing, rounded lines and well-balanced profile. Has been nicely refurbished. Excellent open deck and sunning space. Numerous spacious public rooms with fine-quality furnishings and fabrics throughout, generously trimmed with fine woods. Roomy cabins, many of them beautifully refurbished, have enormous closet and drawer space, and fine wood paneled walls. Generous-sized bathrooms with solid fixtures.

**–** Some cabins have upper and lower berths. Limited wine list. Plastic chairs at lido buffet need cushions.

**Dining** Tiered European-style dining room is really elegant, with old-world traditions and charm, and superb display of 18th-century Chinese porcelain. Good general food and selection that is tailored well for British tastes, and excellent service from the Goan staff. Buffets are very basic, and disappointing, as is the selection of fruits.

**Other Comments** Originally with two funnels, but now only one. Good British entertainment. Altogether a very professional operation. You'll have a most enjoyable cruise experience on this ship, with some attention to detail and some European finesse, at an appropriate price. Mainly British passengers, a good proportion of whom smoke, making it difficult to escape. She is an ideal ship for long voyages. Insurance and gratuities are extra, but port taxes are included.

# ms Seabourn Pride ★★★★★+

***Principal Cruising Areas***

*Caribbean/Europe/South America (7/14 nights)*

***Base Ports:** various*

| | |
|---|---|
| Cruise Line | *Seabourn Cruise Line* |
| Former Names | *n/a* |
| Gross Tonnage | *9,975* |
| Builder | *Seebeckwerft (Germany)* |
| Original Cost | *$50 million* |
| Christened By | *Mrs Shirley Temple Black* |
| First Entered Service | *Dec 4, 1988* |
| Interior Design | *Yran & Storbraaten* |
| Country of Registry | *Norway (LALT2)* |
| Tel No *131-1351* | Fax No *131-1352* |
| Length (ft/m) | *439.9/134.10* |
| Beam (ft/m) *62.9/19.20* | Draft (ft/m) *16.8/5.15* |
| Engines | *2x12-cyl+ 2x8-cyl Bergen diesels* |
| Propellers | *2 (CP)* |
| Decks *6* | Crew *140* |
| Pass. Capacity (basis 2) *204* | (all berths) *204* |
| Pass. Space Ratio (basis 2) *48.8* | (all berths) *48.8* |
| Officers *Norwegian* | Dining Staff *European* |
| Total Cabins | *106* |
| Size (sq ft/m) *277-575/25.7-53.4* | Door Width *28"* |
| Outside Cabins *106* | Inside Cabins *0* |
| Single Cabins *0* | Supplement *10-100%* |
| Balcony Cabins *6* | Wheelchair Cabins *4* |
| Cabin Current *110/220 AC* | Refrigerator *Yes* |
| Cabin TV *Yes* | VCR *Yes* |
| Dining Rooms *1* | Sittings *Open* |
| Elevators *3* | Door Width *31.5"* |
| Casino *Yes* | Slot Machines *Yes* |

| | |
|---|---|
| Swimming Pools (outside) | *1 (+ aft marina-pool)* |
| (inside) | *0* |
| Whirlpools *3* | Gymnasium *Yes* |
| Sauna/Steam Rm *Yes/Yes* | Massage *Yes* |
| Self-Service Launderette | *Yes* |
| Movie Theater/Seats | *No* |
| Library *Yes* | Children's Facilities *No* |
| Watersports Facilities | *Aft platform, marina pool, banana boat, scuba, snorkel, windsurf, waterski* |
| Classification Society | *Det Norske Veritas* |

| RATINGS | SCORE |
|---|---|
| Ship: Condition/Cleanliness | 9.2 |
| Ship: Space/Flow/Comfort | 9.3 |
| Ship Facilities | 9.0 |
| Ship: Decor/Furnishings | 8.9 |
| Ship: Fitness/Watersports Facilities | 9.2 |
| Cabins: Comfort/Facilities | 9.4 |
| Cabins: Software | 9.0 |
| Food: Dining Room/Cuisine | 9.0 |
| Food: Buffets/Informal Dining | 9.0 |
| Food: Quality of Ingredients | 9.2 |
| Service: Dining Room | 8.7 |
| Service: Bars/Lounges | 9.0 |
| Service: Cabins | 9.2 |
| Cruise: Entertainment/Lecture Program | 9.0 |
| Cruise: Hospitality Standard | 9.1 |
| OVERALL RATING | 136.2 |

**+** Sleek styling with swept-back, rounded lines. All-outside suites are beautifully equipped, with large, walk-in closet, personal safe, and plenty of space. Beautiful wooden cabinetry has softly rounded edges. Large, marble bathrooms have two washbasins, decent sized bathtub, plenty of storage areas, and bathrobe. Suite room doors are neatly angled away from passageway. Attention to quality and detail evident everywhere. Features the finest in furnishings and fittings, with superb wood craftsmanship throughout. Observation lounge has great views.

**–** There's no wrap-around outdoor promenade deck. Ceilings are very plain. Drinks are extra (except at beginning of the cruise, when your refrigerator is stocked), but they are low-priced.

**Dining** Marble and carpet dining room features portholes and elegant decor, but is not as intimate as on the *Sea Goddesses*. Culinary excellence prevails, however, and both food quality and presentation are outstanding. Special orders are welcome. Service is impeccable.

**Other Comments** Beautiful, contemporary outer styling for this lovely, luxuriously equipped cruise vessel, sister to *Seabourn Spirit*. Not for the budget-minded, this ship is for those desiring the utmost in supremely elegant, stylish, small-ship surroundings, but just a little too small for a world cruise. Utterly civilized cruising. This ship receives my highest recommendations. Port taxes and insurance are extra. Gratuities are included, and no further tipping is allowed.

# ms Seabourn Spirit ★★★★★+

***Principal Cruising Areas***

*Europe/Orient (7/14 nights)*

***Base Ports:** London/Singapore*

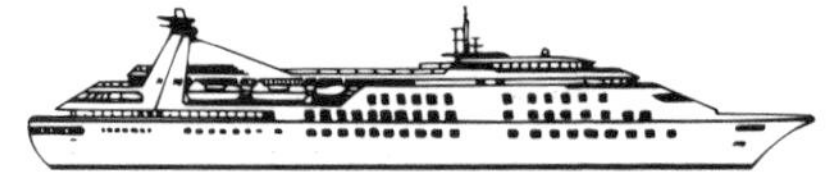

| | | | |
|---|---|---|---|
| Cruise Line | | | *Seabourn Cruise Line* |
| Former Names | | | *n/a* |
| Gross Tonnage | | | *9,975* |
| Builder | | | *Seebeckwerft (Germany)* |
| Original Cost | | | *$50 million* |
| Christened By | | | *Mrs Audun Brynestad* |
| First Entered Service | | | *Nov 10, 1989* |
| Interior Design | | | *Yran & Storbraaten* |
| Country of Registry | | | *Norway (LAOW2)* |
| Tel No | *131-0464* | Fax No | *131-0527* |
| Length (ft/m) | | | *439.9/134.10* |
| Beam (ft/m) | | | *62.9/19.20* |
| Draft (ft/m) | | | *16.8/5.15* |
| Engines/Propellers | | | *2x12-cyl+2x8-cyl diesels/2(CP)* |
| Decks | *6* | Crew | *140* |
| Pass. Capacity (basis 2) | *204* | (all berths) | *204* |
| Pass. Space Ratio (basis 2) | *48.8* | (all berths) | *48.8* |
| Officers | *Norwegian* | Dining Staff | *European* |
| Total Cabins | | | *106* |
| Size (sq ft/m) | *277-575/25.6-53.4* | Door Width | *28"* |
| Outside Cabins | *106* | Inside Cabins | *0* |
| Single Cabins | *0* | Supplement | *10-100%* |
| Balcony Cabins | *6* | Wheelchair Cabins | *4* |
| Cabin Current | *110/220 AC* | Refrigerator | *Yes* |
| Cabin TV | *Yes* | VCR | *Yes* |
| Dining Rooms | *1* | Sittings | *Open* |
| Elevators | *3* | Door Width | *31.5"* |
| Casino | *Yes* | Slot Machines | *Yes* |

| | | | |
|---|---|---|---|
| Swimming Pools (outside) | *1 (+ aft marina-pool)* | (inside) | *0* |
| Whirlpools | *3* | Gymnasium | *Yes* |
| Sauna/Steam Rm | *Yes/Yes* | Massage | *Yes* |
| Self-Service Launderette | | | *Yes* |
| Movie Theater/Seats | | | *No* |
| Library | *Yes* | Children's Facilities | *No* |
| Watersports Facilities | | | *Aft platform, marina pool, banana boat, scuba, snorkel, windsurf, waterski* |
| Classification Society | | | *Det Norske Veritas* |

| RATINGS | SCORE |
|---|---|
| Ship: Condition/Cleanliness | 9.2 |
| Ship: Space/Flow/Comfort | 9.3 |
| Ship Facilities | 9.0 |
| Ship: Decor/Furnishings | 8.9 |
| Ship: Fitness/Watersports Facilities | 9.2 |
| Cabins: Comfort/Facilities | 9.4 |
| Cabins: Software | 9.0 |
| Food: Dining Room/Cuisine | 9.0 |
| Food: Buffets/Informal Dining | 9.0 |
| Food: Quality of Ingredients | 9.2 |
| Service: Dining Room | 8.7 |
| Service: Bars/Lounges | 9.0 |
| Service: Cabins | 9.2 |
| Cruise: Entertainment/Lecture Program | 9.0 |
| Cruise: Hospitality Standard | 9.1 |
| OVERALL RATING | 136.2 |

**+** Sleek styling with swept-back, rounded lines. All-outside suites are beautifully-equipped, with large walk-in closet, personal safe, and plenty of space. Beautiful wooden cabinetry has softly rounded edges. Large, marble bathrooms have two washbasins, decent sized bathtub, plenty of storage areas, and bathrobe. Suite room doors are neatly angled away from passageway. Attention to quality and detail evident everywhere. Features the finest in furnishings and fittings, with superb wood craftsmanship throughout. Observation lounge has great views.

**–** There's no wrap-around outdoor promenade deck. Ceilings are very plain. Drinks are extra (except at beginning of the cruise, when your refrigerator is stocked), but they are low-priced.

**Dining** Marble and carpet dining room features portholes and elegant decor, but is not as intimate as on the *Sea Goddesses.* Culinary excellence prevails, however, and both food quality and presentation are outstanding. Special orders are welcome. Service is impeccable.

**Other Comments** Beautiful, contemporary outer styling for this lovely, luxuriously equipped cruise vessel, sister to *Seabourn Pride.* Not for the budget-minded, this ship is for those desiring the utmost in supremely elegant, stylish, small-ship surroundings, but just a little too small for a world cruise. Utterly civilized cruising. Port taxes and insurance are extra. Gratuities are included, and no further tipping is allowed.

# ss SeaBreeze I ★★★

***Principal Cruising Area***
*Caribbean (7 nights year-round)*
***Base Port:** Miami (Sunday)*

| | | | |
|---|---|---|---|
| Cruise Line | | | *Dolphin Cruise Line* |
| Former Names | | | *Federico "C"/Royale* |
| Gross Tonnage | | | *21,900* |
| Builder | | | *Ansaldo Sestri-Ponente (Italy)* |
| Original Cost | | | *n/a* |
| Christened By | | | *n/a* |
| First Entered Service | | | *Mar 22, 1958/Mar 5, 1989* |
| Interior Design | | | *A&M Katzourakis* |
| Country of Registry | | | *Bahamas (3FGV)* |
| Tel No | *133-6354* | Fax No | *133-6354* |
| Length (ft/m) | | | *605.6/184.61* |
| Beam (ft/m) | | | *78.9/24.06* |
| Draft (ft/m) | | | *29.0/8.84* |
| Engines/Propellers | | | *4 DRG steam turbines/2* |
| Decks | *8* | Crew | *410* |
| Pass. Capacity (basis 2) | *842* | (all berths) | *1,250* |
| Pass. Space Ratio (basis 2) | *26.0* | (all berths) | *17.5* |
| Officers | | | *Greek* |
| Dining Staff | | | *International* |
| Total Cabins | | | *421* |
| Size (sq ft/m) | *65-258/6-24* | Door Width | *25"* |
| Outside Cabins | *263* | Inside Cabins | *158* |
| Single Cabins | *2* | Supplement | *50%* |
| Balcony Cabins | *0* | Wheelchair Cabins | *0* |
| Cabin Current | *110/220 AC* | Refrigerator | *No* |
| Cabin TV | *No* | VCR | *No* |
| Dining Rooms | *1* | Sittings | *2* |
| Elevators | *4* | Door Width | *27"* |

| | | | |
|---|---|---|---|
| Casino | *Yes* | Slot Machines | *Yes* |
| Swimming Pools (outside) | *1* | (inside) | *0* |
| Whirlpools | *3* | Gymnasium | *Yes* |
| Sauna/Steam Rm | *No/No* | Massage | *Yes* |
| Self-Service Launderette | | | *No* |
| Movie Theater/Seats | | | *Yes/110* |
| Library | | | *No* |
| Children's Facilities | | | *Yes* |
| Watersports Facilities | | | *None* |
| Classification Society | | | *Lloyd's Register* |

| RATINGS | SCORE |
|---|---|
| Ship: Condition/Cleanliness | 6.2 |
| Ship: Space/Flow/Comfort | 5.9 |
| Ship: Decor/Furnishings | 6.4 |
| Ship: Fitness Facilities | 4.3 |
| Cabins: Comfort/Facilities | 6.3 |
| Cabins: Software | 6.5 |
| Food: Dining Room/Cuisine | 7.0 |
| Food: Buffets/Informal Dining | 6.8 |
| Food: Quality of Ingredients | 6.5 |
| Service: Dining Room | 6.8 |
| Service: Bars/Lounges | 6.9 |
| Service: Cabins | 7.1 |
| Cruise: Entertainment | 6.2 |
| Cruise: Activities Program | 6.6 |
| Cruise: Hospitality Standard | 6.8 |
| OVERALL RATING | 96.3 |

**+** Classic, old, former ocean liner styling, with forthright white profile and sea-wave stripes in the center of her hull. Neat sail-cloth canopy over aft outdoor area. Public rooms are bright and cheerful, and tastefully decorated, although there are lots of mirrored and chromed surfaces. Wide variety of cabins in many configurations. Many cabins can accommodate five—ideal for families with children. Drawer space is limited but closet space is good.

**–** Open deck and sunning space on this high density ship is quite limited, and thus extremely crowded when full. Disjointed layout, a carry-over from her former three-class ocean liner days, hinders passenger flow. Steep passenger gangway in some ports. She's getting too old.

**Dining** The dining room has bright decor, but tables are much too close together for serving comfort. There are, however, several tables for two. Both food and service are very good for the price paid.

**Other Comments** There's no real finesse, but the staff are very willing to please, and quite attentive. This ship has plenty of life and atmosphere, is quite comfortable, caters well to families, and remains very good value for a first cruise experience. Insurance and gratuities are extra.

# mv SeaSpirit ★★★

***Principal Cruising Areas***

*U.S. Coast/British Virgin Islands (7 nights)*

***Base Ports:** various*

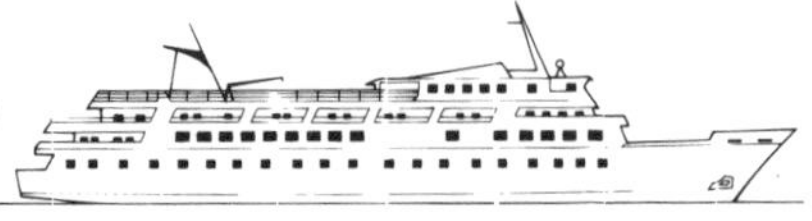

| | | | |
|---|---|---|---|
| Cruise Line | | | *Seaspirit Cruise Line* |
| Former Names | | | *Newport Clipper* |
| Gross Tonnage | | | *1,471* |
| Builder | | | *Jefferson Boatyard (Florida)* |
| Original Cost | | | *$11 million* |
| Christened By | | | *n/a* |
| First Entered Service | | | *1982/Jun 10, 1993* |
| Interior Design | | | *Carl Williams* |
| Country of Registry | | | *USA* |
| Tel No | *n/a* | Fax No | *n/a* |
| Length (ft/m) | | | *207.0/63.09* |
| Beam (ft/m) | | | *37.0/11.27* |
| Draft (ft/m) | | | *8.0/2.40* |
| Engines/Propellers | | | *2 Detroit diesels/2* |
| Decks | *4* | Crew | *32* |
| Pass. Capacity (basis 2) | *102* | (all berths) | *109* |
| Pass. Space Ratio (basis 2) | *14.4* | (all berths) | *13.4* |
| Officers | | | *American* |
| Dining Staff | | | *American* |
| Total Cabins | | | *51* |
| Size (sq ft/m) | *121-138/11.2-12.8* | Door Width | *23"* |
| Outside Cabins | *51* | Inside Cabins | *0* |
| Single Cabins | *0* | Supplement | *100%* |
| Balcony Cabins | *0* | Wheelchair Cabins | *0* |
| Cabin Current | *110 AC* | Refrigerator | *No* |
| Cabin TV | *Yes* | VCR | *Yes* |
| Dining Rooms | *1* | Sittings | *1* |
| Elevators | *0* | Door Width | *n/a* |

| | | | |
|---|---|---|---|
| Casino | *No* | Slot Machines | *No* |
| Swimming Pools (outside) | *0* | (inside) | *0* |
| Whirlpools | *1* | Gymnasium | *Yes* |
| Sauna/Steam Rm | *No/No* | Massage | *No* |
| Self-Service Launderette | | | *No* |
| Movie Theater/Seats | | | *No* |
| Library | | | *No* |
| Children's Facilities | | | *No* |
| Watersports Facilities | | | *None* |
| Classification Society | | | *American Bur. of Shipping* |

| RATINGS | SCORE |
|---|---|
| Ship: Condition/Cleanliness | 6.2 |
| Ship: Space/Flow/Comfort | 4.0 |
| Ship: Decor/Furnishings | 7.6 |
| Ship: Fitness Facilities | 3.5 |
| Cabins: Comfort/Facilities | 5.2 |
| Cabins: Software | 6.3 |
| Food: Dining Room/Cuisine | 7.0 |
| Food: Buffets/Informal Dining | 6.6 |
| Food: Quality of Ingredients | 6.8 |
| Service: Dining Room | 7.4 |
| Service: Bars/Lounges | 7.3 |
| Service: Cabins | 7.7 |
| Cruise: Entertainment | 4.0 |
| Cruise: Activities Program | 6.0 |
| Cruise: Hospitality Standard | 8.1 |
| OVERALL RATING | 93.7 |

**+** This small vessel is specially constructed for close-in coastal and inland cruises. The all-outside cabins are small, but comfortable and very tastefully furnished, although bathrooms are small. Casual and unstructured lifestyle, rather like a small, but not luxurious, country club afloat. Not to be compared with big ship ocean cruising.

**–** It is a high density ship with only three public rooms—the dining room, an observation lounge and aft bar.

**Dining** The dining room is warm and inviting, and has large picture windows. The food is of good quality and very creative, but choice is limited.

**Other Comments** This ship is the world's first gay-owned and operated cruise vessel. Attentive, very friendly service is by young, all-American types. This is most definitely for those seeking to learn more about the coastal ports around the U.S.A. RSVP (the marketing company) will provide a comfortable, warm setting for gay men only. The per diem price is high, and air fare is extra, but she does cater to a very special, highly targeted, and specific market.

# ms Seaward ★★★★

***Principal Cruising Area***
*Bahamas (3/4 nights year-round)*
***Base Port:*** *Miami (Fri/Mon)*

| | | | |
|---|---|---|---|
| Cruise Line | | | *Norwegian Cruise Line* |
| Former Names | | | *n/a* |
| Gross Tonnage | | | *42,276* |
| Builder | | | *Wartsila (Finland)* |
| Original Cost | | | *$120 million* |
| Christened By | | | *Ms Greta Weiss* |
| First Entered Service | | | *Jun 12, 1988* |
| Interior Design | | | *Robert Tillberg* |
| Country of Registry | | | *Bahamas (C6DM2)* |
| Tel No | *110-4601* | Fax No | *110-4602* |
| Length (ft/m) | | | *708.6/216.00* |
| Beam (ft/m) | | | *95.1/29.00* |
| Draft (ft/m) | | | *22.9/7.00* |
| Engines/Propellers | | | *4 Sulzer 8-cyl diesels/2 (CP)* |
| Decks | *9* | Crew | *630* |
| Pass. Capacity (basis 2) | *1,534* | (all berths) | *1,798* |
| Pass. Space Ratio (basis 2) | *27.5* | (all berths) | *23.5* |
| Officers | *Norwegian* | Dining Staff | *International* |
| Total Cabins | | | *767* |
| Size (sq ft/m) | *110-270/10.2-25* | Door Width | *27"* |
| Outside Cabins | *486* | Inside Cabins | *281* |
| Single Cabins | *0* | Supplement | *50-100%* |
| Balcony Cabins | *0* | Wheelchair Cabins | *4* |
| Cabin Current | | | *110 AC* |
| Refrigerator | | | *Category 1/2/3* |
| Cabin TV | *Yes* | VCR | *No* |
| Dining Rooms | *2* | Sittings | *2* |
| Elevators | *6* | Door Width | *35"* |

| | | | |
|---|---|---|---|
| Casino | *Yes* | Slot Machines | *Yes* |
| Swimming Pools (outside) | 2 | (inside) | *0* |
| Whirlpools | 2 | Gymnasium | *Yes* |
| Sauna/Steam Rm | *Yes/No* | Massage | *Yes* |
| Self-Service Launderette | | | *No* |
| Movie Theater/Seats | | | *No* |
| Library | | | *No* |
| Children's Facilities | | | *No* |
| Watersports Facilities | | | *None* |
| Classification Society | | | *Det Norske Veritas* |

| RATINGS | SCORE |
|---|---|
| Ship: Condition/Cleanliness | 8.0 |
| Ship: Space/Flow/Comfort | 7.8 |
| Ship: Decor/Furnishings | 7.7 |
| Ship: Fitness Facilities | 7.8 |
| Cabins: Comfort/Facilities | 7.6 |
| Cabins: Software | 6.2 |
| Food: Dining Room/Cuisine | 7.4 |
| Food: Buffets/Informal Dining | 7.1 |
| Food: Quality of Ingredients | 6.3 |
| Service: Dining Room | 7.4 |
| Service: Bars/Lounges | 7.5 |
| Service: Cabins | 7.2 |
| Cruise: Entertainment | 8.0 |
| Cruise: Activities Program | 7.1 |
| Cruise: Hospitality Standard | 7.4 |
| OVERALL RATING | 110.5 |

**+** Fine teakwood outdoor wrap-around promenade deck. Interior designed to remind you of sea and sky—coral, blue, and mauve are predominant. Excellent gymnasium/fitness center. Striking two-deck-high lobby with unique crystal and water sculpture. Two glass-walled stairways. Striking theater-showroom provides large-scale dazzle and sizzle shows. Most intimate place is mahogany-paneled Oscar's Lounge. Cabins are of average size, but quite tastefully equipped, and quite comfortable. Hairdryers included in bathroom.

**–** Tinny steps on stairways. Too many unnecessary announcements.

**Dining** The two main dining rooms are quite homey, with pastel decor. Gatsby's wine bar is a popular place, with a good wine and champagne list. The cuisine, for a mass-market ship, ranges from adequate to quite good, although it is now being improved. There is a major emphasis on meat dishes with heavy sauces, and overcooked vegetables. However, fish and foul are good. Nothing arrives hot. The service is adequate, nothing more. The selection of wines is excellent.

**Other Comments** Angular, yet attractive, ship with contemporary, European cruise-ferry profile, well-raked bow, and sleek mast and funnel. One of the best in the Caribbean mass-market arena, and popular for first-time cruisegoers, at a sensible, competitive price. The weak spot is the food operation, which needs upgrading. Insurance and gratuities are extra.

# tss Seawind Crown ★★★+

***Principal Cruising Area***
*Caribbean (7 nights year-round)*
***Base Port:*** *Aruba (Sunday)*

| | | | |
|---|---|---|---|
| Cruise Line | | | *Seawind Cruise Line* |
| Former Names | | | *Vasco da Gama/ Infante Dom Henrique* |
| Gross Tonnage | | | *24,568* |
| Builder | | | *Cockerill-Ougree (Belgium)* |
| Original Cost | | | *n/a* |
| Christened By | | | *n/a* |
| First Entered Service | | | *Sep 25, 1961/Oct 6, 1991* |
| Interior Design | | | *Kohnemann/Schindler* |
| Country of Registry | | | *Panama (3EIY6)* |
| Tel No | *133-1251* | Fax No | *133-1252* |
| Length (ft/m) | | | *641.6/195.59* |
| Beam (ft/m) | | | *84.4/25.73* |
| Draft (ft/m) | | | *26.9/8.20* |
| Engines | | | *4 Westinghouse steam turbines* |
| Propellers | | | *2* |
| Decks | *8* | Crew | *311* |
| Pass. Capacity (basis 2) | *626* | (all berths) | *719* |
| Pass. Space Ratio (basis 2) | *39.2* | (all berths) | *34.1* |
| Officers | *Greek* | Dining Staff | *European* |
| Total Cabins | | | *313* |
| Size (sq ft/m) | *118-560/11-52* | Door Width | *23-29"* |
| Outside Cabins | *211* | Inside Cabins | *102* |
| Single Cabins | *0* | Supplement | *0-100%* |
| Balcony Cabins | *2* | Wheelchair Cabins | *2* |
| Cabin Current | *220 AC* | Refrigerator | *All cabins* |
| Cabin TV | *Yes* | VCR | *No* |
| Dining Rooms | *2* | Sittings | *2* |

| | | | |
|---|---|---|---|
| Elevators | *4* | Door Width | *36"* |
| Casino | *Yes* | Slot Machines | *Yes* |
| Swimming Pools (outside) | *2* | (inside) | *0* |
| Whirlpools | *0* | Gymnasium | *Yes* |
| Sauna/Steam Rm | *Yes/No* | Massage | *Yes* |
| Self-Service Launderette | | | *No* |
| Movie Theater/Seats | | | *Yes/209* |
| Library | *Yes* | Children's Facilities | *Yes* |
| Watersports Facilities | | | *None* |
| Classification Society | | | *Lloyd's Register* |

| RATINGS | SCORE |
|---|---|
| Ship: Condition/Cleanliness | 6.5 |
| Ship: Space/Flow/Comfort | 7.8 |
| Ship: Decor/Furnishings | 7.6 |
| Ship: Fitness Facilities | 6.2 |
| Cabins: Comfort/Facilities | 6.8 |
| Cabins: Software | 7.1 |
| Food: Dining Room/Cuisine | 7.4 |
| Food: Buffets/Informal Dining | 7.2 |
| Food: Quality of Ingredients | 7.0 |
| Service: Dining Room | 6.7 |
| Service: Bars/Lounges | 6.5 |
| Service: Cabins | 7.0 |
| Cruise: Entertainment | 6.6 |
| Cruise: Activities Program | 6.0 |
| Cruise: Hospitality Standard | 7.3 |
| OVERALL RATING | 103.7 |

**+** Handsome profile and elegant lines for this former long-distance liner that has been extensively refurbished. Long foredeck and rakish bow. Latest navigation equipment. Two covered indoor teak promenade decks and one outdoor. Surprisingly spacious, classic vessel indeed. Mix of old-world elegance and contemporary features. Host of intimate public rooms feature tasteful decor and pastel tones. Delightful chapel. Superbly equipped hospital. Excellent wood paneling and trim everywhere. Spacious foyers. Bavarian-style taverna. All cabins have excellent closet and drawer space, refrigerator, hairdryer, and cotton bathrobes and towels. Suites are huge. Sports facilities include paddle-tennis and indoor squash courts.

**–** Good cinema, but seats should be staggered for better sightlines. Steep gangway in most ports.

**Dining** Dining room comfortable, and both food and service are very good, although you get what you pay for, and the food budget is low. Poor selection of breads, cheeses, and fruits.

**Other Comments** Underwent a $40 million refit in Greece in 1988. This ship has potential, and will provide you with a very comfortable cruise experience in classic ocean liner surroundings with no glitz, and all at a modest price. A further 110 berths were due to be added in Siptember 1994. Slow immigration in Aruba is a real sore point. Insurance, port taxes, and gratuities are extra.

# ms Sensation ★★★★

***Principal Cruising Area***

*Caribbean (7 nights year-round)*

***Base Port:** Miami (Sunday)*

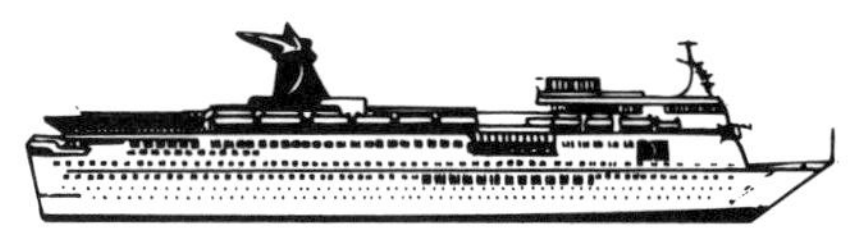

| | | | |
|---|---|---|---|
| Cruise Line | | | *Carnival Cruise Lines* |
| Former Names | | | *n/a* |
| Gross Tonnage | | | *70,367* |
| Builder | | | *Kvaerner Masa-Yards (Finland)* |
| Original Cost | | | *$300 million* |
| Christened By | | | *Geri Donnelly, Vicki Freed, Roberta Jacoby, Cheri Weinstein* |
| First Entered Service | | | *Nov 21, 1993* |
| Interior Design | | | *Joe Farcus* |
| Country of Registry | | | *Liberia (3ESE9)* |
| Tel No | *134-1372* | Fax No | *134-1373* |
| Length (ft/m) | | | *855.0/260.60* |
| Beam (ft/m) | | | *104.0/31.40* |
| Draft (ft/m) | | | *25.9/7.90* |
| Engines/Propellers | | | *2 8-cyl diesel-electrics/2 (CP)* |
| Decks | *10* | Crew | *920* |
| Pass. Capacity (basis 2) | *2,040* | (all berths) | *2,594* |
| Pass. Space Ratio (basis 2) | *34.4* | (all berths) | *26.7* |
| Officers | *Italian* | Dining Staff | *International* |
| Total Cabins | | | *1,020* |
| Size (sq ft/m) | *185-421/17-39* | Door Width | *30"* |
| Outside Cabins | *620* | Inside Cabins | *402* |
| Single Cabins | *0* | Supplement | *50/100%* |
| Balcony Cabins | *54* | Wheelchair Cabins | *20* |
| Cabin Current | | | *110 AC* |
| Refrigerator | | | *Cat. 11/12* |
| Cabin TV | *Yes* | VCR | *No* |
| Dining Rooms | *2* | Sittings | *2* |

| | | | |
|---|---|---|---|
| Elevators | *14* | Door Width | *36"* |
| Casino | *Yes* | Slot Machines | *Yes* |
| Swimming Pools (outside) | *3* | (inside) | *0* |
| Whirlpools | *6* | Gymnasium | *Yes* |
| Sauna/Steam Rm | *Yes/Yes* | Massage | *Yes* |
| Self-Service Launderette | | | *Yes* |
| Movie Theater/Seats | | | *No* |
| Library | *Yes* | Children's Facilities | *Yes* |
| Watersports Facilities | | | *None* |
| Classification Society | | | *Lloyd's Register* |

| RATINGS | SCORE |
|---|---|
| Ship: Condition/Cleanliness | 9.0 |
| Ship: Space/Flow/Comfort | 8.1 |
| Ship: Decor/Furnishings | 8.2 |
| Ship: Fitness Facilities | 7.8 |
| Cabins: Comfort/Facilities | 7.6 |
| Cabins: Software | 7.4 |
| Food: Dining Room/Cuisine | 6.7 |
| Food: Buffets/Informal Dining | 6.4 |
| Food: Quality of Ingredients | 5.3 |
| Service: Dining Room | 7.0 |
| Service: Bars/Lounges | 7.2 |
| Service: Cabins | 6.4 |
| Cruise: Entertainment | 8.2 |
| Cruise: Activities Program | 7.8 |
| Cruise: Hospitality Standard | 6.3 |
| OVERALL RATING | 109.4 |

**+** Almost vibration-free service from diesel-electric propulsion system. Dramatic six-deck-high atrium, with cool marble and hot neon, topped by the largest glass dome afloat. Expansive open deck areas and excellent health spa. 28 outside suites have whirlpool tubs. Public entertainment lounges, bars and clubs galore. Dazzling colors and design themes in handsome public rooms connected by wide indoor boulevards. $1 million art collection. Lavish, but elegant, multi-tiered showroom, and high energy razzle-dazzle shows. Dramatic, three-deck-high glass enclosed health spa. Banked jogging track. Gigantic casino with non-stop action.

**–** Sensory overkill. Large shop, poor merchandise. Too many announcements. Long lines for buffets, shore tenders, embarkation, and disembarkation. Aggressive hustling for drinks.

**Dining** Two huge, noisy dining rooms with usual efficient, assertive service. Cuisine so-so, but it's not *Carnival*'s strong point. Service is attentive, but programed and inflexible.

**Other Comments** Has a bold, angular appearance that is typical of today's space-creative designs. This is the third in a series of five megaships for Carnival that reflects the amazingly creative and dazzling interior design work of Joe Farcus. Poor food, but forget it, the real fun begins at sundown, when Carnival excels. This ship will entertain you well. You'll never be bored, but you may forget to get off in port! Insurance and gratuities are extra.

# ms Shota Rustaveli ★★★

***Principal Cruising Area***
*Europe (various)*
***Base Port:*** *Marseilles*

| | | | |
|---|---|---|---|
| Cruise Line | | | *Black Sea Shipping* |
| Former Names | | | *n/a* |
| Gross Tonnage | | | *20,499* |
| Builder | | | *VEB Mathias Thesen (Germany)* |
| Original Cost | | | *n/a* |
| Christened By | | | *n/a* |
| First Entered Service | | | *Jun 30, 1968* |
| Interior Design | | | *n/a* |
| Country of Registry | | | *Ukraine (UUGF)* |
| Tel No | *140-0253* | Fax No | *140-0253* |
| Length (ft/m) | | | *576.6/175.77* |
| Beam (ft/m) | | | *77.4/23.60* |
| Draft (ft/m) | | | *26.5/8.09* |
| Engines/Propellers | | | *2 Sulzer-Cegielski 7-cyl diesels/2* |
| Decks | *8* | Crew | *350* |
| Pass. Capacity (basis 2) | *493* | (all berths) | *602* |
| Pass. Space Ratio (basis 2) | *41.4* | (all berths) | *34.0* |
| Officers | | | *Russian/Ukrainian* |
| Dining Staff | | | *Russian/Ukrainian* |
| Total Cabins | | | *249* |
| Size (sq ft/m) | *n/a* | Door Width | *26"* |
| Outside Cabins | *244* | Inside Cabins | *5* |
| Single Cabins | *0* | Supplement | *100%* |
| Balcony Cabins | *0* | Wheelchair Cabins | *0* |
| Cabin Current | *220 AC* | Refrigerator | *No* |
| Cabin TV | *No* | VCR | *No* |
| Dining Rooms | *3* | Sittings | *2* |
| Elevators | *3* | Door Width | *32"* |

| | | | |
|---|---|---|---|
| Casino | *No* | Slot Machines | *No* |
| Swimming Pools (outside) | 2 | (inside) | *0* |
| Whirlpools | *0* | Gymnasium | *Yes* |
| Sauna/Steam Rm | *Yes/No* | Massage | *Yes* |
| Self-Service Launderette | | | *Yes* |
| Movie Theater/Seats | | | *Yes/130* |
| Library | | | *Yes* |
| Children's Facilities | | | *Yes* |
| Watersports Facilities | | | *None* |
| Classification Society | | | *RS* |

| RATINGS | SCORE |
|---|---|
| Ship: Condition/Cleanliness | 6.2 |
| Ship: Space/Flow/Comfort | 6.6 |
| Ship: Decor/Furnishings | 6.2 |
| Ship: Fitness Facilities | 5.5 |
| Cabins: Comfort/Facilities | 6.1 |
| Cabins: Software | 6.4 |
| Food: Dining Room/Cuisine | 6.4 |
| Food: Buffets/Informal Dining | 6.3 |
| Food: Quality of Ingredients | 6.5 |
| Service: Dining Room | 6.6 |
| Service: Bars/Lounges | 6.9 |
| Service: Cabins | 7.0 |
| Cruise: Entertainment | 6.0 |
| Cruise: Activities Program | 5.4 |
| Cruise: Hospitality Standard | 6.4 |
| OVERALL RATING | 94.5 |

**+** Good-looking, well-built traditional ship styling with all-white profile. Good teak wood decks and wrap-around open promenade. Good open deck space for sunning, with real wooden deck chairs. Nice inside swimming pool. Spacious interior with quite pleasing decor, although colors are a little dour. Lots of wood paneling and trim. Apart from some deluxe cabins with private balconies, this ship has small, but very comfortable, all-outside cabins, with attractive wood accents, solid fixtures, and pleasing decor. Many portholes actually open—unusual in today's air-conditioned world of ships.

**–** General maintenance needs more attention. Steep, narrow gangway in some ports. Spartan, dated decor. Long lines for embarkation, disembarkation, buffets, and shore tenders.

**Dining** The dining room is quite comfortable. With both French and Russian chefs, the food is quite good, but there is little choice. Limited selection of breads and fruits. Free carafes of wine for lunch and dinner. Service is attentive, but somewhat inflexible.

**Other Comments** This ship, nicely renovated in 1991, is often chartered to a European cruise-tour company. European cruise staff cater well to principally French- and Italian-speaking passengers. Good for the passenger on a low budget who doesn't expect luxury. Insurance, port taxes, and gratuities are extra.

# ms Silver Cloud ★★★★★

***Principal Cruising Areas***

*Worldwide (various)*

***Base Ports:*** *various*

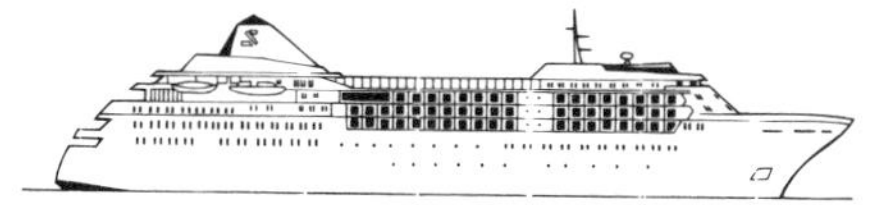

| | |
|---|---|
| Cruise Line | *Silversea Cruises* |
| Former Names | *n/a* |
| Gross Tonnage | *16,800* |
| Builder | *SEC/T. Mariotti (Italy)* |
| Original Cost | *$125 million* |
| Christened By | *Mrs Lefebvre* |
| First Entered Service | *Apr 2, 1994* |
| Interior Design | *Yran & Storbraaten* |
| Country of Registry | *Italy (ICSL)* |
| Tel No | *115-2162/115-2164* |
| Fax No | *115-2163/115-2165* |
| Length (ft/m) | *514.4/155.80* |
| Beam (ft/m) *70.62/21.40* | Draft (ft/m) *17.3/5.30* |
| Engines/Propellers | *2 Wartsila 6-cyl diesels/2 (VP)* |
| Decks *8* | Crew *198* |
| Pass. Capacity (basis 2) *306* | (all berths) *330* |
| Pass. Space Ratio (basis 2) *54.9* | (all berths) *50.9* |
| Officers *Italian* | Dining Staff *European* |
| Total Cabins | *153* |
| Size(sq ft/m) | *240-1,315/22.2-122.17* |
| Door Width | *28"* |
| Outside Cabins *153* | Inside Cabins *0* |
| Single Cabins *0* | Supplement *On request* |
| Balcony Cabins *119* | Wheelchair Cabins *0* |
| Cabin Current *110/220 AC* | Refrigerator *Yes* |
| Cabin TV *Yes* | VCR *Yes* |
| Dining Rooms *1* | Sittings *Open Seating* |
| Elevators *4* | Door Width *35"* |

| | |
|---|---|
| Casino *Yes* | Slot Machines *Yes* |
| Swimming Pools (outside) *1* | (inside) *0* |
| Whirlpools *2* | Gymnasium *Yes* |
| Sauna/Steam Rm *Yes/Yes* | Massage *Yes* |
| Self-Service Launderette | *Yes* |
| Movie Theater/Seats | *Yes/306* |
| Library *Yes* | Children's Facilities *No* |
| Watersports Facilities | *side platform, kayaks, zodiacs, sailfish, snorkel, windsurf, waterski boats* |
| Classification Society | *Lloyd's Register/RINA* |

| RATINGS | SCORE |
|---|---|
| Ship: Condition/Cleanliness | 9.4 |
| Ship: Space/Flow/Comfort | 9.7 |
| Ship: Decor/Furnishings | 9.3 |
| Ship: Fitness Facilities | 8.7 |
| Cabins: Comfort/Facilities | 9.2 |
| Cabins: Software | 9.1 |
| Food: Dining Room/Cuisine | 8.7 |
| Food: Buffets/Informal Dining | 8.6 |
| Food: Quality of Ingredients | 8.6 |
| Service: Dining Room | 8.8 |
| Service: Bars/Lounges | 8.5 |
| Service: Cabins | 9.0 |
| Cruise: Entertainment | 8.8 |
| Cruise: Activities Program | 8.5 |
| Cruise: Hospitality Standard | 8.8 |
| OVERALL RATING | 133.7 |

**+** Sleek, handsome profile, rather like a small version of *Crystal Harmony* or a larger version of the Seabourn ships. Teakwood wrap-around outdoor promenade deck. Excellent outdoor pool deck. Spacious, well planned interior. Elegant decor and the finest quality soft furnishings, with gentle use of brass and fine woods. Useful business center. Fine two-level showroom and beautiful, elegant production shows. All outside suites (75% have private teakwood verandas) have convertible queen-to-twin beds, are beautifully fitted out, and include huge floor-to-ceiling windows, ultra-large closets, dressing table, writing desk, mini-bar, and fresh flowers. Marble floored bathrooms have bathtub. Top suites have CD players.

**–** Not much hanging space in closets. Insulation between cabins could be improved, and a privacy curtain should be installed. Shorter itineraries may be too busy, with not enough days at sea.

**Dining** Lovely dining room, set with fine china and flatware. Features 24-hour in-suite dining service. Fine dining throughout the ship, with choice of formal and informal areas. Not up to the standards of *Sea Goddess* or *Seabourn*, but the potential is excellent.

**Other Comments** Refreshingly, tipping is not allowed. This ship could well become the Rolls Royce (Silver Cloud) of cruise ships if some fine tuning is done. Port taxes, full insurance, and gratuities are included, and no further tipping is allowed.

# ms Silver Wind

***Principal Cruising Areas***

*Worldwide (various)*

***Base Ports:*** *various*

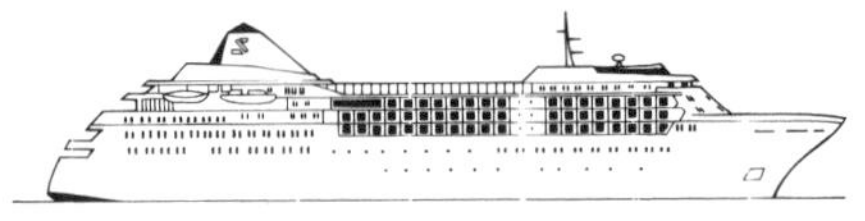

| | | | |
|---|---|---|---|
| Cruise Line | | | *Silversea Cruises* |
| Former Names | | | *n/a* |
| Gross Tonnage | | | *16,800* |
| Builder | | | *Societa Esercizio Cantieri (Italy)* |
| Original Cost | | | *$125 million* |
| Christened By | | | *n/a* |
| First Entered Service | | | *Jan 29, 1995* |
| Interior Design | | | *Yran & Storbraaten* |
| Country of Registry | | | *Italy* |
| Tel No | *n/a* | Fax No | *n/a* |
| Length (ft/m) | | | *514.4/155.80* |
| Beam (ft/m) | | | *70.62/21.40* |
| Draft (ft/m) | | | *17.3/5.30* |
| Engines/Propellers | | | *2 Wartsila 6-cyl diesels/2 (VP)* |
| Decks | *6* | Crew | *197* |
| Pass. Capacity (basis 2) | *306* | (all berths) | *306* |
| Pass. Space Ratio (basis 2) | *54.9* | (all berths) | *54.9* |
| Officers | *Italian* | Dining Staff | *European* |
| Total Cabins | | | *153* |
| Size (sq ft/m) | | | *240-1,315/22.2-122.17* |
| Door Width | | | *28"* |
| Outside Cabins | *153* | Inside Cabins | *0* |
| Single Cabins | *0* | Supplement | *on request* |
| Balcony Cabins | *119* | Wheelchair Cabins | *0* |
| Cabin Current | *110/220 AC* | Refrigerator | *Yes* |
| Cabin TV | *Yes* | VCR | *Yes* |
| Dining Rooms | *1* | Sittings | *Open Seating* |
| Elevators | *4* | Door Width | *35"* |

| | | | |
|---|---|---|---|
| Casino | *Yes* | Slot Machines | *Yes* |
| Swimming Pools (outside) | *1* | (inside) | *0* |
| Whirlpools | *2* | Gymnasium | *Yes* |
| Sauna/Steam Rm | *Yes/Yes* | Massage | *Yes* |
| Self-Service Launderette | | | *Yes* |
| Movie Theater/Seats | | | *Yes/306* |
| Library | | | *Yes* |
| Children's Facilities | | | *No* |
| Watersports Facilities | | | *side platform, kayaks, zodiacs, sailfish, snorkel, windsurf, waterski boats* |

| RATINGS | SCORE |
|---|---|
| Ship: Condition/Cleanliness | NYR |
| Ship: Space/Flow/Comfort | NYR |
| Ship: Decor/Furnishings | NYR |
| Ship: Fitness Facilities | NYR |
| Cabins: Comfort/Facilities | NYR |
| Cabins: Software | NYR |
| Food: Dining Room/Cuisine | NYR |
| Food: Buffets/Informal Dining | NYR |
| Food: Quality of Ingredients | NYR |
| Service: Dining Room | NYR |
| Service: Bars/Lounges | NYR |
| Service: Cabins | NYR |
| Cruise: Entertainment | NYR |
| Cruise: Activities Program | NYR |
| Cruise: Hospitality Standard | NYR |

NYR = Not Yet Rated

**+** Sleek, handsome, and well balanced profile, rather like a small version of *Crystal Harmony* or larger version of the Seabourn ships. Very attractive multi-level atrium has wrap-around staircase. What is most apparent is the incredible amount of space per passenger. Nowhere ever has that "crowded" feeling, and it's always easy to get a chair in any room, which makes cruising on her a real pleasure. Cabins feature round-edged wood-trimmed cabinetry, fresh flowers daily, bathrobes, and fully-stocked mini-bar. Marble-floor bathrooms have bathtubs. Excellent wood (albeit plastic) detailing provides a feeling of warmth everywhere.

**–** None noted at press time. Suite/cabin bathrooms are not quite as elegant as I expected.

**Dining** See comments for sister ship, *Silver Cloud.*

**Other Comments** Same comments as for sister ship, *Silver Cloud*, at present. Operated by "V" Ships, the company that created Sitmar Cruises some years ago. An elegant onboard ambiance is expected. Soft drinks throughout the ship are complimentary—a thoughtful touch. Port taxes, insurance, and gratuities are included, and no further tipping is allowed. The ship was not in service when this book was completed, and so she is not personally rated at press time, but expected to be the same as *Silver Cloud.*

# tss Sky Princess ★★★★+

***Principal Cruising Areas***

*Alaska/Caribbean (7 nights)*

***Base Ports:** Vancouver/Seward/Ft. Lauderdale*

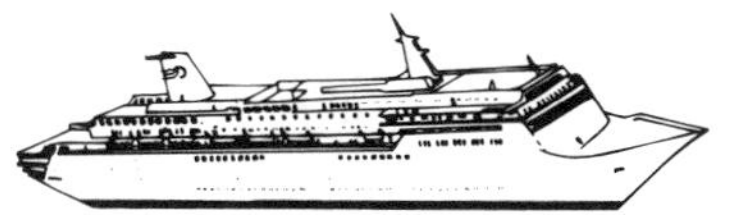

| | | | |
|---|---|---|---|
| Cruise Line | | | *Princess Cruises* |
| Former Names | | | *Fairsky* |
| Gross Tonnage | | | *46,314* |
| Builder | | | *C.N.I.M. (France)* |
| Original Cost | | | *$156 million* |
| Christened By | | | *Mrs Jenny Ueberroth* |
| First Entered Service | | | *Mar 3, 1984* |
| Interior Design | | | *Giacomo Mortola* |
| Country of Registry | | | *Great Britain (GYYP)* |
| Tel No | *144-2264* | Fax No | *144-2266* |
| Length (ft/m) | | | *788.6/240.39* |
| Beam (ft/m) | | | *91.3/27.84* |
| Draft (ft/m) | | | *26.7/8.15* |
| Engines/Propellers | | | *4 steam turbines/2 (CP)* |
| Decks | *11* | Crew | *550* |
| Pass. Capacity (basis 2) | *1,200* | (all berths) | *1,350* |
| Pass. Space Ratio (basis 2) | *38.5* | (all berths) | *34.3* |
| Officers | *British* | Dining Staff | *European* |
| Total Cabins | | | *600* |
| Size (sq ft/m) | *169-520/15.7-48.3* | Door Width | *23"* |
| Outside Cabins | *385* | Inside Cabins | *215* |
| Single Cabins | *0* | Supplement | *25-100%* |
| Balcony Cabins | *10* | Wheelchair Cabins | *10* |
| Cabin Current | | | *110 AC* |
| Refrigerator | | | *AA and B* |
| Cabin TV | *Yes* | VCR | *No* |
| Dining Rooms | *2* | Sittings | *2* |
| Elevators | *6* | Door Width | *43"* |

| | | | |
|---|---|---|---|
| Casino | *Yes* | Slot Machines | *Yes* |
| Swimming Pools (outside) | *3* | (inside) | *0* |
| Whirlpools | *1* | Gymnasium | *Yes* |
| Sauna/Steam Rm | *Yes/No* | Massage | *Yes* |
| Self-Service Launderette | | | *Yes* |
| Movie Theater/Seats | | | *Yes/237* |
| Library | | | *Yes* |
| Children's Facilities | | | *Yes* |
| Watersports Facilities | | | *None* |
| Classification Society | | | *Lloyd's Register* |

| RATINGS | SCORE |
|---|---|
| Ship: Condition/Cleanliness | 8.1 |
| Ship: Space/Flow/Comfort | 8.0 |
| Ship: Decor/Furnishings | 8.1 |
| Ship: Fitness Facilities | 7.7 |
| Cabins: Comfort/Facilities | 8.2 |
| Cabins: Software | 8.2 |
| Food: Dining Room/Cuisine | 7.6 |
| Food: Buffets/Informal Dining | 7.2 |
| Food: Quality of Ingredients | 7.0 |
| Service: Dining Room | 7.6 |
| Service: Bars/Lounges | 7.7 |
| Service: Cabins | 7.8 |
| Cruise: Entertainment | 8.1 |
| Cruise: Activities Program | 7.7 |
| Cruise: Hospitality Standard | 7.9 |
| OVERALL RATING | 116.9 |

**+** Well designed contemporary vessel has short, sharply-raked bow and swept-back funnel. First cruise ship to have steam turbine machinery since the *QE2* debuted in 1969, which means virtually no vibration. Comfortable, easy layout. Good, enclosed promenade deck. Improved showroom, with good visibility from all seats. Horizon Lounge is restful at night. Popular pizzeria. Good health spa facilities. Spacious, very comfortable, well-equipped cabins, with all the essentials and good-sized showers. Lido Deck suites are outstanding. All cabins have bathrobes.

**–** No wrap-around outdoor promenade deck. Clean, bland, clinical, yet tasteful, minimalist interior lacks warmth—perhaps more greenery would help. The Veranda Café, a popular outdoor buffet area, is poorly designed and always congested. Long lines for embarkation, disembarkation, buffets, and shore tenders.

**Dining** Two dining rooms are very brightly lit. No tables for two. The food is adequate, but creative presentation is lacking, as are the garnishes. Pasta is excellent, but other food lacks quality, flair, and presentation. Service, while quite attentive, is somewhat impersonal and superficial.

**Other Comments** Fine array of public rooms, including expansive shops. This well-designed ship provides a well-balanced, very pleasing cruise experience for the mature passenger, with plenty of space and little crowding. Insurance and gratuities are extra.

# ms Song of America ★★★★

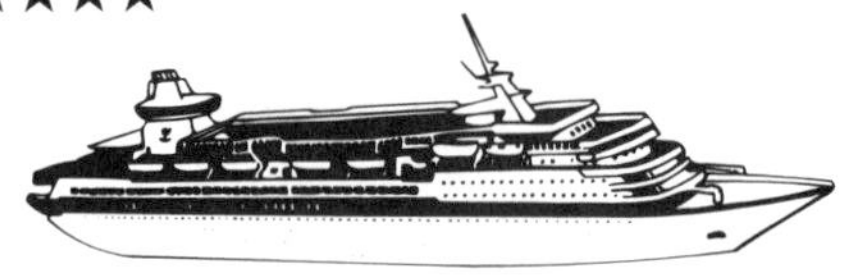

***Principal Cruising Areas***
*Bermuda/Caribbean (7 nights)*
***Base Ports:*** *New York/San Juan*

| | | | |
|---|---|---|---|
| Cruise Line | | | *Royal Caribbean Cruises* |
| Former Names | | | *n/a* |
| Gross Tonnage | | | *37,584* |
| Builder | | | *Wartsila (Finland)* |
| Original Cost | | | *$140 million* |
| Christened By | | | *Ms Beverly Sills* |
| First Entered Service | | | *Dec 5, 1982* |
| Interior Design | | | *Njal Eide* |
| Country of Registry | | | *Norway (LENA)* |
| Tel No | *131-3507* | Fax No | *131-3507* |
| Length (ft/m) | | | *705.0/214.88* |
| Beam (ft/m) | | | *93.1/28.40* |
| Draft (ft/m) | | | *22.3/6.80* |
| Engines/Propellers | | | *4 Sulzer 8-cyl diesels/2 (CP)* |
| Decks | *11* | Crew | *535* |
| Pass. Capacity (basis 2) | *1,402* | (all berths) | *1,552* |
| Pass. Space Ratio (basis 2) | *26.8* | (all berths) | *24.2* |
| Officers | *Norwegian* | Dining Staff | *International* |
| Total Cabins | | | *701* |
| Size (sq ft/m) | *120-425/11-39.5* | Door Width | *25"* |
| Outside Cabins | *406* | Inside Cabins | *295* |
| Single Cabins | *0* | Supplement | *50-100%* |
| Balcony Cabins | *0* | Wheelchair Cabins | *0* |
| Cabin Current | | | *110 AC* |
| Refrigerator | | | *Owner's suite* |
| Cabin TV | *Yes* | VCR | *No* |
| Dining Rooms | *1* | Sittings | *2* |
| Elevators | *7* | Door Width | *35"* |

| | | | |
|---|---|---|---|
| Casino | *Yes* | Slot Machines | *Yes* |
| Swimming Pools (outside) | 2 | (inside) | *0* |
| Whirlpools | *0* | Gymnasium | *Yes* |
| Sauna/Steam Rm | *Yes/No* | Massage | *Yes* |
| Self-Service Launderette | | | *No* |
| Movie Theater/Seats | | | *No* |
| Library | | | *Yes* |
| Children's Facilities | | | *No* |
| Watersports Facilities | | | *None* |
| Classification Society | | | *Det Norske Veritas* |

| RATINGS | SCORE |
|---|---|
| Ship: Condition/Cleanliness | 8.2 |
| Ship: Space/Flow/Comfort | 7.9 |
| Ship: Decor/Furnishings | 8.2 |
| Ship: Fitness Facilities | 7.8 |
| Cabins: Comfort/Facilities | 5.8 |
| Cabins: Software | 7.7 |
| Food: Dining Room/Cuisine | 6.8 |
| Food: Buffets/Informal Dining | 6.6 |
| Food: Quality of Ingredients | 7.1 |
| Service: Dining Room | 6.7 |
| Service: Bars/Lounges | 6.5 |
| Service: Cabins | 6.1 |
| Cruise: Entertainment | 7.8 |
| Cruise: Activities Program | 7.6 |
| Cruise: Hospitality Standard | 7.4 |
| OVERALL RATING | 108.2 |

**+** Contemporary-looking ship has rounded lines and sharply-raked bow. Public rooms are spacious. Striking Viking Crown Lounge wrapped around funnel is the line's trademark, and incorporates a bar. Good open deck and sunning space. Beautifully polished wooden decks and rails. New conference center and Schooner Bar—good for meetings and group business. Better shopping center provided, and the casino is now enlarged. The Veranda Café has improved flow and better weather protection. Attentive, polished service throughout.

**–** High level of noise in the dining room. The cabins and bathrooms (with wrap-around shower curtains) are very small, yet most passengers seem happy with them. Too many announcements.

**Dining** The Madame Butterfly Dining Room has tables for four to eight (no tables for two) and smoking and nonsmoking sections. Service is consistently good. French, Italian, Oriental, Caribbean, or American themes, complete with decorations and costumes. The food is of a generally high quality, and portions are reasonable. Bottled water (extra cost) is offered (pushed); drinking water is not provided unless requested!

**Other Comments** In typical RCCL fashion, the ship caters superbly to passengers in the public entertainment rooms. Recommended for first-time and repeat passengers. A consistently good product in comfortable surroundings. Port taxes, insurance, and gratuities are included.

# ms Song of Flower ★★★★★

***Principal Cruising Areas***
*Indonesia/Europe (7 nights)*
***Base Ports:*** *Singapore/London*

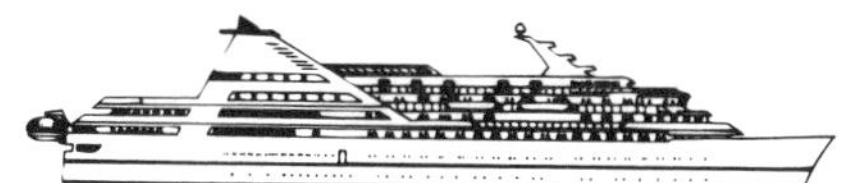

| | | | |
|---|---|---|---|
| Cruise Line | *Seven Seas Cruise Line/"K" Line* | | |
| Former Names | *Explorer Starship* | | |
| Gross Tonnage | *8,282* | | |
| Builder | *KMV (Norway)/Lloyd Werft (Germany)* | | |
| Original Cost | *n/a* | | |
| Christened By | *Ms Mamiko Matsunari* | | |
| First Entered Service | *1986/Feb 11, 1990* | | |
| Interior Design | *Yran & Storbraaten* | | |
| Country of Registry | *Norway (LATY2)* | | |
| Tel No | *131-0152* | Fax No | *131-0153* |
| Length (ft/m) | *407.4/124.20* | | |
| Beam (ft/m) | *52.4/16.00* | Draft (ft/m) | *16.0/4.90* |
| Engines | *2 Wichman 10-cyl diesels* | | |
| Propellers | *2 (CP)* | | |
| Decks | 6 | Crew | *144* |
| Pass. Capacity (basis 2) | *214* | (all berths) | *214* |
| Pass. Space Ratio (basis 2) | *38.7* | (all berths) | *38.7* |
| Officers | *Norwegian* | | |
| Dining Staff | *European/Filipino* | | |
| Total Cabins | *107* | | |
| Size (sq ft/m) | 183-398/17-37 | Door Width | 28" |
| Outside Cabins | 107 | Inside Cabins | 0 |
| Single Cabins | *0* | Supplement | *25%* |
| Balcony Cabins | *10* | Wheelchair Cabins | *0* |
| Cabin Current | *220 AC* | Refrigerator | *All cabins* |
| Cabin TV | *Yes* | VCR | *Yes* |
| Dining Rooms | *1* | Sittings | *Open* |
| Elevators | 2 | Door Width | *31"* |

| | | | |
|---|---|---|---|
| Casino | *Yes* | Slot Machines | *Yes* |
| Swimming Pools (outside) | *1* | (inside) | *0* |
| Whirlpools | *1* | Gymnasium | *Yes* |
| Sauna/Steam Rm | *Yes/No* | Massage | *Yes* |
| Self-Service Launderette | *No* | | |
| Movie Theater/Seats | *No* | | |
| Library | *Yes* | Children's Facilities | *No* |
| Watersports Facilities | *jet skis, snorkel equipment, waterski boat, windsurfers* | | |
| Classification Society | *Det Norske Veritas* | | |

| RATINGS | SCORE |
|---|---|
| Ship: Condition/Cleanliness | 9.0 |
| Ship: Space/Flow/Comfort | 9.2 |
| Ship Facilities | 9.0 |
| Ship: Decor/Furnishings | 8.9 |
| Ship: Fitness/Watersports Facilities | 8.7 |
| Cabins: Comfort/Facilities | 9.0 |
| Cabins: Software | 9.0 |
| Food: Dining Room/Cuisine | 9.0 |
| Food: Buffets/Informal Dining | 9.0 |
| Food: Quality of Ingredients | 8.6 |
| Service: Dining Room | 8.6 |
| Service: Bars/Lounges | 8.8 |
| Service: Cabins | 8.8 |
| Cruise: Entertainment/Lecture Program | 8.7 |
| Cruise: Hospitality Standard | 8.9 |
| OVERALL RATING | 133.2 |

**+** This is an excellent small cruise ship, with tall, twin funnels that give a somewhat squat profile. Well maintained and spotlessly clean. Good sheltered open deck and sunning space. Very elegant interior, with soft, appealing decor and well chosen colors. The finest furnishings and fabrics are used throughout. Tiered showroom is very comfortable, and has good sightlines. Great staff,who really do anticipate your every need.

**–** The bow should be 15 ft. longer to give a sleeker appearance!

**Dining** Delightful dining room has warm colors and ambiance. Very creative food and presentation, but small portions. All drinks included, with the exception of some premium wines. Outstanding personal service. Several tables for two, and plenty of space around each table. The menu is highly creative and beautifully hand-scripted. Freshly squeezed orange juice at any time. Superb cappucino/espresso machine.

**Other Comments** Compact health spa. Well equipped suites, complete with bathrobes and slippers. Superb closet and drawer space. Many cabins have bathtubs, but they are tiny. An outstanding, destination-intensive, yet relaxing, cruise experience. The hardware could look prettier, but the software is outstanding and the personal attention unbeatable. Gratuities are included, and no further tipping is allowed. Port charges are extra.

# ms Song of Norway ★★★+

***Principal Cruising Areas***

*Caribbean/Europe (various/12 nights)*

***Base Ports:*** *San Juan/Stockholm*

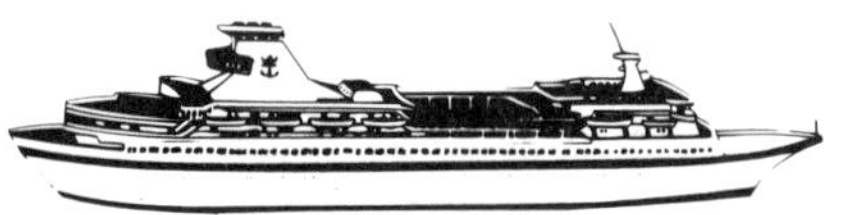

| | | | |
|---|---|---|---|
| Cruise Line | | | *Royal Caribbean Cruises* |
| Former Names | | | *n/a* |
| Gross Tonnage | | | *23,005* |
| Builder | | | *Wartsila (Finland)* |
| Original Cost | | | *$13.5 million* |
| Christened By | | | *Mrs Magnhild Borten* |
| First Entered Service | | | *Nov 7, 1970* |
| Interior Design | | | *Njal Eide* |
| Country of Registry | | | *Norway (LNVP)* |
| Tel No | *131-0562* | Fax No | *131-0562* |
| Length (ft/m) | | | *637.5/194.32* |
| Beam (ft/m) | | | *78.8/24.03* |
| Draft (ft/m) | | | *21.9/6.70* |
| Engines/Propellers | | | *4 Sulzer 9-cyl diesels/2 (CP)* |
| Decks | *8* | Crew | *423* |
| Pass. Capacity (basis 2) | *1,004* | (all berths) | *1,138* |
| Pass. Space Ratio (basis 2) | *22.5* | (all berths) | *20.2* |
| Officers | *Norwegian* | Dining Staff | *International* |
| Total Cabins | | | *502* |
| Size (sq ft/m) | *120-266/11-24.7* | Door Width | *25"* |
| Outside Cabins | *325* | Inside Cabins | *177* |
| Single Cabins | *0* | Supplement | *50-100%* |
| Balcony Cabins | *0* | Wheelchair Cabins | *0* |
| Cabin Current | | | *110 AC* |
| Refrigerator | | | *Owner's suite* |
| Cabin TV | *No* | VCR | *No* |
| Dining Rooms | *1* | Sittings | *2* |
| Elevators | *4* | Door Width | *35"* |

| | | | |
|---|---|---|---|
| Casino | *Yes* | Slot Machines | *Yes* |
| Swimming Pools (outside) | *1* | (inside) | *0* |
| Whirlpools | *0* | Gymnasium | *Yes* |
| Sauna/Steam Rm | *No/No* | Massage | *No* |
| Self-Service Launderette | | | *No* |
| Movie Theater/Seats | | | *No* |
| Library | | | *No* |
| Children's Facilities | | | *No* |
| Watersports Facilities | | | *None* |
| Classification Society | | | *Det Norske Veritas* |

| RATINGS | SCORE |
|---|---|
| Ship: Condition/Cleanliness | 7.4 |
| Ship: Space/Flow/Comfort | 6.7 |
| Ship: Decor/Furnishings | 7.0 |
| Ship: Fitness Facilities | 6.6 |
| Cabins: Comfort/Facilities | 5.8 |
| Cabins: Software | 7.7 |
| Food: Dining Room/Cuisine | 6.8 |
| Food: Buffets/Informal Dining | 6.6 |
| Food: Quality of Ingredients | 7.1 |
| Service: Dining Room | 6.7 |
| Service: Bars/Lounges | 6.5 |
| Service: Cabins | 6.1 |
| Cruise: Entertainment | 7.8 |
| Cruise: Activities Program | 7.6 |
| Cruise: Hospitality Standard | 7.4 |
| OVERALL RATING | 103.8 |

**+** Dated seventies look, with sleek lines, sharply-raked bow, and distinctive cantilevered Viking Crown Lounge high up around the ship's funnel. Stretched sister to *Nordic Prince*. Has wrap-around outdoor polished wood deck. Has a good, but now dated, interior layout. Scandinavian decor—clean and bright. Good open deck space, but it does get crowded when the ship is full (always). Good wood trim in passageways.

**–** High-density ship with expansive open deck and sunning space that becomes cramped when full. Beautifully polished, though slippery, wooden decks. Narrow passageways. The cabins, which need refurbishing, are very small and have very limited closet and drawer space. There are too many irritating announcements, and they are delivered in poor English. More like a crowded, floating summer camp.

**Dining** Attractive dining room, and a good operation, but food and service are disappointing.

**Other Comments** Stretched in 1978. This ship caters to novice and repeat passengers with well-programed flair, and consistently provides a fine-tuned cruise product in comfortable, but very crowded, surroundings. For the same or similar cruise price, I would opt for one of the company's newer megaships, where there is more space. Insurance and gratuities are extra.

# ms Southward ★★★

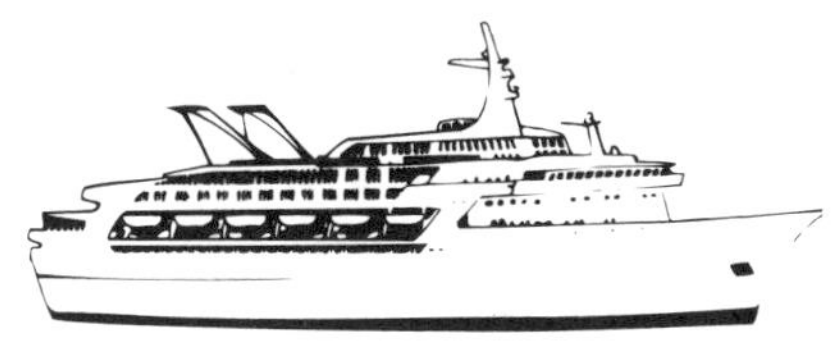

***Principal Cruising Area***

*Mexican Riviera (3/4 nights year-round)*

***Base Port:** San Juan (Fri/Mon)*

| | | | |
|---|---|---|---|
| Cruise Line | | | *Norwegian Cruise Line* |
| Former Names | | | *n/a* |
| Gross Tonnage | | | *16,607* |
| Builder | | | *Cantieri Navale Del Tirreno et Riuniti* |
| Original Cost | | | *n/a* |
| Christened By | | | *n/a* |
| First Entered Service | | | *Nov 16, 1971* |
| Interior Design | | | *Tage Wandborg* |
| Country of Registry | | | *Bahamas (C6CM6)* |
| Tel No | *110-4165* | Fax No | *110-4165* |
| Length (ft/m) | | | *535.7/163.30* |
| Beam (ft/m) | | | *74.7/22.79* |
| Draft (ft/m) | | | *21.3/6.50* |
| Engines | | | *4 GMT-Fiat 10-cyl diesels* |
| Propellers | | | *2 (CP)* |
| Decks | *7* | Crew | *320* |
| Pass. Capacity (basis 2) | *754* | (all berths) | *976* |
| Pass. Space Ratio (basis 2) | *22.0* | (all berths) | *17.0* |
| Officers | *Norwegian* | Dining Staff | *International* |
| Total Cabins | | | *377* |
| Size (sq ft/m) | *90-256/8.3-23.7* | Door Width | *23"* |
| Outside Cabins | *262* | Inside Cabins | *115* |
| Single Cabins | *0* | Supplement | *50-100%* |
| Balcony Cabins | *0* | Wheelchair Cabins | *0* |
| Cabin Current | *110 AC* | Refrigerator | *Cat1/2* |
| Cabin TV | *No* | VCR | *No* |
| Dining Rooms | *1* | Sittings | *2* |
| Elevators | *4* | Door Width | *26"* |

| | | | |
|---|---|---|---|
| Casino | *Yes* | Slot Machines | *Yes* |
| Swimming Pools (outside) | *1* | (inside) | *0* |
| Whirlpools | *0* | Gymnasium | *Yes* |
| Sauna/Steam Rm | *Yes/No* | Massage | *Yes* |
| Self-Service Launderette | | | *No* |
| Movie Theater/Seats | | | *Yes/198* |
| Library | | | *Yes* |
| Children's Facilities | | | *No* |
| Watersports Facilities | | | *None* |
| Classification Society | | | *Det Norske Veritas* |

| RATINGS | SCORE |
|---|---|
| Ship: Condition/Cleanliness | 6.5 |
| Ship: Space/Flow/Comfort | 6.7 |
| Ship: Decor/Furnishings | 6.9 |
| Ship: Fitness Facilities | 5.6 |
| Cabins: Comfort/Facilities | 6.2 |
| Cabins: Software | 6.7 |
| Food: Dining Room/Cuisine | 6.7 |
| Food: Buffets/Informal Dining | 6.2 |
| Food: Quality of Ingredients | 6.1 |
| Service: Dining Room | 7.1 |
| Service: Bars/Lounges | 7.0 |
| Service: Cabins | 7.1 |
| Cruise: Entertainment | 6.4 |
| Cruise: Activities Program | 6.7 |
| Cruise: Hospitality Standard | 6.6 |
| OVERALL RATING | 98.5 |

**+** Comfortable public rooms with bright, contemporary decor. Favorite is the nightclub, set high atop the forward mast. Nice balconied theater. Ten suites are quite spacious and well-equipped, and have full bathtubs; other cabins are compact but clean and tidy, with good closet space for these short cruises.

**–** High density ship means crowds and lines, especially for buffets. Open deck and sunning space is limited. Poor sightlines in showroom. There are too many cabin categories, and too many repetitive announcements. Rowdy.

**Dining** The dining room is quite charming, with warm colors. The food is adequate but not memorable, so don't expect gourmet fare. Bread rolls and fruits are poor. There's no finesse in the service from a mainly Caribbean staff. The wine list is good.

**Other Comments** Clean, reasonably modern profile with rakish superstructure, dual funnels, and inboard lifeboats. All the right ingredients for an active, fun-filled, short cruise vacation for sun-loving couples and families at the right price. Insurance and gratuities are extra.

# ms Sovereign of the Seas ★★★★+

***Principal Cruising Area***

*Caribbean (7 nights year-round)*

***Base Port:*** *Miami (Saturday)*

| | | | |
|---|---|---|---|
| Cruise Line | *Royal Caribbean Cruises* | | |
| Former Names | *n/a* | | |
| Gross Tonnage | *73,192* | | |
| Builder | *Chantiers de l'Atlantique (France)* | | |
| Original Cost | *$183.5 million* | | |
| Christened By | *Mrs Roslyn Carter* | | |
| First Entered Service | *Jan 16, 1988* | | |
| Interior Design | *Njal Eide* | | |
| Country of Registry | *Norway (LAEB2)* | | |
| Tel No | *131-0711* | Fax No | *131-0711* |
| Length (ft/m) | *873.6/266.30* | | |
| Beam (ft/m) | *105.6/32.20* | | |
| Draft (ft/m) | *24.7/7.55* | | |
| Engines/Propellers | *4 Pielstick 9-cyl diesels/2 (VP)* | | |
| Decks | *12* | Crew | *808* |
| Pass. Capacity (basis 2) | *2,276* | (all berths) | *2,524* |
| Pass. Space Ratio (basis 2) | *32.1* | (all berths) | *28.9* |
| Officers | *Norwegian* | Dining Staff | *International* |
| Total Cabins | *1,138* | | |
| Size (sq ft/m) | *120-446/11-41.5* | Door Width | *23"* |
| Outside Cabins | *722* | Inside Cabins | *416* |
| Single Cabins | *0* | Supplement | *50-100%* |
| Balcony Cabins | *0* | Wheelchair Cabins | *0* |
| Cabin Current | *110 AC* | | |
| Refrigerator | *Category R/A* | | |
| Cabin TV | *Yes* | VCR | *No* |
| Dining Rooms | *2* | Sittings | *2* |
| Elevators | *18* | Door Width | *39"* |

| | | | |
|---|---|---|---|
| Casino | *Yes* | Slot Machines | *Yes* |
| Swimming Pools (outside) | 2 | (inside) | *0* |
| Whirlpools | *1* | Gymnasium | *Yes* |
| Sauna/Steam Rm | *Yes/No* | Massage | *Yes* |
| Self-Service Launderette | *No* | | |
| Movie Theater/Seats | *Yes-2/146 each* | | |
| Library | *Yes* | | |
| Children's Facilities | *Yes* | | |
| Watersports Facilities | *None* | | |
| Classification Society | *Det Norske Veritas* | | |

| RATINGS | SCORE |
|---|---|
| Ship: Condition/Cleanliness | 8.0 |
| Ship: Space/Flow/Comfort | 8.0 |
| Ship: Decor/Furnishings | 7.9 |
| Ship: Fitness Facilities | 7.6 |
| Cabins: Comfort/Facilities | 7.6 |
| Cabins: Software | 7.7 |
| Food: Dining Room/Cuisine | 7.9 |
| Food: Buffets/Informal Dining | 7.6 |
| Food: Quality of Ingredients | 7.1 |
| Service: Dining Room | 7.7 |
| Service: Bars/Lounges | 7.6 |
| Service: Cabins | 7.6 |
| Cruise: Entertainment | 8.2 |
| Cruise: Activities Program | 7.9 |
| Cruise: Hospitality Standard | 8.0 |
| OVERALL RATING | 116.4 |

**+** Handsome megaship has well-balanced profile, nicely rounded lines, and high superstructure. Striking Viking Crown Lounge wrap-around funnel has superb views. Wrap-around outdoor polished wood deck. Impressive array of spacious and elegant public rooms. Stunning five-deck-high centrum lobby. Two-level showroom is good. Two movie screening rooms. Delightful array of shops. Excellent on-board shopping. 12 suites on Bridge Deck are quite large and nicely furnished. Good children's/teens' programs and counselors.

**–** Open deck space is adequate, no more. The layout is awkward, with the "cake-layer" stacking of public rooms aft. Having just one whirlpool is ridiculous. Congested passenger flow in some areas. Too much waiting for elevators. Needs more intimate spaces. Little closet and drawer space. The dress code is extremely casual. Far too many announcements.

**Dining** The two dining rooms feature well-presented food and service, but Gigi has better decor than Kismet. No tables for two. All the food tastes similar. Poor breads, rolls, and fruit selection. Decent, middle-of-the-road wine list and prices. The staff are overly friendly, even intrusive.

**Other Comments** Well-tuned, yet somewhat sterile, service from a tip-hungry staff. Too many passenger participation events, although you might enjoy getting involved in them. Too large for those who prefer intimate surroundings. Insurance and gratuities are extra.

# ib Sovetskiy Soyuz ★★★+

***Principal Cruising Areas***

*Polar expedition cruises (various)*

***Base Port:*** *Murmansk*

| | | | |
|---|---|---|---|
| Cruise Line | *Murmansk Shipping* | | |
| Former Names | *n/a* | | |
| Gross Tonnage | *20,646* | | |
| Builder | *Baltic Shipyard, Murmansk (Russia)* | | |
| Original Cost | *$150 million* | | |
| Christened By | *Ms Olga Guseva* | | |
| First Entered Service | *Dec 1989* | | |
| Country of Registry | *Russia (UUQL)* | | |
| Tel No | *140-2512* | Fax No | *140-2511* |
| Length (ft/m) | *492.1/150.00* | | |
| Beam (ft/m) | *98.4/30.00* | Draft (ft/m) | *36.0/11.00* |
| Engines | *Nuclear-powered turbo-electrics* | | |
| Propellers | *3* | | |
| Decks | *4* | Crew | *130* |
| Pass. Capacity (basis 2) | *100* | (all berths) | *100* |
| Pass. Space Ratio (basis 2) | *206.4* | (all berths) | *206.4* |
| Officers | *Russian/Ukrainian* | | |
| Dining Staff | *European/Ukrainian* | | |
| Total Cabins | *50* | | |
| Size (sq ft/m) | *155-300/14.3-27.8* | Door Width | *24"* |
| Outside Cabins | *50* | Inside Cabins | *0* |
| Single Cabins | *0* | Supplement | *Fixed rates* |
| Balcony Cabins | *0* | Wheelchair Cabins | *0* |
| Cabin Current | *220 AC* | Refrigerator | *Yes* |
| Cabin TV | *Yes* | VCR | *No* |
| Dining Rooms | *1* | Sittings | *Open Seating* |
| Elevators | *0* | Door Width | *n/a* |
| Casino | *No* | Slot Machines | *No* |

| | | | |
|---|---|---|---|
| Swimming Pools | | (inside) | *1* |
| Whirlpools | *0* | Gymnasium | *Yes* |
| Sauna/Steam Rm | *Yes-2/No* | Massage | *No* |
| Self-Service Launderette | *Yes* | | |
| Lecture/Film Room | *Yes (seats 100)* | | |
| Library | *Yes* | | |
| Zodiacs | *4* | | |
| Helicopters | *2 available for passenger use* | | |
| Watersports Facilities | *None* | | |
| Classification Society | *RS* | | |

| RATINGS | SCORE |
|---|---|
| Ship: Age/Condition/Cleanliness | 7.7 |
| Ship: Space/Flow/Comfort | 6.1 |
| Ship: Expedition Equipment | 9.0 |
| Ship: Decor/Furnishings | 5.6 |
| Cabins: Comfort/Facilities | 6.0 |
| Cabins: Software | 6.0 |
| Food: Dining Room Experience | 7.2 |
| Food: Buffets/Informal Dining | 6.6 |
| Food: Quality of Ingredients | 7.0 |
| Service: Dining Room | 6.8 |
| Service: Bars/Lounges | 6.7 |
| Service: Cabins | 6.9 |
| Cruise: Itineraries/Operations | 7.8 |
| Cruise: Lecture Program | 7.6 |
| Cruise: Hospitality Standard | 7.8 |
| OVERALL RATING | 104.8 |

**+** An incredible ship! This vessel has a three-inch-thick reinforced bow for ice conditions. Very comfortable. Tiered lecture theater with stage is the setting for the biologists, scientists, geologists, and other expert lecturers. Heated indoor pool. All cabins are generously sized, outside, and have private facilities. Good service throughout. The ultimate in technology accompanies this special icebreaker. Passengers are allowed on the bridge at all times.

**–** Limited closet/drawer space; small, utilitarian bathrooms. Limited public rooms. Almost no art/decoration (and limited carpeting) as this is a working ice-breaker. Steep interior stairways.

**Dining** European chefs oversee all meals.

**Other Comments** Fuel for four years without refuelling! Just one of a fleet of the world's most powerful icebreakers. Try the incredible trans-polar voyage via the North Pole. Other vessels of like capabilities, all featuring nuclear-powered turbo-electric propulsion, are listed below.

| Name | Grt | Built | Length | Beam |
|---|---|---|---|---|
| *Arctica* | 20,905 | 1975 | 485.2ft/147.9m | 98.0ft/29.9m |
| *Lenin* | 17,810 | 1959 | 439.6ft/134.0m | 90.5ft/27.6m |
| *Rossiya* | 22,920 | 1985 | 492.1ft/150.0m | 98.4ft/30.0m |
| *Siberia* | 21,120 | 1977 | 485.2ft/147.9m | 98.0ft/29.9m |
| *Taimir* | 20,000 | 1989 | 498.0ft/151.8m | 95.8ft/29.2m |

# ms Star Odyssey ★★★★+

***Principal Cruising Areas***

*Alaska/New England (7 nights)*

***Base Ports:** Vancouver/New York*

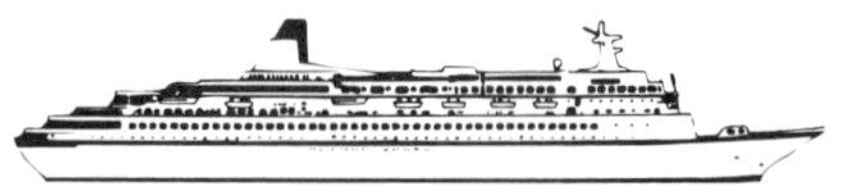

| | | | |
|---|---|---|---|
| Cruise Line | | | *Royal Cruise Line* |
| Former Names | | | *Westward/Royal Viking Star* |
| Gross Tonnage | | | *28,492* |
| Builder | | | *Wartsila (Finland)* |
| Original Cost | | | *$22.5 million* |
| Christened By | | | *Mrs Thor Heyerdahl* |
| First Entered Service | | | *Jun 26, 1972/May 9, 1994* |
| Interior Design | | | *Njal Eide* |
| Country of Registry | | | *Bahamas (C6CN2)* |
| Tel No | *110-4507* | Fax No | *110-4554* |
| Length (ft/m) | | | *674.1/205.47* |
| Beam (ft/m) | | | *82.6/25.20* |
| Draft (ft/m) | | | *24.7/7.55* |
| Engines/Propellers | | | *4 Sulzer 9-cyl diesels/2 (CP)* |
| Decks | *8* | Crew | *325* |
| Pass. Capacity (basis 2) | *790* | (all berths) | *790* |
| Pass. Space Ratio (basis 2) | *36.0* | (all berths) | *36.0* |
| Officers | *Greek* | Dining Staff | *International* |
| Total Cabins | | | *404* |
| Size (sq ft/m) | *136-580/12.6-53.8* | Door Width | *24"* |
| Outside Cabins | *356* | Inside Cabins | *48* |
| Single Cabins | *33* | Supplement | *50-100%* |
| Balcony Cabins | *9* | Wheelchair Cabins | *0* |
| Cabin Current | | | *110/220 AC* |
| Refrigerator | | | *Cat.1-6* |
| Cabin TV | *Yes* | VCR | *No* |
| Dining Rooms | *1* | Sittings | *1* |
| Elevators | *5* | Door Width | *35"* |

| | | | |
|---|---|---|---|
| Casino | *Yes* | Slot Machines | *Yes* |
| Swimming Pools (outside) | *2* | (inside) | *0* |
| Whirlpools | *0* | Gymnasium | *Yes* |
| Sauna/Steam Rm | *Yes/No* | Massage | *Yes* |
| Self-Service Launderette | | | *No* |
| Movie Theater/Seats | | | *Yes/156* |
| Library | | | *No* |
| Children's Facilities | | | *Yes* |
| Watersports Facilities | | | *None* |
| Classification Society | | | *Det Norske Veritas* |

| RATINGS | SCORE |
|---|---|
| Ship: Condition/Cleanliness | 8.3 |
| Ship: Space/Flow/Comfort | 8.7 |
| Ship: Decor/Furnishings | 7.9 |
| Ship: Fitness Facilities | 8.1 |
| Cabins: Comfort/Facilities | 7.7 |
| Cabins: Software | 7.8 |
| Food: Dining Room/Cuisine | 7.8 |
| Food: Buffets/Informal Dining | 7.6 |
| Food: Quality of Ingredients | 7.0 |
| Service: Dining Room | 7.9 |
| Service: Bars/Lounges | 7.8 |
| Service: Cabins | 7.8 |
| Cruise: Entertainment | 6.8 |
| Cruise: Activities Program | 7.0 |
| Cruise: Hospitality Standard | 7.7 |
| OVERALL RATING | 115.9 |

**+** This handsome, sleek white ship with sharply raked bow and distinctive lines is a welcome addition to the Royal Cruise Line fleet. Excellent open deck and sunning space. Tasteful, but dated, seventies decor has been upgraded. Spacious public rooms with high ceilings. Good cinema. Lovely observation lounge high atop ship has commanding views and is very comfortable.

**–** Some cabin bathrooms have awkward access. Sadly, there's no library.

**Dining** Very spacious, high-ceilinged dining room features good cuisine in a relaxed, one-sitting operation. The food is Continental in style, but the quality of ingredients is not first-rate. Waiter service is very friendly (overly friendly) in true Greek style. Poor breads and fruits. The wine list, although varied, has few decent vintages and caters mainly to those with a taste for Californian.

**Other Comments** Stretched in 1981. Excellent health-fitness spa and basketball court set high atop ship. Cabins are well equipped, and have good closet, drawer, and storage space. Several new cabins. Action-packed casino. This ship will provide a good cruise experience, with plenty of activities, at a decent price. Truly good style, but sadly not as good as when operated by the Royal Viking Line division of Kloster Cruise. Insurance and gratuities are extra.

# ms Star Princess ★★★★+

***Principal Cruising Areas***

*Alaska/Caribbean (various)*

***Base Ports:** Vancouver/San Juan*

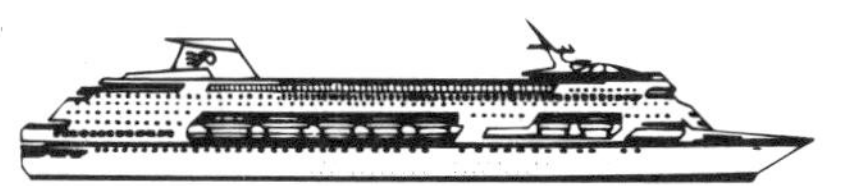

| | | | |
|---|---|---|---|
| Cruise Line | | | *Princess Cruises* |
| Former Names | | | *FairMajesty* |
| Gross Tonnage | | | *63,564* |
| Builder | | | *Chantiers de L'Atlantique (France)* |
| Original Cost | | | *$200 million* |
| Christened By | | | *Ms Audrey Hepburn* |
| First Entered Service | | | *Mar 24, 1989* |
| Interior Design | | | *Ellerbe Becket* |
| Country of Registry | | | *Liberia (ELIR8)* |
| Tel No | *124-0247* | Fax No | *124-0236* |
| Length (ft/m) | | | *805.7/245.60* |
| Beam (ft/m) | | | *105.6/32.20* |
| Draft (ft/m) | | | *25.0/7.62* |
| Engines | | | *4 MAN-B&W diesel-electrics* |
| Propellers | | | *2 (CP)* |
| Decks | *12* | Crew | *600* |
| Pass. Capacity (basis 2) | *1,470* | (all berths) | *1,620* |
| Pass. Space Ratio (basis 2) | *43.2* | (all berths) | *39.2* |
| Officers | *Italian* | Dining Staff | *European* |
| Total Cabins | | | *735* |
| Size (sq ft/m) | | | *180-530/16.7-49.2* |
| Door Width | | | *23-32"* |
| Outside Cabins | *570* | Inside Cabins | *165* |
| Single Cabins | *0* | Supplement | *25-100%* |
| Balcony Cabins | *50* | Wheelchair Cabins | *10* |
| Cabin Current | *110/220 AC* | Refrigerator | *Yes* |
| Cabin TV | *Yes* | VCR | *No* |
| Dining Rooms | *1* | Sittings | *2* |

| | | | |
|---|---|---|---|
| Elevators | *9* | Door Width | *43"* |
| Casino | *Yes* | Slot Machines | *Yes* |
| Swimming Pools (outside) | *3* | (inside) | *0* |
| Whirlpools | *4* | Gymnasium | *Yes* |
| Sauna/Steam Rm | *Yes/No* | Massage | *Yes* |
| Self-Service Launderette | | | *Yes* |
| Movie Theater/Seats | | | *Yes/205* |
| Library | *Yes* | Children's Facilities | *Yes* |
| Watersports Facilities | | | *None* |
| Classification Society | | | *Lloyd's Register* |

| RATINGS | SCORE |
|---|---|
| Ship: Condition/Cleanliness | 8.1 |
| Ship: Space/Flow/Comfort | 8.3 |
| Ship: Decor/Furnishings | 8.1 |
| Ship: Fitness Facilities | 7.7 |
| Cabins: Comfort/Facilities | 8.2 |
| Cabins: Software | 8.2 |
| Food: Dining Room/Cuisine | 7.6 |
| Food: Buffets/Informal Dining | 7.2 |
| Food: Quality of Ingredients | 7.0 |
| Service: Dining Room | 7.6 |
| Service: Bars/Lounges | 7.7 |
| Service: Cabins | 8.0 |
| Cruise: Entertainment | 8.1 |
| Cruise: Activities Program | 7.7 |
| Cruise: Hospitality Standard | 7.9 |
| OVERALL RATING | 117.4 |

**+** Innovative styling mixed with traditional shipboard features. Spacious public rooms have tasteful decor. Excellent selection of artwork. Horseshoe-shaped balconied showroom. Spacious three-deck-high foyer highlighted by kinetic sculpture. Neat wine bar and pizzeria. Characters Bar serves colorful drinks in crazy glasses. Popular in-pool bar. Multi-tiered main restaurant has two-deck-high center ceiling. Spacious, superbly equipped cabins with large, modular bathrooms (crew cabins on this ship are larger than passenger cabins on *Sovereign of the Seas*). Plenty of closet, drawer, and storage space. Interactive cabin video system. Bathrobes for all.

**–** No wrap-around outdoor promenade deck. Domed observation lounge is out of traffic flow. Noisy dining room. Poor outdoor promenade area. Long lines for embarkation, disembarkation, shore tenders, and buffets.

**Dining** The dining room is attractive, but noisy, and there are no tables for two. The food is adequate, but presentation is lacking. Poor bread rolls and fruits. Good pasta dishes. Service is so-so, but could be much improved. Pasta dishes, created by head waiters, are good. The indoor-outdoor buffet restaurant becomes crowded and needs expanding.

**Other Comments** Traditional approach to cruising for repeat passengers who like a large ship, plenty of children, and some degree of anonymity. Insurance and gratuities extra.

# Star/Ship Atlantic ★★★★

***Principal Cruising Area***
*Bahamas (3/4 nights year-round)*
***Base Port:*** *Port Canaveral*

| | | | |
|---|---|---|---|
| Cruise Line | | | *Premier Cruise Lines* |
| Former Names | | | *Atlantic* |
| Gross Tonnage | | | *36,500* |
| Builder | | | *C.N.I.M. (France)* |
| Original Cost | | | *$100 million* |
| Christened By | | | *n/a* |
| First Entered Service | | | *Apr 17, 1982/Jan 13, 1989* |
| Interior Design | | | *A&M Katzourakis* |
| Country of Registry | | | *Liberia (ELAJ4)* |
| Tel No | *n/a* | Fax No | *n/a* |
| Length (ft/m) | | | *671.9/204.81* |
| Beam (ft/m) | | | *89.7/27.36* |
| Draft (ft/m) | | | *25.5/7.80* |
| Engines/Propellers | | | *2 GM-Fiat 10-cyl diesels/2 (CP)* |
| Decks | *9* | Crew | *550* |
| Pass. Capacity (basis 2) | *972* | (all berths) | *1,600* |
| Pass. Space Ratio (basis 2) | *37.5* | (all berths) | *22.8* |
| Officers | | | *Greek* |
| Dining Staff | | | *International* |
| Total Cabins | | | *549* |
| Size (sq ft/m) | *137-427/12.7-39.5* | Door Width | *24"* |
| Outside Cabins | *380* | Inside Cabins | *169* |
| Single Cabins | *0* | Supplement | *75%* |
| Balcony Cabins | *0* | Wheelchair Cabins | *Yes* |
| Cabin Current | *110 AC* | Refrigerator | *No* |
| Cabin TV | *No* | VCR | *No* |
| Dining Rooms | *1* | Sittings | *2* |
| Elevators | *4* | Door Width | *30"* |

| | | | |
|---|---|---|---|
| Casino | *Yes* | Slot Machines | *Yes* |
| Swimming Pools (outside) | *1* | (inside) | *1* |
| Whirlpools | *3* | Gymnasium | *Yes* |
| Sauna/Steam Rm | *Yes/No* | Massage | *Yes* |
| Self-Service Launderette | | | *No* |
| Movie Theater/Seats | | | *Yes/251* |
| Library | | | *Yes* |
| Children's Facilities | | | *Yes* |
| Watersports Facilities | | | *None* |
| Classification Society | | | *American Bur. of Shipping* |

| RATINGS | SCORE |
|---|---|
| Ship: Condition/Cleanliness | 8.0 |
| Ship: Space/Flow/Comfort | 8.0 |
| Ship: Decor/Furnishings | 8.1 |
| Ship: Fitness Facilities | 7.6 |
| Cabins: Comfort/Facilities | 7.8 |
| Cabins: Software | 8.1 |
| Food: Dining Room/Cuisine | 7.6 |
| Food: Buffets/Informal Dining | 7.1 |
| Food: Quality of Ingredients | 6.7 |
| Service: Dining Room | 7.3 |
| Service: Bars/Lounges | 7.2 |
| Service: Cabins | 7.4 |
| Cruise: Entertainment | 6.6 |
| Cruise: Activities Program | 6.7 |
| Cruise: Hospitality Standard | 6.8 |
| OVERALL RATING | 111.0 |

**+** This ship has a short, stubby bow and squat funnel, coupled with a distinctive red hull. Has an excellent amount of outdoor deck space. Spacious interior, with plenty of public rooms. Good indoor-outdoor pool area. Good duty-free shopping. Spacious cabins are generously equipped and very comfortable.

**–** The decor is somewhat garish in places, but there's a generous amount of stainless steel and teak wood trim. Good observation lounge. No cushion pads are provided for deck lounge chairs. The cabin insulation is very poor.

**Dining** The dining room, located on a lower deck, is attractive, but the tables are too close together, so noise level is high. Generally good food quality. Good basic service provided by an attentive, multi-national staff.

**Other Comments** Plenty of children's and teens' counselors. This ship will provide a good cruise experience for families with children, at the right price, in typical Premier Cruise Lines style. Insurance and gratuities are extra.

# Star/Ship Majestic ★★★+

***Principal Cruising Area***

*Mexico (3/4 nights year-round)*

***Base Port:** Tampa*

| | | | |
|---|---|---|---|
| Cruise Line | | | *Premier Cruise Lines* |
| Former Names | | | *Sun Princess/Spirit of London* |
| Gross Tonnage | | | *17,270* |
| Builder | | | *Cantieri Navale Del Tirreno & Riuniti* |
| Original Cost | | | *n/a* |
| Christened By | | | *Mrs Beatrice Marriott* |
| First Entered Service | | | *Nov 11, 1972/May 28, 1989* |
| Interior Design | | | *A&M Katzourakis* |
| Country of Registry | | | *Bahamas (C6HK9)* |
| Tel No | *110-4553* | Fax No | *110-4553* |
| Length (ft/m) | | | *536.0/163.40* |
| Beam (ft/m) | | | *81.4/24.82* |
| Draft (ft/m) | | | *21.3/6.52* |
| Engines/Propellers | | | *4 GMT 10-cyl diesels/2 (CP)* |
| Decks | *7* | Crew | *370* |
| Pass. Capacity (basis 2) | *760* | (all berths) | *983* |
| Pass. Space Ratio (basis 2) | *22.7* | (all berths) | *17.5* |
| Officers | | | *British* |
| Dining Staff | | | *International* |
| Total Cabins | | | *380* |
| Size (sq ft/m) | *99-237/9-22* | Door Width | *24"* |
| Outside Cabins | *256* | Inside Cabins | *124* |
| Single Cabins | *0* | Supplement | *75%* |
| Balcony Cabins | *0* | Wheelchair Cabins | *2* |
| Cabin Current | *110 AC* | Refrigerator | *No* |
| Cabin TV | *Yes* | VCR | *No* |
| Dining Rooms | *1* | Sittings | *2* |
| Elevators | *4* | Door Width | *22-35"* |

| | | | |
|---|---|---|---|
| Casino | *Yes* | Slot Machines | *Yes* |
| Swimming Pools (outside) | *1* | (inside) | *0* |
| Whirlpools | *0* | Gymnasium | *Yes* |
| Sauna/Steam Rm | *No/No* | Massage | *Yes* |
| Self-Service Launderette | | | *No* |
| Movie Theater/Seats | | | *Yes/186* |
| Library | | | *Yes* |
| Children's Facilities | | | *Yes* |
| Watersports Facilities | | | *None* |
| Classification Society | | | *Lloyd's Register* |

| RATINGS | SCORE |
|---|---|
| Ship: Condition/Cleanliness | 7.2 |
| Ship: Space/Flow/Comfort | 6.6 |
| Ship: Decor/Furnishings | 7.3 |
| Ship: Fitness Facilities | 5.0 |
| Cabins: Comfort/Facilities | 6.6 |
| Cabins: Software | 7.0 |
| Food: Dining Room/Cuisine | 7.6 |
| Food: Buffets/Informal Dining | 7.3 |
| Food: Quality of Ingredients | 6.8 |
| Service: Dining Room | 7.3 |
| Service: Bars/Lounges | 7.2 |
| Service: Cabins | 7.4 |
| Cruise: Entertainment | 6.4 |
| Cruise: Activities Program | 6.5 |
| Cruise: Hospitality Standard | 6.6 |
| OVERALL RATING | 102.8 |

**+** Reasonable amount of open deck and sunning space for ship size, but it is cramped. Upgraded interior decor features tasteful earth tones mixed with use of reflective surfaces. Comfortable public rooms, except when full. The deluxe suites are quite spacious; other cabins are on the small side, but quite well equipped, especially for these short cruises. Walls are very thin.

**–** Constant announcements are irritating. No cushion pads are provided for deck lounge chairs. The strong odor of cleansing chemicals is irritating.

**Dining** Charming dining room with high ceiling has a light and airy feel, but is extremely noisy, and tables are close together. Reasonably good service throughout. Good food quality and presentation, with some excellent pasta dishes. Buffets are good.

**Other Comments** Reasonably smart contemporary profile with rakish superstructure, and unmistakable scarlet hull. Fairly well maintained. Inboard lifeboats. Soft furnishings get much use, and need refurbishing constantly. Antiquated cabin telephone system. Reggae music played constantly in passageways. This ship will provide families with children with a very comfortable cruise experience in decent surroundings (there are lots of children's counselors), with a real fun atmosphere, at a moderate price, and the Disney package is an added bonus. Insurance and gratuities are extra.

# Star/Ship Oceanic ★★★★

***Principal Cruising Area***

*Bahamas (3/4 nights year-round)*

***Base Port:*** *Port Canaveral*

| | | | |
|---|---|---|---|
| Cruise Line | | | *Premier Cruise Lines* |
| Former Names | | | *Oceanic* |
| Gross Tonnage | | | *39,241* |
| Builder | | | *Cantieri Riuniti dell' Adriatico (Italy)* |
| Original Cost | | | *$35 million* |
| Christened By | | | *Ms Minnie Mouse* |
| First Entered Service | | | *Apr 3, 1965/Mar 25, 1986* |
| Interior Design | | | *A&M Katzourakis* |
| Country of Registry | | | *Bahamas (C62F7)* |
| Tel No | *112-0520* | Fax No | *112-0520* |
| Length (ft/m) | | | *782.1/238.40* |
| Beam (ft/m) | | | *96.5/29.44* |
| Draft (ft/m) | | | *28.2/8.60* |
| Engines/Propellers | | | *4 De Laval steam turbines/2* |
| Decks | *10* | Crew | *530* |
| Pass. Capacity (basis 2) | *1,180* | (all berths) | *1,500* |
| Pass. Space Ratio (basis 2) | *33.2* | (all berths) | *26.1* |
| Officers | *Greek* | Dining Staff | *International* |
| Total Cabins | | | *590* |
| Size (sq ft/m) | *139-455/13-42.2* | Door Width | *28"* |
| Outside Cabins | *261* | Inside Cabins | *329* |
| Single Cabins | *0* | Supplement | *75%* |
| Balcony Cabins | *8* | Wheelchair Cabins | *0* |
| Cabin Current | | | *110 AC* |
| Refrigerator | | | *No* |
| Cabin TV | *No* | VCR | *No* |
| Dining Rooms | *1* | Sittings | *2* |
| Elevators | *5* | Door Width | *30"* |

| | | | |
|---|---|---|---|
| Casino | *Yes* | Slot Machines | *Yes* |
| Swimming Pools (outside) | *2* | (inside) | *0* |
| Whirlpools | *3* | Gymnasium | *Yes* |
| Sauna/Steam Rm | *No/No* | Massage | *Yes* |
| Self-Service Launderette | | | *No* |
| Movie Theater/Seats | | | *Yes/420* |
| Library | | | *No* |
| Children's Facilities | | | *Yes* |
| Watersports Facilities | | | *None* |
| Classification Society | | | *American Bur. of Shipping* |

| RATINGS | SCORE |
|---|---|
| Ship: Condition/Cleanliness | 7.7 |
| Ship: Space/Flow/Comfort | 7.9 |
| Ship: Decor/Furnishings | 7.6 |
| Ship: Fitness Facilities | 6.6 |
| Cabins: Comfort/Facilities | 6.8 |
| Cabins: Software | 7.1 |
| Food: Dining Room/Cuisine | 7.6 |
| Food: Buffets/Informal Dining | 7.3 |
| Food: Quality of Ingredients | 6.8 |
| Service: Dining Room | 7.3 |
| Service: Bars/Lounges | 7.2 |
| Service: Cabins | 7.5 |
| Cruise: Entertainment | 6.6 |
| Cruise: Activities Program | 6.7 |
| Cruise: Hospitality Standard | 6.8 |
| OVERALL RATING | 107.5 |

**+** Expansive open deck space for sunning. Swimming pool atop ship has a magrodome roof for inclement weather. Contemporary interior decor and cheerful, bright colors. Delightful enclosed promenades. Balconied Sun Deck suites are superb and spacious. Wide choice of other cabins. All have heavy-duty furniture and are well equipped, although some need refurbishing. Many feature double beds. This ship does a wonderful job for families with children, with counselors galore. Cruise-and-stay packages are well designed.

**–** Long lines for embarkation, disembarkation, buffets, and shore tenders. Constant repetitive announcements. No cushion pads are provided for deck lounge chairs.

**Dining** The dining room is cheerful, but noisy when crowded. Good food and service considering the cruise fare, but limited selection of breads, cheeses, and fruits.

**Other Comments** Sleek-looking ship with classic, flowing lines has earned a fine reputation. Distinctive red hull. Recent refit and refurbishment. Busy casino action, but access for children should be better controlled. An excellent, family oriented, fun-filled cruise at an attractive price. Insurance and gratuities are extra.

# ms Starward ★★★

***Principal Cruising Area***
*Caribbean (7 nights year-round)*
***Base Port:*** *San Juan (Sunday)*

| | | | |
|---|---|---|---|
| Cruise Line | | | *Norwegian Cruise Line* |
| Former Names | | | *n/a* |
| Gross Tonnage | | | *16,107* |
| Builder | | | *A.G. Weser (Germany)* |
| Original Cost | | | *n/a* |
| Christened By | | | *n/a* |
| First Entered Service | | | *Dec 1, 1968* |
| Interior Design | | | *Tage Wandborg* |
| Country of Registry | | | *Bahamas (C6CM4)* |
| Tel No | *110-4163* | Fax No | *110-4163* |
| Length (ft/m) | | | *525.3/160.13* |
| Beam (ft/m) | | | *74.9/22.84* |
| Draft (ft/m) | | | *20.4/6.22* |
| Engines/Propellers | | | *2 MAN 16-cyl diesels/2 (CP)* |
| Decks | *7* | Crew | *315* |
| Pass. Capacity (basis 2) | *758* | (all berths) | *1,022* |
| Pass. Space Ratio (basis 2) | *21.2* | (all berths) | *15.7* |
| Officers | *Norwegian* | Dining Staff | *International* |
| Total Cabins | | | *379* |
| Size (sq ft/m) | *90-225/8.3-21* | Door Width | *24"* |
| Outside Cabins | *229* | Inside Cabins | *150* |
| Single Cabins | *0* | Supplement | *50-100%* |
| Balcony Cabins | *0* | Wheelchair Cabins | *0* |
| Cabin Current | | | *110 AC* |
| Refrigerator | | | *Category 1* |
| Cabin TV | *No* | VCR | *No* |
| Dining Rooms | *1* | Sittings | *2* |
| Elevators | *4* | Door Width | *32"* |

| | | | |
|---|---|---|---|
| Casino | *Yes* | Slot Machines | *Yes* |
| Swimming Pools (outside) | 2 | (inside) | *0* |
| Whirlpools | *0* | Gymnasium | *Yes* |
| Sauna/Steam Rm | *Yes/No* | Massage | *Yes* |
| Self-Service Launderette | | | *No* |
| Movie Theater/Seats | | | *Yes/204* |
| Library | | | *Yes* |
| Children's Facilities | | | *No* |
| Watersports Facilities | | | *None* |
| Classification Society | | | *Det Norske Veritas* |

| RATINGS | SCORE |
|---|---|
| Ship: Condition/Cleanliness | 6.3 |
| Ship: Space/Flow/Comfort | 6.1 |
| Ship: Decor/Furnishings | 6.7 |
| Ship: Fitness Facilities | 4.2 |
| Cabins: Comfort/Facilities | 6.1 |
| Cabins: Software | 6.4 |
| Food: Dining Room/Cuisine | 6.7 |
| Food: Buffets/Informal Dining | 6.2 |
| Food: Quality of Ingredients | 6.1 |
| Service: Dining Room | 7.1 |
| Service: Bars/Lounges | 7.0 |
| Service: Cabins | 7.1 |
| Cruise: Entertainment | 6.4 |
| Cruise: Activities Program | 6.7 |
| Cruise: Hospitality Standard | 6.6 |
| OVERALL RATING | 95.7 |

**+** Has a reasonably sharp looking upper profile with dual, swept-back funnels. Fair choice of public rooms with clean, modern furnishings. Upbeat, cheerful decor throughout. Good balconied theater. Except for five good-sized suites, the cabins are compact units that are comfortable, with bright, contemporary colors.

**–** Less-than-handsome, duck-tailed sponson stern. Reasonable open deck and sunning space, but this high-density vessel is crowded when full. Cabin closet and drawer space is poor.

**Dining** Charming dining room, with some tables overlooking the stern. Reasonably good cruise food, and service comes with a smile, but without finesse.

**Other Comments** Although it's hard for this ship to compete against the newcomers, NCL features a well tried Caribbean cruise experience in comfortable, though not elegant, surroundings, at a decent price. But for almost the same money, your cruise would be better on the company's newer and larger *Seaward*. Insurance and gratuities are extra.

# ms Statendam ★★★★+

***Principal Cruising Areas***

*Caribbean/Europe (various)*

***Base Ports:** Ft. Lauderdale/various*

| | | | |
|---|---|---|---|
| Cruise Line | *Holland America Line* | | |
| Former Names | *n/a* | | |
| Gross Tonnage | *55,451* | | |
| Builder | *Fincantieri (Italy)* | | |
| Original Cost | *$215 million* | | |
| Christened By | *Lin Arison* | | |
| First Entered Service | *Jan 25, 1993* | | |
| Interior Design | *VFD Interiors/Joe Farcus* | | |
| Country of Registry | *Bahamas (C6TV)* | | |
| Tel No | *130-5566* | Fax No | *130-5567* |
| Length (ft/m) | *719.4/219.30* | | |
| Beam (ft/m) | *101.0/30.80* | | |
| Draft (ft/m) | *24.6/7.50* | | |
| Engines/Propellers | *2 Sulzer V12-cyl diesels/2 (VP)* | | |
| Decks | *10* | Crew | *588* |
| Pass. Capacity (basis 2) | *1,264* | (all berths) | *1,627* |
| Pass. Space Ratio (basis 2) | *43.8* | (all berths) | *34.0* |
| Officers | *Dutch* | Dining Staff | *Filipino/Indonesian* |
| Total Cabins | *632* | | |
| Size (sq ft/m) | *187-1,126/17.3-104.5* | | |
| Door Width | *26"* | | |
| Outside Cabins | *501* | Inside Cabins | *131* |
| Single Cabins | *0* | Supplement | *50-100%* |
| Balcony Cabins | *150* | Wheelchair Cabins | *6* |
| Cabin Current | *110/220 AC* | Refrigerator | *PS/S/A/B* |
| Cabin TV | *Yes* | VCR | *No* |
| Dining Rooms | *1* | Sittings | *2* |
| Elevators | *12* | Door Width | *40"* |

| | | | |
|---|---|---|---|
| Casino | *Yes* | Slot Machines | *Yes* |
| Swimming Pools (outside) | *1* | (inside) | *1* |
| Whirlpools | *2* | Gymnasium | *Yes* |
| Sauna/Steam Rm | *Yes/No* | Massage | *Yes* |
| Self-Service Launderette | *Yes* | | |
| Movie Theater/Seats | *Yes/249* | | |
| Library | *Yes* | | |
| Children's Facilities | *No* | | |
| Watersports Facilities | *None* | | |
| Classification Society | *Lloyd's Register* | | |

| RATINGS | SCORE |
|---|---|
| Ship: Condition/Cleanliness | 8.7 |
| Ship: Space/Flow/Comfort | 8.2 |
| Ship: Decor/Furnishings | 8.3 |
| Ship: Fitness Facilities | 7.7 |
| Cabins: Comfort/Facilities | 8.1 |
| Cabins: Software | 7.9 |
| Food: Dining Room/Cuisine | 7.8 |
| Food: Buffets/Informal Dining | 7.6 |
| Food: Quality of Ingredients | 7.2 |
| Service: Dining Room | 7.7 |
| Service: Bars/Lounges | 7.6 |
| Service: Cabins | 8.1 |
| Cruise: Entertainment | 7.0 |
| Cruise: Activities Program | 7.2 |
| Cruise: Hospitality Standard | 8.1 |
| OVERALL RATING | 117.2 |

**+** One of three sister ships. All outdoor decks are teakwood, and include a traditional wrap-around promenade deck. Magrodome roof covers indoor-outdoor pool, whirlpools, and central lido area. Elegant, yet eclectic, interior design. Three-deck-high atrium foyer with 8-meter-high statue is lovely. Lovely reference library and card room. $2 million art collection. 28 suites for four feature in-suite dining and free laundry/dry-cleaning. Other cabins are spacious, tastefully decorated, and well laid out. Most feature daytime sitting area. Excellent flower displays.

**–** Long lines for embarkation, disembarkation, shore tenders, and buffets. The Crows Nest observation lounge/disco is uninviting. Standard cabins have little closet spaces. Showroom has pretentious decor, low ceilings, and poor sightlines. Poor entertainment. The library lacks hard-back fiction books (there are paperbacks but they become dog-eared quickly and look awful).

**Dining** Two-level dining room (with smoking/nonsmoking levels) is elegant, with panoramic windows on three sides and Indonesian-themed decor. Music balcony. Two small wings are good for groups. Fine china and silverware. Open seating for breakfast/lunch, two seatings for dinner. Food and service are typical of HAL's generally good standards. Tasteless entrees.

**Other Comments** Port taxes, insurance, and gratuities are extra (gratuities are not "required," according to the brochure, but they are expected).

# ms Stella Maris ★★★

***Principal Cruising Areas***

*Aegean/Mediterranean (7 nights)*

***Base Port:*** *Piraeus*

| | | | |
|---|---|---|---|
| Cruise Line | | | *Sun Line Cruises* |
| Former Names | | | *Bremerhaven* |
| Gross Tonnage | | | *4,000* |
| Builder | | | *Alder Werft (Germany)* |
| Original Cost | | | *n/a* |
| Christened By | | | *Mrs Daniela Caneli* |
| First Entered Service | | | *1960* |
| Interior Design | | | *Mrs Isabella Kousseouglou* |
| Country of Registry | | | *Greece (SMAR)* |
| Tel No | *113-0322* | Fax No | *113-0323* |
| Length (ft/m) | | | *289.4/88.22* |
| Beam (ft/m) | | | *45.9/14.00* |
| Draft (ft/m) | | | *14.4/4.40* |
| Engines/Propellers | | | *2 Koeln 8-cyl diesels/2* |
| Decks | *4* | Crew | *110* |
| Pass. Capacity (basis 2) | *180* | (all berths) | *180* |
| Pass. Space Ratio (basis 2) | *22.2* | (all berths) | *22.2* |
| Officers | *Greek* | Dining Staff | *Greek* |
| Total Cabins | | | *93* |
| Size (sq ft/m) | *96-151/9-14* | Door Width | *24"* |
| Outside Cabins | *80* | Inside Cabins | *13* |
| Single Cabins | *0* | Supplement | *50-100%* |
| Balcony Cabins | *0* | Wheelchair Cabins | *0* |
| Cabin Current | | | *220 AC* |
| Refrigerator | | | *No* |
| Cabin TV | *No* | VCR | *No* |
| Dining Rooms | *1* | Sittings | *1* |
| Elevators | *0* | Door Width | *n/a* |

| | | | |
|---|---|---|---|
| Casino | *No* | Slot Machines | *No* |
| Swimming Pools (outside) | *1* | (inside) | *0* |
| Whirlpools | *0* | Gymnasium | *No* |
| Sauna/Steam Rm | *No/No* | Massage | *No* |
| Self-Service Launderette | | | *No* |
| Movie Theater/Seats | | | *No* |
| Library | | | *Yes* |
| Children's Facilities | | | *No* |
| Watersports Facilities | | | *None* |
| Classification Society | | | *Lloyd's Register* |

| RATINGS | SCORE |
|---|---|
| Ship: Condition/Cleanliness | 6.7 |
| Ship: Space/Flow/Comfort | 6.0 |
| Ship: Decor/Furnishings | 7.1 |
| Ship: Fitness Facilities | 3.0 |
| Cabins: Comfort/Facilities | 6.7 |
| Cabins: Software | 7.4 |
| Food: Dining Room/Cuisine | 7.3 |
| Food: Buffets/Informal Dining | 7.0 |
| Food: Quality of Ingredients | 6.4 |
| Service: Dining Room | 7.6 |
| Service: Bars/Lounges | 7.4 |
| Service: Cabins | 7.6 |
| Cruise: Entertainment | 5.3 |
| Cruise: Activities Program | 5.7 |
| Cruise: Hospitality Standard | 7.7 |
| OVERALL RATING | 98.9 |

**+** Charming little ship has an intimate, yacht-like atmosphere. Superbly maintained, spotlessly clean, and tidy. Fresh flower arrangements throughtout add a splash of color. Excellent service from attentive, considerate staff. Cabins are quite spacious for ship size, and tastefully equipped, but there is not much drawer space. Very warm and intimate ambiance. Good for close-in destination cruising among the Greek Islands and Turkey, which Sun Line does well.

**–** There are limited public rooms and open spaces, and the swimming pool is tiny—really just a "dip" pool. Cabin bathrooms are small. Being small, she does not sail well in open waters.

**Dining** Charming dining room. The food is quite good, though loaded with oil and olives. Good wine list. Limited selection of breads, fruits, and cheeses.

**Other Comments** This ship will provide you with sophisticated, comfortable surroundings, and attention to detail that makes for a personable experience. Insurance, port taxes, and gratuities are extra.

# ms Stella Oceanis ★★★

***Principal Cruising Areas***

*Aegean/Mediterranean (3/4 nights)*

***Base Port:*** *Piraeus*

| | | | |
|---|---|---|---|
| Cruise Line | | | *Sun Line Cruises* |
| Former Names | | | *Aphrodite* |
| Gross Tonnage | | | *6,000* |
| Builder | | | *Cantieri Riuniti dell' Adriatico (Italy)* |
| Original Cost | | | *n/a* |
| Christened By | | | *Mrs Isabella Kousseoglou* |
| First Entered Service | | | *1965/1967* |
| Interior Design | | | *Mrs Isabella Kousseoglou* |
| Country of Registry | | | *Greece (SOCE)* |
| Tel No | *113-0471* | Fax No | *113-0471* |
| Length (ft/m) | | | *344.9/105.14* |
| Beam (ft/m) | | | *55.5/16.92* |
| Draft (ft/m) | | | *14.9/4.56* |
| Engines/Propellers | | | *2 Sulzer 7-cyl diesels/1 (CP)* |
| Decks | *6* | Crew | *140* |
| Pass. Capacity (basis 2) | *300* | (all berths) | *369* |
| Pass. Space Ratio (basis 2) | *20.0* | (all berths) | *16.2* |
| Officers | *Greek* | Dining Staff | *Greek* |
| Total Cabins | | | *159* |
| Size (sq ft/m) | 96-208/9-19.3 | Door Width | 24" |
| Outside Cabins | 113 | Inside Cabins | 46 |
| Single Cabins | *0* | Supplement | *50-100%* |
| Balcony Cabins | *0* | Wheelchair Cabins | *0* |
| Cabin Current | | | *220 AC* |
| Refrigerator | | | *No* |
| Cabin TV | *No* | VCR | *No* |
| Dining Rooms | *1* | Sittings | *2* |
| Elevators | *1* | Door Width | *30"* |

| | | | |
|---|---|---|---|
| Casino | *No* | Slot Machines | *No* |
| Swimming Pools (outside) | *1* | (inside) | *0* |
| Whirlpools | *0* | Gymnasium | *No* |
| Sauna/Steam Rm | *No/No* | Massage | *No* |
| Self-Service Launderette | | | *No* |
| Movie Theater/Seats | | | *No* |
| Library | | | *Yes* |
| Children's Facilities | | | *No* |
| Watersports Facilities | | | *None* |
| Classification Society | | | *Lloyd's Register* |

| RATINGS | SCORE |
|---|---|
| Ship: Condition/Cleanliness | 6.5 |
| Ship: Space/Flow/Comfort | 6.0 |
| Ship: Decor/Furnishings | 7.0 |
| Ship: Fitness Facilities | 3.0 |
| Cabins: Comfort/Facilities | 6.5 |
| Cabins: Software | 7.2 |
| Food: Dining Room/Cuisine | 7.3 |
| Food: Buffets/Informal Dining | 7.0 |
| Food: Quality of Ingredients | 6.4 |
| Service: Dining Room | 7.5 |
| Service: Bars/Lounges | 7.4 |
| Service: Cabins | 7.6 |
| Cruise: Entertainment | 5.2 |
| Cruise: Activities Program | 5.5 |
| Cruise: Hospitality Standard | 7.6 |
| OVERALL RATING | 97.7 |

**+** Tidy, well-maintained ship with clean, rounded lines. Intimate atmosphere. Public rooms are limited, but nicely decorated; a favorite is the Plaka Taverna, decorated in rich woods. The cabins (eight categories) are small, and plainer than on the smaller sister. They have limited closet and drawer space, but those on Lido and Stella decks have interconnecting doors. Some have full bathtub, while others have shower only, but all have private bathrooms.

**–** Few public rooms and not much open deck and sunning space. Narrow, steep gangway.

**Dining** Tastefully decorated, charming dining room. Good food, but little choice.

**Other Comments** This ship lacks the sophistication of the other ships in the fleet, but is nonetheless quite charming. Sun Line provides a fine destination-intensive cruise experience, made better by the charming, friendly officers and staff. Insurance and gratuities are extra.

# ss Stella Solaris ★★★★

***Principal Cruising Areas***

*Caribbean/Europe/South America (various)*

***Base Ports:** Galveston/Piraeus*

| | | | |
|---|---|---|---|
| Cruise Line | | | *Sun Line Cruises* |
| Former Names | | | *Stella V/Camboge* |
| Gross Tonnage | | | *17,832* |
| Builder | | | *Ateliers et Chantiers de France (France)* |
| Original Cost | | | *n/a* |
| Christened By | | | *Mrs Isabella Kousseoglou* |
| First Entered Service | | | *Jul 31, 1953/Jun 25, 1973* |
| Interior Design | | | *Mrs Isabella Kousseouglou* |
| Country of Registry | | | *Greece (SSOL)* |
| Tel No | *113-0403* | Fax No | *113-0403* |
| Length (ft/m) | | | *545.1/166.15* |
| Beam (ft/m) | | | *72.4/22.08* |
| Draft (ft/m) | | | *25.8/7.88* |
| Engines/Propellers | | | *6 Parsons steam turbines/2* |
| Decks | *8* | Crew | *330* |
| Pass. Capacity (basis 2) | *620* | (all berths) | *700* |
| Pass. Space Ratio (basis 2) | *28.7* | (all berths) | *25.4* |
| Officers | *Greek* | Dining Staff | *Greek* |
| Total Cabins | | | *329* |
| Size (sq ft/m) | 96-225/9-21 | Door Width | 24" |
| Outside Cabins | *250* | Inside Cabins | *79* |
| Single Cabins | *0* | Supplement | *50-100%* |
| Balcony Cabins | *0* | Wheelchair Cabins | *0* |
| Cabin Current | | | *110/220 AC* |
| Refrigerator | | | *No* |
| Cabin TV | *No* | VCR | *No* |
| Dining Rooms | *1* | Sittings | *2* |
| Elevators | *3* | Door Width | *31"* |

| | | | |
|---|---|---|---|
| Casino | *Yes* | Slot Machines | *Yes* |
| Swimming Pools (outside) | *1* | (inside) | *0* |
| Whirlpools | *0* | Gymnasium | *Yes* |
| Sauna/Steam Rm | *Yes/No* | Massage | *Yes* |
| Self-Service Launderette | | | *No* |
| Movie Theater/Seats | | | *Yes/275* |
| Library | | | *Yes* |
| Children's Facilities | | | *No* |
| Watersports Facilities | | | *None* |
| Classification Society | | | *Lloyd's Register* |

| RATINGS | SCORE |
|---|---|
| Ship: Condition/Cleanliness | 7.7 |
| Ship: Space/Flow/Comfort | 7.0 |
| Ship: Decor/Furnishings | 7.2 |
| Ship: Fitness Facilities | 5.1 |
| Cabins: Comfort/Facilities | 7.1 |
| Cabins: Software | 7.8 |
| Food: Dining Room/Cuisine | 7.6 |
| Food: Buffets/Informal Dining | 7.1 |
| Food: Quality of Ingredients | 6.6 |
| Service: Dining Room | 7.8 |
| Service: Bars/Lounges | 7.7 |
| Service: Cabins | 7.7 |
| Cruise: Entertainment | 6.1 |
| Cruise: Activities Program | 5.7 |
| Cruise: Hospitality Standard | 7.8 |
| OVERALL RATING | 106.0 |

**+** Traditional ship profile, with attractive funnel amidships. Spotlessly clean and well maintained throughout. Well-planned itineraries. Expansive open deck space. Attractive twin pools and sunning area. Elegant public rooms have quality furniture and fixtures. Nice feeling of space and grace. Fresh flowers everywhere. Cabins are spacious and very well equipped—many have full bathtub. Lido Deck suites are delightful.

**–** The decor is somewhat dated. No observation lounge. Cabins located on Sapphire Deck and midships on Emerald Deck are subject to engine noise.

**Dining** Delightful dining room, excellent food, good wines, and old world, European service.

**Other Comments** This ship is for the older passenger who seeks a relaxed, unhurried, and gracious cruise experience in fine surroundings, at reasonable cost, and without the hype of the more contemporary ships. Insurance and gratuities are extra.

# ms Sun Princess

***Principal Cruising Areas***
*Alaska/Caribbean (7 nights)*
***Base Ports:*** *Vancouver/Ft. Lauderdale*

| | | | |
|---|---|---|---|
| Cruise Line/Operator | | | *Princess Cruises* |
| Former Names | | | *n/a* |
| Gross Tonnage | | | *77,000* |
| Builder | | | *Fincantieri (Italy)* |
| Original Cost | | | *$300 million* |
| Christened By | | | *n/a* |
| First Entered Service | | | *Jan 1996* |
| Interior Design | | | *Giacomo Mortola* |
| Country of Registry | | | *Italy* |
| Tel No | *n/a* | Fax No | *n/a* |
| Length (ft/m) | | | *856.2/261.0* |
| Beam (ft/m) | | | *105.8/32.25* |
| Draft (ft/m) | | | *26.0/7.95* |
| Engines/Propellers | | | *4 diesel-electrics/2 (FP)* |
| Decks | *14* | Crew | *900* |
| Pass. Capacity (basis 2) | *1,950* | (all berths) | *n/a* |
| Pass. Space Ratio (basis 2) | *39.4* | (all berths) | *n/a* |
| Officers | *Italian* | Dining Staff | *International* |
| Total Cabins | | | *975* |
| Size (sq ft/m) | *159-611/14.7-56.7* | Door Width | *24"* |
| Outside Cabins | *652* | Inside Cabins | *398* |
| Single Cabins | *0* | Supplement | *25-100%* |
| Balcony Cabins | *446* | Wheelchair Cabins | *20* |
| Cabin Current | | | *110/220 AC* |
| Refrigerator | | | *Yes* |
| Cabin TV | *Yes* | VCR | *Suites only* |
| Dining Rooms | | | *2 main/3 others* |
| Sittings | | | *2 (main dining rooms)* |

| | | | |
|---|---|---|---|
| Elevators | - | Door Width | - |
| Casino | *Yes* | Slot Machines | *Yes* |
| Swimming Pools (outside) | *3* | (inside) | *0* |
| Whirlpools | *5* | Gymnasium | Yes |
| Sauna/Steam Rm | *Yes* | Massage | *Yes* |
| Self-Service Launderette | | | *Yes* |
| Movie Theater/Seats | | | *Yes* |
| Library | *Yes* | Children's Facilities | *Yes* |
| Watersports Facilities | | | *None* |
| Classification Society | | | *Lloyd's Register of Shipping* |

| RATINGS | SCORE |
|---|---|
| Ship: Condition/Cleanliness | NYR |
| Ship: Space/Flow/Comfort | NYR |
| Ship: Decor/Furnishings | NYR |
| Ship: Fitness Facilities | NYR |
| Cabins: Comfort/Facilities | NYR |
| Cabins: Software | NYR |
| Food: Dining Room/Cuisine | NYR |
| Food: Buffets/Informal Dining | NYR |
| Food: Quality of Ingredients | NYR |
| Service: Dining Room | NYR |
| Service: Bars/Lounges | NYR |
| Service: Cabins | NYR |
| Cruise: Entertainment | NYR |
| Cruise: Activities Program | NYR |
| Cruise: Hospitality Standard | NYR |

NYR = Not Yet Rated

**+** Wide range of public rooms, including more intimate rooms. Plenty of space, and passenger flow is very good. The health spa complex surrounds a swimming pool suspended between two decks (there are two other pools). There is a conference center for up to 300. Excellent collection of art. Expect the cabins to be extremely functional; many outside cabins (70%) have private verandas (more than any other Princess ship to date). Has several showrooms for a wide choice of entertainment and social functions.

**–** None known at press time. As on any large ship, expect long lines for embarkation, disembarkation, buffets, shore tenders, and shore excursions.

**Dining** There are two dining rooms, each with its own galley. Each is split into multi-tier sections. A patisserie, wine/caviar bar, and pizzeria are additional informal dining areas.

**Other Comments** The design is quite handsome for this large ship and is indicative of more to come in the future, and is the latest enhancement of the *Crown/Regal Princess* design. Lots of glass area on the upper decks. Insurance, port taxes, and gratuitites are extra.

# ms Sun Viking ★★★+

***Principal Cruising Areas***

*Alaska/Caribbean (10/11 nights/various)*

***Base Ports:** Vancouver/San Juan*

| | | | |
|---|---|---|---|
| Cruise Line | | | *Royal Caribbean Cruises* |
| Former Names | | | *n/a* |
| Gross Tonnage | | | *18,556* |
| Builder | | | *Wartsila (Finland)* |
| Original Cost | | | *$17.5 million* |
| Christened By | | | *Mrs Sigurd Skaugen* |
| First Entered Service | | | *Dec 9, 1972* |
| Interior Design | | | *Njal Eide* |
| Country of Registry | | | *Norway (LIZA)* |
| Tel No | *131-2151* | Fax No | *131-2151* |
| Length (ft/m) | | | *563.2/171.69* |
| Beam (ft/m) | | | *78.8/24.03* |
| Draft (ft/m) | | | *20.6/6.30* |
| Engines/Propellers | | | *2 Sulzer 9-cyl diesels/2 (CP)* |
| Decks | *8* | Crew | *341* |
| Pass. Capacity (basis 2) | *714* | (all berths) | *818* |
| Pass. Space Ratio (basis 2) | *25.9* | (all berths) | *22.6* |
| Officers | *Norwegian* | Dining Staff | *International* |
| Total Cabins | | | *357* |
| Size (sq ft/m) | *120-237/11-22* | Door Width | *25"* |
| Outside Cabins | *240* | Inside Cabins | *117* |
| Single Cabins | *0* | Supplement | *50-100%* |
| Balcony Cabins | *0* | Wheelchair Cabins | *0* |
| Cabin Current | | | *110 AC* |
| Refrigerator | | | *Owner's suite* |
| Cabin TV | *No* | VCR | *No* |
| Dining Rooms | *1* | Sittings | *2* |
| Elevators | *4* | Door Width | *35"* |

| | | | |
|---|---|---|---|
| Casino | *Yes* | Slot Machines | *Yes* |
| Swimming Pools (outside) | *1* | (inside) | *0* |
| Whirlpools | *0* | Gymnasium | *Yes* |
| Sauna/Steam Rm | *Yes/No* | Massage | *Yes* |
| Self-Service Launderette | | | *No* |
| Movie Theater/Seats | | | *No* |
| Library | | | *Yes* |
| Children's Facilities | | | *No* |
| Watersports Facilities | | | *None* |
| Classification Society | | | *Det Norske Veritas* |

| RATINGS | SCORE |
|---|---|
| Ship: Condition/Cleanliness | 7.4 |
| Ship: Space/Flow/Comfort | 6.3 |
| Ship: Decor/Furnishings | 6.9 |
| Ship: Fitness Facilities | 5.6 |
| Cabins: Comfort/Facilities | 5.8 |
| Cabins: Software | 7.7 |
| Food: Dining Room/Cuisine | 6.8 |
| Food: Buffets/Informal Dining | 6.6 |
| Food: Quality of Ingredients | 7.1 |
| Service: Dining Room | 6.7 |
| Service: Bars/Lounges | 6.5 |
| Service: Cabins | 6.1 |
| Cruise: Entertainment | 7.2 |
| Cruise: Activities Program | 6.7 |
| Cruise: Hospitality Standard | 7.4 |
| OVERALL RATING | 100.8 |

**+** Well-proportioned ship with contemporary styling. Cantilevered Viking Crown Lounge set atop funnel housing provides an impressive view. Smallest and most intimate ship in the RCCL fleet—a real gem. Good open deck and sunning space, with wrap-around, outdoor, polished wood deck. Public rooms decorated in modern Scandinavian style and colors, and named after musicals. Charming, friendly ambiance throughout.

**–** High density ship means public rooms are always busy. Long wait for elevator, buffet, and disembarkation. Small, moderately comfortable cabins with little storage space.

**Dining** Attractive dining room with large picture windows has tables for four, six, or eight (no tables for two). Consistently good food and service, although there's little flexibility. Poor breads, rolls, and fruit selection. Good wine list, but limited vintages.

**Other Comments** This company wants its passengers out and about the public rooms, not in their small cabins, and caters to passengers wanting a more intimate cruise, with all the Royal Caribbean Cruises trimmings at a fair price. Insurance and gratuities are extra.

# ms Taras Shevchenko ★★★

***Principal Cruising Area***

*Europe (various)*

***Base Port:*** *Toulon*

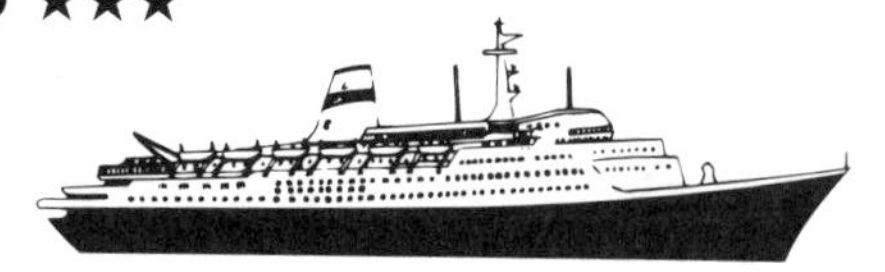

| | | | |
|---|---|---|---|
| Cruise Line | *Black Sea Shipping* | | |
| Former Names | *n/a* | | |
| Gross Tonnage | *20,027* | | |
| Builder | *VEB Mathias Thesen (Germany)* | | |
| Original Cost | *n/a* | | |
| Christened By | *n/a* | | |
| First Entered Service | *Apr 26, 1967* | | |
| Interior Design | *n/a* | | |
| Country of Registry | *Ukraine (UKSA)* | | |
| Tel No | *140-0266* | Fax No | *140-0266* |
| Length (ft/m) | *577.4/176.00* | | |
| Beam (ft/m) | *77.4/23.60* | | |
| Draft (ft/m) | *26.7/8.16* | | |
| Engines/Propellers | 2 *Sulzer-Cegielski 7-cyl diesels/2* | | |
| Decks | *8* | Crew | *370* |
| Pass. Capacity (basis 2) | *574* | (all berths) | *712* |
| Pass. Space Ratio (basis 2) | *34.8* | (all berths) | *28.1* |
| Officers | *Russian/Ukrainian* | | |
| Dining Staff | *East European* | | |
| Total Cabins | *287* | | |
| Size (sq ft/m) | *n/a* | Door Width | *26"* |
| Outside Cabins | *287* | Inside Cabins | *0* |
| Single Cabins | *0* | Supplement | *100%* |
| Balcony Cabins | *0* | Wheelchair Cabins | *0* |
| Cabin Current | *220 AC* | Refrigerator | *No* |
| Cabin TV | *No* | VCR | *No* |
| Dining Rooms | *3* | Sittings | *1* |
| Elevators | *3* | Door Width | *32"* |

| | | | |
|---|---|---|---|
| Casino | *No* | Slot Machines | *No* |
| Swimming Pools (outside) | *2* | (inside) | *1* |
| Whirlpools | *1* | Gymnasium | *Yes* |
| Sauna/Steam Room | *Yes/No* | Massage | *No* |
| Self-Service Launderette | *No* | | |
| Movie Theater/Seats | *Yes/130* | | |
| Library | *Yes* | | |
| Children's Facilities | *Yes* | | |
| Watersports Facilities | *None* | | |
| Classification Society | *RS* | | |

| RATINGS | SCORE |
|---|---|
| Ship: Condition/Cleanliness | 6.2 |
| Ship: Space/Flow/Comfort | 6.6 |
| Ship: Decor/Furnishings | 6.2 |
| Ship: Fitness Facilities | 5.5 |
| Cabins: Comfort/Facilities | 6.1 |
| Cabins: Software | 6.4 |
| Food: Dining Room/Cuisine | 6.4 |
| Food: Buffets/Informal Dining | 6.3 |
| Food: Quality of Ingredients | 6.5 |
| Service: Dining Room | 6.6 |
| Service: Bars | 6.9 |
| Service: Cabins | 7.0 |
| Cruise: Entertainment | 6.0 |
| Cruise: Activities Program | 5.4 |
| Cruise: Hospitality Standard | 6.4 |
| OVERALL RATING | 94.5 |

**+** Solidly-constructed vessel with nicely rounded lines, a classic profile, and an all-white, ice-hardened hull. Good open deck and sunning space. Wrap-around outdoor promenade deck. Pleasant, but very plain, interior decor that could do with more tropical greenery to enhance it. Recent substantial refurbishment has upgraded the vessel considerably and added more color. Spacious music salon. Has all-outside cabins that are very comfortable, each with private facilities. Ten suites are very spacious, and tastefully equipped.

**–** Very plain ceilings throughout, as well as spartan decor that is quite dated. Narrow, steep gangway in most ports. No cushioned pads on deck chairs.

**Dining** Adequate, but there's little menu choice. Service is attentively provided. Poor selection of bread rolls, cheeses, and fruits.

**Other Comments** While this ship is not yet up to Western standards, it was renovated in 1988 and will provide a reasonable cruise experience at a modest rate, for a mostly French and Italian clientele. Often operates under charter, but there's no finesse. Insurance, port taxes, and gratuities are extra.

# mv The Azur ★★★+

***Principal Cruising Area***
*Southern Europe (various)*
***Base Ports:*** *Genoa/Venice*

| | | | |
|---|---|---|---|
| Cruise Line | | | *Festival Cruises* |
| Former Names | | | *Eagle/Azur* |
| Gross Tonnage | | | *14,717* |
| Builder | | | *Dubigeon-Normandie (France)* |
| Original Cost | | | *n/a* |
| Christened By | | | *n/a* |
| First Entered Service | | | *May 18, 1971/Apr 23, 1994* |
| Interior Design | | | *A&M Katzourakis* |
| Country of Registry | | | *Panama (3EPR5)* |
| Tel No | *133-2515* | Fax No | *133-2515* |
| Length (ft/m) | | | *465.8/142.00* |
| Beam (ft/m) | | | *71.8/21.90* |
| Draft (ft/m) | | | *18.7/5.73* |
| Engines/Propellers | | | *2 Pielstick 16-cyl diesels/2 (VP)* |
| Decks | *7* | Crew | *325* |
| Pass. Capacity (basis 2) | *665* | (all berths) | *750* |
| Pass. Space Ratio (basis 2) | *22.1* | (all berths) | *19.6* |
| Officers | *Greek* | Dining Staff | *International* |
| Total Cabins | | | *335* |
| Size (sq ft/m) | *n/a* | Door Width | *24"* |
| Outside Cabins | *152* | Inside Cabins | *183* |
| Single Cabins | *10* | Supplement | *50%* |
| Balcony Cabins | *0* | Wheelchair Cabins | *2* |
| Cabin Current | | | *220 AC* |
| Refrigerator | | | *No* |
| Cabin TV | *No* | VCR | *No* |
| Dining Rooms | *1* | Sittings | *2* |
| Elevators | *3* | Door Width | *27"* |

| | | | |
|---|---|---|---|
| Casino | *Yes* | Slot Machines | *Yes* |
| Swimming Pools (outside) | *2* | (inside) | *0* |
| Whirlpools | *0* | Gymnasium | *Yes* |
| Sauna/Steam Rm | *No/No* | Massage | *No* |
| Self-Service Launderette | | | *No* |
| Movie Theater/Seats | | | *Yes/175* |
| Library | | | *Yes* |
| Children's Facilities | | | *Yes* |
| Watersports Facilities | | | *none* |
| Classification Society | | | *Bureau Veritas* |

| RATINGS | SCORE |
|---|---|
| Ship: Condition/Cleanliness | 8.0 |
| Ship: Space/Flow/Comfort | 6.8 |
| Ship: Decor/Furnishings | 7.6 |
| Ship: Fitness Facilities | 7.9 |
| Cabins: Comfort/Facilities | 6.7 |
| Cabins: Software | 7.1 |
| Food: Dining Room/Cuisine | 7.1 |
| Food: Buffets/Informal Dining | 6.5 |
| Food: Quality of Ingredients | 6.4 |
| Service: Dining Room | 7.4 |
| Service: Bars/Lounges | 6.7 |
| Service: Cabins | 7.4 |
| Cruise: Entertainment | 6.3 |
| Cruise: Activities Program | 6.1 |
| Cruise: Hospitality Standard | 6.7 |
| OVERALL RATING | 104.7 |

**+** Generous open deck space for sunning, but rather crowded when full. Good selection of public rooms, and numerous bars, with light, well chosen, contemporary decor and abundant mirrored surfaces. Fine, two-level cinema—good for seminars. Most cabins are plain, but nicely furnished, and decorated in earth tones. Two new outside cabins for the physically challenged. Lively action in the casino. Excellent sports facilities include indoor squash and volleyball courts.

**–** Very small swimming pools. The showroom has very poor sightlines and low ceiling, but is good for meetings. Many inside cabins. Constant announcements in several languages are irritating, but typical of European operations that try to cater for everyone.

**Dining** Charming, low-ceilinged, aft dining room has ocean-view windows on three sides, and chairs are comfortable. Outdoor barbecue and buffet is popular. Typically decent food, but presentation lacks finesse. Poor selection of breads, fruits, and cheeses. Courteous staff.

**Other Comments** Smart, though stubby-looking, with a short bow and twin tall funnels set well aft. This ship will appeal to the young, active set looking for a good first cruise experience to a host of destinations, at a very reasonable price, as well as to those seeking a venue for meetings and incentive cruises. Festival Cruises took over operation in 1994. Currency aboard: lire. Insurance and gratuities are extra.

# ms Triton ★★★+

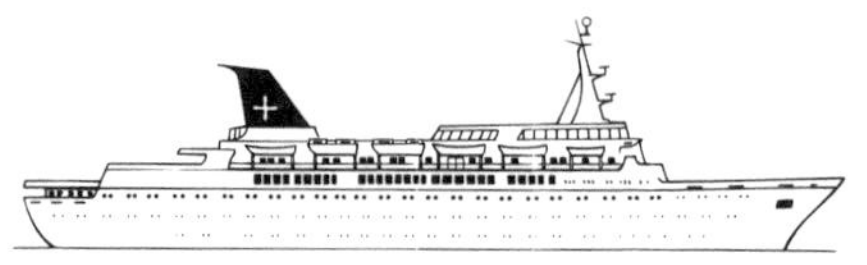

***Principal Cruising Areas***
*Aegean/Mediterranean (3/4/7 nights)*
***Base Port:** Piraeus*

| | | | |
|---|---|---|---|
| Cruise Line | | | *Epirotiki Lines* |
| Former Names | | | *Cunard Adventurer/Sunward II* |
| Gross Tonnage | | | *14,155* |
| Builder | | | *Rotterdamsche Dry Dock (Holland)* |
| Original Cost | | | *n/a* |
| Christened By | | | *n/a* |
| First Entered Service | | | *Oct 9, 1971/Spring 1992* |
| Interior Design | | | *Arminio Lozzi* |
| Country of Registry | | | *Greece (SVKR)* |
| Tel No | *113-1266* | Fax No | *113-1266* |
| Length (ft/m) | | | *491.1/149.70* |
| Beam (ft/m) | | | *70.5/21.50* |
| Draft (ft/m) | | | *20.9/6.4* |
| Engines | | | *4 Stork-Werkspoor 12-cyl diesels* |
| Propellers | | | *2 (CP)* |
| Decks | *7* | Crew | *265* |
| Pass. Capacity (basis 2) | *704* | (all berths) | *898* |
| Pass. Space Ratio (basis 2) | *20.1* | (all berths) | *15.7* |
| Officers | *Greek* | Dining Staff | *Greek* |
| Total Cabins | | | *352* |
| Size (sq ft/m) | *118-132/11-12.2* | Door Width | *22"* |
| Outside Cabins | *235* | Inside Cabins | *117* |
| Single Cabins | *0* | Supplement | *50%* |
| Balcony Cabins | *0* | Wheelchair Cabins | *0* |
| Cabin Current | *110/220 AC* | Refrigerator | *No* |
| Cabin TV | *No* | VCR | *No* |
| Dining Rooms | *1* | Sittings | *2* |
| Elevators | *2* | Door Width | *32"* |

| | | | |
|---|---|---|---|
| Casino | *Yes* | Slot Machines | *Yes* |
| Swimming Pools (outside) | *1* | (inside) | *0* |
| Whirlpools | *0* | Gymnasium | *Yes* |
| Sauna/Steam Rm | *Yes/No* | Massage | *Yes* |
| Self-Service Launderette | | | *No* |
| Movie Theater/Seats | | | *Yes/96* |
| Library | | | *Yes* |
| Children's Facilities | | | *Yes* |
| Watersports Facilities | | | *None* |
| Classification Society | | | *Lloyd's Register* |

| RATINGS | SCORE |
|---|---|
| Ship: Condition/Cleanliness | 7.5 |
| Ship: Space/Flow/Comfort | 6.4 |
| Ship: Decor/Furnishings | 7.2 |
| Ship: Fitness Facilities | 5.2 |
| Cabins: Comfort/Facilities | 6.6 |
| Cabins: Software | 7.9 |
| Food: Dining Room/Cuisine | 7.0 |
| Food: Buffets/Informal Dining | 6.1 |
| Food: Quality of Ingredients | 6.0 |
| Service: Dining Room | 7.2 |
| Service: Bars/Lounges | 6.8 |
| Service: Cabins | 7.1 |
| Cruise: Entertainment | 6.2 |
| Cruise: Activities Program | 6.1 |
| Cruise: Hospitality Standard | 7.7 |
| OVERALL RATING | 101.0 |

**+** Handsome, sleek profile and deep clipper bow. The most contemporary ship in the Epirotiki fleet. Excellent, destination-intensive itineraries. Wrap-around outdoor promenade deck. Fine nightclub with forward observation views. Good open deck space for sunning. Well-equipped cabins for ship size, even though they are rather small. Friendly staff and ambiance.

**–** High density ship means crowded public areas. Small cabins and bathrooms. Long lines for buffets. Too many announcements for tours when in ports of call.

**Dining** While the dining room is quite attractive and has contemporary colors and ambiance, it is also very noisy. The cuisine is Continental—much use of oils. Choice is adequate, but presentation is inconsistent. Poor bread rolls and fruits. Service is attentive but hurried.

**Other Comments** Well maintained, although now showing its age. Excellent ship for short cruises, however. Good layout and passenger flow, with ample public rooms and delightful, contemporary interior decor, but very crowded when full. Excellent value for money. A well delivered product on which to cruise around the Greek islands. Insurance and gratuities are extra.

# ms Tropicale ★★★★

***Principal Cruising Area***
*Caribbean (7 nights year-round)*
***Base Port:*** *Tampa (Saturday)*

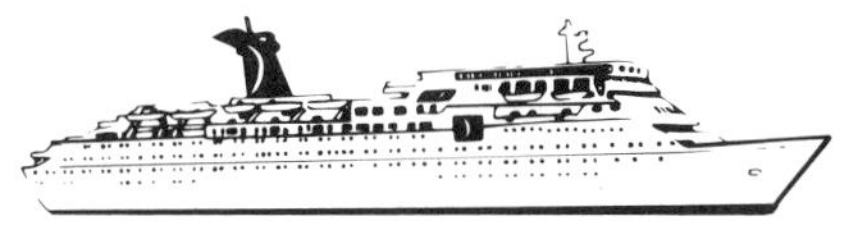

| | | | |
|---|---|---|---|
| Cruise Line | | | *Carnival Cruise Lines* |
| Former Names | | | *n/a* |
| Gross Tonnage | | | *36,674* |
| Builder | | | *Aalborg Vaerft (Denmark)* |
| Original Cost | | | *$100 million* |
| Christened By | | | *Mrs Madeleine Arison* |
| First Entered Service | | | *Jan 16, 1982* |
| Interior Design | | | *Joe Farcus* |
| Country of Registry | | | *Liberia (ELBM9)* |
| Tel No | *124-0561* | Fax No | *124-0561* |
| Length (ft/m) | | | *671.7/204.76* |
| Beam (ft/m) | | | *86.7/26.45* |
| Draft (ft/m) | | | *23.3/7.11* |
| Engines/Propellers | | | *2 Sulzer 7-cyl diesels/2 (CP)* |
| Decks | *10* | Crew | *550* |
| Pass. Capacity (basis 2) | *1,022* | (all berths) | *1,400* |
| Pass. Space Ratio (basis 2) | *35.8* | (all berths) | *26.1* |
| Officers | *Italian* | Dining Staff | *International* |
| Total Cabins | | | *511* |
| Size (sq ft/m) | *180/9.2* | Door Width | *30"* |
| Outside Cabins | *324* | Inside Cabins | *187* |
| Single Cabins | *0* | Supplement | *50%/100%* |
| Balcony Cabins | *12* | Wheelchair Cabins | *11* |
| Cabin Current | | | *110 AC* |
| Refrigerator | | | *(Suites only)* |
| Cabin TV | *Yes* | VCR | *No* |
| Dining Rooms | *1* | Sittings | *2* |
| Elevators | *8* | Door Width | *36"* |

| | | | |
|---|---|---|---|
| Casino | *Yes* | Slot Machines | *Yes* |
| Swimming Pools (outside) | *3* | (inside) | *0* |
| Whirlpools | *0* | Gymnasium | *Yes* |
| Sauna/Steam Rm | *Yes/No* | Massage | *Yes* |
| Self-Service Launderette | | | *Yes* |
| Movie Theater/Seats | | | *No* |
| Library | | | *Yes* |
| Children's Facilities | | | *Yes* |
| Watersports Facilities | | | *None* |
| Classification Society | | | *Lloyd's Register* |

| RATINGS | SCORE |
|---|---|
| Ship: Condition/Cleanliness | 7.7 |
| Ship: Space/Flow/Comfort | 7.0 |
| Ship: Decor/Furnishings | 6.8 |
| Ship: Fitness Facilities | 7.8 |
| Cabins: Comfort/Facilities | 7.5 |
| Cabins: Software | 7.4 |
| Food: Dining Room/Cuisine | 6.7 |
| Food: Buffets/Informal Dining | 6.4 |
| Food: Quality of Ingredients | 5.3 |
| Service: Dining Room | 7.0 |
| Service: Bars/Lounges | 7.2 |
| Service: Cabins | 6.4 |
| Cruise: Entertainment | 7.5 |
| Cruise: Activities Program | 7.8 |
| Cruise: Hospitality Standard | 6.6 |
| OVERALL RATING | 105.1 |

**+** Distinctive, contemporary look, with large, wing-tipped funnel. Well laid-out interior, with good passenger flow. Well maintained. Very lively casino action. 12 cabins have verandas. Good for families: Carnival goes out of its way to entertain young cruisers and their parents.

**–** Noisy dining room. Long lines for embarkation, disembarkation, shore tenders, and buffets. Too many repetitive announcements. Aggressive hustling for drinks (in plastic glasses).

**Dining** The dining room is located on a lower deck. It is colorful, cheerful, brightly lit, but very noisy (maybe that's "atmosphere"), and there are no tables for two. The food is typical Americana—quantity, not quality. The selection of bread rolls, fresh fruits, cheeses, and pastries is poor. Service lacks finesse. The food is adequate, but consistently uninspiring despite being upgraded. Service is hurried and inflexible, but cheerful.

**Other Comments** Public rooms are decorated in stimulating colors. Cabins are quite spacious, well equipped, and decorated in contemporary colors. Stunning discotheque. This ship will provide novice cruisers with a well-proven product that is attractively packaged, at a reasonable price. It is not a luxury cruise by any means, nor does it pretend to be. Insurance and gratuities are extra.

# ss Universe ★★★

***Principal Cruising Area***
*Alaska (14 nights)*
***Base Port:** Vancouver*

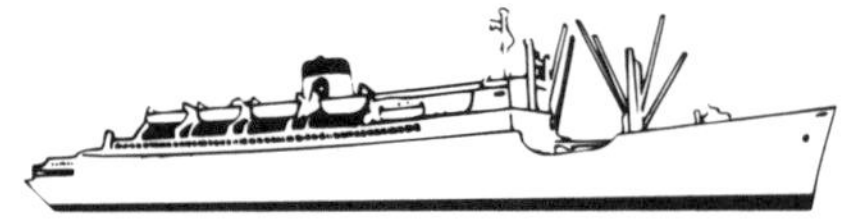

| | | | |
|---|---|---|---|
| Cruise Line | | | *World Explorer Cruises* |
| Former Names | | | *Atlantic Universe Campus/ Badger Mariner* |
| Gross Tonnage | | | *18,100* |
| Builder | | | *Sun Shipbuilding (USA)* |
| Original Cost | | | *n/a* |
| Christened By | | | *n/a* |
| First Entered Service | | | *Nov 1953/1976* |
| Interior Design | | | *Ocean Craft Interiors* |
| Country of Registry | | | *Liberia (5LGK)* |
| Tel No | *124-0713* | Fax No | *124-0713* |
| Length (ft/m) | | | *563.6/171.81* |
| Beam (ft/m) | | | *76.3/23.27* |
| Draft (ft/m) | | | *28.6/8.72* |
| Engines | | | *2 General Electric steam turbines* |
| Propellers | | | *1* |
| Decks | *7* | Crew | *200* |
| Pass. Capacity (basis 2) | *542* | (all berths) | *833* |
| Pass. Space Ratio (basis 2) | *33.5* | (all berths) | *21.7* |
| Officers | *Chinese* | Dining Staff | *Chinese/Filipino* |
| Total Cabins | | | *314* |
| Size (sq ft/m) | *63-180/5.8-16.7* | Door Width | *24"* |
| Outside Cabins | *138* | Inside Cabins | *176* |
| Single Cabins | *25* | Supplement | *None* |
| Balcony Cabins | *0* | Wheelchair Cabins | *0* |
| Cabin Current | *110 AC* | Refrigerator | *No* |
| Cabin TV | *No* | VCR | *No* |
| Dining Rooms | *1* | Sittings | *2* |

| | | | |
|---|---|---|---|
| Elevators | *1* | Door Width | *26"* |
| Casino | *No* | Slot Machines | *No* |
| Swimming Pools (outside) | *1* | (inside) | *0* |
| Whirlpools | *0* | Gymnasium | *Yes* |
| Sauna/Steam Rm | *No/No* | Massage | *Yes* |
| Self-Service Launderette | | | *Yes* |
| Movie Theater/Seats | | | *Yes/200* |
| Library | *Yes* | Children's Facilities | *No* |
| Watersports Facilities | | | *None* |
| Classification Society | | | *American Bur. of Shipping* |

| RATINGS | SCORE |
|---|---|
| Ship: Condition/Cleanliness | 5.9 |
| Ship: Space/Flow/Comfort | 5.7 |
| Ship: Decor/Furnishings | 6.8 |
| Ship: Fitness Facilities | 4.6 |
| Cabins: Comfort/Facilities | 5.9 |
| Cabins: Software | 6.4 |
| Food: Dining Room/Cuisine | 6.3 |
| Food: Buffets/Informal Dining | 5.6 |
| Food: Quality of Ingredients | 5.8 |
| Service: Dining Room | 6.5 |
| Service: Bars/Lounges | 6.2 |
| Service: Cabins | 6.8 |
| Cruise: Entertainment | 5.2 |
| Cruise: Activities Program | 6.1 |
| Cruise: Hospitality Standard | 6.5 |
| OVERALL RATING | 90.3 |

**+** Solidly-constructed ship with cargo-liner profile. Part floating campus (fall/winter) and part cruise ship (spends summers in Alaska). On-board life and ambiance is very casual and unpretentious. Recent refurbishment of all public rooms and cabins has improved the decor. Spacious public rooms feature comfortable, conservative decor. Excellent, recently-enlarged library and reference center contains over 13,000 books. Goes to more ports of call than any other cruise line going to Alaska. Culture without glitz.

**–** Limited number of public rooms and open deck space. Lifeboats/tenders are old and well worn. Narrow, steep gangway.

**Dining** The informal dining room is set low down, but is cozy and quite comfortable. The cuisine is Asian-American, but there's little choice of breads, cheeses, and fruits. Very attentive service with a smile.

**Other Comments** Cultured, tasteful entertainment consists of lectures and semi-classical music. Good lecture and life-enrichment programs. Caters well to passengers of wisdom years seeking a leisurely two-week destination-intensive Alaska cruise, at an extremely attractive price. Also has gentleman "hosts" on selected sailings. Insurance and gratuities are extra.

# ms Viking Serenade ★★★★

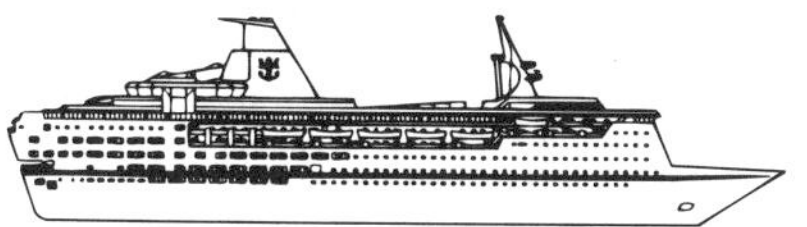

***Principal Cruising Area***

*Mexican Riviera (3/4 nights year-round)*

***Base Port:*** *Los Angeles (Fri/Mon)*

| | |
|---|---|
| Cruise Line | *Royal Caribbean Cruises* |
| Former Names | *Stardancer/Scandinavia* |
| Gross Tonnage | *40,132* |
| Builder | *Dubigeon-Normandie (France)* |
| Original Cost | *$100 million* |
| Christened By | *Ms Liv Ullmann/ Ms WhoopiGoldberg* |
| First Entered Service | *Oct 1981/Jan 27, 1990* |
| Interior Design | *Njal Eide/Petter Yran/ Snoweiss Group* |
| Country of Registry | *Bahamas (C6CP)* |
| Tel No *110-3132* | Fax No *110-3132* |
| Length (ft/m) | *623.0/189.89* |
| Beam (ft/m) | *88.6/27.01* |
| Draft (ft/m) | *22.6/6.90* |
| Engines/Propellers | *2 B&W 9-cyl diesels/2 (CP)* |
| Decks *7* | Crew *612* |
| Pass. Capacity (basis 2) *1,512* | (all berths) *1,863* |
| Pass. Space Ratio (basis 2) *26.5* | (all berths) *21.5* |
| Officers *International* | Dining Staff *International* |
| Total Cabins | *756* |
| Size (sq ft/m) *144-400/13.3-37* | Door Width *23"* |
| Outside Cabins *478* | Inside Cabins *278* |
| Single Cabins *0* | Supplement *50-100%* |
| Balcony Cabins *8* | Wheelchair Cabins *4* |
| Cabin Current *110 AC* | Refrigerator *R/A* |
| Cabin TV *Yes* | VCR *No* |
| Dining Rooms *2* | Sittings *2* |

| | |
|---|---|
| Elevators *5* | Door Width *35"* |
| Casino *Yes* | Slot Machines *Yes* |
| Swimming Pools (outside) *1* | (inside) *0* |
| Whirlpools *0* | Gymnasium *Yes* |
| Sauna/Steam Rm *Yes/No* | Massage *Yes* |
| Self-Service Launderette | *No* |
| Movie Theater/Seats | *No* |
| Library *Yes* | Children's Facilities *Yes* |
| Watersports Facilities | *None* |
| Classification Society | *Det Norske Veritas* |

| RATINGS | SCORE |
|---|---|
| Ship: Condition/Cleanliness | 7.9 |
| Ship: Space/Flow/Comfort | 6.4 |
| Ship: Decor/Furnishings | 7.2 |
| Ship: Fitness Facilities | 7.5 |
| Cabins: Comfort/Facilities | 6.3 |
| Cabins: Software | 7.7 |
| Food: Dining Room/Cuisine | 6.8 |
| Food: Buffets/Informal Dining | 6.6 |
| Food: Quality of Ingredients | 7.1 |
| Service: Dining Room | 6.7 |
| Service: Bars/Lounges | 6.5 |
| Service: Cabins | 6.1 |
| Cruise: Entertainment | 7.8 |
| Cruise: Activities Program | 7.6 |
| Cruise: Hospitality Standard | 7.4 |
| OVERALL RATING | 105.6 |

**+** This high-sided ship underwent an extensive reconstruction and internal enlargement which changed two former car decks to accommodations. A new cutter-type bow and ducktail stern were added, as were a second dining room, a larger casino, children's playroom, teen nightclub, piano bar, conference center, and a Viking Crown Lounge cantilevered high around the funnel. Public rooms are chic, with soft contemporary decor and quality furnishings. The compact cabins are quite well equipped and have reasonable closet space for short cruises. Good open deck and sunning space. Good health spa facilities. Attentive service. Good for families with children.

**–** Many inside cabins. Expect long lines for embarkation, disembarkation, shore tenders, and buffets. Poor drawer space. Too many announcements.

**Dining** The two dining rooms are quite large, but very attractive, and well laid out, although there are no tables for two. The food is typical standard hotel banquet food, perfectly portioned, with robotic presentation, but everything seems to taste the same. Poor bread rolls and fruits. The staff are overly friendly, even intrusive.

**Other Comments** This medium-density ship provides a fine cruise experience in tasteful surroundings, at a decent cruise rate. Discounting has brought down the quality of passenger lately. Insurance and gratuities are extra.

# ms Vistafjord ★★★★★+

***Principal Cruising Areas***

*Worldwide (various)*

***Base Ports:** various*

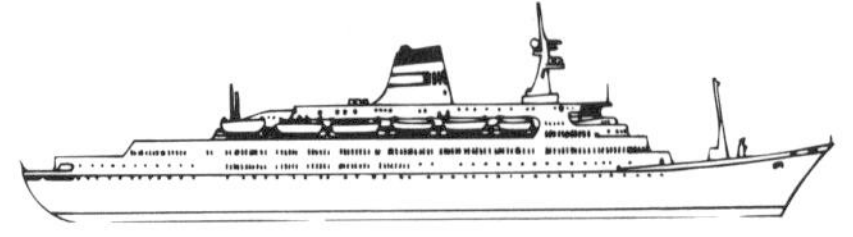

| | |
|---|---|
| Cruise Line | *Cunard* |
| Former Names | *n/a* |
| Gross Tonnage | *24,492* |
| Builder | *Swan, Hunter (UK)* |
| Original Cost | *$35 million* |
| Christened By | *Mrs Agnes Cecille Henrikson* |
| First Entered Service | *May 22, 1973/May 1984* |
| Interior Design | *Platou Design* |
| Country of Registry | *Bahamas (CPZV)* |
| Tel No *110-4114* | Fax No *130-5630* |
| Length (ft/m) | *626.9/191.09* |
| Beam (ft/m) | *82.1/25.05* |
| Draft (ft/m) | *27.0/8.23* |
| Engines/Propellers | *2 Sulzer 9-cyl diesels/2 (CP)* |
| Decks *9* | Crew *384* |
| Pass. Capacity (basis 2) *732* | (all berths) *732* |
| Pass. Space Ratio (basis 2) *33.4* | (all berths) *33.4* |
| Officers | *Norwegian* |
| Dining Staff | *European/Asian* |
| Total Cabins | *384* |
| Size (sq ft/m) *67-325/6.2-30* | Door Width *26"* |
| Outside Cabins *326* | Inside Cabins *58* |
| Single Cabins *36* | Supplement *75%* |
| Balcony Cabins *25* | Wheelchair Cabins *0* |
| Cabin Current *110/220 AC* | Refrigerator *I/II* |
| Cabin TV *Yes* | VCR *No* |
| Dining Rooms *1* | Sittings *1* |
| Elevators *6* | Door Width *29"* |

| | |
|---|---|
| Casino *Yes* | Slot Machines *Yes* |
| Swimming Pools (outside) *1* | (inside) *1* |
| Whirlpools *2* | Gymnasium *Yes* |
| Sauna/Steam Rm *Yes/No* | Massage *Yes* |
| Self-Service Launderette | *Yes* |
| Movie Theater/Seats | *Yes/250* |
| Library | *Yes* |
| Children's Facilities | *No* |
| Watersports Facilities | *None* |
| Classification Society | *Lloyd's Register* |

| RATINGS | SCORE |
|---|---|
| Ship: Condition/Cleanliness | 9.2 |
| Ship: Space/Flow/Comfort | 9.0 |
| Ship: Decor/Furnishings | 9.2 |
| Ship: Fitness Facilities | 8.8 |
| Cabins: Comfort/Facilities | 9.0 |
| Cabins: Software | 9.1 |
| Food: Dining Room/Cuisine | 9.3 |
| Food: Buffets/Informal Dining | 9.1 |
| Food: Quality of Ingredients | 9.2 |
| Service: Dining Room | 9.2 |
| Service: Bars/Lounges | 8.8 |
| Service: Cabins | 8.8 |
| Cruise: Entertainment | 8.7 |
| Cruise: Activities Program | 8.6 |
| Cruise: Hospitality Standard | 9.1 |
| OVERALL RATING | 135.1 |

**+** Well maintained and spotlessly clean, stable and smooth as a swan. Expansive open deck and sunning space (sometimes a little sooty). Built with the finest materials. Wrap-around promenade deck. Spacious, elegant public rooms with high ceilings. Very tasteful Scandinavian decor. Bathrobes for all. Excellent stewardesses. Conservative, sophisticated, classically-oriented entertainment. Wide interior stairwells. Suites with balconies are superbly equipped, but all cabins are extremely well equipped and tastefully decorated, although smaller than on *Sagafjord*. All have excellent closet and drawer space. Refreshingly few announcements and interruptions.

**–** Operates in two languages, English and German, which may be a negative factor for some.

**Dining** The dining room is a grand room, with tables for two, four, six, or eight. Senior officers host tables for dinner each evening. International cuisine. Highest quality ingredients. Outstanding variety of breads, cheeses, salads, dressings, and juices. Silver-service and plate-service. European-style service in the best tradition. Sophisticated management structure. Unhurried single-sitting dining in style, with menus that are never repeated, even on the longest voyages.

**Other Comments** This ship has classic liner styling and profile. Finely-proportioned with beautiful, rounded, flowing lines and classic, sleek profile from any angle. Port taxes and insurance are extra. Gratuities are extra, but can be pre-paid.

# ms Vistamar ★★★★

***Principal Cruising Areas***

*Mediterranean/South America (various)*

***Base Ports:** various*

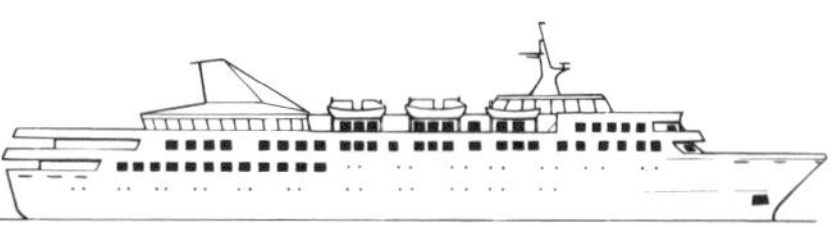

| | | | |
|---|---|---|---|
| Cruise Line | | | *Jahn Reisen/Mar Line Shipping* |
| Former Names | | | *n/a* |
| Gross Tonnage | | | *7,478* |
| Builder | | | *Union Navale de Levante (Spain)* |
| Original Cost | | | *$45 million* |
| Christened By | | | *n/a* |
| First Entered Service | | | *Sep 1989* |
| Interior Design | | | *Oliver Design* |
| Country of Registry | | | *Spain (3EKG7)* |
| Tel No | *133-2275* | Fax No | *133-2275* |
| Length (ft/m) | | | *385.1/117.40* |
| Beam (ft/m) | | | *55.1/16.82* |
| Draft (ft/m) | | | *14.9/4.55* |
| Engines/Propellers | | | *2 Ecchevarria diesels/2* |
| Decks | *6* | Crew | *100* |
| Pass. Capacity (basis 2) | *295* | (all berths) | *340* |
| Pass. Space Ratio (basis 2) | *25.3* | (all berths) | *21.9* |
| Officers | *Spanish* | Dining Staff | *European* |
| Total Cabins | | | *150* |
| Size (sq ft/m) | *n/a* | Door Width | *24"* |
| Outside Cabins | *126* | Inside Cabins | *24* |
| Single Cabins | *5* | Supplement | *Fixed rates* |
| Balcony Cabins | *0* | Wheelchair Cabins | *0* |
| Cabin Current | | | *220 AC* |
| Refrigerator | | | *No* |
| Cabin TV | *Yes* | VCR | *No* |
| Dining Rooms | *1* | Sittings | *1* |
| Elevators | *3* | Door Width | *36"* |

| | | | |
|---|---|---|---|
| Casino | *No* | Slot Machines | *Yes* |
| Swimming Pools (outside) | *1* | (inside) | *0* |
| Whirlpools | *0* | Gymnasium | *Yes* |
| Sauna/Steam Rm | *Yes/No* | Massage | *Yes* |
| Self-Service Launderette | | | *No* |
| Movie Theater/Seats | | | *No* |
| Library | | | *Yes* |
| Children's Facilities | | | *No* |
| Watersports Facilities | | | *None* |
| Classification Society | | | *Det Norske Veritas* |

| RATINGS | SCORE |
|---|---|
| Ship: Condition/Cleanliness | 8.1 |
| Ship: Space/Flow/Comfort | 7.8 |
| Ship: Decor/Furnishings | 7.8 |
| Ship: Fitness Facilities | 5.8 |
| Cabins: Comfort/Facilities | 7.6 |
| Cabins: Software | 7.9 |
| Food: Dining Room/Cuisine | 6.8 |
| Food: Buffets/Informal Dining | 6.1 |
| Food: Quality of Ingredients | 6.2 |
| Service: Dining Room | 7.1 |
| Service: Bars/Lounges | 7.0 |
| Service: Cabins | 7.1 |
| Cruise: Entertainment | 6.2 |
| Cruise: Activities Program | 6.4 |
| Cruise: Hospitality Standard | 7.3 |
| OVERALL RATING | 105.2 |

**+** Small, rather smart, but squat, ship, with more conservative striping along her sides than before. Central staircase. All passenger accommodations are forward, while public rooms are located aft in a "cake-layer" stacking. Lots of wood trim. Contemporary interior decor is attractive and warm, but mirrored metallic ceilings a distraction. Outdoor pool has splash surround and excellent water fountain. A very jazzy nightclub/disco, with acres of glass, is set around funnel base. Contemporary four-deck-high atrium with skydome has a glass-walled elevator and wrap-around staircase, giving the whole a feelng of inner spaciousness. Cabins are extremely comfortable and very well equipped, although the bathrooms are a little small.

**–** Narrow, steep gangway. Cabin closet and drawer space is limited.

**Dining** The single sitting dining is attractive, with warm, contemporary colors and decor. The food is moderate, but the selection of breads, cheeses, and fruits is very limited.

**Other Comments** Spanish-speaking passengers should enjoy this new, intimate ship which features very attractively priced cruises with comfort, style, and flair. Insurance and gratuities extra.

# ms Westerdam ★★★★

***Principal Cruising Area***
*Caribbean (7 nights)*
***Base Port:*** *Ft. Lauderdale*

| | | | |
|---|---|---|---|
| Cruise Line | | | *Holland America Line* |
| Former Names | | | *Homeric* |
| Gross Tonnage | | | *53,872* |
| Builder | | | *Meyer Werft (Germany)* |
| Original Cost | | | *$150 million* |
| Christened By | | | *n/a* |
| First Entered Service | | | *May 31, 1986/Nov 12, 1988* |
| Interior Design | | | *Robert Tillberg/VFD Interiors* |
| Country of Registry | | | *Bahamas (C6HE2)* |
| Tel No | *110-4521* | Fax No | *110-4520* |
| Length (ft/m) | | | *797.9/243.23* |
| Beam (ft/m) | | | *95.1/29.00* |
| Draft (ft/m) | | | *23.6/7.20* |
| Engines/Propellers | | | *2 MAN 10-cyl diesels/2* |
| Decks | *9* | Crew | *642* |
| Pass. Capacity (basis 2) | *1,494* | (all berths) | *1,773* |
| Pass. Space Ratio (basis 2) | *36.0* | (all berths) | *30.3* |
| Officers | *Dutch* | Dining Staff | *Filipino/Indonesian* |
| Total Cabins | | | *747* |
| Size (sq ft/m) | *131-425/12-39.5* | Door Width | *25"* |
| Outside Cabins | *495* | Inside Cabins | *252* |
| Single Cabins | *0* | Supplement | *50-100%* |
| Balcony Cabins | *0* | Wheelchair Cabins | *4* |
| Cabin Current | | | *110 AC* |
| Refrigerator | | | *No* |
| Cabin TV | *Yes* | VCR | *No* |
| Dining Rooms | *1* | Sittings | *2* |
| Elevators | *7* | Door Width | *39"* |

| | | | |
|---|---|---|---|
| Casino | *Yes* | Slot Machines | *Yes* |
| Swimming Pools (outside) | 2 | (inside) | *0* |
| Whirlpools | 2 | Gymnasium | *Yes* |
| Sauna/Steam Rm | *Yes/No* | Massage | *Yes* |
| Self-Service Launderette | | | *Yes-5* |
| Movie Theater/Seats | | | *Yes/237* |
| Library | | | *Yes* |
| Children's Facilities | | | *Yes* |
| Watersports Facilities | | | *None* |
| Classification Society | | | *Lloyd's Register* |

| RATINGS | SCORE |
|---|---|
| Ship: Condition/Cleanliness | 8.0 |
| Ship: Space/Flow/Comfort | 8.0 |
| Ship: Decor/Furnishings | 7.9 |
| Ship: Fitness Facilities | 6.9 |
| Cabins: Comfort/Facilities | 7.7 |
| Cabins: Software | 7.9 |
| Food: Dining Room/Cuisine | 7.6 |
| Food: Buffets/Informal Dining | 7.4 |
| Food: Quality of Ingredients | 7.2 |
| Service: Dining Room | 7.6 |
| Service: Bars/Lounges | 7.6 |
| Service: Cabins | 8.1 |
| Cruise: Entertainment | 7.0 |
| Cruise: Activities Program | 7.4 |
| Cruise: Hospitality Standard | 8.2 |
| OVERALL RATING | 114.5 |

**+** Quality construction throughout. All outside decks are teakwood, and include a traditional, wrap-around promenade deck. Elegant, functional interior, with restful public rooms decorated in pastel tones, though some decor is looking dated. Absorbs passengers well. Caribbean cruises year-round in 1995. High quality furnishings and fabrics throughout. Good open deck space for sunning. Fine health and fitness center. Cabins are generously proportioned, well equipped, and well equipped. Ample closet, drawer, and storage space, and generous-sized bathrooms.

**–** Too many inside cabins. Long lines for embarkation, disembarkation, buffets, and shore tenders. Magrodome-covered swimming pool deck is far too small. Low-budget entertainment.

**Dining** Traditional dining room, located on a low deck, with portholes, highlighted at night by special lighting effects, and a raised central dome. Very comfortable. Open seating for breakfast/lunch, two seatings for dinner. The food, while attractive, is not memorable, and entrees all taste the same—tasteless! Poor bread rolls, pastries, and fresh fruits. Indonesian service is excellent, though communication is sometimes frustrating.

**Other Comments** Traditional features and a sleek profile. Entertainment has improved but is still staid. Elegant, comfortable setting, but she carries too many passengers. Port taxes, insurance, and gratuities are extra (gratuities are not "required," but are expected by the staff).

# ms Windward ★★★★+

***Principal Cruising Areas***

*Alaska/Caribbean (7 nights)*

***Base Ports:** Vancouver/San Juan*

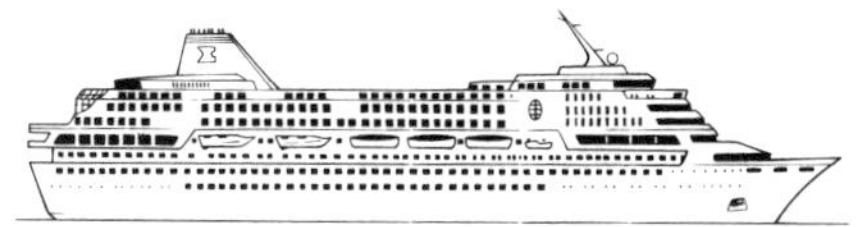

| | | | |
|---|---|---|---|
| Cruise Line | | | *Norwegian Cruise Line* |
| Former Names | | | *n/a* |
| Gross Tonnage | | | *39,217* |
| Builder | | | *Chantiers de l'Atlantique (France)* |
| Original Cost | | | *$240 million* |
| Christened By | | | *Mrs Barbara Bush* |
| First Entered Service | | | *May 23, 1993* |
| Interior Design | | | *Yran & Storbraaten* |
| Country of Registry | | | *Bahamas (C6LG6)* |
| Tel No | | | *130-5713/130-5715* |
| Fax No | | | *130-5714/130-5716* |
| Length (ft/m) | | | *623.3/190.00* |
| Beam (ft/m) | | | *93.5/28.50* |
| Draft (ft/m) | | | *22.3/6.80* |
| Engines/Propellers | | | *2 MAN 8-cyl diesels/2 (CP)* |
| Decks | *11* | Crew | *483* |
| Pass. Capacity (basis 2) | *1,246* | (all berths) | *1,450* |
| Pass. Space Ratio (basis 2) | *32.9* | (all berths) | *28.2* |
| Officers | *Norwegian* | Dining Staff | *International* |
| Total Cabins | | | *623* |
| Size (sq ft/m) | *140-350/13-32.5* | Door Width | *26.5"* |
| Outside Cabins | *531* | Inside Cabins | *92* |
| Single Cabins | *0* | Supplement | *50-100%* |
| Balcony Cabins | | | *48* |
| Wheelchair Cabins | | | *6 (+ 30 for hearing impaired)* |
| Cabin Current | *110 AC* | Refrigerator | *1/2/3* |
| Cabin TV | *Yes* | VCR | *No* |
| Dining Rooms | *2* | Sittings | *2* |

| | | | |
|---|---|---|---|
| Elevators | *7* | Door Width | *31.5"* |
| Casino | *Yes* | Slot Machines | *Yes* |
| Swimming Pools (outside) | *1* | (inside) | *0* |
| Whirlpools | *2* | Gymnasium | *Yes* |
| Sauna/Steam Rm | *Yes/No* | Massage | *Yes* |
| Self-Service Launderette | | | *No* |
| Movie Theater/Seats | | | *No* |
| Library | *Yes* | Children's Facilities | *Yes* |
| Watersports Facilities | | | *None* |
| Classification Society | | | *Det Norske Veritas* |

| RATINGS | SCORE |
|---|---|
| Ship: Condition/Cleanliness | 8.7 |
| Ship: Space/Flow/Comfort | 7.9 |
| Ship: Decor/Furnishings | 8.3 |
| Ship: Fitness Facilities | 8.1 |
| Cabins: Comfort/Facilities | 7.8 |
| Cabins: Software | 8.0 |
| Food: Dining Room/Cuisine | 7.2 |
| Food: Buffets/Informal Dining | 6.3 |
| Food: Quality of Ingredients | 6.4 |
| Service: Dining Room | 7.7 |
| Service: Bars/Lounges | 7.6 |
| Service: Cabins | 7.6 |
| Cruise: Entertainment | 8.4 |
| Cruise: Activities Program | 7.8 |
| Cruise: Hospitality Standard | 7.6 |
| OVERALL RATING | 115.4 |

**+** Almost identical sistership to *Dreamward,* typical of the contemporary exterior design. Delightful, aft sun terraces overlooking aft swimming pool (quieter than the one atop ship). Nice array of public rooms, and spacious, open lobby area. Fine showlounge and colorful, pizazz-filled shows. 85% outside cabins. All are warm and cozy, with soft colors and wood accents. Fairly good layout and passenger flow.

**–** No wine waiters. Cabins have almost no drawer space, and storage space is minimal. Very disappointing cuisine. Long lines for buffets.

**Dining** Four dining rooms (nicest is The Terraces), all with the same menu and food. Casual Sports Bar for breakfast, luncheon, and teatime buffets. The cuisine has been a weak point, but is slowly improving. Best described as family diner food, with an emphasis on thick, non-descript sauces, and salad dressings. Service is perfunctory, at best, by waiters who speak little English; they are willing, but need more training. Good wine list. 19 types of beer. Good cutlery, but no fish knives. Afternoon tea is not served anywhere.

**Other Comments** Outdoor pool deck is always busy and noisy, but fun. Special cabins for the hearing impaired. Together with *Dreamward,* she's more expensive than NCL's other ships, but worth it for first-time cruisegoers not seeking fine cuisine. Insurance and gratuities are extra.

# ms World Discoverer ★★★★+

***Principal Cruising Areas***

*Worldwide expedition cruises (various)*

***Base Ports:*** *various*

| | | | |
|---|---|---|---|
| Cruise Line | | | *Clipper Cruise Line* |
| Former Names | | | *Bewa Discoverer* |
| Gross Tonnage | | | *3,153* |
| Builder | | | *Schichau Unterweser (Germany)* |
| Original Cost | | | *n/a* |
| Christened By | | | *n/a* |
| First Entered Service | | | *Apr 7, 1977* |
| Interior Design | | | *Carleton Varney* |
| Country of Registry | | | *Liberia (ELDU3)* |
| Tel No | *124-2744* | Fax No | *124-2744* |
| Length (ft/m) | | | *287.1/87.51* |
| Beam (ft/m) | | | *49.6/15.12* |
| Draft (ft/m) | | | *14.6/4.46* |
| Engines/Propellers | | | *2 MAK 8-cyl diesels/1 (CP)* |
| Decks | *4* | Crew | *75* |
| Pass. Capacity (basis 2) | *138* | (all berths) | *138* |
| Pass. Space Ratio (basis 2) | *22.8* | (all berths) | *22.8* |
| Officers | *European* | Dining Staff | *European/Filipino* |
| Total Cabins | | | *71* |
| Size (sq ft/m) | *89-218/8.2-20.2* | Door Width | *30"* |
| Outside Cabins | *71* | Inside Cabins | *0* |
| Single Cabins | *0* | Supplement | *Fixed rates* |
| Balcony Cabins | *0* | Wheelchair Cabins | *0* |
| Cabin Current | *110/220 AC* | Refrigerator | *No* |
| Cabin TV | *No* | VCR | *No* |
| Dining Rooms | | | *1 (open seating)* |
| Elevators | *1* | Door Width | *36"* |
| Casino | *No* | Slot Machines | *No* |

| | | | |
|---|---|---|---|
| Swimming Pools (outside) | *1* | (inside) | *0* |
| Whirlpools | *0* | Gymnasium | *Yes* |
| Sauna/Steam Rm | *No/No* | Massage | *Yes* |
| Self-Service Launderette | | | *No* |
| Lecture Room/Theater | | | *No* |
| Library | *Yes* | Zodiacs | *Yes* |
| Helicopter Pad | | | *No* |
| Watersports Facilities | | | *Scuba diving, snorkeling, fishing, waterski and windsurf equipment* |
| Classification Society | | | *American Bur. of Shipping* |

| RATINGS | SCORE |
|---|---|
| Ship: Condition/Cleanliness | 8.0 |
| Ship: Space/Flow/Comfort | 7.8 |
| Ship: Expedition Equipment | 7.9 |
| Ship: Decor/Furnishings | 8.0 |
| Cabins: Comfort/Facilities | 7.7 |
| Cabins: Software | 7.8 |
| Food: Dining Room/Cuisine | 7.8 |
| Food: Buffets/Informal Dining | 7.2 |
| Food: Quality of Ingredients | 7.1 |
| Service: Dining Room | 7.7 |
| Service: Bars/Lounges | 7.5 |
| Service: Cabins | 7.8 |
| Cruise: Itineraries/Operations | 8.0 |
| Cruise: Lecture Program | 7.6 |
| Cruise: Hospitality Standard | 7.8 |
| OVERALL RATING | 115.7 |

**+** Ice-hardened hull. Extremely maneuverable. Well maintained. Well-equipped for in-depth expedition cruising in comfort. Elegant and impressive public rooms and interior decor. Cabins have good proportions, are comfortable, and are very tastefully furnished. Naturalists, expert lecturers, and nature specialists on every expedition. One of the best expedition cruise vessels of its type in service today.

**–** Steep passenger gangway. Closet space is limited.

**Dining** Very attractive, cozy dining room (some tables for two). Big picture windows and comfortable chairs make for an elegant setting. Excellent cuisine and service, although it relies heavily on dairy products. Limited selection of breads and fruits.

**Other Comments** Sophisticated, small, but very comfortable, vessel built expressly for adventure cruising has sleek, well-proportioned profile with contemporary swept-back funnel. This ship provides a fine setting for expedition cruising to some of the most remote destinations in the world. It's quite expensive, but worth it for discerning, well-traveled passengers yearning for a sense of adventure and who enjoy learning about the world around us and its fascinating peoples. Gratuities are not included.

# ms World Renaissance ★★★+

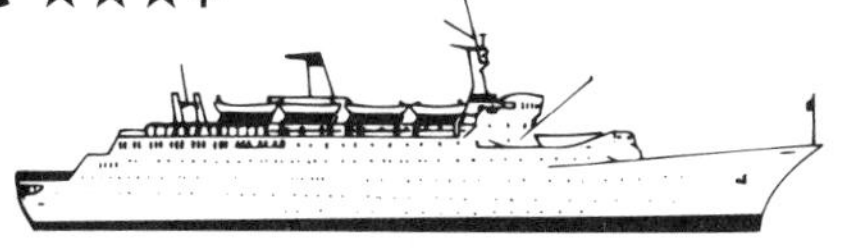

***Principal Cruising Areas***

*Aegean/Mediterranean (14 nights)*

***Base Ports:*** *Genoa/Venice*

| | | | |
|---|---|---|---|
| Cruise Line | *Epirotiki Lines* | | |
| Former Names | *Renaissance/Homeric Renaissance* | | |
| Gross Tonnage | *11,724* | | |
| Builder | *Chantiers de l'Atlantique (France)* | | |
| Original Cost | *n/a* | | |
| Christened By | *n/a* | | |
| First Entered Service | *May 10, 1966/1978* | | |
| Interior Design | *n/a* | | |
| Country of Registry | *Greece (SYXQ)* | | |
| Tel No | *113-0440* | Fax No | *113-0440* |
| Length (ft/m) | *492.1/150.02* | | |
| Beam (ft/m) | *69.0/21.06* | | |
| Draft (ft/m) | *22.9/7.00* | | |
| Engines/Propellers | *2 B&W 6-cyl diesels/2* | | |
| Decks | *8* | Crew | *204* |
| Pass. Capacity (basis 2) | *536* | (all berths) | *609* |
| Pass. Space Ratio (basis 2) | *21.8* | (all berths) | *19.2* |
| Officers | *Greek* | Dining Staff | *Greek* |
| Total Cabins | *268* | | |
| Size (sq ft/m) | *110-270/10.2-25* | Door Width | *25"* |
| Outside Cabins | *228* | Inside Cabins | *40* |
| Single Cabins | *5* | Supplement | *50%* |
| Balcony Cabins | *0* | Wheelchair Cabins | *0* |
| Cabin Current | *110 AC* | | |
| Refrigerator | *No* | | |
| Cabin TV | *No* | VCR | *No* |
| Dining Rooms | *1* | Sittings | *2* |
| Elevators | *2* | Door Width | *33"* |

| | | | |
|---|---|---|---|
| Casino | *Yes* | Slot Machines | *Yes* |
| Swimming Pools (outside) | *2* | (inside) | *0* |
| Whirlpools | *0* | Gymnasium | *Yes* |
| Sauna/Steam Rm | *Yes/No* | Massage | *Yes* |
| Self-Service Launderette | *No* | | |
| Movie Theater/Seats | *Yes/110* | | |
| Library | *Yes* | | |
| Children's Facilities | *No* | | |
| Watersports Facilities | *None* | | |
| Classification Society | *Lloyd's Register* | | |

| RATINGS | SCORE |
|---|---|
| Ship: Condition/Cleanliness | 6.8 |
| Ship: Space/Flow/Comfort | 6.4 |
| Ship: Decor/Furnishings | 6.9 |
| Ship: Fitness Facilities | 6.4 |
| Cabins: Comfort/Facilities | 7.0 |
| Cabins: Software | 8.1 |
| Food: Dining Room/Cuisine | 7.1 |
| Food: Buffets/Informal Dining | 6.7 |
| Food: Quality of Ingredients | 6.2 |
| Service: Dining Room | 7.2 |
| Service: Bars/Lounges | 7.4 |
| Service: Cabins | 7.3 |
| Cruise: Entertainment | 7.0 |
| Cruise: Activities Program | 6.3 |
| Cruise: Hospitality Standard | 7.0 |
| OVERALL RATING | 103.8 |

**+** Charming vessel has yacht-like intimacy and ambiance. Generous open deck and sunning space. Beautiful wood paneling in cabins, which are homey and quite spacious for ship size, though not luxurious. Tiled bathrooms. The library room is restful. Friendly staff and ambiance.

**–** Steep passenger gangway. No wrap-around outdoor promenade deck.

**Dining** The dining room is pleasant, but there are no tables for two. Continental cuisine is predominantly Mediterranean, with too many oils used. Poor bread, pastry, and fruit. Good basic service throughout, but there's no finesse.

**Other Comments** This ship has traditional sixties styling and profile topped by a slender funnel. Public rooms are few, but the main lounge is very comfortable. Xenia Tavern is colonial in style and decor, and functions as the setting for both intimate classical concerts and the disco. This ship will cruise you in comfort at a very fair price. Insurance and gratuities are extra.

# ib Yamal ★★★+

***Principal Cruising Areas***

*Antarctica/Transpolar expeditions (various)*

***Base Port:** Murmansk*

| | | | |
|---|---|---|---|
| Cruise Line | | | *Murmansk Shipping* |
| Former Names | | | *n/a* |
| Gross Tonnage | | | *20,646* |
| Builder | | | *Baltic Shipyard, Murmansk (Russia)* |
| Original Cost | | | *$150 million* |
| Christened By | | | *n/a* |
| First Entered Service | | | *Dec 1989* |
| Interior Design | | | *n/a* |
| Country of Registry | | | *Russia* |
| Tel No | *n/a* | Fax No | *n/a* |
| Length (ft/m) | | | *492.1/150.00* |
| Beam (ft/m) | *98.4/30.00* | Draft (ft/m) | *36.0/11.00* |
| Engines | | | *nuclear-powered turbo-electrics* |
| Propellers | | | *3* |
| Decks | *4* | Crew | *130* |
| Pass. Capacity (basis 2) | *100* | (all berths) | *100* |
| Pass. Space Ratio (basis 2) | *206.4* | (all berths) | *206.4* |
| Officers | | | *Russian/Ukrainian* |
| Dining Staff | | | *European/Ukrainian* |
| Total Cabins | | | *50* |
| Size (sq ft/m) | *155-300/14.3-27.8* | Door Width | *24"* |
| Outside Cabins | *50* | Inside Cabins | *0* |
| Single Cabins | *0* | Supplement | *80%* |
| Balcony Cabins | *0* | Wheelchair Cabins | *0* |
| Cabin Current | *220 AC* | Refrigerator | *Yes* |
| Cabin TV | *Yes* | VCR | *Yes* |
| Dining Rooms | *1* | Sittings | *open seating* |
| Elevators | *0* | Door Width | *n/a* |

| | | | |
|---|---|---|---|
| Casino | *No* | Slot Machines | *No* |
| Swimming Pools | (inside) *1* | (outside) | - |
| Whirlpools | *0* | Gymnasium | *Yes* |
| Sauna/Steam Rm | *Yes-2/No* | Massage | *No* |
| Self-Service Launderette | | | *Yes* |
| Lecture/Film Room | | | *Yes (seats 100)* |
| Library | *Yes* | Zodiacs | *4* |
| Helicopters | | | *2 for passenger use* |
| Watersports Facilities | | | *None* |
| Classification Society | | | *RS* |

| RATINGS | SCORE |
|---|---|
| Ship: Condition/Cleanliness | 7.6 |
| Ship: Space/Flow/Comfort | 6.0 |
| Ship: Expedition Equipment | 9.0 |
| Ship: Decor/Furnishings | 5.8 |
| Cabins: Comfort/Facilities | 5.7 |
| Cabins: Software | 6.0 |
| Food: Dining Room/Cuisine | 6.8 |
| Food: Buffets/Informal Dining | 6.4 |
| Food: Quality of Ingredients | 7.0 |
| Service: Dining Room | 6.6 |
| Service: Bars/Lounges | 6.6 |
| Service: Cabins | 6.6 |
| Cruise: Itineraries/Operations | 7.8 |
| Cruise: Lecture Program | 7.7 |
| Cruise: Hospitality Standard | 7.6 |
| OVERALL RATING | 103.2 |

**+** The ultimate in technology accompanies this special ice-breaker. Zodiacs for shore landings. Two helicopters for reconnaissance and sightseeing. Very comfortable. Team of biologists, scientists, geologists, and other expert lecturers. European chefs and catering. Two lounges. Heated indoor pool. Generously sized cabins, all outside, private facilities. Attentive and friendly Russian service throughout. Access to the bridge at all times.

**–** Limited closet/drawer space; small, utilitarian bathrooms. Limited public rooms. Almost no art/decoration (and limited carpeting) as this is a working ice-breaker. Steep interior stairways.

**Dining** Nicely equipped dining room. The catering is surprisingly hearty, with plenty of meat and potato dishes, but little fruit and cheese. Remember, this is not a gourmet cruise.

**Other Comments** Three-inch-thick reinforced bow for negotiating tough ice conditions. Nuclear-powered expedition vessel with 75,000 shaft horsepower and enough fuel for four years! Try the incredible trans-polar voyage via the North Pole. Similar vessels are listed below.

| Name | Grt | Built | Length | Beam |
|---|---|---|---|---|
| *Arctica* | 20,905 | 1975 | 485.2ft/147.9m | 98.0ft/29.9m |
| *Lenin* | 17,810 | 1959 | 439.6ft/134.0m | 90.5ft/27.6m |
| *Rossiya* | 22,920 | 1985 | 492.1ft/150.0m | 98.4ft/30.0m |
| *Siberia* | 21,120 | 1977 | 485.2ft/147.9m | 98.0ft/29.9m |
| *Taimir* | 20,000 | 1989 | 498.0ft/151.8m | 95.8ft/29.2m |

# Yorktown Clipper ★★★

*Principal Cruising Areas*

*American Coast/Caribbean (various)*

***Base Ports:*** *various*

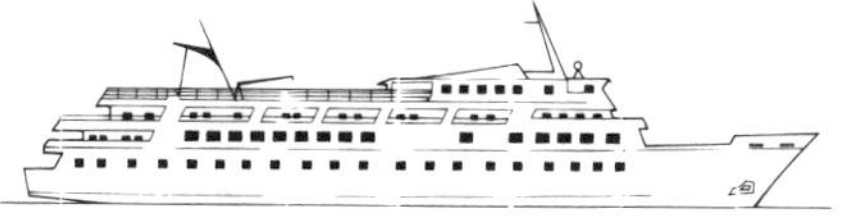

| | | | |
|---|---|---|---|
| Cruise Line | | | *Clipper Cruise Line* |
| Former Names | | | *n/a* |
| Gross Tonnage | | | *2,354* |
| Builder | | | *First Coast Shipbuilding (USA)* |
| Original Cost | | | *$12 million* |
| Christened By | | | *Mrs Richard Wilson* |
| First Entered Service | | | *Apr 30, 1988* |
| Interior Design | | | *Christner Partnership* |
| Country of Registry | | | *USA (WTA4768)* |
| Tel No | *n/a* | Fax No | *n/a* |
| Length (ft/m) | | | *257.0/78.30* |
| Beam (ft/m) | *43.0/13.10* | Draft (ft/m) | *8.0/2.43* |
| Engines/Propellers | | | *2 Detroit diesels/2* |
| Decks | *4* | Crew | *37* |
| Pass. Capacity (basis 2) | *138* | (all berths) | *149* |
| Pass. Space Ratio (basis 2) | *17.0* | (all berths) | *15.9* |
| Officers | | | *American* |
| Dining Staff | | | *American* |
| Total Cabins | | | *69* |
| Size (sq ft/m) | | | *121-138/11.2-12.8* |
| Door Width | | | *24"* |
| Outside Cabins | *69* | Inside Cabins | *0* |
| Single Cabins | *0* | Supplement | *Fixed rates* |
| Balcony Cabins | *0* | Wheelchair Cabins | *0* |
| Cabin Current | | | *110 AC* |
| Refrigerator | | | *No* |
| Cabin TV | *No* | VCR | *No* |
| Dining Rooms | *1* | Sittings | *1* |

| | | | |
|---|---|---|---|
| Elevators | *0* | Door Width | *n/a* |
| Casino | *No* | Slot Machines | *No* |
| Swimming Pools (outside) | *0* | (inside) | *0* |
| Whirlpools | *0* | Gymnasium | *No* |
| Sauna/Steam Rm | *No/No* | Massage | *No* |
| Self-Service Launderette | | | *No* |
| Movie Theater/Seats | | | *No* |
| Library | *Yes* | Children's Facilities | *No* |
| Watersports Facilities | | | *None* |
| Classification Society | | | *American Bur. of Shipping* |

| RATINGS | SCORE |
|---|---|
| Ship: Condition/Cleanliness | 7.3 |
| Ship: Space/Flow/Comfort | 4.0 |
| Ship: Decor/Furnishings | 7.2 |
| Ship: Fitness Facilities | 3.0 |
| Cabins: Comfort/Facilities | 6.1 |
| Cabins: Software | 6.5 |
| Food: Dining Room/Cuisine | 7.1 |
| Food: Buffets/Informal Dining | 6.2 |
| Food: Quality of Ingredients | 7.0 |
| Service: Dining Room | 7.1 |
| Service: Bars/Lounges | 7.0 |
| Service: Cabins | 7.3 |
| Cruise: Entertainment | 4.0 |
| Cruise: Activities Program | 5.6 |
| Cruise: Hospitality Standard | 7.4 |
| OVERALL RATING | 92.8 |

**+** This neat-looking, small vessel is specially built for coastal and inland cruises. Well maintained and tidy throughout. Carries rubber zodiac craft for close-in excursions. Glass-walled observation lounge, with rattan chairs. The all-outside cabins, in five categories, are small, with lots of wood-accented trim and pleasant colors. They are quite comfortable and tastefully furnished. This ship provides an "Americana" experience for those seeking to learn more about the coastal ports around the USA. Casual and totally unregimented lifestyle, rather like a small, congenial country club. No mindless activities or corny games.

**–** High density ship with only two public rooms, a dining room, and a lounge. High engine and generator noise when underway.

**Dining** The dining room is warm and inviting, and has large picture windows, but no tables for two. Friendly, attentive service is provided by young, friendly, all-American Mid-Western college types. The food is of good quality, made from locally purchased fresh ingredients, but choice is limited, as is the selection of breads and fruits. The chef is from the Culinary Institute of America.

**Other Comments** This ship cannot be compared with big ship ocean cruising. The per diem price is high for what you get, and air fare is extra, but it does appeal to the older American passenger who doesn't want to be on the megaships. Insurance and gratuities are extra.

# mv Zenith ★★★★★

***Principal Cruising Area***

*Caribbean (7 nights year-round)*

***Base Port:*** *Ft. Lauderdale (Saturday)*

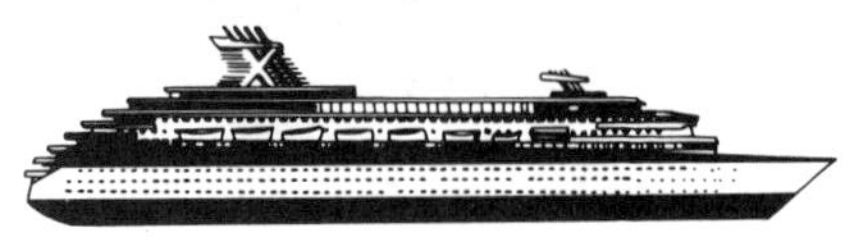

| | | | |
|---|---|---|---|
| Cruise Line | | | *Celebrity Cruises* |
| Former Names | | | *n/a* |
| Gross Tonnage | | | *47,255* |
| Builder | | | *Meyer Werft (Germany)* |
| Original Cost | | | *$210 million* |
| Christened By | | | *Mrs Antony Chandris* |
| First Entered Service | | | *Apr 4, 1992* |
| Interior Design | | | *Katzourakis/McNeece* |
| Country of Registry | | | *Liberia (ELOU5)* |
| Tel No | *124-5564* | Fax No | *124-5567* |
| Length (ft/m) | | | *681.0/207.59* |
| Beam (ft/m) | | | *95.1/29.00* |
| Draft (ft/m) | | | *23.6/7.20* |
| Engines/Propellers | | | *2 MAN-B&W 9-cyl diesels/2* |
| Decks | *9* | Crew | *628* |
| Pass. Capacity (basis 2) | *1,374* | (all berths) | *1,796* |
| Pass. Space Ratio (basis 2) | *34.3* | (all berths) | *26.3* |
| Officers | | | *Greek* |
| Dining Staff | | | *International* |
| Total Cabins | | | *687* |
| Size (sq ft/m) | *185-334/17-31* | Door Width | *24"* |
| Outside Cabins | *541* | Inside Cabins | *146* |
| Single Cabins | *0* | Supplement | *50%* |
| Balcony Cabins | *0* | Wheelchair Cabins | *4* |
| Cabin Current | *110 AC* | Refrigerator | *No* |
| Cabin TV | *Yes* | VCR | *No* |
| Dining Rooms | *1* | Sittings | *2* |
| Elevators | *7* | Door Width | *35.5"* |

| | | | |
|---|---|---|---|
| Casino | *Yes* | Slot Machines | *Yes* |
| Swimming Pools (outside) | 2 | (inside) | *0* |
| Whirlpools | *3* | Gymnasium | *Yes* |
| Sauna/Steam Rm | *Yes/No* | Massage | *Yes* |
| Self-Service Launderette | | | *No* |
| Movie Theater/Seats | | | *Yes/850* |
| Library | | | *Yes* |
| Children's Facilities | | | *Yes* |
| Watersports Facilities | | | *None* |
| Classification Society | | | *Lloyd's Register* |

| RATINGS | SCORE |
|---|---|
| Ship: Condition/Cleanliness | 9.2 |
| Ship: Space/Flow/Comfort | 8.7 |
| Ship: Decor/Furnishings | 9.0 |
| Ship: Fitness Facilities | 8.4 |
| Cabins: Comfort/Facilities | 8.3 |
| Cabins: Software | 8.1 |
| Food: Dining Room/Cuisine | 8.5 |
| Food: Buffets/Informal Dining | 8.2 |
| Food: Quality of Ingredients | 8.1 |
| Service: Dining Room | 8.4 |
| Service: Bars/Lounges | 8.1 |
| Service: Cabins | 8.3 |
| Cruise: Entertainment | 8.7 |
| Cruise: Activities Program | 8.3 |
| Cruise: Hospitality Standard | 8.4 |
| OVERALL RATING | 126.7 |

**+** Smart and handsome. Double-wide indoor promenade. Meeting center. Well chosen art throughout. Art-deco, hotel-like lobby. Soothing pastel colors and fine quality furnishings throughout. Lovely library. Well insulated cabins are well equipped and spacious, with plenty of closet and drawer space. Bathrooms are practical, with large shower areas. The 22 suites are very tastefully decorated, and butler service is provided. Highly creative productions, and one of the best showrooms at sea. Good, seasonal, and unobtrusive children's program.

**–** Long lines for embarkation, disembarkation, shore excursions, and buffets. Heavy doors to public restrooms and outdoor decks. Most outside cabins on Bermuda Deck have lifeboat-obstructed views. Too many announcements. No cushioned pads for deck lounge chairs.

**Dining** The dining room is large and elegant, yet feels small, and there are a number of tables for two. Chairs have no armrests. Two buffet lines (one for smokers, one for nonsmokers) in the Windsurf Cafe feature an excellent array for breakfast and luncheon, with indoor and outdoor seating. Outstanding cuisine. Finest quality ingredients. Pastries are superb. Service is very professional. Separate menu for vegetarians and children. Midnight buffets are excellent.

**Other Comments** The benchmark for mainstream cruises. Value for money is unsurpassed in the cruise industry today. Insurance and gratuities are extra.

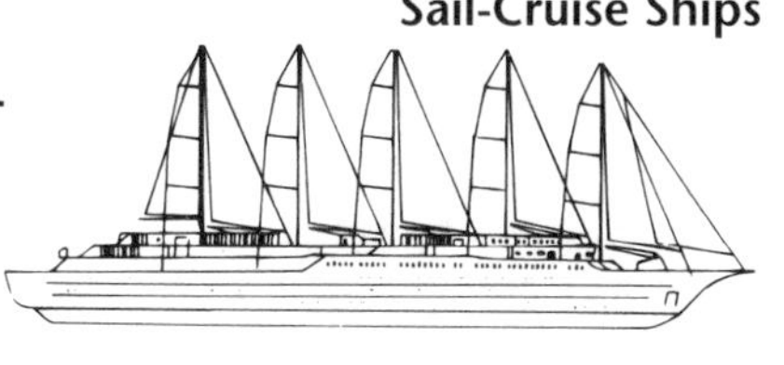

# mys Club Med I ★★★★+

*Principal Cruising Areas*

*Caribbean/Europe (7 nights)*

***Base Ports:*** *Martinique/Nice*

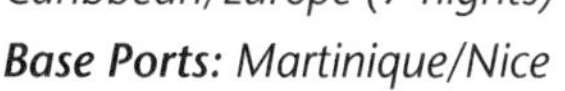

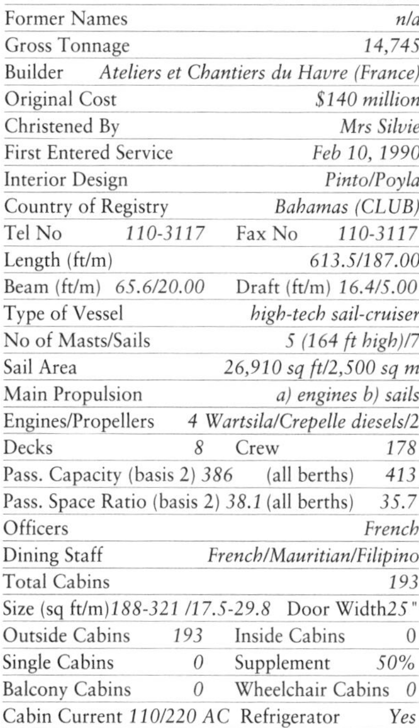

| | | | |
|---|---|---|---|
| Cruise Line | *Club Mediterranée* | | |
| Former Names | *n/a* | | |
| Gross Tonnage | *14,745* | | |
| Builder | *Ateliers et Chantiers du Havre (France)* | | |
| Original Cost | *$140 million* | | |
| Christened By | *Mrs Silvie* | | |
| First Entered Service | *Feb 10, 1990* | | |
| Interior Design | *Pinto/Poyla* | | |
| Country of Registry | *Bahamas (CLUB)* | | |
| Tel No | *110-3117* | Fax No | *110-3117* |
| Length (ft/m) | *613.5/187.00* | | |
| Beam (ft/m) | *65.6/20.00* | Draft (ft/m) | *16.4/5.00* |
| Type of Vessel | *high-tech sail-cruiser* | | |
| No of Masts/Sails | *5 (164 ft high)/7* | | |
| Sail Area | *26,910 sq ft/2,500 sq m* | | |
| Main Propulsion | *a) engines b) sails* | | |
| Engines/Propellers | *4 Wartsila/Crepelle diesels/2* | | |
| Decks | *8* | Crew | *178* |
| Pass. Capacity (basis 2) | *386* | (all berths) | *413* |
| Pass. Space Ratio (basis 2) | *38.1* | (all berths) | *35.7* |
| Officers | *French* | | |
| Dining Staff | *French/Mauritian/Filipino* | | |
| Total Cabins | *193* | | |
| Size (sq ft/m) | *188-321 /17.5-29.8* | Door Width | *25"* |
| Outside Cabins | *193* | Inside Cabins | *0* |
| Single Cabins | *0* | Supplement | *50%* |
| Balcony Cabins | *0* | Wheelchair Cabins | *0* |
| Cabin Current | *110/220 AC* | Refrigerator | *Yes* |

| | | | |
|---|---|---|---|
| Cabin TV | *Yes* | VCR | *No* |
| Dining Rooms | *2* | Library | *Yes* |
| Elevators | *2* | Door Width | *40"* |
| Casino | *Yes* | Slot Machines | *Yes* |
| Swimming Pools (outside) | *2* | | |
| Whirlpools | *0* | Gymnasium | *Yes* |
| Sauna/Steam Rm | *Yes/No* | Massage | *Yes* |
| Watersports Facilities | *Aft platform, windsurfers, sailboats, waterski boats, scuba tanks, snorkels* | | |
| Classification Society | *Bureau Veritas* | | |

| RATINGS | SCORE |
|---|---|
| Ship: Condition/Cleanliness | 8.4 |
| Ship: Space/Flow/Comfort | 8.0 |
| Ship: Decor/Furnishings | 8.5 |
| Ship: Watersports Facilities | 9.0 |
| Cabins: Comfort/Facilities | 8.5 |
| Cabins: Software | 8.0 |
| Food: Dining Room/Cuisine | 7.7 |
| Food: Buffets/Informal Dining | 7.7 |
| Food: Quality of Ingredients | 7.4 |
| Service: Dining Room | 7.4 |
| Service: Bars/Lounges | 7.6 |
| Service: Cabins | 8.2 |
| Cruise: Sail-Cruise Experience | 7.4 |
| Cruise: Entertainment/Activities | 5.6 |
| Cruise: Hospitality Standard | 7.4 |
| OVERALL RATING | 116.8 |

**+** Extensive watersports facilities and superb aft marina platform. Computer workshop. Golf simulator (extra charge). Cabins are beautifully equipped, have mini-bars, 24-hour room service (but you pay for food), safe, TV, plenty of storage space, bathrobes, and hairdryers. Odyssey Restaurant has lovely open terrace. Continental and Japanese cuisine, but presentation needs improving. Complimentary wine with meals. Afternoon tea is a delight.

**–** Activities are under the direction of a large team of young, energetic GOs (Gentils Organisateurs), who, like their compatriots on land, have the full run of the ship. Entertainment is clown-like and very amateurish.

**Dining** Two lovely dining rooms have tables for one, two, or more. Open seating for all meals. Open air dining terrace for informal meals. The cuisine is mainly French and Continental. Beer and standard wine included for lunch and dinner.

**Other Comments** One of a pair of the world's largest sail-cruisers—part cruise ship, part yacht. A larger version of the *Windstar* vessels. Five huge masts provide seven computer-controlled sails. Six four-person cabins, and some 35 doubles are fitted with an extra pullman berth. Superb for the more upscale active singles and couples who like casual elegance. Port taxes and insurance are extra. No gratuities are expected or accepted, as at all Club Med resorts.

# mys Club Med II ★★★★+

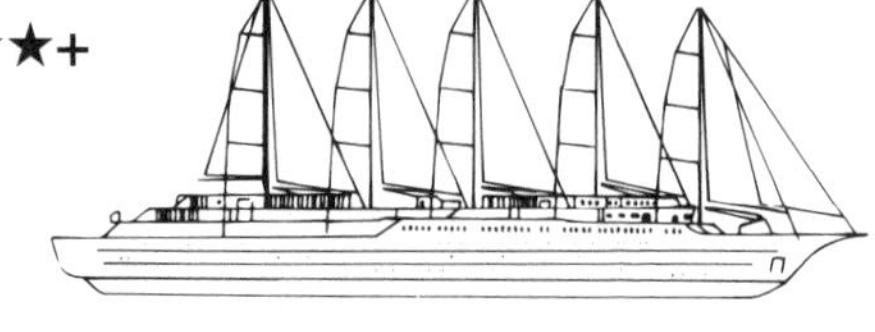

***Principal Cruising Areas***

*Tahiti/South Pacific (various)*

***Base Ports:*** *Noumea/Guam*

| | | | |
|---|---|---|---|
| Cruise Line | | | *Club Mediterranée* |
| Former Names | | | *n/a* |
| Gross Tonnage | | | *14,745* |
| Builder | | | *Ateliers et Chantiers du Havre (France)* |
| Original Cost | | | *$145 million* |
| Christened By | | | *n/a* |
| First Entered Service | | | *Dec 15, 1992* |
| Interior Design | | | *Pinto/Poyla* |
| Country of Registry | | | *Wallis & Fortuna (France)* |
| Tel No | *110-2173* | Fax No | *110-2173* |
| Length (ft/m) | | | *613.5/187.00* |
| Beam (ft/m) | *65.6/20.00* | Draft (ft/m) | *16.4/5.00* |
| Type of Vessel | | | *high-tech sail-cruiser* |
| No of Masts/Sails | | | *5 (164 ft)/7* |
| Sail Area | | | *26,910 sq ft/2,500 sq m* |
| Main Propulsion | | | *a) engines b) sails* |
| Engines/Propellers | | | *4 Wartsila/Crepelle diesels/2* |
| Decks | *8* | Crew | *181* |
| Pass. Capacity (basis 2) | *392* | (all berths) | *419* |
| Pass. Space Ratio (basis 2) | *37.6* | (all berths) | *35.1* |
| Total Cabins | *196* | Officers | *French* |
| Dining Staff | | | *French/Mauritian/Filipino* |
| Size (sq ft/m) | *188-321 /17.5-29.8* | Door Width | *25"* |
| Outside Cabins | *196* | Inside Cabins | *0* |
| Single Cabins | *0* | Supplement | *50%* |
| Balcony Cabins | *0* | Wheelchair Cabins | *0* |
| Cabin Current | *110/220 AC* | Refrigerator | *Yes* |
| Cabin TV | *Yes* | VCR | *No* |

| | | | |
|---|---|---|---|
| Dining Rooms | *2* | Library | *Yes* |
| Elevators | *2* | Door Width | *40"* |
| Casino | *Yes* | Slot Machines | *Yes* |
| Swimming Pools (outside) | | | *2* |
| Whirlpools | *0* | Gymnasium | *Yes* |
| Sauna/Steam Rm | *Yes/No* | Massage | *Yes* |
| Watersports Facilities | | | *Aft platform, windsurfers, sailboats, waterski boats, scuba tanks, snorkels, motorized watersport boats* |
| Classification Society | | | *Bureau Veritas* |

| RATINGS | SCORE |
|---|---|
| Ship: Condition/Cleanliness | 8.4 |
| Ship: Space/Flow/Comfort | 8.0 |
| Ship: Decor/Furnishings | 8.5 |
| Ship: Watersports Facilities | 9.0 |
| Cabins: Comfort/Facilities | 8.5 |
| Cabins: Software | 8.0 |
| Food: Dining Room/Cuisine | 7.7 |
| Food: Buffets/Informal Dining | 7.7 |
| Food: Quality of Ingredients | 7.4 |
| Service: Dining Room | 7.4 |
| Service: Bars/Lounges | 7.6 |
| Service: Cabins | 8.2 |
| Cruise: Sail-Cruise Experience | 7.4 |
| Cruise: Entertainment/Activities | 5.6 |
| Cruise: Hospitality Standard | 7.4 |
| OVERALL RATING | 116.8 |

**+** Extensive watersports facilities and superb aft marina platform. Computer workshop. Golf simulator (extra charge). Cabins are beautifully equipped, have mini-bars, 24-hour room service (but you pay for food), safe, TV, plenty of storage space, bathrobes, and hairdryers. Odyssey Restaurant has lovely open terrace. Continental and Japanese cuisine, but presentation needs improving. Complimentary wine with meals. Afternoon tea is a delight.

**–** Activities, under the direction of a large team of young, energetic GOs (Gentils Organisateurs), is clown-like and very amateurish.

**Dining** Two lovely dining rooms have tables for one, two, or more. Open seating for all meals. Open air dining terrace for informal meals. The cuisine is mainly French and Continental. Beer and standard wine included for lunch and dinner.

**Other Comments** One of a pair of the world's largest sail-cruisers—part cruise ship, part yacht. It is a larger version of the *Windstar* vessels. Five huge masts provide seven computer-controlled sails. There are six four-person cabins, and some 35 doubles are fitted with an extra pullman berth. Superb for the more upscale active singles and couples who might like casual elegance rather than the wilder vacation experience one might find at some Club Med resorts. Port taxes and insurance are extra. No gratuities are expected or accepted, as at all Club Med resorts.

# mys Le Ponant ★★★★+

***Principal Cruising Area***

*Caribbean (7 nights year-round)*

***Base Port:*** *Guadeloupe*

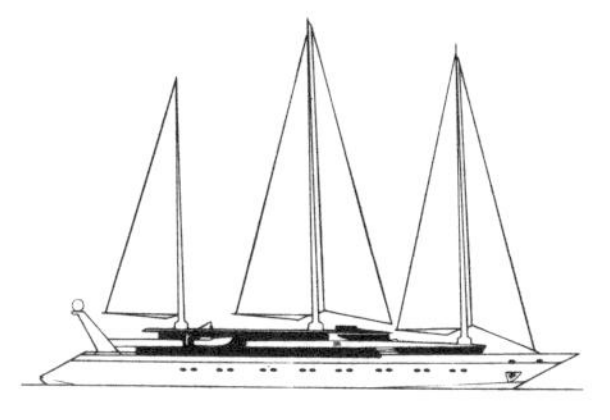

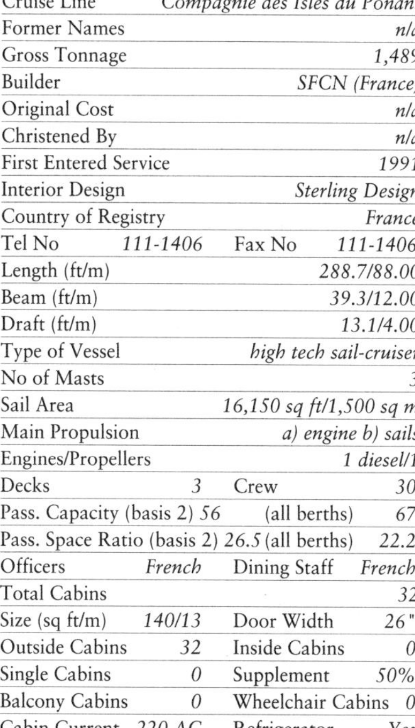

| | | | |
|---|---|---|---|
| Cruise Line | | | *Compagnie des Isles du Ponant* |
| Former Names | | | *n/a* |
| Gross Tonnage | | | *1,489* |
| Builder | | | *SFCN (France)* |
| Original Cost | | | *n/a* |
| Christened By | | | *n/a* |
| First Entered Service | | | *1991* |
| Interior Design | | | *Sterling Design* |
| Country of Registry | | | *France* |
| Tel No | *111-1406* | Fax No | *111-1406* |
| Length (ft/m) | | | *288.7/88.00* |
| Beam (ft/m) | | | *39.3/12.00* |
| Draft (ft/m) | | | *13.1/4.00* |
| Type of Vessel | | | *high tech sail-cruiser* |
| No of Masts | | | *3* |
| Sail Area | | | *16,150 sq ft/1,500 sq m* |
| Main Propulsion | | | *a) engine b) sails* |
| Engines/Propellers | | | *1 diesel/1* |
| Decks | *3* | Crew | *30* |
| Pass. Capacity (basis 2) | *56* | (all berths) | *67* |
| Pass. Space Ratio (basis 2) | *26.5* | (all berths) | *22.2* |
| Officers | *French* | Dining Staff | *French* |
| Total Cabins | | | *32* |
| Size (sq ft/m) | *140/13* | Door Width | *26"* |
| Outside Cabins | *32* | Inside Cabins | *0* |
| Single Cabins | *0* | Supplement | *50%* |
| Balcony Cabins | *0* | Wheelchair Cabins | *0* |
| Cabin Current | *220 AC* | Refrigerator | *Yes* |

| | | | |
|---|---|---|---|
| Cabin TV | *No* | VCR | *No* |
| Dining Rooms | *1* | Library | *Yes* |
| Elevators | *No* | Door Width | *n/a* |
| Casino | *No* | Slot Machines | *No* |
| Swimming Pools (outside) | *0* | | |
| Whirlpools | *0* | Gymnasium | *Yes* |
| Sauna/Steam Rm | *No/No* | *Massage* | *No* |
| Watersports Facilities | | | *Aft marina platform, windsurf, waterski boat, scuba, snorkel* |
| Classification Society | | | *Lloyd's Register* |

| RATINGS | SCORE |
|---|---|
| Ship: Condition/Cleanliness | 8.8 |
| Ship: Space/Flow/Comfort | 7.4 |
| Ship: Decor/Furnishings | 9.0 |
| Ship: Watersports Facilities | 8.8 |
| Cabins: Comfort/Facilities | 8.7 |
| Cabins: Software | 8.1 |
| Food: Dining Room/Cuisine | 8.5 |
| Food: Buffets/Informal Dining | 8.1 |
| Food: Quality of Ingredients | 8.0 |
| Service: Dining Room | 8.0 |
| Service: Bars/Lounges | 7.7 |
| Service: Cabins | 8.0 |
| Cruise: Sail-Cruise Experience | 7.7 |
| Cruise: Activities Program | 7.6 |
| Cruise: Hospitality Standard | 8.0 |
| OVERALL RATING | 122.4 |

**+** This captivating ship has plenty of room on her open decks for sunbathing.Watersports platform at the stern. Very elegant—no glitz. Interior design is clean, stylish, and functional, and ultra high-tech throughout. Three public lounges have pastel decor, soft colors, and great European flair. Crisp, clean, blond woods and pristine white cabins feature double or twin beds, mini-bar, personal safe, and private bathroom. All cabins feature portholes and crisp artwork.

**–** Cabin bathrooms are quite small. Cabins have limited storage space and few drawers.

**Dining** The lovely Karukera dining room features complimentary wines and good food. There is fresh fish every day, and meals are true *affaires gastonomiques*. Charming outdoor cafEe under canvas sail-cloth awning.

**Other Comments** Ultra-sleek and very efficient, this latest generation of sail-cruise ship has three masts that rise 54.8 ft. (16.7 m.) above the water line. One price fits all. Marketed mainly to young, sophisticated French-speaking passengers who love yachting and the sea. Port taxes and insurance are extra. Gratuities are not "required" but they are expected.

# sy Sea Cloud ★★★★★

***Principal Cruising Areas***

*Caribbean/Europe (7 days)*

***Base Ports:*** *Antigua/various*

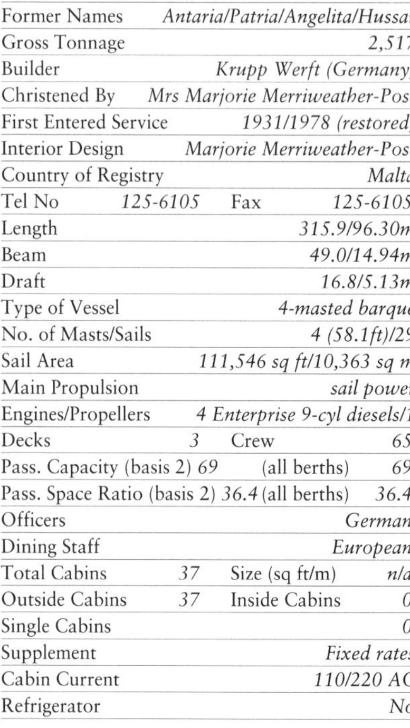

| | | | |
|---|---|---|---|
| Cruise Line | *Sea Cloud Cruises/Deilmann Reederei* | | |
| Former Names | *Antaria/Patria/Angelita/Hussar* | | |
| Gross Tonnage | *2,517* | | |
| Builder | *Krupp Werft (Germany)* | | |
| Christened By | *Mrs Marjorie Merriweather-Post* | | |
| First Entered Service | *1931/1978 (restored)* | | |
| Interior Design | *Marjorie Merriweather-Post* | | |
| Country of Registry | *Malta* | | |
| Tel No | *125-6105* | Fax | *125-6105* |
| Length | *315.9/96.30m* | | |
| Beam | *49.0/14.94m* | | |
| Draft | *16.8/5.13m* | | |
| Type of Vessel | *4-masted barque* | | |
| No. of Masts/Sails | *4 (58.1ft)/29* | | |
| Sail Area | *111,546 sq ft/10,363 sq m* | | |
| Main Propulsion | *sail power* | | |
| Engines/Propellers | *4 Enterprise 9-cyl diesels/1* | | |
| Decks | *3* | Crew | *65* |
| Pass. Capacity (basis 2) | *69* | (all berths) | *69* |
| Pass. Space Ratio (basis 2) | *36.4* | (all berths) | *36.4* |
| Officers | *German* | | |
| Dining Staff | *European* | | |
| Total Cabins | *37* | Size (sq ft/m) | *n/a* |
| Outside Cabins | *37* | Inside Cabins | *0* |
| Single Cabins | *0* | | |
| Supplement | *Fixed rates* | | |
| Cabin Current | *110/220 AC* | | |
| Refrigerator | *No* | | |

| | | | |
|---|---|---|---|
| Cabin TV | *No* | VCR | *No* |
| Dining Rooms | *1 (open seating)* | | |
| Elevators | *0* | | |
| Casino | *No* | Slot Machines | *No* |
| Swimming Pools (outside) | *0* | | |
| Whirlpools | *0* | Gymnasium | *No* |
| Sauna/Steam Rm | *No/No* | Massage | *No* |
| Library | *Yes* | | |
| Watersports Facilities | *No* | | |
| Classification Society | *Germanischer Lloyd* | | |

| RATINGS | SCORE |
|---|---|
| Ship: Condition/Cleanliness | 8.8 |
| Ship: Space/Flow/Comfort | 8.2 |
| Ship: Decor/Furnishings | 8.8 |
| Ship: Watersports Facilities | 7.6 |
| Cabins: Comfort/Facilities | 8.1 |
| Cabins: Software | 8.5 |
| Food: Dining Room/Cuisine | 8.6 |
| Food: Buffets/Informal Dining | 8.1 |
| Food: Quality of Ingredients | 8.4 |
| Service: Dining Room | 8.3 |
| Service: Bars/Lounges | 8.1 |
| Service: Cabins | 8.2 |
| Cruise: Sail-Cruise Experience | 9.2 |
| Cruise: Activities Program | 7.8 |
| Cruise: Hospitality Standard | 8.4 |
| OVERALL RATING | 125.1 |

**+** Plenty of deck space under the expanse of sail. Incredibly fine handcrafted interior, with antique furniture, original oil paintings, and gorgeous, carved oak paneling everywhere. Two owner's suites are lavish, with Chippendale furniture, gilt detailing, a real fireplace, and Italian marble bathrooms.

**–** Steep interior staircase, as on most sailing vessels.

**Dining** Elegant dining room (which is also the ship's library) has wood paneled walls and a wood beam ceiling. German chefs. Excellent Continental food and presentation, although the choice is limited. Good breakfast and lunch buffets. Wines are included with lunch and dinner.

**Other Comments** The oldest and most beautiful tall ship sailing, and the largest private yacht ever built. Her masts reach as high as a very tall building. Originally built for Marjorie Merriweather Post (the American cereal heiress), this lovely working sailing ship is now owned by a consortium of nine German yachtsmen and chartered to various operators. Assisted by diesel engines when not under sail. Unlike any other ship. Uncompromising comfort and elegance of a bygone era. A stately home afloat, this is one of the world's most delightful travel and vacation experiences. I cannot recommend it highly enough. Gratuities are extra.

# sy Sir Francis Drake ★★

***Principal Cruising Areas***

*UK, US Virgin Islands/Caribbean Cruise (3/4/7 nights)*

***Base Ports:*** *St. Marten/St. Thomas*

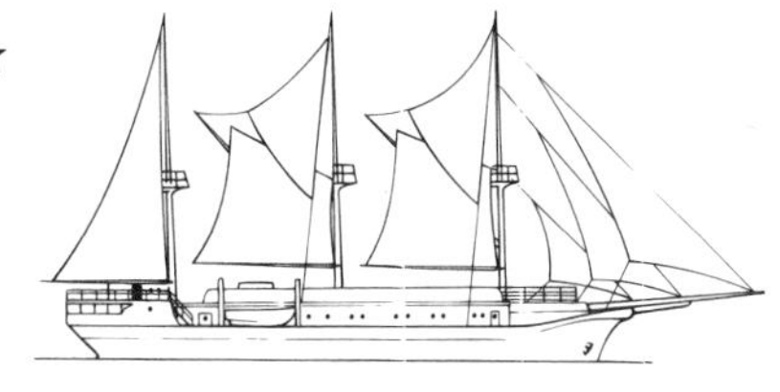

| | | | |
|---|---|---|---|
| Cruise Line | | | *Tall Ship Adventures* |
| Former Names | | | *n/a* |
| Gross Tonnage | | | 450 DWT |
| Builder | | | 1917 |
| Original Cost | | | n/a |
| Christened By | | | n/a |
| First Entered Service | | | 1917 |
| Interior Design | | | n/a |
| Country of Registry | | | Honduras |
| Tel No | | | 809-496-0914 (cellular) |
| Length (ft/m) | | | *162.4/49.50* |
| Beam (ft/m) | | | *22.9/7.00* |
| Draft (ft/m) | | | *9.1/2.80* |
| Type of Vessel | | | *topsail schooner* |
| No of Masts/Sails | | | *3/9 (manually-furled)* |
| Sail Area | | | *6,456 sq ft/600 sq m* |
| Main Propulsion | | | *sail power* |
| Engines/Propellers | | | *1 diesel/1* |
| Decks | 2 | Crew | 14 |
| Pass. Capacity (basis 2) | *28* | (all berths) | *30* |
| Pass. Space Ratio (basis 2) | *16.0* | (all berths) | *15.0* |
| Officers | | | *British* |
| Dining Staff | | | *International* |
| Total Cabins | | | *14* |
| Size (sq ft/m) | *n/a* | Door Width | *n/a* |
| Outside Cabins | *14* | Inside Cabins | *0* |
| Single Cabins | *0* | Supplement | *100%* |
| Balcony Cabins | *0* | Wheelchair Cabins | *0* |

| | | | |
|---|---|---|---|
| Cabin Current | *110/220 AC* | Refrigerator | *No* |
| Cabin TV | *No* | VCR | *No* |
| Dining Rooms | | | *1 (open seating)* |
| Casino | *No* | Slot Machines | *No* |
| Swimming Pools (outside) | | | *0* |
| Whirlpools | *0* | Gymnasium | *No* |
| Sauna/Steam Rm | *No/No* | Massage | *No* |
| Library | | | *No* |
| Watersports Facilities | | | *None* |
| Classification Society | | | *Germanischer Lloyd* |

| RATINGS | SCORE |
|---|---|
| Ship: Condition/Cleanliness | 6.3 |
| Ship: Space/Flow/Comfort | 4.4 |
| Ship: Decor/Furnishings | 6.1 |
| Ship: Watersports Facilities | 3.8 |
| Cabins: Comfort/Facilities | 4.3 |
| Cabins: Software | 4.6 |
| Food: Dining Room/Cuisine | 5.4 |
| Food: Buffets/Informal Dining | 5.1 |
| Food: Quality of Ingredients | 5.8 |
| Service: Dining Room | 6.0 |
| Service: Bars/Lounges | 6.0 |
| Service: Cabins | 6.2 |
| Cruise: Sail-Cruise Experience | 6.8 |
| Cruise: Activities Program | 5.7 |
| Cruise: Hospitality Standard | 6.0 |
| OVERALL RATING | 82.5 |

**+** An authentic topsail schooner, lovingly restored to her original condition. More than a Windjammer (Windjammer Barefoot Cruises vessels are not certified by the U.S. Coast Guard), yet not as upmarket as the Star Clipper ships, this tall ship is a real treasure for those who don't expect the service finesse offered aboard more contemporary ships. Passengers can, and often do, participate in hoisting the sails.

**–** Very steep interior stairways, as on most true sailing vessels.

**Dining** Charming, dark-wood paneled dining room with wood-trimmed chairs and picture windows. The cuisine is decidedly casual fast-food Americana fare. Not much choice for non-meat eaters, and food quality is barely adequate.

**Other Comments** You'll have a very relaxing vacation aboard one of the last tall ships. For people who really like sailing ships and the hands-on experience this kind of vessel can provide.

# sv Star Clipper ★★★★+

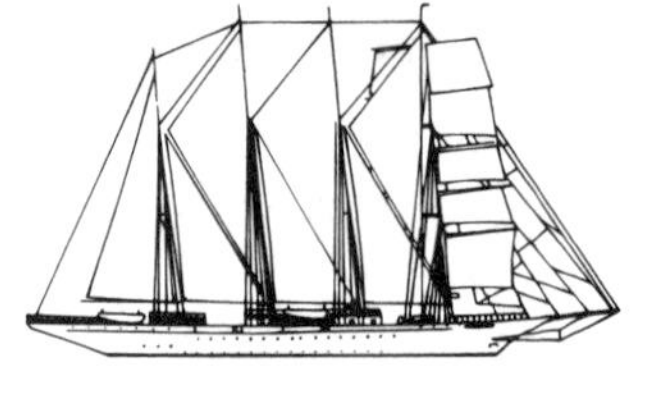

***Principal Cruising Area***

*Caribbean (7/14 nights)*

***Base Port:*** *Barbados (Saturday)*

| | | | |
|---|---|---|---|
| Cruise Line | | | *Star Clippers* |
| Former Names | *n/a* | Gross Tonnage | *3,025* |
| Builder | | | *Scheepswerven van Langerbrugge* |
| Original Cost | | | *$30 million* |
| Christened By | | | *Ms Maria Krafft* |
| First Entered Service | | | *May 16, 1992* |
| Interior Design | | | *Struik & Hammerslag* |
| Country of Registry | | | *Luxembourg (LXST)* |
| Tel No | *125-3210* | Fax No | *125-3206* |
| Length (ft/m) | | | *366.1/111.60* |
| Beam (ft/m) | *49.2/15.00* | Draft (ft/m) | *17.7/5.60* |
| Type of Vessel | | | *barkentine schooner* |
| No of Masts/Sails | | | *4 (208 ft)/16 (manually-furled)* |
| Sail Area | | | *36,221 sq ft/3,365 sq m* |
| Main Propulsion | | | *sail power* |
| Engines | | | *1 Caterpillar V16-cyl diesel* |
| Propellers | | | *1 (CP)* |
| Decks | *4* | Crew | *72* |
| Pass. Capacity (basis 2) | *170* | (all berths) | *182* |
| Pass. Space Ratio (basis 2) | *17.7* | (all berths) | *16.6* |
| Officers | *European* | Dining Staff | *International* |
| Total Cabins | | | *79* |
| Size (sq ft/m) | *95-150/8.8-14* | Door Width | *26"* |
| Outside Cabins | *85* | Inside Cabins | *6* |
| Single Cabins | *0* | Supplement | *50%* |
| Balcony Cabins | *0* | Wheelchair Cabins | *0* |
| Cabin Current | *110 AC* | Refrigerator | *Cat. 1* |
| Cabin TV | *Yes* | VCR | *No* |

| | | | |
|---|---|---|---|
| Dining Rooms | | | *1 (open seating)* |
| Elevators | *0* | Door Width | *n/a* |
| Casino | *No* | Slot Machines | *No* |
| Swimming Pools (outside) | | | *2* |
| Whirlpools | *0* | Gymnasium | *No* |
| Sauna/Steam Rm | *No/No* | Massage | *No* |
| Library | | | *Yes* |
| Watersports Facilities | | | *Waterski boat, sunfish, scuba, snorkel, zodiacs* |
| Classification Society | | | *Lloyd's Register* |

| **RATINGS** | **SCORE** |
|---|---|
| Ship: Condition/Cleanliness | 8.7 |
| Ship: Space/Flow/Comfort | 7.6 |
| Ship: Decor/Furnishings | 8.6 |
| Ship: Watersports Facilities | 6.6 |
| Cabins: Comfort/Facilities | 8.2 |
| Cabins: Software | 8.1 |
| Food: Dining Room/Cuisine | 7.4 |
| Food: Buffets/Informal Dining | 6.7 |
| Food: Quality of Ingredients | 6.4 |
| Service: Dining Room | 7.6 |
| Service: Bars/Lounges | 7.4 |
| Service: Cabins | 7.8 |
| Cruise: Sail-Cruise Experience | 9.5 |
| Cruise: Activities Program | 6.8 |
| Cruise: Hospitality Standard | 8.5 |
| OVERALL RATING | 115.9 |

**+** Second of a pair, this brand new, true sailing ship with cruise accommodations evokes memories of the 19th-century clipper ships. Accurate, four-masted, barkentine-rigged vessel with graceful lines and superbly-shaped hull. Absolutely breathtaking! Good for watersports lovers—this vessel has excellent sea manners. Sports directors provide basic dive instruction—for a fee. Classic Edwardian nautical decor throughout is clean, warm, and intimate. The paneled library has a fireplace, and chairs that are supremely comfortable. Well-equipped, comfortable, contemporary cabins. No lines. No hassle.

**–** Not for the physically-impaired, nor children. The internal stairs are steep, as in most sailing vessels. No room service. Pooled tipping system needs modification.

**Dining** Charming dining room. Rather unimaginative buffet breakfasts and lunches, and a mix of buffet and à la carte dinners. Poor seating arrangement. Cuisine is not gourmet, but is quite creative. A pasta dish would be a welcome addition. Poor bread rolls, pastries and fruits. Tea and coffee (in paper cups) should be available 24 hours (in china). No cabin food service at all.

**Other Comments** Staff are very casual, and often mix in areas that should be reserved for passengers. Carefree and casual (no jacket or tie). Totally unstructured setting at a modest price. Very highly recommended for even the most jaded cruisegoer. Insurance and gratuities are extra.

# sv Star Flyer ★★★★+

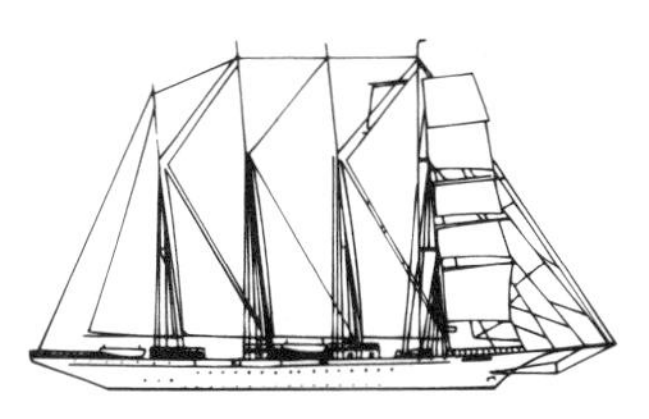

***Principal Cruising Areas***

*Caribbean/Europe (7 nights)*

***Base Ports:*** *St Maarten/Cannes*

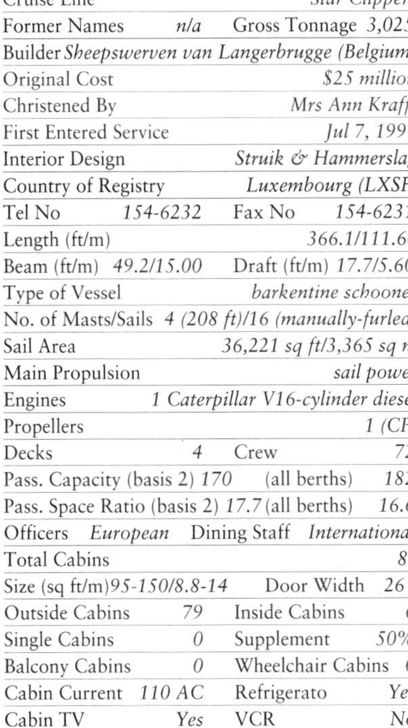

| | | | |
|---|---|---|---|
| Cruise Line | | | *Star Clippers* |
| Former Names | *n/a* | Gross Tonnage | *3,025* |
| Builder | | | *Sheepswerven van Langerbrugge (Belgium)* |
| Original Cost | | | *$25 million* |
| Christened By | | | *Mrs Ann Krafft* |
| First Entered Service | | | *Jul 7, 1991* |
| Interior Design | | | *Struik & Hammerslag* |
| Country of Registry | | | *Luxembourg (LXSF)* |
| Tel No | *154-6232* | Fax No | *154-6231* |
| Length (ft/m) | | | *366.1/111.60* |
| Beam (ft/m) | *49.2/15.00* | Draft (ft/m) | *17.7/5.60* |
| Type of Vessel | | | *barkentine schooner* |
| No. of Masts/Sails | | | *4 (208 ft)/16 (manually-furled)* |
| Sail Area | | | *36,221 sq ft/3,365 sq m* |
| Main Propulsion | | | *sail power* |
| Engines | | | *1 Caterpillar V16-cylinder diesel* |
| Propellers | | | *1 (CP)* |
| Decks | *4* | Crew | *72* |
| Pass. Capacity (basis 2) | *170* | (all berths) | *182* |
| Pass. Space Ratio (basis 2) | *17.7* | (all berths) | *16.6* |
| Officers | *European* | Dining Staff | *International* |
| Total Cabins | | | *85* |
| Size (sq ft/m) | *95-150/8.8-14* | Door Width | *26"* |
| Outside Cabins | *79* | Inside Cabins | *6* |
| Single Cabins | *0* | Supplement | *50%* |
| Balcony Cabins | *0* | Wheelchair Cabins | *0* |
| Cabin Current | *110 AC* | Refrigerato | *Yes* |
| Cabin TV | *Yes* | VCR | *No* |

| | | | |
|---|---|---|---|
| Dining Rooms | | | *1 (open seating)* |
| Elevators | *0* | Door Width | *n/a* |
| Casino | *No* | Slot Machines | *No* |
| Swimming Pools (outside) | | | *2* |
| Whirlpools | *0* | Gymnasium | *No* |
| Sauna/Steam Rm | *No/No* | Massage | *No* |
| Library | | | *Yes* |
| Watersports Facilities | | | *Waterski boat, sunfish, scuba, snorkel, zodiacs* |
| Classification Society | | | *Lloyd's Register* |

| RATINGS | SCORE |
|---|---|
| Ship: Condition/Cleanliness | 8.7 |
| Ship: Space/Flow/Comfort | 7.6 |
| Ship: Decor/Furnishings | 8.6 |
| Ship: Watersports Facilities | 6.6 |
| Cabins: Comfort/Facilities | 8.2 |
| Cabins: Software | 8.1 |
| Food: Dining Room/Cuisine | 7.4 |
| Food: Buffets/Informal Dining | 6.7 |
| Food: Quality of Ingredients | 6.4 |
| Service: Dining Room | 7.6 |
| Service: Bars/Lounges | 7.4 |
| Service: Cabins | 7.8 |
| Cruise: Sail-Cruise Experience | 9.5 |
| Cruise: Activities Program | 6.8 |
| Cruise: Hospitality Standard | 8.5 |
| OVERALL RATING | 115.9 |

**+** First of a pair of two new, real, tall sailing ships. Graceful hull that evokes memories of the 19th-century clipper sailing ships. Good watersports program. Classic Edwardian nautical decor throughout. Very well equipped, comfortable, contemporary, mostly outside cabins. Paneled library has supremely comfortable chairs, and even a fireplace. Cabins are of a generous size, and feature wood-trimmed cabinetry.

**–** Not for the physically-impaired, nor children. Internal stairs are steep.

**Dining** Charming dining room is used for rather unimaginative buffet breakfasts and lunches, and a mix of buffet and à la carte dinners. Poor seating arrangement. Cuisine is not gourmet, but quite creative given the incredibly small galley space. A pasta dish would be a welcome—and simple—addition. Poor bread rolls, pastries, and fruits. Tea and coffee should be made available 24 hours a day (in china, not paper, cups), particularly in view of the fact that there is no cabin food service at all.

**Other Comments** This ship is casual (leave all formal and informal wear at home), but provides an outstanding sailing cruise experience at a very modest price, for those that don't need much entertainment beyond the wind and the sea. Truly breathtaking, intimate, and very affordable! Insurance and gratuities are extra.

# mys Wind Song ★★★★+

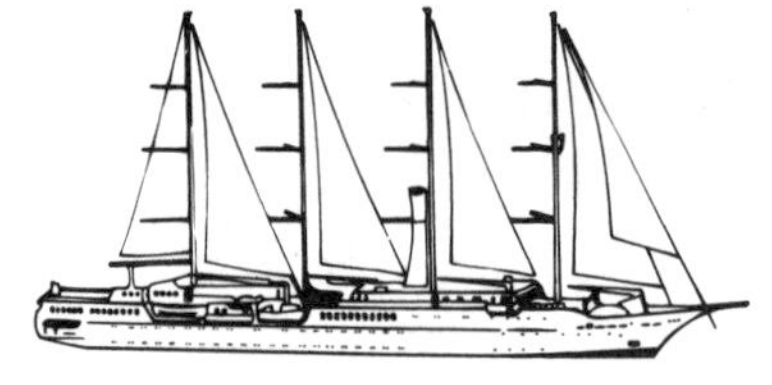

***Principal Cruising Area***

*French Polynesia (7 nights year-round)*

***Base Port:** Papeete (Sunday)*

| | | | |
|---|---|---|---|
| Cruise Line | | | *Windstar Cruises* |
| Former Names | *n/a* | Gross Tonnage | *5,703* |
| Builder | | | *Ateliers et Chantiers du Havre (France)* |
| Original Cost | | | *$34.2 million* |
| Christened By | | | *Mrs Nadia Stolt-Nielsen* |
| First Entered Service | | | *Jul 24, 1987* |
| Interior Design | | | *Archiform Design/Marc Held* |
| Country of Registry | | | *Bahamas (C6CB2)* |
| Tel No | *110-4270* | Fax No | *110-4271* |
| Length (ft/m) | | | *440.2/134.20* |
| Beam (ft/m) | *51.8/15.80* | Draft (ft/m) | *13.4/4.10* |
| Type of Vessel | | | *computer-controlled sail-cruiser* |
| No of Masts/Sails | | | *4 (204 ft)/6 (self-furling)* |
| Sail Area | | | *21,489 sq ft/1,996.4 sq m* |
| Main Propulsion | | | *a) engines b) sails* |
| Engines | | | *2 Wartsila diesel-electrics* |
| Propellers | | | *1 (VP)* |
| Decks | *5* | Crew | *91* |
| Pass. Capacity (basis 2) | *148* | (all berths) | *159* |
| Pass. Space Ratio (basis 2) | *38.5* | (all berths) | *34.1* |
| Officers | *British* | Dining Staff | *Indonesian/Filipino* |
| Total Cabins | | | *74* |
| Size (sq ft/m) | *185-220/17-20.5* | Door Width | *27"* |
| Outside Cabins | *74* | Inside Cabins | *0* |
| Single Cabins | *0* | Supplement | *50-100%* |
| Balcony Cabins | *0* | Wheelchair Cabins | *0* |
| Cabin Current | *110 AC* | Refrigerator | *Yes* |
| Cabin TV | *Yes* | VCR | *Yes* |
| Dining Rooms | | | *1 (open seating)* |
| Casino | *Yes* | Slot Machines | *Yes* |
| Swimming Pools (outside) | | | *1 (dip pool)* |
| Whirlpools | *1* | Gymnasium | *Yes* |
| Sauna/Steam Rm | *Yes/No* | Massage | *Yes* |
| Library | | | Yes |
| Watersports Facilities | | | *Aft marina platform, kayaks, sunfish sailboats, windsurf boards, waterski boat, scuba, snorkel, zodiacs* |
| Classification Society | | | *Bureau Veritas* |

| RATINGS | SCORE |
|---|---|
| Ship: Condition/Cleanliness | 8.2 |
| Ship: Space/Flow/Comfort | 7.8 |
| Ship: Decor/Furnishings | 8.3 |
| Ship: Watersports Facilities | 8.0 |
| Cabins: Comfort/Facilities | 8.2 |
| Cabins: Software | 8.3 |
| Food: Dining Room/Cuisine | 7.4 |
| Food: Buffets/Informal Dining | 7.0 |
| Food: Quality of Ingredients | 7.2 |
| Service: Dining Room | 7.6 |
| Service: Bars/Lounges | 7.7 |
| Service: Cabins | 7.8 |
| Cruise: Sail-Cruise Experience | 8.1 |
| Cruise: Activities Program | 7.4 |
| Cruise: Hospitality Standard | 8.1 |
| OVERALL RATING | 117.1 |

**+** Beautifully-crafted interior with fine, blond woods and soft, complementary colors. Open deck and sunning space is adequate. Cabins are all-outside, one-price suites, and come completely equipped. Bathrooms are a neat figure-of-eight shape. At the stern is a watersports platform. No scheduled activities make this a real relaxing vacation. This ship will cruise you in extremely comfortable surroundings that are bordering on contemporary luxury.

**–** Constant whine from the ship's engine can be heard in most cabins. No bathtubs. Tiny dip pool. Interior colors are a little cold. The library needs more hardback fiction. Communication with Indonesian crew can prove frustrating. Drinks prices are high.

**Dining** Charming, elegant dining room, with ocean views from large picture windows. Features nouvelle cuisine, which is creative and attractively presented, but not up to the standard of the small luxury ships. The quality of ingredients should be upgraded. Attentive, friendly service throughout, but communication proves frustrating at times. Poor pastries, breads, and fruits.

**Other Comments** Long, sleek-looking craft, part yacht, part cruise ship, with four giant masts and computer-controlled sails. Ambiance could be warmer. A relaxing, unstructured cruise experience, just right for seven idyllic nights in sheltered areas. Unwind in style and see the beautiful islands of Tahiti. Port taxes and insurance are extra. Gratuities not "required," but expected.

# mys Wind Spirit ★★★★+

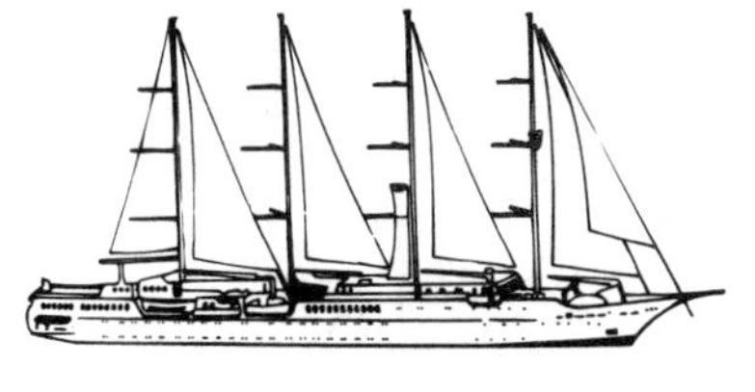

***Principal Cruising Areas***

*Caribbean/Mediterranean (7 nights)*

***Base Ports:** Antigua/Nice*

| | | | |
|---|---|---|---|
| Cruise Line | | | *Windstar Cruises* |
| Former Names | *n/a* | Gross Tonnage | *5,736* |
| Builder | | | *Ateliers et Chantiers du Havre (France)* |
| Original Cost | | | *$34.2 million* |
| Christened By | | | *Mrs Clara van der Vorm* |
| First Entered Service | | | *Apr 9, 1988* |
| Interior Design | | | *Archiform Design/Marc Held* |
| Country of Registry | | | *Bahamas (C6CY9)* |
| Tel No | *110-4434* | Fax No | *110-4435* |
| Length (ft/m) | | | *440.2/134.20* |
| Beam (ft/m) | *51.8/15.80* | Draft (ft/m) | *13.4/4.10* |
| Type of Vessel | | | *computer-controlled sail-cruiser* |
| No of Masts/Sails | | | *4 (204 ft)/6 (self-furling)* |
| Sail Area | | | *21,489 sq ft/1,996.4 sq m* |
| Main Propulsion | | | *a) engines b) sails* |
| Engines | | | *2 Wartsila diesel-electrics* |
| Propellers | | | *1 (VP)* |
| Decks | *5* | Crew | *91* |
| Pass. Capacity (basis 2) | *148* | (all berths) | *159* |
| Pass. Space Ratio (basis 2) | *38.7* | (all berths) | *36.0* |
| Officers | | | *British/Dutch* |
| Dining Staff | | | *Indonesian/Filipino* |
| Total Cabins | | | *74* |
| Size (sq ft/m) | *185-220/17-22.5* | Door Width | *27"* |
| Outside Cabins | *74* | Inside Cabins | *0* |
| Single Cabins | *0* | Supplement | *50-100%* |
| Balcony Cabins | *0* | Wheelchair Cabins | *0* |
| Cabin Current | *110 AC* | Refrigerator | *Yes* |

| | | | |
|---|---|---|---|
| Cabin TV | *Yes* | VCR | *Yes* |
| Dining Rooms | *1* | Library | *Yes* |
| Casino | *Yes* | Slot Machines | *Yes* |
| Swimming Pools (outside) | | | *1 (dip pool)* |
| Whirlpools | *1* | Gymnasium | *Yes* |
| Sauna/Steam Rm | *Yes/No* | Massage | *Yes* |
| Watersports Facilities | | | *Aft marina platform, kayaks, windsurf boards, sunfish sailboats, water ski boat, scuba, snorkel, zodiacs* |
| Classification Society | | | *Bureau Veritas* |

| RATINGS | SCORE |
|---|---|
| Ship: Condition/Cleanliness | 8.2 |
| Ship: Space/Flow/Comfort | 7.8 |
| Ship: Decor/Furnishings | 8.3 |
| Ship: Watersports Facilities | 8.0 |
| Cabins: Comfort/Facilities | 8.2 |
| Cabins: Software | 8.3 |
| Food: Dining Room/Cuisine | 7.4 |
| Food: Buffets/Informal Dining | 7.0 |
| Food: Quality of Ingredients | 7.2 |
| Service: Dining Room | 7.6 |
| Service: Bars/Lounges | 7.7 |
| Service: Cabins | 7.8 |
| Cruise: Sail-Cruise Experience | 8.1 |
| Cruise: Activities Program | 7.4 |
| Cruise: Hospitality Standard | 8.1 |
| OVERALL RATING | 117.1 |

**+** Nicely-crafted, high quality, elegant, nautical-themed interior. Light woods used extensively throughout. No lines, no hassle. Outdoor deck space is quite good unless full. All-outside suites are one price, well equipped and finished, have two portholes, and have CD players. Lots of wood trim. Elegant main lounge, with crisp, but stark, colors. Good indoor-outdoor eatery. Recommended for watersports fans.

**–** Constant whine from the ship's generator heard in most cabins. Not much deck space, due to the complex sail machinery. No bathtubs in cabins. Tiny "dip" pool. Interior colors are a little cold. Communicating with Indonesian crew can prove frustrating. High drinks prices.

**Dining** Charming, elegant dining room, with ocean views from large picture windows. Nouvelle cuisine, which is creative and attractively presented, but just not up to the standard of the small luxury ships. The quality of ingredients should be upgraded. Attentive, friendly service throughout. Poor pastries. Food budget should be higher.

**Other Comments** Identical to *Wind Song* and *Wind Spirit*. Part yacht, part cruise ship, with four giant masts and computer-controlled sails. Staff are very casual. Relaxed, fairly refined surroundings. Seven nights of unstructured living at sea, but only partly under sail. Port taxes and insurance are extra. Gratuities are "not required," but they are expected.

# mys Wind Star ★★★★+

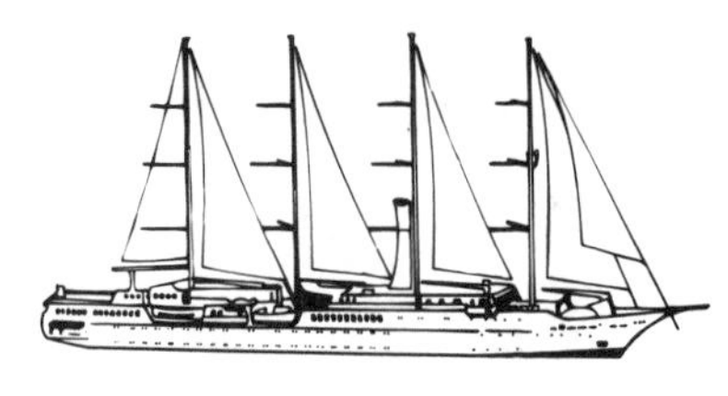

***Principal Cruising Areas***

*Caribbean/Europe (7 nights)*

***Base Ports:*** *Nassau/Nice*

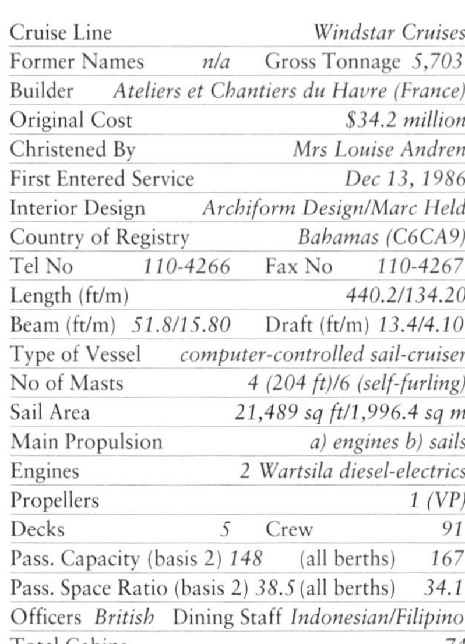

| | | | |
|---|---|---|---|
| Cruise Line | *Windstar Cruises* | | |
| Former Names | *n/a* | Gross Tonnage | *5,703* |
| Builder | *Ateliers et Chantiers du Havre (France)* | | |
| Original Cost | *$34.2 million* | | |
| Christened By | *Mrs Louise Andren* | | |
| First Entered Service | *Dec 13, 1986* | | |
| Interior Design | *Archiform Design/Marc Held* | | |
| Country of Registry | *Bahamas (C6CA9)* | | |
| Tel No | *110-4266* | Fax No | *110-4267* |
| Length (ft/m) | *440.2/134.20* | | |
| Beam (ft/m) | *51.8/15.80* | Draft (ft/m) | *13.4/4.10* |
| Type of Vessel | *computer-controlled sail-cruiser* | | |
| No of Masts | *4 (204 ft)/6 (self-furling)* | | |
| Sail Area | *21,489 sq ft/1,996.4 sq m* | | |
| Main Propulsion | *a) engines b) sails* | | |
| Engines | *2 Wartsila diesel-electrics* | | |
| Propellers | *1 (VP)* | | |
| Decks | *5* | Crew | *91* |
| Pass. Capacity (basis 2) | *148* | (all berths) | *167* |
| Pass. Space Ratio (basis 2) | *38.5* | (all berths) | *34.1* |
| Officers | *British* | Dining Staff | *Indonesian/Filipino* |
| Total Cabins | *74* | | |
| Size (sq ft/m) | *185-220/17-22.5* | Door Width | *27"* |
| Outside Cabins | *74* | Inside Cabins | *0* |
| Single Cabins | *0* | Supplement | *50-100%* |
| Balcony Cabins | *0* | Wheelchair Cabins | *0* |
| Cabin Current | *110 AC* | | |
| Refrigerator | *Yes* | | |

| | | | |
|---|---|---|---|
| Cabin TV | *Yes* | VCR | *Yes* |
| Dining Rooms | *1* | Library | *Yes* |
| Casino | *Yes* | Slot Machines | *Yes* |
| Swimming Pools (outside) | *1 (dip pool)* | | |
| Whirlpools | *1* | Gymnasium | *Yes* |
| Sauna/Steam Rm | *Yes/No* | Massage | *Yes* |
| Watersports Facilities | *Aft marina platform, kayaks, windsurf boards, sunfish sailboats, waterski boat, scuba, snorkel, zodiacs* | | |
| Classification Society | *Bureau Veritas* | | |

| RATINGS | SCORE |
|---|---|
| Ship: Condition/Cleanliness | 8.2 |
| Ship: Space/Flow/Comfort | 7.8 |
| Ship: Decor/Furnishings | 8.3 |
| Ship: Watersports Facilities | 8.0 |
| Cabins: Comfort/Facilities | 8.2 |
| Cabins: Software | 8.3 |
| Food: Dining Room/Cuisine | 7.4 |
| Food: Buffets/Informal Dining | 7.0 |
| Food: Quality of Ingredients | 7.2 |
| Service: Dining Room | 7.6 |
| Service: Bars/Lounges | 7.7 |
| Service: Cabins | 7.8 |
| Cruise: Sail-Cruise Experience | 8.1 |
| Cruise: Activities Program | 7.4 |
| Cruise: Hospitality Standard | 8.1 |
| OVERALL RATING | 117.1 |

**+** Elegant, high quality interior is beautifully crafted. Light woods used extensively throughout. No lines, no hassle. Outdoor deck space is quite good. All-outside suites are one price, and come well equipped and finished, with two portholes and even a CD player. Lots of wood trim everywhere. Elegant main lounge, with crisp, but stark, colors. Recommended for watersports fans.

**–** Constant whine from the ship's engine heard in most cabins. No bathtubs in cabins. Tiny pool. Interior colors are a little cold. Communication with Indonesian crew can prove frustrating. High drink prices.

**Dining** Charming, elegant dining room, with ocean views from large picture windows. Nouvelle cuisine, which is creative and attractively presented, but just not up to the standard of the small luxury ships. The quality of ingredients should be upgraded. Attentive, friendly service throughout. Poor pastries, breads, and fruits.

**Other Comments** One of three identical sisters that is part yacht, part cruise ship, this high-tech vessel has four tall masts with computer-controlled sails. She's a very comfortable ship throughout, and, with the emphasis on refined privacy, will provide you with a very relaxing, casual cruise experience, but only partly under sail. Port taxes and insurance are extra. Gratuities are "not required," but they are expected.

# The Rating Results

## The Ratings by Points and Stars

| Ship | Cruise Line | Rating | Stars |
|---|---|---|---|
| Royal Viking Sun | Royal Viking Line | 137.2 | ★★★★★+ |
| Royal Viking Queen | Royal Viking Line | 137.1 | ★★★★★+ |
| Sea Goddess I | Cunard | 137.1 | ★★★★★+ |
| Sea Goddess II | Cunard | 137.1 | ★★★★★+ |
| Seabourn Pride | Seabourn Cruise Line | 136.2 | ★★★★★+ |
| Seabourn Spirit | Seabourn Cruise Line | 136.2 | ★★★★★+ |
| Queen Elizabeth 2 | Cunard (Grill Class) | 135.5 | ★★★★★+ |
| Crystal Harmony | Crystal Cruises | 135.3 | ★★★★★+ |
| Europa | Hapag-Lloyd Cruises | 135.3 | ★★★★★+ |
| Sagafjord | Cunard | 135.2 | ★★★★★+ |
| Vistafjord | Cunard | 135.1 | ★★★★★+ |
| Silver Cloud | Silversea Cruises | 133.7 | ★★★★★ |
| Hanseatic | Hanseatic Tours | 133.5 | ★★★★★ |
| Song of Flower | Seven Seas Cruise Line | 133.2 | ★★★★★ |
| Asuka | NYK Cruises | 128.7 | ★★★★★ |
| Zenith | Celebrity Cruises | 126.7 | ★★★★★ |
| Radisson Diamond | Diamond Cruises | 126.3 | ★★★★★ |
| Horizon | Celebrity Cruises | 126.1 | ★★★★★ |
| Sea Cloud | Sea Cloud Cruises | 125.1 | ★★★★★ |
| Queen Elizabeth 2 | Cunard (First Class) | 124.8 | ★★★★+ |
| Hebridean Princess | Hebridean Island Cruises | 124.2 | ★★★★+ |
| Bremen | Hanseatic Tours | 123.1 | ★★★★+ |
| Le Ponant | Compagnie des Isles du Ponant | 122.4 | ★★★★+ |
| Fedor Dostoyevsky | Black Sea Shipping | 120.4 | ★★★★+ |
| Royal Princess | Princess Cruises | 120.3 | ★★★★+ |
| Oceanic Grace | Oceanic Cruises | 120.0 | ★★★★+ |
| Aurora I | Classical Cruises | 119.5 | ★★★★+ |
| Aurora II | Classical Cruises | 119.5 | ★★★★+ |
| CostaRomatica | Costa Cruise Lines | 119.3 | ★★★★+ |
| Golden Princess | Princess Cruises | 119.1 | ★★★★+ |
| Meridian | Celebrity Cruises | 117.9 | ★★★★+ |
| Crown Odyssey | Royal Cruise Line | 117.8 | ★★★★+ |

**THE RATINGS BY POINTS AND STARS**

| Ship | Cruise Line | Rating | Stars |
|---|---|---|---|
| Ryndam | Holland America Line | 117.8 | ★★★★+ |
| Berlin | Deilmann Reederei | 117.6 | ★★★★+ |
| Maasdam | Holland America Line | 117.6 | ★★★★+ |
| Star Princess | Princess Cruises | 117.4 | ★★★★+ |
| Statendam | Holland America Line | 117.2 | ★★★★+ |
| Wind Song | Windstar Cruises | 117.1 | ★★★★+ |
| Wind Spirit | Windstar Cruises | 117.1 | ★★★★+ |
| Wind Star | Windstar Cruises | 117.1 | ★★★★+ |
| Sky Princess | Princess Cruises | 116.9 | ★★★★+ |
| Club Med I | Club Mediterranée | 116.8 | ★★★★+ |
| Club Med II | Club Mediterranée | 116.8 | ★★★★+ |
| Monarch of the Seas | Royal Caribbean Cruises | 116.6 | ★★★★+ |
| Majesty of the Seas | Royal Caribbean Cruises | 116.4 | ★★★★+ |
| Regal Princess | Princess Cruises | 116.4 | ★★★★+ |
| Sovereign of the Seas | Royal Caribbean Cruises | 116.4 | ★★★★+ |
| Renaissance Five | Renaissance Cruises | 116.3 | ★★★★+ |
| Renaissance Six | Renaissance Cruises | 116.3 | ★★★★+ |
| Renaissance Seven | Renaissance Cruises | 116.3 | ★★★★+ |
| Renaissance Eight | Renaissance Cruises | 116.3 | ★★★★+ |
| Crown Princess | Princess Cruises | 116.1 | ★★★★+ |
| Star Odyssey | Royal Cruise Line | 115.9 | ★★★★+ |
| Star Clipper | Star Clippers | 115.9 | ★★★★+ |
| Star Flyer | Star Clippers | 115.9 | ★★★★+ |
| World Discoverer | Clipper Cruise Line | 115.7 | ★★★★+ |
| Americana | Ivaran Lines | 115.5 | ★★★★+ |
| Windward | Norwegian Cruise Line | 115.4 | ★★★★+ |
| Dreamward | Norwegian Cruise Line | 115.3 | ★★★★+ |
| Royal Odyssey | Royal Cruise Line | 115.3 | ★★★★+ |
| Columbus Caravelle | Odessa Cruise Company | 115.1 | ★★★★+ |
| Nieuw Amsterdam | Holland America Line | 115.1 | ★★★★+ |
| Noordam | Holland America Line | 115.1 | ★★★★+ |
| Sea Princess | P&O Cruises | 115.1 | ★★★★+ |
| CostaClassica | Costa Cruise Lines | 114.7 | ★★★★ |
| Nordic Empress | Royal Caribbean Cruises | 114.7 | ★★★★ |
| Westerdam | Holland America Line | 114.5 | ★★★★ |
| Marco Polo | Orient Lines | 114.1 | ★★★★ |
| Orient Venus | Japan Cruise Line | 114.0 | ★★★★ |

| Ship | Cruise Line | Rating | Stars |
|---|---|---|---|
| American Adventure | American Family Cruises | 113.6 | ★★★★ |
| Crown Dynasty | Cunard Crown Cruises | 113.3 | ★★★★ |
| Renaissance One | Renaissance Cruises | 113.3 | ★★★★ |
| Renaissance Two | Renaissance Cruises | 113.3 | ★★★★ |
| Renaissance Three | Renaissance Cruises | 113.3 | ★★★★ |
| Renaissance Four | Renaissance Cruises | 113.3 | ★★★★ |
| Island Princess | Princess Cruises | 113.2 | ★★★★ |
| Pacific Princess | Princess Cruises | 113.2 | ★★★★ |
| Royal Majesty | Majesty Cruise Line | 112.8 | ★★★★ |
| Crown Monarch | Cunard Crown Cruises | 112.7 | ★★★★ |
| Crown Jewel | Cunard Crown Cruises | 112.1 | ★★★★ |
| Norway | Norwegian Cruise Line | 111.0 | ★★★★ |
| Star/Ship Atlantic | Premier Cruise Lines | 111.0 | ★★★★ |
| Seaward | Norwegian Cruise Line | 110.5 | ★★★★ |
| Arkona | Deutsche Seerederei | 110.0 | ★★★★ |
| Nippon Maru | Mitsui OSK Passenger Line | 109.7 | ★★★★ |
| Fascination | Carnival Cruise Lines | 109.5 | ★★★★ |
| Sensation | Carnival Cruise Lines | 109.4 | ★★★★ |
| Queen Elizabeth 2 | (Transatlantic Class) | 109.3 | ★★★★ |
| Polaris | Special Expeditions | 108.5 | ★★★★ |
| Maxim Gorki | Phoenix Seereisen | 108.4 | ★★★★ |
| Song of America | Royal Caribbean Cruises | 108.2 | ★★★★ |
| Star/Ship Oceanic | Premier Cruise Lines | 107.5 | ★★★★ |
| Langkapuri Star Aquarius | Star Cruise | 107.4 | ★★★★ |
| Fuji Maru | Mitsui OSK Passenger Line | 106.7 | ★★★★ |
| Ecstasy | Carnival Cruise Lines | 106.5 | ★★★★ |
| Fantasy | Carnival Cruise Lines | 106.5 | ★★★★ |
| Stella Solaris | Sun Line Cruises | 106.0 | ★★★★ |
| Celebration | Carnival Cruise Lines | 105.7 | ★★★★ |
| Viking Serenade | Royal Caribbean Cruises | 105.6 | ★★★★ |
| Holiday | Carnival Cruise Lines | 105.5 | ★★★★ |
| Jubilee | Carnival Cruise Lines | 105.2 | ★★★★ |
| Vistamar | Mar Line Shipping | 105.2 | ★★★★ |
| CostaAllegra | Costa Cruise Lines | 105.1 | ★★★★ |
| Tropicale | Carnival Cruise Lines | 105.1 | ★★★★ |
| Caledonian Star | Noble Caledonian | 104.9 | ★★★+ |
| Rotterdam | Holland America Line | 104.9 | ★★★+ |

**THE RATINGS BY POINTS AND STARS**

| Ship | Cruise Line | Rating | Stars |
|---|---|---|---|
| Sovetskiy Soyuz | Murmansk Shipping | 104.8 | ★★★+ |
| Black Prince | Fred Olsen Cruises | 104.7 | ★★★+ |
| The Azur | Festival Cruises | 104.7 | ★★★+ |
| CostaMarina | Costa Cruise Lines | 104.5 | ★★★+ |
| EugenioCosta | Costa Cruises | 104.5 | ★★★+ |
| Nordic Prince | Royal Caribbean Cruises | 103.8 | ★★★+ |
| Odessa | Black Sea Shipping | 103.8 | ★★★+ |
| Pearl | Pearl Cruises | 103.8 | ★★★+ |
| Song of Norway | Royal Caribbean Cruises | 103.8 | ★★★+ |
| World Renaissance | Epirotiki Lines | 103.8 | ★★★+ |
| Seawind Crown | Seawind Cruise Line | 103.7 | ★★★+ |
| FiestaMarina | FiestaMarina Cruises | 103.6 | ★★★+ |
| Canberra | P&O Cruises | 103.4 | ★★★+ |
| Illiria | Blue Aegean Cruises | 103.4 | ★★★+ |
| Festivale | Carnival Cruise Lines | 103.3 | ★★★+ |
| Yamal | Murmansk Shipping | 103.2 | ★★★+ |
| Daphne | Costa Cruises | 102.9 | ★★★+ |
| Star/Ship Majestic | Premier Cruise Lines | 102.8 | ★★★+ |
| Monterey | Starlauro Cruises | 102.3 | ★★★+ |
| Cunard Princess | Cunard Crown Cruises | 101.8 | ★★★+ |
| Kazakhstan II | Delphin Seereisen | 101.7 | ★★★+ |
| Cunard Countess | Cunard Crown Cruises | 101.1 | ★★★+ |
| Triton | Epirotiki Lines | 101.0 | ★★★+ |
| Argonaut | Epirotiki Lines | 100.8 | ★★★+ |
| Sun Viking | Royal Caribbean Cruises | 100.8 | ★★★+ |
| Aegean Dolphin | DolphinHellas Shipping | 100.3 | ★★★+ |
| Delfin Star | Effjohn International | 100.3 | ★★★+ |
| Kapitan Khlebnikov | Murmansk Shipping | 99.6 | ★★★ |
| EnricoCosta | Costa Cruises | 99.5 | ★★★ |
| Fair Princess | Princess Cruises | 99.4 | ★★★ |
| Albatros | Phoenix Seereisen | 99.4 | ★★★ |
| Orpheus | Epirotiki Lines | 99.4 | ★★★ |
| Funchal | Fritidskryss | 99.2 | ★★★ |
| Stella Maris | Sun Line Cruises | 98.9 | ★★★ |
| Southward | Norwegian Cruise Line | 98.5 | ★★★ |
| Regent Sun | Regency Cruises | 98.2 | ★★★ |
| Britanis | Fantasy Cruises | 98.1 | ★★★ |

| Ship | Cruise Line | Rating | Stars |
|---|---|---|---|
| Amerikanis | Fantasy Cruises | 97.7 | ★★★ |
| Stella Oceanis | Sun Line Cruises | 97.7 | ★★★ |
| OceanBreeze | Dolphin Cruise Line | 97.6 | ★★★ |
| Explorer | Abercrombie & Kent | 97.5 | ★★★ |
| Dolphin IV | Dolphin Cruise Line | 97.3 | ★★★ |
| Mermoz | Paquet Cruises | 97.0 | ★★★ |
| Royal Star | Star Line | 97.0 | ★★★ |
| Regent Sea | Regency Cruises | 96.7 | ★★★ |
| Atalante | Paradise Cruises | 96.6 | ★★★ |
| SeaBreeze I | Dolphin Cruise Line | 96.3 | ★★★ |
| Odysseus | Epirotiki Lines | 96.2 | ★★★ |
| Ausonia | Ausonia Cruises | 95.7 | ★★★ |
| Starward | Norwegian Cruise Lines | 95.7 | ★★★ |
| Regent Rainbow | Regency Cruises | 95.3 | ★★★ |
| Constitution | AmericanHawaii Cruises | 95.2 | ★★★ |
| Independence | AmericanHawaii Cruises | 95.2 | ★★★ |
| Regent Star | Regency Cruises | 95.0 | ★★★ |
| Regent Spirit | Regency Cruises | 94.7 | ★★★ |
| Ivan Franko | Black Sea Shipping | 94.5 | ★★★ |
| Shota Rustaveli | Black Sea Shipping | 94.5 | ★★★ |
| Taras Shevchenko | Black Sea Shipping | 94.5 | ★★★ |
| Achille Lauro | Starlauro Cruises | 94.1 | ★★★ |
| Sea Spirit | SeaSpirit Cruise Lines | 93.7 | ★★★ |
| Andaman Princess | Siam Cruise | 93.4 | ★★★ |
| Ilich | Baltic Line | 93.1 | ★★★ |
| Yorktown Clipper | Clipper Cruise Line | 92.8 | ★★★ |
| Neptune | Epirotiki Lines | 92.6 | ★★★ |
| La Palma | Intercruise | 92.5 | ★★★ |
| Jason | Epirotiki Lines | 92.4 | ★★★ |
| Leisure World | Ace Casindo Ltd | 92.1 | ★★★ |
| Fairstar | P&O Holidays | 91.4 | ★★★ |
| Nantucket Clipper | Clipper Cruise Line | 91.4 | ★★★ |
| Enchanted Seas | Commodore Cruise Line | 91.0 | ★★★ |
| Kristina Regina | Kristina Cruises Baltic | 91.0 | ★★★ |
| Regal Empress | Regal Cruises | 91.0 | ★★★ |
| Universe | World Explorer Cruises | 90.3 | ★★★ |
| Princesa Victoria | Louis Cruise Lines | 89.4 | ★★+ |

**THE RATINGS BY POINTS AND STARS**

| Ship | Cruise Line | Rating | Stars |
|---|---|---|---|
| Princesa Marissa | Louis Cruise Lines | 88.7 | ★★+ |
| Astra | Neckermann Seereisen | 88.5 | ★★+ |
| Gruziya | OdessaAmerica Cruise Co. | 88.3 | ★★+ |
| Fedor Shalyapin | Black Sea Shipping | 88.2 | ★★+ |
| Kareliya | CTC Cruise Lines | 87.7 | ★★+ |
| Azerbaydzhan | CTC Cruise Lines | 87.1 | ★★+ |
| Kazakhstan | Black Sea Shipping | 86.6 | ★★+ |
| Dimitri Shostakovich | Black Sea Shipping | 84.8 | ★★ |
| Konstantin Simonov | Baltic Line | 84.8 | ★★ |
| Lev Tolstoi | Black Sea Shipping | 84.8 | ★★ |
| Mikhail Sholokhov | Far Eastern Shipping | 84.8 | ★★ |
| Princesa Cypria | Louis Cruise Lines | 84.5 | ★★ |
| Romantica | Ambassador Cruises | 84.3 | ★★ |
| Princesa Amorosa | Louis Cruise Lines | 83.4 | ★★ |
| Antonina Nezhdanova | Far East Shipping | 83.0 | ★★ |
| Sir Francis Drake | Tall Ship Adventures | 82.5 | ★★ |
| Leonid Sobinov | Black Sea Shipping | 81.7 | ★★ |
| City of Rhodos | Cycladic Cruises | 79.8 | ★ |
| Klaudia Yelanskaya | Murmansk shipping | 79.2 | ★ |
| Ayvasovskiy | Soviet Danube Shipping | 78.1 | ★ |
| Century | Celebrity Cruises | Not Yet Rated | |
| Crystal Symphony | Crystal Cruises | Not Yet Rated | |
| Imagination | Carnival Cruise Lines | Not Yet Rated | |
| Italia Prima | Nina Cruise Lines | Not Yet Rated | |
| Legend of the Seas | Royal Caribbean Cruises | Not Yet Rated | |
| Olympic | Epirotiki Lines | Not Yet Rated | |
| Oriana | P&O Cruises | Not Yet Rated | |
| Orient Star | American Pacific Cruises | Not Yet Rated | |
| Regent Jewel | Regency Cruises | Not Yet Rated | |
| St. Helena | Curnow Shipping | Not Yet Rated | |
| Silver Wind | Silversea Cruises | Not Yet Rated | |
| Sun Princess | Princess Cruises | Not Yet Rated | |

## The Ratings in Alphabetical Order

| Ship | Cruise Line | Rating | Stars |
|---|---|---|---|
| Achille Lauro | Starlauro Cruises | 94.1 | ★★★ |
| Aegean Dolphin | Dolphin Hellas Shipping | 100.3 | ★★★+ |
| Albatros | Phoenix Seereisen | 99.4 | ★★★ |
| American Adventure | American Family Cruises | 113.6 | ★★★★ |
| Americana | Ivaran Lines | 115.5 | ★★★★+ |
| Amerikanis | Fantasy Cruises | 97.7 | ★★★ |
| Andaman Princess | Siam Cruise | 93.4 | ★★★ |
| Antonina Nezhdanova | Far East Shipping | 83.0 | ★★ |
| Argonaut | Epirotiki Lines | 100.8 | ★★★+ |
| Arkona | Deutsche Seerederei | 110.0 | ★★★★ |
| Astra | Neckermann Seereisen | 88.5 | ★★+ |
| Asuka | NYK Cruises | 128.7 | ★★★★★ |
| Atalante | Paradise Cruises | 96.6 | ★★★ |
| Aurora I | Classical Cruises | 119.5 | ★★★★+ |
| Aurora II | Classical Cruises | 119.5 | ★★★★+ |
| Ausonia | Ausonia Cruises | 95.7 | ★★★ |
| Ayvasovskiy | Soviet Danube Shipping | 78.1 | ★ |
| Azerbaydzhan | CTC Cruise Lines | 87.1 | ★★+ |
| Berlin | Deilmann Reederei | 117.6 | ★★★★+ |
| Black Prince | Fred Olsen Cruises | 104.7 | ★★★+ |
| Bremen | Hanseatic Tours | 123.1 | ★★★★+ |
| Britanis | Fantasy Cruises | 98.1 | ★★★ |
| Caledonian Star | Noble Caledonian | 104.9 | ★★★+ |
| Canberra | P&O Cruises | 104.6 | ★★★+ |
| Celebration | Carnival Cruise Lines | 105.7 | ★★★★ |
| Century | Celebrity Cruises | Not Yet Rated | |
| City of Rhodos | Cycladic Cruises | 79.8 | ★ |
| Columbus Caravelle | Odessa Cruise Company | 115.1 | ★★★★+ |
| Constitution | American Hawaii Cruises | 95.2 | ★★★ |
| CostaAllegra | Costa Cruises | 105.1 | ★★★★ |
| CostaClassica | Costa Cruises | 114.7 | ★★★★+ |
| CostaMarina | Costa Cruises | 104.5 | ★★★+ |
| CostaRomatica | Costa Cruises | 119.3 | ★★★★+ |
| Crown Dynasty | Cunard Crown Cruises | 113.3 | ★★★★ |
| Crown Jewel | Cunard Crown Cruises | 112.1 | ★★★★ |
| Crown Monarch | Cunard Crown Cruises | 112.7 | ★★★★ |

**THE RATINGS IN ALPHABETICAL ORDER**

| Ship | Cruise Line | Rating | Stars |
|---|---|---|---|
| Crown Odyssey | Royal Cruise Line | 117.8 | ★★★★+ |
| Crown Princess | Princess Cruises | 116.1 | ★★★★+ |
| Crystal Harmony | Crystal Cruises | 135.3 | ★★★★★+ |
| Crystal Symphony | Crystal Cruises | Not Yet Rated | |
| Cunard Countess | Cunard Crown Cruises | 101.1 | ★★★+ |
| Cunard Princess | Cunard Crown Cruises | 101.8 | ★★★+ |
| Daphne | Costa Cruises | 102.9 | ★★★+ |
| Delfin Star | Effjohn International | 100.3 | ★★★+ |
| Dimitri Shostakovich | Black Sea Shipping | 84.8 | ★★ |
| Dolphin IV | Dolphin Cruise Line | 97.3 | ★★★ |
| Dreamward | Norwegian Cruise Line | 115.3 | ★★★★+ |
| Ecstasy | Carnival Cruise Lines | 106.5 | ★★★★ |
| Enchanted Seas | Commodore Cruise Line | 91.0 | ★★★ |
| EnricoCosta | Costa Cruises | 99.5 | ★★★ |
| EugenioCosta | Costa Cruises | 104.5 | ★★★+ |
| Europa | Hapag-Lloyd Cruises | 135.3 | ★★★★★+ |
| Explorer | Abercrombie & Kent | 97.5 | ★★★ |
| Fair Princess | Princess Cruises | 99.4 | ★★★ |
| Fairstar | P&O Holidays | 91.4 | ★★★ |
| Fantasy | Carnival Cruise Lines | 106.5 | ★★★★ |
| Fascination | Carnival Cruise Lines | 109.5 | ★★★★ |
| Fedor Dostoyevsky | Black Sea Shipping | 120.4 | ★★★★+ |
| Fedor Shalyapin | Black Sea Shipping | 88.2 | ★★+ |
| Festivale | Carnival Cruise Lines | 103.3 | ★★★+ |
| FiestaMarina | FiestaMarina Cruises | 99.7 | ★★★ |
| Fuji Maru | Mitsui OSK Passenger Line | 106.7 | ★★★★ |
| Funchal | Fritidskryss | 99.2 | ★★★ |
| Golden Princess | Princess Cruises | 119.1 | ★★★★+ |
| Gruziya | OdessaAmerica Cruise Co. | 88.3 | ★★+ |
| Hanseatic | Hanseatic Tours | 133.5 | ★★★★★ |
| Hebridean Princess | Hebridean Island Cruises | 124.2 | ★★★★+ |
| Holiday | Carnival Cruise Lines | 105.5 | ★★★★ |
| Horizon | Celebrity Cruises | 126.1 | ★★★★★ |
| Ilich | Baltic Line | 93.1 | ★★★ |
| Illiria | New Frontier Cruises | 103.4 | ★★★+ |
| Imagination | Carnival Cruise Lines | Not Yet Rated | |
| Independence | American Hawaii Cruises | 95.2 | ★★★ |

| Ship | Cruise Line | Rating | Stars |
|---|---|---|---|
| Island Princess | Princess Cruises | 113.2 | ★★★★ |
| Italia Prima | Nina Cruise Lines | Not Yet Rated | |
| Ivan Franko | Black Sea Shipping | 94.5 | ★★★ |
| Jason | Epirotiki Lines | 92.4 | ★★★ |
| Jubilee | Carnival Cruise Lines | 105.2 | ★★★★ |
| Kapitan Khlebnikov | Murmansk Shipping | 99.6 | ★★★ |
| Kareliya | CTC Cruise Lines | 87.7 | ★★+ |
| Kazakhstan | Black Sea Shipping | 86.6 | ★★+ |
| Kazakhstan II | Delphin Seereisen | 101.7 | ★★★+ |
| Klaudia Yelanskaya | Murmansk Shipping | 79.2 | ★ |
| Konstantin Simonov | Baltic Line | 84.8 | ★★ |
| Kristina Regina | Kristina Cruises | 91.0 | ★★★ |
| La Palma | Intercruise | 92.5 | ★★★ |
| Langkapuri Star Aquarius | Star Cruise | 107.4 | ★★★★ |
| Legend of the Seas | Royal Caribbean Cruises | Not Yet Rated | |
| Leisure World | New Century Tours | 92.1 | ★★★ |
| Leonid Sobinov | Black Sea Shipping | 81.7 | ★★ |
| Lev Tolstoi | Black Sea Shipping | 84.8 | ★★ |
| Maasdam | Holland America Line | 117.6 | ★★★★+ |
| Majesty of the Seas | Royal Caribbean Cruises | 116.4 | ★★★★+ |
| Marco Polo | Orient Lines | 114.1 | ★★★★ |
| Maxim Gorki | Phoenix Seereisen | 108.4 | ★★★★ |
| Meridian | Celebrity Cruises | 117.9 | ★★★★+ |
| Mermoz | Paquet Cruises | 97.0 | ★★★ |
| Mikhail Sholokhov | Far Eastern Shipping | 84.8 | ★★ |
| Monarch of the Seas | Royal Caribbean Cruises | 116.6 | ★★★★+ |
| Monterey | Starlauro Cruises | 102.3 | ★★★+ |
| Nantucket Clipper | Clipper Cruise Line | 91.4 | ★★★ |
| Neptune | Epirotiki Lines | 92.6 | ★★★ |
| Nieuw Amsterdam | Holland America Line | 115.1 | ★★★★+ |
| Nippon Maru | Mitsui OSK Passenger Line | 109.7 | ★★★★ |
| Noordam | Holland America Line | 115.1 | ★★★★+ |
| Nordic Empress | Royal Caribbean Cruises | 114.7 | ★★★★ |
| Nordic Prince | Royal Caribbean Cruises | 103.8 | ★★★+ |
| Norway | Norwegian Cruise Line | 111.0 | ★★★★ |
| OceanBreeze | Dolphin Cruise Line | 97.6 | ★★★ |
| Oceanic Grace | Oceanic Cruises | 120.0 | ★★★★+ |

## THE RATINGS IN ALPHABETICAL ORDER

| Ship | Cruise Line | | Rating | Stars |
|---|---|---|---|---|
| Odessa | Black Sea Shipping | | 103.8 | ★★★+ |
| Odysseus | Epirotiki Lines | | 96.2 | ★★★ |
| Olympic | Epirotiki Lines | | Not Yet Rated | |
| Oriana | P&O Cruises | | Not Yet Rated | |
| Orient Star | American Pacific Cruises | | Not Yet Rated | |
| Orient Venus | Japan Cruise Line | | 114.0 | ★★★★ |
| Orpheus | Epirotiki Lines | | 99.4 | ★★★ |
| Pacific Princess | Princess Cruises | | 113.2 | ★★★★ |
| Pearl | Pearl Cruises | | 103.8 | ★★★+ |
| Polaris | Special Expeditions | | 108.5 | ★★★★ |
| Princesa Amorosa | Louis Cruise Lines | | 83.4 | ★★ |
| Princesa Cypria | Louis Cruise Lines | | 84.5 | ★★ |
| Princesa Marissa | Louis Cruise Lines | | 88.7 | ★★+ |
| Princesa Victoria | Louis Cruise Lines | | 89.4 | ★★+ |
| Queen Elizabeth 2 | Cunard | Grill Class | 135.5 | ★★★★★+ |
| | | First Class | 124.8 | ★★★★+ |
| | | Transatlantic Class | 109.3 | ★★★★ |
| Radisson Diamond | Diamond Cruises | | 126.3 | ★★★★★ |
| Regal Empress | Regal Cruises | | 91.0 | ★★★ |
| Regal Princess | Princess Cruises | | 116.4 | ★★★★+ |
| Regent Jewel | Regency Cruises | | Not Yet Rated | |
| Regent Rainbow | Regency Cruises | | 95.3 | ★★★ |
| Regent Sea | Regency Cruises | | 96.7 | ★★★ |
| Regent Spirit | Regency Cruises | | 94.7 | ★★★ |
| Regent Star | Regency Cruises | | 95.0 | ★★★ |
| Regent Sun | Regency Cruises | | 98.2 | ★★★ |
| Renaissance One | Renaissance Cruises | | 113.3 | ★★★★ |
| Renaissance Two | Renaissance Cruises | | 113.3 | ★★★★ |
| Renaissance Three | Renaissance Cruises | | 113.3 | ★★★★ |
| Renaissance Four | Renaissance Cruises | | 113.3 | ★★★★ |
| Renaissance Five | Renaissance Cruises | | 116.3 | ★★★★+ |
| Renaissance Six | Renaissance Cruises | | 116.3 | ★★★★+ |
| Renaissance Seven | Renaissance Cruises | | 116.3 | ★★★★+ |
| Renaissance Eight | Renaissance Cruises | | 116.3 | ★★★★+ |
| Romantica | Ambassador Cruises | | 84.3 | ★★ |
| Rotterdam | Holland America Line | | 104.9 | ★★★+ |
| Royal Majesty | Majesty Cruise Line | | 112.8 | ★★★★ |

## THE RATINGS IN ALPHABETICAL ORDER

| Ship | Cruise Line | Rating | Stars |
|---|---|---|---|
| Royal Odyssey | Royal Cruise Line | 115.3 | ★★★★ |
| Royal Princess | Princess Cruises | 120.3 | ★★★★+ |
| Royal Star | Star Line | 97.0 | ★★★ |
| Royal Viking Queen | Royal Viking Line | 137.1 | ★★★★★+ |
| Royal Viking Sun | Royal Viking Line | 137.2 | ★★★★★+ |
| Ryndam | Holland America Line | 117.8 | ★★★★+ |
| St. Helena | Curnow Shipping | Not Yet Rated | |
| Sagafjord | Cunard | 135.2 | ★★★★★+ |
| Sea Goddess I | Cunard | 137.1 | ★★★★★+ |
| Sea Goddess II | Cunard | 137.1 | ★★★★★+ |
| Sea Princess | P&O Cruises | 115.1 | ★★★★+ |
| Seabourn Pride | Seabourn Cruise Line | 136.2 | ★★★★★+ |
| Seabourn Spirit | Seabourn Cruise Line | 136.2 | ★★★★★+ |
| SeaBreeze I | Dolphin Cruise Line | 96.3 | ★★★ |
| SeaSpirit | SeaSpirit Cruise Lines | 93.7 | ★★★ |
| Seaward | Norwegian Cruise Line | 110.5 | ★★★★ |
| Seawind Crown | Seawind Cruise Line | 103.7 | ★★★+ |
| Sensation | Carnival Cruise Lines | 109.4 | ★★★★ |
| Shota Rustaveli | Black Sea Shipping | 94.5 | ★★★ |
| Silver Cloud | Silversea Cruises | 133.7 | ★★★★★ |
| Silver Wind | Silversea Cruises | Not Yet Rated | |
| Sky Princess | Princess Cruises | 116.9 | ★★★★+ |
| Song of America | Royal Caribbean Cruises | 108.2 | ★★★★ |
| Song of Flower | Seven Seas Cruise Line | 133.2 | ★★★★★ |
| Song of Norway | Royal Caribbean Cruises | 103.8 | ★★★+ |
| Southward | Norwegian Cruise Line | 98.5 | ★★★ |
| Sovereign of the Seas | Royal Caribbean Cruises | 116.4 | ★★★★+ |
| Sovetskiy Soyuz | Murmansk Shipping | 104.8 | ★★★+ |
| Star Odyssey | Royal Cruise Line | 115.9 | ★★★★+ |
| Star Princess | Princess Cruises | 117.4 | ★★★★+ |
| Star/Ship Atlantic | Premier Cruise Lines | 111.0 | ★★★★ |
| Star/Ship Majestic | Premier Cruise Lines | 102.8 | ★★★+ |
| Star/Ship Oceanic | Premier Cruise Lines | 107.5 | ★★★★ |
| Starward | Norwegian Cruise Line | 95.7 | ★★★ |
| Statendam | Holland America Line | 117.2 | ★★★★+ |
| Stella Maris | Sun Line Cruises | 98.9 | ★★★ |
| Stella Oceanis | Sun Line Cruises | 97.7 | ★★★ |

| THE RATINGS IN ALPHABETICAL ORDER | | | |
|---|---|---|---|
| **Ship** | **Cruise Line** | **Rating** | **Stars** |
| Stella Solaris | Sun Line Cruises | 106.0 | ★★★★ |
| Sun Princess | Princess Cruises | Not Yet Rated | |
| Sun Viking | Royal Caribbean Cruises | 100.8 | ★★★+ |
| Taras Shevchenko | Black Sea Shipping | 94.5 | ★★★ |
| The Azur | Festival Cruises | 104.7 | ★★★+ |
| Triton | Epirotiki Lines | 101.0 | ★★★+ |
| Tropicale | Carnival Cruise Lines | 105.1 | ★★★★ |
| Universe | World Explorer Cruises | 90.3 | ★★★ |
| Viking Serenade | Royal Caribbean Cruises | 105.6 | ★★★★ |
| Vistafjord | Cunard | 135.1 | ★★★★★+ |
| Vistamar | Mar Line Shipping | 105.2 | ★★★★ |
| Westerdam | Holland America Line | 114.5 | ★★★★ |
| Windward | Norwegian Cruise Line | 115.4 | ★★★★+ |
| World Discoverer | Clipper Cruise Line | 115.7 | ★★★★+ |
| World Renaissance | Epirotiki Lines | 103.8 | ★★★+ |
| Yamal | Murmansk Shipping | 103.2 | ★★★+ |
| Yorktown Clipper | Clipper Cruise Line | 92.8 | ★★★ |
| Zenith | Celebrity Cruises | 126.7 | ★★★★★ |

## Sail-Cruise Ships

| Ship | Cruise Line | Rating | Stars |
|---|---|---|---|
| Club Med I | Club Mediterranée | 116.8 | ★★★★+ |
| Club Med II | Club Mediterranée | 116.8 | ★★★★+ |
| Le Ponant | Compagnie des Isles du Ponant | 122.4 | ★★★★+ |
| Sea Cloud | Sea Cloud Cruises | 125.1 | ★★★★★ |
| Sir Francis Drake | Tall Ship Adventures | 82.5 | ★★ |
| Star Clipper | Star Clippers | 115.9 | ★★★★+ |
| Star Flyer | Star Clippers | 115.9 | ★★★★+ |
| Wind Song | Windstar Cruises | 117.1 | ★★★★+ |
| Wind Spirit | Windstar Cruises | 117.1 | ★★★★+ |
| Wind Star | Windstar Cruises | 117.1 | ★★★★+ |

# Appendixes

## World's 10 Largest Cruise Ships Currently in Service

| Ship | Cruise Line | Built | GRT |
|---|---|---|---|
| Norway | Norwegian Cruise Line | 1962 | 76,049 |
| Majesty of the Seas | Royal Caribbean Cruise Line | 1992 | 73,941 |
| Monarch of the Seas | Royal Caribbean Cruise Line | 1991 | 73,941 |
| Sovereign of the Seas | Royal Caribbean Cruise Line | 1988 | 73,192 |
| Ecstasy | Carnival Cruise Lines | 1991 | 70,367 |
| Fantasy | Carnival Cruise Lines | 1990 | 70,367 |
| Fascination | Carnival Cruise Lines | 1994 | 70,367 |
| Sensation | Carnival Cruise Lines | 1993 | 70,367 |
| Crown Princess | Princess Cruises | 1990 | 70,000 |
| Regal Princess | Princess Cruises | 1991 | 70,000 |

## World's 10 Longest Cruise Ships Currently in Service

| Ship | Shipping Line | Length (ft) |
|---|---|---|
| Norway | Norwegian Cruise Line | 1,035 |
| Queen Elizabeth 2 | Cunard | 963 |
| Majesty of the Seas | Royal Caribbean Cruise Line | 873 |
| Monarch of the Seas | Royal Caribbean Cruise Line | 873 |
| Sovereign of the Seas | Royal Caribbean Cruise Line | 873 |
| Ecstasy | Carnival Cruise Lines | 855 |
| Fantasy | Carnival Cruise Lines | 855 |
| Fascination | Carnival Cruise Lines | 855 |
| Sensation | Carnival Cruise Lines | 855 |
| Canberra | P&O Cruises | 810 |

## World's 12 Largest Passenger Ships (Past and Present)

| Ship | Shipping Line | GRT | Length (ft) |
|---|---|---|---|
| Queen Elizabeth | Cunard Line | 83,673 | 1,031 |
| Normandie | French Line | 82,799 | 1,029 |
| Queen Mary | Cunard Line | 81,237 | 1,019 |
| Norway (ex-France) | Norwegian Cruise Line | 76,069 | 1,035 |
| Majesty of the Seas | Royal Caribbean Cruise Line | 73,941 | 873 |
| Monarch of the Seas | Royal Caribbean Cruise Line | 73,941 | 873 |
| Sovereign of the Seas | Royal Caribbean Cruise Line | 73,192 | 873 |
| Ecstasy/Fantasy | Carnival Cruise Lines | 70,367 | 855 |
| Fascination/Sensation | Carnival Cruise Lines | 70,367 | 855 |
| Queen Elizabeth 2 | Cunard | 69,053 | 963 |

## World's 10 Largest Cruise Companies (by tonnage, July 1994*)

| COMPANY<br>Cruise Line | Number<br>of Ships | Name<br>of Ship | GRT | Total<br>Cabins | Berths |
|---|---|---|---|---|---|
| 1 CARNIVAL CORP | 22 | | 956,304 | | |
| Carnival Cruise Line | 10 | | 567,260 | 8,404 | 21,522 |
| | | Celebration | 47,262 | 743 | 1,896 |
| | | Ecstasy | 70,367 | 1,020 | 2,594 |
| | | Fantasy | 70,367 | 1,022 | 2,634 |
| | | Fascination | 70,367 | 1,022 | 2,634 |
| | | Festivale | 38,175 | 580 | 1,400 |
| | | Holiday | 46,052 | 726 | 1,800 |
| | | Jubilee | 47,262 | 743 | 1,896 |
| | | Imagination | 70,367 | 1,022 | 2,634 |
| | | Sensation | 70,367 | 1,022 | 2,634 |
| | | Tropicale | 36,674 | 511 | 1,400 |
| FiestaMarina Cruises | 1 | | 27,250 | 482 | 1,350 |
| | 1 | FiestaMarina | 27,250 | 482 | 1,350 |
| Holland America Line | 7 | | 326,733 | 4,428 | 10,604 |
| | | Maasdam | 55,451 | 632 | 1,627 |
| | | Nieuw Amsterdam | 33,930 | 605 | 1,350 |
| | | Noordam | 33,930 | 605 | 1,350 |
| | | Rotterdam | 38,645 | 575 | 1,250 |
| | | Ryndam | 55,451 | 632 | 1,627 |
| | | Statendam | 55,451 | 632 | 1,627 |
| | | Westerdam | 53,875 | 747 | 1,773 |
| Seabourn Cruise Line | 2 | | 19,950 | 212 | 408 |
| | | Seabourn Pride | 9,975 | 106 | 204 |
| | | Seabourn Spirit | 9,975 | 106 | 204 |
| Windstar Cruises | 3 | | 15,111 | 222 | 510 |
| | | Wind Song | 5,307 | 74 | 170 |
| | | Wind Spirit | 5,307 | 74 | 170 |
| | | Wind Star | 5,307 | 74 | 170 |
| **2 P&O GROUP** | **12** | | **530,176** | **7,211** | **16,506** |
| P&O Cruises | 3 | | 139,477 | 2,045 | 4,159 |
| | | Canberra | 44,807 | 780 | 1,441 |
| | | Oriana | 67,000 | 900 | 1,975 |
| | | Sea Princess | 27,670 | 365 | 743 |

*These figures were compiled immediately before going to press, and take account of Cunard's purchase of *Royal Viking Sun* and the brand name Royal Viking Line in June 1994.

| COMPANY Cruise Line | Number of Ships | Name of Ship | GRT | Total Cabins | Berths |
|---|---|---|---|---|---|
| P&O Holidays | 1 | | 23,764 | 488 | 1,598 |
| | | Fairstar | 23,764 | 488 | 1,598 |
| Princess Cruises | 8 | | 366,935 | 4,678 | 10,749 |
| | | Crown Princess | 70,000 | 795 | 1,910 |
| | | Fair Princess | 24,724 | 445 | 1,100 |
| | | Golden Princess | 28,078 | 402 | 867 |
| | | Island Princess | 19,907 | 305 | 717 |
| | | Regal Princess | 70,000 | 795 | 1,910 |
| | | Royal Princess | 44,348 | 600 | 1,275 |
| | | Sky Princess | 46,314 | 600 | 1,350 |
| | | Star Princess | 63,564 | 735 | 1,620 |
| **3 ROYAL CARIBBEAN** | **10** | | **478,814** | **8,016** | **18,598** |
| Royal Caribbean Cruises | 10 | | 478,814 | 8,016 | 18,598 |
| | | Legend of the Seas | 66,700 | 902 | 2,068 |
| | | Majesty of the Seas | 73,941 | 1,177 | 2,744 |
| | | Monarch of the Seas | 73,941 | 1,177 | 2,744 |
| | | Nordic Empress | 48,563 | 800 | 2,020 |
| | | Nordic Prince | 23,200 | 506 | 1,127 |
| | | Song of America | 37,584 | 701 | 1,552 |
| | | Song of Norway | 23,005 | 502 | 1,13 |
| | | Sovereign of the Seas | 73,192 | 1,138 | 2,524 |
| | | Sun Viking | 18,556 | 357 | 818 |
| | | Viking Serenade | 40,132 | 756 | 1,863 |
| **4 KLOSTER CRUISE** | **10** | | **312,331** | **5,314** | **12,139** |
| Norwegian Cruise Line | 6 | | 229,473 | 3,872 | 9,066 |
| | | Dreamward | 39,217 | 623 | 1,450 |
| | | Norway | 76,049 | 1,013 | 2,370 |
| | | Seaward | 42,276 | 767 | 1,798 |
| | | Southward | 16,607 | 377 | 976 |
| | | Starward | 16,107 | 379 | 1,022 |
| | | Windward | 39,217 | 623 | 1,450 |
| Royal Cruise Line | 4 | | 82,858 | 1,442 | 3,073 |
| | | Crown Odyssey | 34,242 | 516 | 1,221 |
| | | Queen Odyssey | 9,975 | 106 | 212 |
| | | Royal Odyssey | 28,078 | 410 | 820 |
| | | Star Odyssey | 28,078 | 410 | 820 |

| COMPANY<br>Cruise Line | Number<br>of Ships | Name<br>of Ship | GRT | Total<br>Cabins | Berths |
|---|---|---|---|---|---|
| 5 CUNARD | 11 | | **252,821** | **5,105** | **10,902** |
| Cunard QE2 | 1 | | 69,053 | 957 | 1,870 |
| | | Queen Elizabeth 2 | 69,053 | 957 | 1,870 |
| Cunard Crown Cruises | 5 | | 88,451 | 1,879 | 4,274 |
| | | Crown Dynasty | 19,046 | 410 | 900 |
| | | Crown Jewel | 19,046 | 410 | 900 |
| | | Crown Monarch | 15,271 | 255 | 556 |
| | | Cunard Countess | 17,593 | 398 | 956 |
| | | Cunard Princess | 17,495 | 402 | 959 |
| Cunard Royal Viking | 5 | | 95,317 | 1,191 | 2,398 |
| | | Royal Viking Sun | 37,845 | 370 | 814 |
| | | Sagafjord | 24,474 | 321 | 620 |
| | | Sea Goddess I | 4,253 | 58 | 116 |
| | | Sea Goddess II | 4,253 | 58 | 116 |
| | | Vistafjord | 24,492 | 384 | 732 |
| 6 COSTA CROCIERE | 7 | | **229,949** | **3,167** | **8,410** |
| Costa Cruises | 7 | | 229,949 | 3,167 | 8,410 |
| | | CostaAllegra | 28,430 | 405 | 1,066 |
| | | CostaClassica | 53,700 | 654 | 1,766 |
| | | CostaMarina | 25,441 | 386 | 1,025 |
| | | CostaRomantica | 56,800 | 678 | 1,782 |
| | | Daphne | 16,330 | 206 | 508 |
| | | EnricoCosta | 16,495 | 332 | 845 |
| | | EugenioCosta | 32,753 | 506 | 1,418 |
| 7 BLASCO | 13 | | **215,426** | **3,087** | **8,037** |
| Black Sea Shipping | 13 | | 215,426 | 3,087 | 8,037 |
| | | Azerbaydzhan | 15,065 | 230 | 635 |
| | | Dimitri Shostakovich | 9,878 | 139 | 494 |
| | | Fedor Dostoyevsky | 20,158 | 295 | 650 |
| | | Fedor Shalyapin | 21,406 | 292 | 800 |
| | | Gruziya | 15,402 | 226 | 640 |
| | | Ivan Franko | 20,064 | 290 | 714 |
| | | Kareliya | 15,065 | 236 | 644 |
| | | Kazakhstan | 15,410 | 235 | 640 |
| | | Kazakhstan II | 16,600 | 237 | 640 |
| | | Lev Tolstoi | 12,600 | 132 | 290 |
| | | Odessa | 13,252 | 241 | 570 |
| | | Shota Rustaveli | 20,499 | 247 | 608 |
| | | Taras Shevchenko | 20,027 | 287 | 712 |

| COMPANY Cruise Line | Number of Ships | Name of Ship | GRT | Total Cabins | Berths |
|---|---|---|---|---|---|
| 8 CHANDRIS GROUP | **5** | | **170,551** | **2,690** | **6,434** |
| **Celebrity Cruises** | 3 | | 124,506 | 1,917 | 4,854 |
| | | Horizon | 46,811 | 677 | 1,660 |
| | | Meridian | 30,440 | 553 | 1,398 |
| | | Zenith | 47,255 | 687 | 1,796 |
| **Fantasy Cruises** | 2 | | 46,045 | 773 | 1,580 |
| | | Amerikanis | 19,904 | 310 | 620 |
| | | Britanis | 26,141 | 463 | 960 |
| 9 REGENCY | **6** | | **117,783** | **2,198** | **5,008** |
| **Regency Cruises** | 6 | | 117,783 | 2,198 | 5,008 |
| | | Regent Jewel | 8,000 | 251 | 618 |
| | | Regent Rainbow | 24,851 | 484 | 1,168 |
| | | Regent Sea | 22,785 | 358 | 760 |
| | | Regent Spirit | 12,433 | 211 | 532 |
| | | Regent Star | 24,214 | 474 | 1,000 |
| | | Regent Sun | 25,500 | 420 | 930 |
| 10 EPIROTIKI | **8** | | **68,728** | **1,582** | **3,426** |
| **Epirotiki Lines** | 8 | | 68,728 | 1,582 | 3,426 |
| | | Argonaut | 4,007 | 88 | 183 |
| | | Jason | 5,250 | 139 | 310 |
| | | Neptune | 4,000 | 93 | 208 |
| | | Odysseus | 12,000 | 226 | 486 |
| | | Olympic | 12,500 | 263 | 600 |
| | | Orpheus | 5,092 | 153 | 318 |
| | | Triton | 14,155 | 352 | 712 |
| | | World Renaissance | 11,724 | 268 | 609 |

# OCEAN-GOING SHIPS TO DEBUT 1995/6/7

| Debut Date | Cruise Line | Name of Ship | Tonnage | Cost millions | Length feet | Passengers | Builder |
|---|---|---|---|---|---|---|---|
| Apr 1995 | P&O Cruises | Oriana | 67,000 | $358 | 853.0 | 1,975 | Meyer Werft (Germany) |
| Apr 1995 | Royal Caribbean Cruises | Legend of the Seas | 66,700 | $325 | 867.0 | 1,800 | Chantiers de l'Atlantique (France) |
| Jul 1995 | Crystal Cruises | Crystal Symphony | 49,000 | $250 | 778.0 | 960 | Kvaerner-Masa Yards (Finland) |
| Late 1995 | Regency Cruises | Regent Sky | 50,000 | $170 | 726.7 | 1,400 | Avlis Shipyards (Greece) |
| Dec 1995 | Carnival Cruise Lines | Imagination | 70,367 | $330 | 864.8 | 2,594 | Kvaerner-Masa Yards (Finland) |
| Dec 1995 | Celebrity Cruises | Century | 70,000 | $320 | 807.0 | 1,740 | Meyer Werft (Germany) |
| Jan 1996 | Princess Cruises | Sun Princess | 76,500 | $300 | 856.0 | 1,740 | Fincantieri (Italy) |
| Mar 1996 | Carnival Cruise Line | Inspiration | 70,367 | $270 | 864.8 | 1,950 | Kvaerner-Masa Yards (Finland) |
| Spring 1996 | Holland America Line | Veendam | 55,451 | $225 | 715.2 | 2,594 | Fincantieri (Italy) |
| Spring 1996 | Royal Caribbean Cruises | Splendor of the Seas | 66,700 | $325 | 867.0 | 1,266 | Chantiers de l'Atlantique (France) |
| July 1996 | Celebrity Cruises | Century II | 77,000 | $320 | 852.0 | 1,800 | Meyer Werft (Germany) |
| July 1996 | Costa Cruises | unnamed | 70,000 | $300 | n/a | 2,200 | Bremer Vulkan (Germany) |
| Late 1996 | Carnival Cruise Lines | unnamed | 95,000 | $400 | n/a | 2,600 | Fincantieri (Italy) |
| Late 1996 | Royal Caribbean Cruises | unnamed | 73,000 | $300 | 915.2 | 1,950 | Kvaerner-Masa Yards (Finland) |
| Late 1996 | Silversea Cruises | unnamed | 18,000 | $125 | 514.0 | 306 | Francesco Visentini Shipyard (Italy) |
| Late 1996 | Silversea Cruises | unnamed | 18,000 | $125 | 514.0 | 306 | Francesco Visentini Shipyard (Italy) |
| Feb 1997 | Royal Caribbean Cruises | unnamed | 65,000 | $330 | 834.0 | 1,800 | Chantiers de l'Atlantique (France) |
| Spring 1997 | Princess Cruises | unnamed | 77,000 | $295 | 856.0 | 1,950 | Fincantieri (Italy) |
| July 1997 | Celebrity Cruises | Century III | 77,000 | $320 | 852.0 | 1,800 | Meyer Werft (Germany) |
| Sep 1997 | Royal Caribbean Cruises | unnamed | 73,000 | $300 | 915.2 | 1,950 | Kvaerner-Masa Yards (Finland)-option |
| Fall 1997 | Princess Cruises | unnamed | 100,000 | $385 | 935.0 | 2,600 | Fincantieri (Italy) |

# Cruise Line Addresses

As this book is marketed principally in the United States and the U.K., only the offices and head offices of the principal cruise lines are listed, due to space limitations. Telephone and fax numbers are not given, as these can change frequently.

Note: Please mention the *Berlitz Complete Guide to Cruising and Cruise Ships* when writing to the cruise lines for information or brochures.

## United States

**Abercrombie & Kent**
1520 Kensington Road
Oak Brook
IL 60521

**American Family Cruises**
World Trade Center
80 SW 8th Street
Miami
FL 33130-3097

**American Hawaii Cruises**
2 North Riverside Plaza
Chicago
IL 60606

**Carnival Cruise Lines**
5225 NW 87th Avenue
Miami
FL 33178-2428

**Celebrity Cruises**
5200 Blue Lagoon Drive
Miami
FL 33126

**Classical Cruises**
132 East 70 Street
New York
NY 10021

**Clipper Cruise Line**
7711 Bonhomme Avenue
St. Louis
MO 63105

**Club Mediterranée**
40 West 57 Street
New York
NY 10019

**Commodore Cruise Line**
800 Douglas Road
Coral Gables
FL 33134

**Costa Cruises**
World Trade Center
80 SW 8th Street
Miami
FL 33130-3097

**Crystal Cruises**
2121 Avenue of the Stars
Los Angeles
CA 90067

**Cunard**
555 Fifth Avenue
New York
NY 10017

**Cunard Crown Cruises**
(See Cunard)

**Diamond Cruise**
600 Corporate Drive
Suite 410
Ft. Lauderdale
FL 33180

**Dolphin Cruise Line**
901 South America Way
Miami
FL 33132-2073

**Epirotiki Lines**
(See Dolphin Cruise Line)

**Fantasy Cruises**
5200 Blue Lagoon Drive
Miami
FL 33126

**Fiesta Marina Cruises**
(See Carnival Cruise Lines)

**Holland America Line**
300 Elliott Avenue West
Seattle
WA 98119

**Ivaran Lines**
Ivaran Agencies
111 Pavonia Avenue
Jersey City
NJ 07310

**Majesty Cruise Line**
901 South America Way
Miami
FL 33132-2073

**Norwegian Cruise Line**
2 Alhambra Plaza
Coral Gables
FL 33134

**Orient Lines**
1710 S.E. 17th Street
Ft. Lauderdale
FL 33316

**Paquet French Cruises**
6301 N.W. 5th Way
Suite 4000
Ft. Lauderdale
FL 33309

**Pearl Cruises**
(See Paquet French Cruises)

**Premier Cruise Lines**
400 Challenger Road
Cape Canaveral
FL 32920

**Princess Cruises**
10100 Santa Monica Blvd
Los Angeles
CA 90067

**RSVP Cruises**
2800 University Avenue S.E.
Minneapolis
MN 55414-3293

**Regency Cruises**
260 Madison Avenue
New York
NY 10016

**Renaissance Cruises**
110 East Broward Blvd
Suite 1801
Ft. Lauderdale
FL 33301

**Royal Caribbean Cruises**
1050 Caribbean Way
Miami
FL 33132-2601

**Royal Cruise Line**
One Maritime Plaza, Suite 660
San Francisco
CA 94111

**Royal Viking Line**
95 Merrick Way
Coral Gables
FL 33134

**Seabourn Cruise Line**
55 Francisco Street
Suite 210
San Francisco
CA 94133

**Seawind Cruises**
1750 Coral Way
Coral Gables
FL 33145

**Seven Seas Cruise Line**
333 Market Street
Suite 2600
San Francisco
CA 94105-2102

**Silversea Cruises**
110 Broward Boulevard
Ft. Lauderdale
FL 33301

**Special Expeditions**
720 Fifth Avenue
Suite 605
New York
NY 10019

**Star Clippers**
4101 Salzedo Avenue
Coral Gables
FL 33146

**Sun Line Cruises**
One Rockefeller Plaza
Suite 315
New York
NY 10020

**Windstar Cruises**
300 Elliott Avenue West
Seattle
WA 98119

**World Explorer Cruises**
555 Montgomery Avenue
San Francisco
CA 94111

## United Kingdom

**CTC Cruise Lines**
1 Regent Street
London SW1Y 4NN

**Celebrity Cruises**
17 Old Park Lane
London W1Y 3LH

**Cunard**
30A Pall Mall
London SW1Y 5LS

**Fred Olsen Cruises**
Crown House
Crown Street
Ipswich
Suffolk IP1 3HB

**Hebridean Island Cruises**
Acorn Park
Skipton
North Yorkshire
BD23 2UE

**Jubilee Sailing Trust**
Test Road
Eastern Docks
Southampton SO1 1GD

**Orient Lines**
38 Park Street
London W1Y 3PF

**P&O Cruises**
77 New Oxford Street
London WC1A 1PP

**Swan Hellenic Cruises**
77 New Oxford Street
London WC1A 1PP

## Headquarters – Other Countries

**Aegean Oceanic SA**
12 Akti Possidonos
Piraeus 185 31
GREECE

**Ausonia Cruises**
Via C. D'Andrea
80133 Naples
ITALY

**Cycladic Cruises**
81 Patission Street
104 34 Athens
GREECE

**Deilmann Reedereri**
Am Hafensteig 19
D-2430 Neustadt in Holstein
GERMANY

**Dolphin Hellas Shipping**
71 Akti Miaouli
185 37 Piraeus
GREECE

**Epirotiki Lines**
87 Miaouli Akti
185 38 Piraeus
GREECE

**Festival Cruises**
99 Akti Miaouli
GR 185 38, Piraeus
GREECE

**Fritidskryss**
Soder Malarstrand 29
10444 62 Stockholm
SWEDEN

**Hanseatic Tours**
Nagelsweg 55
D-20097 Hamburg
GERMANY

**Hapag-Lloyd Cruises**
Gustav-Deetjen-Allee 2/6/D
2800 Bremen-1
GERMANY

**Hurtig-Ruten Coastal Express**
Ofotens og Vesteraalens DS
N-8500 Narvik
NORWAY

**Intercruise**
126 Kolokotroni Street
185 35 Piraeus
GREECE

**Kristina Cruises**
Rannikolininjat OY
Korkeavouenkatu 2
SF-48100 Helsinki
FINLAND

**Louis Cruise Lines**
P.O. Box 5612
Limassol
CYPRUS

**Mediterranean Queen Lines**
5 Sachtouri Street
Piraeus
GREECE

**Mitsui OSK (Passenger Line) Ltd**
Syosen Mitsui Building
2-1-1 Toranomon
Minato-Ku
Tokyo 105
JAPAN

**NYK Cruises**
Yusen Building
3-2 Marunouchi 2-Chome
Chiyoda-Ku
Tokyo
JAPAN

**Paquet French Cruises**
5 Boulevard Malesherbes
F-7500-B Paris
FRANCE

**Paradise Cruises**
P.O. Box 157
Limassol
CYPRUS

**Starlauro Cruises**
Via Cristoforo Colombo 45
I-80133 Naples
ITALY

**Peace Boat Foundation**
Arai Building 1-6-15 Takadanobaba Sinjuku-ku
Tokyo 169
JAPAN

**Star Line Kreutzfahrten**
Monchstrasse 32
7000 Stuttgart 1
GERMANY

# Dear Cruisegoer

*The author invites you to complete this comments section. Useful suggestions will be taken into consideration during compilation of the next edition of this handbook, due for publication in September 1996.*

**Did you buy this book:**

☐ because it contains comparative and analytical cruise ship ratings?

☐ after seeing it in a bookstore? If so, where?

.......................................................

☐ after reading about it in a newspaper or periodical. If so, which?

.......................................................

☐ on the recommendation of your travel agent?

**Have you taken a cruise before?**

☐ Yes ☐ No

If yes, how many? ................................

**In which areas have you cruised?**

.......................................................

**Which is your favorite area?**

.......................................................

**Which is your favorite ship?**

.......................................................

**Which is your favorite cruise line?**

.......................................................

**Which cruise line did you cruise with last?**

.......................................................

**Did these revised ratings help you decide which ship to take on your next cruise vacation?**

☐ Yes ☐ No

**If space is available, what other information would you like to see included in future editions?**

.......................................................

.......................................................

.......................................................

.......................................................

.......................................................

*Thank you for your valued time in completing this questionnaire. Please note that absolutely* ***no*** *correspondence will be entered into concerning ship evaluations and ratings. If you would like to know more about the bi-monthly color magazine,* **PortHole Magazine**, *please send a stamped self-addressed envelope to:*

**Douglas Ward**, *PortHole Magazine*,
10 Fairway Drive, Suite 200, Deerfield Beach,
FL 33441-1854, USA. Tel. 305-426-0046.